W9-DCY-793

INTENTIONAL FORGETTING: INTERDISCIPLINARY APPROACHES

INTENTIONAL FORGETTING: INTERDISCIPLINARY APPROACHES

Edited by

Jonathan M. Golding
University of Kentucky

Colin M. MacLeod
University of Toronto at Scarborough

LEA LAWRENCE ERLBAUM ASSOCIATES, PUBLISHERS
1998   Mahwah, New Jersey   London

Copyright © 1998 by Lawrence Erlbaum Associates, Inc.
All rights reserved. No part of the book may be reproduced in
any form, by photostat, microform, retrieval system, or any
other means, without the prior written consent of the publisher.

Lawrence Erlbaum Associates, Inc., Publishers
10 Industrial Avenue
Mahwah, NJ 07430

Library of Congress Cataloging in Publication Data

Intentional forgetting: interdisciplinary approaches / edited by
Jonathan M. Golding, Colin M. MacLeod.
     p. cm.
   Includes bibliographicical references and index
   ISBN 0-8058-2211-9 (cloth : alk. paper). — ISBN 0-
8058-2212-7 (pbk. : alk. paper)
   1. Human information processing. 2. Selectivity (Psychology). 3. Memory. 4. Human information processing. I. Golding, Jonathan M. II. MacLeod, Colin M.
   BF378.S45I58 1998
   153.1'25—dc21   97–10293
                                        CIP

Books published by Lawrence Erlbaum Associates are printed on
acid-free paper, and their bindings are chosen for strength and
durability.

Printed in the United States of America
10 9 8 7 6 5 4 3 2 1

For our parents,
Samuel & Eleanor Golding and Clary & Anne MacLeod,
and for our graduate supervisors,
Janice M. Keenan and Thomas O. Nelson,
with thanks for everything they taught us.

CONTENTS

PREFACE

This volume explores the psychological phenomenon of intentional forgetting. For both of us, the first research project we ever undertook in graduate school examined directed forgetting, and it was our continuing interest in this phenomenon that led to our research collaboration and friendship. The book grew out of our desire to understand the breadth of this phenomenon, which has tendrils into surprisingly many areas of psychological inquiry. The 17 chapters examine the effect on memory of instructions to forget, think of as false, disregard, discredit, discount, not think about, or ignore information in a wide variety of contexts. These contexts range from the animal laboratory to the courtroom, with the methodologies employed in each domain varying dramatically.

Research on intentional forgetting has been conducted in various forms and under various names for at least 30 years, but until now no effort has been made to present these different perspectives in one place. That is our main goal: Using both review chapters and new empirical studies, this book brings together the many research paradigms investigating intentional forgetting, highlighting the commonalities that link these seemingly disparate areas of research. We think of the book as a sort of "case study" of one phenomenon in memory—the intention to forget, or to modify memory.

Why is research on intentional forgetting important? Such work helps to increase our understanding of how memory functions, especially with regard to its updating. In William James' (1890) "blooming, buzzing confusion" (p. 488), we frequently are unable to process adequately all of the information that we experience; online forgetting of some information is necessary. Moreover, we must often replace existing information with new information, as when someone we know relocates and acquires a new address and telephone number. Investigating this updating ability has been the main thrust of research on intentional forgetting, specifically those studies on the directed forgetting effect (see the opening review chapter of this volume by MacLeod). As you will read, cognitive experiments on directed forgetting have shown that we are able to deal more effectively with large amounts of information by following instructions to treat some of the information as "to be forgotten." In this way, interference is reduced and we are able to devote all of our resources to the remaining to-be-remembered information. The mechanisms (e.g., selective rehearsal, retrieval inhibition) that lead to this reduction continue to promote new experiments, but more than a quarter century of research leaves no doubt that the directed-forgetting effect is robust.

The interest in memory updating is also partly a function of the fact that even when we can adequately process the information presented to us, there remain instances when specific information should not be processed. The most typical example of this is an instruction to disregard inadmissible evidence presented in a courtroom. The aim of an instruction to disregard is to inform jurors that this particular evidence should not be incorporated into memory or used in rendering a verdict. There are numerous other related experiences (see Golding & Long's review chapter in this volume), ranging from advertisements that convey incorrect or deceptive information to behavioral descriptions that should be kept confidential. Despite the intent of the instructions in these studies—and unlike the findings in studies of directed forgetting—much of this research has shown that we are apt not to heed the instruction to disregard, and instead to use to-be-disregarded information to make a "contaminated" judgment.

The organization of the book reflects both of the previous points regarding the importance of research on intentional forgetting. After the directed-forgetting review (chap. 1) and the review on related intentional-forgetting phenomena (chap. 2), the book is divided into several separable but related sections. The first section includes chapters that describe recent research on directed forgetting in humans. Chapters 3 through 6 examine the mechanisms responsible for directed forgetting (i.e., selective rehearsal vs. retrieval inhibition); chapter 7 presents research on disregarding information in text. The second section (chaps. 8 & 9) describes research on directed forgetting in animals. The third section describes research on social and clinical psychological phenomena, at both the individual (chaps. 10, 11, & 12) and group levels (chap. 13), ending with a treatment (chap. 14) of recent clinical work. The fourth section focuses on psychology and law, presenting both a research overview (chap. 15) and a legal guide (chap. 16). The book concludes with a chapter (chap. 17) by Robert Bjork, putting research on intentional forgetting into perspective.

As with any book, we owe a debt of gratitude to many people for their contributions, and we are happy to acknowledge them. First and foremost, we thank the authors of the chapters for their enthusiasm regarding the project and for hewing closer to our production schedule than we had any right to expect. We especially thank Robert Bjork for writing the final overview chapter, a wonderfully personal account from the one researcher who has contributed continuously to the study of intentional forgetting from its earliest days. We are also grateful to Rebecca Polley Sanchez for the fine work she did in constructing the indexes. Finally, we owe a considerable debt of gratitude to the team at Lawrence Erlbaum Associates—most notably our Acquisitions Editor, Judith Amsel, her Editorial Assistant, Kathy Dolan, and our Book Production Editor, Larry Hayden—for an excellent job in making this book a reality. The contributions of all of these colleagues have helped to make editing this volume an even more edifying and enjoyable activity for us.

Jonathan M. Golding
Colin M. MacLeod

REFERENCE

James, W. (1890). *Principles of psychology* (Vol. 1). New York: Holt.

1

DIRECTED FORGETTING

Colin M. MacLeod
University of Toronto at Scarborough

When people experience failures of memory, they often express the desire for a panacea to prevent such failures from ever happening again. Of course, what they usually want is a "memory pill" to eliminate the need to exert any effort toward developing this vastly improved memory. Most people apparently believe that memory improvement should be effortless, despite recognizing that improvement of other skills such as squash or bridge requires intensive practice and dedication. Moreover, they do not seem to consider the negative consequences of never forgetting anything. We do not want to remember the loss of family and friends, the embarrassing moments, or indeed the old telephone numbers of our personal past. We need to forget, just as we need to remember.

The value of forgetting has long been understood by those who study memory. Ribot (1882, p. 61) said that "Forgetfulness, except in certain cases, is not a disease of memory, but a condition of its health and life." Similarly, James (1890, p. 680) wrote that "if we remembered everything, we should on most occasions be as ill off as if we remembered nothing."[1] Much earlier, Cicero talked in *De Oratore* of a professor offering to teach the skill of mnemonics to the very wise Themistocles. "The professor asserted that it would enable him to remember everything; and Themistocles replied that he would be doing him a greater kindness if he taught him to forget what

---

[1]These two quotations from Ribot (1882) and James (1890) were initially cited in the introduction to an article by Geiselman (1977, p. 323).

he wanted than if he taught him to remember" (cited in Herrmann & Chaffin, 1988). Forgetting is important to successful remembering. This chapter is about one aspect of forgetting: the forgetting that we intend to do.

INTRODUCTION

In 1954, John Brown published an article in which he used an unusual procedure to study interference in short-term retention. Had he called his manipulation *directed forgetting*, this article probably would be highly cited today. Instead, it is essentially unknown.[2] Here is what Brown did in his first experiment. Subjects saw four rapidly presented arrow–number pairs on each trial. Either before or just after the stimuli were presented, instructions were given to recall only the arrows, only the numbers, or both, in a specified order. Recall of the arrows was unaffected by condition. For the numbers, however, being told in advance what to recall was much better: This was true for numbers only (.78 before, .51 after), for numbers first (.61 before, .36 after), and for numbers second (.48 before, .39 after).[3] What is especially noteworthy is that instructions to recall only the numbers led to better memory even when the instructions were given *after* encoding. Brown (1954, p. 147) concluded that "Some of the difference may be due to selective rehearsal of the numbers during presentation" but believed this to be an unlikely account (given the rapid presentation).

A decade later, Muther (1965) employed a similar manipulation: Subjects saw several lists of 20 letters but were told that, for some lists, only 10 of the letters would have to be recalled later. The 10 to-be-omitted letters were cued by either a preceding or a succeeding blank field. Compared to control lists of only 10 letters, where recall accuracy was .74, accuracy for cued lists averaged .61, a significant reduction. Thus, the letters that did not have to be recalled still interfered with those that did. This interference was not surprising. More interesting, however, was the comparison to 20-letter lists with no cuing. Here, correct recall was only .46. Quite clearly, being allowed to omit half of the letters from recall resulted in significantly improved performance on the remaining ones.

From these modest beginnings, a new technique arose for studying what Bjork (1972) soon characterized as the "updating of memory." Initially known

---

[2]Intriguingly, this is the same John Brown who reported his research on forgetting from short-term memory (Brown, 1958) a year before the better known work of Peterson and Peterson (1959).

[3]In reporting data, the values in parentheses are always mean proportions correct, except in the very few cases indicated otherwise. I have occasionally collapsed over means, and have sometimes had to estimate values from figures. Hopefully, this does not do too much violence to the actual findings.

as instructions to forget (e.g., Bjork, LaBerge, & Legrand, 1968), and variously called positive, voluntary, motivated, or intentional forgetting, the name investigators eventually settled on was *directed forgetting* (see the early literature reviews by Bjork, 1972; Epstein, 1972), arguing that it was the most general (and the least theory-dependent) label. Oddly, there were no further reviews until Johnson's (1994), itself fairly selective (see also Bjork, 1978, 1989, for extended discussions). The aim of this chapter is to provide a comprehensive overview of the memory literature that has addressed directed forgetting in the past 30 years. The next chapter (Golding & Long) surveys the rest of the relevant literature outside memory research where intentional forgetting has been studied.

Here is my plan. First, I examine the studies of directed forgetting, organizing them as shown in Table 1.1. I attempt to extract the most fundamental and reliable findings to provide a clear set of phenomena to be explained. Often, I present short summaries of actual data in the form of mean proportion correct in each condition, hopefully providing more archival value. The studies are presented largely in chronological order, in this case a reasonable sequence with the advantage of making individual studies easy to locate. Once the literature is covered, I examine the existing theories against

TABLE 1.1
Organization of the Chapter

this database. My goal is to arrive at the best explanation currently possible for the existing set of data. But first, as a "start vector," I introduce the rudiments of the technique and define the key terms used in this chapter.

THE BASIC PARADIGM

Consider a simple prototype experiment. My only shorthand will be to call the to-be-remembered material the *R items* and the to-be-forgotten material the *F items*, with the instruction referred to as the "cue." In this minimalist experiment, the studied material consists of a list of unrelated words. However, the technique is applicable to a wide variety of materials and situations, as the experiments reviewed here—and in the other chapters in this book—ably demonstrate.

The Muther (1965) study illustrates one basic procedure for conducting a directed-forgetting study. There are three conditions. The directed-forgetting condition consists of equal numbers of R and F words, say 12 of each. This condition is "bracketed" by conditions representing the two logical extremes; specifically, a list of only the 12 R words, and a list of 24 words in which all items are to be remembered. In the critical list containing F cues, the subject is told that only the R items will ever be tested, though more often than not experimenters break this promise.

If the subject is instructed to forget 12 of 24 words and edits those words out of study and recall, then recall ought to be better on the remaining 12 R words than on the corresponding 12 words in a list where all 24 must be remembered. Why? There are many possible reasons, including lowered attentional demands, reduced proactive interference, more focused rehearsal, easier organization, and the like, all of which I consider along the way. Note, however, that unless the memory editing is perfectly effective, the 12 R words from the list of 24 should not be as well remembered as the 12 words from a list of only 12. That is exactly what Muther (1965) found.

How does one administer a cue to forget? There have been two basic tactics. The *item procedure*, still the most prevalent, is similar to the one Muther used. The words are presented one at a time at a fixed rate. For each F item, the subject is given an explicit cue, such as "forget" or "FFFF." As well, researchers usually signal each R item with a complementary cue, such as "remember" or "RRRR." Occasionally, the cue is presented before the word to which it applies, but generally the cue comes after the relevant word, ensuring that the subject registers the word.

The other procedure for delivering the cue is called the *list procedure*. This involves only one cue, ordinarily presented at the middle of the list. In my example, the subject would be presented with the first 12 words and then told either to remember those 12 words or to forget them. The remaining 12 words would then be presented, always to be remembered. Variations between these two procedures are possible, such as presenting a few words before each cue (e.g., MacLeod, 1975), but these are less commonly used.

It is common to refer to a "directed-forgetting effect" when the instructional cues affect memory. However, some potential for confusion exists because there are two logical candidate measures of the basic "directed-forgetting effect." One compares the critical 12 R words across the three conditions. I describe such effects in terms of a *cost/benefit* analysis. To the extent that the critical 12 R words do better when coupled with an equal number of F words as opposed to an equal number of R words, then the *directed-forgetting benefit* is large. To the extent that the critical 12 R words do worse when coupled with an equal number of F words as opposed to being presented alone in a 12-word list, then the *directed-forgetting cost* is large. So, the "directed-forgetting effect" can be measured by treating the difference in performance between 12 R words presented alone (the cost baseline) and 24 R words (the benefit baseline) as the entire range, and then determining where performance on the 12 R words in the critical condition (i.e., 12 R + 12 F) lies in that range. Benefit plus cost must always sum to the difference between the two end points of the range.

This cost/benefit analysis considers only the R items. Yet we generally look at performance on the F words as well (much to the subject's consternation). Thus, in the critical condition, one can also directly examine the difference in performance between the 12 R and the 12 F words as another measure of the "directed-forgetting effect," common in studies where the two baseline conditions are omitted. Indeed, this has come to be the preferred measure. To the extent that the F words are successfully edited out, then the difference between the R and F items should be large. I refer to this difference as the *remember–forget (R–F) difference*. Introduction of these new terms may help to reduce the confusion of labeling two different phenomena as the "directed-forgetting effect."

This thumbnail sketch characterizes the directed-forgetting paradigm. The only other feature to note is that the dependent variable is virtually always accuracy, typically the proportion of items correct on a memory test that the subject had been told would occur. Occasionally, response latency has been recorded, but exploration of other dependent variables has been minimal. With this sketch in mind, I now review the literature.

OFT-FORGOTTEN ANTECEDENTS

Investigators thought about lightening a subject's memory load "on line" before the directed-forgetting procedure became prevalent (e.g., Brown, 1954). In particular, there was a longstanding interest in "repression" (for reviews, see MacKinnon & Dukes, 1962; Weiner, 1966; for experimental work, see Glucksberg & King, 1967; Zeller, 1950). Could subjects prevent specific information in memory from becoming conscious and, if so, what were the consequences for remembering other information? Some of the relevant repression literature is examined in this chapter; some is covered in the next chapter by Golding and Long.

The idea of controlling remembering was in the air in memory research when directed forgetting was born, no doubt due to the emergence of the two-state memory models (Atkinson & Shiffrin, 1968; Waugh & Norman, 1965) and the resulting concern with transfer from short-term memory to long-term memory. This can be seen most plainly in the work on the monitoring and control of rehearsal (e.g., Atkinson & Shiffrin, 1971). Investigators were intrigued by what happened when material received differing amounts of rehearsal either freely under a person's own control (e.g., Rundus, 1971) or as instructed by the experimenter (e.g., Hellyer, 1962).

There were other relevant manipulations as well, the most directly pertinent being part-list cuing (Slamecka, 1968; for a review, see Nickerson, 1984). Here, subjects studied a list and then were given part of that list at the time of the retention test and asked to remember the rest. Remembering was poorer on the rest of the list when subjects were given the part-list cues than when they were left on their own. This cost due to the part-list cues is reminiscent of the cost due to F items in the list. But over the last 30 years, directed forgetting has created its own niche in memory research. Let us begin by examining the seminal studies in the late 1960s and early 1970s.

THE GOLDEN AGE: 1968–1974

This first epoch of directed-forgetting research begins with the study that really established directed forgetting (Bjork et al., 1968). Because a few investigators were predominant in this early work, I organize my discussion in part by researcher rather than by topic, although the two overlap. As these studies heavily influenced what was to follow, I consider them in some detail.

Bjork, LaBerge, and Legrand (1968)

Although they cited the Muther study, it was Bjork et al. (1968) who really brought directed forgetting to the attention of memory researchers. They reported a single experiment. Subjects were presented with 48 lists of digits, each list also containing one or two target consonant strings (e.g., BKNR). Subjects were to name the digits and consonants targets, and then to recall them after each list. In some lists, subjects were warned just before the second consonant string target that the first one could be forgotten. When both targets had to be remembered, only about .15 of second targets were recalled, whereas approximately .39 were recalled from lists with only one target. When the first of two could be forgotten, recall accuracy for the second was about .30, a pattern like Muther's.

Bjork et al. concluded that allowing people to forget the first of two items reduced the proactive interference on the second one, improving its recall. In a way, this was another technique for producing "release from proactive interference" (cf. Wickens, 1970). Indeed, they even suggested that the case where the first item could be forgotten was more like that of a single item than of two items. They called their procedure "instructions to forget."

Most important, Bjork et al. set out four possible explanations. First, subjects might be able to *actively erase* items from short-term memory; like Muther, though, they saw this possibility as "intriguing but highly unlikely" (p. 56). Muther reported that F letters appeared more often as intrusions than did unpresented letters, indicating that the F items could not have been deleted. Thus, the erasure view never found favor. Second, Bjork et al. thought that not having to remember the first item might lead subjects to rehearse the second item more. Because their rapid presentation was intended to minimize rehearsal opportunities, they also saw this *selective rehearsal* account as "unlikely." Interestingly, Bjork (1972) would come to prefer this explanation in his review. Both of these accounts emphasized encoding differences between R and F words.

Their third account seems to have been a sort of *output interference* idea, with the extra load of other R items impairing recall of a target item when the whole list had to be remembered. Here, the analogy to part-list cuing resurfaces. This load could at least be reduced when part of the list was to be forgotten. Such an explanation segues nicely into their final account, the one Muther (1965) preferred. Subjects might be able to segregate or partition R items from F items by "actively tagging" them, the precursor to the *set differentiation–selective search* hypothesis that Epstein (1972) favored in his review. These two approaches shift the emphasis away from encoding and toward retrieval. The stage was set for the testing of these hypotheses to begin.

Bjork and Colleagues: Segregation and Selective Rehearsal

From the beginning, Robert Bjork emphasized the utility of directed forgetting as a sort of "model" (in the sense used in the animal literature) of the updating of memory. How we deal with new information that renders old information irrelevant is one of the major insights that he sees as coming from directed-forgetting research.

Bjork (1970) examined the reduction in proactive interference caused by a cue to forget prior material. Subjects studied 64 lists, each made up of one to eight syllable–word pairs presented on colored slides. Some subjects were told that, when the color of slides changed (once or not at all in a list), they could forget all prior pairs in that list. Other subjects were not told the significance of the cue. The number of precue pairs ranged from zero to three, thereby varying proactive interference.

For subjects not told to forget, performance on postcue pairs dropped as the number of precue pairs increased, demonstrating increasing proactive interference. Furthermore, precue pairs intruded on the recall of postcue pairs. For subjects given a forget cue, the number of F pairs prior to the cue did not matter and precue F pairs rarely intruded. Thus, F pairs caused virtually no proactive interference. Recall of F pairs (measured on the last four lists only) was poor but not zero. Thus, although they caused no proactive interference, F items were not entirely forgotten.

In Bjork's third experiment, the F cue could occur either before or after the R items. He used four-pair lists with one cue in the middle and one at the end. Consider recall of the second two pairs. When told to remember both sets, subjects recalled about .57; the same was true when they were initially told to remember and then later told to forget the first set (.62). But when told to forget the first set and remember the second, recall increased (.89), a clear directed-forgetting benefit. Now consider first-set recall. When both sets had to be remembered, recall was .54; when the first set was to be remembered and the second set could be forgotten, recall improved to about .65. Intrusion results also told a consistent story: Forgetting some items helped in remembering the others.

Bjork argued that subjects used F cues in two ways: to segregate R from F items (set differentiation) and to then rehearse only R items (selective rehearsal). He saw these two processes as demanding each other in that keeping sets differentiated would require different processing, and different processing would tend to keep sets separated. This view explained why the cue first to remember and later to forget the initial set failed in Experiment 3: Subjects had grouped the sets, but had not differentially rehearsed them.

Bjork's account also explained the findings of a related study by Reitman, Malin, Bjork, and Higman (1973).[4] They occasionally tested F pairs and showed two things: (a) Although F pairs did not intrude or interfere with recall of R pairs, they were quite often present in memory, and (b) F pairs did interfere with each other. When the F pair immediately before the cue to forget was preceded by no other F pairs, it was recalled .54 of the time; this value fell to .49 for one prior F pair and to .24 for two prior F pairs. Bjork saw this study as evidence that selective rehearsal alone could not explain directed forgetting. The F and R items appeared to behave as quite independent sets.

---

[4]This research actually was carried out earlier and was frequently cited as a 1971 technical report (see e.g., Bjork, 1972; Epstein, 1972). The reason this is worthy of note is that, even in its early form, this paper bore the title "Strategy control and directed forgetting," making it the first to introduce what would become the common name for the paradigm and the phenomenon.

Woodward and Bjork (1971) switched to longer lists and used the item procedure (colored dots) to signal the cue after each word. Subjects studied six 24-word lists, attempting to recall just the R words after each list. They earned 1¢ for each R word recalled and lost 1¢ for each F word recalled. Subjects recalled about .50 of R words, intruding only about .02 of F words. After all six lists, subjects were given a final recall test and earned 1¢ for every word recalled—whether F or R. Here, they recalled .23 of R words and .05 of F words. Manipulating presentation time from 1 to 4 sec had little effect, probably because subjects waited for the cue before processing an item. When asked to circle F words on a list of all studied words, subjects correctly circled .45 of the F words and only incorrectly circled .06 of the R words. This was the first use of a measure of cue retention.

In Experiment 2, each 24-word list was composed of six 4-word semantic categories. Each category could be all R, all F, or a mixture (cf. Horton & Petruk, 1980). Categorization had an interesting effect. As the number of R words in a category increased, recall of *both* R and F words improved: For the case of 2 R and 2 F words in a category, as recall of R words rose from 0 to 1 to 2 words, recall of F words rose from .03 to .46 to .54. Finally, cue retention was better in Experiment 2, with .74 of F words correctly identified and only .08 of R words incorrectly identified.

Woodward and Bjork (1971) offered several conclusions. First, they were impressed by the subjects' ability to avoid intruding F items, given random cues within lists. Second, although F items did not intrude in recall, they were still present in memory to some extent. In particular, when F items were categorically related to R items, facilitating their retrieval, they were much more likely to be remembered (see also Halmiova & Sipos, 1976). They were also surprised that differential grouping of R and F words could be done even within a semantic category. They retained Bjork's emphasis on selective rehearsal, but viewed rehearsal as having its impact on retrieval, not encoding. F items did not interfere because they were segregated via rehearsal, hence relatively unretrievable.

In a follow-up study, Bjork and Woodward (1973) made one change: Only three of the six lists were tested immediately for R items (a distractor task filled the test interval), and an additional one was tested for both F and R items. Subjects recalled many R words (.60) but intruded few F words (.02) on the immediate test. Recall of F words only went up to .05 on the single list where subjects had to recall all words, so F words were not just suppressed. What is intriguing, though, is their conclusion that "the results implicate rehearsal and organizational processes *at input* rather than suppression or selective retrieval processes during output" (p. 22, italics added), in contrast to their earlier conclusion that "the differential rehearsal devoted to R words operates primarily *on retrieval* rather than on storage" (Woodward & Bjork, 1971, p. 109, italics added). This "about-face" aside, they still favored the explanation that rehearsal led to set differentiation of the R and F items.

Woodward, Bjork, and Jongeward (1973) went on to argue that there was a type of rehearsal that simply maintained items in memory until the cue appeared. Subjects studied four 36-word lists, half R and half F items, using the item procedure. Each word was presented for 1 sec followed by a variable blank period prior to the 1-sec cue. Three R words and three F words were followed by each of six blank periods—0, 1, 2, 4, 8, or 12 sec— included to encourage differential rehearsal of the items.

The immediate and final recall data closely replicated Woodward and Bjork (1971; Bjork & Woodward, 1973). Intriguingly, the duration of the rehearsal interval prior to the cue had very little effect on immediate or final recall. Only when they measured final recognition in their third experiment did they find a beneficial effect of precue rehearsal interval duration. They concluded from these recognition data that any rehearsal, whether maintenance or elaborative, led to improved long-term retention of an item. However, only elaborative rehearsal benefited recall because it encouraged interitem association. Elaborative rehearsal was much more likely to occur for R items than for F items.

Woodward, Park, and Seebohm (1974) focused on the impact of an F cue at encoding versus retrieval. Subjects saw six 24-word lists, with one color cue designating the 8 F items in a list and two other color cues indicating the two sets of 8 R items. After each list, subjects were told what to recall. In immediate recall, two main findings emerged: (a) F words intruded very little, even when subjects were told to recall them, and (b) R words that subjects were told not to recall intruded considerably more than F words. In final recall, where subjects were to ignore previous instructions, there were again two main findings: (a) F words were still very difficult to recover, and (b) having had to recall F words immediately did not help them, but did somewhat reduce R-word recall. In final Yes–No recognition, there was a strong R–F difference, but memory for F items was evident.

Overall, Woodward et al. (1974) concluded that explicit cues to forget an item were quite different from implicit cues to not recall that item, both in recall and in recognition. They believed that it was the immediate contingency of the explicit F cue that made the difference. Subjects ceased rehearsal of explicit F items, whereas they only tried to edit recall of implicit F items. Thus "true" forget items were much less available in memory than were items simply not to be recalled.

In his review of this era, Bjork (1972) emphasized that we often need to change the priority of information in memory, and that a mechanism like directed forgetting may be one of the tactics we use to do so. His explanation of directed forgetting in this period is best put in his own words: "subjects take advantage of an F-cue in two ways: (a) They devote all further rehearsal, mnemonic, and integrative activities exclusively to R-items, and (b) they differentially group, organize, or code R-items in a way that functionally segregates them from F-items in memory" (p. 229).

Epstein and Colleagues: Segregation and Selective Search

William Epstein was the other dominant influence early on. He began by telling subjects the order in which to output items after list presentation (Epstein, 1969a), and was not surprised that recalling the beginning of a list before the end lowered recall of the end relative to recalling the end first; that was expected as a consequence of proactive and output interference. But, when told to output *only* the end part, subjects' performance on the end part was better than when they output the end part first, followed by the beginning. The obvious difference was that the beginning could be disregarded in the "only" case, analogous to a forget cue. He decided to explore this more closely.

Epstein (1969b) constructed eight 16-item lists, half of each list consisting of two-digit numbers and half consisting of words. Subjects were tested four times, after lists 2, 4, 6, and 8. On each test, subjects were cued to recall only words, only numbers, or one before the other. The results were similar for words and numbers, so I summarize just the word data. For the second half of the list, recalling only words (.70) was better than recalling words first (.62) or second (.49). For the first half of the list, output instruction made no difference (about .50 in all three cases). Experiments 2 and 3 confirmed this pattern for longer lists and equal recall time for different cues.

Experiments 4 and 5 switched to the item procedure, randomizing words and numbers in the list. This change eliminated the advantage for the "only" condition over the "first" condition. Epstein concluded that, to be effective, directed forgetting required discrete subsets of items. He offered two explanations for the advantage of the forget (only) condition. Put in the terminology of directed forgetting,[5] these were: (a) When the F cue is given, the F set is deleted from short-term memory, minimizing interference, and (b) because the F half of the list need not be rehearsed, it causes minimal inhibition on retrieval of the R half. The first idea corresponds to the erasure hypothesis and Epstein, too, rejected it. But the second hypothesis, which Epstein opted for, is apparently the first mention of what would eventually become the *retrieval inhibition* explanation.

Shebilske, Wilder, and Epstein (1971) had subjects study 24 lists, each made up of four syllable–word pairs presented for 2 sec each. For half of

---

[5] Briefly, Epstein and his colleagues referred to directed forgetting as the "only effect" (e.g., Shebilske, Wilder, & Epstein, 1971). Unless you were a directed-forgetting researcher, though, this label might seem a little "exclusionary," so they began using the term *directed forgetting* in 1972.

the subjects, the four words in a list were unrelated; for the other half, the first two words were from a different category than the second two. The cue was presented after presenting all four pairs and just before testing one pair. The procedure was equivalent to instructing subjects to remember all of the pairs or to forget the first two or the second two pairs. The advantage for the lists with both F and R items over those with only R items was greater for categorized (.23) than for uncategorized (.10) lists.

Intrusions were much less frequent for F items (.20 of intrusions) than for R items (.43). Also, intrusions of F items were less common in categorized lists (.12) than in uncategorized lists (.28), but there was no corresponding difference in R-item intrusion. Epstein et al. saw their findings as supporting a selective search account. In particular, distraction-filled versus unfilled intervals had little impact on the size of the directed-forgetting benefit. Filled intervals should prevent rehearsal, so this result seemed inconsistent with a selective rehearsal account. It is also noteworthy that their study showed that Bjork's findings generalized to the case of a cue given after all of the items in a set had been studied, a finding which also led Shebilske et al. to prefer the selective search account.

Epstein, Massaro, and Wilder (1972) attempted to pit the selective search and selective rehearsal accounts against each other. Their lists contained 6 pairs, with three response words from each of two categories. After each list, the cue was given and then a 3-sec filled or unfilled interval occurred. The selective rehearsal account predicts a larger directed-forgetting benefit for the unfilled intervals. Two tests were used: Half the time, subjects had to recall the response word of a critical pair; half the time, they had to pick it from the three R possibilities. Epstein et al. argued that the selection test made the search set for lists with F pairs equivalent to the search set for lists without F pairs. Therefore, directed forgetting should be evident only in recall and not in selection.

In Experiment 1, there was a directed-forgetting benefit for R words of about .13 in recall but only about .03 in selection, and this was true for both the filled and the unfilled intervals. (Note that R intrusions at .41 again vastly outnumbered F intrusions at .11.) However, when the selection test was modified in Experiment 2 to include all six possible responses—both the R and the F responses—the magnitude of the selection effect (.13) was virtually identical to that in the first experiment. Epstein et al. maintained that F cues provided tags to differentiate items at the time of retrieval, permitting subjects to search only among the R items.

Epstein and Wilder (1972) added a new wrinkle. On 8 of the 24 lists, they tested an F pair instead of an R pair, informing subjects of this on half of those trials. As always, they found higher R recall when a list contained F items (.70) than when it did not (.52). In contrast to Epstein et al., however, this advantage tended to be larger for unfilled intervals, implicating a role for selective rehearsal. Subjects correctly recalled the F items .44 of the time when informed but only .15 of the time when uninformed. F items intruded into the recall of R items only when subjects were trying to recover another F item. Otherwise, most intrusions were other R items.

The results were seen as strong support for selective search. Two new results buttressed this claim: (a) Subjects rarely recalled an F item when they did not know that an F item was being tested, and (b) when subjects did know that they were to recall an F item, their recall of F items improved dramatically, though not to the level of R items. However, Epstein and Wilder (1972) allowed that selective rehearsal also seemed to be operating, assigning it the role of maintaining the R set's readiness to be searched, thus enhancing the effect of selective search. This is a rather different interpretation than Bjork's that both processes are necessary and working in tandem.

Instead of testing only one pair from a short list containing F items, Shebilske and Epstein (1973) sometimes unexpectedly tested all of the pairs from the list in succession. This procedure was designed to abolish the opportunity for using selective search. They reasoned that this sort of "catch trial" would not eliminate the cue effect if the relevant operations had been done prior to retrieval (i.e., if the mechanism had to do with encoding). If, on the other hand, the cue effect was largely a retrieval phenomenon due to selective search, then it should disappear because the subject could not restrict search when all items were to be tested.

As always, memory was better for R items from a list containing F items (.69) than from one containing only R items (.53). However, for trials containing F items, the directed-forgetting benefit was smaller on "test all" trials (.06) than on trials where only R items were tested (.16). As usual, there also were fewer intrusions from F items but when subjects had to recall all of the items from a list, F items made up about half of the intrusions. Because the "test all" trials virtually eliminated the cue effect, Shebilske and Epstein (1973) concluded that selective search was the key mechanism. When conditions prevented this mechanism from operating, the effect essentially vanished. In their experiments, manipulations of rehearsal opportunities did not produce such dramatic effects.

In his review, Epstein (1972, p. 187) strongly advocated the selective search hypothesis, stating that "the data are sufficient grounds for concluding that selective search can account for many of the findings of directed forgetting experiments." He noted, though, that "unequivocal positive findings of erasure have not emerged" (p. 188), and allowed that this view still might have "genuine merit." He rejected a perceptual-encoding explanation on the basis that the cues came after perception and encoding, though this does imply quite a narrow definition of encoding. Most provocative, though, was his position on rehearsal: "We consider as uninteresting those effects of forget cues that are fully accountable in terms of differential rehearsal"

(p. 151). To Epstein, the mnemonic benefits of rehearsal were not "news-worthy," a view shared by Johnson (1994) in her recent review.

Elmes and Colleagues: Segregation and Short-Term Memory

David Elmes was one of the first to study directed forgetting in short-term memory. In Elmes (1969a, Experiment 2), subjects studied 12 lists where tests of some word pairs were interspersed with presentation of the other pairs. After either 8 or 10 pairs (from lists of 12 or 14 pairs, respectively), half of the subjects knew that they could "disregard" all prior pairs, and half did not. Although not explicitly told to forget, subjects could trust the cue because precue pairs were never tested. Contrary to Bjork et al. (1968), Elmes reported no reliable recall advantage on a subsequent critical pair for the group that could forget earlier pairs (.42) compared to the group that could not forget them (.37). Elmes (1969a) argued that the "isolation or emphasis" of the single critical item in the Bjork et al. lists, not the reduction in proactive interference, was the crucial element. Elmes' view is in essence a version of the tagging or selective search account.

Elmes (1969b) manipulated the amount of information to be forgotten. Subjects studied 24 lists of seven or eight pairs. This time, the cue was explicit and more obvious than in Elmes (1969a), and amounted to a cue to forget either three, four, or five untested prior pairs. As it turned out, the number of pairs prior to the cue did not matter, but recall of a subsequent critical pair was better following an F cue (.59) than following an R cue (.40). Elmes (1969b) held that the more explicit cue caused the stronger effect than in his prior study (Elmes, 1969a), now attributing this to selective rehearsal of the critical pair. The idea was that all items resided in short-term memory only as long as they were rehearsed, and that the F cue basically was a cue to discontinue rehearsal of the designated items, which then were not transferred to long-term memory. Tagging or isolation could not be the important feature because the same events transpired for both groups prior to the critical item.

In Elmes, Adams, and Roediger (1970), after half of the list was presented, half of the subjects were cued to forget prior pairs. Subsequent recall of the critical pair that followed the cue did not differ for the two groups. In Experiments 3 and 4, a cue was presented to both groups, with only one group told that this meant to forget all prior pairs. Now the directed-forgetting benefit reappeared in recall. In Experiment 4, the advantage was .24, with the cued group recalling .51 of critical pairs and the uncued group recalling only .27. Furthermore, intrusions from prior F items made up only .08 of all responses for cued subjects, but .25 of the responses for uncued subjects.

Elmes et al. (1970) added a four-alternative recognition test for the pairs. Of the correctly recognized items, .24 were precue items for the cued group and .26 were precue items for the uncued group, so there appeared to be no directed-forgetting benefit in recognition despite the clear advantage in recall. Unfortunately, Elmes et al. did not report postcue performance. Nevertheless, along with the study by Gross, Barresi, and Smith (1970), described later, this appears to have been the first published use of a recognition test to measure directed forgetting.

Elmes et al. considered four possible explanations for directed forgetting. First, they argued against active erasure and selective rehearsal because recognition did not differ for R and F items, showing that the F items were still in memory. Although they considered repression of F items, they were not impressed with the support for such a view. Instead, they favored *set differentiation*, closely allied to the selective search idea. They maintained that items in the F set were suppressed whereas those in the R set were selected. The mention of suppression would appear to be, following Epstein (1969b), an early version of what would become the *retrieval inhibition* account.

The final study in this set was a change of pace. Elmes and Wilkinson (1971, Experiment 1) showed subjects lists containing a four-word category, an eight-word category, and two eight-word categories in which four words were designated as F items. In Experiment 2, an uncategorized set of eight words was added, half cued to be forgotten. Collapsing over the experiments, recall of the four-item R-only categories (.43) exceeded that for the four R items from the F-cued category (.36), as expected. But performance for the eight-item R-only categories (.48) was best of all. Oddly, then, there was a directed-forgetting cost without a corresponding benefit. This may be because scoring appears to include the first four items in the eight-item categories; a better comparison would have been to only the last four of the eight. The uncategorized items from Experiment 2 also differed (R: .28, F: .05). Finally, despite being asked not to remember the precue items in F categories, subjects still recalled .20 of the categorized F items. The size of the remember–forget difference was similar for the categorized (.16) and uncategorized (.23) items despite overall better recall for the categorized items. Once again, a subsequent recognition test on just the last list (with twice as many distractors as targets) showed no effect of cue. This recognition–recall difference, together with a preliminary analysis of clustering in recall, was taken as confirming set differentiation of R and F items, but now there was evidence that such differentiation could occur even within a category.

The Elmes studies teach us several things. First, the F cue must be distinctive, and explicit use of the word "forget" seems to make a difference. Second, it is apparently valuable to compare recognition and recall. Third, both the directed-forgetting cost/benefit and the remember–forget difference are robust (but not guaranteed) effects, at least in recall. Fourth, these effects obtain for relatively short lists as well as for longer lists; the phenomenon is not limited to short-term memory.

Weiner and Colleagues: Repression

Because of his interest in repression (cf. Weiner, 1966), Bernard Weiner (1968) took a different tack in studying directed forgetting in short-term memory. In Experiment 1, he showed subjects letter trigrams and tested each 3, 9, or 17 sec after its presentation; number shadowing filled each retention interval. In Experiment 2, half of the subjects were asked to forget the trigrams between presentation and test on each trial whereas half were told to remember them. Forgetting rate was much more precipitous for the F group (.93 at 3 sec, .64 at 9 sec, and .40 at 17 sec) than for the R group (.97, .84, and .71, respectively). When, in Experiment 4, Weiner switched to a within-subject design and cued subjects immediately before each presentation whether to remember or forget that item, he replicated this pattern: for the F group (.87, .48, and .36) and for the R group (.93, .78, and .65). Giving the cue after presentation of the trigram also generated the same pattern in Experiment 5.

Further experiments in this series examined the situation where a shock was used to motivate forgetting. This procedure originated with Glucksberg and King (1967), who had subjects learn a 10-pair nonsense trigram–word list. Each word had a remote associate, as in the example pair *cef–stem*, where the remote associate *smell* can be reached through the sequence *stem–flower–smell*. Once subjects knew the initial pairs, they then studied a new list of pairs where the responses were the remote associates (e.g., *cef–smell*). Subjects were shocked each time 1 of 3 of the 10 pairs appeared until they could correctly anticipate those shocked pairs. Then, they had a single relearning trial on the original list. Recall of word responses from the original list was poorer after relearning if the response word's associate had been shocked (.71) than if it had not been shocked (.94). Glucksberg and King saw this as an experimental analog of repression caused by shock.

Weiner and Higgins (1969) maintained that the effects observed by Glucksberg and King were due to differential original learning, not to repression. In their Experiment 1, Weiner and Higgins failed to replicate Glucksberg and King: Forgetting was almost equivalent for both the shocked (.80) and unshocked (.82) pairs. They claimed that the pairs associated with shock in the Glucksberg and King study coincidentally were the hardest pairs to learn (although their Experiment 3 did replicate Glucksberg and King's original difference). In a reply, Glucksberg and Ornstein (1969) argued that shock and original learning level interacted, but that shock certainly affected recall.

Returning to Weiner's (1968) study, he incorporated shock for his final three experiments. In Experiment 6, he observed more forgetting for items associated with shock cues during both encoding and retrieval (.80, .57, .46 over the 3-, 9-, and 17-sec retention intervals) than for items that had an initial shock cue dispelled by a subsequent shock cue (.87, .55, .53) or for items that had no shock cue (.87, .58, .52). Weiner (1968, p. 223) maintained that his results supported "a process of active forgetting which is attributed to differences in memory storage as opposed to differences in trace formation." He explicitly rejected differential rehearsal, and also pointed out a concern that has not always received sufficient consideration in the directed-forgetting literature: "Perhaps the most serious experimental problem … is differential withholding (suppression)" (p. 223). Were subjects simply being cooperative, and how often is this a potential alternative to the more exciting idea of forgetting on cue? Demand characteristics (Orne, 1962) loom large as a threat to this paradigm.

Weiner and Reed (1969) attempted to test whether directed forgetting affected encoding or retrieval in short-term memory. They followed Weiner's (1968) procedure but used three cues, delivering one just prior to each stimulus: remember and rehearse, remember but do not rehearse, and forget. Because the results were similar, I present just their within-subject version of the experiment. Over the three retention intervals (3, 9, and 17 sec), recall declined differentially: for remember-and-rehearse (.97, .88, .82), for remember without rehearsing (.95, .77, .60), and for forget (.94, .64, .51). Forgetting rate was enhanced by nonrehearsal, but even more so by an F cue. Their second experiment tackled rehearsal directly. Subjects studied each item with the goal "to remember the stimuli without rehearsing, unless signalled to forget" (p. 228). All items were tested after 13 sec, but the F versus R cue could appear at 3, 6, 9, or 13 sec. If rehearsal is crucial, delaying the cue should reduce its effectiveness. Although F items were recalled about 8–10% less than R items, there was no effect of cue timing, which Weiner and Reed saw as further evidence against differential initial learning.

Their third experiment tackled retrieval directly. Here, each of 12 trigrams was shown twice, once in set 1 (trials 1–12) and once in set 2 (trials 13–24). All possible cue combinations were used. A large overall remember–forget difference (about .25) occurred in each set, as usual. More interesting, though, was the effect of the cue staying the same or changing on individual items over the two sets. On second presentation, performance was just as high for F–R items as for R–R items, and performance was just as low for R–F items as for F–F items. Weiner and Reed argued that memory for the first presentation of an F item was available but not used unless "released" when that item became an R item on the second presentation. Retrieval of a former F item was completely disinhibited when that item became an R item, neatly presaging Bjork's (1989) argument.

Weiner and Reed's final question concerned the extent to which directed forgetting was due to suppression (conscious) or repression (unconscious). They repeated Experiment 3, interviewing subjects extensively afterward. Two groups were isolated—suppressors (one third) who consciously used differential retrieval for R and F items, and repressors (two thirds) who did not. Weiner and Reed took the very similar patterns of data in these two groups as evidence that their findings did not depend on conscious strategies; I am not convinced. It seems as reasonable to argue that the demand characteristics that led subjects to withhold F items also led many of them to deny having "cheated," so that the apparent consistency in the two strategies really could reflect only one strategy.

Reed (1970) focused on retroactive interference (see also Decker, 1976). Many prior short-term memory studies gave the F cue after the first but before the second of two items, which he reasoned might have influenced encoding of the second item. So he moved the cue after the second item, following it by a 10-sec distraction interval. In Experiment 1, Reed contrasted recall of a single trigram studied alone (.91) to that when followed by an additional R trigram (.69) to that when followed by an additional F trigram (.94). The postencoding forget cue appeared to eliminate retroactive interference. In Experiment 2, Reed contrasted an F cue before versus after the filled interval and found that the "late" forget cue reduced recall from .54 to .44, the latter value being the same as in a control condition where only the first trigram was to be recalled. This suggests that a major function of a prerecall F cue is to eliminate retroactive interference.

But why does the F cue before the retention interval have an even larger effect? To discount a rehearsal explanation, Reed examined repeated presentation of the same items under changing instructions (cf. Weiner & Reed, 1969). Experiment 3 captures his idea. He ran a single trial in each of the conditions of Experiments 1 and 2 (except for the late forget condition), replicating the previous patterns. Then, all of the items from these trials were re-presented as R items. Now, recall of the trigrams did not differ as a function of original condition. Apparently, the conditions had not led to differential learning, so Reed concluded that the F cue affected retrieval from short-term memory, not storage. Interestingly, he argued that rehearsal played the role of maintaining items, not learning them, a view that would soon resurface (Woodward et al., 1973).

With the exception of Roediger and Crowder (1972; see later), Weiner was alone in his early emphasis on repression, which he also called retrieval inhibition; even his coauthor Reed did not use the term in subsequent writings. Yet repression would return in the work of Geiselman, Bjork, and Basden. Setting aside the problem of demand characteristics, the results of Weiner and Reed did seem to fit with the idea that F items and R items were equally well learned but that F items were difficult to recover. With selective search and differential rehearsal, retrieval inhibition would eventually become one of the three major explanatory mechanisms for directed forgetting.

Other Short-Term Memory Studies

Turvey and Wittlinger (1969) were among the first to examine the placement of the F cue. In Experiment 1, subjects saw a trigram for 2 sec, counted backward for 1 sec, and then tried to recall. For one group, F cues appeared at encoding, simultaneously with the trigram. For another group, all items were R items. Recall accuracy for R items in the two groups differed by about .20, favoring the group with F cues. In Experiment 2, locating the F cue at retrieval instead of encoding almost eliminated the difference between groups. Turvey and Wittlinger opted for a selective rehearsal explanation: Critical R items were rehearsed more only in Experiment 1, where rehearsal of other items could be avoided. They did admit, though, that not having to recall the items in Experiment 2 might have been crucial, recognizing the possible impact of differences in output interference.

Block's (1971) study is reminiscent of Reed's (1970). Following Bjork et al. (1968), he cued subjects to forget either the first or the second of two trigrams on some trials. When the second item was tested, subjects told to forget the first (.81) did much better than those not so instructed (.69). In fact, performance in the F-cued condition was no different from a single-item control (.84). However, when the first item was tested, subjects told to forget the second item (.46) were no better than those who had to remember it (.47), both substantially poorer than the single-item control (.76). Directed forgetting alleviated proactive interference but not retroactive interference. Because he had included a shadowing task to minimize rehearsal, Block favored a selective search or segregation account.

In Experiment 2, Block had subjects either remember or forget the first 6 words of a 12-word list; they always had to remember the last 6 words. Recall of the last 6 words was almost equivalent for subjects told to forget the first 6 (.58) as for those who did not see the first 6 (.60), but considerably worse for those told to remember all 12 words (.41). Block was among the first not only to test F items, but also to add a recognition test. The virtually identical recognition for the last 6, whether after an F cue ($d' = .60$) or an R cue ($d' = .63$), led him to argue against erasure and selective rehearsal because all memory tests ought to have been affected. This recognition–recall contrast came to be a standard argument in favor of the segregation explanation.

Roediger and Crowder (1972) investigated whether selective rehearsal could explain the short-term memory effects that Weiner (1968) took as evidence for repression. They thought Weiner's constant rate for his interpolated task might have prevented rehearsal only in some subjects, so they adopted the familiar Peterson and Peterson (1959) procedure. On each trial, subjects read a trigram and then counted backward from a 3-digit number for 3, 9, or 17 sec before attempting recall. A cue at encoding told subjects that, during number counting, they should either rehearse the item without disrupting number counting, remember the item without rehearsing, or forget the item. A final Yes–No recognition test followed all 54 trials. Separate counting-only blocks provided a baseline for counting performance on the critical trials.

Both main effects—cue and retention interval—were significant, as was the interaction. Thus, trigram recall was better with rehearsal (.91, .79, .78) than without rehearsal (.80, .72, .49), and worse for F items (.70, .52, .38). The counting data concurred, with counting fastest in the F condition, intermediate in the no rehearsal condition, and slowest in the rehearsal condition. Turning to recognition, the two R conditions hardly differed (.44 for rehearsal, .41 for no rehearsal), but both were more accurate than the F condition (.33). Roediger and Crowder maintained that there was no evidence in support of a retrieval inhibition account. Rehearsal was the critical mechanism.

Spector, Laughery, and Finkelman (1973) also worried whether prior attempts to prevent rehearsal (e.g., Shebilske et al., 1971) had been successful. They used trigram–word pairs in 32 lists of either 4 or 8 pairs with or without a filled or unfilled rehearsal opportunity following the list. Subjects studied each pair for 2 sec, then, halfway through the list, a 3-sec blank occurred, then the second half of the list was presented, followed by a 3-sec rehearsal/no rehearsal period. In Experiment 1, the cue always preceded the rehearsal interval; in Experiment 2, the cue either preceded or followed the rehearsal interval, which was always unfilled. The cue could indicate a test from only the first half of the list, only the second half, or either, like the procedure of Shebilske et al. (1971).

In Experiment 1, rehearsal definitely helped cued recall, as did being allowed to recall only half of a list. For four-item lists, having to recall all words resulted in accuracies of .50 for the rehearsed and .32 for the unrehearsed pairs. Only having to recall half of the list boosted recall to .68 for rehearsed and .39 for unrehearsed pairs. A muted version of this same result was evident for eight-item lists. The directed-forgetting benefit was considerably greater for rehearsed than for unrehearsed items, and about twice as large for shorter lists as for longer lists. This is in keeping with the critical role of rehearsal because there was about twice as much opportunity to rehearse in short lists. Experiment 2 supported this claim: When the cue preceded the rehearsal interval, recall was better if only half of the list was tested (.60) than if the whole list was tested (.50); when the cue followed the rehearsal interval, this directed-forgetting benefit vanished (both conditions at .50). Making differential rehearsal impossible by delaying the cue until after the rehearsal interval ended caused all evidence of a cue effect to disappear. Once again, selective rehearsal seemed to be the key.

Timmins (1973) closely followed Bjork's (1970) procedures. Subjects studied trigram–word pairs for 4 sec each in lists of eight R pairs, four R pairs, or eight pairs with a midlist cue to forget the first four. In a novel twist, an item from the F set was sometimes repeated in the R set. For just the comparable last four R items across conditions, the standard pattern obtained: Recall was better for the four-item list (.57) than for the eight-item list (.48), but the list containing an F cue showed no cost (.59). Most important, repeated items (.67) were better recalled than all others. If set differentiation was perfect, the probability of recalling this repeated F item should be no greater than that of the unrepeated R items because the prior instance of the repeated item was in the F set, and hence segregated. However, if rehearsal was the key, then the repeated item should be better recalled than its companion R items.

Waugh (1972; see later) previously reported a similar finding using free, rather than cued recall. Timmins argued that subjects were concentrating their rehearsal on the repeated items. But perhaps they had noticed the repeated items and directed rehearsal to them. Timmins (1975) tried to address this possibility, but a probable ceiling effect prevents straightforward interpretation.

In a close replication of Bjork et al.'s (1968) procedure, Yinger and Johnson (1973) extended the retention interval, measuring the effect of the forget cue at 6, 15, and 40 sec. They found a reliable directed-forgetting benefit at 6 sec and at 15 sec (both about .25 better when allowed to forget the first trigram vs. having to remember both), but no such difference after 40 sec. They attributed this to the short-term/long-term distinction, arguing that directed forgetting was limited to short-term retention intervals. Unfortunately, they did not explain why recall in the F condition dramatically *improved* (by about .30) from the 15-sec to the 40-sec interval, which calls their study into question.

Homa and Spieker (1974) predicted that, if selective search was operative, recall RTs should increase as the number of R items increased, and decrease in lists where an F cue allowed some items to be omitted from search. Subjects studied lists of either four, six, or eight word pairs. The use of pairs permitted timing from the onset of the stimulus term at the time of test. After half of each list was presented, a filler slide appeared, then the rest of the list was presented, followed by another filler slide, the cue, and the test slide. Items were presented for 2 sec with a 1-sec gap. Turning to the data, as predicted from the selective search view, RTs increased with list length for all lists and cue conditions, and subjects recalled R responses faster for lists containing an F cue (1.53 sec) than for all-R lists (1.73 sec). These results also fit with the accuracy data of Shebilske et al. (1971). Homa and Spieker concluded in favor of a selective search or retrieval account, but noted that this might only apply when a single F cue followed the list.

The last three studies in this section moved farther afield. Johnson (1971) used a new dependent measure, pupillary response. He gave five-word lists to subjects at a 2-sec rate. One group received midlist F cues for all prior words in that list; the other group did not. Johnson observed a highly contingent dilation–constriction pattern immediately after the F cue, with no corresponding change in the control group. Oddly, however, he did not report the recall data, so it is difficult to evaluate his finding. Furthermore, he pointed out the perennial problem with measures such as pupil response, specifically that "in many cases such pupil changes reflect the influence of information processing confounded with motivational effects" (p. 318). Although the pupil pattern suggested a change in information load given an F cue, it is hard to know whether this is motivational, cognitive, or both.

Martin and Kelly (1974) closely followed up Johnson (1971). In place of pupil dilation, they used a secondary simple RT task: While doing the memory task, subjects had to press a button as quickly as possible to turn off a light. In Experiment 1, they found only a small accuracy advantage for R words in lists with an F cue (.97) versus no F cue (.94), but a ceiling effect could be occurring here. The RT data are more interesting. For all-R lists, RTs increased as encoding progressed through the five studied items, and then decreased as retrieval progressed through the five items. Subjects seemed to load up and then unload. When an F cue occurred, secondary RTs dropped sharply, much like the pupil dilation effect. Furthermore, the fewer items that had to be remembered, the faster the RT. Martin and Kelly hypothesized a reduced search set in lists containing an F cue, although the data could also reflect reduced need for resource-demanding rehearsal of F items.

Burwitz (1974) extended the domain of directed forgetting to short-term memory for simple motor responses. Subjects had to learn lever displacements without visual feedback, and then reproduce them as accurately as possible following either a short (5 sec) or long (90 sec) retention interval. In the control condition, the test followed one movement. In the R condition, four other movements preceded the critical one; at test, subjects had to reproduce the critical movement first, then the others. In the F case, the four prior movements were cued to be forgotten right before or right after the critical movement. Error in reproduction of the critical final movement was the dependent measure. At the 5-sec retention interval, the R case and the F-after case were less accurate than the F-before and the control cases. At the 90-sec retention interval, the effects magnified and spread, with accuracy of reproduction still equivalent in the control and F-before case, but both F-after and R were even less accurate. Burwitz argued that there was clearly a strong role for cognitive control of interference in motor learning, as illustrated by the effect of an F cue.

Overall, the evidence for a directed-forgetting effect in short-term memory is considerable. If subjects are permitted or encouraged to cease thinking about an item, that item causes sharply reduced interference on other items that the subject must remember. Furthermore, the F item is rather poorly recalled, although its recognition may suffer little decrement. With the decline of short-term memory studies, directed-forgetting research moved toward studies of more extended learning and remembering. This trend was already becoming evident even in this first epoch.

Other Long-Term Memory Studies

This section features studies that are not all closely interrelated, but that involve directed forgetting of items in longer lists, outside the usual realm of short-term memory. Investigators began to explore the boundary conditions and susceptibilities of the novel directed-forgetting procedure.

Bruce and Papay (1970) explored the source of primacy in free recall: Was reduced proactive interference or more rehearsal the key? Subjects studied five lists of words at 2.5 sec per word. In two lists, all words were to be remembered; one list contained 20 words and one contained 35 words. In two other lists, an F cue appeared after 15 words, then either 20 or 35 more R words were presented. For these four lists, subjects were to recall only the R words. Finally, for half of the subjects, the fifth list had 15 words before an F cue and 20 words after it, and subjects were asked to recall both R and F words. Control subjects had a fifth list containing 35 words without a cue.

Over the first four lists, primacy was equivalent for lists with versus without prior F words. Under the proactive interference account, lists with prior F items should have shown reduced primacy. Now consider the final list. For subjects given an F cue, words were recalled more poorly in positions 1–5, just as well in positions 6–11, and more poorly in positions 12–15 compared to subjects without an F cue. Apparently, rehearsal of the last few words prior to the cue—the words presumably in short-term memory—was interrupted. Perhaps, too, continued rehearsal of the earliest items was curtailed. Interestingly, these patterns were not evident on a four-alternative recognition test. Both tests did show, however, much better memory after the cue for those subjects given an F cue. Bruce and Papay replicated this pattern with an auditorily presented list (Experiment 1) and also demonstrated that simply including an odd item (the von Restorff effect; see Wallace, 1965) in the position of the F cue did not lead to the same pattern (Experiment 3). They concluded that primacy was the result of differential rehearsal of early list items.

Archer and Margolin (1970) examined whether the arousal properties of white noise would affect the action of R versus F cues. Subjects studied lists of 16 two-digit numbers, half followed randomly by each cue. Crossed with cue was the presence versus absence of a burst of 100 dB white noise before or after the list. Numbers and cues were presented for 3 sec each, with white noise for 1 sec. The test involved selecting from a complete list all those numbers that had been shown with an R cue versus an F cue. There was a strong effect of R (.74) versus F (.17) cues on digit identification, probably enhanced by the fact that F items were not identified until after R items. Noise did improve performance for R items (.81 with, .69 without), but had no effect on F items. They argued that the F cue terminated both further processing of the item and any advantage due to arousal.

Bugelski (1970) examined what he called "anti-intentional learning" (a term that did not catch on). Subjects read each of 32 words in a list aloud four times. Half of the words had a plus sign above them. One group was told to learn only those words with the plus sign, and to inhibit, not learn, or "tune out" the words without the plus sign; the plus sign was not explained to the other group. The control group recalled .42 of the signed words and .45 of the unsigned words. The experimental group, who had the "forget" cue, recalled .56 of the signed words but only .26 of the unsigned words. Thus, there was a benefit of .14 for R items and a cost of .19 for F words.

Bugelski also explored imagery. Of primary interest, a group instructed to image all words but to then inhibit those without signs recalled almost the same proportion of signed (.49) and unsigned (.46) words (although it is odd that imaging conferred no advantage over the control group). A group instructed to image only the signed words and to inhibit the others showed an advantage for signed words (.61) over unsigned words (.22)—a benefit of .12 and a cost of .24. Overall, imagery instructions hardly altered the standard pattern. To my knowledge, there has been no further exploration of imagery and directed forgetting. Because of the absence of an imagery effect here, it is not clear whether we can draw any conclusion about the interplay between these two instructional manipulations. However, it is interesting that the group told to image all words and inhibit half of them could not do so. Perhaps a strong encoding is less subject to directed forgetting.

Gross et al. (1970) studied what might be described as "shared forgetting." Subjects heard a list of 18 word pairs, with one word in each pair assigned a value of 50 times the other (25¢ vs. ½¢). Subjects took part in dyads, with one member of the dyad determining which word in each pair was to be remembered by each subject. After study, subjects were tested on either their own words or those of their partner. In essence, there were really two R versus F cues at encoding: Remember the more valuable items, and remember your own items. In Experiment 1, subjects did recall their own words (.49 high value, .39 low value) better than their partner's words (.24 high value, .19 low value), also showing an effect of value. This was not the case in Experiment 2: Neither manipulation mattered when the test was three-alternative recognition using related distractors (all means around .46). Gross et al. concluded that the critical mechanism was differential rehearsal, which subjects used primarily when they expected a recall test.

An important study for several reasons is that of Davis and Okada (1971). Subjects studied three 64-word lists at 1 sec per word, followed by 1 sec per cue, with half R words and half F words in each list. For the first two lists, recall of F words was discouraged and recall of R items (.26) was much higher than that of F items (.03). For the third list, subjects were asked to recall both the R items (.27) and the F items (.05), making little difference. It is noteworthy that the R words showed a standard bowed serial position curve, but the function for the F words was flat (although a floor effect may have been responsible).

The main goal of Davis and Okada was to examine Yes–No recognition performance following directed forgetting. The result was clear: There was a strong advantage for R items (.70) over F items (.50). Davis and Okada were also among the first to test retention of the cues originally associated with each word. Of the words correctly recognized, .83 of R words versus only .64 of F words were correctly labeled. So subjects had decent ability to discriminate R from F items, at least for correctly recognized words. But the key result in Davis and Okada's study was the strong remember–forget difference in recognition, which they claimed was inconsistent with any retrieval-based account (e.g., inhibition), and more in keeping with a selective rehearsal effect on encoding.

Waugh (1972, Experiment 2) used directed forgetting to investigate why long lists are harder to remember than short ones. Subjects studied normal 20-word and 40-word lists, plus 40-word lists with a midlist cue to "erase" the first 20 words. Recall accuracy was .26 in the 20-word list. For the normal 40-word list, recall accuracy was .10 for the first 20 words and .19 for the second 20 words. For the "erase" 40-word list, recall accuracy was .03 for the first 20 words and .24 for the second 20 words. Thus, there was almost no directed-forgetting cost. In her third experiment, Waugh showed that the erase condition was essentially unchanged if half of the items in the second half of the list were repetitions of items in the first (or "erased") half of the list (cf. Timmins, 1973, 1975). Her conclusion was that information had to be re-rehearsed periodically to remain accessible, and that the likelihood of such rehearsal was greater in shorter lists, including lists where subjects were permitted to forget some of the items, thereby leading to a functionally shorter list.

Timmins (1974) explored variations in processing time on the effect of an F cue. In each list, subjects saw 15 words, each set of 5 followed by a cue. "Forget set 1" could appear after 5, 10, or 15 words; "forget set 2" could appear after 10 or 15 words; otherwise, the cue was "continue." Then, just prior to testing, subjects were cued to recall sets 1 and 3 or sets 2 and 3. (Unfortunately, Timmins did not report recall of F words or recognition of R words.) Recall of set 3 was uniformly good (.80 to .86) and unaffected by the presence or location of the F cue. For set 2, recall accuracy was .41 without a set 1 F cue, and declined from .74 to .51 to .43 as the F cue for set 1 moved to later in the list. For set 1, recall was .49 without a cue to forget set 2, and declined from .61 to .47 as the F cue for set 2 moved to later in the list. Thus, F words interfered less when subjects could act on the cue right away. Indeed, placing the F cue after the list eliminated its value (see also Spector et al., 1973). These claims were supported by the recognition data for F words: Recognition improved for both set 1 items (.45, .66, .64) and set 2 items (.42, .59) as the F cue moved to later in the list, presumably because those items benefited from more processing with later F cues.

Woodward et al. (1973) showed that items are minimally rehearsed until their cue appears in the item method. What Timmins added is that when the F cue is delayed in the list method, subjects cannot suspend processing so they rehearse as they would for R items, eroding the potential value of the F cue. Holding words in memory that will eventually be designated as F words improves memory for those words, but at the expense of the R words in the list. This pattern is entirely consistent with a rehearsal account.

Finally, taking a more indirect approach, Kausler and Settle (1974) used homophones (e.g., kernel, colonel) to investigate false alarms in recognition. Subjects studied 22 F words and 38 R words for 3 sec each using the item method. Among the 60 recognition test items were 12 studied words, 12 F-word homophones, 12 R-word homophones, and 24 unrelated words. Homophones produced more false alarms for R words (.16) than for F words (.12), relative to control items (.10), averaging over experiments. Thus, even an indirect test suggests that F items are less accessible, undermining demand characteristic concerns that subjects simply withhold F items on the test.

Summary of the Golden Age

Over the first decade of directed-forgetting research, several things became clear. First, the effect of an F cue was consistently quite powerful, independent of the specific procedures used. The effect was apparent in both short-term and long-term memory. However, its consistency in recall was not reflected in recognition. Many of these early studies contrasted the case where a list contained an F cue to the case where all items were to be remembered. Thus, the comparison was between R items accompanied by other R items or by F items. Both benefits for R items and costs for F items were reported, primarily in accuracy of recall (and sometimes recognition) but also in latency.

This first epoch also introduced all of the major theoretical accounts that would come to dominate subsequent explorations of directed forgetting right up to the present. The erasure idea—that F items were culled from memory—was quite quickly discarded. Apart from the work of Weiner and his colleagues, few investigators subscribed to the notion that F items were repressed (or inhibited) at the time of retrieval. But the ideas of segregation and differential rehearsal, advocated by Bjork, and of selective search, advocated by Epstein, garnered much attention and support. The stage was set to expand the study of directed forgetting, a promising new memory tool.

THE SILVER AGE: 1975–1985

Over the next decade, directed forgetting became more of a subject of study in its own right. What made directed forgetting work? How did the encodings of R and F items differ? To what situations might the manipulation be extended? How did directed forgetting differentially influence the emerging new types of memory tests? These were a few of the questions that guided research on directed forgetting through the formative years of its "adolescence." As in the early years, there was also one investigator who was featured in this era, so I end with an overview of his work. This work is especially relevant because it also laid the foundation for a shift in the preferred explanation of directed-forgetting effects toward inhibitory mechanisms, a shift that was occurring throughout cognitive psychology (see, e.g., Arbuthnott, 1995). To begin, though, I consider the last of the short-term studies before turning to the burgeoning long-term memory research.

Last of the Short-Term Memory Studies

Most work on short-term effects of directed forgetting is tied to the Golden Age. But a few short-term memory studies using response latency trickled over into the more eclectic Silver Age.

Using recognition latency as the dependent measure, Epstein, Wilder, and Robertson (1975) tested whether the search set was smaller when a list contained F items. Subjects studied four-pair trigram–word lists with each pair presented for 4 sec. F cues appeared either before or after the list (remember only the first two or the last two pairs); R cues always followed the list. Each of the 96 lists was followed with a one-pair test to which the subject responded yes (for studied pairs) or no (for re-paired items) as quickly as possible. On "no" trials, the re-pairing could be within set or across set, but was always within list. Averaging over response types (because they behaved alike), performance was slowest and most accurate on R trials (2002 ms, .23), intermediate on F-after trials (1890 ms, .17), and fastest and least accurate on F-before trials (1606 ms, .10). Epstein et al. concluded that the presence of an F cue reduces the search set more for a prior than for a subsequent F cue. The fact that a postlist F cue nonetheless led to more rapid search suggested to them that the R and F items are separated and can be searched at least partially independently.[6]

Howard (1976) reported much the same pattern (Epstein et al., 1975, had modeled their study on an earlier Howard technical report). She used shape–picture pairs, presenting four in each block at a rate of 6 sec per pair, with the first two distinguished from the second two by slide color. Cues were delivered either at the middle of the block or after it. Once again averaging over similarly behaved response types, R trials were the slowest and most accurate (1773 ms, .13); however, F-after (1615 ms, .10) and F-during (1547 ms, .03) were more comparable. Presumably because subjects now

---

[6]A cautionary note must be sounded: The speed–accuracy tradeoff pattern evident in this study and the next one complicate interpretation.

had to encode and process the first two items at least until they received the midlist cue, which they did not have to do in the F-before condition of Epstein et al., the F-after and F-during conditions differed less. As in many directed-forgetting studies (see especially Epstein's early work), being able to avoid encoding is quite different from encoding and then trying to forget. Howard argued that the R and F items were segregated, possibly with the aid of selective rehearsal.

Virtually all directed-forgetting studies have used verbal materials: Cruse and Jones (1976) used auditory tones instead. If differential rehearsal alone caused directed forgetting, and if tones could not be rehearsed, then directed forgetting should not affect tones. They modified the Sternberg (1969) memory-scanning paradigm, following the lead of Kaminsky and DeRosa (1974), who showed that when the search set was divided into two subsets (letters and digits), subjects could restrict their search to one of the subsets. Cruse and Jones' idea was that, for a memory set of both R and F items, subjects would only have to search the R items. Using set sizes of one to four tones, with one to three of those to be remembered, they tested subjects with R items (yes) versus new items (no) as probes. They also included a few F probes, also "no" responses. Study tones were presented for 500 ms each with a 500 ms R or F cue between successive tones and a test tone after a 1200 ms gap.

When only one tone had to be remembered, response times were faster (in the range of 325 ms) than when more than one tone had to be remembered (425–450 ms). Thus, there was a cue effect, but limited to a single R item. Furthermore, there was still an effect of the F items: The search slope with a single R item, although shallow, was nonzero. Cruse and Jones argued that because they observed directed forgetting for a single R item, and assuming that rehearsal was not possible for tones, then selective rehearsal was not an adequate explanation. They preferred a selective search explanation, noting that ability to segregate the search in short-term memory might suffer as more items in the R set increased the memory load, disrupting the segregation.

The Growth of Long-Term Memory Studies

Most of the studies after the first 10 years involved longer lists. In part, this was no doubt due to the increasing impact of the levels of processing framework (Craik & Lockhart, 1972), with its emphasis on the processing and retention of larger amounts of material.

Rakover (1975) manipulated test expectations. Subjects studied a list of nine trigrams and nine 3-digit numbers, with one group told to remember trigrams only, and the other told to remember numbers only. This cue was given prior to study, nonoptimal because subjects can simply ignore the F set, instead of encoding and then having to forget them. The list was shown 1, 3, 5, 7, or 14 times. After study, all subjects were required to free recall the trigrams only. For the digits group, accuracy was only about .22 overall, and was relatively unaffected by number of study trials: .14, .19, .24, .30, and .20. However, for the trigram group, recall was much better overall (.73) and rose with number of presentations: .44, .71, .64, .87, and .98. Rakover concluded that F items were dropped from short-term memory whereas R items continued to be processed, essentially a selective rehearsal account.

In a follow-up study, Rakover (1976) manipulated list length (3 vs. 12 of each type of item). Lists were made up either of digits and trigrams, only digits, or only trigrams, and subjects were told in advance which to remember. When tested, all subjects had to recall trigrams only. For lists containing both types of items, trigram recall was much better for the R group (.91 and .50 for 3 and 12 item lists, respectively) than for the F group (.11 and .05, respectively). For lists containing only one type of item, the pattern was similar: for the R group, .83 and .47; for the F group, .29 and .14. Once again, Rakover argued that F items received less postpresentation rehearsal.

Rakover and Kaminer (1978) tested the rehearsal idea in one more study. Subjects studied 15 trigrams at a rate of one every 2 sec. In one condition, they saw each trigram once and were to remember all of them. In three other conditions, they saw each trigram twice, with the lag between repetitions manipulated. One condition required remembering all of the trigrams, one required remembering any underlined trigram, and one required forgetting any underlined trigram (always on its second presentation). Recall accuracy for F items rose from about .08 to .21 with lag in the group told to forget underlined trigrams. Recall accuracy was a steady .20 to .30 for the three other groups. Recognition showed a similar lag pattern. Rakover and Kaminer suggested that the increase with lag in the F condition was due to F items being increasingly more rehearsed with longer gaps between successive presentations. With a long enough gap, there was almost no cost for F items.

Jongeward, Woodward, and Bjork (1975) promoted the idea of segregation. Subjects saw five 32-word lists divided into 8 four-word blocks, with each block followed by a cue that either preceded or succeeded a 3-sec rehearsal period. That cue required remembering all four words in the block, only the first two, only the last two, or none of them. After all five lists had been studied and tested, there was a final recall test for all words from all lists. For the rehearsal group, recall of R words from lists containing F cues (.38 immediate; .18 final) was better than recall of the corresponding words from lists of only R words (.30 immediate; .13 final); for the no rehearsal group, these two conditions did not differ (F cues: .36 and .16; R cues: .34 and .15). Both groups recalled F items poorly, at less than .10. Selective rehearsal benefited R items, even given identical search set sizes for R and F items. Jongeward et al. were especially impressed at the ability of subjects to keep the R and F items apart, arguing that segregation was the critical mechanism.

In contrast, MacLeod (1975) argued for a selective rehearsal interpretation based on the effects of F cues over a long retention interval, in this case 1 or 2 weeks. In Experiment 1, subjects studied 60 words made up of 3 each from 20 semantic categories. The setup was 3 sec for the category name, 3 sec each for the words, and 6 sec for the cue, with half of the categories being R cued and half F cued. Either immediately after study or 1 week later, subjects completed category-cued recall and three-alternative recognition tests. The R–F difference was the same regardless of test type or retention interval: There was a constant .10 advantage for R over F items on both tests at both retention intervals. Assuming that set-differentiating information would be lost before item-specific information, then a selective search account predicts that the R–F difference should diminish with retention interval; it does not. Moreover, the effect is constant in recall and recognition. Both results are inconsistent with selective search, but quite in keeping with selective rehearsal.

In Experiment 2, MacLeod switched to unrelated items. Subjects saw each of the 38 studied words for 3 sec, followed by its cue for 3 sec. A three-alternative recognition test was administered 1 or 2 weeks later. For each item, subjects either were told the original cue associated with that item or they had to recall that item's original cue. There was a strong R–F difference, and recognition declined with retention interval (R-1 = .68; F-1 = .53; R-2 = .64; F-2 = .47). Providing subjects with the original cues did not matter, conflicting with the selective search account. Overall, MacLeod favored a selective rehearsal explanation because of the persistence of the effects over long retention intervals.

To examine rehearsal more closely, Wetzel and colleagues manipulated the timing of F cues. In the first of this series, Wetzel (1975) combined a levels-of-processing manipulation of encoding with directed forgetting. Subjects heard three lists of 16 words each under one of two encoding conditions:[7] They were either to write down the word, or to write down an adjective to modify the word. In Experiment 1, each word was presented for 5 sec and then an R or F cue was presented, with 1 sec before the next word appeared. In Experiment 2, this timing was reversed. Cues were randomized through the list, with half of the words receiving each cue. Subjects recalled each list immediately, and then had an unmentioned final recall and a final Yes–No recognition test after all of the lists.

---

[7]There were actually three conditions, the third being a rhyme encoding, but because the rhyme-encoding and adjective-encoding conditions did not differ, and because the rhyme-encoding condition was not included in Experiment 2, I deleted it.

The patterns over experiments were virtually identical, so I only report Experiment 1. On immediate recall, there was a large R–F difference for both rehearse words (R: .61, F: .13) and adjective words (R: .36, F: .12). Serial position analyses showed recency for both R and F words but primacy for R words only. Most intriguing, the levels-of-processing manipulation affected only R words. Final recall showed a similar, though muted, pattern (rehearse, R: .33, F: .13; adjective, R: .21, F: .12). Final recognition showed an even more muted pattern (rehearse, R: .75, F: .64; adjective, R: .67, F: .59). Wetzel argued that the potential of differential processing prior to the cue was only realized for R words: The F cue stopped further processing of F words. This was entirely consistent with a selective rehearsal account, with items held in limbo until the instruction tells the subject what to do, so that only R items benefit from prior processing. The fact that the duration of the cue interval had little impact is also consistent with subjects waiting for the instruction.

To delve into cue delay, Wetzel and Hunt (1977, Experiment 2) again manipulated the time between successive words. For half of the subjects, this was done within list. In the long-delay group, subjects had 1, 4, 8, or 12 sec before the cue and 1 sec after it; in the short-delay group, they had 1 sec before the cue and 1, 4, 8, or 12 sec after it, thereby keeping the total interval between words comparable. For the other half of the subjects, the rehearsal intervals were the same, but were manipulated between lists, such that a given list had only one of the four intervals. Subjects heard four 32-word lists, with a random half of the words in each list followed by each cue.

In the within-list case, there was little effect of the four rehearsal intervals, with short-delay R words (.64) showing better immediate recall than long-delay R words (.46) regardless of delay. In the between-list case, performance rose steadily as a function of rehearsal interval: Short-delay R words (.36, .57, .75, .84) again were better recalled than long-delay R words (.38, .47, .60, .61). F words showed the opposite pattern: Long-delay words (between list: .07, .10, .13, .14; within list: .17, .10, .11, .18) showed some benefit of rehearsal compared to short-delay words (all around .04). Presumably, the short delay helped R items by reducing interference before further processing; the long delay helped F items by permitting a little rehearsal prior to suspension of processing. Final recall showed similar although attenuated effects. Recognition also showed a strong R advantage, but all of the long-delay performance shifted upward, demonstrating the important role of maintenance rehearsal in recognition. Also, recognition of F words was relatively better than was recall of F words, although still far from the level of R-word recognition. Wetzel and Hunt saw these results as strong evidence of selective rehearsal in directed forgetting. The contrasting impact of delay on the R and F items is a particularly nice illustration of the importance of duration versus kind of rehearsal.

Tzeng, Lee, and Wetzel (1979) looked at how well subjects could judge when R versus F items had appeared in a list. In Experiment 1, subjects studied a 40-word list at 2 sec per word and 3 sec per cue, with half of the words randomly assigned R and F cues. Recall was much better for the R words (.65) than for the F words (.17); recognition showed a less dramatic but still reliable difference (R: .95; F: .87), perhaps limited by a ceiling effect. But the focus was on the last test, where subjects judged the serial position of each word they had recognized in terms of five-item successive blocks of the list. Position judgments were very accurate for R words, but extremely poor for F words.

In Experiment 2, Tzeng et al. used another measure of temporal judgment. On the same list, recall of R words (.61) was again better than recall of F words (.22). Subjects then judged for pairs of words which one had appeared earlier or later in the list. Accuracy declined from .83 for R–R pairs to .71 for R–F pairs to .60 for F–R and F–F pairs, where the first member of each pair was the one that actually appeared first in the list. Tzeng et al. argued that accessibility of the first item at the time of encoding the second one is crucial for the pairwise judgment, explaining the advantage of an R item being first in the pair. Overall, Tzeng et al. saw their studies as evidence that temporal coding occurs quite automatically for R items but not for F items. Temporal information could even be part of the basis for the segregation of the R- and F-item sets that must underlie selective rehearsal (cf. Bjork, 1972).

Deviating from strict chronological order, a later study by Jackson and Michon (1984) is relevant here. First, they nicely replicated the Tzeng et al. (1979, Experiment 1) order results using both concrete and abstract words. Then, based on an examination of the correlations between judged position and actual position, they went on to argue that unrecalled R items, like F items, might not have been entered into the rehearsal set, which apparently is crucial for good retention of temporal order, and therefore usually favors R words. In arguing that temporal order information is not automatically encoded, they made it clear that there is very little temporal information for F items, consistent with F items not being rehearsed at the time of encoding.

Like Wetzel (1975), Horton and Petruk (1980) focused on the type of encoding that subjects engaged in and the timing of the cue. Each word in the three 24-word lists was presented for 2 sec followed by a 2-sec cue. A further 5 sec was assigned to encoding task—structural (write a word starting with the same letter), phonemic (write a rhyming word), or semantic (write a word from the same category). For half of the subjects, cues preceded encoding tasks; for half of the subjects, cues followed encoding tasks. For one third of each of these groups, the words were unrelated; for one third, the words were categorized and the cues honored the categories (e.g., forget all fruits, remember all animals), and for one third, the lists were categorized but the cues divided categories (e.g., forget half of the fruits and half of the animals, remember the other half of each).

In immediate recall, R words (.51) were better remembered than F words (.23). As well, unlike Wetzel (1975), there was a typical levels-of-processing effect, with semantic (R: .50; F: .31) better than phonemic (R: .35; F: .20) and structural (R: .36; F: .20). Note that the R advantage was greatest in the semantic condition. Collapsing over encoding condition, unrelated lists were more poorly recalled (R: .28; F: .13) than lists of honored categories (R: .44; F: .29) or divided categories (R: .49; F: .29). As for cue location, R items benefited from prior cues (.54) versus subsequent cues (.48), but this manipulation did not matter for F items (.22 and .23, respectively). Final recall data patterns were quite similar. Recognition also showed a reliable effect of instructional cue.

Horton and Petruk emphasized the relation between set differentiation and level of processing. The R and F sets were better separated, allowing a greater advantage for R items, when the cues preceded the words and when the words were processed more semantically. Under selective rehearsal, more semantic processing should have improved memory for both R and F items, undermining segregation. In fact, the opposite happened. Horton and Petruk argued that R and F items were stored separately, casting their vote for selective search (cf. Epstein, 1972).

At the outset, I mentioned Slamecka's (1968) part-list cuing effect as related to directed forgetting. When shown part of the studied list at the time of testing, subjects recall the remainder of the list more poorly than without such cues. Roediger and Tulving (1979) bridged these two topics. In Experiment 1, subjects studied two 64-word lists made up of eight items from each of eight categories, with the words from every category beginning with the same eight letters. The lists were presented at a 2-sec rate, one category at a time. Following study, subjects received either a standard free recall test or one of two "exclusion" tests on both lists. In one exclusion test, subjects were told not to recall items from four specified categories; in the other, they were told not to recall items beginning with four specified letters. The two lists were studied and tested one at a time.

In contrast to the usual pattern in directed forgetting, recall was slightly poorer when subjects had to exclude some items (.29) than when they were free to recall any items at all (.33). Switching to excluding two or six categories or letters in Experiment 2 hardly changed the pattern. In Experiment 3, subjects studied either a 30-word list (six categories) or a 60-word list (12 categories). They then recalled all of the words or, in the 60-word list, only a specified half of the categories corresponding to the 30-word list. Not surprisingly, more words were recalled from the 60-word list, about .53. But recall of the 30-word list was about .62 whereas recall of only a specified 30 of the words in the 60-word list was .47. Exclusion of part of the list resulted in poorer recall than was observed for a corresponding shorter list, analogous to their earlier part-list cuing experiments.

In directed forgetting, the cue is given during study. In part-list cuing, the cue is given at the time of retrieval. Roediger and Tulving's main claim was that a cue to forget will ordinarily be successful only when given during encoding. If given at the time of testing, the cue would have to uniquely specify what was to be recalled (e.g., one of only two categories) in such a way as to permit rapid recall, thereby benefiting by avoiding output interference.

In a more naturalistic study related to the upcoming Geiselman studies of text recall, Golding and Keenan (1985) gave subjects a set of verbal directions to remember. One group received the basic directions, a second received the basic directions plus an extra item, and the third received the basic directions, the extra item, and an instruction to forget the extra item. On an immediate recall test, performance on R information was worse for the two groups with the extra item (R: .30; F: .28) than for the group with just the basic directions (.35), but there was no R–F difference. The same pattern occurred on a verbal recognition test (R: .58; F: .64; basic: .72). Furthermore, neither recall nor recognition showed any difference in performance on the F items. It was only when subjects drew the map that the F cue helped memory for the R items by reducing the memory load (R: .53; F: .74; basic: .69). They concluded that subjects encode F information together with R information and mark the F information as wrong, to help keep track of what is in fact correct.

Geiselman and Colleagues: From Selective Rehearsal to Repression

Edward Geiselman was the most active researcher in the area of directed forgetting during this middle era. It is probably not surprising that he was a colleague of Bjork's at UCLA during much of this time. Initially, his explanation of directed forgetting relied primarily on selective rehearsal, but his perspective changed quite dramatically over the 10-year period.

Geiselman's early work used sentences. In the first study (Geiselman, 1974), subjects studied 10-sentence passages, with each sentence shown for 5 sec, followed by a 1-sec R or F cue and a 5-sec blank interval. The first two passages were followed by recall tests for R items only, and the last was followed by either a recall test or a sentence completion test of both R and F items. R items from the last passage were better recalled (.74) than the corresponding R items from the first two passages (.57), a directed-forgetting benefit of .17. Furthermore, recall of F items from the last passage (.40) was worse than recall of the corresponding R items, a directed-forgetting cost of .17. On the sentence completion test, R items were completed reliably better (.87) than F items (.75).

Geiselman took the subjective reports of rehearsal during the blank intervals and the symmetry of the cost and benefit results as strongly supporting selective rehearsal. He discounted an explanation in terms of earlier output of R items by replicating the experiment and requiring output of the F items first: The results were unchanged. He also noted that the size of the effect seemed smaller for meaningful materials like sentences than for individual, isolated words. This may have been the result of remembered R sentences serving as retrieval cues for related F items, thereby undermining successful directed forgetting (see Golding, Long, & MacLeod, 1994).

Next, Geiselman (1975) showed subjects 10 sentences from each of two different themes, in random order. In advance, half of the subjects were told to remember all of the sentences from both themes and half were told that they could forget all of the sentences from one of the themes. Sentences within a theme were either ordered or scrambled, with each shown for 7 sec, followed by a 7-sec blank interval. R sentences enjoyed a strong benefit in recall for lists containing F sentences (.50) relative to lists of only R items (.23). Moreover, presenting either the R or the F sentences in order benefited recall of R items. Experiment 2 used eye movements to reveal that easier encoding of the sentences and easier grouping of the themes both contributed to the advantage due to ordered presentation of the sentences. Geiselman concluded that his results supported the need for both the grouping and the selective rehearsal elements of Bjork's (1972) account of directed forgetting.

Geiselman and Riehle (1975) extended this study to show that, like R sentences, recall of F sentences benefited from being presented in order. For just the R sentences in lists containing both R and F sentences from Geiselman's (1975) study, accuracy was .64 when both R and F sentences were ordered versus .36 when both were scrambled. Having just the F sentences ordered (.53) led to slightly better recall than having just the R sentences ordered (.46). Geiselman and Riehle replicated this study, adding results for the F-sentence recall. Recall of F sentences was much better when only the F sentences were ordered (.41) than for the other conditions (all .29 or less). They concluded that ordering the sentences made segregating the two sets of sentences easier.

In the final study in the sentence-memory set, Geiselman (1977) again presented sentences from two themes in random order, this time auditorily. The two themes were hard to understand without a title. Half of the subjects were told the titles and half were not. Order within theme was again either logical or scrambled, and the benefits of order from the prior studies replicated. But for the order effects to appear, it was necessary for the theme of the F sentences to be explicit. Presumably, this permitted the sorting necessary to group the R and F sets. During the study phase, Geiselman also measured time to decide whether a sentence was from the F or the R theme, and found that R recall was better for shorter decisions whereas F recall was better for longer decisions. This suggests that trying to remember benefits from easier comprehension, whereas trying to forget suffers from lengthened study time. Finally, Geiselman found that recognition of individual words from the sentences was better on R sentences than on F sentences only if subjects had been told the theme for the F sentences. Once again, organization was critical to permit sorting by cue.

Geiselman's sentence experiments are instructive in a couple of regards. First, directed forgetting works with meaningfully related information. However, there is the strong suggestion that relatedness among R and F items undermines the success of an F cue. Second, organization of the materials—both of the R and the F materials—helps in successfully using the cue to forget some items and remember others. Geiselman argued that the better grouping of the items under the two cue conditions permitted operations to be applied to the conditions selectively. Distinctiveness appeared to be crucial; even organizing the F items made the R items better remembered.

By the mid 1980s, Geiselman was arguing for a very different interpretation of the directed-forgetting phenomenon, one that emphasized processes operating at the time of retrieval more than those at the time of encoding, thereby restoring interest in the repression account offered early on by Weiner (1968; Weiner & Reed, 1969). Geiselman came to this new perspective through exploration of the link between directed forgetting and posthypnotic amnesia. I only consider the standard memory research here, however; studies relating hypnosis and directed forgetting are discussed in the next chapter by Golding and Long.

The critical study was that of Bjork and Geiselman (1978), in which they aimed to eliminate rehearsal. Their subjects studied two lists of 16 pairs of words for 3 sec each, with 3–12 sec of arithmetic distraction after each pair. The cue followed the distraction interval. One list was followed by immediate recall of R words; the other was followed by distraction only. Then subjects did a final recall of all items, both F and R words, followed by a final Yes–No recognition test.

The immediate recall data showed the usual large advantage for R words (.30) over F words (.06). Unlike the flat performance for F words across the 3–12 sec distraction interval, recall of R words increased from about .20 to .40, in contrast to Woodward et al. (1973). This suggests that differential rehearsal occurred despite efforts to prevent it. Final recall showed a very similar pattern, with prior testing helping R items but not F items, although interpretation is complicated by the apparent floor effect for F items on both recall tests. Final recognition was unaffected by either distraction duration or prior testing, but did show an advantage for R items (.68) over F items (.56).

Bjork and Geiselman argued that only R items are retrieved when their cue appears. If so, then forcing retrieval of F items at the time of their cue should attenuate the effect. In Experiment 2, they required subjects to retrieve every pair upon presentation of its cue. Within-list retrieval accuracy was almost identical for both the R and F items. Immediate recall showed a substantially reduced, although still reliable, advantage for R words (.15) over F words (.11). Once again, the pattern was similar in final recall, but now the recognition difference vanished (.64 for both R and F). Bjork and Geiselman argued that their balancing of retrieval disrupted the normal segregation of R and F items, and shifted their explanation from selective rehearsal to selective retrieval.

Geiselman, Bjork, and Fishman (1983a; see also Geiselman et al., 1983b) provided converging support for this differential retrieval hypothesis. Subjects heard a list of 48 words, one every 7 sec. They were told to learn one word and to judge the pleasantness of the next one, alternating intentional and incidental learning. Halfway through the list, half of the subjects were told to forget the preceding words; the rest were told to continue remembering all of the "learn" words. Recall of the postcue R words was greater in lists with F cues (learn: .72; judge: .42) than in lists without F cues (learn: .57; judge: .30). The reciprocal pattern occurred for precue words: F-cued words (learn: .57; judge: .32) were recalled worse than R-cued words (learn: .74; judge: .47). Indeed, the tradeoff was close to perfect. But in Yes–No recognition, there was no effect of either cue or initial study mode. Geiselman et al. (1983a) argued that although selective rehearsal could explain the difference in the "learn" items, where subjects might reasonably have rehearsed R items more than F items, it was not clear how this view fit judged items. Incidentally learned items should not have attracted any rehearsal, let alone differential rehearsal. Why were judged words affected by the F cue?

One possibility was that somehow the judged and learned words became linked during study. In Experiment 2, the two sets of words were chosen from distinct semantic categories to prevent such linkage, yet the pattern in Experiment 1 persisted. Furthermore, in both experiments, subjects had difficulty identifying the half of the list in which F-cued words were presented. Experiments 3 and 4 evaluated whether subjects tended to recall the second half first for lists containing an F cue, generating output interference for items from the first half (the F items). When subjects were instructed to recall the first half before the second or the second half before the first, it made no difference at all to the other effects, discounting the output interference hypothesis.

Geiselman et al. (1983a) maintained that selective rehearsal could not explain the R–F difference in the judged items, where rehearsal was irrelevant and did not seem to occur. Instead, they argued for an inhibitory process preventing F item retrieval. This retrieval-blocking idea was consistent with three facts: (a) There was no effect of cuing on recognition, (b) subjects could not identify list half for items prior to an F cue, and (c) the correlation between input and output order was very low for items prior to the F cue. They suggested that inhibition made sense: F items would usually not be retrieved, but could be revived if needed, perhaps by re-presentation. Geiselman et al. (1983a) did not note that their study used the list method whereas many prior studies had used the item method to deliver the F cue. This critical connection was made later by Bjork (1989) and by Basden, Basden, and Gargano (1993).

The linchpin study to support retrieval inhibition is that of Geiselman and Bagheri (1985). Surprisingly, they used the item procedure to deliver the F cue, now ordinarily associated with the rehearsal explanation. In Experiment 1, subjects saw 36 words for 5 sec each, each followed by a cue for 5 sec. Subjects recalled many more of the R words (.58) than of the F words (.10). They then studied the same list again (actually four each of the R and F items were changed), but this time all words were to be remembered. Recall rose much more for the formerly F words (.49) than for the formerly R words (.65). Most important, words not recalled on the first test were much more likely to be recalled on the second test if they had initially been F items (.45) rather than R items (.28). Their explanation was that unrecalled F words benefited from a release from retrieval inhibition in addition to the extra rehearsal that both R and F items attracted. The possibility that unrecalled R words were simply harder than unrecalled F words was discounted by showing that yoked subjects recalled these two sets of items equally well after a single study trial.

It could still be argued, however, that this does not address item selection at the *individual* level. In Experiment 2, they included R and F words, plus words judged for pleasantness. The retrieval inhibition view predicts that only the F items can benefit on the second recall from release from inhibition. On the first recall, F words (.07) were poorly recalled relative to judged words (.32) or R words (.46). On the second recall, following a study trial where all words were repeated and were to be remembered, the F words (.50) rose considerably more than either the judged words (.55) or the R words (.66). Furthermore, the conditional probability of recalling a previously unrecalled word was greatest for formerly F words (.54) as compared to formerly judged (.34) or R (.37) words.

Could unrecalled F words from the first trial have been selectively rehearsed on the second trial? In Experiment 3, the second list contained only formerly F items or formerly R items, with all to be remembered. The initial R–F difference (.44 vs. .13) almost disappeared on the second test (.60 vs. .54) and again, unrecalled former F items improved more (.51) than did unrecalled former R items (.34). Selective rehearsal of the formerly F items during the second study sequence seemed unlikely, so the evidence fit a retrieval inhibition account better. But the fact that there were more initially unrecalled F than R items might have helped formerly F items on the second study trial. To test this idea, Experiment 4 replicated Experiment 3 but with only 10 items to be learned. A faster presentation rate (3 sec/word) was used to minimize rehearsal opportunities and to lower overall performance. The initial advantage for R (.29) over F (.05) items disappeared on the second recall, with formerly F words (.70) now better learned than formerly R words (.56).

Geiselman and Bagheri (1985, p. 61) argued that, in addition to encoding factors, "a strong case can also be made for a significant role of memory retrieval inhibition." Presenting unrecalled F and R items a second time as R items helped the F items more. This was taken as evidence that F items, unlike R items, benefited additionally from release of retrieval inhibition on a second study. Whether item selection on the second study trial was completely ruled out is uncertain, but the results have proven to be tantalizing with regard to possible inhibition of F words.

Geiselman and Panting (1985) suggested four possibilities for why repetition of F items from list 1 as R items in list 2 led to equivalent performance for formerly R and formerly F items: (a) Output interference affected F items in list 1; (b) more effort was required on formerly F items on list 2; (c) there was intentional withholding of F items on list 1; and (d) item selection favored formerly F items on list 2. To evaluate these possibilities, in Experiment 1 subjects saw six categories of eight words each, each word presented for 3 sec and each category followed by a 3-sec cue. Subjects then attempted to recall all of the items from one category at a time, with category cues provided by the experimenter. In this way, either all of the F or all of the R categories could be tested first. Following recall, subjects saw all of the R or all of the F words again, and were instructed to remember all of them.

The effect was quite clear on the first test, whether F categories (R: .56; F: .47) or R categories (R: .66; F: .45) were tested first. However, the difference vanished on list 2 (all conditions around .77). As previously, list 2 recall conditional on list 1 nonrecall was greater for formerly F items (.59) than for formerly R items (.34). The basic pattern—a difference on list 1 but not on list 2—was taken as consistent with the retrieval inhibition view, although the larger R–F difference with R recall first did indicate a contribution of output interference. Because a yoked group of subjects, who learned the unrecalled items from list 1, showed no R–F difference, item selection was considered unlikely, although a yoking design does not rule out the possibility of subject-specific item selection. Because only either R or F items were relearned, differential effort was seen as unlikely; because F items and R items were separately cued, suppression of F items was seen as unlikely. Of course, although plausible, these arguments are speculative: Subjects could still have operated strategically despite these design features.

Finally, a study by Geiselman, Rabow, Wachtel, and MacKinnon (1985) explored strategic processing in directed forgetting at the encoding, forgetting, and retrieval stages. In Experiment 1, subjects saw a list of 28 words, half cued R and half cued F by the item method, with 8 or 16 sec per word and 1.5 sec per cue. One group generated synonyms during study (deep processing); the other group generated homonyms (shallow processing). For both R and F items, more time at study helped in the deep processing condition (R-8: .63; R-16: .81; F-8: .62; F-16: .80) but not in the shallow processing condition (R-8: .45; R-16: .47; F-8: .33; F-16: .28). Not surprisingly, deep processing led to better overall retention, but there was no R–F difference for items processed deeply (cf. Bugelski, 1970; but contrast with Horton & Petruk, 1980).

In Experiment 2, Geiselman et al. (1985) examined the role of encoding strategies. Subjects were given one of three cues:[8] (a) Rehearse R items only, especially when an F cue appears, (b) think about nothing when an F cue appears, or (c) say "stop" repeatedly when an F cue appears. Compared to the "think nothing" control (recall, R: .56, F: .24; recognition, R: .77, F: .57) selective rehearsal benefited only R items (recall, R: .68, F: .24; recognition, R: .89, F: .54). In contrast, the "stop" condition selectively impaired only F items in recall (R: .54, F: .13) but not in recognition (R: .75, F: .55). Clearly "stop" was special, because in Experiment 3 where a nonsense syllable ("dax") replaced "stop," performance was identical to the "think nothing" condition. Geiselman et al. argued that rehearsal affected storage and hence influenced both tests, whereas "stop" affected retrieval and hence affected only the recall test, where retrieval demands were great. They suggested that the "stop" manipulation actually enhanced retrieval inhibition beyond that in the usual F condition.

To discount the possibility that "stop" enhanced demand characteristics to withhold F items, their final experiment manipulated payoff. Subjects studied the 28-word list with item-by-item cues but without strategy instructions. On the test, they received points for recall, either 9 for R and 1 for F, 5 for each, or 9 for F and 1 for R. This payoff manipulation had absolutely no effect on recall, leading Geiselman et al. to reject the idea that subjects were simply withholding F items. Overall, they concluded that both encoding and retrieval were implicated, with selective rehearsal of R items at encoding and inhibition of F items at retrieval, linking Geiselman's original view to his new one.

Summary of the Silver Age

By the middle of this second epoch, directed-forgetting research on short-term memory was at its end. The first era had shown that editing of the brief, active memory we rely on in all cognitive activities could be done

---

[8]A fourth condition—think about riding a down escalator when cued to forget—did not differ from instructions to think about nothing, so I omitted it.

quite successfully. The main new contribution, flowing from the heavy emphasis on scanning of short-term memory (Sternberg, 1969), was on recognition instead of recall, and on latency instead of accuracy. This essentially wrapped up work on short-term memory.

The primary motivating forces in this epoch were the emphases on type of encoding process and opportunity for rehearsal. Directed-forgetting research now involved multiple tests, including immediate and final recall, as well as recognition. Bjork's (1972) "segregate and selectively rehearse" account still dominated the work in this era. Rehearsal obviously mattered. Both the location of rehearsal opportunities and the type of rehearsal had profound influences on memory for R words, but seemed much less influential with regard to F items. Subjects appeared to hold items in abeyance, despite variations in how the items had been processed, until the cue. At that point, processing differences "kicked in" only for R items; processing of F items was suspended. This generalization seemed to apply to everything from type of processing to temporal coding.

Materials also began to change, as is most apparent in Geiselman's use of sentences. But more important was how Geiselman explained his results. Initially, he adhered to the selective rehearsal account, but gradually he came to favor an inhibition account, harkening back to the ideas of Weiner and Reed. By the end of this epoch, selective rehearsal still held sway, but inhibition was closing quickly, forming the crux of the major debate that would dominate the next period.

THE MODERN AGE: 1986–1995

Directed-forgetting research has declined in popularity since its first 20 years, no doubt in part because much of the groundwork had already been laid. But other factors played a role, too. Principal among these was the emergence of a "growth industry"—the implicit/explicit distinction (see Richardson-Klavehn & Bjork, 1988; Roediger & McDermott, 1993). As memory researchers embraced this distinction, many paradigms and questions of earlier times lay fallow, including directed forgetting. As a result, there is a gap in this literature between 1985 and 1989. But directed forgetting remains a viable "cottage industry," with important theoretical issues yet to be resolved, and it would soon be pressed into service to assist in exploring the implicit/explicit distinction.

Directed Forgetting Confronts Implicit Remembering

So far, the tests of memory in the directed-forgetting literature have been explicit tests, usually recall and recognition, that require subjects to be aware that they are remembering. But a new battery of memory measures has emerged since the early 1980s. Implicit tests also involve remembering, but without the need for awareness. Typically, these tests require subjects to perform a task that can be done without conscious recollection but that may still benefit from prior experiences held in memory, a benefit usually referred to as *priming*. Roediger and McDermott (1993) provide a recent review of the literature involving implicit testing of memory.

MacLeod (1989) reported two experiments, each using two tests, one explicit and one implicit. In Experiment 1, subjects studied a 96-word list with 1 sec per word and 3 sec per cue (half R and half F) following each word. In the explicit recognition test, subjects had to circle the 48 studied words from among 96 tests words. In word fragment completion, they had to complete fragments such as C--LIO— with real words (e.g., calliope); half of the 96 test words were in fact studied words. The two tests were administered twice, once immediately and once a week after study, using nonoverlapping sets of studied items. I summarize only the immediate data from when a test was administered first because intertest contamination cannot occur here. Recognition showed a strong remember–forget difference (R: .69, F: .46). I had not expected an effect of instructional cue on the implicit measure, given that other encoding manipulations such as level of processing exert relatively little influence on implicit tests. However, although both R items (.31) and F items (.24) showed priming relative to baseline (.10), there was reliably more priming for R words.

In Experiment 2, subjects studied 40 words. This time, there were only immediate tests: free recall and lexical decision. Recall showed the usual powerful effect of cue (R: .37, F: .04) but lexical decision was also affected. Studied words were faster than unstudied words (560 ms)—repetition priming—but R words (523 ms) were even faster than F words (540 ms). Thus, both implicit tests showed differential priming favoring R words, following the explicit test pattern. The interpretation put forth in the article was that both implicit and explicit tests were similarly affected by inhibition of F words at the time of retrieval, consistent with the Geiselman and Bagheri (1985) explanation.[9]

The next year, Paller (1990) reported conflicting results using as his implicit test word-stem completion, where the task is to finish a word from its first few letters (e.g., BAS for BASEMENT). Subjects studied five 42-word lists, each made up of half R and half F words, with the color of print of the

---

[9]In the originally submitted version, I concluded that there were, in fact, encoding manipulations—notably directed forgetting—that did affect performance on implicit tests. It was a conclusion that ran against the prevailing wisdom, and I was persuaded to explain the results in terms of inhibition instead, thereby not having to conflict with the idea that encoding manipulations generally do not affect priming on implicit tests. Thus, the published interpretation of the results was that F items were inhibited at the time of retrieval, and that inhibition affected all of the tests similarly. In light of subsequent research, I often wish that I had stayed the course on the differential encoding account.

word serving as its cue. Following all of the lists, subjects performed a stem-completion test or a stem-cued recall test, using the same three-letter stems. Thus, only the instructions differed for the two tests. All subjects then did a free recall test. Both explicit tests—free recall (R: .14; F: .05) and cued recall (R: .23, F: .16)—showed a cue effect, albeit small by comparison to the literature. However, there was no effect of cue on the implicit test of stem completion (R: .20, F: .20).[10]

The main thrust of Paller's article focused not on the memory test data but on data from event-related brain potentials (ERPs) recorded during encoding. He showed several interesting results. First, the response to R words took place earlier than the response to F words during study. Second, and more telling, ERPs were more positive during encoding for recalled words than they were for words not recalled. As well, recalled R words tended to show a larger ERP effect than did recalled F words. This pattern was not evident for studied words successfully completed on the implicit stem-completion test, consistent with the behavioral data. Paller concluded that encoding differences underlie the advantage of R over F words, affecting largely only explicit tests of remembering.

The crucial study in the implicit domain was carried out by Basden et al. (1993). Indeed, this study also has important implications for the broader interpretation of directed forgetting, so I devote more space to this study. Building on an idea initially presented by Bjork (1989), Basden et al. (1993) set out to explore a simple, compelling observation: The two usual directed-forgetting methods—item and list—might differ in terms of the mechanism(s) that produce the R–F difference under each. The argument was that the item method led to selective rehearsal of R items whereas the list method led to inhibition of F items. This idea immediately explained two things. First, inhibition was probably a weaker effect than selective rehearsal, so recall differences between F and R items were generally smaller under the list method. Second, unlike recall tests, which consistently showed an R–F difference, recognition tests sometimes did (e.g., Davis & Okada, 1971; MacLeod, 1975) and sometimes did not (e.g., Block, 1971; Elmes et al., 1970). In fact, the item method consistently produced a cue effect on recognition whereas the list method consistently did not! Recall was affected by both selective rehearsal and inhibition whereas recognition was sensitive only to selective rehearsal. For recognition, re-presentation of an item at test essentially lifted or released the inhibition (cf. Bjork, 1989).

Basden et al. then reported a series of experiments. Experiments 1 and 2 differed only in the strength of association of the studied items, so I

---

[10]Paller (1990) did go on to compare stem and fragment completion, replicating both MacLeod's (1989, Experiment 1) finding of differential priming on fragment completion (R: .48, F: .40) and his own finding of no differential priming on stem completion (R: .24, F: .23) in the same experiment. The cause of this difference still has not been established.

describe only Experiment 2. Subjects studied a 16-word list of response words from strongly associated pairs (e.g., bread–BUTTER). Under the item method, words were studied for 8 sec each with cues presented for the final 6 sec; half were R and half were F. Under the list method, each word was presented for 8 sec and subjects were told halfway through the list to forget the first 12 "practice" words. They then did one of four retention tests prior to a recall test. One group did Yes–No recognition; another did word-fragment completion. The other two groups did association tests, where the stimulus words from 48 pairs—16 studied and 32 unstudied—were presented on the test. One group had implicit instructions to generate an association to each test item. The other group was told for each test item whether it was studied or unstudied, and asked to recall the relevant word for studied items.

Under the item method, both recognition (R: .92; F: .77) and explicit association (R: .82; F: .59) showed strong cue effects, whereas implicit association did not (R: .44; F: .40). Fragment completion showed equivalent priming (R: .20; F: .20). In contrast, under the list method, only explicit association (R: .74; F: .65) showed a cue effect, not apparent for either recognition (R: .90; F: .89), implicit association (R: .42; F: .40), or fragment completion (R: .46; F: .45). But the crux was what happened in final recall following recognition: The strong cue effect for the item method (R: .64; F: .15) disappeared for the list method (R: .57; F: .57). This fits with the idea that the inhibition produced by the list method was released by a prior recognition test (Bjork, 1989).

Experiment 3 homed in on the implicit/explicit distinction. Study was much as in Experiment 2, but three groups had different tests. A recall group showed an R–F difference under both methods, larger in the item method (R: .50; F: .05) than in the list method (R: .41; F: .20). Two other groups did word-fragment tests, one explicit (recall the word), and one implicit (complete the word). The explicit test showed a cue effect under the item method (R: .48; F: .36) but not the list method (R: .45; F: .43), consistent with Basden et al.'s notion that an explicit fragment test should behave like an explicit recognition test. Also as predicted, the implicit test did not show a cue effect for either the item method (R: .36; F: .32) or the list method (R: .38; F: .37).

In a final experiment, Basden et al. used MacLeod's (1989, Experiment 1) materials to construct both short (16 word) and long (32 word) lists. As before, recall showed an R–F difference under both methods, although larger under the item method. For recognition, the effect was limited to the item method. In fragment completion, although the advantage for R over F items averaged .07 for both list lengths under both methods, only long lists under the item method—the procedure used by MacLeod—produced a reliable R–F difference. Overall, Basden et al. concluded that their account was entirely plausible: It appears that the mechanism underlying directed-forgetting effects is inhibition for the list method but selective rehearsal for the item method.

The word-fragment completion results were still somewhat muddled, sometimes showing a cue effect, sometimes not. Russo and Andrade (1995) pursued this. In their Experiment 1 (the other two were replications), subjects studied 48 words for 1 sec each, each followed by a 3-sec R or F cue. One group then did a standard implicit word-fragment completion test. Two others did word-fragment completion under instructions either to try to complete the fragments with studied words, but also to complete any fragments they could (inclusion), or to complete fragments only if they had not studied the word (exclusion). On the implicit test, R items showed more priming than F items (R: .25; F: .19), again replicating the MacLeod (1989) result. The exclusion test also showed a reliable R–F difference, but the inclusion test did not. Using Jacoby's (1991) process dissociation procedure, Russo and Andrade argued that the effect of the R or F cue derived largely from intentional use of memory (see also the chapter by Vokey & Allen).

In summary, implicit memory tests have been quite informative with regard to directed forgetting, but much remains to be done. Apparently, some implicit tests are sensitive to directed-forgetting manipulations (e.g., word-fragment completion) and others are not (e.g., word-stem completion). Such discrepancies are well known in the implicit memory literature, so directed forgetting is not unique, but explanations still need to be pursued. It does seem, though, that directed forgetting affects implicit tests less than explicit tests (to the extent that it is reasonable to compare across tests).

The critical study to emerge from this new domain of memory research is that of Basden et al. (1993). This is an important article that helps us both to understand the different directed-forgetting methods and to define the theoretical terrain. Selective rehearsal may underlie the item method effects, where recall shows large effects and recognition also is affected, whereas inhibition may underlie the list method effects, where effects are smaller in recall and absent in recognition.

Studies Using Traditional Explicit Testing Methods

Studies of directed-forgetting effects on explicit tests continue to appear in the literature, although with decreasing regularity. The empirical section of the review ends by describing these.

Tying back to the relation between part-list cuing and directed forgetting (cf. Roediger & Tulving, 1979), Goernert and Larson (1994) investigated the effect of providing within-list retrieval cues at the time of test on the recall of R versus F words. Subjects studied 40 words at a 4-sec rate, with a midlist R or F cue. After study, subjects were instructed to recall the first 20 words and were given 0, 4, or 8 words from the first 20 as cues. To maintain correspondence over conditions, only the data for the 12 never-cued words were analyzed. Whereas there was a strong R–F difference without cues (R:

.44; F: .21), this difference vanished for the 4-cue (R: .29; F: .29) and 8-cue (R: .22; F: .31) conditions. Provision of part-list cues led to reduced recall for R words but not for F words, consistent with the "retrieval blocking" idea (Bjork, 1989; Roediger & Tulving, 1979). Indeed, recall of F words seems to benefit from the presence of within-list cues. Goernert and Larson argued for the retrieval inhibition account, consistent with their use of the list method.

A technique seeing increasing use in the memory literature is the "remember–know" distinction (Tulving, 1985). Subjects indicate for each word they recognize on the test whether they can recall information about the study episode that makes them believe the word was studied, or whether they simply feel that it was. This recollection versus familiarity discrimination has much in common with the process dissociation logic (Jacoby, 1991; Vokey & Allen, this volume). Gardiner, Gawlik, and Richardson-Klavehn (1994) married this procedure to directed forgetting. Subjects studied two 40-word lists with words presented for 1 sec each, followed by a cue. In one list, each word was followed by a 1-sec cue and a 5-sec blank interval (short delay); in the other list, each word was followed by a 5-sec blank and a 1-sec cue (long delay). After a 1-day retention interval, subjects did a 160-word Yes–No recognition test, indicating for each word that they responded yes to whether they did so on the basis of "remembering" or "knowing." For the short delay, there was an R–F difference for "remember" judgments (R: .50; F: .23) but not for "know" judgments (R: .18; F: .20). The same pattern, somewhat attenuated, emerged for long delays ("remember," R: .40; F: .26; "know," R: .27; F: .29). Gardiner et al. argued that the cue effect was largely on conscious recollection.

Golding et al. (1994) illustrated that directed forgetting is not infallible: The items themselves can determine whether directed forgetting will work. Our study lists contained related words (e.g., seat–belt) versus unrelated words (e.g., cheese–suit) made from other related pairs (e.g., cheese–cake and swim–suit). Subjects studied 24 word pairs, 8 related, 8 unrelated, and 8 filler. Each word appeared for 1 sec followed by its cue for 3 sec, with pair members presented consecutively. For each type of pair, the likelihood of each member of the pair being F versus R was equivalent.

Consider just the Experiment 2 recall data (the two experiments replicated well). For related pairs, the pattern was reminiscent of Tzeng et al. (1979) with R–R pairs (.39), R–F pairs (.20), F–R pairs (.08), and F–F pairs (.02). The pattern was different for unrelated pairs: Only R–R pairs (.17) showed an advantage over the others (.03, .01, and .01, respectively). The Yes–No recognition test results concurred; for related words (R–R: 57; R–F: .45; F–R: .31; F–F: .19) versus for unrelated words (R–R: .51; R–F: .25; F–R: .29; F–F: .19). Clearly, the major difference on both tests was in the R–F condition. If the words in a pair were related, having to remember the first provided a bridge to the second that could not be entirely dismantled by an F cue for the second. The availability of strong semantic cues can therefore undermine the ability of an instruction to forget a word in a list.

More recently, Golding, Roper, and Hauselt (1996) varied the cue, not in a binary fashion, but more along a continuum. They told subjects the probability that each item would be tested, which could be either 0 (F) or 1 (R) or .5, which meant that the item had the potential to be either forgotten or remembered. Considering just Experiment 2, subjects studied 24-word lists at a 1-sec rate using the item procedure with each word followed by a number indicating its likelihood of being tested (0, 50, or 100). One group had 8 words associated with each likelihood. Two other groups had no words assigned .5 probabilities; half had 16 R and 8 F words whereas half had 8 R and 16 F words.

The group with only 8 R words showed a much larger effect of cue (R: .65; F: .14) than did the group with 16 R words (R: .38; F: .17), the difference deriving only from the R subset. The group with the .5 probability of test items also produced a strong R–F difference (R: .50; F: .13) with recall of the .5 items close to the midpoint (.28). F words were unaffected by inclusion of the .5 items, whereas recall of R words fell between that of the other two conditions, consistent with a cost–benefit analysis. Subjects who had all three conditions during study reported that they tended to rehearse some .5 words and not others, essentially moving some into the R category and some into the F category. Golding et al. explained their results in terms of differential rehearsal.

Bjork and Bjork (1996; see also Bjork, 1989) described circumstances under which F items that initally did not interfere with R-item recall could be made to do so. Using a standard cost–benefit design, Bjork, Bjork, and Glenberg (1973) had contrasted a 16-word list to a 32-word list that either did or did not contain a midlist F cue. An immediate test showed that the 16 overlapping R words were equally well recalled in the 16-word list (.57) and in the forget-cued 32-word list (.55), both better than in the all-R 32-word list (.44). A delay followed, filled either by an arithmetic distraction task or a recognition test. After arithmetic, the recall pattern was about the same—.46, .49, and .34. But after recognition, the recall pattern changed—.51, .37, .34. Now, the first 16 words in the list interfered just as much when they were F words as when they were R words.

Bjork and Bjork (1996, Experiment 1) replicated this pattern. Recall accuracies were .70, .62, and .48 when tested immediately. When delayed by a recognition test with no distractors from the F set, recall accuracies again were equal for the 16-item list (.64) and the 32-item list with an F cue (.62), but lower for the all-R list (.42). When the distractors on the recognition test were the F items, however, as in the Bjork et al. (1973) study, performance on the F-cued list fell to .44, equal to the all-R list at .39. Apparently, once re-presented via the recognition test, F words return to full strength, as if the inhibition they had previously caused was lifted by re-exposure (cf. Basden et al., 1993). Experiment 3 showed that re-exposing F items on an intervening implicit fragment-completion test did not release inhibition on delayed recall, unlike an intervening recognition test, emphasizing the importance of contact with the initial studied episode to release inhibition.

To sum up this section, in the past few years, directed forgetting has been coupled with other distinctions in the memory literature, such as the explicit–implicit and the remember–know distinctions. In general, these combinations have been informative with regard to both elements. It has also become clear that although it is a highly effective procedure for controlling remembering, directed forgetting is not invulnerable: Item relatedness and precue elaborative processing can seriously undermine the effectiveness of an F cue. Increasingly, as it settles into the toolbox available to memory researchers, directed forgetting is being used to help explore important questions in memory. I strongly suspect that it will continue to be useful in this way for some time to come.

THE BIG PICTURE

In this final section, I set out the major findings to be explained and the major theories available to explain them, arriving at some rapprochement between the two.

The Principal Findings and Explanations

Table 1.2 provides a chronological list of many of the principal findings in the directed-forgetting literature over the past 30 years, and a sample of representative studies in which these findings have been reported and replicated. Once again, I present the information largely in temporal sequence for ease in locating studies, although I have taken the liberty of moving one or two out of order a little to place them closer to related findings. As well, I have placed an asterisk beside those results that appear (to me) most crucial in understanding directed forgetting.

The first theory proposed with reference to directed forgetting was the *active erasure* account, which essentially holds that F items are pruned from memory. This explanation did handle the finding that proactive interference is much diminished by an F cue, but cannot handle many other findings. In particular, it has difficulty with results from the list method that fit an inhibition account better, such as the findings that F items can be perhaps completely revived by re-presentation, and that there is no R–F difference on recognition tests. Numerous other results conflict with the erasure hypothesis as well, such as the priming on implicit tests for F items, sometimes

TABLE 1.2
Chronology of the Principal Findings Regarding Directed Forgetting

Number	Finding	Reference(s)
*1.	Proactive interference on R items is reduced for a list containing F items, but some PI still remains in both short-term and long-term retention	Muther (1965); Bjork et al. (1968); Bjork (1970); Waugh (1972); Turvey & Wittlinger (1969)
*2.	Recalling only part of a list leads to better memory than recalling that part first (before the rest)	Epstein (1969a, 1969b)
*3.	In general, a short item presentation and a longer cue presentation leads to optimal directed forgetting	Epstein (1969a); Wetzel & Hunt (1977)
*4.	Re-presenting former F items as R items all but eliminates the R–F difference under the list method (both for previously recalled and unrecalled items)	Weiner & Reed (1969); Geiselman & Bagheri (1978); Bjork (1989)
5.	An instruction not to rehearse certain items may not be as effective as an instruction to forget them	Weiner & Reed (1969)
6.	A postencoding F cue may or may not reduce retroactive interference	Reed (1970); Block (1971)
7.	Imagery prior to the cue may eliminate the remember–forget difference	Bugelski (1970)
8.	There are few intrusions from F items in short-term memory	Bjork (1970); Shebilske et al. (1971)
*9.	Under the list procedure, recognition tests show R items equivalent to F items	Elmes et al. (1970); Block (1971); Basden et al. (1993)
10.	Arousal increase at the time of encoding helps R items but not F items	Archer & Margolin (1970)
11.	F cues work both during and after study in short-term memory	Shebilske et al. (1971)
*12.	Under the item procedure, recognition tests show R items better than F items	Davis & Okada (1971); MacLeod (1975)
13.	Segregation of R and F items is even possible within the same semantic category	Elmes & Wilkinson (1971); Horton & Petruk (1980)
14.	There is quite good immediate retention of cues, but it is better for R items than for F items	Woodward & Bjork (1971); Davis & Okada (1971)
*15.	Delaying the F cue results in poorer recall of R items and better recall of F items; there is minimal rehearsal until the cue appears	Davis & Okada (1971); Woodward et al. (1973); Timmins (1974); Wetzel (1975)
*16.	A recognition test prior to a recall test does not eliminate the cue effect under the item procedure	Davis & Okada (1971)
17.	Recall of F items is increased by knowledge that the item was in fact an F item	Epstein & Wilder (1972)
18.	F items interfere with each other but not with R items	Reitman et al. (1973); Epstein & Wilder (1972)

(Continued)

TABLE 1.2
(Continued)

Number	Finding	Reference(s)
19.	R items not to be recalled intrude more than F items	Woodward et al. (1974)
*20.	A pretest instruction not to recall (or to forget) certain items is nowhere near as effective as an instruction to forget given during study	Woodward et al. (1974); Roediger & Tulving (1979)
21.	Homophone errors are greater for R items than F items	Kausler & Settle (1974)
22.	Short-term recognition latencies are faster but accuracies are lower if the F cue is given before versus during the item	Epstein et al. (1975); Howard (1976)
23.	Both recall and recognition effects using the item method are constant over long retention intervals	MacLeod (1975)
24.	Sentences and other meaningful material show a smaller F-cue effect than do isolated words	Geiselman (1974); Golding & Keenan (1985)
25.	Organizing F items makes R items easier to remember	Geiselman (1975)
26.	With sentences, knowing the theme is necessary for separately grouping R and F items	Geiselman (1977)
27.	Position and order judgments are poor for F items, but good for R items	Tzeng et al. (1979); Geiselman et al. (1983a)
28.	R items are helped by cues prior to items; F items are not	Horton & Petruk (1980)
29.	F cues do not simply reduce output interference	Geiselman et al. (1983a)
30.	Manipulating the payoff for R and F items does not alter the size of the effect	Geiselman et al. (1985)
31.	Some implicit tests show an R–F difference (e.g., word-fragment completion)	MacLeod (1989); Paller (1990); Russo & Andrade (1995)
32.	Some implicit tests show no R–F difference (e.g., word-stem completion)	Paller (1990); Basden et al. (1993)
33.	Part-list cues given prior to the test eliminate the remember–forget diference	Goernert & Larson (1994)
*34.	F items related meaningfully to preceding R items are difficult to forget on cue	Golding et al. (1994)
*35.	The R item advantage appears in "remember" judgments but not in "know" judgments	Gardiner et al. (1994)
36.	The R item advantage appears to be due to conscious recollection, not automatic retrieval	Russo & Andrade (1995); Vokey & Allen (this volume)
*37.	A filled interval before final recall eliminates the cue effect if the interval is filled with a recognition test containing F items as distractors	Bjork & Bjork (1996)
38.	An intermediate cue—"this item has a .5 probability of being tested"—produces intermediate performance	Golding et al. (1996)

Note. Those results indicated by an asterisk are seen as especially important to understanding directed forgetting.

equivalent to that for R items, and the fact that knowing that certain items were F items improves their recall. This view must be rejected, as even the earliest directed-forgetting investigations acknowledged.

The remaining three accounts—selective rehearsal, selective search, and inhibition—each appear to have a role in explaining the total pattern of results. The explanation of Basden et al. (1993; see also Bjork, 1989) is especially helpful in making these roles clear. First, consider *selective rehearsal*. It appears quite clear that when individual items in a list are followed by R cues versus F cues, subjects use these cues to decide how to process those items during encoding. If there is a delay before the cue, precue processing is held in abeyance until the cue appears. At that time, if the cue is to remember, the potential of the precue processing is realized and further rehearsal, in the form of elaboration, may take place, given time and incentive. If the cue is to forget, precue processing seems to be discarded and further processing is suspended.

Selective rehearsal explains many of the results using the item method. (It may even be a factor in some of the results using the list method, in that opportunities for differential rehearsal may still exist and be used.) F items do not receive the benefits of extended rehearsal, and so are less accessible, interfering less with R items. Immediate cues benefit R items because rehearsal can begin right away; immediate cues correspondingly help to minimize F item acquisition. All explicit tests of memory—notably recall and recognition—are affected because the F items simply are not as firmly planted in memory as the R items. When an F item is related to an earlier R item, it may be entered in the same rehearsal grouping, thereby undermining the success of the F cue. The R item advantage appears to be largely in the realm of conscious, not automatic recollection, as the remember–know judgment data suggest, just as should be the case if R items differ from F items primarily in terms of rehearsal history. And an item that may or may not be an F item behaves like an R item if it is rehearsed and like an F item if it is not. Overall, selective rehearsal is critical in the item method, and explains the large recall difference with this method relative to the list method.

In contrast, the list method produces results incompatible with a selective rehearsal account. In many ways, the F items seem to be as much "in memory" as the R items, but they just do not come through under some circumstances. Instead, the F items are thought to be inhibited in memory; there, but not recoverable without being refreshed. Most notably, a first recall test shows an advantage for R items over F items. However, a recognition test does not show this R advantage because the re-presentation of the item necessitated by the recognition test releases the inhibition suffered on the unsupported recall test. Indeed, even recall will not show an R–F difference if the F items are retrieved or re-presented before the recall test, either via forced within-list retrieval of F items or by the placement of a recognition test that contains the F items as distractors prior to the recall test. Instructions not to rehearse certain items or to stop thinking about them are not as potent as an F cue presumably because they do not invoke inhibition.

Both methods and their corresponding explanations must be augmented, however, by a mechanism like *selective search* or *segregation*. F items intrude with each other but not with R items. F cues can exert an effect even after study, at least in short-term memory tasks, suggesting an organizational influence. F and R items can be kept apart even if both come from the same semantic category. Retention of cues originally associated with items during study is quite good (although better for R items than for F items). Recall of F items improves if subjects know that the target of recall is, in fact, an F item. Organizing F items helps with the retention of R items, presumably because those items are now more easily kept separate. Part-list cues provided prior to the test undermine the advantage of R items over F items, presumably because they break down the segregated organization of the two sets. F items related to prior R items are harder to forget: They cannot readily be kept separate from the R items. All of these results appear to demand some kind of knowledge that there are two sets in memory, the R items and the F items. Thus, segregation serves as a mechanism to support successful directed forgetting under both methods and their correlated underlying processes.

The Past and the Future

Directed forgetting is, after 30 years, an established technique in the set available to memory researchers. It provides us with a previously unavailable way to study the strategies involved in the updating of memory under controlled conditions. We have learned a considerable amount from research on directed forgetting, including that there likely are multiple ways to forget. Unlike many memory phenomena, I believe that we now understand directed forgetting quite well, an important criterion for any procedure to have value in future research. As we develop new tests of memory and new ideas about its operation, directed forgetting will no doubt be called on to help in answering questions along the way. Forgetting is important, perhaps just as important as remembering. As the following chapter by Golding and Long makes even more apparent, intentional forgetting is a key element we use broadly in orchestrating our memories.

REFERENCES

Archer, B. U., & Margolin, R. R. (1970). Arousal effects in intentional recall and forgetting. *Journal of Experimental Psychology, 86*, 8–12.

Arbuthnott, K. D. (1995). Inhibitory mechanisms in cognition: Phenomena and models. *Cahiers de psychologie cognitive/Current Psychology of Cognition, 14*, 3–45.

Atkinson, R. C., & Shiffrin, R. M. (1968). Human memory: A proposed system and its control processes. In K. W. Spence & J. T. Spence (Eds.), *The psychology of learning and motivation* (Vol. 2, pp. 89–195). New York: Academic Press.

Atkinson, R. C., & Shiffrin, R. M. (1971). The control of short-term memory. *Scientific American, 225,* 82–90.

Basden, B. H., Basden, D. R., & Gargano, G. J. (1993). Directed forgetting in implicit and explicit memory tests: A comparison of methods. *Journal of Experimental Psychology: Learning, Memory, and Cognition, 19,* 603–616.

Bjork, E. L., & Bjork, R. A. (1996). Continuing influences of to-be-forgotten information. *Consciousness & Cognition, 5,* 176–196.

Bjork, E. L., Bjork, R. A., & Glenberg, A. (1973, November). *Reinstatement of interference owing to to-be-forgotten items.* Paper presented at the annual meeting of the Psychonomic Society, St. Louis, MO.

Bjork, R. A. (1970). Positive forgetting: The noninterference of items intentionally forgotten. *Journal of Verbal Learning and Verbal Behavior, 9,* 255–268.

Bjork, R. A. (1972). Theoretical implications of directed forgetting. In A. W. Melton & E. Martin (Eds.), *Coding processes in human memory* (pp. 217–235). Washington, DC: Winston.

Bjork, R. A. (1978). The updating of human memory. In G. H. Bower (Ed.), *The psychology of learning and motivation* (Vol. 12). New York: Academic Press.

Bjork, R. A. (1989). Retrieval inhibition as an adaptive mechanism in human memory. In H. L. Roediger III & F. I. M. Craik (Eds.), *Varieties of memory and consciousness: Essays in honour of Endel Tulving* (pp. 309–330). Hillsdale, NJ: Lawrence Erlbaum Associates.

Bjork, R. A., & Geiselman, R. E. (1978). Constituent processes in the differentiation of items in memory. *Journal of Experimental Psychology: Human Learning and Memory, 4,* 347–361.

Bjork, R. A., LaBerge, D., & Legrand, R. (1968). The modification of short-term memory through instructions to forget. *Psychonomic Science, 10,* 55–56.

Bjork, R. A., & Woodward, A. E., Jr. (1973). Directed forgetting of individual words in free recall. *Journal of Experimental Psychology, 99,* 22–27.

Block, R. A. (1971). Effects of instructions to forget in short-term memory. *Journal of Experimental Psychology, 89,* 1–9.

Brown, J. (1954). The nature of set-to-learn and of intra-material interference in immediate memory. *Quarterly Journal of Experimental Psychology, 6,* 141–148.

Brown, J. (1958). Some tests of the decay theory of immediate memory. *Quarterly Journal of Experimental Psychology, 10,* 12–21.

Bruce, D., & Papay, J. P. (1970). Primacy effect in single-trial free recall. *Journal of Verbal Learning and Verbal Behavior, 9,* 473–486.

Bugelski, B. R. (1970). Words and things and images. *American Psychologist, 25,* 1002–1012.

Burwitz, L. (1974). Proactive interference and directed forgetting in short-term motor memory. *Journal of Experimental Psychology, 102,* 799–805.

Craik, F. I. M., & Lockhart, R. S. (1972). Levels of processing: A framework for memory research. *Journal of Verbal Learning and Verbal Behavior, 11,* 671–684.

Cruse, D., & Jones, R. A. (1976). Intentional forgetting of tones in a choice recognition-time task. *Journal of Experimental Psychology: Human Learning and Memory, 2,* 577–585.

Davis, J. C., & Okada, R. (1971). Recognition and recall of positively forgotten items. *Journal of Experimental Psychology, 89,* 181–186.

Decker, W. H. (1976). Instructional set and retroactive inhibition in free recall. *Psychological Reports, 39,* 24.

Elmes, D. G. (1969a). Role of prior recalls and storage load in short-term memory. *Journal of Experimental Psychology, 79,* 468–472.

Elmes, D. G. (1969b). Cueing to forget in short-term memory. *Journal of Experimental Psychology, 80,* 561–562.

Elmes, D. G., Adams, C. A., III, & Roediger, H. L., III. (1970). Cued forgetting in short-term memory: Response selection. *Journal of Experimental Psychology, 86*, 103–107.

Elmes, D. G., & Wilkinson, W. C. (1971). Cued forgetting in free recall: Grouping on the basis of relevance and category membership. *Journal of Experimental Psychology, 87*, 438–440.

Epstein, W. (1969a). Recall of word lists following learning of sentences and of anomalous and random strings. *Journal of Verbal Learning and Verbal Behavior, 8*, 20–25.

Epstein, W. (1969b). Poststimulus output specification and differential retrieval from short-term memory. *Journal of Experimental Psychology, 82*, 168–174.

Epstein, W. (1972). Mechanisms of directed forgetting. In G. H. Bower (Ed.), *The psychology of learning and motivation* (Vol. 6, pp. 147–191). New York: Academic Press.

Epstein, W., & Wilder, L. (1972). Searching for to-be-forgotten material in a directed forgetting task. *Journal of Experimental Psychology, 95*, 349–357.

Epstein, W., Massaro, D. W., & Wilder, L. (1972). Selective search in directed forgetting. *Journal of Experimental Psychology, 94*, 18–24.

Epstein, W., Wilder, L., & Robertson, L. (1975). The effect of directed forgetting on the time to remember. *Memory & Cognition, 3*, 401–404.

Gardiner, J. M., Gawlik, B., & Richardson-Klavehn, A. (1994). Maintenance rehearsal affects knowing, not remembering: Elaborative rehearsal affects remembering, not knowing. *Psychonomic Bulletin & Review, 1*, 107–110.

Geiselman, R. E. (1974). Positive forgetting of sentence material. *Memory & Cognition, 2*, 677–682.

Geiselman, R. E. (1975). Semantic positive forgetting: Another cocktail party phenomenon. *Journal of Verbal Learning and Verbal Behavior, 14*, 73–81.

Geiselman, R. E. (1977). Effects of sentence ordering on thematic decisions to remember and forget prose. *Memory & Cognition, 5*, 323–330.

Geiselman, R. E., & Bagheri, B. (1985). Repetition effects in directed forgetting: Evidence for retrieval inhibition. *Memory & Cognition, 13*, 57–62.

Geiselman, R. E., Bjork, R. A., & Fishman, D. L. (1983a). Disrupted retrieval in directed forgetting: A link with posthypnotic amnesia. *Journal of Experimental Psychology: General, 112*, 58–72.

Geiselman, R. E., MacKinnon, D. P., Fishman, D. L., Jaenicke, C., Larner, B. R., Schoenberg, S., & Swartz, S. (1983b). Mechanisms of hypnotic and nonhypnotic forgetting. *Journal of Experimental Psychology: Learning, Memory, and Cognition, 9*, 626–635.

Geiselman, R. E., & Panting, T. M. (1985). Personality correlates of retrieval processes in intentional and unintentional forgetting. *Personality and Individual Differences, 6*, 685–691.

Geiselman, R. E., Rabow, V. E., Wachtel, S. L., & MacKinnon, D. P. (1985). Strategy control in intentional forgetting. *Human Learning, 4*, 169–178.

Geiselman, R. E., & Riehle, J. P. (1975). The fate of to-be-forgotten sentences in semantic positive forgetting. *Bulletin of the Psychonomic Society, 6*, 19–21.

Glucksberg, S., & King, L. J. (1967). Motivated forgetting mediated by implicit verbal chaining: A laboratory analog of repression. *Science, 158*, 517–518.

Glucksberg, S., & Ornstein, P. A. (1969). Reply to Weiner and Higgins: Motivated forgetting is not attributable to a confounding of original learning with retention. *Journal of Verbal Learning and Verbal Behavior, 8*, 681–685.

Goernert, P. N., & Larson, M. E. (1994). The initiation and release of retrieval inhibition. *Journal of General Psychology, 121*, 61–66.

Golding, J. M., & Keenan, J. M. (1985). Directed forgetting and memory for directions to a destination. *American Journal of Psychology, 98*, 579–590.

Golding, J. M., Long, D. L., & MacLeod, C. M. (1994). You can't always forget what you want: Directed forgetting of related words. *Journal of Memory and Language, 33*, 493–510.

Golding, J. M., Roper, K. L., & Hauselt, J. (1996). To forget or not to forget: The effect of probability of test on directed forgetting. *Quarterly Journal of Experimental Psychology, 49A*, 326–340.

Gross, A. E., Barresi, J., & Smith, E. E. (1970). Voluntary forgetting of a shared memory load. *Psychonomic Science, 20*, 73–75.

Halmiova, O., & Sipos, I. (1976). Intentional forgetting of categorised words. *Studia Psychologica, 18*, 183–189.

Hellyer, S. (1962). Frequency of stimulus presentation and short-term decrement in recall. *Journal of Experimental Psychology, 64*, 650.

Herrmann, D. J., & Chaffin, R. (Eds.). (1988). *Memory in historical perspective: The literature before Ebbinghaus.* New York: Springer-Verlag.

Homa, D., & Spieker, S. (1974). Assessment of selective search as an explanation for intentional forgetting. *Journal of Experimental Psychology, 103*, 10–15.

Horton, K. D., & Petruk, R. (1980). Set differentiation and depth of processing in the directed forgetting paradigm. *Journal of Experimental Psychology: Human Learning and Memory, 6*, 599–610.

Howard, D. V. (1976). Search and decision processes in intentional forgetting: A reaction time analysis. *Journal of Experimental Psychology: Human Learning and Memory, 2*, 566–576.

Jackson, J. L., & Michon, J. A. (1984). Effects of item concreteness on temporal coding. *Acta Psychologica, 57*, 83–95.

Jacoby, L. L. (1991). A process dissociation framework: Separating automatic from intentional uses of memory. *Journal of Memory and Language, 30*, 513–541.

James, W. (1890). *The principles of psychology* (Vol. 2). New York: Holt.

Johnson, D. A. (1971). Pupillary responses during a short-term memory task: Cognitive processing, arousal, or both? *Journal of Experimental Psychology, 90*, 311–318.

Johnson, H. M. (1994). Processes of successful intentional forgetting. *Psychological Bulletin, 116*, 274–292.

Jongeward, R. H., Woodward, A. E., Jr., & Bjork, R. A. (1975). The relative roles of input and output mechanisms in directed forgetting. *Memory & Cognition, 3*, 51–57.

Kaminsky, W., & DeRosa, D. (1974). The influence of retrieval cues and set organization on short-term recognition memory. *Journal of Experimental Psychology, 96*, 449–454.

Kausler, D. H., & Settle, A. V. (1975). The false-recognition effect for homophones of items subjects are cued to forget. *American Journal of Psychology, 88*, 627–634.

MacKinnon, D. W., & Dukes, W. F. (1962). Repression. In L. Postman (Ed.), *Psychology in the making* (pp. 662–744). New York: Knopf.

MacLeod, C. M. (1975). Long-term recognition and recall following directed forgetting. *Journal of Experimental Psychology: Human Learning and Memory, 1*, 271–279.

MacLeod, C. M. (1989). Directed forgetting affects both direct and indirect tests of memory. *Journal of Experimental Psychology: Learning, Memory, and Cognition, 15*, 13–21.

Martin, D. W., & Kelly, R. T. (1974). Secondary task performance during directed forgetting. *Journal of Experimental Psychology, 103*, 1074–1079.

Muther, W. S. (1965). Erasure or partitioning in short-term memory. *Psychonomic Science, 3*, 429–430.

Nickerson, R. S. (1984). Retrieval inhibition from part-set cuing: A persisting enigma in memory research. *Memory & Cognition, 12*, 531–552.

Orne, M. T. (1962). On the social psychology of the psychological experiment. *American Psychologist, 17*, 776–783.

Paller, K. A. (1990). Recall and stem-completion priming have different electrophysiological correlates and are modified differentially by directed forgetting. *Journal of Experimental Psychology: Learning, Memory, and Cognition, 16*, 1021–1032.

Peterson, L. R., & Peterson, M. J. (1959). Short-term retention of individual verbal items. *Journal of Experimental Psychology, 58*, 193–198.

Rakover, S. S. (1975). Voluntary forgetting before and after learning has been accomplished. *Memory & Cognition, 3*, 24–28.

Rakover, S. S. (1976). Voluntary forgetting: The effect of items to be remembered on those to be forgotten. *American Journal of Psychology, 89*, 241–252.

Rakover, S. S., & Kaminer, H. (1978). Voluntary forgetting of the first or second occurrence of an item in free recall and recognition tasks. *American Journal of Psychology, 91*, 51–67.

Reed, H. (1970). Studies of the interference processes in short-term memory. *Journal of Experimental Psychology, 84*, 452–457.

Reitman, W., Malin, J. T., Bjork, R. A., & Higman, B. (1973). Strategy control and directed forgetting. *Journal of Verbal Learning and Verbal Behavior, 12*, 140–149.

Ribot, T. A. (1882). *Diseases of memory: An essay in the positive psychology.* New York: Appleton-Century-Crofts.

Richardson-Klavehn, A., & Bjork, R. A. (1988). Measures of memory. *Annual Review of Psychology, 39*, 475–543.

Roediger, H. L., III, & Crowder, R. G. (1972). Instructed forgetting: Rehearsal control or retrieval inhibition (repression)? *Cognitive Psychology, 3*, 244–254.

Roediger, H. L., III, & McDermott, K. B. (1993). Implicit memory in normal human subjects. In F. Boller & J. Grafman (Eds.), *Handbook of neuropsychology* (Vol. 8, pp. 63–131). Amsterdam: Elsevier.

Roediger, H. L., III, & Tulving, E. (1979). Exclusion of learned material from recall as a postretrieval operation. *Journal of Verbal Learning and Verbal Behavior, 18*, 601–615.

Rundus, D. (1971). Analysis of rehearsal processes in free recall. *Journal of Experimental Psychology, 89*, 63–77.

Russo, R., & Andrade, J. (1995). The directed forgetting effect in word-fragment completion: An application of the process dissociation procedure. *Quarterly Journal of Experimental Psychology, 48A*, 405–423.

Shebilske, W., & Epstein, W. (1973). Effect of forget instructions with and without the conditions for selective search. *Memory & Cognition, 1*, 261–267.

Shebilske, W., Wilder, L., & Epstein, W. (1971). Forget instructions: Effect of selective rehearsal and categorical distinctiveness. *Journal of Experimental Psychology, 89*, 372–378.

Slamecka, N. J. (1968). An examination of trace storage in free recall. *Journal of Experimental Psychology, 76*, 504–513.

Spector, A., Laughery, K. R., & Finkelman, D. G. (1973). Rehearsal and organization in intentional forgetting. *Journal of Experimental Psychology, 98*, 169–174.

Sternberg, S. (1969). Memory scanning: Mental processes revealed by reaction-time experiments. *American Scientist, 57*, 421–457.

Timmins, W. K. (1973). Repetition of intentionally forgotten items. *Journal of Verbal Learning and Verbal Behavior, 12*, 168–173.

Timmins, W. K. (1974). Varying processing time in directed forgetting. *Journal of Verbal Learning and Verbal Behavior, 13*, 539–544.

Timmins, W. K. (1975). Effect of non-recognized repetition in a study of directed forgetting. *Psychological Reports, 37*, 1179–1188.

Tulving, E. (1985). Memory and consciousness. *Canadian Psychologist, 26*, 1–12.

Turvey, M. T., & Wittlinger, R. P. (1969). Attenuation of proactive interference in short-term memory as a function of cuing to forget. *Journal of Experimental Psychology, 80*, 295–298.

Tzeng, O. J. L., Lee, A. T., & Wetzel, C. D. (1979). Temporal coding in verbal information processing. *Journal of Experimental Psychology: Human Learning and Memory, 5*, 52–64.

Wallace, W. P. (1965). Review of the historical, empirical, and theoretical status of the von Restorff phenomenon. *Psychological Bulletin, 63*, 410–424.

Waugh, N. C. (1972). Retention as an active process. *Journal of Verbal Learning and Verbal Behavior, 11*, 129–140.

Waugh, N. C., & Norman, D. A. (1965). Primary memory. *Psychological Review, 72*, 89–97.

Weiner, B. (1966). The effects of motivation on the availability and retrieval of memory traces. *Psychological Bulletin, 65*, 24–37.

Weiner, B. (1968). Motivated forgetting and the study of repression. *Journal of Personality, 36*, 213–234.

Weiner, B., & Higgins, J. (1969). A mediational paradigm for the study of motivated forgetting: A critical analysis. *Journal of Verbal Learning and Verbal Behavior, 8*, 677–680.

Weiner, B., & Reed, H. (1969). Effects of the instructional sets to remember and to forget on short-term retention: Studies of rehearsal control and retrieval inhibition (repression). *Journal of Experimental Psychology, 79*, 226–232.

Wetzel, C. D. (1975). Effect of orienting tasks and cue timing on the free recall of remember- and forget-cued words. *Journal of Experimental Psychology: Human Learning and Memory, 1*, 556–566.

Wetzel, C. D., & Hunt, R. E. (1977). Cue delay and the role of rehearsal in directed forgetting. *Journal of Experimental Psychology: Human Learning and Memory, 3*, 233–245.

Wickens, D. D. (1970). Encoding categories of words: An empirical approach to meaning. *Psychological Review, 77*, 1–15.

Woodward, A. E., Jr., & Bjork, R. A. (1971). Forgetting and remembering in free recall: Intentional and unintentional. *Journal of Experimental Psychology, 89*, 109–116.

Woodward, A. E., Jr., Bjork, R. A., & Jongeward, R. H., Jr. (1973). Recall and recognition as a function of primary rehearsal. *Journal of Verbal Learning and Verbal Behavior, 12*, 608–617.

Woodward, A. E., Jr., Park, D. C., & Seebohm, K. (1974). Directed forgetting as a function of explicit within-list cuing and implicit postlist cuing. *Journal of Experimental Psychology, 102*, 1001–1006.

Yinger, R. J., & Johnson, W. L. (1973). Cued forgetting: Short-term memory effect. *Psychological Reports, 32*, 1197–1198.

Zeller, A. F. (1950). An experimental analogue of repression: The effect of individual failure and success on memory measured by relearning. *Journal of Experimental Psychology, 40*, 411–422.

2

THERE'S MORE TO INTENTIONAL FORGETTING THAN DIRECTED FORGETTING: AN INTEGRATIVE REVIEW

Jonathan M. Golding
University of Kentucky

Debra L. Long
University of California, Davis

It should be clear from chapter 1 that research on intentional forgetting has a long tradition tied to the directed-forgetting paradigm (see MacLeod, this volume). In fact, for many researchers and for many years, "directed forgetting" of words and syllables *was* research on intentional forgetting. Although directed-forgetting research is critical to understanding certain aspects of intentional forgetting, it is now also evident that intentional forgetting means different things to different researchers. For example, Johnson (1994) noted that intentional forgetting does not always mean forgetting in the sense of losing access to information designated to-be-forgotten. In fact, many studies that can be categorized as intentional forgetting studies are not even concerned with the ultimate retrieval of the to-be-forgotten information. Moreover, since the earliest studies of directed forgetting were carried out over 30 years ago (see Muther, 1965; see Bjork, 1972, and Epstein, 1972, for early reviews), the study of intentional forgetting has changed in important ways, employing a variety of methodologies and being driven by a number of theoretical perspectives.

Our purpose in the present chapter is to provide a brief review of some of the literature on intentional forgetting with humans that falls outside the realm of chapter 1. (For a review of directed forgetting in animals, readers should refer to a thorough review by Roper & Zentall, 1993, as well as to chapters by Grant and by Zentall, Roper, Kaiser, & Sherbourne in the present volume.) That is, this chapter shows that intentional forgetting goes well beyond the original domain of standard memory paradigms in cognitive

TABLE 2.1
Areas of Research on Intentional Forgetting

psychology. Other recent reviews have captured some of this literature; Johnson (1994) reviewed some of the issues relating to specific processes of successful intentional forgetting in cognitive and social psychology, and Wilson and Brekke (1994) and Zacks and Hasher (1994) discussed intentional forgetting as it relates to the issue of mental contamination. The present review overlaps with these other reviews to some extent (and with some of the literature discussed in other chapters), but expands to cover other areas of research. We review numerous studies that involve presenting individuals with information and then instructing or cuing them to forget, think of as false, disregard, discredit, discount, not think about, or ignore this information in a variety of contexts. In this way, we demonstrate the relevance of intentional forgetting research for many traditional areas in psychology such as social, developmental, clinical, and cognitive.

As seen in Table 2.1, there are 12 specific areas of research that are covered. These areas can be roughly broken into four major groupings. First, there are those areas of research that deal with social psychological issues such as psychology and the law, and attitudes and beliefs. Next is research on hindsight bias that involves issues of performance. Third, research focusing on developmental issues is examined, both with retardates and normals. Finally, clinical issues are examined through research on thought suppression and posthypnotic amnesia.

PSYCHOLOGY AND THE LAW

Research involving psychology and the law centers on the argument that "in theory, there is no place in a fair trial for evidence that is prejudicial, inherently unreliable, or illegally gathered" (Thompson, Fong, & Rosenhan,

1981, p. 453). If a judge agrees that evidence is inadmissible, the judge must either declare a mistrial or try to neutralize the biasing influence of this evidence by instructing jurors to disregard or to ignore it (Caretta & Moreland, 1983). These instructions are based on the assumption that such instructions are either effective in full or at least in part (i.e., the "cued-error" doctrine), thereby protecting the defendant's rights (see Tanford, 1990; Wrightsman, 1978). In fact, "if jurors are exposed to prejudicial information during a trial and the judge *emphasizes* it by instructing them to disregard it the appellate courts will not consider ordering a new trial because of these mistaken assumptions" (Tanford, 1990, p. 96).

Are instructions to disregard inadmissible evidence successful? The majority of empirical investigations (typically using mock jurors) suggests that such instructions are *ineffective*, especially when individual measures are taken. These investigations vary with regard to what type of information should be disregarded. Some of these studies instruct mock jurors to disregard information that is "external" to the criminal act itself. For example, Broeder (1959), as part of the classic Chicago Jury Project of Kalven and Zeisel (1966), presented mock jurors in a civil trial with information concerning whether or not the defendant had insurance related to the loss in question. Half of the mock jurors that were told he had insurance were told to disregard that information. Mock jurors who were instructed to disregard the information awarded the defendant more money than participants who did not know the defendant had insurance, or who knew that he had insurance but were not told to disregard this information. This overcompensation has been dubbed a "boomerang" effect (see also Wrightsman, 1978).

External information can also involve knowledge about whether or not a defendant had a prior criminal record. In one series of studies, Doob and his colleagues (1976; Doob & Kirshenbaum, 1972; Hans & Doob, 1976) investigated the Canada Evidence Act. This Act states that testimony of the accused on his or her own behalf cannot be entered as evidence; this testimony can be used to determine the credibility of the accused, but not that person's guilt or innocence. Doob found that mock jurors (individually and as a group) did not heed a judge's instructions to disregard the prior criminal record. In fact, Hans and Doob reported that participants who were informed about the defendant's prior record tended to bring up facts that were damaging to the defendant in a group discussion (see also the London School of Economics Jury Project prepared by Cornish & Sealy, 1973). Similar findings were also reported by Pickel (1995; see also Lenehan & O'Neill, 1981), who showed that mock jurors did not heed an instruction to disregard prior conviction evidence ruled inadmissible when the instruction included a specific legal explanation. Her three-experiment study indicated that mock jurors used this evidence because they thought it was "fair" relative to other types of inadmissible evidence, such as hearsay, which they did not use.

Pretrial publicity is another external piece of information. One study (Simon, 1966) reported no effect of pretrial publicity following an instruction to disregard. This study, however, has been criticized on various grounds, including a lack of critical control conditions, such as a condition in which participants did not receive pretrial publicity and a condition in which participants received this publicity but not the judge's instruction (Gerbasi, Zuckerman, & Reis, 1977). A more rigorously designed study, conducted by Sue, Smith, and Gilbert (1974), presented mock jurors with pretrial publicity about a robbery and murder in the form of a newspaper account of the crime. Despite a statement by the judge in a written summary of the trial that warned some mock jurors to disregard the pretrial publicity, the results indicated that the judge's instructions had no effect on verdicts, recommendations for sentencing, or ratings of the prosecution and defense cases compared to participants who did not receive such a warning. The same pattern of results was shown by Kramer, Kerr, and Carroll (1990). Moreover, mock jurors given such an instruction in Kramer et al. were *not* more likely to contest references to this publicity during jury deliberations than were jurors who did not receive the instruction.

Finally, instructions to disregard information external to the crime itself have been investigated in several studies focusing on police searches. Casper, Benedict, and Perry (1989) had students and other adults who had been called for jury duty assess opening and closing arguments in a civil suit against police officers who had allegedly conducted illegal searches. Although the legality of the search should not depend on its outcome, both types of participants were more sympathetic to the plaintiff when the search revealed no incriminating evidence than when the search revealed evidence against the plaintiff. In a related study, Kagehiro, Taylor, Laufer, and Harland (1991) examined third-party consenters (e.g., an apartment building owner) to warrantless police searches. The experimental participants were not supposed to use their knowledge of whether or not incriminating evidence was uncovered. The results showed that if evidence was uncovered, the participants were most likely to think the consenter had the right to permit police entry when the suspect was absent compared to when the suspect was present and protesting. If no evidence was uncovered, however, the participants thought that the consenter did *not* have the right to permit police entry when the suspect was absent compared to when the suspect was present and protesting.

Instructions to disregard evidence specifically pertaining to a crime has also been investigated. In the classic study in this area, Sue, Smith, and Caldwell (1973) presented mock jurors with a robbery trial summary in one of three conditions; (a) no evidence critical to judging the defendant's guilt, (b) evidence critical to judging the defendant's guilt, and (c) evidence critical to judging the defendant's guilt, with an additional instruction to disregard the evidence because it was inadmissible. The results of this study found that jurors used the inadmissible evidence in determining guilt, but only in a "weak" version of the trial summary in which the other evidence did not clearly indicate guilt or innocence. A replication of this study found that authoritarianism increased the likelihood that participants would use incriminating inadmissible evidence to convict a defendant (Werner, Kagehiro, & Strube, 1982).

Other research relating to evidence about the crime itself was conducted by Thompson et al. (1981). This work examined the possibility that a juror's willingness to ignore an instruction to disregard may depend on the view that it is worse to convict an innocent person than to acquit a guilty person. This view would lead jurors to ignore proconviction inadmissible evidence. During a robbery/murder trial, either proconviction or proacquittal evidence was sometimes presented, and was sometimes ruled inadmissible. The results found, in fact, that only proacquittal to-be-disregarded inadmissible evidence affected mock jurors' judgments.

Finally, research has examined courtroom procedure with regard to instructions to disregard inadmissible evidence. Some of these studies focused on the type of instruction given by a judge. Wolf and Montgomery (1977) found that the designation of "inadmissible" alone had no effect on guilt judgments. Only when the "inadmissible" designation was followed by an instruction to disregard were guilt judgments influenced in the direction of the inadmissible testimony. Also, Kassin and Wrightsman (1981; see also Kassin & Wrightsman, 1985) investigated judge's instructions, but in the context of confession evidence. In a case involving a coerced confession (deemed inadmissible as evidence), mock jurors either were directed by the judge to simply "reject any confession they believed to have been coerced," or were given a longer explanation that defined what it meant to have a coerced confession, and made it clear that such elicited confessions were unreliable. The results showed that the mock jurors used the coerced confession, regardless of the judge's instruction. A second experiment found that jurors heeded the instructions, but only if the instructions to disregard emphasized the unfairness of even mildly coercive tactics.

Courtroom procedure has also been the focus in cases of disregarding information in a juror removal situation. Kaplan and Atkins (1982) discussed how in a California armed robbery trial a juror was dismissed the morning after the jury had deliberated for over an hour the previous day. Shortly after the dismissal, an alternate was added to the jury and the defendant was found guilty. The California State Supreme Court upheld the conviction, but defined a new procedure requiring judges to instruct the jury to forget their prior deliberation (the "Collins instruction") and to begin anew on submission of a new juror. Kaplan and Atkins stated that, "This procedure rests on the assumption that jurors exposed to the Collins instruction will be capable of disregarding all that was said during the initial deliberation" (p. 261). Research conducted by Kaplan and Atkins indicated that this assumption was not met, and that mock jurors continued to use information provided by the dismissed juror (see also Clark, 1994).

Why are instructions to disregard inadmissible evidence usually unsuccessful? Various theoretical positions have been developed to answer this question, although they are not necessarily mutually exclusive. We consider three of these. The first, the "juror justice" viewpoint, states that failure to heed a judge's instructions in the courtroom results from different views of justice held by both the court and the jurors (Thompson et al., 1981). Whereas the court views justice with regard to due process, jurors view justice in terms of "right" outcomes. Therefore, it would defy common justice or common sense for juries to ignore relevant, yet inadmissible facts (see also Kadish & Kadish, 1971; Sue et al., 1973; Wolf & Montgomery, 1977).

The second viewpoint, "integrated representation," states that jurors construct an integrated cognitive representation (or story) of the trial events (Devine & Ostrom, 1985; see also Pennington & Hastie, 1981). Jurors try to match the testimony of witnesses to their own evolving conception of the action sequence that occurred during the criminal event. They do this through construction, inference, and credibility evaluation (Hastie, Penrod, & Pennington, 1983). Each item of testimony is evaluated for its credibility and its implications for the developing story. Therefore, if information is to be disregarded but it helps jurors to fill in details of the evolving story, they may continue to use the information (Devine & Ostrom, 1985).

The third idea, Thomas and Hogue's (1976) "decision-making" viewpoint, states that: (a) The apparent weight of evidence to jurors varies randomly over the population of potential jurors; (b) jurors decide for or against a defendant if the apparent weight is less than or greater than a decision criterion (which varies little over the population but may vary over cases, instructions to the jurors, etc.); and (c) decision confidence increases as the absolute difference between apparent weight and decision criterion increases (usually in a linear fashion). The criterion is highest when the standard of proof is "sure and certain" and lowest when it is a "balance of probabilities." On average, the criterion is higher when jurors are told to disregard "damaging evidence" than when they are not, but it is not as high as when no such evidence is mentioned. Thomas and Hogue (1976) argued that this ordering was consistent with Cornish and Sealy's (1973) suggestion that instructions to disregard are effective, but not wholly so.

It should be noted that several researchers have argued that methodological issues complicate conclusions about the ineffectiveness of instructions to disregard. For example, these conclusions may be affected by the length of the trial presentation. Miller (1975) examined the effect of videotaped trials in which inadmissible evidence was presented in varying amounts (i.e., 1–6 pieces of evidence). He deleted varying amounts of inadmissible testimony and found that this did not affect jurors' verdicts. Miller noted that he may not have replicated previous results (e.g., Sue et al., 1973) because the inadmissible evidence was not highly dramatic or extremely damaging, especially because the videotaped trial lasted 3 hours.

In addition, most of the studies reviewed obtained judgments from individual participants. Some research, however, found either no effect or only a partial effect of instructions to disregard on juries as a whole. Caretta and Moreland (1983) had 6-person mock juries read different versions of the Sue et al. (1973) trial summary and then deliberate on a verdict for 30 minutes. They found that (a) the effects of inadmissible evidence were rarely as strong as when the same evidence was ruled admissible, but were much stronger (especially initially) compared to control participants never presented with the evidence; (b) the inadmissible evidence was brought up in the discussion; (c) the issue of admissibility was generally neglected in the discussions; and (d) group discussion sometimes played an important role in helping people to obey a judge's ruling and to resist the effects of inadmissible evidence. A more recent study (Kerwin & Shaffer, 1994) directly compared individual mock jurors who did not deliberate with individual mock jurors who did deliberate. They found that, consistent with previous research, mock jurors who did not deliberate continued to use the inadmissible evidence, whereas the reverse was true for mock jurors who did deliberate. Kerwin and Shaffer stated that this result could be due to the difficulty in justifying one's personal bias (based on the inadmissible evidence) to others during jury deliberations.

Although the vast majority of research in the area of psychology and law has involved inadmissible evidence, research in this domain has also investigated discrediting information in the courtroom. In discrediting studies, a statement is made by a witness that is later discredited by the same witness or by another witness in the trial. The discrediting is not due to the illegal presentation of specific testimony. The classic discrediting study was conducted by Loftus (1974). In this study, either participants were or were not presented with critical eyewitness testimony. Moreover, some of those who received the critical eyewitness testimony also received additional testimony that discredited what was originally presented; a defense attorney pointed out that the eyewitness required eyeglasses and was not wearing them at the time of the crime. Loftus found that participants who received the critical eyewitness testimony had more guilty verdicts than those who did not receive this testimony, regardless of whether they received the discrediting information. These data were interpreted as indicative of the high impact of eyewitness testimony.

Loftus' results (1974), however, have not always been replicated. In one study, Hatvany and Strack (1980) showed that participants virtually ignored eyewitness testimony if it was discredited. The discrediting in this study, however, was quite extreme. The critical witness admitted to not wearing eyeglasses that were needed, apologized for testifying, and then asked the court to ignore her earlier testimony. Weinberg and Baron (1982) avoided the extreme nature of the discrediting and added other manipulations such as whether the discrediting was made by a defense attorney or by another witness. Once again, the results showed that when the eyewitness evidence was discredited, it was ignored (see also Wells, Lindsay, & Tousignant, 1980). Other studies have shown the effectiveness of discrediting an eyewitness, including research by Saunders, Vidmar, and Hewitt (1983), Elliot, Farrington, and Manheimer (1988), and Schul and Manzury (1990).

It should be noted that only one of the above studies, Saunders et al. (1983, Experiment 3), used the discrediting paradigm with jury deliberation and verdicts. In this study, the pattern of jury verdicts was consistent with Loftus (1974); there was support for the failure of discrediting. In this study, however, there was evidence that participants who heard the critical testimony discredited were less accepting of this testimony. This contradiction in results was explained by the fact that jurors who heard the critical testimony, including those who heard it discredited, were more accepting of circumstantial evidence compared to participants who never heard the critical evidence. Thus, it was not a failure in discrediting, per se, that led to the jury verdicts, but the fact that other more circumstantial evidence gained greater importance.

In summary, those studies investigating psychology and the law investigated either instructions to disregard inadmissible testimony or the discrediting of testimony. Of the former, the great majority showed that these instructions are quite *ineffective*. There are several possible explanations for this finding. In addition, some researchers argued that these results were a function of the type of data collected; individual scores rather than group scores. Of the discrediting studies, the empirical evidence appears mixed. More recent research, however, appears to indicate a greater preponderance of evidence in support of individuals' ability to discredit testimony.

ATTITUDES AND BELIEFS

Research on attitudes and beliefs involving intentional forgetting can be broken into several categories. The earliest studies in this domain can be traced to research on debriefing. Sometimes, a participant in an experiment is deceived during the course of the procedure. When deception is used, experimenters debrief the participants at the conclusion of the experiment to explain how and why the deception was used. Experimenters generally believe that such a debriefing accomplishes the goal of returning the participant to his or her preexperimental state (see Walster, Bersheid, Abrahams, & Aronson, 1967). Despite this conviction, research has shown that this goal is probably not achieved as often as is hoped. In the words of Ross, Lepper, and Hubbard (1975, p. 880), "What is done is done and cannot be undone."

Walster et al. (1967) investigated the hypothesis that it is more difficult to successfully debrief (i.e., return to their preexperimental state) participants who received false information on some aspect of themselves about which they are currently concerned compared to participants who received false information on some aspect of themselves about which they are *not* currently concerned. Participants were led to believe that they should be very concerned or less concerned about their own social skills. Then, the participants participated in a deception experiment in which they were led to believe that they had good or bad social skills. This involved presenting participants with scores on various measures, and giving the participants time to "read and think about" their social skills. Finally, participants were debriefed on the experimental procedure, at which time they were informed that the scores they had received were false. Despite the debriefing, participants who were given measures that indicated high social skills rated themselves higher on a sociability scale than those who received measures that indicated low social skills.

The perseverance of participants' attitudes despite debriefing was later examined by Ross et al. (1975) and by Ross, Lepper, Strack, and Steinmetz (1977). In the Ross et al. (1975) study, participants were given false feedback about whether they had succeeded or failed on a novel discrimination task. Following the task, they were debriefed about the nature of the feedback. Then the participants were asked to estimate past and future performance on this task. In Experiment 1, only the person participating in the task was given the feedback and debriefing; in Experiment 2, the participant and a yoked observer were run. Both experiments found a substantial perseverance of initial impressions of performance following debriefing. In Experiment 2, however, a "process" debriefing, in which participants were explicitly informed of the perseverance process, eliminated some of the perseverance, primarily for the actual participants. The Ross et al. (1977) study had participants identify potential antecedents to explain events in various contexts (such as clinical cases, hit-and-run accidents), and replicated the earlier study. Moreover, Ross et al. showed that participants were affected by previous information, even if they knew from the outset that the event to be explained was hypothetical.

Whereas the debriefing studies typically involved instructing participants not to use information about themselves, later research involving attitudes and behaviors looked at instructions to disregard information about other people and other things. Specifically, in these later studies, participants were instructed to disregard information in an impression formation task. The initial study in this domain was conducted by Wyer and Unverzagt (1985) as a test of a general formulation of social information processing called the "bin model." The bin model is quite complex, and is not described in detail here (see Isbell, Smith, & Wyer, this volume, for further discussion of the model). It conceptualizes permanent memory as a set of content-address-able "storage bins." Each bin is of unlimited capacity and is identified by a header that specifies its referent and describes its content. According to the model, the content of a bin depends on the presentation position of the to-be-disregarded and to-be-regarded information. When the to-be-disregarded information is presented before the to-be-regarded information, it is stored separately. Thus, there should be *no* influence (i.e., *no* interference) of one set on another: Each set of behaviors should be recalled well, and the to-be-disregarded information should not influence impression formation. When the to-be-disregarded behaviors are presented after the to-be-regarded behaviors, two bins are also constructed; one contains both the to-be-disregarded and the to-be-regarded information, whereas the other contains only the to-be-regarded information. This type of storage leads to interference, thereby lowering recall of the to-be-disregarded information. In addition, impression formation may be affected by the to-be-disregarded information.

Wyer and Unverzagt (1985; see also Wyer & Budesheim, 1987) empirically tested the bin model. They presented participants with sets of honest, unkind, and neutral behaviors in different positions within a list of characteristics about a person named John Pennebaker. The disregard instruction was cast as an "experimenter error." That is, the experimenter pretended to make an error and followed this error with the disregard instruction. Moreover, the "error" was related to either reading behaviors about a person other than Pennebaker or to reading behaviors about Pennebaker that should not have been read. In general, the results of these studies supported the bin model, especially with regard to the to-be-disregarded behaviors.

At around the same time that Wyer's research was published, Schul and Burnstein (1985) conducted a series of experiments that had the flavor of more recent studies in the cognitive psychology domain (e.g., Basden, Basden, & Gargano, 1993). They were interested in how differences in encoding might promote the successful discounting of knowledge; and how the outcome of discounting might depend on the way the discounting is performed. The results of two experiments showed that discounting was relatively more successful when participants were instructed to ignore under discrete as opposed to integrative encoding, and when the ignore instruction only dealt with a single argument as opposed to a group of behaviors.

Later research by Schul (1993) investigated whether instructions to ignore can be made more effective when a warning is presented prior to receiving the to-be-ignored information that some information they are to receive is invalid. Experiment 1 showed that a warning by itself does not increase the effectiveness of the ignore instruction. Instead, the warning was only successful if it was followed by a bizarre descriptor that had the potential to remind participants of the potential invalidity of information. Subsequent experiments in this study replicated the importance of pairing the warning with the reminder, and showed that once reminded about the warning, people take more time to process the to-be-ignored information.

The effect of explicit cues during impression formation has also been investigated with regard to the use of language in a social context. Golding and his colleagues conducted several studies investigating the effect of pragmatics on the use of and memory for to-be-disregarded information. Pragmatics includes information about the communicative situation, the temporal position of an utterance in the communication, knowledge about the speaker (e.g., intentions, beliefs, and knowledge of and attitude toward the listener), and information about the relationship between the speaker and the listener (see Keenan, MacWhinney, & Mayhew, 1977).

Golding, Fowler, Long, and Latta (1990) reasoned that explicit cues might only be effective to the extent that the pragmatic implication of the cue indicated that the designated information was indeed irrelevant. As an example, Golding et al. presented a scenario in which an individual was instructed to disregard some information. This instruction was followed by the fact that the information was either "confidential" or "incorrect" (i.e., it was about someone else). Although in both cases there was an explicit cue to segregate, the pragmatic implication of the cue was quite different. In the "confidential" case, it might be expected that the listener would continue to process the "irrelevant" information, whereas the "incorrect" information would not be expected to be further processed. This would lead to the confidential information affecting judgments more and being recalled better than the incorrect information.

The prediction for judgments has been supported in several studies. Moreover, support has been found regardless of whether the context involved role-playing (Golding et al., 1990; Golding, Sego, Hauselt, & Long, 1994) or a more naturalistic context (Golding & Hauselt, 1994); whether the task involved person impression or object impression (Golding et al., 1990); whether the to-be-disregarded information was presented before or after the to-be-regarded information (Golding et al., 1990); and whether individual participants (e.g., Golding & Hauselt, 1994) or groups (Golding, Ellis, Hauselt, & Sego, this volume) made judgments about the target. In contrast, the recall results from these studies have generally not supported the effect of pragmatics. That is, the to-be-disregarded information has been recalled relatively well regardless of the type of disregard instruction.

The results of Golding et al. (1990) are important in showing that the use of explicit cues to segregate may be a function of the context in which the cue is presented. Just because information is cued as "to be forgotten" does not mean it will be treated that way (see also Petty & Wegener, 1993; Wegener & Petty, 1995). If participants are presented with other salient information about the relevance or utility of the to-be-forgotten information, the to-be-forgotten information may continue to be used. In Golding et al. (1990), this salient information was labeled "confidential" or "incorrect." In other studies, the labeling of this salient information has differed, but it has still been made clear whether the to-be-forgotten information should be treated as relevant or irrelevant. For example, in the mock-jury studies investigating instructions to disregard inadmissible evidence, the context indicated to participants that the inadmissible evidence was relevant to the trial (see also Golding & Keenan, 1985). Conversely, in typical directed-forgetting studies, participants had no reason to believe that they would be asked to remember any of the to-be-forgotten items, and no reason to think that remembering a to-be-forgotten item would help them remember a to-be-remembered item.

Related to the research on impression formation is the work of Gilbert (Gilbert, 1991; Gilbert, Krull, & Malone, 1990; Gilbert, Tafarodi, & Malone, 1993) dealing with the initial acceptance of propositions about others. For example, in Gilbert et al. (1990, Experiment 1), participants were presented with propositions. After each proposition was presented, the participants were told whether it was true or false. In addition, on some trials, the participants were interrupted prior to the presentation of the true/false designation. Gilbert et al. found that the interruption increased the likelihood that false propositions would be considered true. Additional experiments showed that all propositions were initially represented as true, and that even the designation as false did not easily change this representation. Consistent with this study, Gilbert et al. (1993) found that both high cognitive load and time pressure caused participants to believe and to use false information about a criminal defendant or a college student.

Other areas of intentional-forgetting research have involved changing attitudes and beliefs through persuasive messages. Included in this is research on the "absolute sleeper effect." This effect occurs when a persuasive message is presented, but its effect occurs only after some amount of time. It is as though the persuasive effect of the message is found only after individuals have had a chance to "sleep on it." As a pattern of data, the sleeper effect is opposite to the typical finding that experimentally induced change in opinion dissipates over time (Cook & Flay, 1978).

Studies of the sleeper effect (e.g., Gruder et al., 1978; Pratkanis, Greenwald, Leippe, & Baumgardner, 1988) usually employ experimental and control conditions in much the same way as the other studies in this review. One group receives no persuasive message, and another group receives a persuasive message. In addition, there is a group that receives the persuasive message, but who also receives a "discounting cue" with respect to the message. Gruder et al. (1978) stated that a discounting cue is "any brief signal which indicates that the information in an otherwise persuasive message is not credible" (p. 1062). This cue is presented either before or after the message. Unlike other directed-forgetting studies, however, the discounting cue does not explicitly instruct participants to "forget" or "disregard" the message. Participants who receive the message rate their attitude toward the topic of the message after reading and after a delay, which can be as long as 6 weeks.

Attempts to find evidence of the absolute sleeper effect have not always been successful (e.g., Gillig & Greenwald, 1974). The lack of success, however, has been offset by those studies that have found the sleeper effect to be reliable (e.g., Gruder et al., 1978; Pratkanis et al., 1988). Those studies that have been successful have found that certain conditions must apply for the sleeper effect to occur. According to Pratkanis et al. (1988) these include having the participant note the important arguments in the message; presenting the discounting cue *after* the message; and having the participant rate the trustworthiness of the message communicator immediately after receiving the discounting cue. More recent research on the sleeper effect has also emphasized the availability of the discounted message in memory, sometimes due to greater cognitive elaboration during initial encoding (see Hannah & Sternthal, 1984; Schul & Mazursky, 1990).

Research on corrective advertising also involves changing beliefs and attitudes. Sometimes during the course of marketing a product, a firm may mislead the public in its advertising. If this occurs, the Federal Trade Commission (FTC) has the authority to require the firm to rectify its deception through "corrective advertising" (Wilkie, McNeill, & Mazis, 1984). The goal of the corrective ad is to change or correct erroneous beliefs that were based on the original presentation of the ad (see Jacoby, Nelson, & Hoyer, 1982).

A number of studies have investigated corrective advertising since 1970, the first year that the FTC was given the authority to require these ads (see Wilkie et al., 1984 for a review). These include experiments involving relatively artificial contexts as well as field studies that occurred following FTC-ordered corrective ad campaigns. The earliest study to investigate this issue was conducted by Hunt (1973). In this study, participants were presented with an original ad about gasoline and then with either a typical ad about gasoline produced by a specific company (i.e., "no attack"); a general statement that previous gasoline ads produced by the company were misleading, deceptive, or untrue (i.e., "general attack"); or statements that exposed each point of untruth in a deceptive gasoline ad by the company (i.e., "explicit attack"). Participants then judged how much they liked the gasoline in question. The results showed that the explicit attack was most effective in reducing the favorableness toward the gasoline (see also Dyer & Kuehl, 1974).

Later studies extended Hunt's (1973) original finding using different methodologies. Mazis and Adkinson (1976) were concerned that the presentation of the corrective ad in Hunt (1973) was too artificial, because the ad was presented as an immediate follow-up to an existing ad rather than being incorporated into completely new corrective ads. This artificiality may have exaggerated the impact of the corrective ad. Therefore, participants were presented with the corrective ads within the context of listening to an audiotape of a late-night television interview. The results showed that the corrective ad had a substantial influence on the brand belief it was intended to affect as well as a related belief, which was not the target of the communication. Later research, however, in a field setting showed that belief change following corrective ads only affected beliefs about the product in question. That is, there was no generalization to the overall product category or to general perceptions of the product's company (Bernhart, Kinnear, & Mazis, 1986).

The effectiveness of a corrective ad has been shown to depend on the nature of the correction. Schul and Mazursky (1990) investigated whether corrective ads that instruct individuals to disregard a particular claim (i.e., "ignore" cues) are as effective as those ads that directly refute a claim (i.e., "refute" cues) and provide explicit opposite implications. Participants were presented with stroller advertisements. During presentation of the ads, the attributes of the stroller were either presented in a specific order to facilitate encoding of the durability of the stroller (i.e., elaborative encoding condition) or out of order (i.e., nonelaborative encoding condition). Following the original ad, an ignore or refute cue was presented. The results of Experiment 1 showed that on global judgments (willingness to use the product in future), when participants used elaborative encoding, there was less discounting with ignore cue compared to refute cues. It should be noted, however, that the discounting cue was always successful, (regardless of the type of cue) compared to a condition that did not receive such a cue.

To assess the long-term effects of corrective ads, Dyer and Kuehl (1978) used a longitudinal design. Participants were initially asked to rate their beliefs concerning attributes of a mouthwash after receiving both a deceptive ad for Listerine mouthwash (i.e., "Listerine prevents colds and sore throats") and a nondeceptive ad for another mouthwash. Three weeks later, a second experimental session was conducted in which participants again rated their beliefs about mouthwashes after being presented with ads. Some participants received the same deceptive Listerine ad used in the first session and another mouthwash brand advertisement. The other participants received one of two corrective ads for Listerine and another mouthwash. A third experimental session was scheduled after another 3-week interval. In this last session, no ads were presented, but beliefs about the mouthwashes were again collected. The results indicated that the corrective ad led to less belief that Listerine prevents colds and sore throats after both the second and third sessions compared to the first session. Even after the third session, however, the corrective ad did not fully remove falsely based beliefs about Listerine; compared to other brands, participants still believed to some degree the claims about Listerine and its ability to prevent colds and sore throats. A similar finding concerning the persistence of beliefs over time has been shown by Tyebjee (1982) and by Kinnear, Taylor, and Gur-Arie (1983).

It is interesting to note that although corrective ads are generally effective, research has also shown that the "plain English" developed and proposed by the FTC may be widely misunderstood by large segments of the population. First, Mazis and Adkinson (1976) noted that 39% of their participants misunderstood the corrective message that was used in the study. In addition, in three experiments, Jacoby et al. (1982) showed that remedial statements proposed by the FTC for inclusion in a corrective ad campaign were more often associated with confused or incorrect comprehension than with correct comprehension.

The studies in this section on beliefs and attitudes paint a picture of intentional forgetting that is generally consistent with the prior section on psychology and the law. Specifically, in each of the five sub-sections, it was shown that intentional-forgetting instructions are either not heeded at all or are only partially heeded. Only in very unique contexts, such as designating information as "incorrect" (e.g., Golding et al., 1990), were individuals able to effectively disregard the information. Of course, like the psychology and law research, the implications of this inability to follow instructions for interacting with others and for altering beliefs and attitudes is enormous.

HINDSIGHT BIAS

People who receive knowledge about the outcome of an event exhibit a change in their perceptions of the likelihood of that outcome, even when they are explicitly instructed to disregard that knowledge. This change has been labeled "hindsight bias." Specifically, hindsight bias has been defined operationally as "the tendency for individuals with outcome knowledge (hindsight) to claim that they would have estimated a probability of occurrence for the reported outcome that is higher than they would have estimated in foresight (without the outcome information)" (Hawkins & Hastie, 1990, p. 311). It is worth noting that hindsight bias has been shown with groups as well as with individuals (Stahlberg, Eller, Maass, & Frey, 1995), and that hindsight bias occurs in a wide variety of laboratory tasks (see Hawkins & Hastie, 1990, for a review; and Christensen-Szalanski & Willham, 1991, for a meta-analysis). These tasks include judging the likelihood of historical events (Fischhoff, 1975; Fischhoff & Beyth, 1975), outcomes of scientific experiments (Slovic & Fischhoff, 1977), job performance (Schkade & Kilbourne, 1991), sociopolitical events (Guerin, 1982; Leary, 1982; Pennington, 1981; Powell, 1988; Synodinos, 1986), probability (Hennessey & Edgell, 1991), outcomes of sporting events (Leary, 1981), and correct answers to general knowledge facts (Fischhoff, 1977; Hasher, Attig, & Alba, 1981; Hell, Gigerenzer, Gauggel, Mall, & Muller, 1988; Hoch & Loewenstein, 1989; Wood, 1978). In addition, hindsight bias appears to influence people's judgments in a variety of naturalistic contexts such as in a court of law (see the section in the present chapter on "Psychology and the Law"; see also Bodenhausen, 1990; Cox & Tanford, 1989; Kamin & Rachlinski, 1995), physicians' confidence in their clinical diagnoses (Arkes, 1981; Arkes, Wortmann, Saville, & Harkness, 1981), pregnancy results (Pennington, Rutter, McKenna, & Morley, 1980), and the extent to which victims are blamed for their own misfortune (Janoff-Bulman, Timko, & Carli, 1985).

The majority of these studies involved reporting the outcome of an event to one group of participants (hindsight participants) and comparing their judgments of the likelihood of its occurrence to a group of participants who received no outcome knowledge (foresight participants). For example, Fischhoff (1975) had participants read descriptions of historical events (e.g., a near riot in Atlanta) and clinical cases. Each description included four possible outcomes. Hindsight participants received information about the "true" outcome, whereas foresight participants did not. All participants were asked to predict the likelihood of each of the four outcomes. Fischhoff found that hindsight participants assigned higher probabilities to the outcome they were told had actually occurred than did foresight participants. In addition, Fischhoff found that hindsight participants who were instructed to disregard their outcome knowledge (i.e., to respond "as they would have had they not known the outcome") continued to exhibit a hindsight bias. Fischhoff concluded both that outcome knowledge exaggerates participants' perceptions of the likelihood of the outcome and that participants are unaware of the effects that outcome knowledge has on their perceptions. Thus, participants typically claim that they "would have known it all along" (Fischhoff, 1975).

Several information-processing explanations for hindsight effects have been proposed (Fischhoff, 1975, 1977; Hasher et al., 1981). One such explanation is "creeping determinism": Hindsight effects arise from processes that operate to create a coherent whole out of knowledge about an event. When participants hear the outcome of an event, they integrate the outcome with relevant prior knowledge. This may involve reinterpreting prior knowledge about the topic to make sense of it in light of new knowledge about the outcome or strengthening associations among particular aspects of their knowledge and the reported outcome. Fischhoff (1975) noted that because assimilation occurs automatically, participants underestimate the influence of outcome knowledge on their perceptions. They appear unable to access the state of their knowledge prior to receiving outcome knowledge and thus overestimate how obvious the correct outcome appeared (see also Slovic & Fischhoff, 1977).

Hasher et al. (1981) demonstrated that participants' apparent inability to disregard outcome knowledge does not result from their inability to remember a preoutcome knowledge state (see also Davies, 1987). Participants received a list of general knowledge facts and were asked to rate them on a true-to-false scale. Subsequently, participants received feedback about half of the items that they had rated. Participants were then instructed to rate all of the items again and to ignore the feedback that they had received between the rating trials. Hasher et al. had two critical experimental conditions. In the *wrong* condition, the experimenter told participants prior to the second rating trial that the feedback they had received was wrong. In the *mistake* condition, the experimenter told participants that it looked as if the feedback information list contained a lot of mistakes. Second trial ratings provided by the two critical groups were compared to ratings from a group that received correct feedback (i.e., feedback without disconfirming information) and a no-feedback control group. Hasher et al. found a significant knew-it-all-along effect for the group that received correct feedback. Providing participants with information that some of the feedback they received was mistaken (the mistake group) reduced, but did not eliminate the effect. Finally, participants who were told that the feedback they received was wrong exhibited no hindsight bias. Hasher et al. argued that their results were inconsistent with the view that assimilation of feedback information with prior knowledge leads to an "erasure" of the original knowledge state. Rather, the ability of participants in the wrong condition to disregard the feedback information suggests that participants can retrieve a preoutcome knowledge state when they exert the effort to do so.

With regard to the preoutcome knowledge state, it should be noted that some studies have shown that hindsight bias can be reduced by elaborate encoding of this state. For example, Hell et al. (1988) showed that having participants provide reasons for their responses prior to receiving the outcome led to less hindsight bias. In addition, Arkes et al. (1981) showed that asking physicians to provide reasons for their foresight judgments substantially reduced hindsight bias (see also Pennington et al., 1980).

Although manipulations that increase access to a preoutcome knowledge state appear to reduce hindsight bias, hindsight effects appear to be robust in the face of a variety of other instructional manipulations. For example, Wood (1978) examined the influence of memory instructions on the amount of hindsight bias. Besides providing outcome estimates before and after receiving outcome knowledge, some participants were asked to remember their preoutcome estimate (memory instructions). Although the effect was smaller for participants instructed to remember their preoutcome judgment, there was still a significant hindsight bias even in this memory group.

Hindsight bias also appears to be robust in the face of debiasing instructions. Fischhoff (1977) attempted to minimize hindsight effects by exhorting participants to work harder or by telling them about the bias. Participants answered general knowledge questions taken from almanacs and encyclopedias. Each question had two alternative answers with the correct answer indicated. Participants were asked to estimate their probability of being correct to either the first or the second answer as if they had not received the correct answer. All participants were told that their responses would "enable the experimenters to evaluate the perceived difficulty of the items." Two groups of participants received additional instructions. The warning group was told that their responses were extremely important and that the effort they invested would determine the value of the subsequent study. The debiasing group received an explanation and an example of the I-knew-it-all-along effect. Subsequently, the debiasing group was told to do everything they could to avoid this bias. The results indicated a substantial hindsight effect for all groups. Neither exhorting participants to work harder nor instructing participants to avoid the bias reduced the size of the effect (but see Creyer & Ross, 1993). It should be noted, however, that Sharpe and Adair (1993) did remove hindsight bias by using a debiasing instruction that forewarned participants about a "never-knew-that" effect.

Although most investigations of hindsight bias focused on information-processing explanations (see Hawkins & Hastie, 1990), several researchers investigated the possibility that hindsight effects result from motivational factors. Campbell and Tesser (1983) examined two motivational explanations of hindsight bias. According to a "predictability" motive, people overestimate the likelihood of events in hindsight due to a basic human need to feel control over their environment. According to a "self-presentational" motive, hindsight bias results from a person's desire to impress others or to save face by claiming accurate foresight knowledge. To measure variation in the predictability motive, participants completed an Intolerance of Ambiguity Scale and Rokeach's Dogmatism Scale. Individual differences in the self-presentation motive were assessed by means of the Marlow–Crowne Social Desirability Scale. Campbell and Tesser found measures for both motives to be positively correlated with amount of hindsight bias. In addition, they found that a postexperimental measure of self-reported ego involvement in the task predicted amount of hindsight bias. Campbell and Tesser concluded that motivational factors operate in conjunction with cognitive factors to produce hindsight effects.

Similar studies were conducted to test the relative contribution of information processing and motivational factors in producing hindsight bias (Hell et al., 1988; Leary, 1981, 1982; Synodinos, 1986). Leary (1981, 1982) examined two motivational factors; self-presentation and self-esteem. A self-presentational explanation attributes hindsight effects to participants' beliefs that they will be regarded positively by others as a consequence of accurately predicting an event. Thus, a self-presentational explanation suggests that hindsight effects should be largest when participants' predictions will be known to others. In contrast, a self-esteem explanation attributes hindsight effects to participants' desire to maintain or to enhance self-esteem (i.e., to feel satisfaction about their intelligence, good judgment, or perceptiveness). Leary hypothesized that individuals who perceived themselves as highly knowledgeable about a subject would be motivated to maintain this perception by accurately predicting relevant events. Thus, these individuals would be more likely to exhibit hindsight effects than would less motivated individuals. In one study, Leary (1981) asked students and alumni attending a college football game either to predict the score of the game (foresight) or to estimate what they would have predicted had they not seen the game (hindsight). Participants were classified as high or low in knowledgeability of football (i.e., high or low self-esteem) and were asked to respond publicly or anonymously (i.e., high or low self-presentation). Leary found a significant effect only for timing of prediction. Hindsight predictions were closer to the final score than were foresight predictions. He argued that the failure to obtain significant effects of self-presentation and self-esteem support a nonmotivational, information-processing explanation of hindsight effects. Support for Leary's conclusion was provided by Synodinos (1986) who found no influence of either task specific self-esteem (i.e., amount of knowledge about the task) or global self-esteem (i.e., self-worth, confidence, sense of adequacy) on amount of hindsight bias.

The results of the research on hindsight bias again indicate the relative inability of individuals to follow instructions to ignore specific outcome information. Moreover, this inability is tied to both information-processing and motivational factors. It is not the case that individuals will always use outcome information. But like the previous sections on "Psychology and the Law" and "Attitudes and Behaviors," the conditions necessary to avoid hindsight bias occur infrequently.

MEMORY CONTROL PROCESSES IN RETARDATES

Research conducted with respect to control processes in retardates has been the focus in Bray's laboratory (see Bray, 1979, for an early review of his research). His first study on this issue (Bray, 1973) tested whether retardates would show evidence of directed forgetting, given that retardates were generally considered to rehearse in a nonselective manner. In three experiments, digits alone or digits and pictures were presented to educable retardates ranging in age from 14 to 17 years old. The participants were signaled (through the use of a color change) to "forget" the first block of items presented on certain trials. Comparisons with a control condition, which received the additional block but no cue (i.e., remember condition), showed that the retardates could use an instruction to forget; recall of to-be-remembered items was increased when there was a forget instruction. Moreover, as an indirect way to assess rehearsal, comparisons of the serial position curves indicated that the participants were selectively rehearsing after the forget cue appeared.

Two points should be made concerning the research conducted by Bray. First, although Bray was interested in examining the issue of selective rehearsal with regard to directed forgetting, his methodology (i.e., blocked or list presentation) is consistent with that used to investigate retrieval inhibition, not selective rehearsal (see Basden et al., 1993). Second, none of Bray's studies specifically tested memory for the to-be-forgotten information.

To investigate directed forgetting in younger retardates, Bray and Ferguson (1976) conducted a study in which pictures were presented to educable retardates between 9.5 and 11 years old and IQ-matched normals between 6.9 and 7.4 years old. Consistent with Bray (1973), they found evidence that the forget cue facilitated recall of the to-be-remembered pictures for both the retardates and the normals. In fact, the forget condition was equal to a precued condition (i.e., no pictures in the first block, but pictures in the second block) and both were greater than that on the control trials in which there were only to-be-remembered pictures. Bray and Ferguson (1976) argued that this result suggested that the children processed the pictures following the forget cue more actively than the pictures appearing before the cue; a passive–active strategy.

In both Bray (1973) and Bray and Ferguson (1976), participants received extensive training concerning the significance of the forget cue. To investigate the impact of the amount of task explanation on directed forgetting, Bray, Goodman, and Justice (1982) presented educable retarded adolescents (13–15 years old) with short sequences of picture names under either minimal or extensive task instructions. In addition to measuring memory for the pictures, the amount of time each participant spent between pictures was measured. This latter measure is referred to as "pause time"; participants who use a rehearsal strategy should show a pattern of increasingly longer pause times as they go through a list of items. It was found that only the retardates who received extensive instructions showed evidence of directed forgetting (see also Bray, Justice, & Simon, 1978). However, no evidence of a selective rehearsal strategy on the directed-forgetting task was found for any participant.

Besides being affected by the nature of the task instructions, mentally retarded adolescents have been shown to be affected by the nature of the to-be-remembered and to-be-forgotten information. Bray (1973) described a study in which educable retarded adolescents received minimal task instructions concerning the forget cue. The number of to-be-forgotten or to-be-remembered pictures varied on each trial. He found no directed forgetting when the number of to-be-forgotten pictures varied. This result was interpreted as indicative of retarded adolescents having difficulty keeping track of where the forget cue occurred in the spatial–temporal sequence.

Therefore, these studies indicate that retardates can effectively use explicit cues to segregate to-be-forgotten and to-be-remembered information. The strategy used by the retardates, however, depended on their age. Only the oldest retardates used a selective rehearsal strategy; younger retardates were more apt to use a strategy that involved waiting until after an explicit forget cue was presented before processing the subsequent information. In addition, the degree of intentional forgetting was shown to be a function of various factors including training with the explicit cues and amount of to-be-forgotten information.

DEVELOPMENTAL PROGRESSION

The first published study to investigate the developmental progression in the use of explicit cues was conducted by Posansky (1976). Only Experiment 1 involved explicit cues, and it used the item method of cuing in a within-participants design. (Experiment 2 used a procedure similar to Epstein's [1972] selective search methodology.) Posansky showed that both 3rd and 7th graders could use the explicit cues: Both recalled more to-be-remembered words than to-be-forgotten words. Recognition data were also collected in this study, but no evidence of directed forgetting was found with this measure for any age. This latter result is somewhat surprising, given that the item method of cuing ordinarily leads to directed forgetting on both recall and recognition (see Basden et al., 1993).

Research in this area was later conducted by Bray. Bray and Ferguson (1976) had already shown that children less than 11 years old used a passive–active strategy when presented with a forget cue, whereas adults were known from other directed-forgetting research to use selective rehearsal. Bray investigated these strategy differences with different aged retardates. Bray, Turner, and Hersh (1985, Experiment 1) presented pictures to 11-, 15-, and 18-year-old educable mentally retarded people. It was found that a forget cue improved performance only for the 15- and 18-year-old participants relative to control groups, but the pause time analyses indicated very little selective rehearsal.

Further examination of the developmental progression by Bray involved studies with only normal participants. Using the pause time procedure with 7-, 9-, 11-, and 30-year-old participants (Bray, Justice, & Zahm, 1983), and with

11-, 15-, and 18-year-old participants (Bray, Hersh, & Turner, 1985), studies have shown two developmental transitions in the use of explicit cues. First, between ages 7 and 11, there was a shift from ineffective to effective use of these cues. These children, however, generally used the passive–active strategy instead of selective rehearsal. Second, after age 11, selective rehearsal was used. Bray's conclusions concerning the developmental transitions with normal individuals were supported by research with kindergartners conducted by Howard and Goldin (1979). These researchers noted that in addition to the directed-forgetting research with children, other research (e.g., on metamemory, see Kreutzer, Leonard, & Flavell, 1975) suggests the hypothesis that young children possess selective abilities that they often fail to demonstrate because they have not yet learned that selection would be advantageous for the task at hand.

Other studies investigating the developmental progression in the use of explicit cues with children challenged some of Bray's results. Both Foster and Gavalek (1983) and Lehman and Bavasso (1993) showed that not only can children as young as first-grade students use explicit cues, but that they use a selective rehearsal strategy. The latter was based on participants taking longer to rehearse to-be-remembered items than to-be-forgotten items. In addition, in Lehman and Bavasso (1993), the directed-forgetting effect was found on both recall and recognition. It should be noted, however, that both of these studies used the item method of cueing rather than the list method preferred by Bray.

Recent research has started to investigate retrieval inhibition with regard to developmental progression and intentional forgetting. Harnishfeger and Pope (1996) presented unrelated words to first graders, third graders, fifth graders, and adults using the list method. All participants then received a recall and recognition test. The results showed a developmental progression, such that only the oldest children and the adults showed clear evidence for inhibition; directed forgetting on recall but not on recognition. In Lehman, McKinley-Pace, Wilson, Slavsky, and Woodson (1997), third graders, fourth graders, and adults were presented with unrelated words using the item method of presentation, and were then given an indirect (repetition priming, word-stem completion) or direct (cued recall, word-stem completion) test of memory. There was evidence of directed forgetting for both types of tests for all participants. Lehman et al. argued that their results implicated inhibitory processes, because only retrieval inhibition should affect both types of tests in the same manner (see MacLeod, this volume). It should be noted, however, that because a presentation method was used that is typically thought to lead to selective rehearsal of the to-be-forgotten and to-be-remembered items, Lehman et al. raised the possibility that the inhibition present in their study may be different than that found with the list method of presentation.

Research on the developmental progression of the use of explicit cues has also been extended to older adults. This research examined whether the decrease in certain cognitive abilities found in older adults (e.g., Burke & Light, 1981) extends to the use of explicit cues. The results from these studies, however, have been equivocal. In one study, Kausler and Hakami (1982) presented younger adults (mean age = 20) and older adults (mean age = 65) with words, some of which were underlined because they were to-be-remembered. In addition, the to-be-remembered words could appear with one or two to-be-forgotten words, and the to-be-remembered words appeared from one to three times. The primary dependent measure was frequency judgments of the to-be-remembered words. It was found that the younger and older adults judged frequency equally well when there was one to-be-remembered and one to-be-forgotten word. When there were two to-be-forgotten words, however, older adults gave lower frequency values to the to-be-remembered words than younger adults, indicating more processing and less forgetting of the to-be-forgotten words.

Other researchers investigated the effects of age and categorization. Pavur, Comeaux, and Zeringue (1984) presented adults (mean age = 20 years) and older adults (mean age = 67 years) with two lists of 30 words each in the form of a shopping list. The lists were presented aloud, and each list contained six words from one of five categories. Participants were instructed to forget the words from two categories on each list. Words from one category that had to be forgotten on list 1 (as well as other words) were presented as to-be-remembered items on list 2. It was hypothesized that older adults would not be able to forget the list 1 words from a particular category, thereby leading to interference on other words from this same category on list 2. It was found, however, that both groups of adults reduced interference.

Using different methodologies, Zacks, Radvansky, and Hasher (1995) found that instructions to forget were not effective with categorized or unrelated words. Young adults (mean age = 20 years) and older adults (mean age = 69 years) were presented with either words from various sized categories or with unrelated words using both the item and list methods. In Experiments 1 and 2, after a list of words was presented, participants were asked to recall only the to-be-remembered words. After participants received several lists and a distractor task, they were asked to recall and then to recognize both the to-be-remembered and to-be-forgotten words. The immediate recall results found that the older adults remembered more to-be-forgotten words. In addition, the delayed recall and recognition results found that older adults, although still showing evidence of directed forgetting, remembered fewer to-be-remembered words and more to-be-forgotten words than the younger adults. Finally, in Experiment 3, it took older adults longer to reject a to-be-forgotten word on an immediate timed-recognition task compared to words never presented. Zacks et al. (1995) argued that the increase in the availability of to-be-forgotten words by older adults was due to less inhibition of these words. This view would support Hasher and Zacks' (1988; see also Zacks & Hasher, 1994) view of decreased effectiveness of inhibitory processes accompanying the aging process. However, it is unclear whether these results indicate less inhibition in older adults because the evidence of directed forgetting on both recall and recognition for the younger adults is consistent with an encoding (i.e., differential rehearsal) explanation of directed forgetting.

The research on intentional forgetting and developmental progression indicates that the ability to intentionally forget is acquired at an early age, possibly as young as first grade. Moreover, there is some evidence to indicate that these young children are using effective strategies to forget, namely selective rehearsal. Although this ability remains present for many years, there appears to be a point in later adulthood at which intentional forgetting is not as effective. Whether this decrease in effectiveness is due to an inability to inhibit to-be-forgotten information or an inability to selectively rehearse to-be-forgotten and to-be-remembered information is still an open question.

THOUGHT SUPPRESSION

Thought suppression involves the conscious avoidance of a thought, usually of a traumatic nature (see Wegner, 1989, 1994). The conscious aspect of this act makes suppression different from repression, which has largely been considered an unconscious process (Freud 1915/1957). Therefore, suppression suggests only that we are not thinking of the thought at a particular time, whereas repression implies that we may never get a thought back. Because suppression typically involves an explicit instruction to suppress (either from oneself or from another person), it is very much related to the other types of intentional forgetting discussed thus far. Moreover, like other research described in this book, investigations of suppression are seen as having important applied significance. For example, many psychological disorders are the direct result of our inability to suppress unwanted thoughts, such as obsessions and compulsions, depression, phobias, post-traumatic stress disorder, addictions, eating disorders, and schizophrenia (see Wegner, 1989, for a further discussion of these disorders).

Research on thought suppression comes from two traditions. First, there are laboratory studies that present participants with information they are then told "not to think about" (see Wegner, 1994). Second, there is research involving variations of a therapeutic technique called "thought stopping" (e.g., see Wolpe, 1958) or "thought interruption" (see Lewinsohn, Munoz, Youngren, & Zeiss, 1978). The present review will discuss only the former studies.

Controlled experimentation on thought suppression in a nontherapeutic context was initiated by Daniel Wegner. In the first of his studies (Wegner, Schneider, Carter, & White, 1987, Experiment 1), participants reported into a tape recorder "everything that came to mind" for two 5-minute periods. Instead of having participants suppress traumatic events, they were simply told to "try not to think of a white bear" (initial suppression group) or to "try to think of a white bear" (initial expression group) as they spoke. The instructions were reversed for the two groups in the second period. In addition, for all groups in all periods, the participants were asked to ring a bell if they said "white bear" or if "white bear" came to mind. The results showed that participants were not completely successful in suppressing the "white bear." Moreover, there was a "rebound effect" with regard to suppression, an increase in the frequency of thoughts about the white bear in the second period for the initial suppression group (see also Lavy & van den Hout, 1990). A second experiment found that this rebound effect could be attenuated if participants were given a single distractor item (a red Volkswagen) to think about instead of the white bear.

Subsequent research extended this initial work by examining the relation between thought suppression and affect in various contexts. First, some of these studies focused on depression. Wenzlaff, Wegner, and Roper (1988) had normals and depressives try not to think about stories that conveyed a highly positive or negative event. The thought protocols indicated that depressives failed in suppressing negative thoughts. A similar result was found in a study by Conway, Howell, and Giannopoulos (1991) in which undergraduates were asked not to think about "success" or "failure" feedback regarding test performance. The results found that during a 5-minute suppression period, depressives had reliably more intrusions about failure.

Second, Wenzlaff, Wegner, and Klein (1991) investigated whether the suppression of a thought bonds thought and mood, such that later occurrences of the mood promote the return of the suppressed thought (Experiment 1) or vice versa (Experiment 2). During an initial suppression or expression period, undergraduates were played music that influenced mood in either a positive or negative direction. During a subsequent expression period, participants received the same music they heard initially, or the opposite mood music. The results of the two experiments supported the view that suppression creates a strong bond between suppressed thoughts and their associated moods. There was a particularly strong rebound effect of the thought when the mood music was the same during initial suppression and subsequent expression. Wegner, Erber, and Zanakos (1993) also found that cognitive load can lead to ironic effects when mood is involved. For example, some participants were told to think of an event that was sad, but that they should not feel sad. Participants who had to rehearse a 9-digit number (Experiment 1) or participate in a Stroop task (Experiment 2) produced greater rebound effects than participants who had no such load.

Finally, there have been studies that investigated the suppression of exciting thoughts, and the irony that the suppression of such thoughts can intensify the very excitement that is hoped to be avoided. In Wegner, Shortt, Blake, and Page (1990), undergraduate participants were instructed either to think or not to think about the exciting topic of sex or one of three unexciting topics (e.g., dancing). During the expression or suppression periods, skin conductance level was measured. Three experiments found that the suppression of the exciting thought led to increases in skin conductance level, whether it was during a shorter (e.g., 3-minute) or longer (e.g., 30-minute) suppression period. Wegner, Lane, and Dimitri (1994) found similar results. Using survey data, they showed that if a person ruminated about someone they loved in the past, these feelings were more likely to have been kept a secret (i.e., suppressed) in the past; and if a past relationship was kept secret, it was more likely to have been the target of obsessive preoccupation. Finally, Wegner et al. (1994) showed that if couples played a game in which they had to keep secret the fact that they were in physical contact during the game, they reported greater attraction to one another than if they did not have to keep the contact secret.

Wegner and his colleagues also conducted other thought suppression studies that did not deal specifically with issues of affect. For example, Wegner, Schneider, Knutson, and McMahon (1991) explored the relation between unwanted thoughts and environmental features. They showed that suppressed thoughts were associated with specific environmental distractors (e.g., a slide show on a particular subject). There was a greater rebound effect for participants who initially suppressed thinking about a white bear when the subsequent expression period was in the same context as the suppression. In addition, Wegner and Erber (1993) showed that suppressed thoughts were more readily produced as associates in a word association task when the task involved time constraints, and that these thoughts interfered in a Stroop task. Finally, Wegner, Quillian, and Houston (1996) showed that instructions to not think about a sequence of events in a motion picture led to disruption in memory for the sequence, yet did not disrupt memory for the events themselves.

The Wegner paradigm was also used by other researchers to investigate issues ranging from stereotypes to pain. Macrae, Bodenhausen, Milne, and Jetten (1994) investigated whether stereotypic beliefs, once suppressed, rebound, and then impact perceivers' evaluations and behavior toward another target. In Experiment 1, participants were shown a picture of a skinhead. Some of the participants were encouraged to suppress their stereotypical thoughts about the skinhead during a task in which they described a typical day for the target on paper. After this task, all of the participants were then shown a new picture of a skinhead followed by the same writing task. On this second writing task, however, there were no suppression instructions. The results showed that the content of the stories, when scored for stereotypicality, were lower after picture 1 and higher after picture 2 (i.e., a rebound effect), whereas the participants given no suppression instruction scored the same on both writing tasks. With regard to pain, Cioffi and Holloway (1993) investigated the rebound effect during somatic discomfort. They had participants experience pain by immersing their hand in ice-cold water. Some participants were asked to suppress their thoughts of the pain, whereas others were asked to concentrate on some other object or to pay close attention to the pain. It was shown that participants who suppressed their thoughts of pain rated the pain higher than did the other participants after a delay. That is, those who had suppressed the pain evidenced a slower recovery.

Why is thought suppression not always successful? There are several theoretical positions. Most recent is Wegner's (1994) ironic process theory. He discussed the idea that mental control involves the interaction of two mental processes that work together to promote a certain state; (a) an intentional operating system that searches for the mental contents that will yield a desired state; and (b) an ironic monitoring system that searches for mental contents that signal the failure to achieve the desired state. The former is an effortful process, whereas the latter is relatively automatic. As an example, he stated that when a person is trying to be happy, the intentional operating system searches for mental contents pertinent to happiness, whereas the ironic monitoring system searches for mental contents that indicate happiness has not been achieved. Typically, mental control is achieved. When capacity is reduced for some reason (e.g., cognitive load, stress, or time pressure), however, the intentional operating system is undermined and the contents of the ironic monitoring system will come into consciousness, thereby producing ironic effects (e.g., Wegner & Erber, 1993).

Macrae et al. (1994) evaluated another theoretical position regarding thought suppression; Higgins, Bargh, and Lombardi's (1985) synapse model of construct activation. This model states that constructs function like the synapses of vertebrates: The more a construct is activated, the slower the dissipation of an action potential. In the case of thought suppression, unwanted constructs are continually stimulated or primed, making the action potential dissipate more slowly. In support of their position, Higgins et al. presented (Experiment 3) participants with a lexical decision task after some of the participants had been asked to suppress their thoughts about a specific stereotype. Some of the items in the task were traits specific to the suppressed stereotype. The results showed that, indeed, there were faster reaction times to stereotype traits for the participants who had earlier suppressed their thoughts about the stereotype.

Although there is a great deal of support for the inability to suppress thoughts and the rebound effect, there is some evidence that thought suppression can actually be successful. One set of studies specifically questioned the thought-suppression paradigm used by Wegner. Clark, Ball, and Pape (1991) were concerned that in the Wegner paradigm, thought frequency was compared when the expression period preceded as opposed to followed suppression. Thus, Clark et al. (1991) argued, a higher number of thoughts expressed after suppression might be due to a practice effect of thinking aloud in the first time period. In addition, Clark et al. (1991) argued that the use of expression as the control condition may have made it difficult to detect an immediate enhancement effect for the suppression group, because instructing participants to intentionally think a particular thought was likely to produce a ceiling effect. They felt that a more appropriate and naturalistic control would be to simply mention the target words without requesting participants to express or suppress. To investigate these potential problems, Clark et al. (1991) presented participants with a story about a "green rabbit." During the initial time period participants were instructed either to think about anything except the story (suppression condition), to think about anything, or to think about anything, including the story. During the subsequent time period, all participants were instructed to think about anything. The results found that the suppression group initially had fewer thoughts about the story than either of the other groups. They did, however, show a rebound effect following suppression. Thus, in the short term, the suppression instruction appeared to be successful.

Merckelbach, Muris, van den Hout, and de Jong (1991; see also Muris, Merckelbach, & de Jong, 1993; Muris, Merckelbach, van den Hout, & de Jong, 1992) questioned whether the effects found by Wegner in the laboratory provide an appropriate model for the development of real-life obsessions. Their investigation centered on the explicit expression instruction participants received. Specifically, it was argued that, unlike Wegner's instructions, obsessives are not requested to try and produce obsessions in clinically relevant conditions. Thus, Merckelbach et al. used a more "liberal" expression instruction, in which participants were told that they could think about anything including a white bear. In Experiment 1, although there was evidence that participants could not completely suppress information, no evidence was obtained to suggest that suppression resulted in either a heightened frequency or an accelerated rate of white bear thoughts during a subsequent expression period. Moreover, in Experiment 2, successful suppressors reported fewer white bear thoughts during the expression period. Merckelbach et al. (1991) concluded that the forced-expression instruction in Wegner's studies may have made it easier for participants to concentrate on the target thought.

A second set of studies found that the success of thought suppression may be tied to the type of material being forgotten, or to individual differences. Kelly and Kahn (1994) had people suppress their own intrusive thoughts or other thoughts (e.g., a white bear) and found that there was no rebound effect for personal intrusive thoughts. Thus, it appears that people have more control suppressing their own thoughts, rather than those supplied by the experimenter. Rutledge, Hollenberg, and Hancock (1993, Experiment 1) also found no evidence of a rebound effect for participants instructed to not think about a white bear or an upcoming test. On further investigation (Experiment 2), it was shown, however, that there were some rebounders. Interestingly, these rebounders had high ACT Mathematics scores, which the authors note may be related to visual memory skills and an inability to suppress mental images.

To sum up, research on thought suppression has shown that individuals generally have difficulty following instructions to suppress a variety of information, from "white bears" to stereotypes to previous loves. The to-be-suppressed information is often thought about during a suppression period, and then is thought about in even greater amounts following the attempt to suppress (i.e., a rebound effect). Recent research, however, indicates that the extent of this inability to suppress may be tied to methodological factors in the Wegner paradigm. In addition, thought suppression may be successful with certain types of information, especially those for which individuals may have developed strategies for successful suppression.

POSTHYPNOTIC AMNESIA

Interest in retrieval inhibition as a mechanism involved in intentional forgetting (see MacLeod, this volume) has been enhanced by interesting parallels between studies of directed forgetting and studies of posthypnotic amnesia (e.g., Bjork, 1989; Geiselman & Bagheri, 1985; Geiselman, Bjork, & Fishman, 1983; Kihlstrom, 1983; Weiner, 1968; Weiner & Reed, 1969). Posthypnotic amnesia refers to a participant's inability in the waking state to recall events that occurred while hypnotized. It results from a suggestion (i.e., an explicit cue) that the participant will be unable to remember the events that occurred during hypnosis until the experimenter delivers a prearranged countermand. Participants who score high on tests of hypnotic susceptibility typically exhibit more amnesia than do participants who score low on these tests. Because highly susceptible participants experience no difficulty accessing the "forgotten" information once the amnesia suggestion has been cancelled, posthypnotic amnesia cannot be due to a loss or absence of memories.

In addition to overall recall deficits, posthypnotic amnesia has been associated with reduced memory organization. A number of studies showed that hypnotic participants exhibit less category clustering after learning a list comprised of many relative to few categories during the hypnotic period (Radtke-Bodorik, Spanos, & Haddad, 1979; Spanos & Bodorik, 1977; Spanos, Radtke-Bodorik, & Stam, 1980; Spanos, Stam, D'Eon, Pawlak, & Radtke-Bodorik,

1980). Hypnotic participants are also less likely to recall a list in its input order (i.e., exhibit seriation) during the amnesia period than either before the hypnotic suggestion or after the countermand (Evans & Kihlstrom, 1973; Kihlstrom & Evans, 1976; Kihlstrom & Wilson, 1984; Spanos, McLean, & Bertrand, 1987). Finally, Tkachyk, Spanos, and Bertrand (1985) found that in a list-learning experiment, participants exhibited high levels of subjective organization both before and after the amnesia test period but little subjective organization during the amnesia period.

Disorganized recall in posthypnotic amnesia does not appear to be due to a deliberate attempt on the part of participants to purposefully "mix up" their recall. Spanos and his colleagues investigated the hypothesis that recall deficits and disorganization among partial amnesiacs is due to deliberate response withholding (Spanos, Radtke, Bertrand, Addie, & Drummond, 1982). Response withholding might result due to participants' attempts to balance competing demands to "forget" the target information and to honestly report their recall of some but not all of the target material. Because participants associate forgetting with confusion, they not only withhold some of the information but deliberately disorganize the information they do recall to give the appearance of forgetting. Spanos et al. tested this hypothesis by comparing the pattern of recall exhibited by amnesiacs to the recall pattern of participants who were explicitly instructed to fake amnesia. They found that amnesiacs who learned a list of categorized words exhibited less clustering during the amnesia test period than they did either before they received the amnesia suggestion or after they received the countermand. However, the "simulators" exhibited no reduction in clustering during the amnesia test period. Therefore, they concluded that deliberate response withholding does not account for recall disruption in posthypnotic amnesia.

The recall deficits exhibited by participants in studies of posthypnotic amnesia is somewhat similar to those exhibited by participants in studies of directed forgetting. As discussed earlier, posthypnotic amnesia participants fail to recall many of the events they experience during hypnosis until they receive a countermand, at which time previously unrecalled events become accessible (Kihlstrom & Evans, 1976). Similarly, directed-forgetting participants recall fewer to-be-forgotten items than to-be-remembered items on an initial trial, but exhibit greater improvement for to-be-forgotten items than to-be-remembered items on a second trial in which all items are designated as to-be-remembered (Geiselman & Bagheri, 1985). In addition, those to-be-forgotten items that participants can access at retrieval are not recalled in an order that parallels their input sequence in either posthypnotic amnesia or directed forgetting (Geiselman & Bagheri, 1985).

Although disrupted retrieval appears to be implicated in both directed forgetting and posthypnotic amnesia, it is not clear whether disruption in these two paradigms results from the same or different mechanisms (Coe, Basden, Basden, Fikes, Gargano, & Webb, 1989; Geiselman, MacKinnon, et al., 1983; Horton, Smith, Barghout, & Connolly, 1992; Kihlstrom, 1983). Geiselman, MacKinnon, et al. (1983) investigated the hypothesis that retrieval inhibition is a mechanism common to both directed forgetting and posthypnotic amnesia using a repeated measures design. In a first session, participants were hypnotized, and then instructed to forget the events that had occurred during the session until explicitly instructed to remember them later. Participants were then awakened and their memory for the events that transpired during the hypnotic state was tested (posthypnotic amnesia). Participants were tested again following administration of the countermand (inhibition release). In a second session, participants took part in an item-by-item directed-forgetting procedure. Geiselman, MacKinnon, et al. compared performance in the hypnosis session with performance in the directed-forgetting session. They found that posthypnotic amnesia and inhibition release were significantly correlated with to-be-forgotten item recall but not with to-be-remembered item recall. Participants who exhibited the greatest posthypnotic amnesia showed the lowest to-be-forgotten item recall in the directed-forgetting procedure, and participants who exhibited the greatest inhibition release showed the highest to-be-forgotten item recall. Given the relation between the hypnotic amnesia measures and to-be-forgotten item recall, Geiselman, MacKinnon, et al. argued that it was plausible that posthypnotic amnesia and nonhypnotic intentional forgetting involved common inhibition processes.

Geiselman, MacKinnon, et al.'s (1983) results, however, were not replicated in a study in which directed forgetting and posthypnotic amnesia were assessed in the same experimental paradigm (Coe et al., 1989). In Experiment 1, Coe et al. administered a list-learning task to high- and low-hypnotic susceptibility participants who were hypnotized and assigned to a directed-forgetting or a posthypnotic amnesia condition. Participants in both conditions were asked to recall all of the items that they had learned while hypnotized. After recall, the posthypnotic amnesia participants received the countermand and were again asked to recall all of the items. Recall differed in the two conditions. For participants who received directed-forgetting instructions, low-susceptibility participants recalled more to-be-remembered items than did high-susceptibility participants. However, all of these participants exhibited the same level of to-be-forgotten item recall. In contrast, under posthypnotic amnesia instructions, low-susceptibility participants recalled more to-be-forgotten items than did high-susceptibility participants. Coe et al. argued that the forget instruction interfered with the high-susceptibility participants' ability to learn the to-be-remembered list. In a subsequent experiment, Coe et al. provided evidence that the deficit in recall of the to-be-remembered items exhibited by high-susceptibility participants was not due to hypnotic susceptibility per se. No differences were found between high- and low-susceptibility participants who were administered directed-forgetting instructions outside of the hypnotic context. Rather, the deficit appeared to be due to confusion elicited by the forget instruction in the context of hypnosis. Coe et al. concluded that the retrieval mechanisms involved in directed forgetting and posthypnotic amnesia are not the same: Participant characteristics and instructions interact in the context of hypnosis but do not interact in the context of waking directed forgetting.

Coe et al.'s (1989) results are consistent with other findings suggesting that the retrieval mechanisms involved in directed forgetting and posthypnotic amnesia may not completely overlap. In particular, some researchers argued that posthypnotic amnesia alone is a function of certain social psychological factors. In this vein, Spanos conceptualized posthypnotic amnesia as strategic attention deployment that is dependent on participant expectations (Radtke, Bertrand, & Spanos, 1988; Radtke, Thompson, & Egger, 1987; Spanos & D'Eon, 1980; Spanos, Radtke, & Dubreuil, 1982; Spanos, Stam, et al., 1980; Stam, Radtke-Bodorik, & Spanos, 1980). Participants choose to attend to some events in the testing situation and to ignore other events according to specific social pressures that are present in the experimental context (Coe & Sluis, 1989).

In one study, Spanos, Stam, et al. (1980) hypothesized that participants who exhibit amnesia do so because they interpret the remember instruction during the amnesia period as a request for passive recall. That is, participants respond to the amnesia suggestion by focusing attention on events other than the target material. When they receive the remember challenge during the test period, they interpret the instruction as a request to continue focusing attention away from the target material while reporting any of the target events that "come to mind." In contrast, participants who fail to exhibit amnesia do so because they interpret the remember challenge as a request to "actively" recall the target events.

Spanos, Stam, et al. (1980) tested this hypothesis by manipulating participants' interpretations of the amnesia situation. All participants were told that they would learn a list, receive a suggestion of amnesia for the list, and then receive a challenge to remember the list during the amnesia period. Participants in the active recall group were told that the challenge was a serious request to attend to recalling the list. Participants in the passive recall condition were told that the challenge was not to interfere with the forgetting process. Finally, participants in the control condition were simply told that they would be challenged to recall the list. They found that participants who received active recall instructions exhibited less amnesia than did participants who received passive recall or control instructions. That is, when participants are instructed to interpret the remember challenge as a request to actively attend to the target material, they exhibit significantly less amnesia.

Other studies have also supported the social psychological interpretation of posthypnotic amnesia by attempting to breach amnesia by manipulating participants' expectations about the amnesia testing situation. Investigators admonished participants to be honest, manipulated participants' expectations about their recall behavior during hypnosis, attached participants to lie detectors during recall, and administered retrieval cues during the amnesia test period (Coe & Sluis, 1989; Dubreuil, Spanos, & Bertrand, 1983; Howard & Coe, 1980; Kihlstrom, Evans, Orne, & Orne, 1980; McConkey & Sheehan, 1981; McConkey, Sheehan, & Cross, 1980; Radtke et al., 1987; Schuyler & Coe, 1981; Silva & Kirsch, 1987; Spanos, Radtke, & Bertrand, 1985). For instance, Spanos et al. (1985) conducted a study in which breaching of amnesia was defined to highly susceptible participants as indicative of deep hypnosis. Participants were told that they would learn a word list while hypnotized and receive a hypnotic suggestion to forget the list. They were also told that a "hidden part" of their mind would remain aware of the list throughout the amnesia period and that the experimenter could contact their hidden part to access the list. Subsequently, participants learned the word list, received the amnesia suggestion, and were tested for recall on three successive trials. The first trial consisted of the typical remember challenge. On the second trial, the experimenter contacted the participants' hidden part and instructed the hidden part to recall the words. On the third trial, the experimenter ended contact with the participants' hidden part and again instructed participants to recall the list. The results indicated substantial levels of amnesia on the first and third trials. However, participants breached amnesia completely on the second trial in which breaching was consistent with participants' self-presentation as deeply hypnotized (see also Silva & Kirsch, 1987).

The social psychological interpretation of posthypnotic amnesia does not appear to explain, however, the results of a recent study by Bowers and Woody (1996). For example, in Experiment 1, high- and low-hypnotizable participants received four different trials as part of a 2 × 2 within-participants experiment. The trials represented all combinations of type of instruction (thought suppression vs. amnesia suggestion) and type of hypnotic state (nonhypnotic vs. hypnotic). The results showed that although the thought-suppression instruction did not stop the participants from thinking about a specific object (see the previous section on Thought Suppression), the amnesia suggestion did lead to fewer thoughts about the object, especially for high-hypnotizable participants. Bowers and Woody interpreted these results as supporting the view that thought suppression involves intentional processes (see Wegner, 1994), whereas posthypnotic amnesia does not.

Finally, it should be noted that there is another interpretation of posthypnotic amnesia proposed by Huesmann, Gruder, and Dorst (1987). They argued that posthypnotic amnesia results from output interference, a common mechanism in the early directed-forgetting literature (see MacLeod, this volume). Participants who receive a hypnotic suggestion "tag" the target material as forbidden. During the amnesia testing period, the target information is retrieved into working memory along with the forbidden tag. The information-processing system responds to the tag by inhibiting verbal output of the forbidden material. A countermand functions to delete the tag enabling output routines to report the target information. Because the forbidden information enters into working memory, it has the potential to influence behavior even though it cannot be reported.

Huesmann et al. (1987) tested the output interference model in a study designed to distinguish between the recall of forbidden material and its use in a problem-solving task. Participants were asked to solve a series of problems that required the acquisition of a particular solution algorithm. Subsequently, participants received a hypnotic suggestion to forget the problems and the solution algorithm. During the amnesia test period, participants received new problems to solve, some of which could be solved by a simpler algorithm than the one acquired during the training period. According to Huesmann et al., if a hypnotic suggestion results in participants' failure to retrieve previously learned information into working memory, then participants should apply the simpler solution method used by control participants who never learned the long solution. However, if participants retrieve the old algorithm, then they should be less likely to use a simpler solution algorithm than should control participants. The results indicated that participants who learned the long solution used it to solve the new problem even though they were not able to recall it until after they received a countermand. Huesmann et al. concluded that the previously learned solution clearly entered into working memory. However, participants were not able to report the solution because it was tagged as forbidden.

The research on posthypnotic amnesia appears to offer a view of intentional forgetting that differs from that of traditional directed-forgetting research. Although there is some linkage of posthypnotic amnesia to mechanisms of directed forgetting (e.g., output interference, retrieval inhibition), the theoretical underpinnings of most of the posthypnotic amnesia research relies on social–psychological interpretations. For example, strategic attention deployment (e.g., Spanos et al., 1980) does not appear consistent with the recall behavior of participants in directed-forgetting studies. That is, this account does not appear to explain why the countermand in studies of posthypnotic amnesia typically results in full recall of the to-be-forgotten material, but the command to remember the to-be-forgotten items in studies of directed forgetting does not. Of course, future research is necessary to determine whether there are, in fact, greater similarities between posthypnotic amnesia and intentional forgetting in other contexts.

CONCLUSIONS

The goal of this chapter was to show the breadth of intentional forgetting beyond that originally proposed in research on directed forgetting. After reviewing the broad range of research domains covered by intentional forgetting, we believe that this goal has been met, and that we have shown how many of the pieces of the puzzle fit together. Intentional forgetting may mean different things to different researchers, but in many respects researchers who investigate intentional forgetting examine a common phenomenon. That is, these researchers are examining how individuals in various situations attempt to segregate relevant and irrelevant information in memory based on explicit cues. Theoretically, investigating intentional forgetting allows researchers to better understand how memory operates. In addition, research on intentional forgetting offers a bridge to various applied issues (e.g., psychology and the law) that have important implications outside of the laboratory.

Our review also serves to make two points extremely clear. First, unlike many of the studies on directed forgetting, intentional forgetting is often difficult. Individuals do not always segregate relevant and irrelevant information. Moreover, even when segregation occurs, individuals are apt to use irrelevant information to perform a task. This may be due to the perceived relevance of the to-be-disregarded information (e.g., inadmissible evidence), as well as the inability to stave off automatic processing of the irrelevant information (e.g., suppressing certain thoughts). Second, there is no consensus on the mechanisms that affect intentional forgetting. As with directed forgetting (see chapter 1), researchers discuss intentional forgetting with regard to selective rehearsal and retrieval inhibition. In addition, other processes (e.g., "creeping determinism") find their way into the literature.

Much of the disagreement among intentional-forgetting researchers with regard to mechanisms is likely due to the isolated nature of the research across domains. An examination of the literature indicates that researchers investigating the issues described in this chapter do not even know about directed-forgetting research, let alone research in the other domains of intentional forgetting. This point has rarely been noted (but see Golding et al., 1990), and over time, there has only been a slight progress toward removing the barriers that exist between domains (e.g., Coe et al., 1989; Geiselman, MacKinnon, et al., 1983; Golding et al., 1990). Hopefully, the present review will help to bring together researchers who study intentional forgetting, and will lead to a greater understanding of how memory can be managed.

REFERENCES

Arkes, H. R. (1981). Impediments to accurate clinical judgment and possible ways to minimize their impact. *Journal of Consulting and Clinical Psychology, 49,* 323–330.

Arkes, H. R., Wortmann, R. L., Saville, P. D., & Harkness, A. R. (1981). Hindsight bias among physicians weighing the likelihood of diagnoses. *Journal of Applied Psychology, 66*, 252–254.

Basden, B. H., Basden, D. R., & Gargano, G. J. (1993). Directed forgetting in implicit and explicit memory tests: A comparison of methods. *Journal of Experimental Psychology: Learning, Memory, and Cognition, 19*, 603–616.

Bernhart, K. L., Kinnear, T. C., & Mazis, M. B. (1986). A field study of corrective advertising effectiveness. *Journal of Public Policy and Marketing, 5*, 146–162.

Bjork, R. A. (1972). Theoretical implications of directed forgetting. In A. W. Melton & E. Martin (Eds.), *Coding processes in human memory* (pp. 217–235). Washington DC: Winston.

Bjork, R. A. (1989). Retrieval inhibition as an adaptive mechanism in human memory. In H. L. Roediger & F. I. M. Craik (Eds.), *Varieties of memory and consciousness: Essays in honour of Endel Tulving* (pp. 309–330). Hillsdale, NJ: Lawrence Erlbaum Associates.

Bodenhausen, G. V. (1990). Second-guessing the jury: Stereotypic and hindsight biases in the perception of court cases. *Journal of Applied Social Psychology, 20*, 1112–1121.

Bowers, K. S., & Woody, E. Z. (1996). Hypnotic amnesia and the paradox of intentional forgetting. *Journal of Abnormal Psychology, 105*, 381–390.

Bray, N. W. (1973). Controlled forgetting in the retarded. *Cognitive Psychology, 5*, 288–309.

Bray, N. W. (1979). Strategy production in the retarded. In N. E. Ellis (Ed.), *Handbook of mental deficiency: Psychological theory and research* (2nd ed., pp. 699–726). Hillsdale, NJ: Lawrence Erlbaum Associates.

Bray, N. W., & Ferguson, R. P. (1976). Memory strategies used by young normal and retarded children in a directed forgetting paradigm. *Journal of Experimental Child Psychology, 22*, 200–215.

Bray, N. W., Goodman, M. A., & Justice, E. M. (1982). Task instructions and strategy transfer in the directed forgetting performance of mentally retarded adolescents. *Intelligence, 6*, 187–200.

Bray, N. W., Hersh, R. E., & Turner, L. A. (1985). Selective remembering during adolescence. *Developmental Psychology, 21*, 290–294.

Bray, N. W., Justice, E. M., & Simon, D. L. (1978). The sufficient conditions for directed forgetting in normal and educable mentally retarded children. *Intelligence, 2*, 153–167.

Bray, N. W., Justice, E. M., & Zahm, D. N. (1983). Two developmental transitions in selective remembering strategies. *Journal of Experimental Child Psychology, 36*, 43–55.

Bray, N. W., Turner, L. A., & Hersh, R. E. (1985). Developmental progressions and regressions in the selective remembering strategies of EMR individuals. *American Journal of Mental Deficiency, 90*, 198–205.

Broeder, D. (1959). The University of Chicago jury project. *Nebraska Law Review, 38*, 744–760.

Burke, D. M., & Light, L. L. (1981). Memory and aging: The role of retrieval processes. *Psychological Bulletin, 90*, 513–546.

Campbell, J. D., & Tesser, A. (1983). Motivational interpretations of hindsight bias: An individual difference analysis. *Journal of Personality, 51*, 605–620.

Caretta, T. R., & Moreland, R. L. (1983). The direct and indirect effects of inadmissible evidence. *Journal of Applied Social Psychology, 13*, 291–309.

Casper, J. D., Benedict, K., & Perry, J. L. (1989). Juror decision making, attitudes, and the hindsight bias. *Law and Human Behavior, 13*, 291–310.

Christensen-Szalanski, J. J. J., & Willham, C. F. (1991). The hindsight bias: A meta-analysis. *Organizational Behavior and Decision Processes, 48*, 147–168.

Cioffi, D., & Holloway, J. (1993). Delayed costs of suppressed pain. *Journal of Personality and Social Psychology, 64*, 274–282.

Clark, D. M., Ball, S., & Pape, D. (1991). An experimental investigation of thought suppression. *Behaviour Research and Therapy, 29*, 253–257.

Clark, R. D. (1994). The role of censorship in minority influence. *European Journal of Social Psychology, 24*, 331–338.

Coe, W. C., Basden, B. H., Basden, D., Fikes, T., Gargano, G. J., & Webb, M. (1989). Directed forgetting and posthypnotic amnesia: Information processing and social contexts. *Journal of Personality and Social Psychology, 56,* 189–198.

Coe, W. C., & Sluis, A. S. E. (1989). Increasing contextual pressures to breach posthypnotic amnesia. *Journal of Personality and Social Psychology, 57,* 885–894.

Conway, M., Howell, A., & Giannopoulos, C. (1991). Dysphoria and thought suppression. *Cognitive Therapy and Research, 15,* 153–166.

Cook, T. D., & Flay, B. R. (1978). The persistence of experimentally induced attitude change. In L. Berkowitz (Ed.), *Advances in experimental social psychology* (Vol. 11, pp. 1–57). New York: Academic Press.

Cornish, W. R., & Sealy, A. P. (1973, April). Juries and the rules of evidence. *Criminal Law Review,* 208–223.

Cox, M., & Tanford, S. (1989). Effects of evidence and instructions in civil trials: An experimental investigation of the rules of admissibility. *Social Behavior, 4,* 31–55.

Creyer, E., & Ross Jr., W. T. (1993). Hindsight bias and inferences in choice: The mediating effect of cognitive effort. *Organizational Behavior and Human Processes, 55,* 61–77.

Davies, M. F. (1987). Reduction of hindsight bias by restoration of foresight perspective: Effectiveness of foresight-encoding and hindsight-retrieval strategies. *Organizational Behavior and Human Decision Processes, 40,* 50–68.

Devine, P. G., & Ostrom, T. M. (1985). Cognitive mediation in inconsistency discounting. *Journal of Personality and Social Psychology, 49,* 5–21.

Doob, A. N. (1976). Evidence, procedure, and psychological research. In G. Bermant, C. Nemeth, & N. Vidmar (Eds.), *Psychology and law* (pp. 135–147). Lexington, MA: Lexington Books.

Doob, A. N., & Kirshenbaum, H. M. (1972). Some empirical evidence on the effects of Section 12 of the Canada Evidence Act upon the accused. *Criminal Law Quarterly, 15,* 88–96.

Dubreuil, D. L., Spanos, N. P., & Bertrand, L. D. (1983). Does hypnotic amnesia dissipate with time. *Imagination, Cognition and Personality, 2,* 103–113.

Dyer, R. F., & Kuehl, P. G. (1974). The corrective advertising remedy of the FTC: An experimental evaluation. *Journal of Marketing, 38,* 48–54.

Dyer, R. F., & Kuehl, P. G. (1978). A longitudinal study of corrective advertising. *Journal of Marketing Research, 15,* 39–48.

Elliot, R., Farrington, B., & Manheimer, H. (1988). Eyewitness credible and discredible. *Journal of Applied Social Psychology, 18,* 1411–1422.

Epstein, W. (1972). Mechanisms of directed forgetting. In G. H. Bower (Ed.), *The psychology of learning and motivation* (Vol. 6, pp. 147–191). New York: Academic Press.

Evans, F. J., & Kihlstrom, J. F. (1973). Posthypnotic amnesia as disrupted retrieval. *Journal of Abnormal Psychology, 82,* 317–323.

Fischhoff, B. (1975). Hindsight ≠ foresight: The effect of outcome knowledge on judgment under uncertainty. *Journal of Experimental Psychology: Human Perception and Performance, 1,* 288–299.

Fischhoff, B. (1977). Perceived informativeness of facts. *Journal of Experimental Psychology: Human Perception and Performance, 3,* 349–358.

Fischhoff, B., & Beyth, R. (1975). "I knew it would happen"—Remembered probabilities of once-future things. *Organizational Behavior and Human Performance, 13,* 1–16.

Foster, R. N., & Gavalek, J. R. (1983). Development of intentional forgetting in normal and reading-delayed children. *Journal of Educational Psychology, 75,* 431–440.

Freud, S. (1957). Repression. In J. Strachey (Ed.), *The standard edition of the complete psychological works of Sigmund Freud* (Vol. 14). London: Hogarth Press. (Original work published 1915)

Geiselman, R. E., & Bagheri, B. (1985). Repetition effects in directed forgetting: Evidence for retrieval inhibition. *Memory and Cognition, 13,* 57–62.

Geiselman, R. E., Bjork, R. A., & Fishman, D. L. (1983). Disrupted retrieval in directed forgetting: A link with posthypnotic amnesia. *Journal of Experimental Psychology: General, 112,* 58–72.

Geiselman, R. E., MacKinnon, D. P., Fishman, D. L., Jaenicke, C., Larner, B. R., Schoenberg, S., & Swartz, S. (1983). Mechanisms of hypnotic and nonhypnotic forgetting. *Journal of Experimental Psychology: Learning, Memory, and Cognition, 9,* 626–635.

Gerbasi, K. C., Zuckerman, M., & Reis, H. T. (1977). Justice needs a new blindfold: A review of mock jury research. *Psychological Bulletin, 84,* 323–345.

Gilbert, D. T. (1991). How mental systems believe. *American Psychologist, 46,* 107–119.

Gilbert, D. T., Krull, D. S., & Malone, P. S. (1990). Unbelieving the unbelievable: Some problems in the rejection of false information. *Journal of Personality and Social Psychology, 59,* 601–613.

Gilbert, D. T., Tafarodi, R. W., & Malone, P. S. (1993). You can't not believe everything you read. *Journal of Personality and Social Psychology, 65,* 221–233.

Gillig, P. M., & Greenwald, A. G. (1974). Is it time to lay the sleeper effect to rest? *Journal of Personality and Social Psychology, 29,* 132–139.

Golding, J. M., Fowler, S. B., Long, D. L., & Latta, H. (1990). Instructions to disregard potentially useful information: The effects of pragmatics on evaluative judgments and recall. *Journal of Memory and Language, 29,* 212–227.

Golding, J. M., & Hauselt, J. (1994). When instructions to forget become instructions to remember. *Personality and Social Psychology Bulletin, 20,* 178–183.

Golding, J. M., & Keenan, J. M. (1985). Directed forgetting and memory for directions to a destination. *American Journal of Psychology, 98,* 579–590.

Golding, J. M., Sego, S. A., Hauselt, J., & Long, D. L. (1994). Pragmatics and the effect of instructions to forget information that varies in the magnitude of a trait. *The American Journal of Psychology, 107,* 223–243.

Gruder, C. L., Cook, T. D., Hennigan, K. M., Flay, B. R., Alessis, C., & Halamaj, J. (1978). Empirical tests of the absolute sleeper effect predicted from the discounting cue hypothesis. *Journal of Personality and Social Psychology, 36,* 1061–1074.

Guerin, B. (1982). Salience and hindsight biases in judgments of world events. *Psychological Reports, 50,* 411–414.

Hannah, D. B., & Sternthal, B. (1984). Detecting and explaining the sleeper effect. *Journal of Consumer Research, 11,* 632–642.

Hans, V. P., & Doob, A. N. (1976). Section 12 of the Canada Evidence Act and the deliberations of simulated jurors. *Criminal Law Quarterly, 18,* 235–253.

Harnishfeger, K. K., & Pope, R. S. (1996). Intending to forget: The development of cognitive inhibition in directed forgetting. *Journal of Experimental Child Psychology, 62,* 292–315.

Hasher, L., Attig, M. S., & Alba, J. A. (1981). I knew it all along: Or, did I? *Journal of Verbal Learning and Verbal Behavior, 20,* 86–96.

Hasher, L., & Zacks, R. T. (1988). Working memory, comprehension, and aging: A review with a new view. In G. H. Bower (Ed.), *The psychology of learning and motivation* (Vol. 22, pp. 193–225). San Diego: Academic Press.

Hastie, R., Penrod, S. D., & Pennington, N. (1983). *Inside the jury.* Cambridge, MA: Harvard University Press.

Hatvany, N., & Strack, F. (1980). The impact of a discredited key witness. *Journal of Social Psychology, 10,* 490–506.

Hawkins, S. A., & Hastie, R. (1990). Hindsight: Biased judgments of past events after the outcomes are known. *Psychological Bulletin, 107,* 311–327.

Hell, W., Gigerenzer, G., Gauggel, S., Mall, M., & Muller, M. (1988). Hindsight bias: An interaction of automatic and motivational factors? *Memory and Cognition, 16,* 533–538.

Hennessey, J. E., & Edgell, S. E. (1991). Hindsight bias in a very sparse environment. *Bulletin of the Psychonomic Society, 29,* 433–436.

Higgins, E. T., Bargh, J. A., & Lombardi, W. (1985). The nature of priming on categorization. *Journal of Experimental Psychology: Learning, Memory, and Cognition, 11,* 59–69.

Hoch, S. J., & Loewenstein, G. F. (1989). Outcome feedback: Hindsight and information. *Journal of Experimental Psychology: Learning, Memory, and Cognition, 4*, 605–619.

Horton, K. D., Smith, S. A., Barghout, N. K., & Connolly, D. A. (1992). The use of indirect memory tests to assess malingered amnesia: A study of metamemory. *Journal of Experimental Psychology: General, 121*, 326–351.

Howard, D. V., & Goldin, S. E. (1979). Selective processing in encoding and memory: An analysis of resource allocation by kindergarten children. *Journal of Experimental Child Psychology, 27*, 87–95.

Howard, M. L., & Coe, W. C. (1980). The effects of context and subjects' perceived control in breaching posthypnotic amnesia. *Journal of Personality, 48*, 342–359.

Huesmann, R., Gruder, C. L., & Dorst, G. (1987). A process model of posthypnotic amnesia. *Cognitive Psychology, 19*, 33–62.

Hunt, H. K. (1973). Effects of corrective advertising. *Journal of Advertising Research, 13*, 15–22.

Jacoby, J., Nelson, M. C., & Hoyer, W. D. (1982). Corrective advertising and affirmative disclosure statements: Their potential for confusing and misleading the consumer. *Journal of Marketing, 46*, 61–72.

Janoff-Bulman, R., Timko, C., & Carli, L. L. (1985). Cognitive biases in blaming the victim. *Journal of Experimental Social Psychology, 21*, 161–177.

Johnson, H. (1994). Processes of successful intentional forgetting. *Psychological Bulletin, 116*, 274–292.

Kadish, M. R., & Kadish, S. H. (1971). The institutionalization of conflict: Jury acquittals. *Journal of Social Issues, 27*, 199–217.

Kagehiro, D. K., Taylor, R. B., Laufer, W. S., & Harland, A. T. (1991). Hindsight bias and third-party consenters to warrantless police searches. *Law and Human Behavior, 15*, 305–314.

Kalven, H., & Zeisel, H. (1966). *The American jury.* Boston: Little, Brown.

Kamin, K. A., & Rachlinski, J. J. (1995). Ex post ≠ ex ante: Determining liability in hindsight. *Law and Human Behavior, 19*, 89–104.

Kaplan, R. M., & Atkins, C. J. (1982). Psychological issues raised in the California Supreme Court case *People vs. Collins. Psychological Reports, 50*, 259–266.

Kassin, S. M., & Wrightsman, L. S. (1981). Coerced confessions, judicial instruction, and mock juror verdicts. *Journal of Applied Social Psychology, 11*, 489–511.

Kassin, S. M., & Wrightsman, L. S. (Eds.). (1985). *The psychology of evidence and trial procedure.* Beverly Hills, CA: Sage.

Kausler, D. H., & Hakami, M. K. (1982). Frequency judgments by young and elderly adults for relevant stimuli with spontaneously present irrelevant stimuli. *Journal of Gerontology, 37*, 438–442.

Keenan, J. M., MacWhinney, B., & Mayhew, D. (1977). Pragmatics in memory: A study of natural conversation. *Journal of Verbal Learning and Verbal Behavior, 16*, 549–560.

Kelly, A. E., & Kahn, J. H. (1994). Effects of suppression of personal intrusive thoughts. *Journal of Personality and Social Psychology, 66*, 998–1006.

Kerwin, J., & Shaffer, D. R. (1994). Mock jurors versus mock juries: The role of deliberations in reactions to inadmissible testimony. *Personality and Social Psychology Bulletin, 20*, 153–162.

Kihlstrom, J. F. (1983). Instructed forgetting: Hypnotic and nonhypnotic. *Journal of Experimental Psychology: General, 112*, 73–79

Kihlstrom, J. F., & Evans, F, J. (1976). Recovery of memory after posthypnotic amnesia. *Journal of Abnormal Psychology, 85*, 564–569.

Kihlstrom, J. F., Evans, F. J., Orne, E. C., & Orne, M. T. (1980). Attempting to breach posthypnotic amnesia. *Journal of Abnormal Psychology, 89*, 603–616.

Kihlstrom, J. F., & Wilson, L. (1984). Temporal organization of recall during posthypnotic amnesia. *Journal of Abnormal Psychology, 93*, 200–208.

Kinnear, T. C., Taylor, J., & Gur-Arie, O. (1983). Affirmative disclosure: Long-term monitoring of residual effects. *Journal of Business Policy and Marketing, 2,* 38–45.

Kramer, G. P., Kerr, N. L., & Carroll, J. S. (1990). Pretrial publicity, judicial remedies, and jury bias. *Law and Human Behavior, 14,* 409–438.

Kreutzer, M. A., Leonard, C., & Flavell, J. H. (1975). An interview study of children's knowledge about memory. *Monographs of the Society for Research in Child Development, 40,* 1–58.

Lavy, E. H., & van den Hout, M. (1990). Thought suppression induces intrusions. *Behavioural Psychotherapy, 18,* 251–258.

Leary, M. R. (1981). The distorted nature of hindsight. *The Journal of Social Psychology, 115,* 25–29.

Leary, M. R. (1982). Hindsight distortion and the 1980 presidential election. *Personality and Social Psychology Bulletin, 8,* 257–263.

Lehman, E. B., & Bovasso, M. (1993). Development of intentional forgetting in children. In M. L. Howe & R. Pasnak (Eds.), *Emerging themes in cognitive development* (Vol. 1, pp. 214–233). New York: Springer-Verlag.

Lehman, E. B., McKinley-Pace, M. J., Wilson, J., Slavsky, M. D., & Woodson, M. E. (1997). Direct and indirect measures of intentional forgetting in children and adults: Evidence for retrieval inhibition and reinstatement. *Journal of Experimental Child Psychology, 64,* 295–316.

Lenehan, G. E., & O'Neill, P. (1981). Reactance and conflict as determinants of judgment in a mock jury experiment. *Journal of Applied Social Psychology, 11,* 231–239.

Lewinsohn, P. M., Munoz, R., Youngren, M. A., & Zeiss, A. M. (1978). *Control your depression.* Englewood Cliffs, NJ: Prentice-Hall.

Loftus, E. F. (1974). Reconstructing memory: The incredible eyewitness. *Psychology Today, 8,* 116–119.

Macrae, C. N., Bodenhausen, G. V., Milne, A. B., & Jetten, J. (1994). Out of mind but back in sight: Stereotypes on the rebound. *Journal of Personality and Social Psychology, 67,* 808–817.

Mazis, M. B., & Adkinson, J. E. (1976). An experimental evaluation of a proposed corrective advertising remedy. *Journal of Marketing Research, 13,* 178–183.

Mazursky, D., & Schul, Y. (1988). The effects of advertisement encoding on the failure to discount information: Implications for the sleeper effect. *Journal of Consumer Research, 15,* 24–36.

McConkey, K. M., & Sheehan, P. W. (1981). The impact of videotape playback of hypnotic events on posthypnotic amnesia. *Journal of Abnormal Psychology, 90,* 46–54.

McConkey, K. M., Sheehan, P. W., & Cross, D. G. (1980). Post-hypnotic amnesia: Seeing is not remembering. *British Journal of Social and Clinical Psychology, 19,* 99–107.

Merckelbach, H., Muris, P., van den Hout, M., & de Jong, P. (1991). Rebound effects of thought suppression: Instruction-dependent? *Behavioural Psychotherapy, 19,* 225–238.

Miller, G. R. (1975). Jurors' responses to videotaped trial materials: Some recent findings. *Personality and Social Psychology Bulletin, 1,* 561–569.

Muris, P., Merckelbach, H., & De Jong, P. (1993). Case histories and shorter communications: Verbalization and environmental cuing in thought suppression. *Behavior Research Therapy, 31,* 609–612.

Muris, P., Merckelbach, H., van den Hout, M., & de Jong, P. (1992). Case histories and shorter communications: Suppression of emotional and neutral material. *Behavior Research Therapy, 30,* 639–642.

Muther, W. S. (1965). Erasure or partitioning in short-term memory. *Psychonomic Science, 3,* 429–430.

Pavur, E. J., Comeaux, J. M., & Zeringue, J. A. (1984). Younger and older adults' attention to relevant and irrelevant stimuli in free recall. *Experimental Aging Research, 10,* 59–60.

Pennington, D. C. (1981). The British firemen's strike of 1977/78: An investigation of judgements in foresight and hindsight. *British Journal of Social Psychology, 20,* 89–96.

Pennington, D. C., Rutter, D. R., McKenna, K., & Morley, I. E. (1980). Estimating the outcome of a pregnancy test: Women's judgements in foresight and hindsight. *British Journal of Social and Clinical Psychology, 19,* 317–324.

Pennington, N., & Hastie, R. (1981). Juror decision-making models: The generalization gap. *Psychological Bulletin, 89,* 246–287.

Petty, R. E., & Wegener, D. T. (1993). Flexible correction processes in social judgment: Correcting for context-induced contrast. *Journal of Experimental Social Psychology, 40,* 137–165.

Pickel, K. L. (1995). Inducing jurors to disregard inadmissible evidence. *Law and Human Behavior, 19,* 407–424.

Posansky, C. J. (1976). Directed forgetting among third and seventh graders. *Contemporary Educational Psychology, 1,* 247–256.

Powell, J. L. (1988). A test of the knew-it-all-along effect in the 1984 presidential and statewide elections. *Journal of Applied Social Psychology, 18,* 760–773.

Pratkanis, A. R., Greenwald, A. G., Leippe, M. R., & Baumgardner, M. H. (1988). In search of reliable persuasion effects: III. The sleeper effect is dead, long live the sleeper effect. *Journal of Personality and Social Psychology, 54,* 203–218.

Radtke, H. L, Bertrand, L. D., & Spanos, N. P. (1988). Hypnotic amnesia and temporal organization: Effects of learning set, stimulus type, number of presentations, and hypnotic susceptibility. *Canadian Journal of Behavioral Science, 20,* 201–220.

Radtke, H. L., Thompson, V. A., & Egger, L. A. (1987). Use of retrieval cues in breaching hypnotic amnesia. *Journal of Abnormal Psychology, 4,* 335–340.

Radtke-Bodorik, H. L., Spanos, N. P., & Haddad, M. G. (1979). The effects of spoken versus written recall on suggested amnesia in hypnotic and task-motivated subjects. *American Journal of Clinical Hypnosis, 22,* 8–16.

Roper, K. L., & Zentall, T. R. (1993). Directed forgetting in animals. *Psychological Bulletin, 113,* 513–532.

Ross, L., Lepper, M. R., & Hubbard, M. (1975). Perseverance in self-perception and social perception: Biased attributional processes in the debriefing paradigm. *Journal of Personality and Social Psychology, 32,* 880–892.

Ross, L., Lepper, M. R., Strack, F., & Steinmetz, J. (1977). Social explanation and social expectation: Effects of real and hypothetical explanations on subjective likelihood. *Journal of Personality and Social Psychology, 35,* 817–829.

Rutledge, P. C., Hollenberg, D., & Hancock, R. A. (1993). Individual differences in the Wegner rebound effect: Evidence for a moderator variable in the thought rebound following thought suppression. *Psychological Reports, 72,* 867–880.

Saunders, D. M., Vidmar, N., & Hewitt, E. C. (1983). Eyewitness testimony and the discrediting effect. In S. M. A. Lloyd-Bostock & B. R. Clifford (Eds.), *Evaluating witness evidence.* New York: Wiley.

Schkade, D. A., & Kilbourne, L. M. (1991). Expectation-outcome consistency and hindsight bias. *Organizational Behavior and Decision Processes, 49,* 105–123.

Schul, Y. (1993). When warning succeeds: The effect of warning on success in ignoring invalid information. *Journal of Experimental Social Psychology, 29,* 42–62.

Schul, Y., & Burnstein, E. (1985). When discounting fails: Conditions under which individuals use discredited information in making a judgment. *Journal of Personality and Social Psychology, 49,* 894–903.

Schul, Y., & Mazursky, D. (1990). Conditions facilitating successful discounting in consumer decision making. *Journal of Consumer Research, 16,* 442–451.

Schul, Y., & Manzury, F. (1990). The effects of type of encoding and strength of discounting appeal on the success of ignoring an invalid testimony. *European Journal of Social Psychology, 20,* 337–349.

Schuyler, B. A., & Coe, W. C. (1981). A physiological investigation of volitional and nonvolitional experience during posthypnotic amnesia. *Journal of Personality and Social Psychology, 40,* 1160–1169.

Sharpe, D., & Adair, J. G. (1993). Reversibility of the hindsight bias: Manipulation of experimental demands. *Organizational Behavior and Human Decision Processes, 56,* 233–245.

Silva, C. E., & Kirsch, I. (1987). Breaching hypnotic amnesia by manipulating expectancy. *Journal of Abnormal Psychology, 96,* 325–329.

Simon, R. J. (1966). Murder, juries and the press: Does sensational reporting lead to verdicts of guilty. *Trans-Action, 3,* 40–42.

Slovic, P., & Fischhoff, B. (1977). On the psychology of experimental surprises. *Journal of Experimental Psychology: Human Perception and Performance, 3,* 544–551.

Spanos, N. P., & Bodorik, H. L. (1977). Suggested amnesia and disorganized recall in hypnotic and task-motivated subjects. *Journal of Abnormal Psychology, 86,* 295–305.

Spanos, N. P., & D'Eon, J. L. (1980). Hypnotic amnesia, disorganized recall, and inattention. *Journal of Abnormal Psychology, 89,* 744–750.

Spanos, N. P., McLean, J. M., & Bertrand, L. D. (1987). Serial organization during hypnotic amnesia under two conditions of item presentation. *Journal of Research in Personality, 21,* 361–374.

Spanos, N. P., Radtke, H. L., & Bertrand, L. D. (1985). Hypnotic amnesia as a strategic enactment: Breaching amnesia in highly susceptible participants. *Journal of Personality and Social Psychology, 47,* 1155–1169.

Spanos, N. P., Radtke, H. L., Bertrand, L. D., Addie, D. L., & Drummond, J. (1982). Disorganized recall, hypnotic amnesia and participants' faking: More disconfirmatory evidence. *Psychological Reports, 50,* 383–389.

Spanos, N. P., Radtke, H. L., & Dubreuil, D. L. (1982). Episodic and semantic memory in posthypnotic amnesia: A reevaluation. *Journal of Personality and Social Psychology, 43,* 565–573.

Spanos, N. P., Radtke-Bororik, H. L., & Stam, H. J. (1980). Disorganized recall during suggested amnesia: Fact not artifact. *Journal of Abnormal Psychology, 89,* 1–19.

Spanos, N. P., Stam, H. J., D'Eon, J. L., Pawlak, A. E., & Radtke-Bodorik, H. L. (1980). The effects of social psychological variables on hypnotic amnesia. *Journal of Personality and Social Psychology, 39,* 737–750.

Stahlberg, D., Eller, F., Maass, A., & Frey, D. (1995). We knew it all along: Hindsight bias in groups. *Organizational Behavior and Decision Processes, 63,* 46–58.

Stam, H. J., Radtke-Bodorik, H. L., & Spanos, N. P. (1980). Repression and hypnotic amnesia: A failure to replicate and an alternative formulation. *Journal of Abnormal Psychology, 89,* 551–559.

Sue, S., Smith, R. E., & Caldwell, C. (1973). Effects of inadmissible evidence on the decisions of simulated jurors: A moral dilemma. *Journal of Applied Social Psychology, 3,* 345–353.

Sue, S., Smith, R. E., & Gilbert, R. (1974). Biasing effects of pretrial publicity on judicial decisions. *Journal of Criminal Justice, 2,* 163–171.

Synodinos, N. E. (1986). Hindsight distortion: "I knew-it-all along and I was sure about it." *Journal of Applied Social Psychology, 16,* 107–117.

Tanford, J. A. (1990). The law and psychology of jury instructions. *Nebraska Law Review, 69,* 71–111.

Thomas, E. A. C., & Hogue, A. (1976). Apparent weight of evidence, decision criteria, and confidence ratings in juror decision making. *Psychological Review, 83,* 442–465.

Thompson, W. C., Fong, G. T., & Rosenhan, D. L. (1981). Inadmissible evidence and juror verdicts. *Journal of Personality and Social Psychology, 40,* 453–463.

Tkachyk, M. E., Spanos, N. P., & Bertrand, L. D. (1985). Variables affecting subjective organization during posthypnotic amnesia. *Journal of Research in Personality, 19,* 95–108.

Tyebjee, T. T. (1982). The role of publicity in FTC corrective advertising remedies. *Journal of Marketing and Public Policy, 1,* 111–122.

Walster, E., Bersheid, E., Abrahams, D., & Aronson, V. (1967). Effectiveness of debriefing following deception experiments. *Journal of Personality and Social Psychology, 6*, 371–380.

Wegener, D. T., & Petty, R. E. (1995). Flexible correction processes in social judgment: The role of naive theories in corrections for perceived bias. *Journal of Personality and Social Psychology, 68*, 36–51.

Wegner, D. M. (1989). *White bears and other unwanted thoughts*. New York: Viking/Penquin.

Wegner, D. M. (1994). Ironic processes of mental control. *Psychological Review, 101*, 34–52.

Wegner, D. M., & Erber, R. (1993). Social foundations of mental control. In D. M. Wegner & J. W. Pennebaker (Eds.), *Handbook of mental control* (pp. 37–56). Englewood Cliffs, NJ: Prentice-Hall.

Wegner, D. M., Erber, R., & Zanakos, S. (1993). Ironic processes in the mental control of mood and mood-related thought. *Journal of Personality and Social Psychology, 65*, 1093–1104.

Wegner, D. M., Lane, J. D., & Dimitri, S. (1994). The allure of secret relationships. *Journal of Personality and Social Psychology, 66*, 287–300.

Wegner, D. M., Quillian, F., & Houston, C. E. (1996). Memories out of order: Thought suppression and the disturbance of sequence memory. *Journal of Personality and Social Psychology, 71*, 680–691.

Wegner, D. M., Schneider, D. J., Carter, S. R., III, & White, T. L. (1987). Paradoxical effects of thought suppression. *Journal of Personality and Social Psychology, 53*, 5–13.

Wegner, D. M., Schneider, D. J., Knutson, B., & McMahon, S. R. (1991). Polluting the stream of consciousness: The effect of thought suppression on the mind's environment. *Cognitive Therapy and Research, 15*, 141–152.

Wegner, D. M., Shortt, J. W., Blake, A. W., & Page, M. S. (1990). The suppression of exciting thoughts. *Journal of Personality and Social Psychology, 58*, 409–418.

Weinberg, H. I., & Baron, R. S. (1982). The discredible witness. *Personality and Social Psychology Bulletin, 8*, 60–67.

Weiner, B. (1968). Motivated forgetting and the study of repression. *Journal of Personality, 36*, 213–234.

Weiner, B., & Reed, H. (1969). Effects of the instructional sets to remember and forget on short-term retention: Studies of rehearsal control and retrieval inhibition (repression). *Journal of Experimental Psychology, 79*, 226–232.

Wells, G. L., Lindsay, R. C. L., & Tousignant, J. P. (1980). Effects of expert psychological advice on human performance in judging the validity of eyewitness testimony. *Law and Human Behavior, 4*, 275–285.

Wenzlaff, R. M., Wegner, D. M., & Klein, S. B. (1991). The role of thought suppression in the bonding of thought and mood. *Journal of Personality and Social Psychology, 60*, 500–508.

Wenzlaff, R. M., Wegner, D. M., & Roper D. (1988). Depression and mental control: The resurgence of unwanted negative thoughts. *Journal of Personality and Social Psychology, 55*, 882–892.

Werner, C. M., Kagehiro, D. K., & Strube, M. J. (1982). Conviction proneness and the authoritarian juror: Inability to disregard information or attitudinal bias? *Journal of Applied Psychology, 67*, 629–636.

Wilkie, W. L., McNeill, D. L., & Mazis, M. B. (1984). Marketing's "Scarlet Letter": The theory and practice of corrective advertising. *Journal of Marketing, 48*, 11–31.

Wilson, T. D., & Brekke, N. (1994). Mental contamination and mental correction: Unwanted influences on judgments and evaluations. *Psychological Bulletin, 116*, 117–142.

Wolf, S., & Montgomery, D. A. (1977). Effects of inadmissible evidence and level of judicial admonishment to disregard on the judgments of mock jurors. *Journal of Applied Social Psychology, 7*, 205–219.

Wolpe, J. (1958). *Psychotherapy by reciprocal inhibition*. Stanford, CA: Stanford University Press.

Wood, G. (1978). The knew-it-all-along effect. *Journal of Experimental Psychology: Human Perception and Performance, 4*, 345–353.

Wrightsman, L. S. (1978). The American jury on trial: Empirical evidence and procedural modifications. *The Journal of Social Issues, 34*, 137–164.

Wyer, R. S., & Budesheim, T. L. (1987). Person memory and judgments: The impact of information that one is told to disregard. *Journal of Personality and Social Psychology, 53*, 14–29.

Wyer, R. S., & Unverzagt, W. H. (1985). Effects of instructions to disregard information on its subsequent recall and use in making judgments. *Journal of Personality and Social Psychology, 48*, 533–549.

Zacks, R. T., & Hasher, L. (1994). Directed ignoring: Inhibitory regulation of working memory. In D. Dagenbach & T. Carr (Eds.), *Inhibitory processes in attention, memory, and language* (pp. 241–264). San Diego: Academic Press.

Zacks, R. T., Radvansky, G., & Hasher, L. (1995). Studies of directed forgetting in older adults. *Journal of Experimental Psychology: Learning, Memory, and Cognition, 32*, 143–156.

3

VARIETIES OF GOAL-DIRECTED FORGETTING

Elizabeth Ligon Bjork
Robert A. Bjork
University of California, Los Angeles

Michael C. Anderson
University of Oregon

If asked, most of us would probably say that our biggest memory problem is forgetting things we want to remember. Frequently, however, forgetting is exactly what we need to do to function efficiently. For example, to avoid disabling emotions or dysfunctional personal relationships, we may want to forget past events in our lives that are painful or embarrassing. Another motivation to forget is the need to contend with a changing world: We need to remember our *current* phone number, not the one we had a few years back; how the operating system on *this* computer works, not the one on our old machine, and so forth. Also, when we search our memories for desired information such as someone's name, we continually—in a kind of "online" fashion—need to "forget" or inhibit closely related, but incorrect, information.

Our goal in the present chapter is to examine several varieties of what might be termed *goal-directed forgetting*—that is, situations where forgetting serves some implicit or explicit personal need. Specifically, we summarize the evidence that a particular mechanism—retrieval inhibition—is common to these several situations, and we speculate on some broader implications of retrieval inhibition as a forgetting mechanism. We exclude from our analysis those situations where we are instructed to ignore or disregard information that is confidential, not permissible in a courtroom, and so forth, because such instructions to "forget" are not necessarily consistent with our personal goals and needs (excellent analyses of the "disregard" literature are provided by Johnson, 1994, and in the chapters by Golding, Ellis,

Hauselt, & Sego; Golding & Long; Isbell, Smith, & Wyer; Kassin & Studebaker; Schul & Burnstein; and Thompson & Fuqua in the present volume).

Cues to Forget: Implicit and Explicit

Implicit Cues. In both real-world situations and analogous research paradigms, cues to forget, although clear, are typically implicit. As we park our car in the morning, for example, we do not tend to instruct ourselves to forget the event of having parked our car in a different spot the preceding morning, nor do there tend to be signs posted that instruct us to do so. Similarly, in the various paradigms that incorporate an intrinsic updating requirement, such as the Brown–Peterson short-term-memory paradigm and the A–B, A–D list-learning paradigm of interference research, the cue to forget, although clear, is implicit. As each successive to-be-remembered set of items is presented in the Brown–Peterson paradigm, for example, the structure of the task itself makes it clear to subjects that the items from the preceding trial should now be forgotten, that continuing to remember them is a potential source of errors.

In other research paradigms, such as the retrieval–induced-forgetting paradigm (Anderson, Bjork, & Bjork, 1994), there is also an implied cue to forget, but the cue, as defined by the task itself, is more subtle and differs qualitatively from the implied cue in updating paradigms such as the Brown–Peterson or A–B, A–D paradigms. In the retrieval–induced-forgetting paradigm, a study phase is followed by a retrieval–practice phase, during which subjects are cued to retrieve some of the studied items multiple times and then, after a delay, are asked to recall all the items from the study phase. Typically, the to-be-remembered items are category-exemplar pairs where multiple exemplars are paired with each of a small number of category labels during the study phase. During the retrieval–practice phase, when subjects are cued via a category name and a letter stem to retrieve the particular studied exemplar that fits that combined cue, there is an implied cue to suppress or inhibit other exemplars that were paired with that category during the study phase. The need to suppress or inhibit serves an immediate rather than a long-term need, however, because during the retrieval–practice phase, it remains the subject's goal to remember as many items from the study phase as possible. In contrast, from the standpoint of a subject in a Brown–Peterson or an A–B, A–D experiment, items or associations that were to be learned, but that now are out of date, are history; inhibiting or suppressing those items is consistent with the long-term interests of the subject, as defined by the experimental task.

Explicit Cues. In other real-world and laboratory situations, the cue to forget can be more direct. For example, we have probably all been told something like: "Forget what I just said. I was reading the wrong number.

Here's the correct one." Or, "Forget those directions. It's too hard to get there that way. Here's the way you should go instead." Similarly, a defining characteristic of the directed-forgetting research paradigm, at least with human subjects, is that the cue to forget is explicit. Subjects are instructed at the beginning of such studies that, on occasion, they may receive an instruction to forget some of the material previously presented to them for study, and, if so, their memory for that material will not be tested later. Or, subjects might be unexpectedly told that materials they had just been studying for a later memory test will not be tested after all (e.g., they might be told that incorrect materials had been presented by mistake), and they are then presented with the "correct" materials to study for a later memory test.

Inhibitory Processes in Goal-Directed Forgetting

In a great variety of real-world and laboratory settings, then, we are cued, implicitly or explicitly, to get rid of, set aside, suppress, or inhibit, either permanently or temporarily, something that resides in our memories. Although the nature of the cue to forget or inhibit and the details of the task-defined motivation to forget or inhibit may differ substantially across such settings, we think that three distinct but related bodies of research suggest that a common mechanism—retrieval inhibition—may be involved. By retrieval inhibition, we mean the loss of retrieval access to information that is, in fact, still stored in memory as can be demonstrated by indices other than recall measures, such as recognition tests, relearning, or certain indirect tests.

Terminology. Because the term inhibition is used in multiple ways in the literature, often simply as a description of empirical effects that are the opposite of facilitation, we need to clarify what we mean by *retrieval inhibition* as a "mechanism." Unless modified, as in *retrieval inhibition/blocking* or *retrieval inhibition/suppression* (see R. A. Bjork, 1989), we mean that term to refer, collectively, to the set of possible mechanisms that result in loss of retrieval *access* to inhibited items, without a commensurate loss, if any, in the *availability* of those items (Tulving & Pearlstone, 1966), as measured by tests such as recognition. For a discussion of the full range of possible mechanisms, we refer the reader to Anderson and Bjork (1994).

Following a convention that goes back to the interference theorists of another era, then, we reserve *some* theoretical meaning for the word *inhibition*, and we use *interference* or *impairment* as terms that are simply descriptive of empirical effects. It should be emphasized, however, that some of the mechanisms that result in retrieval inhibition in its general sense do not involve an inhibition in what R. A. Bjork (1989) referred to as its "strong sense," that is, as a suppression type of process that is directed at the to-be-inhibited information, resulting in a suppression or deactivation of that information's representation in memory.

Relevant Research Paradigms. The three bodies of research that are the focus of the present chapter span the last 60 or so years of research on human learning and memory. One, research on "unlearning" and "spontaneous recovery," dates back to the 1930s, when questions having to do with interference and forgetting began to dominate experimental research on memory; another, research on "starting over" in the intentional-forgetting tradition, dates back to the 1960s; and the third, research on "retrieval-induced forgetting," represents a relatively new approach to the study of forgetting. In the three sections that follow, we summarize the phenomena in each of these areas that seem to implicate retrieval inhibition as a forgetting mechanism. We then conclude with a discussion of some remaining issues and some speculations about the potential relevance of retrieval-inhibition mechanisms to the inhibition and recovery of memories in clinical contexts.

UNLEARNING AND SPONTANEOUS RECOVERY

Historical Background

Although experimental research on the causes of forgetting dates back to the turn of the century when Muller and Pilzecker (1900) first reported evidence of retroactive interference, we begin our discussion of such research from the time of McGeoch's classical work on the causes of forgetting. In a seminal and devastating critique of the two dominant theories of forgetting of the time—Muller and Pilzecker's (1900) perseveration–consolidation theory and Thorndike's (1914) law of disuse—McGeoch (1932, 1936, 1942) proposed instead that forgetting was a consequence of interference and competition rather than the loss of memory traces per se.

Briefly, McGeoch's framework assumed that memory is fundamentally associative and that retrieval is guided by cues to which items in memory are associated. Thus, when applied to the A–B, A–D interpolated-learning paradigm, where the learning of a first A–B list of paired associates is followed by the learning of a second A–D list (that is, new responses to the same stimuli), both the B and the D responses are assumed to become associated in memory to the same A cue. Although McGeoch asserted that the availability of the original A–B association was not reduced by the interpolated learning of the A–D association, he assumed that competition occurring between the B and D responses at the time of a recall test would result in reproductive inhibition, with a consequent impairment in recall performance. More specifically, he assumed that at the time of the recall test, whichever response was momentarily dominant would displace the other, or, that both might compete and block one another at an implicit level so that neither could be overtly reported.

McGeoch's proposal was the subject of intense empirical research and theoretical analysis over the next several decades, resulting in a wealth of empirical findings and the development of what has come to be called interference theory, considered by many to be the most significant and systematic theoretical formulation in the field of human learning and memory. The history of this endeavor is a fascinating one (for a summary, see R. A. Bjork, 1992) and we recommend to the interested reader the detailed and scholarly accounts by Postman (1971); Postman and Underwood (1973); Crowder (1976); and Anderson and Neely (1996).

The important point about McGeoch's original theory for present purposes is that what he meant by reproductive inhibition is one theoretical instantiation of retrieval inhibition. With respect to the role of retrieval inhibition in goal-directed forgetting, the subsequent work by Melton and Irwin (1940) and others on "unlearning," as summarized in the next section, is highly relevant.

The Evidence for "Unlearning" and Spontaneous Recovery

In a now classic study, Melton and Irwin (1940) tested McGeoch's assumption of response inhibition by manipulating the degree of interpolated learning of a second list before subjects were asked to relearn the first list, and then measuring the number of list-2 items that were intruded during list-1 relearning. They found that list-2 intrusions increased to a point and then decreased as a function of the degree of list-2 learning. Given that such intrusions might be considered a straightforward measure of response inhibition, Melton and Irwin argued that another factor must be involved in retroactive interference and proposed unlearning as that factor. More specifically, they suggested that the retroactive interference suffered by first-list items during their relearning resulted from the action of two factors. First, during the interpolated learning of list-2 items, the original B responses are subject to unlearning (analogous to response extinction in classical conditioning), with the extent of such unlearning an increasing function of the degree of list-2 learning. Second, those list-1 responses still remaining at the end of list-2 learning are then, as McGeoch proposed, subject to competition from the newly learned list-2 responses.

It is important for present purposes to emphasize that what was encouraged in Melton and Irwin's experiment, if only implicitly, was a type of goal-directed forgetting. From their subjects' standpoint, list 1 became only a nuisance, so to speak, once the learning of list 2 began. List 1 should thus be erased, set aside, suppressed, or otherwise inhibited during list-2 learning. What Melton and Irwin actually proposed, however, was "unlearning," which, in the stimulus–response tradition of the time, they interpreted as analogous to the experimental extinction of conditioned responses in animals. Also, in the spirit of the times, they phrased their theory without reference to the subjects' intent with respect to the first list. Rather, unlearning was presumed to be an automatic consequence of changes in associate strength that resulted from list-2 learning. An implication of Melton and Irwin's unlearning proposal, given the assumed similarities to experimental extinction, is that list-1 items should show spontaneous recovery over time, analogous to conditioned responses that have undergone extinction. In that sense, it is the access to the unlearned list that is inhibited, or, in our terms, unlearning results in retrieval inhibition.

Early attempts to demonstrate spontaneous recovery produced mixed results, creating some doubt as to its actual occurrence. In an analysis of these discrepant results, however, Postman, Stark, and Fraser (1968) were able to characterize the conditions under which spontaneous recovery should be detectable if, in fact, it does occur, and were then able convincingly to demonstrate absolute increases in the recall of first-list B responses under such conditions; namely, when there is little extraexperimental forgetting of materials, as measured by the performance of a control group that learns only one list. (See also, Wheeler, 1995, for recent research demonstrating spontaneous recovery.) Additionally, in the Postman et al. studies, evidence was obtained for systematic changes in recall order of first- and interpolated-list responses with time. Specifically, when recall of both B and D responses was required and the recall test immediately followed the period of interpolated learning, the interpolated D responses were likely to be recalled first; with delay of the test, however, order of recall changed to favor first-list B responses.

The Response-Set Suppression Hypothesis

The response-set suppression hypothesis was proposed by Postman et al. (1968) to explain both retroactive interference effects and the conditions under which items suffering retroactive interference would exhibit spontaneous recovery. In the context of the A–B, A–D list-learning paradigm, spontaneous recovery refers to an increase over time, following A–D learning, in subjects' ability to recall first-list responses.

The response-set suppression hypothesis accounts for both these effects as follows. When interpolated learning of the A–D list begins, covert or overt intrusions of the previously learned B responses are evoked, triggering the onset of a selector mechanism that suppresses the entire set of first-list responses. Such suppression facilitates second-list learning by allowing subjects to limit their responses to the currently correct set of D responses. At the end of interpolated learning, however, although the entire set of B responses is suppressed making B responses less accessible than D responses, which thus accounts for the observation of retroactive interference or the impaired recall of B responses, the specific A–B associations still remain intact. Furthermore, because the proposed suppression mechanism is assumed to be reversible and to diminish in effectiveness with the passage of time, B responses should become more accessible with time, resulting in the increased recall of B responses with test delay. That is, spontaneous recovery of first-list responses should occur.

Thus, as described by Postman and his colleagues, response-set suppression is clearly, in contrast to unlearning as characterized by Melton and Irwin (1940), a *goal-directed* inhibitory mechanism. The assumed suppression is directed at the to-be-inhibited items themselves—that is, the memory representation of the entire set of B responses—and the forgetting produced by that suppression serves the adaptive goal of facilitating second list or A–D learning by reducing the proactive interference attributable to the previously learned B responses. Again, response-set suppression is an example of retrieval inhibition, because, although the subject has lost retrieval access to the B responses, their representations continue to exist in memory as demonstrated by their spontaneous recovery under certain conditions and by other findings, such as the virtual disappearance of retroactive interference effects when a multiple-choice recognition test is given rather than a recall test (Postman & Stark, 1969).

INHIBITION IN DIRECTED FORGETTING

As the chapters in this volume so amply demonstrate, intentional forgetting can be studied using a wide variety of procedures and subject populations. For our purposes, however, one procedure is most relevant; namely, the so-called "list method" in which subjects, after trying to learn a set of items of some type, are then cued that those items are to be forgotten. Typically, then, the "true" to-be-remembered items are presented to replace the to-be-forgotten ones. The cue to forget is explicit rather than implicit, and there are other differences as well, but the list method of directed forgetting shares one strong similarity to procedures such as the Brown–Peterson and A–B, A–D paradigms: The need for a subject to update his or her memory creates a motivation to forget or inhibit the now out-of-date items. (For descriptions of alternative directed-forgetting methodologies in human memory research, see R. A. Bjork, 1972, or MacLeod in this volume.)

Basic Procedures

In a typical directed-forgetting experiment of the list-method variety, illustrated in Fig. 3.1, subjects are presented with a list of items to study for a later memory test, with the items presented one at a time. At some point, usually halfway through the list, the presentation of items is interrupted with a cue either to forget the preceding items (middle list of Fig. 3.1) or to keep on remembering the preceding items (left list of Fig. 3.1). In addition to these two types of lists, a control list or condition (right side of Fig. 3.1)

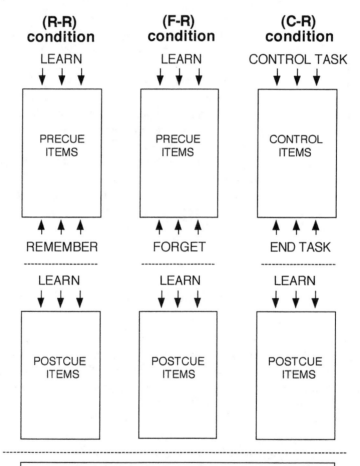

FIG. 3.1. Types of lists or conditions typically employed in the list-method paradigm of directed-forgetting research.

is also sometimes employed. In such a list, the precue items are replaced by a control task of some kind. For example, subjects might be asked to judge the similarity of pairs of shapes, with each pair presented at the same rate as the precue items in the other types of lists. Such a control condition permits a baseline measure of the recall of postcue items when there are no to-be-remembered or to-be-forgotten precue items. In the remainder of the present chapter, we refer to these three types of lists as forget–remember (F–R), remember–remember (R–R), and control–remember (C–R) lists or conditions.

The list method of directed forgetting can be used in either a within- or between-subjects design. When used in a within-subjects design, subjects are informed prior to the presentation of any lists that if a forget cue occurs, they will not be tested for their memory of the preceding items, only for their memory of the items to follow the forget cue; whereas, if a remember cue occurs, they need to keep remembering the preceding items for a later memory test. As long as these instructions are not violated, each of the different types of lists (R–R, F–R, and C–R) can be presented to the same subject multiple times. It needs to be emphasized, however, that in such designs, although subjects are informed at the beginning of the experiment that a cue to forget or a cue to remember can occur on any list, there is no way to anticipate which type of cue will occur during presentation of the precue items. Thus, until the cue occurs, subjects must process all presented items in the same way; namely, as items that they need to learn for a later memory test.

The effectiveness of the forget cue in this type of design is assessed by comparing the recall of postcue items in F–R lists to that of postcue items in R–R lists, and the forget cue is assumed to have been effective if proactive interference effects owing to precue items is significantly decreased in the F–R condition. Additionally, if a control condition was also employed, recall of postcue items from R–R and F–R lists can be compared to that of postcue items from C–R lists. Although subjects are not asked to recall forget items in experiments using this type of design, they are sometimes asked to try to recall any forget items that they can at the very end of the experiment when no further lists are to be presented. (An interesting exception to this rule is a study by Reitman, Malin, Bjork, and Higman, 1973, in which subjects were forewarned that they would occasionally be asked to try to recall forget items, but that they would be informed when they were being asked to do so, and that they should try not to let the possibility of such occasional tests influence what they typically did in response to a forget cue.)

When the list method of directed forgetting is used in a between-subjects design, the forget cue is usually introduced as a surprise. For example, in the F–R condition, presentation of the list may be stopped at the midpoint, at which time the experimenter explains that the preceding items were just for practice and can thus be forgotten, and that the subjects should now try to learn the real list, which is then presented. Or, in what is sometimes called the "whoops" procedure, presentation of items is stopped halfway through the list, at which time the experimenter explains that the preceding items had been presented by mistake, that the subject should thus try to forget those "incorrect" items and to learn the "correct" list of items that will now be presented. Then, following presentation of the next or second list, subjects are tested on the items they were instructed to forget as well as on those they were instructed to remember, and the effectiveness of the forget cue is assessed by comparing the recall of to-be-forgotten items to that of to-be-remembered items. Such misleading use of the forget instruction can, of course, only be used once for any given subject, explaining the need for the F–R versus the R–R condition to be manipulated as a between-subjects variable in these types of directed-forgetting studies.

Finally, we need to mention that there is another basic type of directed-forgetting paradigm, labeled *item-by-item cuing* by Bjork (1972), in which the presentation of each individual item is accompanied, either simultaneously or after a delay, by a cue to forget or to remember that item (see, e.g., Muther, 1965; Woodward & Bjork, 1971). Although there are many similarities between the effects obtained with these two paradigms, and originally it was thought that the processes initiated by the cue to forget were the same in both, there is accumulating evidence that this is not the case. That is, there are compelling reasons to believe that the impaired recall of to-be-forgotten items observed in these two paradigms arises as a consequence of somewhat different processes; in particular, that item-by-item cuing induces differential encoding and rehearsal of to-be-remembered and to-be-forgotten items, which creates a problem of separating the consequences of those differential processes from the consequences of retrieval inhibition (if any) per se.

Given our present focus, then, we limit our analysis to effects obtained with the list method, but we encourage the interested reader to see articles by MacLeod (1975, 1989), Paller (1990), and Basden, Basden, and Gargano (1993) and the chapters by MacLeod, Basden and Basden, and Hauselt in the present volume for results obtained with item-by-item cuing and for discussions of the differences between these two methods. We also encourage the interested reader to see the important work of Hasher, Zacks, and their colleagues, carried out using several variants of item-by-item cuing, on how the pattern of those results changes with aging (e.g., Hartman & Hasher, 1991; Zacks & Hasher, 1994; Zacks, Radvansky, & Hasher, 1996).

Basic Phenomena

Directed-forgetting effects obtained across many studies employing list-method procedures can be summarized in terms of three basic and robust findings. First, postcue to-be-remembered items are recalled better in F–R lists than in R–R lists. That is, the recall of to-be-remembered items appears to suffer less from proactive interference effects owing to precue items in F–R lists than in R–R lists. Second, recall of postcue items in F–R lists is often not different from that of postcue items in C–R lists in which no items are presented in the first half of the list. That is, the recall of postcue items in F–R lists often shows no evidence of suffering from any proactive interference effects owing to the presentation of precue items. In terms of the subjects' ability to recall the postcue to-be-remembered items, it is as though the preceding to-be-forgotten items had never been presented. Third, if subjects are unexpectedly asked to recall items that they were instructed to forget, their ability to recall such to-be-forgotten material is impaired compared to their ability to recall equivalent material that they were instructed to remember.

The reader is referred to R. A. Bjork (1972, 1989), Johnson (1994), and the chapter by MacLeod in the present volume for a review of the studies from which we have extrapolated this basic pattern of directed-forgetting results.

Evidence for Retrieval Inhibition in Directed Forgetting

The first suggestion that retrieval inhibition played a primary role in the production of the pattern of directed-forgetting results just described was reported by Geiselman, Bjork, and Fishman (1983). Until this time, the predominant theoretical account of directed-forgetting effects, proposed by R. A. Bjork (1970, 1972) during the early years of research on directed forgetting, attributed such effects to processes that had nothing to do with inhibition or suppression[1] or even forgetting. Instead, Bjork's model explained such effects in terms of two positive actions taken by subjects in response to a forget cue, namely, focusing all of their postcue rehearsal and other mnemonic activities on the to-be-remembered items and somehow segregating or differentiating in memory the to-be-remembered items from the earlier to-be-forgotten items.

In the Geiselman et al. (1983) study, subjects were presented with a list of two different types of items: intentional items they were asked to learn for a later memory test and incidental items they were asked to judge on a pleasantness scale rather than learn. These two types of items were presented auditorily and in strict alternation throughout the list, with each word being preceded by the appropriate cue, for example, the subject would hear "learn" hand, "judge" rake, "learn" bell, and so forth. Then, midway through the list, subjects either received an instruction that the to-be-learned words presented thus far were practice and should be forgotten

---

[1]Research by Roediger and Crowder (1972), Weiner (1968), and Weiner and Reed (1969) represent notable exceptions to this early reluctance to assume that inhibitory or suppression-like processes played a role in the production of directed-forgetting effects.

(i.e., the F–R condition), or subjects were instructed that the to-be-learned words presented thus far were the first half of the list and should be remembered (i.e., the R–R condition). Following presentation of the second half of the list, however, subjects in either condition were given a free-recall test and asked to recall all of the words that they could remember from the experiment; that is, judge words as well as learn words, and first-half list words as well as second-half list words.

Subjects' recall of the learn words showed the typical directed-forgetting result: lowered recall of precue to-be-forgotten words and enhanced recall of postcue to-be-remembered words. The important and surprising results, however, and the results leading to the postulation of a role for retrieval inhibition in producing directed-forgetting effects, were those obtained for the judge items. Namely, subjects' recall of these words showed the same directed-forgetting pattern as that obtained for the learn words. Although the results obtained for the learn words could continue to be explained in terms of the old assumptions of differential rehearsal and grouping of the second-half list words following the forget cue, the effects of the forget cue on the judge words could not be explained in those terms. Subjects were not trying to learn or rehearse the judge items. Nor was the forget cue directed at the judge words. Nonetheless, simply by being intertwined with the learn words, or being part of the same episode as the learn words, it appeared that the judge words had also been inhibited or rendered inaccessible by the forget cue. By being in the same place as the learn words, the judge words had, so to speak, suffered the same fate as the learn words.

Alternative explanations of these results, such as subjects becoming confused about what were learn words and what were judge words or that the impaired recall of to-be-forgotten words arose from output interference owing to to-be-remembered words tending to be output first on the recall test, were ruled out by additional analyses and experiments performed by Geiselman et al. (1983). For example, in additional studies, subjects were able to sort the words they recalled into judge and learn categories with high accuracy and, even when learn and judge words were drawn from different categories, the same pattern of results obtained. Similarly, controlling for output order during recall did not change the basic pattern of results.

Thus, on the basis of these findings as well as other considerations that we elaborate in a later section, the explanation of directed-forgetting effects obtained with the list method that we and others have come to prefer includes the additional mechanism of retrieval inhibition. More specifically, we believe that when subjects are told to forget preceding information and are then presented with new information to learn, a process is initiated that inhibits the subsequent retrieval of the to-be-forgotten information. Because such to-be-forgotten items are not retrievable, they do not interfere with the recall of to-be-remembered information. Furthermore, whereas this updating process inhibits the retrieval of the to-be-forgotten information, it leaves its strength in memory—as indicated by other measures—unaffected.

Evidence for this last assumption comes from the following findings: (a) When measured by a recognition test, memory for to-be-forgotten items is unimpaired as compared to that for to-be-remembered items (e.g., Block, 1971; Elmes, Adams, & Roediger, 1970; Geiselman et al., 1983; Gross, Barresi, & Smith, 1970); (b) in a relearning paradigm, to-be-forgotten items are relearned as readily as to-be-remembered items (e.g., Geiselman & Bagheri, 1985;[2] Reed, 1970); and (c) the proactive interference of precue items that is eliminated by the forget instruction can, under certain circumstances, be reinstated at full strength. Evidence for this last effect, obtained in a series of studies conducted by E. L. Bjork, R. A. Bjork, and various collaborators, is described in a later section.

Necessary Conditions for Retrieval Inhibition in Directed Forgetting

Although considerable evidence suggests that people can intentionally forget previously learned items in such a way that their retrieval access to them is inhibited, there also appear to be limitations to this ability. One limitation concerns the timing of the forget instruction. A forget instruction seems to be most effective if given immediately after the to-be-forgotten items have been presented for study. If the cue to forget is delayed until after additional study material has been presented, there is both less forgetting of the to-be-forgotten information and little or no reduction in the proactive interference owing to such items on the recall of the later studied items (e.g., R. A. Bjork, 1970; Epstein, Massaro, & Wilder, 1972; Roediger & Tulving, 1979).

Another constraint on the effectiveness of the forget cue appears to be that new learning needs to occur after the forget instruction is given in order to produce retrieval inhibition. Evidence for this possible necessary condition comes from an experiment by Gelfand and R. A. Bjork (1985; described in R. A. Bjork, 1989). In the critical aspect of this experiment for the present issues, an initial study list of nouns was followed by instructions either to forget or to remember the preceding items, after which (a) some subjects did nothing while the experimenter fumbled around killing time; (b) some subjects received a list of adjectives for which they had to perform a rating task; and (c) some subjects received a second study list of nouns to learn. Then, after each type of activity, all subjects—that is, both those given the

---

[2]Although we cite the Geiselman and Bagheri (1985) study here, the relevance of these findings for assumptions regarding retrieval inhibition is somewhat questionable as they were obtained using the item-by-item cuing procedure as opposed to the list method of directed forgetting.

forget instruction and those given the remember instruction—were tested for their recall of the first study list of nouns.

Consistent with the results of previous studies, Gelfand and Bjork found that recall for to-be-forgotten items was impaired for subjects given a second list of nouns to learn following the forget instruction. However, instructing people to forget the first study list of nouns did not impair later recall of such to-be-forgotten items when this instruction was followed by either the unfilled interval or the adjective-rating task. On the basis of this pattern of results, it would seem that the instruction to forget, in and of itself, is not sufficient to inhibit retrieval of the to-be-forgotten items; rather, a resetting of the learning process initiated by the presentation of a new list of to-be-remembered items is necessary for inhibition of the prior to-be-forgotten items to occur.

Nature of the Retrieval Inhibition Involved in Directed Forgetting

We turn now to a discussion of a series of studies dating back to 1973 in which E. L. Bjork, R. A. Bjork, and various collaborators (e.g., E. L. Bjork, Bjork, & Glenberg, 1973; E. L. Bjork, Bjork, & White, 1984) tried to characterize more fully the underlying processes involved in directed-forgetting effects by investigating the conditions under which the proactive interference owing to to-be-forgotten items is or is not reinstated. Or, expressed in terms of the theoretical processes presently under consideration, these studies tried to characterize more fully the nature of the retrieval inhibition involved in directed-forgetting effects by investigating the conditions under which such inhibition is or is not released.

The basic procedure used in this series of studies was to present the three list types described in Fig. 3.1 and then to measure subjects' ability to recall postcue to-be-remembered items by a free-recall test that was either immediate or delayed by different types of interpolated activities. Across the various studies conducted, the different types of interpolated tasks included solving arithmetic problems, a forced-choice recognition test, and a yes/no recognition test. When the interpolated task was a forced-choice recognition test, subjects were shown pairs of words and asked to judge which word had been presented in the postcue part of the list; thus, for all list types, the correct choice was always a to-be-remembered item. On a subset of the pairs, however, the distractor item was a word that had appeared in the precue part of the list; thus, for F–R lists, such pairs contained a to-be-forgotten item as a distractor. When the interpolated task was a yes/no recognition test, subjects were shown individual words and asked to indicate whether each had been presented in the postcue part of the list; thus, again, for all list types, subjects were only required to recognize to-be-remembered words. On some yes/no recognition tests, all distractors were new items; however, on others, a subset of the distractors came from the precue part of the list; thus, for F–R lists, these were to-be-forgotten items. The recall performance obtained in these studies, which was based only on words that had *not* been re-presented in any of the interpolated tasks, can be summarized as follows. On the immediate recall test, the basic directed-forgetting pattern was obtained: Recall of postcue items from R–R lists was significantly poorer than that from F–R lists, which did not differ from that obtained in the C–R condition. When recall was delayed by the solving of arithmetic problems, performance levels were depressed, but the same basic directed-forgetting pattern was obtained as in the immediate recall condition. When, however, recall was delayed by either the forced-choice recognition test or the yes/no recognition test in which some of the distractors were precue items, a dramatically different pattern of results was obtained: Now, recall performance in the F–R condition decreased to the level of the R–R condition, with both being poorer than performance in the C–R condition. In contrast, when recall was delayed by a recognition test that did *not* re-present precue items as distractors, the basic directed-forgetting pattern of results (i.e., the pattern observed in the immediate recall condition) was again obtained.

Couched in the present theoretical terms, these results demonstrate that when a free-recall test is delayed by some dissimilar task, such as the solving of arithmetic problems, there is no spontaneous recovery of the proactive interference owing to to-be-forgotten items; that is, the retrieval inhibition imposed on such items is not released. When, however, the free-recall test is delayed by a recognition test of postcue to-be-remembered items on which only a small subset of the to-be-forgotten items appear as distractors, the retrieval inhibition of the entire set is apparently released, as evidenced by the drop in recall of postcue to-be-remembered items to the level of that obtained when subjects do not receive instructions to forget the precue list. It is not, however, the recognition test per se that releases the inhibition of the to-be-forgotten items. When the recognition test for postcue to-be-re-membered items does not re-present any to-be-forgotten items as distractors, then the entire set remains inhibited, as evidenced by the lack of any proactive interference effects on the recall of the postcue to-be-remembered items.

Such a pattern of results raises questions of exactly what is inhibited as a consequence of instructions to forget and then released by certain tasks, such as a recognition task involving to-be-forgotten items as distractors. For example, does an instruction to forget cause inhibited overall access to the to-be-forgotten items in memory, or, rather, inhibited access to those items because they are part of an episode that is inhibited—namely, the learning of the list that subjects were instructed to forget? Additionally, would inhib-ited to-be-forgotten items, as indicated by recall measures and the absence of proactive interference effects, nonetheless continue to have indirect or unconscious effects on other types of performance?

To answer such questions, the same list types (R–R, F–R, and C–R) were again presented to participants and followed by a free-recall test of the postcue to-be-remembered words that was either immediate or delayed by an interpolated task (E. L. Bjork & Bjork, 1996, Experiment 2). In this study, however, the interpolated task was a word-fragment-completion task, which included a subset of precue and postcue items, and, thus, for F–R lists, some fragments were based on to-be-forgotten items. As in the earlier studies, on the immediate free-recall test (again, based only on the recall of words not re-presented on the intervening task), the basic directed-forgetting pattern was obtained. Given that it could thus be inferred that the to-be-forgotten items were inhibited, as evidenced by their lack of interference on the recall of the to-be-remembered items, two critical questions concerning the nature of this inhibition could be asked.

First was the question of whether access to the to-be-forgotten items to serve as appropriate completions on the word-fragment-completion task would also be inhibited. That is, would the completion rate for precue to-be-forgotten words be less than that for precue to-be-remembered words and, possibly, not different from the completion rate for the new, or un-primed, words? A positive answer to this question would imply that the effects of the inhibitory processes initiated by the forget cue were not limited to inhibiting conscious access to the precue list-learning episode, but that they also extended to the inhibition of specific item representations in semantic memory. The answer to this question was that the priming effect of the to-be-forgotten words was equal to that of the to-be-remembered words, indicating that indirect access to the to-be-forgotten items was either not inhibited by the directed-forgetting instructions or that possibly the original inhibition had been released during the word-fragment-completion task.

Thus, the second critical question to be asked was whether the interven-ing word-fragment-completion task had reinstated the proactive interference of the to-be-forgotten items on the recall of postcue to-be-remembered items. The answer was "no": The overall pattern of performance, although lower, remained the same as in the immediate recall condition; that is, the basic pattern of directed-forgetting results was obtained. Thus, despite no sign that the to-be-forgotten items were inhibited on the word-fragment-comple-tion task (priming effects were just as strong for them as for the to-be-re-membered words), that they were inhibited in some way was indicated by the lack of any proactive interference effects on the delayed recall test for the to-be-remembered items.

Considered together, the results obtained in this series of studies reveal several important characteristics concerning the nature of the inhibition involved in directed forgetting. Clearly, special conditions are necessary to release the inhibition imposed on items in response to the instruction to forget them, or to reinstate the proactive interference that would normally arise from such items. One such condition is that at least some subset of the to-be-forgotten items must be re-exposed to subjects. Mere exposure, however, is not sufficient. During this exposure, the forgotten material must be processed in a manner that accesses, or makes contact with, the initial learning episode. This necessary condition for release would seem to indicate that the inhibition involved in directed forgetting is not a general inhibition of the to-be-forgotten items as lexical entries. If that were the case, the to-be-forgotten items should have primed their completions less well than the to-be-remembered items primed their completions on the intervening word-fragment-completion task. Although the word-fragment-completion task does involve a type of retrieval in that only some letters of each word are presented, the type of retrieval involved is largely data driven. That is, it is not a task that directs or refers the subject back to the initial learning event or episode. On the other hand, the intervening recognition test is just such a task; indeed, when subjects encountered to-be-forgotten items in the context of this type of task, proactive interference owing to the forgotten items was reinstated.

In conclusion, the inhibition involved in the directed-forgetting situation appears to be a type of retrieval inhibition that impairs conscious access to original learning episodes that are the object of a forget instruction; that is, the episode in which the information was first learned and then intentionally forgotten. This inhibition does not, however, seem to inhibit the activation level of the to-be-forgotten information in semantic memory or to prevent it from having indirect or unconscious influences on behavior. Indeed, in some research in progress in which we are using a variant of Jacoby's famous-name task (e.g., Jacoby, Kelley, Brown, & Jasechko, 1989; Jacoby, Woloshyn, & Kelley, 1989) in a directed-forgetting design, we appear to be obtaining evidence that information subjects have intentionally forgotten can have greater indirect or unconscious influences on their judgments than information they have been instructed to remember (E. L. Bjork, Bjork, Stallings, & Kimball, 1996).

RETRIEVAL-INDUCED FORGETTING

The retrieval-practice paradigm (as instantiated in Anderson et al., 1994) was initially developed to assess the effects of increasing the retrieval strength of some items on the retrieval strength of other related items. This question was motivated, in part, to test predictions of what these effects should be according to the "new theory of disuse" proposed by R. A. Bjork and E. L. Bjork (1992). The relevant assumptions of the new theory of disuse are (a) that an item's representation in memory can be characterized by two types of "strengths," a storage strength and a retrieval strength; (b) that storage strength grows as a pure accumulation process and is unlimited in the sense that a given item's storage strength is not decreased by increases in the storage strength of other items; but (c) retrieval strength is assumed to be a limited resource—that is, if the retrieval strength of a given item associated with a cue of some type is increased via study or retrieval practice, the retrieval of other items associated with that cue is assumed to decrease. Anderson et al. obtained results consistent with those assumptions and inconsistent with spreading-activation theories, which predict that the benefits of practicing the retrieval of a given item should spread to other closely related items.

Beyond addressing that initial motivating question, the retrieval-practice paradigm has proven to be a rich source of other findings; in particular, findings that clarify the underlying mechanisms by which increasing the retrieval strength of one item decreases the retrieval strength of similar items. The results obtained by Anderson and Spellman (1995), which suggest that inhibitory mechanisms may play quite a general role in higher-order cognitive processes, have especially broad implications. How the logic of this paradigm has permitted the investigation of such questions and issues is explained in the next section.

The Basic Paradigm and Results

The logic of the retrieval-practice paradigm is most easily illustrated in the context of a simple semantic network, as shown in Fig. 3.2. Here, two category nodes are depicted, *Fruit* and *Drink*, each with two studied exemplars. In the context of this network, the basic questions addressed by the retrieval-practice paradigm concern the effects of giving retrieval practice to one exemplar, such as *Orange*, on the later recall of *Orange* itself, and on the later recall of other exemplars that are associated with the same category cue but that are not given specific retrieval practice, such as *Banana*. These effects can be assessed by comparing the later recall of *Orange* and *Banana* to the retrieval cue *Fruit* to the later recall of corresponding exemplars from an unpracticed category, depicted in Fig. 3.2 by the exemplars *Scotch* and *Gin* of the category *Drink*.

The basic procedure used in the retrieval-practice paradigm involves four phases: a study phase, a directed retrieval-practice phase, a distractor (retention interval) phase, and a final, surprise recall test. In the first phase, subjects are presented with a list of category-exemplar pairs, with the pairs being presented individually and in mixed order. After this study phase, subjects engage in directed retrieval practice on half of the items for half of the categories. Retrieval practice is directed by presenting a category

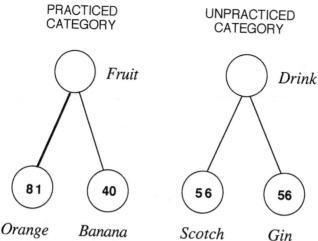

PRACTICED CATEGORY

UNPRACTICED CATEGORY

Fruit

Drink

81   40   56   56

Orange   *Banana*   *Scotch*   *Gin*

FIG. 3.2. A semantic network illustrating the logic of the retrieval-practice paradigm. The circles represent nodes for categories and exemplars, and the lines represent the associative links between them. Giving retrieval practice to *Fruit–Orange* (indicated by the heavier line connecting *Fruit* and *Orange*), but not to *Fruit–Banana* creates practiced and unpracticed exemplars from a practiced category, respectively. The unpracticed exemplars *Scotch* and *Gin* from the unpracticed category *Drink* serve as baseline controls. The numbers depicted inside the exemplar nodes illustrate a typical pattern of results obtained in this paradigm (e.g., Anderson et al., 1994, Experiment 1). The recall of *Orange*, a practiced exemplar, has been facilitated compared to the baseline of unpracticed controls (*Scotch* and *Gin*); whereas the recall of *Banana*, an unpracticed exemplar of a practiced category, has been impaired compared to the same baseline.

name, such as *Fruit*, together with a two-letter stem, such as "Or___" for the exemplar *Orange*, and subjects are instructed to retrieve the previously studied exemplar that fits the combined category-stem cue. To maximize the effectiveness of this retrieval practice, each pair is usually given three such retrieval-practice tests separated by expanding intervals filled with the retrieval practice of other items (Landauer & R. A. Bjork, 1978).

The retrieval-practice phase is followed by a distractor phase, typically lasting 20 minutes. A surprise recall test is then given for all category-exemplar pairs presented in the original study list. In this final test, subjects are presented with each category cue and asked to free recall any exemplars that they can remember from any part of the experiment. (A category-plus-stem cued-recall test has also been employed to control for output interference effects.) On the final test, recall of the three types of exemplars depicted in Fig. 3.2 are of interest: (a) exemplars given retrieval practice (e.g., *Orange*); (b) unpracticed exemplars from practiced categories (e.g., *Banana*); and (c) unpracticed exemplars from unpracticed categories (e.g., *Scotch* or *Gin*).

The results of a typical experiment using this paradigm (Anderson et al., 1994, Experiment 1) are also shown in Fig. 3.2, where the numbers inside the exemplar nodes represent the percentage of exemplars of that type correctly recalled on a final category-cued free-recall test. Practicing the retrieval of *Orange* to the category cue *Fruit*, compared to the baseline recall of unpracticed controls, facilitated its final recall (in this case, by 25 percentage points), consistent with many prior studies (for a sample, see Allen, Mahler, & Estes, 1969; R. A. Bjork, 1975; Landauer & Bjork, 1978; Whitten & Bjork, 1977). The recall of *Banana*, however, compared to the same baseline, was clearly impaired (in this case, by 16 percentage points).

Findings That Implicate Suppression

The impaired recall of unpracticed members of practiced categories, illustrated by the recall of *Banana* in Fig. 3.2, is what we have called *retrieval-induced forgetting*, and our conception of the mechanism producing such forgetting is as follows (see also Anderson et al., 1994). During the retrieval practice of *Orange*, *Banana* is activated causing interference. To retrieve *Orange* selectively in the presence of such competition, *Banana* must be inhibited or suppressed, which is then reflected in its impaired recall on the final recall test. According to this view, inhibitory processes facilitate momentary coherence in cognition and action, in that they serve to decouple competing representations from response-production mechanisms and prevent accidental, misdirected responding. This proposed function of inhibitory processes is compatible with the selection-for-action view of selective attention (see Allport, 1989), although the critical need for selection derives from competition among competing memory traces rather than from external percepts.

Given just the findings shown in Fig. 3.2, other explanations that do not appeal to inhibition in the strong sense, such as blocking (e.g., Blaxton & Neely, 1983; Roediger, 1974; Roediger & Neely, 1982; Rundus, 1973; Tulving & Hastie, 1972; Watkins, 1975) or response competition (e.g., McGeoch, 1942; Mensink & Raajimakers, 1988; Raajimakers & Shiffrin, 1981) owing to the strengthening of the practiced pairs, are consistent with the observed retrieval-induced forgetting. To test between these alternative explanations, we have conducted a number of studies using the following basic strategy. First, we construct a situation in which competitors would not be expected to interfere and thus be suppressed during the retrieval practice of other category-exemplar pairs. Then, we ask the question: Will the later recall of such competitors be nonetheless impaired, consistent with blocking or response-competition or strength-dependence explanations, or will their later recall *not* be impaired, consistent with the suppression hypothesis?

In one such study (Anderson et al., 1994, Experiment 3), we manipulated the taxonomic strength of the practiced and unpracticed exemplars. According to our suppression hypothesis, taxonomically strong, unpracticed exemplars should compete during the retrieval practice of other pairs and, thus, have to be suppressed. In contrast, taxonomically weak, unpracticed exemplars would be unlikely to compete during retrieval practice and, thus, should escape being inhibited. Most noninhibitory explanations, however, would have to predict that the recall of either type of exemplar would be impaired owing to the strengthening of the practiced pairs, and certain specific theories of that type predict that practice of weak exemplars should *cause* more retrieval-induced forgetting and/or that weak exemplars should *suffer* more retrieval-induced forgetting. What we found was that the recall of taxonomically strong exemplars (exemplars that should compete during retrieval practice of other exemplars) was impaired whether the practiced exemplars were taxonomically strong (e.g., *Orange*) or taxonomically weak (e.g., *Papaya*). In contrast, recall of taxonomically weak exemplars (exemplars that would be less likely to compete during retrieval practice of other exemplars) was not impaired and perhaps even facilitated, whether the practiced items were taxonomically strong or weak. This pattern of results was obtained even though large positive effects of retrieval practice were obtained for both strong and weak exemplars.

Additional support for the suppression hypothesis was obtained when we manipulated the type of retrieval practice given subjects (Anderson, Bjork, & Bjork, 1993, Experiment 2). In this experiment, all subjects studied the same list of category-exemplar pairs, but some subjects then engaged in a type of retrieval practice that we assumed to be competitive, whereas others engaged in a variation of retrieval practice that we assumed not to be competitive. To illustrate, subjects given competitive retrieval practice were cued, as before, with *Fruit–Or___*, whereas subjects given noncompetitive retrieval practice were cued with *Fr___–Orange* as a cue to recall "Fruit." Thus, in both cases, subjects engaged in retrieval practice of the critical category-exemplar associations and, in both cases, that association was very likely to be strengthened by these additional processing occasions. We assumed, however, that, in the former case, retrieving *Orange* would be subject to competition from other strong exemplars, such as *Banana*, which would then need to be suppressed during the retrieval-practice phase. In contrast, during the noncompetitive retrieval practice, there should be no such competition among exemplars.

The results obtained in this study were consistent with the suppression hypothesis. Both types of retrieval practice resulted in the strengthening of practiced category-exemplar pairs: Recall of *Orange* was facilitated by both the *Fruit–Or___* and *Fr___–Orange* types of practice; but it was only in the competitive retrieval-practice condition that the recall of unpracticed exemplars, such as *Banana*, was impaired. Again, these results provide strong support for the idea that retrieval-induced forgetting results from the need to select against potentially interfering competitors in order to achieve the goal of retrieving the target defined by the retrieval-practice cue.

Evidence of Cue-Independent Forgetting

Although the results just reviewed constitute strong support for the suppression hypothesis, the most compelling evidence that retrieval practice triggers *inhibition* in the strong sense of that term comes from research by Anderson and Spellman (1995). Using what they have called the *independent-probe technique*, they conducted an experiment using categories and exemplars related as illustrated in Fig. 3.3.

Thus, on the study list of category-exemplar pairs, there were categories, such as *Red* items and *Food* items, for which some exemplars studied under only one of the categories were also semantic members of the other category. Suppose now that *Red–Blood* is given retrieval practice. Both inhibitory and noninhibitory accounts would predict that retrieval practice of *Red–Blood* should impair the later recall of *Red–Cherry*. The crucial question that allows separation of these two types of accounts is what effect practicing *Red–Blood* should have on the later recall of *Food–Radish*. Only the suppres-

PRACTICED   UNPRACTICED
CATEGORY   CATEGORY

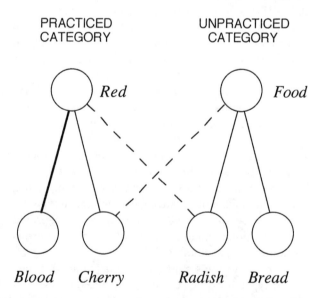

Blood   Cherry   Radish   Bread

FIG. 3.3. Illustration of how related categories were constructed in Anderson and Spellman (1995, Experiment 1). *Blood* and *Cherry* are practiced and unpracticed exemplars, respectively, of a practiced category, and *Radish* and *Bread* are unpracticed exemplars from an unpracticed category. However, as illustrated by the dashed lines, *Radish*, although never studied as such in the experiment, is a semantic member of the *Red* category.

sion/inhibition account of retrieval-induced forgetting predicts that later recall of *Radish* to the retrieval cue *Food* might be impaired.

Such an impairment is predicted because *Radish's* implicit semantic link to the category cue *Red* should cause it to be activated and to compete during the retrieval practice of *Red–Blood*. That is, even though *Radish* was not paired with *Red* in the study list, it is a potential competitor when members of the *Red* category are retrieved during the retrieval-practice phase. If *Radish* does compete in this way, then to retrieve the desired target *Blood*, *Radish* will have to be inhibited, just like *Cherry*. Furthermore, if *Radish's* representation in memory is truly inhibited by being selected against during the retrieval practice of *Red–Blood*, then performance decrements arising from that inhibition should generalize to any cue used to test it.

The results obtained in this study replicated the basic pattern shown in Fig. 3.2; that is, facilitated later recall of practiced exemplars (e.g., *Blood* to *Red*) and impaired later recall of unpracticed exemplars from practiced categories (e.g., *Cherry* to *Red*). Additionally, the final recall of exemplars like *Radish* to the retrieval cue *Food* was also impaired significantly. The impaired recall of *Radish* was assessed by comparing performance on that item in the key experimental condition just described to the recall of that same item in a control condition where it was again presented as a *Food* but the category *Red* was neither studied nor practiced.

Anderson and Spellman's results provide strong support for an inhibitory account of retrieval-induced forgetting, because the mechanisms proposed by the noninhibitory accounts to explain within-category impairment (e.g., the impaired recall of *Cherry* to *Red*) are not applicable to the recall of items in response to a separate retrieval cue (e.g., *Radish* to *Food*). What is not so clear yet, however, is whether the inhibition observed is *retrieval* inhibition. Experiments on the recognition, relearning, or recovery of the inhibited exemplars, analogous to those in the directed-forgetting domain, have yet to be carried out. It is possible, at least in principle, that retrieved-induced forgetting does not simply impair the retrieval of the inhibited items, but also impairs some aspect of their episodic/semantic representation per se.

SIMILARITIES AND DIFFERENCES AMONG MECHANISMS

We have reviewed three research paradigms that involve what we describe as goal-directed forgetting, and we have indicated the evidence that leads us to think that the forgetting observed in each case is best explained in terms of inhibitory mechanisms. By doing so, we mean to assert that the forgetting observed in these situations reflects an impairment arising from a suppression-type process directed at the to-be-inhibited information for some adaptive purpose or goal. We do not, however, mean to assert that the processes by which such inhibition is invoked are necessarily the same, nor that the goal-directed nature of the forgetting is the same in each case. Indeed, we now turn to a discussion of issues concerning similarities and differences among the inhibitory mechanisms implicated in unlearning, directed forgetting, and retrieval-induced forgetting.

Does Intention Matter?

At a general level, the goal of the forgetting observed in all three paradigms is the same; namely, to avoid interference. One potentially significant difference, however, is the degree to which this goal is explicit. Of the three situations, the goal to forget seems most explicit in the directed-forgetting paradigm. In fact, in that paradigm, it may be the case that without an explicit intent on the part of the subject "to forget," inhibition of the to-be-forgotten items does not occur.

Such a possibility is suggested by the Gelfand and Bjork (1985) study described earlier. On the one hand, intent by itself did not seem to produce inhibition of the to-be-forgotten items; rather, new learning seemed necessary for the production of retrieval inhibition. On the other hand, new learning did not appear to be sufficient to produce inhibition. When subjects were given the list of adjectives to rate after being told to forget the previously studied list of items, one might have expected some inhibition of those items if new learning was a sufficient condition, because this type of adjective rating task produces good incidental learning. Thus, it may well be that both intent to update the system—that is, to forget some prior information—and the process of storing new information in memory—in particular, information that is looked upon as replacing the previously stored information—are necessary conditions for retrieval inhibition to occur.

Similarly, in the A–B, A–D paradigm, it is not clear the degree to which subjects' intentions play a role in causing the inhibitory mechanism of response-set suppression to be invoked during the interpolated learning of the A–D list. In fact, to our knowledge, there are no data that directly bear on this issue.[3] To the degree subjects realize that they need to replace the previously learned responses with the new set of responses, and that keep-

---

[3] A study by Postman and Gray (reported as a personal communication in R. A. Bjork, 1978) could be of relevance here. When, in an A–B, A–D paradigm, subjects were given explicit instructions not to give any thought to the first list during acquisition of the second list, second-list acquisition was both speeded up and there was little or no recovery of PI—that is, in our terms, little or no evidence of release from any inhibition imposed on the first-list items. In a more recent study by Wheeler (1995, Experiment 3), subjects were told that the A–B list had just been for practice and that they would not be tested on it. Whether such instructions contributed to inhibition of the A–B items, however, cannot be assessed as there was no comparable group given instructions to continue remembering the A–B list.

ing the old responses from intruding during the acquisition of the new responses will aid this process, one might speculate that subjects' intent could play a role, as in the directed-forgetting paradigm. Indeed, one could argue that although not explicitly instructed to forget the previously learned B responses and replace them with the D responses, there is nonetheless a very clear implicit cue to forget in this paradigm.

In contrast to these situations, however, it seems clear that in retrieval-induced forgetting, there is no explicit goal on the part of the subject to forget any of the materials presented in the previous study list. Rather, the goal during retrieval practice is selectively to retrieve the desired target exemplar when presented with its cue, a process that might be thought of as being analogous to selection for action or selective attention (see, Anderson et al., 1994, and, particularly, Anderson & Spellman, 1995, for a detailed discussion of the similarities between selective retrieval and selective attention). Nonetheless, the operations invoked to satisfy that goal result in the forgetting of similar or competing information, in particular the information that is selected against.

Recovery From Retrieval Inhibition

Our conjecture that there is an implicit instruction to forget in the A–B, A–D paradigm suggests that the processes involved in creating retrieval inhibition in that situation might be very similar to, if not the same as, those involved in the directed-forgetting paradigm. Certainly, the assumption that the suppression invoked in that paradigm applies to the entire set of first-list responses is similar to our assumption that the inhibition invoked in the directed-forgetting paradigm acts on the entire precue list-learning episode. On the other hand, whereas there does seem to be convincing evidence for spontaneous recovery of first-list B responses in the A–B, A–D paradigm, there is no such corresponding evidence in the directed-forgetting paradigm. Indeed, what direct evidence exists relevant to this issue, such as the results from the previously described studies in which recall was delayed by various intervening tasks or from studies reported by Gilliland, Basden, and Basden (1995, as cited in Basden & Basden in the present volume), indicates the opposite: Retrieval inhibition imposed by an instruction to forget does not diminish simply as a function of delay.

In coming to this inference, one might well wonder about the relevance of results obtained by Wheeler (1995) in his studies investigating spontaneous recovery. His subjects did show improved recall with delay for a target list that, after studying, they were told was just for practice and would not be tested. Indeed, Wheeler concluded from these results that effects due to retrieval inhibition dissipate over time or with delay from the interpolated learning of additional lists. A problem with this conclusion, however, is that none of his experiments incorporated what would be comparable to an R–R condition. Thus, we cannot really know whether the items in his target list were actually inhibited either in terms of subjects' ability to access or retrieve them or in terms of their not exhibiting proactive interference effects. That is, although when given a surprise test for the target list, subjects' ability to recall items from the list improved with time, we cannot really infer if this improvement was due to a release from retrieval inhibition or to other factors, such as a relative decrease with delay in the competitive dominance of items from the interference lists studied later. Clearly, this is an issue needing further research.

It also seems to be the case that the inhibition evoked in the retrieval-practice paradigm does not undergo spontaneous recovery. Moreover, based on preliminary results from our laboratory, it seems likely that different conditions may be necessary for the release of inhibition created by the retrieval-practice paradigm as compared to that created in the directed-forgetting paradigm.

Finally, we should point out that although the inhibition proposed by the response-set suppression hypothesis and that proposed to be invoked in the directed-forgetting situation seem more similar to one another than to that proposed to explain retrieval-induced forgetting, this is only true with respect to the response-set suppression hypothesis as formulated by Postman et al. (1968). If the possibility of stimulus-specific response suppression, as well as suppression of the entire set of list-1 responses, is assumed possible, as suggested by Postman and Underwood (1973) to account for results from studies using mixed-list interpolation, then the proposed inhibitory mechanism becomes more similar to that proposed by Anderson et al. (1994).

Shortly after the original proposal of response-set suppression, problematical results were reported from studies in which both A–D and C–D items were mixed together in the same interpolated lists (e.g., Delprato, 1971; Weaver, Rose, & Campbell, 1971; Wichawut & Martin, 1971). In these studies, half of the items in the interpolated list were C–D pairs for which neither the stimulus nor the response term had been on the A–B study list. The other half of the items, however, were A–D pairs. Thus, half the A–B pairs from the original study list had specific retroactive-interference pairs on the interpolated list whereas the other half did not. In such studies, recall on a subsequent MMFR test (i.e., a recall test in which subjects are free to give all responses associated to the same cue in any order, thus presumably eliminating response competition effects on recall) showed greater impairment for those A–B pairs with specific retroactive-interference pairs on the interpolated list than for those without such pairs. In essence, then, these results were inconsistent with the original notion of response-set suppression in which the mechanism of suppression was assumed to act on the entire set of first-list B responses.

In addressing the problem created by such findings for the response-set suppression hypothesis, Postman and Underwood (1973) proposed that "differential suppression of subgroups of items" (p. 25) within a list might be possible. Although they did not suggest a mechanism for such stimulus-specific response suppression, certainly one feasible mechanism would be that proposed by Anderson et al. (1994) to account for retrieval-induced forgetting. (A more detailed discussion and critical analysis of this suggested modification to the original response-set suppression hypothesis as a consequence of mixed-list interpolation findings can be found in Anderson & Neely, 1996; Brown, 1976; and Crowder, 1976.)

RELEVANCE TO INHIBITION AND RECOVERY OF TRAUMATIC MEMORIES: SOME SPECULATIONS

We end this chapter with some speculations concerning the possible relevance of the inhibitory processes that we have reviewed for an issue of considerable current concern: the forgetting and recovery of traumatic memories. We were asked to address this issue at a recent symposium of the Second International Conference on Memory (E. L. Bjork, Bjork, & Anderson, 1996). More specifically, in a symposium entitled "Inhibitory processes in memory: Clinical and experimental perspectives," we were asked what implications inhibitory processes identified in the laboratory might have for understanding clinical observations of the forgetting and recovery of traumatic memories.

Replacing Unpleasant Memories With Pleasant Ones

Here and elsewhere (e.g., R. A. Bjork, 1989; E. L. Bjork & Bjork, 1988; R. A. Bjork & Bjork, 1992), we have stressed the importance of forgetting in memory updating. The argument is that the type of retrieval inhibition demonstrated by directed-forgetting results plays an adaptive role in keeping readily accessible information that we need in our present situations by preventing information that is no longer needed (but still in memory) from interfering. It does not, therefore, seem too far fetched to assume that the same or similar processes could be involved in the replacing of unpleasant memories with more pleasant ones. Just as with the to-be-forgotten items in the present directed-forgetting research, such negative memories would still reside in memory, but one's access to them would be inhibited.

Furthermore, whereas such memories would not tend to recover spontaneously (that is, become accessible on their own), as implied by the lack of recovery of to-be-forgotten items when recall was delayed by the arithmetic task, they could continue to influence behavior in indirect ways, as implied by the finding that to-be-forgotten items continue to prime, although still inhibited in terms of retrieval access. One's access to such memories, however, could possibly be reinstated under certain conditions, such as encountering or being supplied with cues that formed part of, or were a subset of, the inhibited episodic event or memory.

With respect to this possible means of reinstatement, it is interesting to consider a possible connection between the results obtained in the previously described directed-forgetting studies involving some to-be-forgotten items as distractors and the results obtained by Myers and Brewin (1994) using the semi-structured interview technique to assess the recollections of subjects classified as repressors. Repressors are individuals who score low on a measure of trait anxiety but high on a measure of defensiveness, and who are believed to possess a repressive coping style in that they typically report fewer negative memories than nonrepressors. When interviewed using this technique, however, Myers and Brewin found repressors to report more memories of parental antipathy and indifference than did nonrepressors. Perhaps the direct questions or probes used in this interviewing technique functioned like the to-be-forgotten foils in the interpolated recognition tests of the directed-forgetting studies, resulting in a reinstatement of retrieval access to inhibited unpleasant memories for the repressors.

Implications of Retrieval-Induced Forgetting

Although both the paradigm and findings from the area of directed-forgetting research seem the most directly applicable to the possible forgetting and recovery of traumatic memories, it is also possible to imagine how the hypothesized process of retrieval-induced inhibition could be a mechanism for the forgetting of traumatic memories. To illustrate, it seems reasonable to us to assume that in most abusive situations, the individuals being abused would have both positive and negative memories associated with their abusers. Furthermore, it seems reasonable that there would be both external and internal pressures for victims of abuse to want to retrieve only the positive memories associated with the perpetrator of the abuse. If so, then whenever such victims think about their abusers, they would tend to engage in retrieval practice for the positive memories.

Under that assumption, as victims practice retrieving positive memories, those memories—like practiced exemplars—would become more and more likely to be retrieved in the future, whereas the negative memories—being selected against and thus inhibited again and again—would become less and less likely to be retrieved in the future. As long as victims continue to practice retrieving positive memories, access to unpracticed negative memories will remain inhibited. Moreover, as Anderson and Spellman's (1995) results indicate, this impaired recall of negative memories might well extend to other possible retrieval cues.

The question thus arises as to how negative memories would *ever* be recovered if their inhibition was occurring as a result of this type of retrieval practice. Because we have little data addressing the issue of how the inhibition created in the retrieval-practice paradigm might be released, this remains an open question.

Does Intent Matter?

Finally, the role of intent would seem relevant in relating laboratory-defined inhibitory mechanisms to clinical observations of the forgetting of traumatic memories. That is, it seems reasonable to assume that the intent to forget traumatic memories would be an important aspect of successfully doing so. As reviewed earlier, however, it is unclear the degree to which intent plays any role in the production of the retrieval inhibition observed in any of the paradigms we have considered.

Corresponding to the directed-forgetting paradigm, where intent to forget, as well as new learning, may be necessary for inhibition of to-be-forgotten items to occur, both intent and new learning could also be necessary for the inhibition of traumatic memories. That is, simply having the intent to forget might not be sufficient; it would need to be coupled with new learning. Similarly, although intent seems not to play a role in the inhibition of unpracticed exemplars in the retrieval-practice paradigm (where, instead, inhibition seems to occur as a by-product of competitors being selected against during selective retrieval of a desired target), one could speculate that intention to retrieve only positive memories helps to discriminate positive competitors for retrieval from negative ones and, thereby, indirectly promotes the inhibition of negative memories.

In conclusion, although such possible linkages between the goal-directed forgetting observed in the laboratories of experimental psychologists and the real-world repression/recovery phenomena of interest to clinicians remain tenuous and highly speculative, they do suggest that there may be more common ground in clinical and experimental approaches to inhibitory processes than might have been thought some years ago.

CONCLUDING COMMENTS

Toward the end of the last decade, in a chapter on "Retrieval inhibition as an adaptive mechanism in human memory," R. A. Bjork (1989) blamed the computer metaphor and an "unappealing association to poorly understood clinical phenomena, such as repression" for the fact that "inhibitory processes have played little or no role" in our theories of human memory (p. 310). He argued that inhibitory mechanisms, although well represented in theories of lower-order cognitive processes, such as sensation and attention, were underrepresented in theories of higher-order cognitive processes, such as memory and language. At the end of that chapter, however, he predicted that the role of inhibitory processes in memory would seem "incontestable in the near future," and that the emerging "brain metaphor . . . and neural/connectionist approaches to the simulation of cognitive processes" would "push us towards" recognizing the role of inhibition in higher-order cognitive processes (p. 328).

Looking back at those arguments from the perspective of the present chapter, several comments seem warranted. First, as far as recognizing the role of inhibitory processes in memory and cognition, the field would seem to have been "pushed" even farther and faster than that chapter anticipated. Over a relatively brief time, as evidenced by the present volume, other recent volumes on inhibitory processes in attention, memory, language, and other cognitive processes (see, e.g., Dagenbach & Carr, 1994a; Dempster & Brainerd, 1995), and the current empirical and theoretical literature more generally, the picture has changed markedly. Much current theorizing, whether behavioral or neurobiological, and whether stated verbally or in formal/quantitative terms, is characterized by a presumed interplay of excitatory and inhibitory processes.

It seems safe to say, however, that the increased emphasis on inhibitory mechanisms is more a product of hard data than it is of any change of metaphor or style of formal modeling. A variety of behavioral, neuropsychological, and neurobiological findings have provided compelling evidence for inhibitory processes of one type or another. In part, those findings have emerged from new paradigms in behavioral research, such as the retrieval-practice paradigm discussed here and the "negative priming" paradigm (see, e.g., Tipper, 1985), and new procedures in neuroscience.

Our second comment is that the specific assertion that *retrieval* inhibition/suppression is a unique and broadly useful mechanism for avoiding interference and competition in human memory may, in a sense, have been an understatement. We have argued here that the retrieval-inhibition processes that underlie retrieval-induced forgetting are similar, in a formal sense, to those that underlie the updating of memory. Anderson and Spellman (1995) argued that the inhibition/suppression processes that give rise to retrieval-induced forgetting are formally similar to the inhibition/suppression processes identified long ago in selective attention. And analogous inhibition/suppression mechanisms have been implicated in perceptual encoding (as in the "negative priming" paradigm), perceptual recognition (see, e.g., Dagenbach & Carr, 1994b), the control of working memory (e.g., Zacks & Hasher, 1994), and the disambiguation of meaning in the comprehension of text and speech (e.g., Eberhard, 1994; Gernsbacher & Faust, 1991; Simpson & Kang, 1994).

To perhaps now overstate the case, it may be that retrieval inhibition is *the* primary solution in the functional architecture of the human as an information-processing device to the problem of avoiding interference and competition at various levels of cognitive processing. In a broad range of motor and cognitive activities, *selecting* appears to involve *inhibiting*. The formal properties of selection/inhibition processes may have much in common across domains; Anderson and Spellman (1995, p. 94), for example, interpret the total pattern of retrieval-induced forgetting results as evidence that retrieval is best regarded as "conceptually focused selective attention." The common goal of such selection/inhibition mechanisms is to enhance the selection of task-relevant percepts, movements, and stored information by inhibiting competing percepts, movements, and information. The importance of selection/inhibition mechanisms is also underscored by the accumulating evidence that the efficiency of such mechanisms may play a significant role in developmental changes in cognitive abilities (e.g., Bjorklund & Harnishfeger, 1990; Dempster, 1992), deficits in information processing that accompany aging (e.g., Hasher, Stoltzfus, Zacks, & Rypma, 1991; Hasher & Zacks, 1988), and even, possibly, psychopathologies, such as schizophrenia (e.g., Beech, Powell, McWilliams, & Claridge, 1989).

Finally, a somewhat ironic comment seems called for with respect to the uniquely human and adaptive character of retrieval inhibition as an updating/selection mechanism. It is "uniquely human" because it differs so markedly from the overwriting/scanning mechanisms typical of nonliving information-processing devices, such as a computer. It is "adaptive" because it enhances updating/selection without erasing the representation of the inhibited information, should that information be needed later. As an adaptive solution to the updating/selection problems faced by humans as information processors, however, it is important to note that retrieval inhibition is the product of evolution and the living organism, not the product of the human intellect. Where the human intellect *has* played a role is in the design of the less flexible and less sophisticated updating/selection mechanisms characteristic of computers, tape recorders, and other inanimate information-processing devices.

REFERENCES

Allen, G. A., Mahler, W. A., & Estes, W. K. (1969). Effects of recall tests on long-term retention of paired associates. *Journal of Verbal Learning and Verbal Behavior, 8,* 463–470.

Allport, A. (1989). Visual attention. In M. I. Posner (Ed.), *Foundations of cognitive science* (pp. 631–682). Cambridge, MA: MIT Press.

Anderson, M. C., Bjork, E. L., & Bjork, R. A. (1993, November). *Strengthening is not enough: Evidence against the blocking theory of retrieval inhibition.* Paper presented at the Psychonomic Society, Washington, DC.

Anderson, M. C., & Bjork, R. A. (1994). Mechanisms of inhibition in long-term memory: A new taxonomy. In D. Dagenbach & T. H. Carr (Eds.), *Inhibitory processes in attention, memory, and language* (pp. 265–325). San Diego, CA: Academic Press.

Anderson, M. C., Bjork, R. A., & Bjork, E. L. (1994). Remembering can cause forgetting: Retrieval dynamics in long-term memory. *Journal of Experimental Psychology: Learning, Memory, and Cognition, 20,* 1063–1087.

Anderson, M. C., & Neely, J. H. (1996). Interference and inhibition in memory retrieval. In E. L. Bjork & R. A. Bjork (Eds.), *Handbook of perception and cognition: Vol. 10. Memory* (pp. 237–313). San Diego: Academic Press.

Anderson, M. C., & Spellman, B. A. (1995). On the status of inhibitory mechanisms in cognition: Memory retrieval as a model case. *Psychological Review, 102,* 68–100.

Basden, B. H., Basden, D. R., & Gargano, G. J. (1993). Directed forgetting in implicit and explicit memory tests: A comparison of methods. *Journal of Experimental Psychology: Learning, Memory, and Cognition, 19,* 603–616.

Beech, A., Powell, T., McWilliams, J., & Claridge, G. (1989). Evidence for reduced "cognitive inhibition" in schizophrenia. *British Bulletin of Clinical Psychology, 28,* 109–116.

Bjork, E. L., & Bjork, R. A. (1988). On the adaptive aspects of retrieval failure in autobiographical memory. In M. M. Gruneberg, P. E. Morris, & R. N. Sykes (Eds.), *Practical aspects of memory: Current research and issues: Vol. 1. Memory in everyday life* (pp. 283–288). London: Wiley.

Bjork, E. L., & Bjork, R. A. (1996). Continuing influences of to-be-forgotten information. *Consciousness and Cognition, 5,* 176–196.

Bjork, E. L., Bjork, R. A., & Anderson, M. R. (July, 1996). *Inhibition and suppression: Intentional and unintentional.* Paper presented at the International Conference on Memory, Abano Terme, Italy.

Bjork, E. L., Bjork, R. A., & Glenberg, A. (1973, November). *Reinstatement of interference owing to to-be-forgotten items.* Paper presented at the meeting of the Psychonomic Society, St. Louis, MO.

Bjork, E. L., Bjork, R. A., Stallings, L., & Kimball, D. R. (1996, November). *Enhanced false fame owing to instructions to forget.* Paper presented at the meeting of the Psychonomic Society, Chicago, IL.

Bjork, E. L., Bjork, R. A., & White, S. A. (1984, November). *On the induced recovery of proactive interference.* Paper presented at the meeting of the Psychonomic Society, San Antonio, TX.

Bjork, R. A. (1970). Positive forgetting: The noninterference of items intentionally forgotten. *Journal of Verbal Learning and Verbal Behavior, 9,* 255–268.

Bjork, R. A. (1972). Theoretical implications of directed forgetting. In A. W. Melton & E. Martin (Eds.), *Coding processes in human memory* (pp. 217–235). Washington, DC: Winston.

Bjork, R. A. (1975). Retrieval as a memory modifier. In R. Solso (Ed.), *Information processing and cognition: The Loyola symposium* (pp. 123–144). Hillsdale, NJ: Lawrence Erlbaum Associates.

Bjork, R. A. (1978). The updating of human memory. In G. H. Bower (Ed.), *The psychology of learning and motivation* (Vol. 12., pp. 235–259). New York: Academic Press.

Bjork, R. A. (1989). Retrieval inhibition as an adaptive mechanism in human memory. In H. L. Roediger & F. I. M. Craik (Eds.), *Varieties of memory and consciousness: Essays in honour of Endel Tulving* (pp. 309–330). Hillsdale, NJ: Lawrence Erlbaum Associates.

Bjork, R. A. (1992). Interference and memory. In L. R. Squire (Ed.), *Encyclopedia of learning and memory* (pp. 283–288). New York: Macmillan.

Bjork, R. A., & Bjork, E. L. (1992). A new theory of disuse and an old theory of stimulus fluctuation. In A. Healy, S. Kosslyn, & R. Shiffrin (Eds.), *From learning processes to cognitive processes: Essays in honor of William K. Estes* (Vol. 2, pp. 35–67). Hillsdale, NJ: Lawrence Erlbaum Associates.

Bjorklund, D. F., & Harnishfeger, K. K. (1990). The resources construct in cognitive development: Diverse sources of evidence and a theory of inefficient inhibition. *Developmental Review, 10,* 48–71.

Blaxton, T. A., & Neely, J. H. (1983). Inhibition from semantically related primes: Evidence of a category-specific inhibition. *Memory & Cognition, 11,* 500–510.

Block, R. A. (1971). Effects of instructions to forget in short-term memory. *Journal of Experimental Psychology, 89,* 1–9.

Brown, A. A. (1976). Spontaneous recovery in human learning. *Psychological Bulletin, 83,* 321–328.

Crowder, R. G. (1976). *Principles of learning and memory.* Hillsdale, NJ: Lawrence Erlbaum Associates.

Dagenbach, D., & Carr, T. H. (Eds.). (1994a). *Inhibitory processes in attention, memory, and language.* Orlando, FL: Academic Press.

Dagenbach, D., & Carr, T. H. (1994b). Inhibitory processes in perceptual recognition: Evidence for a center-surround attentional mechanism. In D. Dagenbach & T. H. Carr (Eds.), *Inhibitory processes in attention, memory, and language* (pp. 327–357). Orlando, FL: Academic Press.

Delprato, R. G. (1971). Specific-pair interference on recall and associative matching retention tests. *American Journal of Psychology, 84,* 185–193.

Dempster, F. N. (1992). The rise and fall of the inhibitory mechanism: Toward a unified theory of cognitive development and aging. *Developmental Review, 12,* 45–75.

Dempster, F. N., & Brainerd, C. J. (Eds.). (1995). *Interference and inhibition in cognition.* San Diego, CA: Academic Press.

Eberhard, K. M. (1994). Phonological inhibition in auditory word recognition. In D. Dagenbach & T. H. Carr (Eds.), *Inhibitory processes in attention, memory, and language* (pp. 383–407). Orlando, FL: Academic Press.

Elmes, F. J., Adams, C., & Roediger, H. L. (1970). Cued forgetting in short-term memory: Response selection. *Journal of Experimental Psychology, 86,* 103–107.

Epstein, W., Massaro, D. W., & Wilder, L. (1972). Selective search in directed forgetting. *Journal of Experimental Psychology, 95,* 18–24.

Geiselman, R. E., & Bagheri, B. (1985). Repetition effects in directed forgetting: Evidence for retrieval inhibition. *Memory & Cognition, 13,* 51–62.

Geiselman, R. E., Bjork, R. A., & Fishman, D. (1983). Disrupted retrieval in directed forgetting: A link with posthypnotic amnesia. *Journal of Experimental Psychology: General, 112,* 58–72.

Gelfand, H., & Bjork, R. A. (1985, November). *On the locus of retrieval inhibition in directed forgetting.* Paper presented at the meeting of the Psychonomic Society, Boston, MA.

Gernsbacher, M. A., & Faust, M. E. (1991). The mechanism of suppression: A component of general comprehension skill. *Journal of Experimental Psychology: Learning, Memory, & Cognition, 117,* 245–262.

Gross, A. E., Barresi, J., & Smith, E. E. (1970). Voluntary forgetting of a shared memory load. *Psychonomic Science, 20,* 73–75.

Hartman, M., & Hasher, L. (1991). Aging and suppression: Memory for previously relevant information. *Psychology and Aging, 6,* 587–594.

Hasher, L., Stoltzfus, E. R., Zacks, R. T., & Rypma, B. (1991). Age and inhibition. *Journal of Experimental Psychology: Learning, Memory, and Cognition, 17,* 163–169.

Hasher, L., & Zacks, R. T. (1988). Working memory, comprehension, and aging: A review and a new view. *The psychology of learning and motivation* (Vol. 22, pp. 193–225). New York: Academic Press.

Jacoby, L. L, Kelley, C., Brown, J., & Jasechko, J. (1989). Becoming famous overnight: Limits on the ability to avoid unconscious influences of the past. *Journal of Personality and Social Psychology, 56,* 326–338.

Jacoby, L. L., Woloshyn, V., & Kelley, C. (1989). Becoming famous without being recognized: Unconscious influences of memory produced by dividing attention. *Journal of Experimental Psychology: General, 118,* 115–125.

Johnson, H. M. (1994). Processes of successful intentional forgetting. *Psychological Bulletin, 116,* 274–292.

Landauer, T. K., & Bjork, R. A. (1978). Optimal rehearsal patterns and name learning. In M. M. Gruneberg, P. E. Morris, & R. N. Sykes (Eds.), *Practical aspects of memory* (pp. 625–632). London: Academic Press.

MacLeod, C. M. (1975). Long-term recognition and recall following directed forgetting. *Journal of Experimental Psychology: Human Learning and Memory, 104,* 271–279.

MacLeod, C. M. (1989). Directed forgetting affects both direct and indirect tests of memory. *Journal of Experimental Psychology: Learning, Memory, and Cognition, 15,* 13–21.

McGeoch, J. A. (1932). Forgetting and the law of disuse. *Psychological Review, 39,* 352–370.

McGeoch, J. A. (1936). Studies in retroactive inhibition: VII. Retroactive inhibition as a function of the length and frequency of presentation of the interpolated lists. *Journal of Experimental Psychology, 19,* 674–693.

McGeoch, J. A. (1942). *The psychology of human memory.* New York: Longman.

Melton, A. W., & Irwin, J. M. (1940). The influence of degree of interpolated learning on retroactive inhibition and the overt transfer of specific responses. *American Journal of Psychology, 3,* 173–203.

Mensink, G. J. M., & Raaijmakers, J. W. (1988). A model of interference and forgetting. *Psychological Review, 95,* 434–455.

Muller, G. E., & Pilzecker, A. (1900). Experimentelle beitrage zur lehre von gedachtnis. *Zeitschrift fur Psychologie, 1,* 1–300.

Muther, W. S. (1965). Erasure or partitioning in short-term memory. *Psychonomic Science, 3,* 429–430.

Myers, L. B., & Brewin, C. R. (1994). Recall of early experience and the repressive copying style. *Journal of Abnormal Psychology, 103,* 288–292.

Paller, K. A. (1990). Recall and stem-completion priming have different electrophysiological correlates and are modified differentially by directed forgetting. *Journal of Experimental Psychology: Learning, Memory, and Cognition, 16,* 1021–1032.

Postman, L. (1971). Transfer, interference and forgetting. In J. W. Kling & L. A. Riggs (Eds.), *Woodworth and Schlosberg's experimental psychology* (3rd ed., pp. 1019–1132). New York: Holt, Rinehart & Winston.

Postman, L., & Stark, K. (1969). The role of response availability in transfer and interference. *Journal of Experimental Psychology, 79,* 168–177.

Postman, L., Stark, K., & Fraser, J. (1968). Temporal changes in interference. *Journal of Verbal Learning and Behavior, 7,* 672–694.

Postman, L., & Underwood, B. J. (1973). Critical issues in interference theory. *Memory & Cognition, 1,* 19–40.

Raaijmakers, J. W., & Shiffrin, R. M. (1981). Search of associative memory. *Psychological Review, 88,* 93–134.

Reed, H. (1970). Studies of the interference processes in short-term memory. *Journal of Experimental Psychology, 84,* 452–457.

Reitman, W., Malin, J. T., Bjork, R. A., & Higman, B. (1973). Strategy control and directed forgetting. *Journal of Verbal Learning and Verbal Behavior, 12,* 140–149.

Roediger, H. L. (1974). Inhibiting effects of recall. *Memory & Cognition, 2,* 261–269.

Roediger, H. L., & Crowder, R. G. (1972). Instructed forgetting: Rehearsal control or retrieval inhibition (repression)? *Cognitive Psychology, 3,* 244–254.

Roediger, H. L., & Neely, J. H. (1982). Retrieval blocks in episodic and semantic memory. *Canadian Journal of Psychology, 36,* 213–242.

Roediger, H. L., & Tulving, E. (1979). Exclusion of learned material from recall as a postretrieval operation. *Journal of Verbal Learning and Verbal Behavior, 18,* 601–615.

Rundus, D. (1973). Negative effects of using list items as retrieval cues. *Journal of Verbal Learning and Verbal Behavior, 12,* 43–50.

Simpson, G. B., & Kang, H. (1994). Inhibitory processes in the recognition of homograph meanings. In D. Dagenbach & T. H. Carr (Eds.), *Inhibitory processes in attention, memory, and language* (pp. 369–381). Orlando, FL: Academic Press.

Thorndike, E. L. (1914). *The psychology of learning.* New York: Teachers College Press.

Tipper, S. P. (1985). The negative priming effect: Inhibitory effects of ignored primes. *Quarterly Journal of Experimental Psychology, 37A,* 571–590.

Tulving, E., & Hastie, R. (1972). Inhibition effects of intralist repetition in free recall. *Journal of Experimental Psychology, 92,* 297–304.

Tulving, E., & Pearlstone, Z. (1966). Availability versus accessibility of information in memory for words. *Journal of Verbal Learning and Verbal Behavior, 5,* 381–391.

Watkins, M. J. (1975). Engrams as cuegrams and forgetting as cue-overload: A cueing approach to the structure of memory. In C. R. Puff (Ed.), *The structure of memory* (pp. 347–372). New York: Academic Press.

Weaver, G. E., Rose, R. G., & Campbell, N. R. (1971). Item-specific retroactive inhibition in mixed-list comparisons of the A-B, A-C, and A-B, D-C paradigms. *Journal of Verbal Learning and Verbal Behavior, 10,* 488–498.

Weiner, B. (1968). Motivated forgetting and the study of repression. *Journal of Personality, 36,* 213–234.

Weiner, B., & Reed, H. (1969). Effects of the instructional sets to remember and to forget on short-term retention: Studies of rehearsal control and retrieval inhibition (repression). *Journal of Experimental Psychology, 79,* 226–232.

Wheeler, M. A. (1995). Improvement in recall over time without repeated testing: Spontaneous recovery revisited. *Journal of Experimental Psychology: Learning, Memory, and Cognition, 21,* 173–184.

Whitten, W. B., & Bjork, R. A. (1977). Learning from tests: The effects of spacing. *Journal of Verbal Learning and Verbal Behavior, 16,* 465–478.

Wichawut, C., & Martin, E. (1971). Independence of A-B and A-C associations in retroaction. *Journal of Verbal Learning and Verbal Behavior, 10,* 316–321.

Woodward, A. E., Jr., & Bjork, R. A. (1971). Forgetting and remembering in free recall: Intentional and unintentional. *Journal of Experimental Psychology, 89,* 109–116.

Zacks, R. T., & Hasher, L. (1994). Directed ignoring: Inhibitory regulation of working memory. In D. Dagenbach & T. H. Carr (Eds.), *Inhibitory processes in attention, memory, and language* (pp. 241–264). Orlando, FL: Academic Press.

Zacks, R. T., Radvansky, G. A., & Hasher, L. (1996). Studies of directed forgetting in older adults. *Journal of Experimental Psychology: Learning, Memory, and Cognition, 22,* 143–156.

4

DIRECTED FORGETTING: A CONTRAST OF METHODS AND INTERPRETATIONS

Barbara H. Basden
David R. Basden
California State University, Fresno

When told we can forget some of the information we have studied, our memory for that information is impaired. This is the phenomenon of directed forgetting. Two methods are commonly used to study this phenomenon in the memory laboratory; the list method and the item method. In the first section of this chapter, we review evidence that the mechanisms underlying directed forgetting differ for these two methods, arguing that the list method more clearly involves retrieval inhibition than does the item method. In the second section, we present research on a new directed-forgetting phenomenon we refer to as the warning effect. Consistent with our idea that the mechanisms underlying directed forgetting differ according to method, the warning effect occurs with the list method but not with the item method. In the third section, we briefly contrast the theories of retrieval inhibition that may apply to directed forgetting in general and to the warning effect in particular. The purpose of this chapter is to clarify empirical and theoretical issues associated with retrieval inhibition in directed forgetting.

COMPARISONS OF THE LIST AND ITEM METHODS

In 1972, R. A. Bjork distinguished between the list and item methods of directed forgetting. Although both methods involve having subjects study a list of items containing an instruction to forget some of them, the methods differ in the way this instruction is delivered. With the item method, the exposure of a target item is followed closely by the instruction either to remember it or to forget it. With the list method, an entire list is presented before the instruction is given to forget that list and to concentrate on remembering the upcoming list. Bjork (1970, 1972) also distinguished between two mechanisms that may underlie directed forgetting; the differential rehearsal of remember and forget items and the segregation of remember items from forget items. In 1989, he added retrieval inhibition as a third mechanism that may underlie directed forgetting. Bjork's summary of the empirical work and his evaluation of the theoretical approaches to inhibitory phenomena have served as a benchmark for subsequent research in this field.

The retrieval-inhibition interpretation has been applied to both item-method directed forgetting (Geiselman & Bagheri, 1985) and list-method directed forgetting (e.g., Geiselman, Bjork, & Fishman, 1983a). We, on the other hand, argue that retrieval inhibition underlies directed forgetting only with the list method (Basden & Basden, 1996; Basden, Basden, & Gargano, 1993; Basden, Basden, Coe, Decker, & Crutcher, 1994). When the list method is used, we maintain that the two lists undergo separate (segregated) relational processing to produce two retrieval units. We argue here that, at the time of testing, the research subject implements a conscious strategy that favors retrieval of the remember unit. We maintain that the scenario is quite different when the item method is used. Our view is that providing forget or remember cues for individual items encourages item-specific processing rather than relational processing. Remember words would, of course, be processed more extensively than forget words, resulting in their better storage and retrieval. However, remember words and forget words would not be interrelated and recalled together as a unit with the item method.

Relational Versus Item-Specific Processing in Directed Forgetting. According to the distinction between relational and item-specific processing (Einstein & Hunt, 1980; Hunt & Einstein, 1981), procedures that focus the subject's attention on the list as a whole (or on large units within the list) encourage the identification of relations among the items, whereas procedures that focus the subject's attention on individual items encourage the identification of item-specific information. If we accept this view, use of the list method should encourage relational processing whereas use of the item method should encourage item-specific processing. Furthermore, relational processing should facilitate list-method directed forgetting whereas item-specific processing should facilitate item-method directed forgetting. This follows because, with the list method, an already-processed list must be forgotten as a unit whereas, with the item method, individual targets must be forgotten at the time they undergo processing. We tested this idea by manipulating study format as a means of encouraging either relational or item-specific processing (Basden & Basden, 1996, Experiment 1). We expected the relative magnitude of directed forgetting, that is, the retention of remember minus forget words, to vary with study format with the two methods.

According to Hunt and his colleagues, item-specific processing can be encouraged either by forming images of the targets (Hunt & Marschark, 1989) or by studying pictures corresponding to the targets (Hunt & McDaniel, 1993). Hunt and McDaniel also argued that relational processing is encouraged by presentation of categorized lists. These distinctions between item-specific and relational processing provided the basis for the hypotheses tested in Experiment 1 reported by Basden and Basden (1996). One group of subjects studied a set of animal pictures and two other groups of subjects studied a list of names for those pictures. The subjects in one of the two latter groups were given simple learning instructions and those in the other group were told to form a mental image of the referent of each target. Of course, studying pictures or forming mental images of referents emphasizes information specific to individual items, rather than information suggesting relations among items. Thus, we predicted that the magnitude of item-method directed forgetting would be greater when subjects studied pictures or studied words with imagery instructions than when they studied words alone. In fact, that is precisely what we observed. These results are shown in Fig. 4.1, with directed forgetting expressed as difference scores between the mean proportions of remember and forget (R–F) targets recalled. Because a manipulation that influences type of processing differentially affected directed forgetting with the two methods, our position (i.e., that relational processing underlies directed forgetting with the list method whereas item-specific processing underlies it with the item method) was supported. Next, we turn to evidence that retrieval inhibition underlies list-method directed forgetting but not item-method directed forgetting.

Recall Versus Recognition Tests.   Most would agree that retrieval plays more of a major role in recall than in recognition. If this is true, then retrieval inhibition should affect recall more than recognition. Evidence critical to the role of retrieval inhibition in directed forgetting could reasonably be expected to derive from a comparison of recall and recognition with each of the two methods.

A review of the relevant research supports the generalization that directed forgetting occurs in both recall and recognition with the item method but only in recall with the list method. Many of the studies reviewed used only one or the other of the two methods. For example, both Elmes, Adams, and Roediger (1970) and Block (1971) used the list method with relatively short lists and observed directed forgetting in free recall but not in recognition. Subsequent research with longer lists replicated these findings (e.g., Geiselman et al., 1983a). In contrast, directed forgetting was observed in

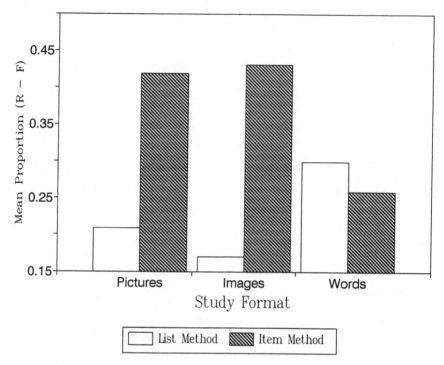

FIG. 4.1. Mean proportion of directed forgetting (R–F) as function of method and study format (from Basden & Basden, 1996, Experiment 1).

both recall and recognition when the item method was used (Bjork & Geiselman, 1978; Davis & Okada, 1971; Geiselman, Rabow, Wachtel, & MacKinnon, 1985; Golding, Long, & MacLeod, 1994; Horton & Petruk, 1980; MacLeod, 1975, 1989; Paller, 1990; Wetzel, 1975; Woodward, Bjork, & Jongeward, 1973). Thus, directed forgetting in recognition occurs only when the item method is used.

An early attempt to directly compare the effect of item- and list-method directed forgetting on recall and recognition tests was made by Woodward, Park, and Seebohm (1974). Unfortunately, these investigators failed to obtain list-method directed forgetting on the recall test. More recently, Basden et al. (1993) directly compared recall and recognition performance with the item and list methods in three experiments. As expected, directed forgetting occurred in both recall and recognition with the item method but only in recall with the list method.

Basden et al. (1994) extended this to a comparison of the influence of directed forgetting and posthypnotic amnesia procedures on recall and recognition. The subjects were all highly susceptible to hypnosis, as demonstrated by showing posthypnotic amnesia on Form A of the Harvard Group Scale of Hypnotic Susceptibility. Under the posthypnotic amnesia procedure, subjects are told in advance that they will be tested for all words studied. While under hypnosis, they are told that they will be unable to remember the forget words no matter how hard they try, but that they will be able to recall the forget words again when amnesia is canceled by the instruction, "Now you will be able to remember all the words you studied earlier." The study phase occurs while subjects are hypnotized, but tests are given after subjects are awakened from hypnosis. Two tests are given in succession—one is given before posthypnotic amnesia is canceled, and one is given afterward.

In Experiment 1 (Basden et al., 1994), both the item and list methods were used, and subjects were given either recall or recognition tests after completing the study session using either the directed-forgetting or posthypnotic amnesia procedure. Both procedures yielded differential recall of remember and forget items on the initial free recall test, with the difference being somewhat greater under the posthypnotic amnesia procedure than under the directed-forgetting procedure. This replicated results with the list method reported by Coe et al. (1989). After the forget (or amnesia) cue was canceled, forget-word recall increased significantly under the posthypnotic amnesia procedure but not under the directed-forgetting procedure. Better recognition of remember than of forget words occurred only with the item method and then only when that method was used in conjunction with the directed-forgetting procedure. The results of the initial recall and recognition tests are shown in Fig. 4.2; these results are reported in terms of the difference between the mean proportions of remember and forget words retained.

These results, like those summarized earlier, support our generalization that directed forgetting occurs in recognition only when the item method is used. If directed forgetting is produced by retrieval inhibition, it should not occur in recognition, where retrieval is less influential. The fact that directed forgetting does occur in recognition with the item method supports our position that retrieval inhibition does not underlie item-method directed forgetting. If, when the item method is used, remember and forget words receive differential item-specific processing, differential recognition performance is to be expected.

It is worth noting that, when the list method is used, retrieval inhibition under posthypnotic amnesia procedures is more profound than under directed-forgetting procedures, as shown in Table 4.1, fewer forget words are recalled under the former rather than under the latter procedure. Furthermore, under posthypnotic amnesia procedures, retrieval inhibition was released when the forget (amnesia) cue was canceled, resulting in an increase in forget-word recall. In contrast, under directed-forgetting procedures, forget-word recall did not increase when the forget cue was canceled. These and other differences between directed forgetting and posthypnotic amnesia led Coe et al. (1989) to conclude that the processes underlying retrieval

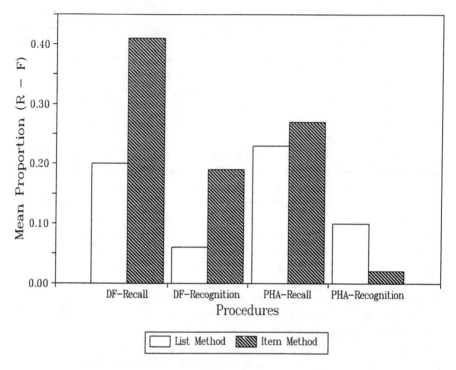

FIG. 4.2. Mean proportion of directed forgetting (R–F) as a function of method and instructional procedure (from Basden et al., 1994, Experiment 1).

TABLE 4.1
Mean Proportions of Remember (R) and Forget (F) Words Recalled
Before and After the Forget (or Amnesia) Cue Was Canceled

	Method			
	Item		*List*	
	R	*F*	*R*	*F*
Directed Forgetting				
Test 1	.53	.12	.44	.24
Test 2	.46	.13	.42	.25
Posthypnotic Amnesia				
Test 1	.39	.12	.37	.14
Test 2	.40	.18	.40	.22

Note. Data come from Basden et al., 1994, Experiment 1.

inhibition differ for the two procedures. Subjects who are highly susceptible to hypnosis accede to the demands of hypnotic suggestion, possibly withholding responses they are in fact able to retrieve. However, directed forgetting does not appear to result from deliberate withholding of forget words (see Basden et al., 1994, Experiment 2).

Release of Retrieval Inhibition. As just mentioned, posthypnotic amnesia can be reversed by simply canceling the forget cue, but directed forgetting cannot. On the other hand, directed forgetting can be reversed through reexposure to some or all of the forget items. Bjork (1989) referred to this phenomenon as release of retrieval inhibition. This reexposure manipulation does not seem to affect posthypnotic amnesia (Basden et al., 1994).

In an experiment using the list method, Geiselman et al. (1983a) reported directed forgetting on an initial recall test. However, forget words were recognized as well as remember words on a subsequent recognition test. Bjork (1989, p. 317) referred to this as "release of retrieval inhibition." Of course, we do not expect retrieval inhibition in recognition in any case, so we do not think of it that way. Nonetheless, the Geiselman et al. study does serve quite well to demonstrate our point that retrieval inhibition-based directed forgetting does not occur in recognition because the influence of retrieval is minimized on recognition tests.

According to this reasoning, it is doubtful that the absence of directed forgetting in recognition should be considered a "release." However, there was clearly a genuine release of retrieval inhibition in two of our experiments (Basden et al., 1993, Experiments 1 and 2). In those experiments, we administered a recall test both before and after a recognition test. For the list method, we observed directed forgetting on the initial recall test but not on the final recall test. For the item method, directed forgetting was still in evidence on the final recall test. It does appear that reexposure to all of the items effects a release of directed forgetting with the list method but not with the item method. This is to be expected if list- but not item-method directed forgetting is based on retrieval inhibition.

Release of retrieval inhibition in list-method directed forgetting was also reported by Goernert and Larson (1994). Subjects were assigned either to a control condition in which list 1 was to be remembered or to an experimental condition in which list 1 was to be forgotten. Just prior to the recall test, subjects were shown either 0, 4, or 8 items randomly selected from list 1. At the beginning of the recall test, subjects were instructed to recall as many of the remaining members of list 1 as they could. Reexposure to some of the remember items in list 1 significantly decreased the recall of the remaining items in list 1 for subjects in the control condition. However, reexposure to some of the forget items significantly increased recall of the remaining items in list 1 for subjects in the directed-forgetting condition.

Release of inhibition has also been observed indirectly when only some of the forget items are reexposed. Bjork, Bjork, and Glenberg (1973, as cited in Bjork, 1989) reported a list-method experiment demonstrating this phenomenon. Three groups were tested; Group FR (the directed-forgetting group), which was told to forget list 1; Group RR (the control group), which studied both lists but did not receive a forget instruction, and Group -R (the rest control), which studied only the second list. Recall of the second list was equivalent in Groups FR and -R, and both groups were superior to Group RR. The implication is that Group RR experienced proactive inhibition from the first list, but Group FR did not. The directed-forgetting instruction appears to have prevented forget words from interfering with the retrieval of the remember words. The study phase was followed by a forced choice recognition test in which subjects were exposed to just 4 of the 16 forget items. On a final recall test, performance of Groups RR and FR was equivalent, and both groups performed significantly worse than Group -R. Here, the implication is that the reexposure to some forget words in Group FR released all of them from retrieval inhibition, and that this resulted in the same level of proactive interference in Group FR as in Group RR. Apparently the forget words are treated as a unit, which either enters into the retrieval process and causes interference or is inhibited from entering into that process and so does not cause interference.

The results reported by Bjork et al. (1973) were later replicated (Bjork & Bjork, 1996, Experiment 1). In a follow-up experiment (Experiment 2), Bjork & Bjork once again compared recall in the R-R, F-R, and -R conditions, but subjects were required to perform a word fragment completion test rather than a recognition test prior to final recall. Changing the intervening test from recognition (explicit) in Experiment 1 to word fragment completion (implicit) in Experiment 2, drastically altered the findings. Retrieval inhibition was *not* released in Experiment 2. Bjork and Bjork's interpretation of the difference between the results is that retrieval inhibition impairs conscious access to the original learning episode, and that reexposure unaccompanied by "conscious access" does not reinstate the forget list in memory. However, subjects were reexposed to only an average of about two forget words in Bjork and Bjork's Experiment 2. Subjects were given only three word fragments and solved only 60% of those. Because subjects were reexposed to fewer forget words in Experiment 2 than in Experiment 1, the critical variable in obtaining release of retrieval inhibition may have been the number of items that were reexposed rather than the nature of the intervening task.

To test this idea, Wright, Burke, and Basden (1997) measured list-method directed forgetting before and after subjects completed one of two different tasks, recognition or pleasantness judgments. Each subject responded to 48 words comprising list members intermingled with distractors. Separate

TABLE 4.2
Mean Directed Forgetting (R–F) as a Function of
Percentage Reexposure and Type of Intervening Task

		Percentage Reexposure				
		0	*25*	*50*	*75*	*100*
Recognition	Test 1	. . .	.21	.12	.16	.17
	Test 2	. . .	.14	.07	.01	.03
Pleasantness	Test 1	.17	.17	.11	.15	.21
	Test 2	.15	.13	.02	.02	.04

Note. Results come from Wright, Burke, and Basden (1997).

groups of subjects were reexposed to 25%, 50%, 75%, or 100% of the target words (both R and F items) during the intervening tasks. An additional group of subjects judged the pleasantness of 0% of the target words, responding only to distractor items. Results of this experiment are shown in Table 4.2. On the final recall test, only the 0% and 25% pleasantness judgment groups and the 25% recognition group showed directed forgetting. Thus, it would appear that the variable critical to release of retrieval inhibition is the number of items to which the subjects are reexposed and not the nature of the intervening task. Because directed forgetting was unaffected by intermediate percentages of item reexposure, it appears that the entire list is either accessible or inaccessible.

As mentioned earlier, if retrieval inhibition does not occur with the item method, then release of retrieval inhibition also should not occur with that method. To our knowledge, there has been only one report (Geiselman & Bagheri, 1985) claiming release of retrieval inhibition with the item method. Geiselman and Bagheri reported that their subjects recalled more remember than forget words on an initial free recall test, which the authors attributed to the combination of better encoding of remember words and inhibition of forget words. After the initial test, the subjects were given an additional study trial in which unrecalled remember and forget words were re-presented, and the subjects were instructed to learn both types of items. Forget-word recall improved more than remember-word recall on the subsequent test, and the authors interpreted this as release of inhibition. Of course, unrecalled but fully processed remember items are likely to be more difficult than unrecalled and less adequately processed forget items. It is therefore not surprising that there was greater improvement in the recall of re-presented forget items than in the recall of re-presented remember items. In subsequent research, Geiselman and Panting (1985) attempted to control for such item selection effects, but their procedures did not control for idiosyncratic differences in item difficulty. To our knowledge, there has not yet been an adequate test of the hypothesis that differential difficulty of remember and forget items underlies the results reported by Geiselman and Bagheri.

Our results (Basden et al., 1993) indicated that although simple re-exposure to forget words was adequate to bring about release of retrieval inhibition with the list method, it was not adequate to bring about such a release with the item method. We remain unconvinced that retrieval inhibition occurs and is released when the item method is used.

Know and Recollect Judgments. Tulving (1985) distinguished between two bases for judging an item as "old" on a recognition test: (a) The subject specifically remembers studying the item, or (b) the subject finds the item somewhat familiar. These have been referred to as remember and know judgments, respectively. To reduce confusion with directed forgetting, we refer to these memory judgments as recollect and know, respectively. The distinction between memory judgments has been extensively developed by Gardiner (e.g., Gardiner, 1988; Gardiner & Java, 1993). The claim is that the basis for recognition can be obtained simply by asking subjects to indicate for each recognized item whether its actual occurrence in the study list is remembered or whether it merely seems familiar. For example, Gardiner (1988, Experiment 1) observed a levels-of-processing effect with recollect judgments but not with know judgments. Thus, a study task that focused attention on semantic rather than structural characteristics of the items influenced the subject's ability to remember the study event but did not influence the subject's feeling of familiarity.

If item-method directed forgetting does indeed involve differential rehearsal of remember and forget words, then levels of processing and item-method directed-forgetting procedures should have parallel effects on recognition judgments. Gardiner, Gawlik, and Richardson-Klavehn (1994) tested this idea and found item-method directed forgetting with recollect but not with know judgments. Furthermore, they varied the delay of the forget or remember cue and found that increased cue delay was associated with an increase in know judgments for items accompanied by either cue. Increasing the delay of the cue decreased the time available for elaborative rehearsal of the item after the cue resulted in a *decrease* in recollect judgments for remember-cued targets. Gardiner et al.'s interpretation was that maintenance rehearsal influences familiarity, and hence, know judgments whereas elaborative rehearsal influences conscious remembering, and hence, recollect judgments.

Basden and Basden (1996, Experiment 3) contrasted the influence of item- and list-method directed forgetting on know and recollect judgments. If differential processing of remember and forget targets underlies directed forgetting with the item method but not with the list method, then directed forgetting should occur for recollect judgments with the item method but not with the list method. Neither method should yield directed forgetting with know judgments. This is precisely what we observed. The mean pro-

TABLE 4.3
Mean Recollect and Know Judgments for
Remember (R), Forget (F), and Distractor (D) Items

	Recollect			Know		
Method	R	F	D	R	F	D
List	.72	.71	.04	.17	.18	.08
Item	.67	.48	.04	.18	.20	.07

Note. Results are taken from Basden and Basden (1996, Experiment 3).

portions of remember, forget, and distractor words judged as recollect and know are shown in Table 4.3.

We also found that the difference in correct recollect judgments between forget and distractor items was greater with the list method than with the item method, but that the corresponding difference between remember and distractor items was equivalent with the two methods. Thus, forget words appear to receive less extensive processing with the item method than with the list method, but remember words appear to receive equivalent processing with the two methods.

In summary, when recognition was decomposed into conscious remembering (recollect judgments) and familiarity (know judgments), directed forgetting was observed only with recollect judgments and only then with the item method. These results thus demonstrate another dissociation between the list and item methods, further strengthening the distinction that we have proposed.

Implicit Tests.   Explicit tests require subjects to intentionally remember studied information whereas implicit tests require only incidental remembering. Although directed forgetting has been reported on implicit tests with the item method, it has never been reported on implicit tests with the list method (Basden et al., 1993; Basden & Basden, 1996; Bjork & Bjork, 1996; MacLeod, 1989). This may be because, with the list method, there is no reason for retrieval inhibition to influence performance, because subjects are not consciously attempting to remember or forget information.

In previous experiments that obtained item-method directed forgetting on implicit tests (e.g., MacLeod, 1989), perceptual tests such as word-fragment completion were used. According to the transfer appropriate processing theory of implicit memory, such tests are typically less sensitive to differential processing than are conceptual tests, which rely on meaning (see Roediger & McDermott, 1993). It follows then, that item-method directed forgetting might be more likely to occur on implicit conceptual tests than on implicit perceptual tests.

In research reported earlier (Basden et al., 1993, Experiments 1 & 2) we failed to observe item-method directed forgetting with a conceptual test (word association), and we attributed this to a floor effect. However, subsequent research (McDermott & Roediger, 1996) showed that priming on conceptual implicit tests may vary with type of test, that is, that not all conceptual tests are equally sensitive to various types of conceptual processing. Our recent findings are consistent with that conclusion, because we did observe item-method directed forgetting when we used a different type of implicit conceptual test (Basden & Basden, 1996, Experiment 2). After studying a list of low frequency words with either item- or list-method directed-forgetting instructions, subjects were asked to provide words in response to general knowledge questions. Definitions of targets and distractors were provided at the time of the test, and subjects were instructed to respond to each definition with the first word that came to mind. Because this test, like other implicit tests, includes item-by-item cuing, it is regarded as sensitive to differential processing of remember and forget items of the sort we believe the item method encourages. After completing this implicit general knowledge test, subjects were asked to recall the remember and forget targets.

Directed forgetting was significant on the implicit general knowledge test with the item method, but not with the list method. Mean proportions of targets given in response to remember, forget, and distractor word definitions for each group are shown in Table 4.4. Directed forgetting was also significant on the recall test. Mean proportions of recalled remember and forget words were .14 and .11 with the list method, and .17 and .06 with the item method. Although directed forgetting was significant in recall with both methods, the difference in recall was greater with the item method than with the list method. If release of retrieval inhibition was affected by reexposure to target items during the general knowledge test, the extent of that release was not sufficient to eliminate directed forgetting on the final test. Because subjects produced only a small proportion of R and F items on the general knowledge test, this failure to release retrieval inhibition is consistent with the analysis provided in the section on Release of Retrieval Inhibition.

TABLE 4.4

Mean Proportions of Remember (R), Forget (F), and Distractor (D)
Terms Produced on the General Knowledge Test as a Function of Method

	Word Type		
Method	Remember	Forget	Distractor
List	.32	.30	.14
Item	.28	.20	.15

Note. Results from Basden and Basden, 1996, Experiment 2.

To summarize, Basden and Basden (1996, Experiment 2) found item-method directed forgetting both on the implicit conceptual test and on the explicit free recall test, but list-method directed forgetting only on the explicit test. These results are consistent with our hypotheses that remember targets are more extensively processed than forget targets under the item method but not under the list method, and tests of implicit memory are sensitive to the effects of differential processing but not to those of retrieval inhibition. When subjects are given retrieval cues, that is, word definitions, on an item-by-item basis, inhibition of the entire forget list is unlikely to occur.

Golding et al. (1994) suggested that, because directed-forgetting instructions may result in differential processing of remember and forget words, the underlying basis for directed forgetting on implicit tests may be differential levels of processing. Although this is in accordance with our position, Golding et al. did not distinguish between item- and list-method directed forgetting. If differential processing underlies directed forgetting with *both* the list and item methods, then both methods should yield directed forgetting on implicit tests. Furthermore, if we can assume that the differential processing with item-method directed forgetting parallels that with levels of processing manipulations, the magnitude of directed forgetting should be greater with the list method than with the item method. This follows from the finding in mixed-list designs (Challis & Brodbeck, 1992; Thapar & Greene, 1994) that the levels of processing effect is larger when targets are blocked at presentation, as in the list method, rather than randomly intermingled, as in the item method. The fact that list-method directed forgetting does not even occur on implicit tests is consistent with our position that differential processing of remember and forget items is not responsible for list-method directed forgetting.

It could be argued that item-method directed forgetting on implicit tests results from the contamination by intentional retrieval. Toth, Reingold, and Jacoby (1994) recently applied the process dissociation procedure to levels-of-processing findings. They claimed that conscious recollection accounted for the advantage of semantically processed targets over nonsemantically processed targets on certain implicit tests. If the differential processing of remember and forget words with the item method parallels levels of processing, then item-method directed forgetting on implicit tests may be mediated by conscious retrieval. This suggestion is not easily dismissed. In fact, both Basden et al. (1993) and Paller (1990) argued that the directed forgetting observed on an implicit test by MacLeod (1989) may have resulted from intentional retrieval. Russo and Andrade (1995) recently applied the process dissociation procedure to word fragment completion data. They showed a directed-forgetting effect on the inclusion test, which could arguably be termed an implicit test. Their estimate of the contribution of conscious recollection on this test was greater for remember than for forget targets.

In summary, directed forgetting on implicit tests has sometimes been observed with the item method, but has never been observed with the list method. We suggest that this difference between directed-forgetting methods occurs because implicit tests typically involve item-by-item cuing that is relatively more sensitive to the effects of differential processing than to the effects of retrieval inhibition. To our knowledge, even explicit tests, which provide item-by-item cues (e.g., word-fragment cued recall, stem-cued recall, recognition, and word association) produce little or no list-method directed forgetting. List-method directed-forgetting instructions appear to act on the remember and forget items as two integrated, relationally processed units rather than on individual items. Looked at another way, list-method directed forgetting seems only to occur reliably when the subject controls the output order.

In conclusion, results with implicit tests support the distinction between list and item methods. Although item-method directed forgetting is occasionally present on implicit tests, list-method directed forgetting is consistently absent on such tests. In the next section, we report a new phenomenon, the warning effect, which also differentiates between the list and item methods of directed forgetting.

DELAY AND WARNING EFFECTS

The starting point for this line of research was the suggestion by Geiselman and his colleagues that retrieval inhibition in directed forgetting occurs because "an F cue serves to initiate a process that inhibits the accessibility of a space in time in episodic memory" (Geiselman et al., 1983a, p. 63). Perhaps subjects are unable to recall forget words because the context of that information is inaccessible to them. In other words, remember and forget words may be equally well learned but forget words may not be as readily retrieved. According to Tulving and Pearlstone (1966), a set of available words may not be accessible without the appropriate retrieval cue. Perhaps when the list method is used, subjects use temporal or order information, for example, "list 2" or "later list," to selectively retrieve remember words. If subjects can no longer differentiate between the remember and forget words on the basis of time or serial order, then directed forgetting should disappear. More specifically, if differentiation between remember and forget words (or between list 1 and list 2) decreases over time, then directed forgetting should also decrease over time.

MacLeod (1975) tested the influence of recall delay on directed forgetting. In Experiment 1, subjects studied categorized items that were preceded by the category name; each target consisted of a group of three instances from a given category. Each such target was followed by either a forget or remember cue. In other words, the item method was used, but in this case, each "item" was a category comprising three exemplars. Category-cued recall and recognition were tested immediately or after a 1-week delay. Directed forgetting was present on both the cued-recall and the recognition tests, and remained constant over the delay. In his second experiment, MacLeod's subjects studied a list of unrelated words again presented via the item method. Performance was assessed on a forced choice recognition test administered either immediately, after a 1-week delay, or after a 2-week delay. As in Experiment 1, directed forgetting was present and did not decrease over the delay.

If, as we have assumed, item-method directed forgetting results from differential rehearsal of remember and forget words, then item-method directed forgetting would not be expected to decrease with delay. On the other hand, source information may be more critical for list-method directed forgetting. If remember and forget words are equally well learned, then retrieval inhibition would fail if subjects could not discriminate between the source of remember and forget words and so could not suppress retrieval of the latter. In fact, in their list-method experiments, Geiselman et al. (1983a) reported that subjects were less accurate in identifying the list membership of forget than remember words. They used that observation as support for their hypothesis that retrieval inhibition results from lack of access to a particular source of information, that is, all information occurring during presentation of list 1. If a failure of source memory underlies list method but not item-method directed forgetting, then list-method directed forgetting might be expected to decrease on a delayed test. Because MacLeod (1975) used only the item method in his experiments, his research does not bear on list-method directed forgetting. However, in the experiments reported here, we included both the list and item methods, and tested recall immediately or after a delay. Because we were concerned that delay subjects might differentially rehearse the remember and forget items, we also included an additional delay condition in which the subjects were warned at the conclusion of the study phase that both remember and forget words would be tested after the delay.

In Experiment 1, reported by Gilliland, McLaughlin, Wright, Basden, and Basden (1996), the delayed test was given after 1 week had elapsed. That particular delay was chosen on the basis of results reported by Riccio, Rabinowitz, and Axelrod (1994). Riccio et al. presented substantial evidence suggesting that discrimination of contextual information breaks down in approximately 1 week. On this basis, Gilliland et al. predicted that for the list method, subjects would not be able to discriminate between the source of remember and forget words after the delay. However, for the item method, recall of remember and forget words would be unaffected by the delay, as reported by MacLeod (1975).

All subjects studied a list of unrelated high frequency words, attempted to recall both the remember and forget words, and then identified each word on a recognition test as remember, forget, or new. Results from the recall test are shown in Fig. 4.3. Directed forgetting was greater with the item method than with the list method. However, to our surprise, both the item and list methods showed decreased directed forgetting on the delayed free recall test. Because recall performance was generally quite poor after the delay, the decrease in directed forgetting may have been artificially induced by a floor effect on forget word recall.

On the recognition test, each remember and forget word was counted as a hit if the subject did not identify it as a new word. We also counted forget items as hits whether identified by the subject as remember items or forget items. This essentially converted the subject's choices on the recognition test to standard old versus new judgments. As shown in Fig. 4.4, with this measure of retention, directed forgetting remained constant over the delay with both methods, replicating and extending the results reported by MacLeod (1975). Furthermore, directed forgetting on the recognition test

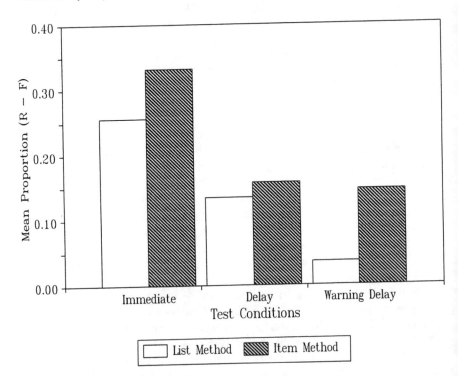

FIG. 4.3. Mean proportion of directed forgetting (R–F) in free recall as a function of method and test conditions with a 1-week delay (from Gilliland et al., 1996, Experiment 1).

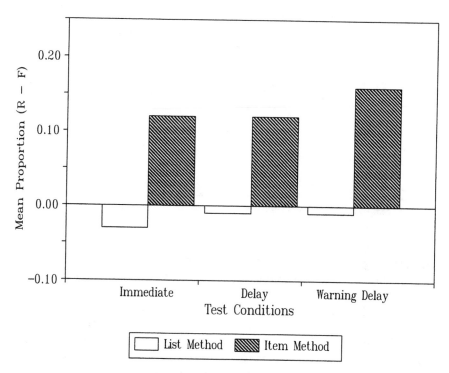

FIG. 4.4. Mean proportion of directed forgetting (R–F) in recognition as a function of method and test conditions with a 1-week delay (from Gilliland et al., 1996, Experiment 1).

was significant with the item method but not with the list method, replicating our previous results (e.g., Basden et al., 1993).

Accuracy of source memory was indexed by the subjects' confusions between remember and forget words, or R–F or F–R confusions (i.e., the tendency to call remember words forget and vice versa). As shown in Table 4.5, overall source confusions were reliably greater with the list method than with the item method, and there was no increase in source errors with delay. These results are consistent with MacLeod (1975, Experiment 2), who reported that source errors remained constant over a 2-week delay. Our list-method subjects were more likely to misclassify forget words as remember rather than vice versa, that is, F–R confusions were more frequent than R–F confusions. Thus, we found with the list method, as did Geiselman et al. (1983a), that subjects are less accurate in remembering the source of forget words than of remember words.

The surprising finding in Experiment 1, shown in Fig. 4.3, was that directed forgetting was not significant when a warning preceded the delayed test. This warning effect is of theoretical importance because it occurs with the

TABLE 4.5
Mean Proportions of Remember–Forget (R–F) and Forget–Remember (F–R)
Confusions in the Recognition/Source Identification Test

	Method			
	Item		List	
	R–F	F–R	R–F	F–R
Type of Test				
Immediate	.19	.25	.16	.33
Delay	.27	.28	.18	.52
Warning Delay	.31	.34	.37	.38

Note. Results from Gilliland et al., 1996, Experiment 1.

list but not the item method, and because it further supports the retrieval-inhibition explanation of list-method directed forgetting. Because this is a new finding, we conducted additional research to verify that it is reliable.

Because delay did not seem to be associated with a breakdown in source memory in Experiment 1, we reduced the length of the retention interval to 20 minutes in Experiment 2. We hoped this would eliminate the floor effect on forget-word recall we observed in Experiment 1. To increase relational processing, we switched from the list of unrelated words used in Experiment 1 to a list comprising instances of a single category—animal names.

These changes were successful. As shown in the results from the recall and recognition tests from Gilliland et al. (1996, Experiment 2), illustrated in Figs. 4.5 and 4.6, there was an overall decrease in recall performance with delay, but floor was not approached in this experiment. Directed forgetting in the delay conditions did not differ significantly from directed forgetting in the immediate condition with either method, confirming our suspicion that the decrease in directed forgetting in Experiment 1 resulted from a floor effect on forget word recall. Directed forgetting in recognition was significant with the item method but not with the list method, again replicating our previous results (Basden et al., 1993). As in Experiment 1, source confusions were more frequent with the list method than with the item method, and neither R–F nor F–R confusions increased with delay.

Most importantly, we were able to replicate the warning effect, that is, list-method directed forgetting was eliminated when subjects were warned before the delay that they would be tested on both remember and forget words. Note that subjects are *always* told just prior to the retention test that they are to attempt to recall both the remember and the forget words. The warning effect occurs only when subjects are told they will have to remember both the remember and forget words *before* the delay. Thus, the warning effect requires both a delay as well as a warning.

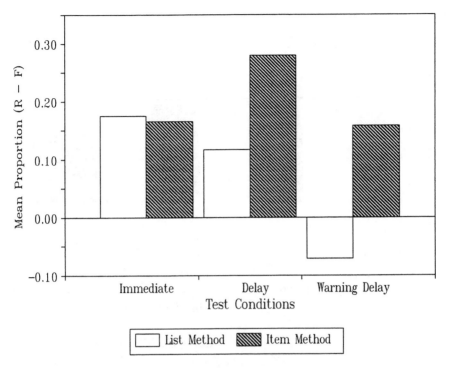

FIG. 4.5. Mean proportion of directed forgetting (R–F) in recall as a function of method and test conditions with a 20-min delay (from Gilliland et al., 1996, Experiment 2).

It could be argued, of course, that warned subjects rehearse the forget words during the delay. We investigated this possibility in Gilliland et al. (1996) Experiment 1. At the conclusion of the experiment, we asked delay subjects whether they had rehearsed forget words, remember words, or both. Subjects rarely reported rehearsing either remember or forget words during the delay and rehearsal was no more frequent for warned subjects than for unwarned subjects. In Experiment 2, rehearsal was prevented during the delay by a distractor task. We are fairly confident that increased rehearsal of forget words cannot explain the warning effect. It could also be argued that source memory is somehow rendered less accessible by the warning; that is, subjects remove remember and forget tags when warned. Because R–F and F–R confusions were no greater for warned than for unwarned delay subjects, this does not seem likely.

For these reasons, a retrieval-inhibition explanation is most appropriate. The mechanism we prefer is one emphasizing a change in retrieval strategy. When subjects are told to forget list 1 but to remember list 2, they presumably formulate a retrieval strategy that favors list 2. When warned that they

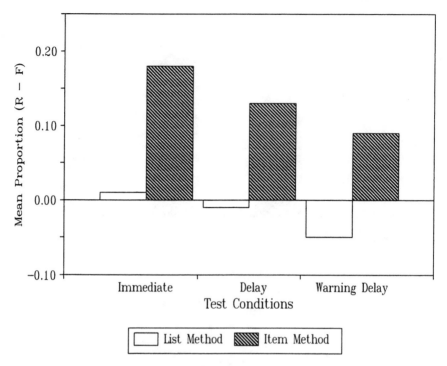

FIG. 4.6. Mean proportion of directed forgetting (R–F) in recognition as a function of method and test conditions with a 20-min delay (from Gilliland et al., 1996, Experiment 2).

are to recall both lists of items, subjects may alter their retrieval strategy so that list 1 and list 2 are emphasized equally. To determine if retrieval strategy was affected by the warning, we analyzed individual recall protocols from Experiment 2, calculating the mean proportions of remember and forget words recalled in each half of output. As shown in Table 4.6, all subjects recalled a higher proportion of remember words in the first half of the test than in the second half with the single exception of list-method subjects who had been warned. These subjects had apparently implemented a retrieval strategy that integrated remember and forget words. Reorganization of recall is probably an option only for list-method subjects, because only these subjects have segregated items into two sets of relationally processed items. Reorganization is probably not an option with the item method, because item-method subjects are engaged in item-specific processing.

Because subjects show directed forgetting when remember words are recalled before forget words, it might be argued that output interference rather than type of retrieval strategy could account for these data. Geisel-

TABLE 4.6
Mean Proportions of Remember Words Recalled in the
First Half (R1) and Second Half of Recall (R2)

	Method			
	Item		List	
	R1	R2	R1	R2
Type of Test				
Immediate	.71	.57	.70	.55
Delay	.82	.64	.57	.46
Warning Delay	.77	.60	.49	.47

Note. Results come from Gilliland et al., 1996, Experiment 2.

man et al. (1983a) also found that more remember than forget words are recalled in the first half of output. They investigated the possibility that output interference accounts for directed forgetting by measuring directed forgetting when subjects were instructed to recall list 1 first versus list 2 first. Because directed forgetting was significant with recall in either order, it is clear that output interference cannot account for directed forgetting. If presence of output interference cannot account for directed forgetting, its absence cannot account for the elimination of directed forgetting when a warning is given.

It would be interesting to learn how much delay is necessary for the occurrence of the warning effect and to determine how the warning influences retrieval inhibition. Because this is a new phenomenon, more research is needed to answer these questions. One variable of interest to us is whether explicit instructions to intermingle list 1 and list 2 items might influence the magnitude of directed forgetting.

Our retrieval strategy interpretation of the warning effect is a retrieval-inhibition theory, because it assumes that the information is stored but cannot be accessed without a change in retrieval strategy. In the next section, we evaluate this interpretation along with the various alternative theories of retrieval inhibition that apply to directed-forgetting phenomena.

INTERPRETATIONS OF RETRIEVAL INHIBITION

In this section of the chapter, we briefly describe several alternative theoretical accounts of retrieval inhibition, including a few we have already introduced. We evaluate each of these as it applies to list- and item-method directed forgetting in general and to the warning effect in particular.

Loss of Source Information

Retrieval inhibition in directed forgetting may occur because subjects lose access to that episode in their lives that included presentation of list 1. Geiselman et al. (1983a) referred to this as loss of access to a space in time in episodic memory. These researchers applied this description to their finding that both incidentally learned (judge for pleasantness) and intentionally learned (learn) forget words were recalled less well than corresponding remember words. In comparison with controls who were not given the forget instruction, subjects in the experimental condition were less accurate in identifying the list membership of list 1 words, and this was true regardless of the judge or learn status of those words. These results suggest that subjects lose access to all of the events occurring during presentation of list 1.

Source memory has also been tested by asking subjects to indicate the remember or forget status of target words (e.g., Davis & Okada, 1971; MacLeod, 1975). Unfortunately, neither indicating remember or forget status nor indicating list membership is an entirely satisfactory measure of source memory, because either of them could be affected by item accessibility. If items are readily retrieved, subjects may well attribute that retrieval to the items' membership in the to-be-remembered set.

As mentioned in conjunction with the delay and warning effect experiments (Gilliland et al., 1996) reported earlier, we found little evidence in support of a source memory interpretation of the warning effect in directed forgetting. Subjects in those experiments were more likely to misjudge forget words as remember words with the list method than with the item method. However, the disappearance of directed forgetting that occurred with the warning was not associated with a change in source memory performance, and neither F–R nor R–F confusions increased with delay.

A measure of source memory that is perhaps less influenced by item availability in directed forgetting was suggested by Tzeng, Lee, and Wetzel (1979). They used the item method and asked subjects to provide judgments of the approximate serial position of each recalled item. They found serial position judgments to be more accurate for remember than for forget words. Unfortunately for our purposes, these researchers neither included a control condition in which subjects did not receive directed-forgetting instructions, nor did they test subjects with the list method. To determine what would happen when these conditions were met, Basden and Basden (1996, Experiment 1) used serial position judgments to measure source memory when subjects were given either list- or item-method directed forgetting instructions or no instructions. After subjects had completed their recall test, they were asked to go back through the words they had recalled, indicating in which sixth of the 24-word list each item was presented. If subjects actually do lose access to information about the context in which the words occur, then experimental subjects should be less accurate than control subjects in judging the serial positions of forget words. We found experimental subjects to be as accurate as control subjects in identifying the serial positions of forget words, and this held true for both the list and the item methods. Furthermore, only the item method yielded more accurate serial position estimates for remember than forget words. We feel more confident of these results than of measures used by previous investigators, because serial position judgments such as these are less likely to be influenced by accessibility than are judgments of remember and forget status. These results are supportive of our position that measures of source memory are not predictive of magnitude of directed forgetting.

Recollect judgments may also reflect source memory because they measure the subject's conscious ability to remember that target words occurred in the experimental context. Basden and Basden (1996, Experiment 3) found recollect judgments to be lower for forget than for remember words with the item method but not with the list method. These results suggest that directed forgetting does not reduce source memory with the list method.

In summary, disruption of source memory does not appear to be consistently associated with list-method directed forgetting, contrary to the hypothesis presented by Geiselman et al. (1983a). When subjects are tested with the list method, measures of source memory in the form of either recollect judgments or estimates of serial position are as accurate for forget as for remember targets. Although subjects tested with the list method show greater confusion between remember and forget targets than do subjects tested with the item method, F–R and R–F confusions do not seem to be related to levels of directed forgetting on recall tests, including delayed tests preceded by a warning. Subjects tested with the list method may be more likely to show F–R confusions than subjects tested with the item method, simply because forget items are processed more elaborately with the list method.

Finally, in the delayed recall research reported by Gilliland et al. (1996) and MacLeod (1975), it was assumed that source information is lost more rapidly than item information. However, a recent article by Bornstein and LeCompte (1995) called this basic assumption into question because their research showed that item and source memory were lost at the same rate. Thus, disrupted source memory interpretations of directed forgetting appear to have little supporting evidence.

Response-Set Suppression

In the classic retroactive interference paradigm, experimental subjects study list 1 and then list 2, whereas control subjects study list 1 and then rest. Retroactive interference was demonstrated if list 1 retention was poorer for the experimental subjects than for the control subjects. Spontaneous recovery was demonstrated if retroactive interference was lower on a delayed retention test. That recovery was said to be absolute if the retention of experimental subjects actually increased after a delay. According to response-set suppression theory (Postman & Underwood, 1973), retroactive interference occurs because the experimental subjects employ a response selector, which favors the recall of list 2 over that of list 1. Spontaneous recovery occurs because inertia in this response selector is overcome with time, improving access to list 1.

Wheeler (1995) employed the retroactive interference paradigm in conjunction with directed-forgetting instructions. In Experiments 1a and 1b, the experimental subjects studied list 1 for three trials, but were then told to forget it and to learn two subsequent lists. They received one study–test trial on each of these two interpolated lists. Control subjects were also told to forget list 1, but rested in lieu of interpolated learning. List 1 retention was tested either immediately or after a delay. The delay was 16 minutes in Experiment 1a and 36 minutes in Experiment 1b. When the results of the two experiments were combined, absolute recovery was observed for the experimental subjects; that is, recall of list 1 was greater after the delay than on the immediate test. Wheeler attributed the retroactive interference he observed to retrieval inhibition produced by the interpolated learning, and the absolute recovery he observed to dissipation of retrieval inhibition with the delay. Wheeler suggested that this conception of retrieval inhibition may be operationally indistinguishable from response-set suppression.

If, as Wheeler (1995) suggested, a common retrieval-inhibition process underlies both retroactive interference and directed forgetting, then inhibition should dissipate with delay for both paradigms. Wheeler cited release of retrieval inhibition in directed forgetting (e.g., Bjork, 1989) as evidence that a phenomenon similar to spontaneous recovery does occur in directed forgetting.

A major problem with Wheeler's suggestion is that retrieval inhibition does *not* dissipate with delay in directed forgetting. First, in the Coe et al. (1989) experiments, the magnitude of directed forgetting was as great on the second of two successive free recall tests as on the first, where a delay separated the two tests. Second, Gilliland et al. (1996) reported no reduction in directed forgetting after either a 1-week or a 20-minute delay unless an advance warning was given. On those occasions in which a release of retrieval inhibition has been shown in directed forgetting, it was obtained either on a recognition test (Bjork, 1989; Gilliland et al., 1996) or on a recall test after re-exposure to the forget words (Basden et al., 1993). Given that directed forgetting does not dissipate with time, the similarity between retroactive interference and directed forgetting seems more apparent than real. On the other hand, the concept of selecting a response set does not seem very different from that of selecting a retrieval strategy. A key differ-

TABLE 4.7
Mean Proportions of Remember (R) and Forget (F) Words
Recalled in the Control Conditions With a 20-min. Delay

| | Method | | | |
| | Item | | List | |
	R	F	R	F
Type of Test				
Immediate	.54	.49	.52	.52
Delay	.40	.35	.27	.49

Note. Results are from Gilliland et al., 1996, Experiment 2.

ence between the two approaches is that list integration underlies the absence of directed forgetting in retrieval strategy theory, whereas list differentiation is maintained in response-set suppression theory.

According to response-set suppression theory, the relative dominance of response sets varies with the passage of time (e.g., Postman & Underwood, 1973). Thus, proactive interference may increase on delayed tests. Inertia in the response selector is overcome with time, decreasing the accessibility of list 2 items (Postman, Stark, & Fraser, 1968). Thus, the response selector favors recall of list 2 on the immediate test, but may favor list 1 on a delayed test. As shown in Table 4.7, Gilliland et al. (1996, Experiment 2) found that control subjects recalled the two lists equally on the immediate test, but list 1 better than list 2 after the delay. This implies that list 1 items are more accessible than list 2 items after a delay for subjects given directed-forgetting instructions. This increase in proactive interference with delay may be a crucial factor underlying the warning effect. The attempt to reorganize recall upon receipt of the warning may be successful in part because list 1 members become relatively more accessible during the delay. However, the increase in proactive interference alone cannot account for the decrease in directed forgetting with a warning because directed forgetting does not decrease in the unwarned delay condition. Once again, the warning effect requires not only a warning but also a delay.

Retrieval-Induced Forgetting

Anderson developed an account of retrieval inhibition (Anderson, Bjork, & Bjork, 1994; Anderson & Neely, 1996) that focuses on the effect of retrieval on the strength of previously learned items. Anderson et al. reported evidence that items are inhibited if they are retrieved but rejected as inappropriate. They suggested that even acceptable items that compete unsuccessfully for output may be inhibited. Despite the repeated opportunities for retrieval that occur with continued testing, items that are inhibited early in the test may remain inaccessible. This phenomenon, which Anderson et al. referred to as retrieval-induced forgetting, may underlie various types of retrieval inhibition, including directed forgetting. This analysis is appealing because long-lasting inhibition has been obtained with these procedures, and because it may explain why list-method directed forgetting occurs only when subjects learn a second list after having been told to forget the first list. Directed forgetting does not occur in the absence of new learning between the study of the first list and the test for its retention (see Gelfand & Bjork, as cited in Bjork, 1989).

Retrieval-induced forgetting has a few limitations as a complete account of retrieval inhibition in directed forgetting. First, it is difficult to see how it might account for the release of retrieval inhibition that occurs when a recall test is given after a recognition test (Basden et al., 1993) or when some of the forget words are re-exposed (e.g., Bjork & Bjork, 1996). Second, retrieval-induced forgetting does not explain the increase in proactive interference observed in the control conditions in the Gilliland et al. (1996) research. Finally, it is difficult to see how retrieval-induced forgetting can explain the warning effect, except perhaps as an output interference phenomenon; that is, in terms of an alteration in output order. As mentioned earlier, Geiselman et al. (1983a, Experiment 4) directly tested and rejected the idea that output interference accounts for directed forgetting. On the other hand, theirs is the only study providing evidence against an output interference (or re-trieval-induced forgetting) interpretation of list-method directed forgetting. Because it is generally the case that list-method directed forgetting is absent whenever output order is controlled on retention tests (see the earlier section on Implicit Memory), and because controlling output order controls for output interference, there is some indirect evidence in support of an output interference account. There is clearly a need for additional research examining the role of output interference in directed forgetting.

In summary, retrieval-induced forgetting as described by Anderson et al. (1994) may provide a plausible account for list-method directed forgetting in that the learning of list 2 is necessary for retrieval inhibition of list 1. Retrieval-induced forgetting may also explain why list-method directed for-getting is absent on tests in which the order of output is controlled. How-ever, retrieval-induced forgetting does not adequately explain either release of retrieval inhibition or the warning effect.

Attentional Inhibition

Directed forgetting has been described as resulting from inhibition of atten-tion to activated information (Zacks, Radvansky, & Hasher, 1996). An impor-tant index to attentional inhibition is negative priming. In a typical procedure for investigating this phenomenon, subjects are given trials on which they must choose a target item in preference to one or more nontarget (ignored) items. Negative priming occurs when the reaction time to a target item is greater when it was shown previously as an ignored item than when it was not shown previously (e.g., Tipper, 1985). In a recent review of the negative priming literature, May, Kane, and Hasher (1995) concluded that negative priming is diminished in older adults who are described as deficient in memory-based attentional inhibition. Hasher and Zacks (1988) defined attentional inhibition as the suppression of irrelevant information so that it will not enter working memory. Considerable evidence now supports their observation that older adults are deficient in attentional inhibition.

Zacks et al. (1996) compared directed-forgetting performance in young and elderly adults. In Experiments 1a and 1b, the item method was used to present four instances from each of six categories in blocked order. An initial recall test for remember items was followed by a recall test for both remember and forget items and then by a general recognition test. Directed forgetting was observed on both recall and recognition tests, and was greater for young adults than for elderly adults. When asked on the initial test to recall only the remember items, older subjects intruded more forget items than did younger subjects. Zacks et al. interpreted these results as support for the hypothesis that directed forgetting involves a mechanism by which forget items are inhibited, and that the inhibition process is less effective for elderly subjects.

In Experiment 2, Zacks et al. (1996) used a variation of the list method. For each of 15 short lists, subjects were shown 0 to 4 forget items followed by 3 to 7 remember items. Participants were asked to recall only the remember items after each list, but to recall both the remember and forget items after all lists had been studied. Contrary to results in Experiments 1a and 1b, forget-item intrusions were no greater for older adults than for younger adults on the initial remember-only tests. On the final test, older subjects recalled fewer remember words than did younger subjects, but their recall of forget words was equivalent to that of the younger subjects. Zacks et al. interpreted the latter results as evidence that the elderly subjects were not inhibiting the forget words to the same extent as were the younger subjects.

Because Zacks et al. (1996) found that older subjects recalled forget words at higher levels than did younger subjects with the item method (Experiments 1a and 1b) but not with the list method (Experiment 2), their results are consistent with our position that the list and item methods involve different processes. More specifically, although attentional inhibition may explain item-method directed forgetting, results with the list method are less consistent with that interpretation. With the item method, older subjects may perseverate longer in the processing of forget items, which would result in their producing more forget-item intrusions than do younger subjects. Because the list method does not involve differential processing of remember and forget items, the number of forget words produced as intrusions should be no greater for older than for younger subjects with this method. These were precisely the results Zacks et al. reported in Experiment 2 for both tests. The magnitude of directed forgetting was less for the older than for the younger subjects on the final recall test primarily because older subjects as compared with younger subjects showed greater loss of remember words rather than greater recall of forget words.

In summary, attentional inhibition may refer to a reduction in the processing of forget items. Such an account applies better to results obtained with the item method than with the list method. With the item method, attentional inhibition can explain why older subjects show less directed forgetting than do younger subjects and why older subjects provide more forget items than do younger subjects when recall of remember items is solicited. Because attentional inhibition accounts better for item-specific inhibitory processes than for inhibition of an entire list, it does not appear to provide an explanation of the warning effect, which occurs only with the list method.

Retrieval Strategies

Earlier, we explained the warning effect by suggesting that it may induce subjects to alter their retrieval strategies. This interpretation of the warning effect is an extension of our work on part-list cuing inhibition (e.g., Basden & Basden, 1995). Part-list cuing inhibition is poorer recall of the remainder of the study list when some of the items are provided as cues on the recall test. Part-list cuing inhibition and list-method directed forgetting are similar in that release from inhibition occurs with both procedures. In the part-list cuing paradigm, the inhibition disappears on a final uncued recall test given after the cued test. For example, in Basden and Basden (1995, Experiment 1), subjects were shown a 48-word categorized list for two study/test trials. This was followed by a test with 24 of the words filled in for cued subjects, but none filled in for uncued subjects. A final test was uncued for all subjects. As shown in Fig. 4.7, the cued subjects recalled fewer words than uncued subjects on the cued test, but this retrieval inhibition was released when the cues were removed on the final test. Cued and uncued subjects were statistically equivalent in their recall of noncue words on the final test, replicating similar release of retrieval inhibition effects we observed in previous research (e.g., Basden, Basden, & Galloway, 1977).

Our interpretation of part-list cuing inhibition is that cued subjects abandon their whole-list retrieval strategy in favor of a less effective part-list retrieval strategy. Release of retrieval inhibition occurs when subjects revert to their original whole-list retrieval strategy on removal of the cues. Analo-

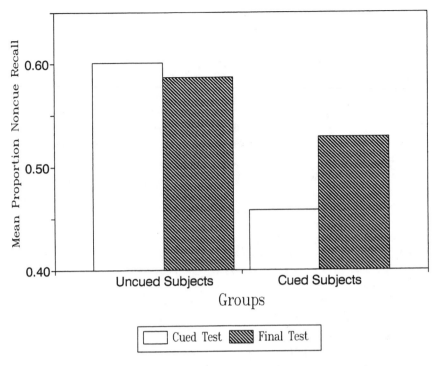

FIG. 4.7. Mean proportion of noncue words recalled on cued and final tests by cued and uncued subjects (from Basden & Basden, 1995, Experiment 1).

gously, list-method directed forgetting may occur because subjects formulate a retrieval strategy that favors list 2. When warned that they will be asked to recall both lists after a delay, subjects may abandon their list 2 retrieval strategy in favor of one that is appropriate for retrieving both lists. Because proactive inhibition for list 2 items increases with delay, list 1 items are relatively more accessible after a delay. This equalization in the accessibility of the items from the two lists should facilitate the implementation of a retrieval strategy in which the two lists are integrated.

Three lines of evidence support the retrieval strategy disruption interpretation of directed forgetting. First, Geiselman et al. (1983a) found little correlation between presentation (input) order and recall (output) order for forget words, but substantial input–output correlations for remember words. Input–output correlations were also high for the control conditions. Input–output correlations were also lower for subjects tested with the post-hypnotic amnesia procedure than without (e.g., Geiselman et al., 1983b). Such results were attributed to disrupted retrieval resulting from reduced source memory (e.g., Evans, 1988; Geiselman et al., 1983a), but could equally well be attributed to the use of different retrieval strategies. A strategy directed toward the retrieval of remember words might make use of the list 2 input order, but might be less systematic with regard to the retrieval of forget words. Similarly, subjects told to be amnesic for a list might avoid using a systematic retrieval strategy until the amnesia is lifted.

A second line of evidence that a retrieval strategy may be altered by directed-forgetting instructions comes from studies in which the subjects' output order is controlled. Evidence cited earlier in connection with the Implicit Memory section showed that list-method directed forgetting is reduced or absent when output order is controlled. Poorer retention of list 1 items has been observed most reliably when subjects are free to output items in any order they choose, presumably because they choose a retrieval strategy that favors the output of list 2. When subjects are prevented from implementing a retrieval strategy, either because output order is controlled or because conscious retrieval is not attempted, list-method directed forgetting diminishes or disappears.

A third line of evidence supporting the retrieval strategy disruption interpretation is provided by the results reported by Goernert and Larson (1994). When subjects were provided with a portion of list 1 items at the time of the recall test, those items served as part-list cues that inhibited retrieval of the remaining list 1 items for control subjects but released retrieval inhibition of the remaining items for the experimental subjects. Forget items apparently function as an intact memory unit.

In summary, the results obtained with list-method directed forgetting and part-list cuing inhibition are similar, which suggests that the same mechanism may underlie both phenomena. We believe that mechanism is the subject's retrieval strategy. Inhibition of forget words appears when conditions result in the use of a retrieval strategy that favors remember words; inhibition disappears when conditions permit integrated retrieval of the forget and remember words. When forget words are increased in accessibility, either through their re-exposure during recognition testing or through increased proactive interference in delayed testing, the implementation of such an integrated retrieval strategy becomes possible.

GENERAL DISCUSSION

In this chapter, we reviewed evidence relevant to the argument that the processes underlying directed forgetting are different for the list and item methods. We argued that item-method directed forgetting results from differential processing of remember and forget items during study, whereas list-method directed forgetting results from retrieval inhibition. Our evidence for this distinction came from the examination of two different phenomena. First, comparisons of recall and recognition performance indicated that although the item method yields directed forgetting on both recall and recognition tests, the list method yields directed forgetting only on recall tests. Second, re-exposure to the forget items results in a release of retrieval inhibition with the list method but not with the item method. Although performance on forget items may improve dramatically with additional study (Geiselman & Bagheri, 1985), simple re-exposure does not reinstate those items in memory when the item method is used.

Furthermore, we argued that the list method emphasizes relational processing whereas the item method emphasizes item-specific processing. We supported that argument with results showing that the magnitude of directed forgetting is influenced by the nature of the study task. With the item method, directed forgetting is greater with materials that facilitate item-specific rather than relational processing; with the list method, directed forgetting is greater with materials that facilitate relational processing.

In support of our argument that remember and forget words are differentially processed with the item method, we cited evidence that tests that are sensitive to differential processing, such as certain implicit tests, show item-method directed forgetting but not list-method directed forgetting. Similarly, item-method directed forgetting occurs with recollect but not with know judgments, whereas list-method directed forgetting occurs with neither of these metamemory measures.

Recent work in our laboratory (Gilliland et al., 1996) was also presented. This research showed that when floor effects are avoided, neither list- nor item-method directed forgetting is reduced when the recall test is delayed. We also observed what we have termed the warning effect when using the list method. When subjects were warned in advance of a delay that their memory for both remember and forget items would be tested, directed forgetting with the list method vanished.

After examining alternative interpretations, we concluded that list-method directed forgetting can best be explained in terms of retrieval strategies. In standard directed-forgetting procedures, the instruction to forget list 1 causes subjects to formulate a retrieval strategy that favors list 2 recall. The warning reduces directed forgetting because it causes subjects to abandon their previously formulated retrieval strategy in favor of one that involves list 1 and list 2 equally. Such an integrated strategy can be implemented only when list 1 items become relatively more accessible; that is, after a delay.

REFERENCES

Anderson, M. C., Bjork, R. A., & Bjork, E. L. (1994). Remembering can cause forgetting: Retrieval dynamics in long-term memory. *Journal of Experimental Psychology: Learning, Memory, and Cognition, 20*, 1063–1087.

Anderson, M. C., & Neely, J. H. (in press). Interference and inhibition in memory retrieval. In E. L. Bjork & R. A. Bjork (Eds.), *Handbook of perception and cognition. Vol 10: Memory* (pp. 237–313). San Diego: Academic Press.

Basden, B. H., & Basden, D. R. (1996). Directed forgetting: A further comparison of the list and item methods. *Memory, 4*, 633–653.

Basden, B. H., Basden, D. R., Coe, W. C., Decker, S., & Crutcher, K. (1994). Retrieval inhibition in directed forgetting and posthypnotic amnesia. *International Journal of Clinical and Experimental Hypnosis, 42*, 184–203.

Basden, B. H., Basden, D. R., & Gargano, G. J. (1993). Directed forgetting in implicit and explicit memory tests: A comparison of methods. *Journal of Experimental Psychology: Learning, Memory, and Cognition, 19*, 603–616.

Basden, D. R., & Basden, B. H. (1995). Part-list cuing: A retrieval strategy disruption interpretation. *Journal of Experimental Psychology: Learning, Memory, and Cognition, 21*, 1656–1669.

Basden, D. R., Basden, B. H., & Galloway (1977). Inhibition with part-list cuing. *Journal of Experimental Psychology: Human Learning and Memory, 3*, 100–108.

Bjork, E. L., & Bjork, R. A. (1996). Continuing influences of to-be-forgotten information. *Consciousness and Cognition, 5*, 176–196.

Bjork, R. A. (1970). Positive forgetting: The noninterference of items intentionally forgotten. *Journal of Verbal Learning and Verbal Behavior, 9*, 255–268.

Bjork, R. A. (1972). Theoretical implications of directed forgetting. In A. W. Melton & E. Martin (Eds.), *Coding processes in human memory* (pp. 217–235). Washington, DC: Winston.

Bjork, R. A. (1989). Retrieval inhibition as an adaptive mechanism in human memory. In H. L. Roediger, III, & F. I. M. Craik (Eds.), *Varieties of memory and consciousness: Essays in honour of Endel Tulving* (pp. 309–330). Hillsdale, NJ: Lawrence Erlbaum Associates.

Bjork, R. A., & Geiselman, R. E. (1978). Constituent processes in the differentiation of items in memory. *Journal of Experimental Psychology: Human Learning and Memory, 4*, 347–361.

Block, R. A. (1971). Effects of instructions to forget in short-term memory. *Journal of Experimental Psychology, 89*, 1–9.

Bornstein, B. H., & LeCompte, D. C. (1995). A comparison of item and source forgetting. *Psychonomic Bulletin and Review, 2*, 254–259.

Challis, B. H., & Brodbeck, D. R. (1992). Level of processing affects priming in word fragment completion. *Journal of Experimental Psychology: Learning, Memory, and Cognition, 18*, 595–607.

Coe, W. C., Basden, B. H., Basden, D. R., Fikes, T., Gargano, G. J., & Webb, M. (1989). Directed forgetting and posthypnotic amnesia: Information processing and social contexts. *Journal of Personality and Social Psychology, 56*, 189–198.

Davis, J. C., & Okada, R. (1971). Recognition and recall of positively forgotten items. *Journal of Experimental Psychology, 89*, 181–186.

Einstein, G. O., & Hunt, R. R. (1980). Levels of processing and organization: Additive effects of individual-item and relational processing. *Journal of Experimental Psychology: Human Learning and Memory, 6*, 588–598.

Elmes, D. G., Adams, C., III, & Roediger, H. L., III (1970). Cued forgetting in short-term memory: Response selection. *Journal of Experimental Psychology, 86*, 103–107.

Evans, F. J. (1988). Posthypnotic amnesia: Dissociation of content and context. In H. M. Pettinati (Ed.), *Hypnosis and memory* (pp. 157–192). New York: Guilford.

Gardiner, J. M. (1988). Functional aspects of recollective experience. *Memory and Cognition, 16*, 309–313.

Gardiner, J. M., Gawlik, G., & Richardson-Klavehn, A. (1994). Maintenance rehearsal affects knowing, not remembering; Elaborative rehearsal affects remembering, not knowing. *Psychonomic Bulletin and Review, 1*, 107–110.

Gardiner, J. M., & Java, R. I. (1993). Recognizing and remembering. In A. Collins, S. Gathercole, M. Conway, & P. Morris (Eds.), *Theories of memory* (pp. 163–188). Hillsdale, NJ: Lawrence Erlbaum Associates.

Geiselman, R. E., & Bagheri, B. (1985). Repetition effects in directed forgetting: Evidence for retrieval inhibition. *Memory and Cognition, 13,* 57–62.

Geiselman, R. E., Bjork, R. A., & Fishman, D. L. (1983a). Disrupted retrieval in directed forgetting: A link with posthypnotic amnesia. *Journal of Experimental Psychology: General, 112,* 58–72.

Geiselman, R. E., MacKinnon, D. P., Fishman, D. L., Jaenicke, C., Larner, B. R., Schoenberg, S., & Swartz, S. (1983b). Mechanisms of hypnotic and nonhypnotic forgetting. *Journal of Experimental Psychology: Learning, Memory, and Cognition, 9,* 626–635.

Geiselman, R. E., & Panting, T. (1985). Personality correlates of retrieval processes in intentional and unintentional forgetting. *Personality & Individual Differences, 6,* 685–691.

Geiselman, R. E., Rabow, V. E., Wachtel, S. L., & MacKinnon, D. P. (1985). Strategy control in intentional forgetting. *Human Learning, 4,* 169–178.

Gilliland, T. R., McLaughlin, K., Wright, M., Basden, B. H., & Basden, D. R. (1996). The *"warning effect"* in directed forgetting. Poster presented at the 76th Annual Convention of the Western Psychological Association, San Jose, CA.

Goernert, P. N., & Larson, M. E. (1994). The initiation and release of retrieval inhibition. *The Journal of General Psychology, 121,* 61–66.

Golding, J. M., Long, D. L., & MacLeod, C. M. (1994). You can't always forget what you want: Directed forgetting of related words. *Journal of Memory and Language, 33,* 493–510.

Hasher, L., & Zacks, R. T. (1988). Working memory, comprehension, and aging: A review and a new view. In G. H. Bower (Ed.), *The psychology of learning and motivation* (Vol. 22, pp. 193–225). San Diego: Academic Press.

Horton, K. D., & Petruk, R. (1980). Set differentiation and depth of processing in the directed forgetting paradigm. *Journal of Experimental Psychology: Human Learning and Memory, 6,* 599–610.

Hunt, R. R., & Einstein, G. O. (1981). Relational and item-specific information in memory. *Journal of Verbal Learning and Verbal Behavior, 20,* 497–514.

Hunt, R. R., & Marschark, M. (1989). Yet another picture of imagery: The roles of shared and distinctive information in memory. In M. A. McDaniel & M. Pressley (Eds.), *Imagery and related mnemonic processes: Theories, individual differences, and applications* (pp. 129–150). New York: Springer-Verlag.

Hunt, R. R., & McDaniel, M. A. (1993). The enigma of organization and distinctiveness. *Journal of Memory and Language, 32,* 421–445.

MacLeod, C. M. (1975). Long-term recognition and recall following directed forgetting. *Journal of Experimental Psychology: Human Learning and Memory, 104,* 271–279.

MacLeod, C. M. (1989). Directed forgetting affects both direct and indirect tests of memory. *Journal of Experimental Psychology: Learning, Memory, and Cognition, 15,* 13–21.

May, C. P., Kane, M. J., & Hasher, L. (1995). Determinants of negative priming. *Psychological Bulletin, 118,* 35–54.

McDermott, K. B., & Roediger, H. L. (1996). Exact and conceptual repetition dissociate conceptual memory tests: Problems for transfer appropriate processing theory. *Canadian Journal of Experimental Psychology, 50,* 57–71.

Melton, A. W., & Irwin, J. M. (1940). Retroactive and proactive inhibition in retention: Evidence for a two-factor theory of retroactive inhibition. *American Journal of Psychology, 3,* 173–203.

Paller, K. A. (1990). Recall and stem-completion priming have different electrophysiological correlates and are modified differentially by directed forgetting. *Journal of Experimental Psychology: Learning, Memory, and Cognition, 16,* 1021–1032.

Postman, L., Stark, K., & Fraser, J. (1968). Temporal changes in interference. *Journal of Verbal Learning and Verbal Behavior, 7,* 672–694.

Postman, L., & Underwood, B. J. (1973). Critical issues in interference theory. *Memory and Cognition, 1,* 19–40.

Riccio, D. C., Rabinowitz, V. C., & Axelrod, S. (1994). Memory: When less is more. *American Psychologist, 49,* 917–926.

Roediger, H. L., III, & McDermott, K. B. (1993). Implicit memory in normal human subjects. In H. Spinnler & F. Boller (Eds.), *Handbook of neuropsychology* (Vol. 8, pp. 63–131). Amsterdam: Elsevier.

Russo, R., & Andrade, J. (1995). The directed-forgetting effect in word fragment completion: An application of the process dissociation procedure. *The Quarterly Journal of Experimental Psychology: Section A: Human Experimental Psychology, 48A*, 405–423.

Thapar, A., & Greene, R. L. (1994). Effects of level of processing on implicit and explicit tasks. *Journal of Experimental Psychology: Learning, Memory, and Cognition, 20*, 671–679.

Tipper, S. P. (1985). The negative priming effect: Inhibitory priming by ignored objects. *Quarterly Journal of Experimental Psychology, 37A*, 571–590.

Toth, J. P., Reingold, E. M., & Jacoby, L. L. (1994). Toward a redefinition of implicit memory: Process dissociations following elaborative processing and self-generation. *Journal of Experimental Psychology: Learning, Memory, and Cognition, 20*, 290–303.

Tulving, E. (1985). Memory and consciousness. *Canadian Psychologist, 26*, 1–12.

Tulving, E., & Pearlstone, Z. (1966). Availability versus accessibility of information in memory for words. *Journal of Verbal Learning and Verbal Behavior, 5*, 381–391.

Tzeng, O. J. L., Lee, A. T., & Wetzel, C. D. (1979). Temporal coding in verbal information processing. *Journal of Experimental Psychology: Human Learning and Memory, 5*, 52–64.

Wetzel, C. D. (1975). Effect of orienting tasks and cue timing on the free recall of remember- and forget-cued words. *Journal of Experimental Psychology: Human Learning and Memory, 1*, 556–566.

Wheeler, M. A. (1995). Improvement in recall over time without repeated testing: Spontaneous recovery revisited. *Journal of Experimental Psychology: Learning, Memory, and Cognition, 21*, 173–184.

Woodward, A. E., Bjork, R. A., & Jongeward, R. H. (1973). Recall and recognition as a function of primary rehearsal. *Journal of Verbal Learning and Verbal Behavior, 12*, 608–617.

Woodward, A. E., Park, D. C., & Seebohm, K. (1974). Directed forgetting as a function of explicit within-list cuing and implicit postlist cuing. *Journal of Experimental Psychology, 102*, 1001–1006.

Wright, M., Burke, A., & Basden, B. H. (1997). *Release of retrieval inhibition as a function of target reexposure.* Poster presented at the 13th annual Central California Research Symposium, California State University, Fresno, CA.

Zacks, R. T., Radvansky, G., & Hasher, L. (1996). Studies of directed forgetting in older adults. *Journal of Experimental Psychology: Learning, Memory and Cognition, 22*, 143–156.

5

DIRECTED FORGETTING AND REHEARSAL ON DIRECT AND INDIRECT MEMORY TESTS

Scott W. Allen
John R. Vokey
University of Lethbridge

Directed forgetting refers to the relatively poorer retrieval following a direction, or instruction, to forget rather than to remember a prior event. Interest in the phenomenon ranges from such effects in simple item recall and recognition experiments with words, to related phenomena in posthypnotic amnesia, and to the efficacy of instructions to jurors to disregard previously heard testimony (e.g., Golding, Fowler, Long, & Latta, 1990; Simon, 1966; Wyer & Unverzagt, 1985). As Kihlstrom (1983) noted, by the mid-1970s the phenomenon seemed to be generally well understood, principally in terms of enhanced retrieval of remember items (See e.g., Bjork, 1972; Epstein, 1972, for reviews of the earlier literature). Some recent research, however, has been taken as generally supportive of the hypothesis that memory for the forget items is suppressed, particularly in the form of retrieval inhibition (e.g., Geiselman & Bagheri, 1985; Geiselman, Bjork, & Fishman, 1983; but see also Weiner & Reed, 1969; see Bjork, 1989, for a general discussion on the adaptive nature of retrieval inhibition).

One interesting line of research seen as providing strong support for the retrieval inhibition explanation of directed forgetting is that using indirect rather than direct tests of memory. MacLeod (1989), for example, demonstrated that item-based directed forgetting could be obtained with such indirect tests of memory as word fragment completion and lexical decision, in addition to the more usual findings with direct tests such as item recall or recognition. The strength of this evidence lies in the assumption that indirect memory tests are not, or at least are very substantially less, susceptible to the kinds of memorial processes (e.g., conceptually driven processing) thought to enhance performance on direct memory tests, particularly for remember items. Rather, indirect tests are thought to reflect the automatic memorial consequences of perceptually based or data-driven processing (e.g., Jacoby, 1983a, 1983b; Roediger, 1990), something both remember and forget items should have in common because the instruction to remember or forget occurs *after* the item has been presented and perceptually processed. If so, then the finding of directed forgetting on indirect tests implies the operation of additional processes that, rather than enhancing the retrieval of remember items, selectively reduce the retrieval of forget items. Some form of retrieval inhibition would be a likely candidate (cf. MacLeod, 1989).

However, the assumption that indirect memory tasks are, in this sense, "process pure" has not gone unchallenged. The essential argument is that the indirect tests of memory, particularly as used by MacLeod (1989), are contaminated to some degree by the same kinds of retrieval processes that mediate the effects of elaborative processing on direct memory tests, namely explicit, recollective processes. Both Paller (1990) and Basden, Basden, and Gargano (1993) successfully replicated MacLeod's (1989) directed-forgetting results with word fragment completion as long as his procedures were followed, but did not otherwise find the effect on indirect memory tests. Paller (1990), for example, reported an effect of directed forgetting on stem-cued recall (a direct test), but not on stem completion (an indirect test). Basden et al. (1993) similarly found effects of directed forgetting on direct tests of memory, particularly recall, but also on recognition if the instruction to remember or forget was on a word-by-word rather than on a list basis, but failed to find an effect on indirect tests, including word fragment completion, unless, in the latter case, the procedure closely followed MacLeod's (1989). Basden et al. reported that the important components of MacLeod's procedure for obtaining directed forgetting with fragment completion were, first, the word-by-word rather than the list method of the instruction to remember or forget and, second, aspects of the test procedure itself that would tend to promote explicit retrieval on the indirect test, such as failing to disguise adequately the relation between the study and test, and the long list of fragment test items used.

Allen and Vokey (1993) and Vokey and Allen (1993) took the contamination argument one step further for a variety of both direct and indirect tests, as did Russo and Andrade (1995) for word fragment completion. We applied variants of Jacoby's (1991; Jacoby, Toth, & Yonelinas, 1993) process dissociation approach with the aim of disentangling the contributions to directed forgetting of explicit, recollective influences (influences of a previously presented item accompanied by explicit awareness of the source of the influence) from those of implicit influences (influences of a previously presented item unaccompanied by such awareness) both on direct memory tests such as item recognition, and on indirect memory tests such as stem completion, fragment completion, and lexical decision. We did so over a series of experiments that used different approaches to process dissociation in an attempt to ensure that the results with directed forgetting were not an artifact of the procedures used to dissociate the influences. We found that when directed forgetting occurred in these tasks, it was a function of differences in explicit, recollective influences of memory, and not implicit influences. In fact, when the effects of explicit recollection were removed using the process dissociation logic, no residual effects of directed forgetting were found, for either direct or indirect memory tasks; the results with indirect tasks confirming the conclusions of Basden et al. (1993). That is, with respect to *implicit retrieval*, access to remember and forget items appears to be equal regardless of whether a direct or indirect test of memory is used. Implicit retrieval inhibition, therefore, at least for these tasks and procedures, is not a likely explanation for directed forgetting.

Of course, eliminating implicit retrieval inhibition as an explanation does not rule out the possibility of some form of inhibition of *explicit* retrieval for forget items. For example, it is possible that directed forgetting is a result, at least in part, of some process at the time of the instruction to forget that subsequently reduces (i.e., inhibits) explicit retrieval of such items while maintaining equivalent levels of indirect or implicit access as that for remember items. However, beyond the possibility of *intentional* inhibition of retrieval (or at least *acknowledgment* thereof, as has been commonly proposed as an explanation for posthypnotic amnesia; e.g., Basden, Basden, & Coe, 1994; Geiselman et al., 1983), it is not at all clear what the mechanism of such an inhibitory process would be.

Alternatively, encoding processes, such as elaborative rehearsal, that subsequently enhance explicit retrieval of information that people have been asked to remember have been the focus of much memory research in recent decades. In fact, the combination of enhanced performance on direct memory tests and unchanged performance on (uncontaminated) indirect memory tests is a common result of simple encoding and rehearsal processes (e.g., Roediger, 1990). Consequently, in this chapter, we explore the possibility that directed forgetting is mediated by processes that enhance the explicit retrieval of remember items rather than by those that suppress or inhibit the retrieval of forget items. Of course, the processes, possibly including those involving inhibition or suppression, that are active in response to other methods of manipulating the instruction to remember and to forget, such as list-based instructions, or responsible for such effects when memory is assessed with other tasks, such as recall, may well be very different from those that are active in response to item-based instructions and memory tests involving item-based cued retrieval, such as recognition and word fragment completion (Basden et al., 1993). Accordingly, the present investigation is restricted to item-based instructions to forget and the kinds of item-based memory tests used in MacLeod (1989) and in Vokey and Allen (1993).

The focal interest in this chapter, then, is the prosaic possibility that directed forgetting in recognition tasks and indirect retrieval tasks such as word fragment completion and lexical decision is a consequence of simple rehearsal differences between remember and forget items, an idea that has been prevalent in the directed-forgetting literature from the outset (e.g., Bjork, 1972; MacLeod, 1975; Wetzel, 1975). For example, Wetzel and Hunt (1977), following up some earlier work by Woodward, Bjork, and Jongeward (1973), found large effects on item recall of the time available for rehearsal. Among other manipulations, they varied the time available to rehearse an item from 1 to 12 secs, following the instruction either to remember or to forget, and found increasing immediate and final free recall as a function of rehearsal time as long as the rehearsal time was constant for all items in a list. Furthermore, as expected by the hypothesis that directed forgetting is a consequence of simple rehearsal differences between remember and forget items, the effect of rehearsal time was larger for remember than for forget items. In contrast, randomly varying rehearsal time following the instruction from item to item within a list showed no such effects of rehearsal time. Of more relevance for our purposes, Wetzel and Hunt also found similar results for a final recognition test. The recognition of both remember and forget items increased with rehearsal time (again, as long as rehearsal time was manipulated between lists), with the effect of rehearsal time being larger for the remember items than for the forget items. Of course, such differential effects of rehearsal time do not mean that such differences, and only such differences, provide a complete account for the effect of directed forgetting in these tasks, only that they could, in principle, do so. It could be, for example, that remember items simply benefit more from subsequent rehearsal than do forget items but that the base difference is due to some other process (cf. Weiner & Reed, 1969), including some other kind of rehearsal process. Even in the Wetzel and Hunt experiments, for example, which showed large differential effects of rehearsal time on the recall and recognition of remember and forget items, there were still pronounced differences in the recall and recognition of remember and forget items at the shortest (i.e., 1 sec) rehearsal times.

Such caveats duly noted, it is still worth investigating whether such effects can be demonstrated in primary recognition tests and indirect memory tests. Informal interviews with subjects in the Vokey and Allen (1993) experiments suggested that a large number of them attempted to follow the training instructions by retrieving and elaboratively rehearsing the remember but not the forget items when instructed to do so. We therefore investigated the possibility that this difference in retrieval and rehearsal between remember and forget items was the source of directed forgetting with a series of experiments using the same direct and indirect memory tasks as we used in Allen and Vokey (1993) and Vokey and Allen (1993).

EXPERIMENT I: DIRECTED FORGETTING AND THE OPPORTUNITY FOR REHEARSAL

In the first experiment, the opportunity for rehearsal was controlled in two ways. The first of these was the time available to rehearse the item during initial exposure subsequent to the instruction to remember or to forget. In the experiments in Vokey and Allen (1993), the exposure times were the same as those used by MacLeod (1989)—and apparently canonical for this literature—a short, 1-sec exposure of each item followed by a 3-sec period in which the instruction to remember or to forget the immediately preceding item was displayed. These same exposure times were used in one of the conditions of this first experiment, but the results with them were contrasted with those obtained with only a 1-sec period for the instruction and, hence, the time available to retrieve and rehearse an item following an instruction to remember it. If Wetzel and Hunt's (1977) effects of the time available for rehearsal following the instruction to remember or to forget generalize from item recall and final recognition to primary recognition and indirect memory tasks such as word fragment completion, then reducing the time available for rehearsal would be expected to reduce the magnitude of the directed-forgetting effect in these tasks.

The second way of controlling rehearsal, and the one used in all subsequent experiments with these materials, is to vary the number of periods in which a remember item arguably could be rehearsed. One simple strategy subjects could be following is to take every instruction to forget as a period in which to retrieve and to rehearse prior remember items. This strategy might apply especially to the most recently presented remember items. If so, then remember items immediately followed by one or more forget items would have more potential rehearsal opportunities than would remember items immediately followed by one or more remember items. If such rehearsal of remember items is the source of the directed-forgetting effect in these tasks, then it might be expected that the size of the effect would vary with the number of such immediate rehearsal periods afforded an item. The memory for remember items ought to increase as a function of immediate rehearsal periods (i.e., the number of immediately subsequent periods with instructions to forget), whereas the memory for forget items ought to remain relatively stable over such periods, reflecting only the memory for items arising from the initial, predirection encoding (or reading) of the item. At an extreme, for example, it might even be expected that remember items immediately followed by a long string of instructions to remember other, subsequent items would be little better remembered than would forget items, particularly in the condition with the shortened (i.e., 1 sec) rehearsal period. In contrast, a remember item followed by a long series of forget items and consequently many uninterrupted opportunities for rehearsal might evince substantially superior memory to that of forget items, particularly in the condition with the long (i.e., 3 sec) rehearsal periods, accounting possibly for the bulk of the directed-forgetting effect in these tasks.

Typically, in item-based directed forgetting experiments, the sequence of remember and forget items is semirandom, and long sequences of remember or forget instructions in a row are consequently quite rare. Furthermore, because such sequencing is not systematic, any attempt at the analysis of sequencing effects on memory is problematic. By judicious use of a few filler (i.e., untested) items associated with instructions of the appropriate type, however, it was possible to construct sequences over items that appeared random to the subjects, yet that maximized the number of long sequences or lags, and balanced the frequencies of remember and forget items that preceded each lag. The longest lag was three subsequent forget instruction periods following an instruction to remember or to forget, and the shortest was a lag of zero (i.e., the next item was a remember item). Although lags of zero were necessarily the most common, lags of 1 next most so, and so on, each of the lags of 0, 1, 2, or 3 subsequent forget trials was associated with equal numbers of remember and forget items.[1] In addition, counterbalanced over subjects, an item associated with a particular lag occurred as both a remember and a forget item, and as a distractor item.

In total, for each subject, there were 180 critical items, 60 followed by an instruction to remember, 60 followed by an instruction to forget, and 60 not shown during study to be used as distractors (new items) on the subsequent memory tests. These items were some of those used in Allen and Vokey (1993), Vokey and Allen (1993), and MacLeod (1989), and consisted of the bulk of the items from the Tulving, Schacter, and Stark (1982) low-frequency, fragment completion word set. The completions provided by Tulving et al. were accepted as canonical for the fragment completion test, and were used as the study and recognition items. One half of the items of each study instruction type of remember, forget, and new were used on the direct memory test of item recognition, with the remaining items of each study instruction type being used as fragments on the indirect memory test of fragment completion.

---

[1]For the 30 items in each instruction category, there were 16 items with a lag of 0, 8 with a lag of 1, 4 with a lag of 2, and 2 with a lag of 3. Because there were so few items with lags of 2 and 3, they were combined into a lag category of "2 or more" for analysis.

The procedure followed that of the first experiment in Vokey and Allen (1993). Briefly, subjects were presented with a study list and two memory tests. Study trials were generated by computer directly to videotape, and then were presented to small groups of subjects via a large-screen video monitor. Each study trial consisted of a ready prompt, followed by the study word for 1 sec in bold, upper-case black letters on a white background, subtending approximately one third of the height of the video display, which was then replaced by the study instruction (the word "Remember" or "Forget") for either 1 or 3 sec, depending on whether the subject was assigned to the short or long rehearsal conditions. With this exception, the 36 subjects in the 1-sec rehearsal condition were otherwise treated identically to the 12 subjects in the 3-sec or standard rehearsal condition.[2] The study phase was followed by the two paper-and-pencil memory tests. The recognition test was always presented first. Subjects were given 5 minutes to circle words they had seen in the study list, and were instructed to do so regardless of whether they had been previously instructed to remember or to forget the word. Subjects were then given 10 minutes to complete the fragment completion test. They were instructed to fill in the missing letters to make an English word, and to use any completion that would fit.

Rather than disguise the relation between the fragment completion test and the study list as is usually done with indirect memory tasks, following the procedures of Vokey and Allen (1993), subjects were encouraged to use any of the remember and forget study words that they could recall as completions for the relevant fragments. Drawing the subjects' attention to a possible relation between the study and test lists, as well as using such long study and test lists, clearly disqualifies fragment completion as a pure measure of implicit memory, but our argument is that the task is often contaminated in just that fashion anyway. However, it is still an indirect memory test in the sense that a subject's ability to correctly complete a word does not *require* the subject to refer to the study list. The concern with contamination of the indirect fragment completion test with explicit use of memory for the prior items is circumvented through the use of the process dissociation procedure in Experiment 2 of this chapter (see Vokey & Allen, 1993, for an investigation of how subjects' awareness of the relationship between study lists and indirect test lists affects directed forget-

---

[2]The imbalance in numbers of subjects in the two rehearsal conditions reflects the fact that the standard or 3-sec condition was intended as a systematic replication of the study conditions used in many of our other experiments with these materials in Allen and Vokey (1993) and Vokey and Allen (1993) and the current chapter; as such, only the 1-sec rehearsal condition was completely novel, and was therefore assigned the bulk of the subjects and, hence, power for statistical testing. Counterbalancing required six different study conditions; thus, there were 5–7 subjects for each of the counterbalancing conditions in the 1-sec rehearsal condition, and 2 for each of the conditions in the 3-sec rehearsal.

ting). The strength of the subsequent process dissociation analysis is that it allows for the algebraic decomposition of performance into two separate components—that arising from explicit retrieval and that arising from implicit retrieval—when performance is thought to be determined by a mixture of the two sources (Jacoby, 1991). In the case of directed forgetting, the argument is that this mixture of sources of retrieval should be as true for indirect tasks such as word fragment completion (Allen & Vokey, 1993; Russo & Andrade, 1995; Vokey & Allen, 1993) as it is for item recognition (Allen & Vokey, 1993; Vokey & Allen, 1993).

The primary results are shown in Fig. 5.1, which depicts the mean hit and false-alarm rates for both rehearsal groups for recognition, and the mean canonical completion rates for fragment completion. Effects were assessed for reliability over both subjects and items; thus, both these data, and all those that follow, were analyzed once with subjects as the random variate and then again with items as the random variate. All effects were assessed at the $p = .05$ level of significance; only those effects reliable over both subjects and items were considered significant, unless otherwise noted. The results are depicted in two ways. In the top panels of each figure, the data are plotted ignoring lag and in the bottom panels, the data are plotted as a function of lag.

Recognition. As can be seen in the top-left panel of Fig. 5.1, which depicts the results ignoring training lag, overall there was a significant effect of item instruction on recognition, due principally to both remember and forget items evincing hit rates significantly greater than the false-alarm rate to new items. Similarly, there was an effect of directed forgetting on recognition in that the hit rate for remember items was significantly greater than that for forget items. However, contrary to expectations, neither of these effects varied as a function of the time available for rehearsal. Simply put, reducing the time available for rehearsal from 3 sec to 1 sec had no effect on either memory for the items or the magnitude of directed forgetting.

The bottom-left panel of Fig. 5.1 depicts the recognition results for both rehearsal groups as a function of training lag, the number of forget items following a critical remember or forget item. As can be seen, there was no effect at all of training lag on recognition, either alone or in interaction with rehearsal condition. Again, the only effects were significant memory for both remember and forget items and directed forgetting, that is, better memory for remember items than for forget items. Neither of these effects varied significantly as a function of training lag.

Fragment Completion. The results for fragment completion are shown in the right-hand panels of Fig. 5.1. As with item recognition, fragment completion evinced significant memory for the items; however, there was no overall significant effect of directed forgetting, although the effect approached significance for the 1-sec rehearsal condition. Although disappointing, the failure

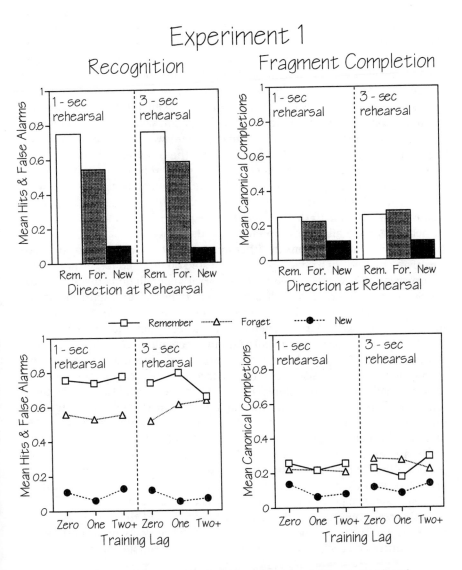

FIG. 5.1. Mean hits and false alarms for recognition (left-hand panels), and canonical completions for word fragment completion (right-hand panels) in the 1- and 3-sec conditions of Experiment 1 plotted as a function of instruction at training. The bottom panels depict the same data as a function of training lag. Subject means are shown in the top panels, and item means in the bottom panels.

to find an effect of directed forgetting on fragment completion is not unusual, even under these conditions that stress the relation between the test and the original training (see Paller, 1990). Indeed, Vokey and Allen (1993) capitalized on just such occasional failures to demonstrate that significant differences between remember and forget items in the explicit component following process dissociation tended to track the effect of directed forgetting.

There was no significant effect of the time available for rehearsal on fragment completion, either alone or in interaction with either memory for the items or directed forgetting. Similarly, there was no effect of training lag, either alone or in interaction with any of the other effects.

In summary, there were no effects of either of the rehearsal manipulations on the results of either the direct or the indirect memory tests. Nor was directed forgetting influenced by either manipulation, suggesting that it is relatively impervious to the memorial consequences of rehearsal. But, as it turned out, there also were no effects of the rehearsal manipulations on simple memory for the items in either memory test, so it is perhaps not too surprising that no such effects were manifested on directed forgetting. What is surprising is how ineffective both rehearsal manipulations turned out to be. Such large differences both in rehearsal time and in opportunities to rehearse normally would be expected to generate large effects on simple memory tests, particularly recognition, as indeed they did in Wetzel and Hunt's (1977) research with recall and final recognition. It is possible that the effects they found with rehearsal time on final recognition occur only following the multiple recall periods that preceded the final recognition task in Wetzel and Hunt's experiments. Furthermore, Wetzel and Hunt (1977) also found that varying the rehearsal time for items within a list—the manipulation of theirs closest in spirit to our lag manipulation (although missing the multiple retrievals that would be associated with effective use of the lag retrieval periods)—was relatively ineffective, and at any rate, the effect of it did not differ for remember and forget items, so perhaps the current results are not as surprising as they first appear. The possibility that the weakness of the rehearsal manipulations reflects the subjects' failure to take advantage of the rehearsal opportunities the manipulations afforded them is explored in Experiment 3. The next experiment investigated the consequences of rehearsal for the process dissociation of explicit and implicit components of memory.

EXPERIMENT 2: PROCESS DISSOCIATIONS OF DIRECTED FORGETTING AND REHEARSAL

If enhanced rehearsal of the remember items is the source of directed forgetting, then it would be expected that explicit retrieval would increase as a function of rehearsal whereas implicit retrieval would remain constant. This possibility was explored in this next experiment by applying the process dissociation approach of Jacoby (1991; Jacoby et al., 1993) that we used in Vokey and Allen (1993) to the lag manipulation used in Experiment 1. We used the procedure not to dissociate processes per se, but to separate two types of retrieval that differ in the level of awareness that accompanies them—acknowledged and unacknowledged retrievals. By acknowledged retrieval, we mean retrieval accompanied by an attribution of the source of the retrieval to the context or elaborations of the original encounter (e.g., "that one was right near the beginning of the list and reminded me of my mother"). Unacknowledged retrieval, on the other hand, refers to the attributions of item-specific familiarity unaccompanied by the retrieval of context or elaborations of the original encounter (e.g., "Gee, it seems familiar but I don't know from where"). Although the terms "acknowledged" and "unacknowledged" capture the distinction we wish to make, for the sake of continuity we use terms that are more commonly used in the literature; explicit and implicit retrieval. Estimates of explicit retrieval in this chapter refer to the proportion of trials on which retrieval is estimated to have been accompanied by awareness of the source of the retrieved information regardless of the retrieval process itself, and regardless of whether the awareness is responsible for the behavior (cf. Richardson-Klavehn, Gardiner, & Java, 1994; Richardson-Klavehn, Lee, Joubran, & Bjork, 1994). Estimates of implicit retrieval, in contrast, refer to the proportion of trials on which retrieval of a specific prior encounter is estimated to have been unaccompanied by awareness of the source of the retrieved information.

The separation between explicit and implicit retrieval is accomplished by comparing performance of trials when subjects are asked to "include" a set of prior items to performance of trials when subjects are asked to "exclude" that set of items. For example, subjects who respond to forget items when asked to include them may respond on the basis of implicit retrieval, explicit retrieval, or some combination of the two. Subjects who respond to forget items when asked to exclude them can be assumed to be responding on the basis of implicit rather than explicit retrieval; explicitly retrieving the items would be grounds for withholding the response. Thus, comparing performance under the two conditions, as detailed later, allows one to estimate the contributions of explicit and implicit retrieval to the memory task.

The materials and basic design for this experiment were identical to those used in the 1-sec rehearsal condition of Experiment 1. The only difference was in the instructions to the subjects at the time of the tests. Instead of instructing them that they could use *any* item they remembered from the training list as selections for recognition or as completions for fragment completion, they were instructed to use only certain items. Subjects in one group (31, at least 5 in each of the 6 counterbalancing conditions) were instructed to use only remember items, and to exclude any forget items from their responses. Those in the other group (35, at least 5 in each of the counterbalancing conditions) were instructed to use only forget items, and to exclude any remember items from their responses. This form of exclusion task was used by Allen and Vokey (1993) and by Vokey and Allen (1993) and was shown to produce results not different in kind from other forms of exclusion. One advantage of this approach is that it does not require a large set of filler items whose sole purpose is to provide the basis for exclusion at test. Rather, items that provide the data for exclusion with one group of subjects provide the data for inclusion with the other group. Thus, both inclusion and exclusion data are obtained, within items, for each training instruction (i.e., remember, forget, and new).

Performance Analyses. The primary results are shown in Fig. 5.2. Referring to the inclusion data for recognition in the top-left panel (i.e., remember items from the exclude forget condition, and forget items from the exclude remember condition), it is clear that, as in Experiment 1, subjects showed significant memory for the items; the hit rate for both remember and forget items was significantly greater than the rate of false alarms to new items. Similarly, comparing the data from the remember items in the exclude forget condition with those of the forget items in the exclude remember condition revealed a significant effect of directed forgetting on recognition. There also was significant memory for both remember and forget items on the fragment completion test, but as in Experiment 1, directed forgetting did not affect fragment completion.

The results as a function of training lag are shown in the bottom panels of Fig. 5.2. As can be seen, and similar to the results of Experiment 1, there was no effect of training lag either alone or in interaction with other effects for either recognition or fragment completion.

Process Dissociation Analyses. Buchner, Erdfelder, and Vaterrodt-Plünnecke (1995) provided a lucid account of the logic of process dissociation, and their extended model is a useful synthesis of model variants. These variants emphasize both the importance of taking into account base rates of responding positively to the items even in the absence of task-specific prior exposure (e.g., Allen & Vokey, 1993; Buchner et al., 1995), and that the assumption of process independence, a central assumption of Jacoby's (1991) original formulation, is not necessary for obtaining meaningful estimates (Buchner et al., 1995; Joordens & Merikle, 1993), and at any rate may not be appropriate for some indirect tests (Curran & Hintzman, 1995). However, figuring in these complications does not detract from the basic principle of deriving estimates of explicit versus implicit retrieval of specific training experiences from the comparison of inclusion and exclusion conditions. We use here a technique of our own devising (Allen & Vokey, 1993; Vokey & Allen, 1993) that we believe to be much closer in spirit to what Jacoby (1991) originally proposed than is the approach espoused by Buchner et al. (1995). Our

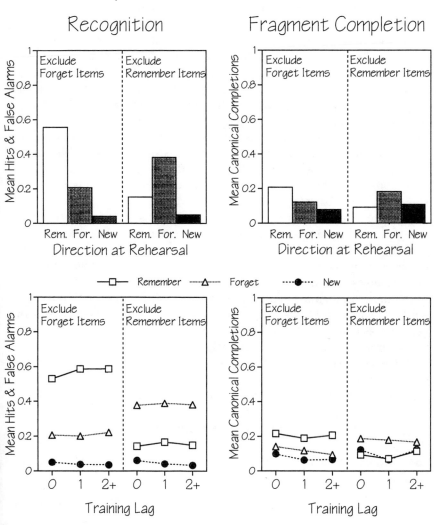

FIG. 5.2. Mean hits and false alarms for recognition (left-hand panels), and canonical completions for word fragment completion (right-hand panels) in the exclude forget and exclude remember conditions of Experiment 2 plotted as a function of instruction at training. The bottom panels depict the same data as a function of training lag. Subject means are shown in the top panels, and item means in the bottom panels.

technique has the advantage that it also incorporates and corrects the estimates for base rates of responding, modeled as a simple additive term within the implicit component arising for reasons other than specific prior exposure (e.g., structural similarity) of the particular test instances.

In brief, elaborating on the process dissociation procedure of Jacoby (1991; Jacoby et al., 1993), the rate of responding in the inclusion conditions, $p(I)$, is given by $p(I) = p(R) + [1 - p(R)][p(S) + p(b_I)]$, in which $p(R)$ is the probability of responding on the basis of explicit recollection; $p(S) + p(b_I)$ is the probability of responding on the basis of independent, implicit memory processes; and $p(b_I)$ is the base rate of responding in the particular inclusion task (for that subject or that item) for reasons other than specific, prior exposure to the test items; $p(S)$, then, is the increase in the rate of responding on the basis of implicit retrieval derived from *specific* familiarity: It is modeled in this approach as simply adding to the probability of responding on the basis of general familiarity.

The rate of responding in the exclusion conditions, $p(E)$, for which explicit retrieval provides the basis for excluding responding, is given by $p(E) = [1 - p(R)][p(S) + p(b_E)]$, in which $p(R)$ and $p(S)$ are as before, and $p(b_E)$ is the corresponding base rate of responding in the particular exclusion task. If, as in Jacoby's formulation, $p(b_I)$ and $p(b_E)$ are assumed to equal a common base rate, $p(b)$, then the estimates of $p(R)$ and $p(S)$ are given by $p(R) = p(I) - p(E)$ and $p(S) = p(E)/[1 - p(R)] - p(b)$, where $p(S)$ can be interpreted more generally as conditional on not-R [i.e., $p(S | {\sim}R)$] if the independence assumption is dropped (cf. Buchner et al., 1995).

If, however, $p(b_I)$ and $p(b_E)$ are assumed not to be equivalent (e.g., because of different response biases over the two conditions), then the estimate of $p(R)$ is given by the more complicated expression:

$$p(R) = [p(I) - p(E) + p(b_E) - p(b_I)]/[1 + p(b_E) - p(b_I)], \qquad (1)$$

and the appropriate base rate for deriving the estimate of $p(S)$ [or $p(S | {\sim}R)$] is $p(b_E)$:

$$p(S | {\sim}R) = p(E)/[1 - p(R)] - p(b_E). \qquad (2)$$

Equations 1 and 2 provide the bases for the process dissociation calculations used in Experiment 2.[3] The base-rate parameters, $p(b_E)$ and $p(b_I)$, are

---

[3]Because the inclusion–exclusion distinction for a given study instruction occurred between subjects, but within items, all process dissociation analyses for Experiment 2 of necessity were conducted with items as the unit of analysis. Occasionally, but rarely, the estimate of $p(R) = 1.0$, which results in a division-by-zero error for the subsequent calculation of $p(S | {\sim}R)$. This error means that for these cases there is no estimate of $p(S | {\sim}R)$ possible and the corresponding cases are therefore treated as missing for analyses calling for those values. More frequently

given by the positive or canonical response rates to new items in the various tasks in the appropriate conditions. In direct comparisons, these equations produce estimates patterned very similarly to those of Buchner et al. (1995) and the signal detection approach of Yonelinas and Jacoby (1996) and Yonelinas, Regehr, and Jacoby (1995).

The results are shown in Fig. 5.3, which depicts the estimates of $p(R)$ and $p(S|\sim R)$ as a function of training lag and item instruction for recognition in the top panel and for fragment completion in the bottom panel. As can be seen, neither estimate varied significantly as a function of training lag, for either memory task; that is, increasing the rehearsal opportunities afforded the items had no effect on the estimates of either explicit or implicit retrieval, which presumably accounts for the failure to find an effect of training lag on the performance measures. Otherwise, the results were similar to those of Allen and Vokey (1993) and Vokey and Allen (1993). No effect of directed forgetting was found on $p(S|\sim R)$ or implicit retrieval for either task, suggesting, as in our previous work, that the effects of directed forgetting that were found on recognition were not a consequence of implicit retrieval suppression of forget items. In contrast, significant effects of directed forgetting were found on $p(R)$ or explicit retrieval for both tasks, suggesting first that directed forgetting is a function of differences in explicit retrieval, and second that it also occurred for fragment completion, but was otherwise masked by the noisy mixture of processes responsible for performance in that task. Finally, both estimates were significantly larger for recognition than for fragment completion, indicating that both explicit and implicit specific memory for the items played a larger role in recognition than in fragment completion performance, even for forget items. In fact, also in agreement with our other work, although substantial implicit retrieval was evident for the recognition task, after correcting for responding for reasons other than specific memory as our process dissociation procedure does, there was virtually no specific, implicit retrieval for the fragment completion task, despite its being the nominal standard for "implicit memory" tests.

In sum, although the experiment provided strong evidence that directed forgetting in these tasks is a function of differences in explicit rather than implicit retrieval (and, hence, is not due to implicit retrieval inhibition), once again no evidence was found that these differences vary as a function of rehearsal or, in this case, opportunities for rehearsal. It is not clear whether the failure to find rehearsal effects on directed forgetting occurs because directed forgetting is not a function of such rehearsal differences or because

---

(especially for the forget items, for which it was expected that the actual values would be closer to zero), the estimates of either or both probabilities, $p(R)$ and $p(S|\sim R)$, are negative. On the assumption that all such estimates are subject to some degree of random error with an expected value of zero (i.e., each estimate is as likely to be inflated as deflated), the negative estimates are retained for analysis so that the estimates of the means will remain unbiased.

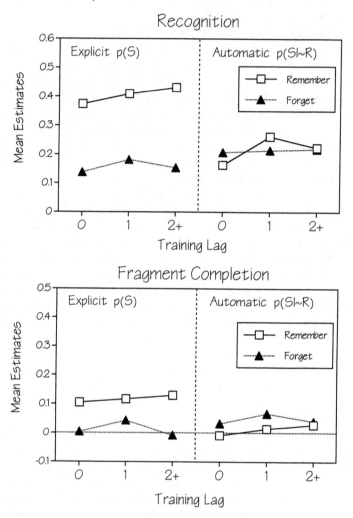

FIG. 5.3. Mean estimates of $p(R)$ and $p(S|\sim R)$ from the process dissociation analysis of Experiment 2 plotted as a function of training instruction and training lag. Items were used as the unit of analysis.

our rehearsal manipulations are merely ineffective. The next experiment investigates the possibility that the rehearsal manipulations were ineffective because subjects failed to capitalize on them.

EXPERIMENT 3: DIRECTED FORGETTING AND INSTRUCTIONS TO REHEARSE

There are at least two reasons why no effect of training lag appeared in the previous studies. One possibility is that the subjects were not really doing what they claimed they were doing. That is, subjects may not have been taking advantage of the additional rehearsal opportunities to retrieve and rehearse the most recent remember item. The other possibility is that they were doing as they claimed but that the additional retrieval/rehearsals added nothing to the memory performance on those items. In this next experiment, rehearsal was controlled through the simple expedient of instructing the subjects to rehearse the items in the same manner that previous subjects had claimed they were doing in response to the instructions to remember and to forget, namely, retrieving and elaboratively rehearsing items they were instructed to remember, and using instructions to forget as periods to retrieve and elaboratively rehearse previous remember items. Subjects were given explicit instructions to use the period following a forget instruction as a retrieval/rehearsal opportunity for the most recent remember item. Thirty-nine subjects participated in this experiment (at least 6 in each of the 6 counterbalancing conditions). Apart from the instructions on how to rehearse, this experiment was identical to the 3-sec condition of the first experiment.

Recognition. The results for recognition are shown in left-hand panels of Fig. 5.4. As in the previous studies, subjects showed substantial memory for the items and a large effect of directed forgetting. Once again, however, there was no interaction of the lag manipulation with the size of the effect of directed forgetting (or any effect of training lag at all).

Fragment Completion. The results for fragment completion are displayed in the right-hand panels of Fig. 5.4. Subjects again showed memory for the old items on this test but did not show an effect of directed forgetting. Analyzed as a function of training lag, there was a reliable interaction between the instruction at training and training lag. However, this interaction was not due to the predicted pattern of results, but rather to a combination of a reliable negative linear trend on the forget items and a reliable quadratic trend on the remember items. Thus, remember items were completed correctly more often than were forget items when two or more additional re-

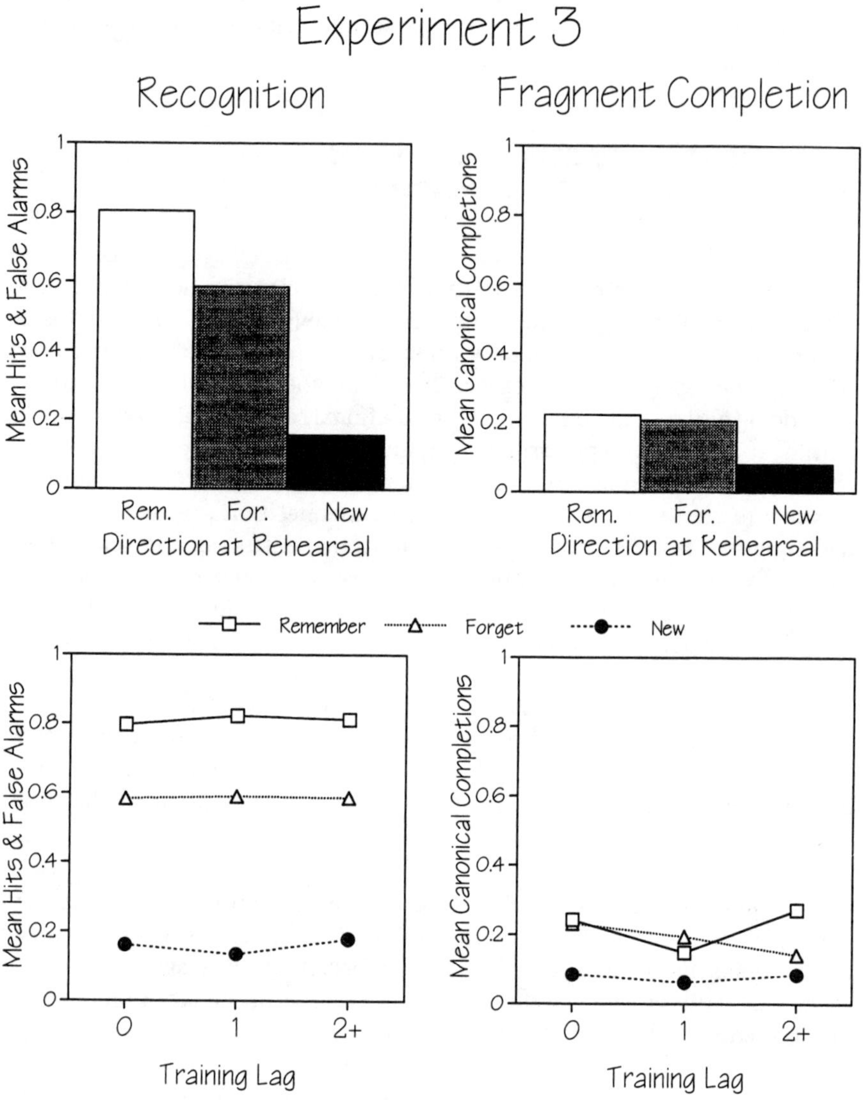

Experiment 3

Recognition
Fragment Completion

FIG. 5.4. Mean hits and false alarms for recognition (left-hand panels), and canonical completions for word fragment completion (right-hand panels) in Experiment 3 plotted as a function of instruction at training. The bottom panels depict the same data as a function of training lag. Subject means are shown in the top panels, and item means in the bottom panels.

hearsal opportunities were provided at training. However, this result was not due to the expected relative increase in completions of remember items given the additional rehearsal, but rather to an inexplicable decrease in the completions of forget items relative to those with no additional rehearsal opportunities.

The results of the experiment as a whole suggest that the failure to find effects of the manipulation of rehearsal opportunities was not due to the subjects' failure to take advantage of such opportunities. Even when subjects were specifically instructed to use the additional rehearsal opportunities, and claimed to be doing so, recognition and fragment completion rates of remember items were not increased by the additional rehearsals. That is, recognition and fragment completion rates for the remember items, those likely to be affected by increased rehearsal, did not increase with rehearsal opportunities and consequently did not increase the effect of directed forgetting. Rather, where a directed-forgetting effect did occur, namely in the recognition test, the size of such an effect was as large at the zero lag level as at any other, suggesting that the mechanism responsible for the directed-forgetting effect was acting at the time of the first instruction to remember or to forget the item, and that additional rehearsal opportunities played no significant role in directed forgetting.

SUMMARY AND CONCLUSION

Throughout the three experiments reported in this chapter, there was no evidence that increased rehearsal opportunities have any effect on the consequences of an instruction to remember or to forget an item, at least for these tasks and procedures. Directed forgetting always occurred on the recognition tests and it occurred to the same degree regardless of whether subjects had 1 or 3 seconds to retrieve and process an item following the instruction, whether subjects had 0, 1, 2 or 3 additional rehearsal opportunities immediately following the instruction, and whether subjects were explicitly instructed to use the rehearsal opportunities provided them and claimed to be doing so. Furthermore, the results of the process dissociation analysis confirmed the findings of Allen and Vokey (1993) and Vokey and Allen (1993) that directed forgetting in these tasks is a function of differences in explicit rather than implicit retrieval of the items, and therefore cannot be due to implicit retrieval inhibition.

This combination of results is curious. On the one hand, directed forgetting has been shown to be a function of explicit retrieval, but on the other, it has been found to be impervious to the influences of the kinds of rehearsal manipulations that normally would be expected to affect explicit retrieval in the first place. As outlined earlier, the source of the effect could be some process at the time of the instruction that results in the suppression of the explicit retrieval of the forget items; that simple differences in rehearsal between remember and forget items cannot account for directed forgetting, and that some inhibitory process is therefore responsible.

To make such an argument assumes that having established that longer and additional rehearsal periods do not influence directed forgetting means that all differences in rehearsal are ineffective, and that the rehearsal differences we manipulated were the only such differences between remember and forget items. However, regardless of what additional rehearsal opportunities we provided or asked our subjects to use for remember items, there was still one rehearsal opportunity that of necessity remained, namely, that provided by the initial instruction to remember or to forget. In fact, because directed forgetting occurred even for items immediately followed by a remember item (i.e., zero lag), and remained constant regardless of the period length or the number of additional periods, the directed forgetting effect must be established relatively quickly in that initial retrieval and rehearsal opportunity. As mentioned, Wetzel and Hunt (1977) also found pronounced differences in the recall and final recognition of remember and forget items in their minimal rehearsal condition. Thus, a mechanism operating at the very first rehearsal opportunity that increases the explicit retrieval of the remember items remains plausible.

One of the possibilities along these lines that we are currently investigating is the idea that a single act of retrieval for the remember items in response to the instruction to remember is itself an act of rehearsal sufficient to establish the phenomenon of directed forgetting. We think, for example, following Jacoby (1978), that this initial retrieval of remember, but not forget items, like the initial solving of a problem, results in the bulk of the explicit memory for the item as a solution (on direct memory tests such as recognition, and on indirect memory tests such as fragment completion). Subsequent retrievals, as we asked for with our lag manipulation, are more akin to subsequent retrievals of a solution in that they are relatively ineffective as rehearsal episodes (Jacoby, 1978); that is, only the first retrieval enhances subsequent recognition. We are investigating this possibility in a number of different ways. In one study, for example, we are replacing the remember and forget prompts of the directed-forgetting experiments with requests to retrieve either the immediately preceding item, or some other (filler) prior item. According to this single retrieval hypothesis of directed forgetting, the request to retrieve the immediately preceding item corresponds to the instruction to remember that item in a directed-forgetting experiment, whereas the request to retrieve a filler item, blocking the retrieval of the immediately preceding item, corresponds to the instruction to forget the immediately preceding item in a directed forgetting experiment. We anticipate that not only will these manipulations produce results analogous to directed forgetting on direct memory tasks, such as recognition, and on indirect memory tasks, such as fragment completion and lexical decision, but that asking for subsequent multiple retrievals within the same training task will prove no more effective than did our lag manipulation in our current experiments. Conversely, in other experiments we will distribute, rather than mass, these retrievals, in a fashion more akin to the multiple recall tests that preceded Wetzel and Hunt's (1977) final recognition task. Under such conditions, we anticipate finding rehearsal effects of directed forgetting similar to those found by Wetzel and Hunt. Thus, despite the ineffectiveness of the common rehearsal manipulations in the experiments in this chapter, in the absence of a clear mechanism for explicit retrieval inhibition, and the presence of such rehearsal possibilities as the single retrieval hypothesis, we remain drawn to a rehearsal explanation for directed forgetting.

ACKNOWLEDGMENTS

This research was supported by operating grants from the Natural Sciences and Engineering Research Council of Canada to each of the authors. We thank especially Brenda Boulton, Margy Hicken, Jennifer Relf, and Chad Martin for their able assistance in collecting the data, and M. Jesse Martin for his contributions to earlier phases of the project. Jonathan Golding and Colin MacLeod deserve thanks for their thorough and insightful review of an earlier draft of this chapter.

REFERENCES

Allen, S. W., & Vokey, J. R. (1993, November). *Process dissociations of directed forgetting: Recognized and unrecognized retrieval*. Paper presented at the annual meeting of the Psychonomic Society, Washington, DC.

Basden, B. H., Basden, D. R., & Coe, W. C. (1994). Retrieval inhibition in directed forgetting and posthypnotic amnesia. *International Journal of Clinical and Experimental Hypnosis, 42,* 184–203.

Basden, B. H., Basden, D. R., & Gargano, G. J. (1993). Directed forgetting in implicit and explicit memory tests: A comparison of methods. *Journal of Experimental Psychology: Learning, Memory, and Cognition, 19,* 603–616.

Bjork, R. A. (1972). Theoretical implications of directed forgetting. In A. W. Melton & E. Martin (Eds.), *Coding processes in human memory* (pp. 217–235). Washington, DC: Winston.

Bjork, R. A. (1989). Retrieval inhibition as an adaptive mechanism in human memory. In H. L. Roediger, III & F. I. M. Craik (Eds.), *Varieties of memory and consciousness: Essays in honour of Endel Tulving* (pp. 309–330). Hillsdale, NJ: Lawrence Erlbaum Associates.

Buchner, A., Erdfelder, E., & Vaterrodt-Plünnecke, B. (1995). Toward unbiased measurement of C and U memory processes within the process dissociation framework. *Journal of Experimental Psychology: General, 124,* 137–160.

Curran, T., & Hintzman, D. (1995). Violations of the independence assumption in process dissociation. *Journal of Experimental Psychology: Learning, Memory, and Cognition, 21*, 531–547.

Epstein, W. (1972). Mechanisms of directed forgetting. In G. H. Bower (Ed.), *The psychology of learning and motivation* (Vol. 6, pp. 147–191). New York: Academic Press.

Geiselman, R. E., & Bagheri, B. (1985). Repetition effects in directed forgetting: Evidence for retrieval inhibition. *Memory & Cognition, 13*, 57–62.

Geiselman, R. E., Bjork, R. A., & Fishman, D. L. (1983). Disrupted retrieval in directed forgetting: A link with posthypnotic amnesia. *Journal of Experimental Psychology: General, 112*, 58–72.

Golding, J. M., Fowler, S. B., Long, D. L., & Latta, H. (1990). Instructions to disregard potentially useful information: The effects of pragmatics on evaluative judgments and recall. *Journal of Memory and Language, 29*, 212–227.

Jacoby, L. L. (1978). On interpreting the effects of repetition: Solving a problem versus remembering a solution. *Journal of Verbal Learning and Verbal Behavior, 17*, 649–667.

Jacoby, L. L. (1983a). Perceptual enhancement: Persistent effects of an experience. *Journal of Experimental Psychology: Learning, Memory, and Cognition, 9*, 21–38.

Jacoby, L. L. (1983b). Remembering the data: Analyzing interactive processes in reading. *Journal of Verbal Learning and Verbal Behavior, 22*, 485–508.

Jacoby, L. L. (1991). A process dissociation framework: Separating automatic from intentional uses of memory. *Journal of Memory and Language, 30*, 513–541.

Jacoby, L. L., Toth, J. P., & Yonelinas, A. P. (1993). Separating conscious and unconscious influences of memory: Measuring recollection. *Journal of Experimental Psychology: General, 122*, 139–154.

Joordens, S., & Merikle, P. (1993). Independence or redundancy? Two models of conscious and unconscious influences. *Journal of Experimental Psychology: General, 122*, 462–467.

Kihlstrom, J. F. (1983). Instructed forgetting: Hypnotic and nonhypnotic. *Journal of Experimental Psychology: General, 112*, 73–79.

MacLeod, C. M. (1975). Long-term recognition and recall following directed forgetting. *Journal of Experimental Psychology: Human Learning and Memory, 1*, 271–279.

MacLeod, C. M. (1989). Directed forgetting affects both direct and indirect tests of memory. *Journal of Experimental Psychology: Learning, Memory, and Cognition, 15*, 13–21.

Paller, K. A. (1990). Recall and stem-completion priming have different electrophysiological correlates and are modified differently by directed forgetting. *Journal of Experimental Psychology: Learning, Memory, and Cognition, 16*, 1021–1032.

Richardson-Klavehn, A., Gardiner, J. M., & Java, R. I. (1994). Involuntary conscious memory and the method of opposition. *Memory, 2*, 1–29.

Richardson-Klavehn, A., Lee, M. G., Joubran, R., & Bjork, R. A. (1994). Intention and awareness in perceptual identification priming. *Memory & Cognition, 22*, 293–312.

Roediger, H. L., III. (1990). Implicit memory: Retention without remembering. *American Psychologist, 45*, 1043–1056.

Russo, R., & Andrade, J. (1995). The directed forgetting effect in word-fragment completion: An application of the process dissociation procedure. *The Quarterly Journal of Experimental Psychology, 48A*, 405–423.

Simon, R. (1966). Murder, juries, and the press: Does sensational reporting lead to verdicts of guilty? *Transaction, 3*, 40–42.

Tulving, E., Schacter, D. L., & Stark, H. A. (1982). Priming effects in word-fragment completion are independent of recognition memory. *Journal of Experimental Psychology: Learning, Memory, and Cognition, 8*, 336–342.

Vokey, J. R., & Allen, S. W. (1993). *Process dissociations of directed forgetting: Recognized and unrecognized retrieval* (Tech. Rep. No. 93-2). University of Lethbridge, Dept. of Psychology. Available: http://www.uleth.ca/~Vokey/

Weiner, B., & Reed, H. (1969). Effects of the instructional sets to remember and to forget on short-term retention: Studies of rehearsal control and retrieval inhibition (repression). *Journal of Experimental Psychology, 79*, 226–232.

Wetzel, C. D. (1975). Effect of orienting tasks and cue timing on the free recall of remember- and forget-cue words. *Journal of Experimental Psychology: Human Learning and Memory, 1,* 556–566.

Wetzel, C. D., & Hunt, R. E. (1977). Cue delay and the role of rehearsal in directed forgetting. *Journal of Experimental Psychology: Human Learning and Memory, 3,* 233–245.

Woodward, A. E., Jr., Bjork, R. A., & Jongeward, R. H., Jr. (1973). Recall and recognition as a function of primary rehearsal. *Journal of Verbal Learning and Verbal Behavior, 12,* 608–617.

Wyer, R., & Unverzagt, W. (1985). Effects of instructions to disregard information on its subsequent recall and use in making judgments. *Journal of Personality and Social Psychology, 48,* 533–549.

Yonelinas, A. P., & Jacoby, L. L. (1996). Response bias and the process-dissociation procedure. *Journal of Experimental Psychology: General, 125,* 422–434.

Yonelinas, A. P., Regehr, G., & Jacoby, L. L. (1995). Incorporating response bias in a dual-process theory of memory. *Journal of Memory and Language, 34,* 821–835.

6

AN ILLUSION OF RETRIEVAL INHIBITION: DIRECTED FORGETTING AND IMPLICIT MEMORY

Jerry Hauselt
Southern Connecticut State University

The retrieval inhibition model of directed forgetting proposes that access to to-be-forgotten (TBF) items is blocked or inhibited as a result of a forget instruction (Bjork, 1989; Geiselman, Bjork, & Fishman, 1983). The value of the model is that it can account for directed forgetting that is unexplainable by the selective rehearsal of to-be-remembered items. Memory is often successfully updated in situations where rehearsal is not common, such as when errors in communication occur and when errata are corrected. For example, suppose that a colleague tells you that a committee meeting has been scheduled for the next day at noon. Later that day, the same colleague stops you in the hall and tells you that she was incorrect and the meeting time actually is 2 hours later. Many of us would be unlikely to rehearse the new meeting time; we would simply thank her, continue on down the hall, and make the meeting on time without rehearsing the new time. Retrieval inhibition provides a way of keeping memory current that makes interference from irrelevant information unlikely.

In experimental situations, selective rehearsal mechanisms have trouble accounting for directed forgetting of incidentally learned material. For example, subjects in a study by Geiselman et al. (1983) performed both an intentional learning task and an incidental learning task (rating pleasantness) alternately on a series of words. Halfway through the list, one group was given a forget instruction. As expected, these subjects recalled fewer intentionally learned words than a control group that was not instructed to forget. However, recall of the incidentally learned (rated) words also displayed a directed-forgetting effect. Fewer rated words were remembered by subjects instructed to forget than by subjects in the control group. As rehearsal was not necessary for the rating task, selective rehearsal mechanisms failed to adequately explain this effect.

Similarly, directed forgetting on implicit memory tests, which can be completed without specific reference to a study episode, (see Roediger, 1990; Schacter, 1987) would seem unexplainable by a selective rehearsal account. In a discussion on this point, MacLeod (1989) noted that; (a) implicit tests of memory are generally immune to manipulations of elaboration (Richardson-Klavehn & Bjork, 1988); thus (b) any directed forgetting on an implicit test is unlikely to have been caused by an elaborative difference between to-be-remembered (TBR) and to-be-forgotten (TBF) words; therefore (c) any directed forgetting on an implicit test of memory is probably retrieval based.

MacLeod (1989) tested this logic in two experiments. In both studies, words were presented to subjects for 1 sec with the memory instruction, either "RRRR" or "FFFF" for "remember" and "forget," respectively, following immediately for 3 secs. Both explicit and implicit tests, recognition and fragment completion in the first experiment, and free recall and lexical decision in the second, were conducted. Reliable directed-forgetting effects were found on both the explicit and the implicit memory tests in both experiments. MacLeod's results are important because they may represent converging evidence for the retrieval inhibition mechanism. In this case, retrieval inhibition was indicated not by a directed-forgetting effect on incidental items, as in Geiselman et al. (1983), but by a directed-forgetting effect on an implicit memory test.

Although MacLeod's (1989) results seem to be compelling evidence for retrieval inhibition, several problems can be identified with his study. First, it should be noted that these results are not entirely consistent with a retrieval inhibition model. That is, despite MacLeod's claim to present evidence in support of retrieval inhibition, there is an inconsistency between his results and other studies that support the retrieval inhibition model. Specifically, MacLeod found a directed-forgetting effect on a recognition test. Geiselman et al. (1983), however, did not find a directed-forgetting effect on a recognition test. Furthermore, Geiselman et al. used the *lack* of a directed forgetting effect in recognition as evidence for a release from inhibition. According to the retrieval inhibition model, presenting the words on a recognition test should be sufficient to remove the inhibitory block that prevents access to the TBF words. Also, MacLeod presented the memory instructions immediately after each word. Later work by Basden, Basden, and Gargano (1993) suggests that retrieval inhibition is likely only when memory instructions are provided after a block of words (list method presentation) and not when item-by-item (word method) instructions are used.

Therefore, retrieval inhibition may not be present in MacLeod's study even though the implicit test results seem to be compelling evidence.

Moreover, the presence of directed-forgetting effects on implicit tests of memory has not turned out to be a consistent finding on studies subsequent to MacLeod's (1989). Paller (1990) did not find such effects when the TBF and TBR instructions were presented to subjects simultaneously with the words to which they were associated. In this study, subjects were told to forget words appearing in one color and to remember words appearing in another. Words were presented individually for 200 ms with a 1300 ms pause between words. To insure that all of the words were processed, subjects were given the task of monitoring the presented words for members of a specific target category (color names). Paller reasoned that the simultaneous presentation of the instruction, along with the semantic search task, was equivalent to the delayed cue presentation used by MacLeod (1989). That is, both procedures required subjects to attend to the TBF words. Subjects were tested with either a cued recall test or a stem-completion task. The cues and stems were the same in both tests; only the instructions on how they were to be used differed, following the logic of Graf and Mandler (1984).

The results indicated that although a directed-forgetting effect was found on the cued recall test, the effect was absent from the stem-completion test. Paller (1990) concluded that retrieval inhibition was not present due to the lack of directed forgetting on the stem-completion test. Instead, he argued that selective rehearsal of the TBR and TBF words was the cause of the observed directed-forgetting effect on the cued recall test. Event-related potential (ERP) data collected during the study also supported this conclusion. These data, which have been correlated with memory performance, assess the electrical activity of the brain in response to environmental stimuli (see Hillyard & Kutas, 1983; Kutas, 1988, for reviews). The ERP data showed differences in the patterns of electrical activity for TBR and TBF words as soon as 250 ms after the words had been presented; electrical activity at this early stage was greater for TBR words than TBF words.

In reconciling his results with those of MacLeod (1989), Paller (1990) suggested that the implicit tests used by MacLeod (fragment completion and lexical decision) may have been subject to explicit memory strategies, thereby transforming them into explicit tests. For the lexical decision test, subjects may have anticipated the presentation of TBR words and this anticipatory retrieval would have given the TBR words a small reaction time advantage over the TBF words. As for the fragment completion test, Paller noted that each word fragment had only one possible completion. The extended search of memory needed to find the correct completion may have "reminded" subjects of the presentation episode. In support of this point, Squire, Shimamura, and Graf (1987) reported that amnesic patients did not perform well on completion tests in which there was only one possible completion for each stem or fragment. This lack of facilitation is similar to what occurs when explicit memory is tested. That is, performance on implicit memory tests with a single possible answer is not different from explicit test performance. Therefore, the difficulty that Squire et al.'s (1987) amnesic patients experienced suggests that explicit memory processes may be needed to perform completion tasks on which unique answers are required.

Further support for the conclusion that directed-forgetting effects on implicit tests are the result of selective rehearsal processes through contamination by explicit memory can also be found in Basden et al. (1993). They tested for directed-forgetting effects following word-method or list-method presentation of the memory instructions using both implicit and explicit memory tests. Basden et al. suggested that the mechanism of directed forgetting may be associated with the type of processing, either item specific (distinctive) or relational (Einstein & Hunt, 1980; Hunt & Einstein, 1981), that each presentation method encourages. Word-method instructions set up distinctive processing, which focuses on the uniqueness of each word in a list. In this case, directed forgetting through a selective rehearsal mechanism may be more likely, as TBR words would be processed more elaboratively than TBF words. A list-method instruction, on the other hand, favors relational processing, or processing each word in terms of characteristics shared with other list words. As the TBR words share the characteristics of memory instruction and of temporal position in the experiment (i.e., to-be-remembered and second half of the list), these words would be processed together. Such processing would make retrieval inhibition a likely means of blocking interference; subjects would only have to inhibit the retrieval of the TBF set, and not each word individually.

The results of the explicit memory tests in the Basden et al. (1993) study supported their hypotheses. As expected from a selective rehearsal model, directed forgetting was found for both recall and recognition following word-method presentation of the memory instructions. List-method memory instructions, however, led to directed forgetting on recall, but not recognition, consistent with a retrieval-inhibition explanation of directed forgetting.

In regard to implicit memory test performance, however, Basden et al. (1993) noted that because MacLeod (1989) used a word-method instruction method, directed forgetting would have been based upon a selective rehearsal mechanism. Therefore, only explicit memory tests, and not implicit memory tests should have been affected. On the implicit tests in three of their four experiments, Basden et al. found no directed forgetting. These experiments used two different implicit memory tests, word association and fragment completion. On the fragment completion tests used in these studies, each item on the test could be completed in at least two ways. For the word association test, subjects were instructed to generate words related to stimulus words presented at testing. The stimulus words were words that had not been presented, but were chosen to be related to those that had been presented. Basden et al. found no differences in the frequency of usage between TBR and TBF words on either of these tests in these three experiments. Only in a fourth experiment, using a fragment completion test on which each fragment had only one possible solution, was directed forgetting found on an implicit test.

The purpose of their fourth experiment was to test the hypothesis that MacLeod's (1989) results were contaminated by explicit memory processes. The words for this experiment were selected from the pool of words used by MacLeod, and were presented using the same word and instruction (hereafter called "trial") times as MacLeod used. Furthermore, the length of the list presented to subjects was varied. Subjects in this study received either 32 words (16 words per memory instruction) or 16 words (8 words per memory instruction). The results found no differences due to memory instructions on the fragment completion test following list-method presentation of the instructions. A directed-forgetting effect was found when the instructions were presented using the word method, but only when the list of words was relatively long.

Because directed forgetting was present only when the list was relatively long, Basden et al. (1993) concluded that explicit retrieval processes were responsible. A long list of words requires that the corresponding implicit memory test also be long, thereby increasing the probability that subjects will notice the correspondence between the presentation and test. If subjects are aware of this relation, they may be likely to use their memory of the words to complete the implicit test. This problem is compounded when, as for the words from the pool used by MacLeod (1989), there is only a single possible answer for each implicit test item.

Despite the logic used by MacLeod (1989), the use of implicit memory tests as an indicator of retrieval inhibition does not seem plausible given the more recent work of Basden et al. (1993) and Paller (1990). These studies suggest that MacLeod's implicit memory tests were not implicit tests at all, but were contaminated by explicit memory processes. The methods and procedures of the various implicit studies vary greatly, however. The major purpose of the present series of experiments was to more closely examine the validity of using implicit memory tests in directed forgetting.

EXPERIMENT I

Experiment 1 was conducted to clarify the role of implicit memory tests in assessing retrieval inhibition. The procedures used by previous research in this area are as widely varied as the conclusions. One purpose of this experiment was to directly compare simultaneous and delayed memory cues. A second purpose was to directly determine the extent to which implicit tests are subject to contamination from explicit memory processes. If implicit tests are completed using implicit memory processes, then subjects should not be aware of the relation between the words presented and the test itself. None of the previous studies directly examined subjects' level of awareness regarding the purpose of the implicit memory tests. In the present study, this was accomplished through the use of a posttest questionnaire.

The present study used the word-method instruction procedure to directly compare the effects of the simultaneous and delayed memory instructions at the intermediate trial presentation times used by Basden et al. (1993) and MacLeod (1989). A search task, to insure that participants fully processed all stimuli, was also used. Following the presentation of the material, both groups received two tests of memory—an implicit test (stem completion) and an explicit test (free recall).

Both instruction conditions in the present study were expected to produce directed-forgetting effects on the recall test (after MacLeod, 1989, and Paller, 1990). The results of greater interest involved the implicit tests of memory. Several outcomes were possible for these results. According to Basden et al. (1993), no directed forgetting was expected to be present because the present experiment utilized an item-method presentation of words and cues. This presentation favored distinctive processing of the words, which should lead to selective rehearsal of the TBR words. However, it remained possible that directed forgetting might still be found. Even with item-method presentation of the memory instructions, directed forgetting may be possible for at least two reasons. First, the stem-completion test may be contaminated by explicit memory processes. In this case, the test would be approached by subjects as a stem-cued recall test and not as a stem-completion test. Second, the test may actually tap implicit memory and indicate the presence of retrieval inhibition. Recall that one of Basden et al.'s (1993) experiments did find directed forgetting on an implicit memory test following word-method presentation. That experiment also utilized the same presentation times as MacLeod (1989). It may be the case that such times allow subjects to engage in relational processing of the presented words. The results of the posttest questionnaire helped to decide between these two alternatives. This questionnaire probed subjects' knowledge of the relation between the stem test and the list presentation. If a large number of subjects reported being aware that the stem test was actually a memory test, explicit contamination of the indirect memory test would be indicated.

This experiment used a 2 (instruction) × 2 (delay) × 2 (test order) mixed-factors design. Half of the words presented to each subject were associated with a "forget" instruction; the other half were associated with a "remember" instruction. There was also a delay factor: Subjects were presented with the memory instructions either simultaneously with each word (immediate) or

1 sec after each word was presented (delayed). After the presentation of all the words, each subject completed a free recall test and a stem-completion test. The order in which these tests were administered was counterbalanced between subjects (test order), but this variable is not considered further because it had little impact and is not related to the key predictions.

The 192 words used in the experiment were selected from the words used by Paller (1990). These were divided into four lists of 48 words each for presentation. Assignment of each list as the 48 TBR words, the 48 TBF words, or as half of the 96 distractors on the stem-completion test was accomplished using a Latin square. Six more words were used as buffer words to prevent primacy and recency effects. All buffer words were associated with the TBR instruction and were not scored. Furthermore, 10 color words were used for the target search words. For each subject, half of the color words were associated with the TBR instruction and half with the TBF instruction. The reason for the use of a predefined semantic category as target words was to make the search-set words distinct from the experimental-set words.

Sixty-four subjects were tested individually. They were told that the purpose of the experiment was to see how well they could remember words while performing a secondary monitoring task. The instructions informed them that a series of words followed by asterisks (e.g., *****) would be presented. Subjects were told to remember the words, and to monitor the list for the specified color names. They were told to say those color words aloud to indicate that they had been seen.

Subjects were also told that the computer would indicate which words were to be remembered. The colors red and green were used for the memory instructions and each color was used equally often across subjects for each memory instruction. Words were presented for 1 second and asterisks were presented for 3 seconds. In the immediate condition, memory instructions were indicated by the color in which the word itself was presented; asterisks were presented in the same color as the preceding word. Thus, the memory instructions were available simultaneously with the presentation of each word. In the delayed condition, the memory instructions were not presented until 1 second after the word had been removed from the screen. In this condition, memory instructions were presented through the color of the asterisks presented after each word. The words were presented in white; the asterisks were either red or green. Subjects were warned that color names would be associated with both TBR and TBF memory instructions and that the instructions also applied to these words.

After the instructions, subjects were given practice according to the delay condition to which they had been assigned. The practice session presented three TBR words, three TBF words, and two color name words (one associated with each memory instruction) in a single random order to all subjects. The purpose of the practice was to familiarize subjects with the presentation, including the semantic search task, and to reinforce the validity of the memory instructions. When practice was concluded, subjects were asked to recall only the words that had been associated with the remember instruction, and were provided with feedback regarding their performance.

The experimental period began once subjects indicated that they understood their task. The experimental words were presented in a different random order for each subject. After the list had been presented, subjects received both a free recall test and a stem-completion test, with order counterbalanced. The free recall test assessed a subject's memory for all of the critical words and not just those that they were instructed to remember. All subjects were given 10 minutes to recall as much as possible.

Several steps were taken to maintain the implicit nature of the stem-completion test. First, subjects were told that the stem-completion test was part of a separate experiment testing the vocabularies of college students. Second, 96 distractor stems not related to the presented words were included to minimize the likelihood of unintentional identification of the experimental words as the source of the answers for the stem completion test. Third, subjects were told that they should write down completions for the stems as rapidly as possible.

After completing both memory tests, subjects were asked the following question: "Did you try to complete the word stems with words that had been presented or just the first word to come to mind?" This question was included to assess whether subjects noticed the relation between the stem-completion test and the list presentation.

The Explicit Free Recall Test

Directed forgetting should be demonstrated by subjects in both the immediate and delayed conditions. To assess this prediction, the proportions of TBR and TBF words correctly recalled were analyzed. Overall, more TBR words ($M = .22$, $SD = .13$) than TBF words ($M = .04$, $SD = .04$) were recalled, but no other effects were significant (all results are significant at $p < .05$, unless otherwise noted). Therefore, the recall results indicate that directed forgetting was present and did not vary between the delay conditions.

The Implicit Stem-Completion Test

The stem-completion results were examined for the presence of priming before directed-forgetting effects were assessed. When the words were not studied, they were rarely used as completions ($M = .09$, $SD = .03$). Compared to this baseline completion rate, priming was evident for words associated with both memory instructions. Reliably more words were used as completions when they were presented as TBR words ($M = .24$, $SD = .08$) or TBF words ($M = .21$, $SD = .07$). Thus, there was evidence that the stem-completion test may have tapped implicit memory; simply presenting words increased the probability that they would be used as completions for the word stems.

To determine if directed forgetting was present on the stem-completion test, an analysis combining instruction and delay was carried out. Reliably more TBR words ($M = .24$, $SD = .08$) were used as completions for the stems than TBF words ($M = .21$, $SD = .07$). Thus, directed forgetting on an implicit memory was present in this experiment. Moreover, directed forgetting did not differ between the immediate and delayed memory instruction conditions.

The Posttest Question

The responses of each subject to the posttest question regarding the stem-completion test were categorized by a scorer who was not informed of each subject's condition. These responses were classified according to how subjects reported their performance on that test. Only 30% of subjects ($n = 19$) reported completing the stems with the first word to come to mind. The remaining 70% reported trying to use words that had been presented ($n = 4$) or some mixture of the previous two strategies ($n = 40$; the questionnaire was accidentally omitted for one of the 64 subjects). From these results, it can be concluded that the majority of subjects were aware that the stem-completion test was related to the words that had been presented. Thus, it seems likely that the stem-completion test was compromised by explicit memory processes.

The results of this experiment showed that, as expected, directed forgetting was present on the explicit test of memory regardless of whether the memory instructions were presented simultaneously with the words or after each word was removed. In each case, subjects were able to use the instructions effectively to prevent interference from the TBF words. This finding was consistent with previous studies of directed forgetting (Basden et al., 1993; MacLeod, 1989; Paller, 1990). Directed-forgetting effects were also found on the stem-completion test regardless of the memory instruction delay condition. Therefore, the present results suggest that the lack of directed forgetting on the stem-completion test in Paller (1990) may have been related to the short trial presentation time and not to the simultaneous memory instructions. Thus, the results for the implicit test replicate the pattern observed by MacLeod and by Basden et al. (Experiment 4) in fragment completion, but not by Basden et al. (Experiments 1–3) in word association and fragment completion or by Paller in stem completion.

In the present study, however, a large majority of subjects reported that they were aware that previously presented words could have been used as completions, and most tried to do so at least some of the time. Given these results, it seems likely that the nominally implicit stem-completion test may have been treated by subjects as if it was an explicit test of memory. If this was the case, then the directed-forgetting effect in stem completion could be due to selective rehearsal intruding via intentional recollection. Even though the results of the posttest question may only indicate that subjects noticed the correspondence after they had written the completions, it is likely that this knowledge affected how subjects completed the subsequent items. Given the importance of this issue for the interpretation of the results, the possibility that the stem-completion tests were contaminated by explicit recollection of the list presentation was examined more closely in Experiment 2.

EXPERIMENT 2

The purpose of Experiment 2 was to determine whether explicit memory processes could be ruled out as the cause of the directed forgetting observed on the stem-completion test in Experiment 1. Through explicit contamination, the implicit test results in Experiment 1 may reflect selective rehearsal and not retrieval inhibition. Previous research investigating selective rehearsal by Wetzel (1975) and Wetzel and Hunt (1977) showed that directed forgetting can be attenuated if the total time for rehearsal of TBR words across a list of words is reduced. In these studies, when the amount of time between words was reduced, TBR memory performance was also reduced, thereby attenuating directed forgetting. Experiment 2 manipulated the time subjects had for rehearsal whereas total list presentation time remained constant. If the directed-forgetting effect on the implicit tests was affected by this manipulation, clear evidence that those effects are rehearsal based would be present. If directed forgetting is based on retrieval inhibition, then manipulating rehearsal time should not affect directed forgetting on the implicit test.

This study required three groups of subjects. Two groups were given the same instructions as the delayed memory instruction condition in Experiment 1. Rehearsal time was varied between these two groups by instructing subjects in one group to count aloud whenever a word was associated with a forget instruction. A selective rehearsal explanation predicts that when subjects are presented with a forget cue, previous TBR words are rehearsed (Bjork, 1972). By forcing subjects to count after the TBF words, rehearsal of the TBR words during this period is prevented, and the total rehearsal time for the TBR words across the list is cut in half. This manipulation should reduce the magnitude of the directed forgetting on the explicit test if the effect is a result of selective rehearsal. Moreover, if the stem-completion test is affected by explicit memory processes, restricting selective rehearsal should attenuate the difference between the TBR and TBF words on this test as well. If, however, directed forgetting is caused by retrieval inhibition, the manipulation of rehearsal time should not affect either test.

A third group of subjects served as a control group. These subjects in this group were told to remember all of the words, and to count aloud after half of the words when instructed. The purpose of the control group was to assess the effects of the counting task alone on memory. Because the instruction to forget was confounded with counting for one of the two groups described earlier, differences in TBR and TBF word memory in this group could be due either to the memory instructions or to counting. If counting has no effect on memory apart from preventing rehearsal, then no differences on either test of memory should be present between TBR words followed as compared to not followed by a counting instruction. If, however, counting interferes with memory for the words that are associated with the counting instruction, counting aloud would negatively affect memory for these words. This would result in differential memory that mimics directed forgetting.

To summarize, then, the three tasks manipulated between subjects were; (a) remember half of the words and forget the other half (the forget group); (b) remember half of the words and forget the other half while counting aloud after the words cued as to-be-forgotten (the count-TBF group); and (c) remember all of the words but count aloud after half (the count-TBR group). The within-subject variable was instruction (remember vs. forget). After the presentation of the words, each subject completed a free recall test, a stem-completion test, and a posttest question. The order in which the two memory tests were administered was again counterbalanced between subjects, but is not considered further.

The words used in this experiment, and the assignment of words to conditions, were the same as in Experiment 1. In this experiment, however, the simultaneous memory instructions were not used, eliminating the need for the detection task. Therefore, the 10 color names were not included. The procedure for this experiment also followed that of Experiment 1, except that three-digit numbers (e.g., 527) appeared in the place of the asterisks. All words were presented in white, whereas the numbers were presented in either red or green.

The instructions for each group of subjects differed depending on the condition to which they had been assigned. Subjects in the directed-forgetting groups (the forget and count-TBF groups) were instructed to use the color of the three-digit numbers as a memory instruction. That is, each subject was told to remember only those words followed by a certain color. In one of these groups, the count-TBF group, the color of the number following each word served not only as a memory instruction (e.g., red–remember; green–forget), but also as a cue to count backwards by 3 from that number. The counting was always associated with the color indicating TBF words. In the final condition, the count-TBR condition, subjects were told to remember all of the words, regardless of the color of the subsequent three-digit number. For these subjects, the color served only as a cue to begin counting backwards. For example, when the number was green, half of the subjects were told to begin counting backwards by 3 from that number.

After the instructions were presented, subjects were given practice according to the task condition to which they had been assigned, and then the experimental period began. The experimental presentation and the testing that followed was the same as in Experiment 1, except that the experimenter remained with the subjects during the presentation period to insure that they followed the counting instructions.

The Explicit Free Recall Test

The main effects of instruction and task were both significant as was the Instruction × Task interaction. As seen in the top half of Table 6.1, differences between the presented words were found only when half of the words were to be forgotten. For the forget condition, more words followed by remember instructions were recalled than words followed by forget instructions. The same was also true of the count-TBF condition, even though subjects were instructed to count after the forget words. From these results, it can also be seen that the counting manipulation reduced the directed- forgetting effect by lowering TBR recall. Subjects in the count-TBF condition recalled reliably fewer TBR words than did subjects in the forget condition, whereas TBF word recall between the groups was not different.

TABLE 6.1
Experiment 2: Mean Proportions and Standard Deviations for the Recall and Stem-Completion Tests as a Function of Task Condition and Instruction

	Task	Instruction	M	SD
Recall				
	Forget	TBR-No Counting	.23	.11
		TBF-No Counting	.04	.04
	Count-TBF	TBR-No Counting	.11	.06
		TBF-Counting	.03	.03
	Count-TBR	TBR-No Counting	.09	.05
		TBR-Counting	.07	.05
Stem Completion				
	Forget	TBR-No Counting	.23	.07
		TBF-No Counting	.16	.05
		Not Presented	.08	.03
	Count-TBF	TBR-No Counting	.20	.06
		TBF-Counting	.18	.07
		Not Presented	.09	.03
	Count-TBR	TBR-No Counting	.20	.08
		TBR-Counting	.19	.06
		Not Presented	.09	.03

The attenuation of the directed-forgetting effect for the count-TBF group appears primarily to have been due to the prevention of rehearsal, and not to interference from the counting task. Counting only marginally affected memory for words in the count-TBR group. The mean for words followed by counting was not reliably different from the mean for words not followed by counting. Therefore, evidence of selective rehearsal was obtained; eliminating the opportunity to rehearse lessened the effect of the remember instruction.

The Implicit Stem-Completion Test

Before the stem-completion test was examined for evidence of directed forgetting, the presence of priming was assessed. The means are presented in the lower half of Table 6.1. For the forget group, reliably more presented words were used as completions than unpresented words, both for TBR words and for TBF words. For the count-TBF group, presented words were also used reliably more often as completions, both for TBR words and for TBF words. This advantage was also evident for the count-TBR condition. Presented words were used more frequently than unpresented words for completions if there was no subsequent counting. Even words that were followed by subsequent counting were used more frequently than unpresented words.

In regard to directed forgetting, it was predicted that if selective rehearsal affected the implicit test results, then stem completion would be differentially affected by the prevention of rehearsal. The relevant analysis found a significant effect of instruction and a significant Instruction × Task interaction, as shown in Table 6.1. More TBR words than TBF words were used on the stem-completion test for the forget group, but not for the count-TBF group. Therefore, the stem-completion test results found that preventing rehearsal attenuated the directed-forgetting effect for the count-TBF group, just as it did on the free recall test. No difference was evident between TBR and TBF words in the count-TBR group. Comparisons between the groups told to forget, however, found that there were no differences between the forget and count-TBF groups in the use of either TBR words or TBF words as completions. Therefore, although there was evidence of attenuation of directed forgetting for the count-TBF group compared to the forget group, the use of TBR and TBF words as completions was not different between these two groups.

The Posttest Question

The responses to the posttest question also support the conclusion that explicit memory processes affect the stem-completion test. These responses were categorized by a scorer who was not informed of each subject's condition and were classified according to how subjects reported their perform-ance. Across the three task conditions, 55% ($n = 53$) of the subjects reported completing the stems with the first word that came to mind. The remaining 45% reported specifically trying to use words that had been presented ($n = 3$) or some mixture of the previous two strategies ($n = 40$). Although fewer subjects in Experiment 2 than Experiment 1 reported being aware of the study–test relation, the overall proportion was still high. Thus, these results indicate that explicit contamination of the stem-completion test was likely for almost half of the subjects.

From the results of this experiment, it can be seen that by preventing rehearsal, the directed-forgetting effect was attenuated on the explicit test of memory. The difference between TBR and TBF words on recall was less for the count-TBF group than for the forget group. The free recall results are consistent with previous research (Wetzel, 1975; Wetzel & Hunt, 1977) that demonstrated the important role of selective rehearsal in directed forgetting. Specifically, these studies showed that as more rehearsal of the TBR words is allowed, the directed-forgetting effect is larger.

The counting manipulation had similar effects on the stem-completion test as well. On this test, directed forgetting was present for the forget group but not the count-TBF group. It was predicted that if these implicit tests were subject to contamination by explicit memory processes, effects of rehearsal prevention would be evident on the stem-completion test. As the counting task did attenuate directed forgetting on the stem-completion test, explicit memory processes can be implicated as the cause of the directed-forgetting effect on this test. The results of the posttest question underscore this conclusion and indicate the difficulty associated with maintaining the implicit nature of these tests, especially when word-method memory instruc-tions are presented.

EXPERIMENT 3

This final experiment was conducted to gain more conclusive evidence that the directed-forgetting effects found on the stem-completion and free recall tests in Experiment 2 were the result of selective rehearsal. Rehearsal was directly manipulated in Experiment 3 by requiring subjects to rehearse the TBR and TBF words aloud equally often. Subjects were required either to repeat each TBR and TBF word aloud three times, or to generate at least three related words aloud (e.g., "tree," "red," and "worm" for the presented word "apple") for each TBR and TBF word. These two rehearsal strategies represent two qualitatively different means by which subjects may rehearse words for a later memory test (Craik & Lockhart, 1972). By constraining the rehearsal of each subject to only one of these methods, it was assumed that rehearsal of TBR and TBF words within each group was both qualitatively and quantitatively equal. That is, both TBR and TBF words were either repeated three times or elaborated three times. Rehearsal in a third condition was unconstrained; subjects were free to rehearse the TBR and TBF words in any fashion, as long as that rehearsal was aloud.

If selective rehearsal is responsible for directed forgetting in this situation, then the constrained rehearsal groups should show no differences between TBR and TBF words on the free recall test. That is, to the extent that directed forgetting is based on the selective rehearsal of TBR words, then the effect should not be found when rehearsal of the TBR and TBF words is equated. The unconstrained rehearsal group subjects, however, should exhibit directed forgetting on this test, as these subjects were free to selectively rehearse only TBR words. If subjects treated the stem-completion test as an explicit test of memory, the rehearsal constraint manipulation should affect the stem-completion test in the same way as the free recall test.

It should be noted that Experiment 3 represented a strong test of retrieval inhibition as a possible mechanism of directed forgetting when memory instructions are presented using the word method. If retrieval inhibition is possible when memory instructions are presented using the word method, subjects in each of the rehearsal conditions should show evidence of directed forgetting. Moreover, these results would be apparent on both the free recall and stem-completion tests. That is, for the constrained rehearsal groups, even though they were forced to rehearse the TBR and TBF words equally often, retrieval inhibition would lead to a difference between the TBR and TBF words. However, if retrieval inhibition is not possible with word-method instructions, no directed-forgetting effects should be seen for the constrained rehearsal groups.

In Experiment 3, there was one within-subjects factor, instruction, and two between-subjects factors, task and test order. As always, the instruction factor refers to the instructions associated with each word, either TBR or TBF. The levels of the task factor were unconstrained rehearsal, rote rehearsal, and elaborative rehearsal. After the presentation of the words, each subject completed a free recall test, a stem-completion test, and a posttest question. The order in which the two memory tests were administered was counterbalanced between subjects.

The experimental and buffer words used in this experiment were the same as in Experiment 2, as was the procedure. In this experiment, however, asterisks followed each word instead of three-digit numbers. All subjects were told that the purpose of the experiment was to determine how people try to remember a list of words; their task was to speak into a tape recorder during the presentation period so that their behavior could be analyzed at a later time. Individual instructions varied depending upon the condition to which subjects had been assigned. Subjects in the unconstrained rehearsal group were instructed to "say aloud whatever you are thinking." Extreme care was taken by the experimenters not to suggest a specific strategy to the subjects in this group. Subjects in the rote and elaborative rehearsal groups also were told to speak aloud, but were instructed to do so in a specific fashion. The rote rehearsal instructions informed subjects that they were to repeat each word aloud three times, and were paced on this task by the asterisks. The asterisks "blinked" once every second during the 3-second period after each word. The elaborative rehearsal instructions informed subjects to generate at least three words related to each presented word during the 3-second period.

After the rehearsal instructions were given, the function of the memory instructions was explained to all of the task groups. Therefore, although each group was given different instructions for rehearsing the words, all subjects were instructed to remember only half of the word list. Subjects were told that not all of the presented words would be on the memory test, and that the computer would signal which words would be tested. Immediately following the instructions, subjects were given practice according to the rehearsal condition to which they had been assigned.

The Explicit Free Recall Test

The operation of selective rehearsal should be prevented by the rehearsal constraints. This would be evident in the results if there was a difference between TBR and TBF words only for the unconstrained rehearsal group; the constrained rehearsal groups should show no such difference. In fact, there were significant main effects of instruction and task, as well as a significant Instruction × Task interaction. As seen in the top half of Table 6.2, more TBR words than TBF words were recalled in the unconstrained rehearsal group and in the rote rehearsal group. The difference between TBR and TBF words was not reliable for the elaborative rehearsal group, however. Thus, although equating rehearsal through rote repetition of TBR and TBF words still led to a directed-forgetting effect, equal elaborative rehearsal of these words removed the effect. It may be that subjects in the rote rehearsal group were able to circumvent the rehearsal constraint. These results suggest that the difference between TBR and TBF words is established through selective rehearsal, which was prevented by requiring elaborative rehearsal of both TBR and TBF words.

The Implicit Stem-Completion Test

Before the predictions regarding directed forgetting were assessed, the stem-completion results were examined for the presence of priming. The means for the TBR words, TBF words, and words not presented in each

TABLE 6.2
Experiment 3: Mean Proportions and Standard Deviations for the Recall
and Stem-Completion Tests as a Function of Task Condition and Instruction

	Task	Instruction	M	SD
Recall				
	Unconstrained	TBR	.23	.07
		TBF	.09	.10
	Rote	TBR	.20	.11
		TBF	.11	.05
	Elaborative	TBR	.23	.06
		TBF	.20	.06
Stem Completion				
	Unconstrained	TBR	.24	.09
		TBF	.20	.07
		Not Presented	.09	.04
	Rote	TBR	.28	.12
		TBF	.29	.10
		Not Presented	.10	.03
	Elaborative	TBR	.30	.13
		TBF	.26	.13
		Not Presented	.09	.03

condition are presented in the lower half of Table 6.2. Subjects in the unconstrained rehearsal group used more TBR and TBF words as completions than unpresented words. Subjects in the rote rehearsal group also used more presented words as completions, both for TBR words and for TBF words. And the elaborative rehearsal group also displayed corresponding evidence of priming. Again, more presented words were used as completions than unpresented words regardless of the memory instruction.

An analysis incorporating task and instruction revealed no significant effects at all. Given the nature of the predictions, however, planned comparisons on the means in the lower half of Table 6.2 were conducted. It was predicted that if the stem-completion test was contaminated by explicit memory processes (i.e., selective rehearsal), these results would have the same pattern as the free recall results. Thus, a difference between TBR and TBF words should only be found for the unconstrained rehearsal group. Indeed, these comparisons found that more TBR words than TBF words were used as completions only in the unconstrained rehearsal group. The difference between the TBR words and the TBF words was not reliable for either the rote rehearsal group or the elaborative rehearsal group. These results indicate that directed forgetting was evident on the stem-completion test, but only for subjects in the unconstrained rehearsal group. As these results generally follow the pattern of the free recall results, it appears that the stem completion test once again was contaminated by explicit memory processes.

The Posttest Question

The responses to the posttest question were categorized by an experimenter who was not informed of each subject's condition. As in the previous two experiments, responses were classified according to how subjects reported performing on the stem-completion test. This analysis found that a majority of subjects were aware of the relation between the presented words and the stem test. Across the three task groups, 40% ($n = 19$) of the subjects reported completing the stem test with only the first words to come to mind. On the other hand, 60% reported using only words that had been presented ($n = 3$) or some mixture of both strategies ($n = 26$). Therefore, the responses to the posttest question suggest that explicit memory processes affected the stem-completion test for a relatively large proportion of subjects. This finding is consistent with the posttest question results of Experiments 1 and 2.

It was predicted that if selective rehearsal processes were responsible for directed forgetting, equating the rehearsal of the TBR and TBF words would not result in directed forgetting. The results of Experiment 3 generally supported this prediction. Whereas the unconstrained rehearsal group demonstrated directed-forgetting effects on both tests, the elaborative rehearsal group demonstrated no directed forgetting at all. The rote rehearsal group, however, did show differential memory of the TBR and TBF words on the explicit free recall test, but not on the implicit stem-completion test. Therefore, it seems that directed-forgetting effects following a word-method presentation procedure are the result of selective rehearsal, and can affect an implicit memory test through explicit contamination.

Even though the free recall performance of the rote rehearsal group seems to argue against this conclusion, this result deserves further discussion. For this group, despite rehearsal of TBR and TBF words being equated, more TBR than TBF words were recalled. Although this may seem to indicate that retrieval inhibition was present, the elaborative rehearsal constraint group results, along with the result of the posttest question, make this conclusion unlikely. Retrieval inhibition should have affected both rehearsal constraint groups similarly, regardless of how rehearsal was equated between TBR and TBF words. In both conditions, subjects' use of selective rehearsal as a mechanism of directed forgetting should have been prevented, making retrieval inhibition necessary. It may be the case, however, that subjects in the rote rehearsal group were still able to selectively rehearse the TBR words. The task of repeating each word three times was paced relatively slowly and may not have been very demanding, thereby allowing subjects to rehearse the TBR words elaboratively. This possibility was examined in a follow-up experiment by repeating the rote rehearsal condition, but instructing subjects to repeat each word as many times as possible in the 3-second period in which the asterisks were presented. Even with this increased rehearsal demand, however, subjects in this fourth group still showed greater recall of the TBR words ($M = .17$, $SD = .06$) than of the TBF words ($M = .09$, $SD = .04$). Postexperiment interviews revealed that subjects were able to rehearse the TBR words in a qualitatively different way than the TBF words, through the use of imagery or elaboration, while repeating the words aloud. Thus, even in the face of a greater attentional demand, subjects were able to differentially rehearse TBR and TBF words. Based on this information, it seems reasonable to conclude that subjects in the original rote rehearsal condition in Experiment 3 may also have been able to circumvent the rehearsal constraints.

CONCLUSION

The study of how individuals update their memory for recent events has focused upon two competing processes, selective rehearsal and retrieval inhibition. Until recently, these two processes have represented mutually exclusive means of reducing interference from irrelevant information in studies of directed forgetting. Basden et al. (1993), however, presented evidence that the mechanisms of directed forgetting are context dependent, relying upon the method by which the instruction to forget is provided.

Although evidence consistent with a retrieval-inhibition interpretation was found in Experiment 1, closer examination indicated that the observed directed forgetting was apparently due to a selective rehearsal mechanism and not to retrieval inhibition. Evidence that explicit retrieval processes affected the implicit tests came from two sources. First, the posttest question results indicated that a large proportion of subjects in each experiment were aware of the correspondence between the studied list and the word stems. By definition, implicit tests are those in which subjects are not aware that their memories are being tested (Schacter, 1987). Second, limiting or preventing selective rehearsal attenuated or removed directed-forgetting effects from both the free recall and stem-completion tests of memory. If directed forgetting through retrieval inhibition was possible in a word-method instruction procedure like the one used here, then the manipulations of rehearsal should not have attenuated directed forgetting.

Therefore, the results of these studies support the operation of a selective rehearsal mechanism when memory instructions are presented in a word-method fashion. This conclusion is consistent with Basden et al. (1993) regarding the relation between the method by which memory instructions are presented and the type of processing that is favored. Although it may seem odd that selective rehearsal would lead to directed forgetting on implicit tests, these tests do not seem to have functioned as implicit tests of memory. Instead, the stem-completion tests were completed as if they were explicit tests of memory. Therefore, it is logical that the stem-completion test was affected by selective rehearsal.

The stem-completion results of this study have implications for the use of implicit memory tests in other contexts. Although implicit tests can be completed without direct reference to the presentation episode, they can also be completed with such reference. Even though subjects may not intentionally refer to the list that was presented, it is extremely difficult to prevent such awareness from developing. Unintentional reminding or involuntary explicit memory (Richardson-Klavehn & Bjork, 1988; Schacter, 1987) seems to have been common in the present study, despite the steps taken to safeguard the nature of the implicit test. These steps included using a large number of distractors, requiring subjects to work as quickly as possible, and explicitly stating that the stem-completion test was part of another experiment. Although steps like these may prevent subjects from initially approaching the stem test as an explicit memory test, there seems to be relatively little a researcher can do to prevent unintentional awareness from developing. One step may be to use smaller lists of words. Basden et al. (1993) suggested that longer lists seem to promote involuntary explicit memory by providing more opportunity for connections to be made. No matter how such reminding occurs, however, future research using implicit tests of memory will have to take into consideration effects due to involuntary explicit memory. The use of a posttest question may prove helpful in indicating when such reminding has occurred.

There are two other issues regarding the present study that need to be discussed. First, it should be noted that although no evidence for retrieval inhibition was found in the present studies, there is substantial evidence for this mechanism from other contexts (e.g., Basden et al., 1993; Geiselman et al., 1983). These studies involved situations in which list-method instructions to forget were provided, and a selective rehearsal explanation was difficult to impose. Moreover, the explanatory power of a retrieval-inhibition model of directed forgetting is appealing when considering more practical, everyday uses of memory, such as remembering that an important meeting has been rescheduled. Therefore, the results of the present experiments can speak only to the context used here; word-method presentation of the memory instructions for a list of words.

The second issue involves the distinctive/relational processing distinction raised by Basden et al. (1993) in regard to directed forgetting. Basden et al. suggested that the word method of presenting memory instructions favors distinctive processing of list words and that it is this processing that favors selective rehearsal. In regard to this issue, it is important to remember that Basden et al. proposed that all words in an experiment experience both types of processing to some degree; the method of presentation only favors one type of processing.

The results of the present study indicate that distinctive processing alone, even though it favors selective rehearsal, is not sufficient for directed forgetting to be found. In Experiment 3, subjects' rehearsal of the TBR and TBF words was constrained such that only individual words were rehearsed. In effect, this manipulation created a situation in which each word was rehearsed in relative isolation from the others and "pure" distinctive processing of each word occurred. The general effect of this manipulation, however, was to erase any differences between TBR and TBF words. The results of the present study highlight the fact that the key to obtaining directed-forgetting effects lies in differential processing of TBR and TBF words (Basden et al., 1993). That is, both TBR and TBF words can be processed distinctively, but the TBR words must be processed differently than the TBF words in some way. The results of the rote rehearsal group in Experiment 3 and the follow-up experiment indicate that subjects can and will go to great lengths to differentially process TBR words through elaboration. It should be noted, however, that when subjects were required to elaborate both the TBR and TBF words in Experiment 3, no memory advantage for the TBR words was found. Apparently, when both TBR and TBF words were elaborated, subjects can find no way to give the TBR words a processing advantage.

In conclusion, this study found evidence that selective rehearsal was the basis for any differences between TBR and TBF words following word-method presentation of memory instructions. Although the implicit test results seemed to indicate retrieval inhibition was present in Experiment 1, the subsequent experiments indicated that this evidence was illusory; the stem-completion tests did not tap implicit memory. Evidence was found that subjects treated these tests as if they were explicit memory tests. In short, the implicit stem-completion test did not accurately reflect implicit memory processes. Therefore, using implicit tests as the only marker for retrieval inhibition may not be warranted, especially when the potential for contamination by explicit memory processes is great.

ACKNOWLEDGMENTS

These studies were conducted as part of a dissertation completed at the University of Kentucky. Parts of this research were presented at the annual meeting of the Eastern Psychological Association, Providence, RI, 1994. I wish to thank Jonathan Golding, Betty Lorch, Bob Lorch, Terry Turner, Suzanne Hauselt, and Colin MacLeod for comments on earlier versions of this paper. I also wish to thank Jackie Premuk and Lorenda Ragland for assistance with data collection.

REFERENCES

Basden, B. H., Basden, D. R., & Gargano, G. J. (1993). Directed forgetting in implicit and explicit memory tests: A comparison of methods. *Journal of Experimental Psychology: Learning, Memory, and Cognition, 19*, 603–616.

Bjork, R. A. (1972). Theoretical implications of directed forgetting. In A. W. Melton & E. Martin (Eds.), *Coding processes in human memory* (pp. 217–235). Washington DC: Winston.

Bjork, R. A. (1989). Retrieval inhibition as an adaptive mechanism in human memory. In H. L. Roediger & F. I. M. Craik (Eds.), *Varieties of memory and consciousness: Essays in honour of Endel Tulving* (pp. 309–330). Hillsdale, NJ: Lawrence Erlbaum Associates.

Craik, F. I. M., & Lockhart, R. S. (1972). Levels of processing: A framework for memory research. *Journal of Verbal Learning and Verbal Behavior, 11*, 671–684.

Einstein, G. O., & Hunt, R. R. (1980). Levels of processing and organization: Additive effects of individual-item and relational processing. *Journal of Experimental Psychology: Human Learning and Memory, 6*, 588–598.

Geiselman, R. E., Bjork, R. A., & Fishman, D. L. (1983). Disrupted retrieval in directed forgetting: A link with posthypnotic amnesia. *Journal of Experimental Psychology: General, 112*, 58–72.

Graf, P., & Mandler, G. (1984). Activation makes words more accessible but not necessarily more retrievable. *Journal of Verbal Learning and Verbal Behavior, 23*, 553–568.

Hillyard, S. A., & Kutas, M. (1983). Electrophysiology of cognitive processing. *Annual Review of Psychology, 34*, 33–61.

Hunt, R. R., & Einstein, G. O. (1981). Relational and item-specific information in memory. *Journal of Verbal Learning and Verbal Behavior, 20*, 497–514.

Kutas, M. (1988). Review of event-related potential studies of memory. In M. Gazzaniga (Ed.), *Perspectives on memory research* (pp. 181–218). Cambridge, MA: MIT Press.

MacLeod, C. M. (1989). Directed forgetting affects both explicit and implicit tests of memory. *Journal of Experimental Psychology: Learning, Memory, and Cognition, 15*, 13–21.

Paller, K. A. (1990). Recall and stem-completion priming have different electrophysiological correlates and are modified differentially by directed forgetting. *Journal of Experimental Psychology: Learning, Memory, and Cognition, 16*, 1021–1032.

Richardson-Klavehn, A., & Bjork, R. A. (1988). Measures of memory. *Annual Review of Psychology, 39*, 475–543.

Roediger, H. L. (1990). Implicit memory: Retention without remembering. *American Psychologist, 45*, 1043–1056.

Schacter, D. L. (1987). Implicit memory: History and current status. *Journal of Experimental Psychology: Learning, Memory, and Cognition, 13*, 501–518.

Squire, L. R., Shimamura, A. P., & Graf, P. (1987). Strength and duration of priming effects in normal subjects and amnesic patients. *Neuropsychologia, 25*, 195–210.

Wetzel, C. D. (1975). Effect of orienting task and cue timing on the free recall of remember- and forget-cued words. *Journal of Experimental Psychology: Human Learning and Memory, 1*, 556–566.

Wetzel, C. D., & Hunt, R. E. (1977). Instruction delay and the role of rehearsal in directed forgetting. *Journal of Experimental Psychology: Human Learning and Memory, 3*, 233–245.

7

DISREGARDING INFORMATION IN TEXT

Hollyn M. Johnson
Washington State University at TriCities

People often face the challenge of disregarding misinformation that they read earlier. For example, someone may read a newspaper account that attributes a family's death to food they had eaten at a Chinese restaurant. Along with the reported facts of the case, one may also store a number of inferences in memory, such as a reminder to avoid this establishment in the future. However, further investigation may reveal that the newspaper's initial speculations were wrong, and the restaurant's food was not responsible for the deaths. In this case, it would be important to disregard the initial misinformation in order to determine what really caused the deaths and who else might be at risk, and to avoid making judgments that have unfair consequences for the innocent restaurant owners. This chapter explores a number of factors that may influence how successful people are in disregarding information presented in text.

Misinformation correction shares a number of characteristics with other tasks that have been considered to involve intentional forgetting. First, a correction provides an overt, unexpected indication that specific material should be disregarded, generally because it is untrue or irrelevant. Some research on directed forgetting (e.g., Bjork, 1970; Epstein, 1969; Geiselman, Bjork, & Fishman, 1983) used similar unexpected, overt disregard instructions,[1] as have

---

[1]This paper focuses mainly on directed-forgetting research that used the list method (Basden, Basden, & Gargano, 1993) rather than the item method. In the list method, participants do not expect to receive a disregard instruction, so they engage in normal processing up to that point. This situation provides a better parallel to misinformation correction than does the item method, in which participants are forewarned that they will receive forget cues for some of the information (see also Johnson, 1994).

a number of studies of social judgments (e.g., Schul & Burnstein, 1985; Thompson, Fong, & Rosenhan, 1981; Wyer & Budesheim, 1987). Second, complying with a correction is likely to involve an intent to forget, so the misinformation does not distort one's understanding of an event or subsequent reasoning about it. Similarly, participants in directed-forgetting studies may intend to forget a cued item from a word list so that it does not interfere with recall or use of other items they should remember. In both of these cases, intentionally forgetting may be more reliable and effective than relying on spontaneous forgetting processes to cope with the undesired information.

For purposes of this chapter, *intentional forgetting* is defined as a motivated attempt to limit the future expression of a specific memory content. This definition goes beyond the traditional view of forgetting as losing access to information stored in memory; it also includes intentional changes in one's decision processes, such as withholding information one has not forgotten in the more traditional sense. The focus on limiting expression of invalid or irrelevant information, by whatever means, seems reasonable in understanding how one disregards information presented in many real-world situations, such as when one is asked to ignore prior misinformation. Accordingly, one may consider a disregard instruction effective if the information it refers to has little further influence on one's subsequent comprehension or judgments. Thus, ideally, people who successfully forget misinformation should report inferences and judgments that are similar to those of people who do not encounter the misinformation at all.

Prior work on disregarding information in text has identified a number of factors that influence how successfully this process occurs, but it has not systematically explored how intentional forgetting might occur in the normal course of text processing. The next section summarizes a number of studies in which people received instructions to disregard textual material. The following section first provides an analysis of representational consequences of processing misinformation and then discusses the potential effectiveness of currently identified intentional-forgetting processes. The section ends with a brief consideration of how postcorrection comprehension tasks may influence intentional forgetting. The final section suggests that readers may use an additional process of selective reconstruction to successfully disregard information while maintaining coherence in the text.

PRIOR FINDINGS ON DISREGARDING TEXT

Prior research on disregarding textual material found limited evidence of intentional forgetting. Early studies (Geiselman, 1974, 1977) used a directed-forgetting paradigm in which each sentence of a text was followed by a cue to either remember or forget it (the item method). The results showed less forgetting when individual sentences were presented as an orderly text rather than intermingled randomly. This advantage for orderly text occurred despite the fact that this paradigm tends to lead to superficial encoding (Johnson, 1994). Other studies (Johnson & Seifert, 1994a; Wilkes & Leatherbarrow, 1988) used a disregard instruction that unexpectedly corrected earlier information by literally negating it. Again, people had little difficulty recalling the information they were told to disregard. In addition to literal recall, these correction studies also had participants answer comprehension questions that required inferences about material not directly presented in the text. These results showed that even after the correction, the initial misinformation continued to influence the inferences made, relative to those made by people who did not receive that information. This suggests that people did not forget the to-be-disregarded information in the sense of retrieval failure, nor did they fully limit its expression in inferences about the account.

The effects described here cannot be attributed to failure to notice the disregard instruction. A number of studies (Baker & Wagner, 1987; Glenberg, Wilkinson, & Epstein, 1982; Otero & Kintsch, 1992) found that people have difficulty in detecting contradictions within text, which could account for people continuing to remember and rely on the information. However, over 90% of participants in the correction studies acknowledged the correction when asked about it directly (Johnson & Seifert, 1994a), which shows that they knew what information they were to disregard. Similarly, participants have little trouble noticing and interpreting the disregard instruction used in directed-forgetting paradigms.

Other evidence suggests that the effects are not due to the simple availability of information that provides plausible inferences. One could argue that forgetting effects did not occur in the correction studies (Johnson & Seifert, 1994a; Wilkes & Leatherbarrow, 1988) because the experimental task required people to provide answers for questions they might not have considered otherwise. According to this argument, people may have understood that the misinformation was not relevant within the story context, but nevertheless, it suggested plausible inferences that allowed them to answer the required questions. If this was the case, one might expect people to make similar inferences if similar information is made available, through whatever means.

To test this, Johnson and Seifert (1994a) manipulated whether a piece of target information (e.g., oil paint and gas cylinders) was either mentioned in a causal context during the story (i.e., near where a fire broke out) and then later corrected, mentioned in a noncausal context during the story (i.e., located in a different building), or introduced in a stem-completion task given after the story. The results showed that people used the target information as a basis for inferences when it was mentioned in a causal context and then corrected, but not when it was made available through the stem-completion task or through a noncausal mention within the story context. This suggests that the influence effects are due to the way a piece of information fits into a story's context before a correction occurs, rather than simply due to its presentation, either within the account or external to it.

These studies also implicated several common properties of texts that contribute to decreased forgetting. Geiselman (1977) examined the effect of thematic knowledge by presenting "texts" composed of intermingled sentences from two passages with distinct themes, with each sentence cued to either be remembered or forgotten. The results showed that people recalled more forget-cued (F-cued) material when they knew the theme of the F-cued passage, and when that passage was presented in order rather than scrambled. In another study using a directed-forgetting paradigm, Geiselman (1974) presented a set of three texts, varying in their degree of connectedness. The results showed that the more connected the text was, the more F-cued material people recalled. These results suggest that the presence of theme and connectedness, both key components of text, can make information harder to disregard.

Johnson and Seifert (1994a) further explored the issue of connectedness by manipulating the likelihood that people would involve initial misinformation in causal inferences before a correction occurred. According to an editing hypothesis (Wilkes & Leatherbarrow, 1988), people may have trouble disregarding initial misinformation because they involved it in a number of inferences before a correction occurred, and they were subsequently unable to trace out and alter these inferences. These inferences would then remain in memory and could potentially be expressed later. Johnson and Seifert (1994a) tested this by manipulating whether misinformation was corrected immediately after it was presented or after a number of intervening messages that allowed for causal inferences. The results showed that misinformation influenced people's inferences, even when immediately corrected. This in turn suggests that disregarding textual information requires attending to elements present in the representation at the time of correction and also preventing new associations between the misinformation and any post-correction text that is processed.

Johnson and Seifert (1994a) also found evidence that people have more trouble disregarding misinformation when that information provides an account with coherence that it would not have had otherwise. First, the results showed that misinformation influenced inferences when it was presented in a causal context, but not when the same information was incidentally mentioned in the text or primed by similar material presented outside of the text (Experiment 2). Second, people showed more ability to disregard initial misinformation when a correction provided a causal alternative rather than simply negating the information (Experiments 3A and 3B). Having a causal alternative would allow one to construct a coherent representation without necessarily relying on the misinformation. On the other hand, merely negating misinformation could disrupt a number of causal links within the account and leave some features of the event unexplained. This suggests that the role information plays within a text's causal structure influences how successfully one can disregard it.

The prior work on disregarding information in text suggests a number of common text features that make intentional forgetting more difficult; however, no one has made an in-depth attempt to relate what is known about processes of successful forgetting to processes involved in text comprehension. The following section provides an analysis of the process by which misinformation becomes part of a representation, the forgetting processes readers could use at the point of correction to limit expression of misinformation, and how their consequences might stand up to and influence both subsequent text processing and question answering. Such a processing framework could aid in understanding correction comprehension and suggest further factors that could influence a comprehender's ultimate success in disregarding misinformation.

FACTORS IN DISREGARDING INFORMATION IN TEXT

Misinformation Encoding

One key influence on processes of intentional forgetting is how people encode the information before the disregard instruction occurs. Comprehenders are likely to use a learning strategy (Johnson, 1994) when they do not expect to receive a disregard instruction. In this case, they assume that they received valid, relevant information, and thus use "normal" comprehension processes to construct a representation in memory. A number of studies (Gilbert, Krull, & Malone, 1990; Gilbert, Tafarodi, & Malone, 1993) argued that people encode what they hear or read as true by default, and they must engage in more effortful processing to represent information as false. The following subsection provides an overview of normal processes used to construct a text representation, which in turn suggests how misinformation may be incorporated into memory before a correction occurs.

A number of comprehension models (Gernsbacher, 1990; Kintsch, 1988) characterized comprehension as a process of constructing a structure in memory, based on propositions that are derived from the presented text and inferences that link and elaborate upon them. The initial text one reads forms the representation's basis (Gernsbacher & Hargreaves, 1988; van Dijk & Kintsch, 1983) and may also lead to the generation of plausible inferences based on its associations with prior knowledge in memory (Kintsch, 1988). As people read the next text segment, they make bridging inferences that establish relations between it and prior text (Haviland & Clark, 1974; Keenan, Baillet, & Brown, 1984; Singer, Halldorson, Lear, & Andrusiak, 1992), thereby adding to the structure. They may also make strategic inferences, depending on their reading goals (Kintsch, 1988). Then, according to construction-integration theory (Kintsch, 1988), an integration phase would follow, in which inferences that cohere with the current representational structure become strengthened and others with less contextual support decrease in strength. These cycles of construction and integration would continue as the reader proceeds through the text, eventually resulting in a text representation in memory.

Additional research has suggested that people often make particular types of inferences during the process of comprehension, whereas other possible inferences are rarely generated spontaneously. Based on converging methodological evidence, Graesser, Singer, and Trabasso (1994) argued that people often make inferences about causal relations, motives, superordinate goals, and emotional reactions on-line, during the course of reading. Table 7.1 provides some examples of the type of inferences made on-line. Additional evidence has also suggested that people may also make predictive inferences on-line when the situation described in the text is highly constrained (McKoon & Ratcliff, 1986). In contrast, as shown in Table 7.1, people more rarely make on-line inferences about noncausal features, specific goal-related actions, and spatial relations (Graesser et al., 1994). Thus, people typically incorporate only a subset of all possible inferences into a text representation in memory as a result of normal comprehension.

Comprehenders are likely to use these same integration and inferencing processes to encode information that is later revealed to be mistaken. As a result, at the point of correction, misinformation may be associated with a number of other text elements and may have spurred a number of inferences that people would not have made otherwise. In particular, misinformation about motives and causes of events could lead to a number of on-line inferences, and thus may be causally central to one's understanding of the event described. Disregarding such misinformation would be important in having an accurate idea of what has really occurred.

Correction Processing

In addition to the way one has encoded misinformation, the scope of the disregard instruction influences the forgetting processes that people can successfully apply. Johnson (1994) proposed a distinction between global

TABLE 7.1
Possible Inferences Made During Reading

Typically Made On-Line

Inferences About Causes
Text: Police are investigating the auto accident. They have found that the driver was
drinking.
Inference: Drunk driving caused the accident.

Inferences About Motives/Superordinate Goals
Text: A 10-year-old girl was not waiting where her mother expected to pick her up. The
mother is contacting the girl's friends.
Inference: The mother wants to find her daughter.

Inferences About Emotions
Text: The student was ready to print the final draft of his research paper. Then the hard
drive on his computer crashed.
Inference: The student is upset.

Rarely Made On-Line

Inferences About Noncausal Features
Text: Police are investigating the auto accident. They have found that the driver was
drinking.
Inference: The car has four tires.

Inferences About Specific Actions
Text: A 10-year-old girl was not waiting where her mother expected to pick her up. The
mother is contacting the girl's friends.
Inference: The mother is dialing the friends' numbers on a telephone.

Inferences About Spatial Relations
Text: The student was ready to print the final draft of his research paper. Then the hard
drive on his computer crashed.
Inference: The student is sitting in front of the computer.

and specific forget instructions.[2] A global forget instruction indicates that
one should forget all of the information presented so far; this allows one to
begin constructing an entirely new representation for any subsequent infor-

---

[2]A similar distinction was used to classify directed-forgetting paradigms (Basden et al., 1993).
In the list method, participants learn an initial word list, receive an instruction to forget it, and
then learn a second list. This paradigm uses what I am terming a global forget instruction.
Other directed-forgetting research has used the item method, in which each individual word
is followed by a cue to either remember or forget it. Elsewhere (Johnson, 1994) I have called
this type of forget instruction a discriminatory one because people are forewarned about the
forgetting task and thus use the cues to discriminate what they need to remember from what
they do not. A few studies of directed forgetting (Rakover, 1975; Roediger & Tulving, 1979) used
what I would term a specific forget instruction. In these studies, participants learned a large
set of items and then received an instruction to forget a subset of them (e.g., forget the animal
names from the list).

mation. However, corrections of text will often involve a specific forget instruction, in which one is asked to disregard only a specific portion of the material presented. This presents a special challenge because other parts of the text will remain valid and should continue to underlie one's understanding of the event being described. Successful forgetting would require more than just altering the misinformation itself in memory. It would also require the additional steps of identifying and evaluating the associations and inferences within the representation to determine which remain valid and which should be forgotten.

Early research on directed forgetting (Epstein & Wilder, 1972; Geiselman et al., 1983; Reitman, Malin, Bjork, & Higman, 1973) proposed several representational changes that could result from processing a disregard instruction, and these could also potentially contribute to disregarding text material. One such change would be segregation (Epstein & Wilder, 1972), which would involve separating the elements to be remembered from those to be disregarded and then storing them as two distinct representations. In text, separating the elements could require disrupting previously made associations between valid and invalid information. One would also need to incorporate any subsequent text information into the valid representation rather than linking it to the misinformation. If successful, one would have a discrete representation of valid information that one could retrieve later without encountering the information to be disregarded.

A second possible representational change would be inhibition of the information to be disregarded. This would involve either blocking access to the cued information itself (Geiselman et al., 1983) or suppressing its activation. Thus, the information to be remembered would be stronger or more accessible than that to be disregarded but would not be stored in a separate representation. If inhibition was successful, this would decrease the likelihood that one would retrieve the inhibited information later and involve it in further reasoning.

A final possible representational change is that the information in memory could be tagged with an explicit cue that it should be forgotten. This would not require people to create a separate representation for information they intend to disregard, as would occur with segregation. Instead, people could maintain their initial representation but tag some portions of it as invalid. Such a tag would not necessarily prevent people from retrieving the invalid information along with the valid information later, as segregation or inhibition might. However, the tag would allow them to evaluate the retrieved information and decide whether to use it. In this case, successful forgetting would occur if these decision processes limited the expression of the invalid information. The rest of this section explores the extent to which these processes might lead to successful forgetting of corrected text material.

Segregation. Previous research involving specific forget instructions has provided little evidence that people successfully use segregation to comply with them. First, studies in both social judgment (Schul & Burnstein, 1985; Wyer & Budesheim, 1987; Wyer & Unverzagt, 1985) and directed forgetting (Epstein, 1969; Rakover, 1975; Roediger & Tulving, 1979) compared patterns of forgetting when people received either a global or a specific forget instruction. With a global forget instruction, one can in essence put aside the F-cued information and begin a new representation with what one subsequently learns. Later, one could retrieve this second representation without encountering the F-cued information. If people could also segregate F-cued and R-cued information after a specific instruction, one would not expect the type of instruction to have an influence. However, the results from social judgment studies (Schul & Burnstein, 1985; Wyer & Budesheim, 1987; Wyer & Unverzagt, 1985) show that F-cued information has a larger influence on judgments made after a specific forget instruction than after a global forget instruction. Similarly, directed-forgetting studies (Epstein, 1969; Rakover, 1975; Roediger & Tulving, 1979) found more interference with recall of list items after a specific forget instruction than after a global one. These findings suggest that specific forget instructions do not result in the same segregated representation that global forget instructions do.

Further, other evidence suggests that people who receive a specific forget instruction do not make later judgments on the basis of a veridical review of only R-cued information. If segregation has occurred, one would expect similar judgments from both those who received the forget instruction and those who only received the R-cued information, because in both conditions people could retrieve a representation that did not contain misinformation. However, a number of studies of juror decision making (Hatvany & Strack, 1980; Thompson et al., 1981) and of person perception (Wyer & Budesheim, 1987) found that people tend to overcorrect when disregarding negative information and to undercorrect when disregarding positive information, relative to those who do not receive the F-cued information. Neither of these patterns would occur if people had segregated F-cued material from their representation and were making a judgment based on a review of R-cued information alone.

Research on working memory suggests further reasons to suspect that people would have difficulty using segregation to disregard misinformation in text. During comprehension, working memory is used to store prior text propositions and to engage in inferencing operations (Fletcher, 1981; Just & Carpenter, 1992). A number of studies found increased difficulty in problem solving (Carpenter, Just, & Shell, 1990; Casey, 1993) and normal text comprehension (Daneman & Carpenter, 1983; Just & Carpenter, 1992; Miyake, Just, & Carpenter, 1994) when the memory load and processing requirements put more demands on people's limited working memory capacity.

There are several ways in which working memory limitations might make a wholesale segregation process difficult. Suppose a reader learns, early in a story, that a boy has been accused of robbing a woman's house, and that a number of other thefts have occurred recently. One may infer that the boy may have committed those too. If a correction later indicates that the boy did not rob the woman's house, it might be wise to reevaluate the inference about the other thefts. However, the reader might not have that information in working memory at the time of correction. The reader would have to search for it in long-term memory, along with other associations and inferences that might have arisen because the misinformation was presented. The reader would also need working memory resources to evaluate associations and inferences to determine whether they remain valid or not. In this example, the reader must decide if it is still reasonable to blame the boy for the other thefts. Finally, working memory may be needed to restructure the remaining valid information into a coherent representation. If the reader decides that the boy was not to blame for the other thefts, this aspect of the story becomes unexplained, and the reader may try to restructure the story to account for it another way. Locating and evaluating potentially invalid inferences could be a daunting task if the misinformation was key to one's understanding of the event and was embedded in a complex network of associations. This suggests that segregation may rarely be a viable method of disregarding textual material.

Inhibition. Inhibition is another representational change that could result from processing a disregard instruction and contribute to successful forgetting. In a strong form, inhibition could block the retrieval path to the misinformation and make it inaccessible. In this case, one would expect a higher rate of memory failure for information one is told to disregard. In a weaker form, inhibition could suppress the activation of the F-cued information, relative to other parts of the representation. In turn, this suppressed activation could influence comprehension of any subsequent text by shifting the misinformation to the background and decreasing the likelihood that one links it to subsequent information. For example, a correction could indicate that a child was not kidnapped by her father, as previously believed. This could suppress activation of information about the father and make it less likely to be linked to subsequent information about the child being seen in a blue car. However, the suppressed activation might not substantially influence people's ability to recall that the misinformation was presented. Similar inhibition processes have been proposed as ways of diminishing intrusions from contextually irrelevant information in the normal course of text comprehension (Gernsbacher & Faust, 1991; Kintsch, 1988). This section examines the extent to which strong and weak forms of inhibition might allow one to disregard text material.

Some evidence against a strong form of inhibition comes from studies in which people show good recall of F-cued material but differ in how much it influences performance in other tasks. Some research on text comprehension (Johnson & Seifert, 1994a; Wilkes & Leatherbarrow, 1988) and on person perception (Golding, Fowler, Long, & Latta, 1990; Wyer & Unverzagt, 1985) found that people have little difficulty recalling the information to be disregarded, but that it can still influence their judgments and inferences. This would suggest that inhibition did not lead to successful forgetting. More interestingly, other studies found cases in which misinformation does not influence juror verdicts (Thompson et al., 1981) or person impressions (Golding et al., 1990), despite the fact that people have little difficulty remembering it. These findings suggest that people can show successful forgetting even without a strong form of inhibition occurring.

Other studies found evidence of differential use of F-cued information, which would also be inconsistent with a strong inhibition hypothesis. One might expect inhibition to affect the F-cued information uniformly and result in retrieval failure, regardless of the later memory or judgment task. However, work on juror decision making (Carretta & Moreland, 1983) asked people to disregard inadmissible evidence, and the results showed that it did not influence verdict decisions but did influence judgments of probable guilt. Such differential influence should not occur if inhibition made the information uniformly inaccessible. Similarly, other work (Golding et al., 1990) manipulated whether a forget instruction was given to correct a mistake or to ask for confidentiality. The results showed more compliance in the mistake condition, which indicates that simply processing a disregard instruction does not uniformly result in inhibition.

In contrast, text research found evidence for the weak form of inhibition in situations involving contextually irrelevant information, although few studies to date involved overt corrections. Swinney (1979) found that people initially activated multiple meanings of ambiguous words such as "bug," but that a contextually inappropriate meaning (e.g., insect) becomes less active over time whereas an appropriate meaning (e.g., spying device) retains its initial activation. Gernsbacher and colleagues found similar effects for semantic associations that are contextually irrelevant (Gernsbacher & Faust, 1991). For example, when people initially read "piano" in a sentence, the associates "music" and "heavy" are activated, but the former quickly decreases in activation when the context refers to moving the instrument. Gernsbacher (1989) also found evidence that this effect occurred due to suppression, or an inhibition of the information, which occurred independent of increases in activation of more contextually relevant information. This evidence, as well as some models of comprehension (Kintsch, 1988), suggest that people can inhibit information that is not relevant to what they are currently reading.

A few text comprehension studies have begun to examine the effects of having information disconfirmed during reading. MacDonald and Just (1989) had people read sentences containing either a conjunction (X and Y) or a denial (X not Y) and tested priming for the X or Y elements at the end of the sentence. They found less activation for the Y term in the denial condition than in the conjunction condition. Similarly, Klin and Myers (1993) manipulated whether an event's potential cause was disconfirmed before participants read text that invited a causal inference. They found more activation for the potential causes when they had not been disconfirmed. Johnson and Seifert (1994b) also presented evidence that disconfirmed referents are not strongly activated when people make anaphoric inferences later in the text. These findings suggest that inhibition, in the sense of decreased activation, occurs and decreases the likelihood that people will make inferences involving disconfirmed information.

However, one might expect inhibition effects to be limited, despite their potential effectiveness in decreasing the influence that corrected misinformation has on processing subsequent text. First, inhibition may have little effect on information that the correction does not directly specify. The studies cited earlier found evidence that information showed decreased activation when it had been directly denied or disconfirmed. However, MacDonald and Just (1989) found that semantic associates of terms that had been denied were just as activated as when those terms had appeared as part of a conjunction. This suggests that inhibition could have a local effect on the misinformation itself, but might not be useful in helping one disregard associations and inferences based on the misinformation. One would need a systematic way to identify which associations and inferences to inhibit, which might require effortful search and evaluation. If inhibition only has a local effect on misinformation itself, rather than more global effects on related inferences as well, it might not be sufficient for successful forgetting because those potentially invalid inferences could still influence one's comprehension and judgments.

The potential for rebound effects could also limit the effectiveness of inhibition processes. Prior research on directed forgetting has found that re-presenting a subset of F-cued items on a recognition test improves later recall of the information to be disregarded (Basden et al., 1993; Geiselman et al., 1983) and increases interference with R-cued items (Bjork, 1989). It has been argued that re-presentation releases the inhibition that had previously blocked access to the F-cued material (Geiselman et al., 1983). Similarly, research on thought suppression (Wegner, Schneider, Carter, & White, 1987) found that people can reduce, although not eliminate, thoughts on a topic when instructed to; however, when instructed to think about the topic after such a suppression period, people report more thoughts than others who did not have an initial suppression period. Thus, ending the suppression period seems to lead to rebound for the suppressed thoughts. Such rebound effects could potentially occur in text comprehension as well, based on text presented after a correction. This subsequent text could mention valid facts that were associated with the misinformation, or additional information that is causally consistent with it. Activating associates or causal features of misinformation might be sufficient to overcome any inhibition that had occurred as a result of the correction.

Discrimination. Discrimination is another proposed representational change that could result from a correction and contribute to disregarding text. This would involve storing discriminatory tags in memory that indicate that particular information is to be disregarded. This could allow successful forgetting even if people retrieved the misinformation because they could evaluate it based on the tag associated with it. This would allow people to reject the information and alter their decision processes so that the information does not influence their reasoning.

Few studies have directly assessed whether people do store discriminatory tags with information in memory as a result of a disregard instruction, although this was suggested by a number of performance measures. First, several studies (Golding et al., 1990; Wyer & Unverzagt, 1985) asked people to recall what they were told to disregard and found that this request in itself led to reliable retrieval of the information. People also spontaneously indicated that particular information was to be disregarded when doing a free recall of a text containing a correction (Johnson & Seifert, 1994a) and during mock jury deliberation (Carretta & Moreland, 1983). These findings suggest that people have stored an association between the information and the disregard instruction. However, as with inhibition, there is little evidence on whether such tagging is a local or global phenomenon. If it is local, people might tag the misinformation but not the associations and inferences based on it. For example, if a correction indicates that a boy did not rob a woman's house, as believed earlier, people could tag this particular information as incorrect. However, they might not tag related inferences, such as the boy's possible involvement in other thefts, as questionable. If people retrieved such untagged inferences later, people might have difficulty disregarding them because they might not realize that they are questionable and should be evaluated.

Consequences of Representational Change. A factor that could further complicate disregarding information in text is that succeeding text could disrupt the coherence of the representation. Text comprehension has been characterized as the process of establishing coherence among text elements (Kintsch, 1988; Trabasso & Suh, 1993). Previous research (Graesser & Clark, 1985; Trabasso & van den Broek, 1985) suggested that causal connections provide structure to an account; without them, the account may seem less coherent. People have more difficulty recalling and answering questions about incoherent texts (Zabrucky, 1986). Problems may occur if misinformation is causally central in a text and provides it with a coherent structure before a correction occurs. For example, in reading about a particular fire, one might construct a causal chain in which electric sparks ignite nearby cans of paint, which in turn cause the explosions and fumes that were reported. Attempting to disregard the information about the presence of paint cans could weaken or eliminate key causal relations within this structure (i.e., if there was no paint, it could not have caused explosions) and leave one with a series of facts that no longer fit together coherently. At this point, one may need either to tolerate decreased coherence and trust that subsequent text will resolve it soon, or attempt to find an alternative way to structure the account coherently. Given the potential costs to coherence, people may be cautious about attempting to disregard corrected material.

Subsequent Task Performance

Postcorrection Comprehension. Several characteristics of text presented after a correction may influence how well one can disregard earlier misinformation. First, people may show more successful disregarding if a correction provides a concrete alternative to the misinformation, especially when the misinformation was causally central to the account. As seen in the preceding example, a potential consequence of disregarding misinformation is the disruption of a causal structure that provides the text with coherence. People might have difficulty maintaining a corrected representation if it is more incoherent than the one based on misinformation. However, providing a causal alternative, such as the presence of cleaning fluids rather than paint, would allow people to construct an alternative causal structure and explain how a few sparks resulted in explosions and fumes. Thus, people could maintain a coherent account without relying on the misinformation. In this case, there would be less cost to disregarding the misinformation.

A second characteristic that could influence how well one can disregard earlier misinformation is the extent to which postcorrection text supports or is inconsistent with the misinformation. As readers process a piece of text, they often make inferences that establish causal or referential relations with earlier text (O'Brien, Duffy, & Myers, 1986; Singer et al., 1992; Trabasso & van den Broek, 1985). For example, reading a sentence such as "witnesses saw several explosions" could lead one to search prior text for a reason why this occurred. In normal texts, this search will generally turn up causal information that allows an inferential link. However, this is less certain when an account contains corrected misinformation. For example, a correction may rule out the presence of gas cylinders, but someone who reads about "explosions" later on in the text will still attempt to relate this to some prior information. If the text contains no other plausible causes, people may activate the misinformation and form a tentative hypothesis that it still might explain the occurrence. In this case, people might be less likely to disregard the misinformation because it is the only thing that makes sense of the story.

Question Answering. Answering later questions about corrected texts may require altering one's decision processes to disregard misinformation. If the question brought misinformation to mind, one would need to forget it, in the sense of limiting its expression in one's answer. Prior research identified several ways to accomplish this, although little work has directly addressed answering questions about corrected text. First, some directed-forgetting research (Roediger & Tulving, 1979) cued people to forget a categorized subset of a list they had already learned. The results showed that the F-cued items interfered with recall of the other items, but people did not produce them directly during the task. This suggests that people recalled the items but decided to withhold them. People could also use such a strategy to reject misinformation as an appropriate answer to a question.

A second strategy would be to use theory-based compensation to "subtract out" the perceived influence of the information to be disregarded. Theory-based compensation would involve estimating how much influence a piece of misinformation might have and altering one's judgments to take this into account. Work in person perception (Wyer & Budesheim, 1987) asked people to ignore either a set of mistakenly presented negative or positive traits about a person. People who were asked to ignore negative traits made ratings that were more positive than ratings made by people who did not hear the negative traits at all. However, people who were asked to ignore positive traits still rated the person more positively than people who did not hear the positive traits. The researchers concluded that people have a theory about potential bias from negative information but not about the impact of positive information. Similar effects have been found in studies of juror decision making (Thompson et al., 1981), in which people feel more biased by prosecution than by defense evidence, but find the former easier to ignore than the latter. The accuracy of the judgments, relative to those of people not exposed to the misinformation, would of course depend on how accurate one's theory about potential influence was. People might use theory-based compensation to answer comprehension questions that require them to consider what they would have believed if they had not been exposed to misinformation.

CONCLUSIONS

The process of disregarding information in text presents several challenges. First, one must disregard not only the misinformation itself, but also other consequences of having processed it, such as associations and inferences.

Determining which parts of the representation remain valid and which should be forgotten could be difficult, especially if the misinformation had a number of causal implications. A second challenge is to prevent the misinformation from influencing how one processes subsequent information about the event. This challenge would arise when the correction occurs within the story context as the information unfolds, rather than after one has completed comprehension. The goal would be to link subsequent text to valid information and not to the misinformation. These challenges suggest that successfully disregarding textual material will be more complicated and difficult than disregarding more traditional verbal learning materials.

Some of the processes that lead to successful forgetting in other domains may also contribute to people's ability to disregard text. First, it seems likely that people can tag the misinformation itself in memory with a discriminatory cue that indicates that the misinformation should be disregarded. This would allow people to retrieve the information later, evaluate the associated cue, and alter their decision processes to avoid expressing the information. In this case, the misinformation would not literally be forgotten, but it would not influence people's judgments, so the result would be functionally equivalent to literal forgetting. Second, processing a correction could result in inhibition that acts to shift the misinformation into the background of one's representation. Several studies found evidence that information shows less activation later in a text when it had been negated (MacDonald & Just, 1989) or disconfirmed (Johnson & Seifert, 1994b; Klin & Myers, 1993). Such inhibition could reduce the likelihood that people link any postcorrection text to the misinformation during further comprehension attempts. However, both discrimination and inhibition might be limited in scope, so they affect the representation of the misinformation itself but not necessarily all the inferences associated with it.

Gaining a further understanding of how people disregard textual information, however, may require exploring additional factors such as the pragmatics of corrections and the search for coherence. Pragmatics has been defined as knowledge about the speaker's intentions, and research shows that people consider the pragmatics that motivate a disregard instruction (Golding et al., 1990). On one hand, conversational convention may support accepting the correction and complying with it due to assumptions that the speaker believes it is informative and more accurate. This would be consistent with a Gricean (1967/1987) perspective on pragmatics. On the other hand, complying with the instruction may disrupt the coherence of one's text representation and leave a number of facts unexplained. In this case, people may want to weigh the pragmatic value of the correction carefully before attempting to comply with the disregard instruction. Prior research on pragmatics (Golding et al., 1990) found that people consider the motives behind a disregard instruction and show more compliance when asked to forget mistaken rather than confidential information. Other pragmatic factors, such as the motive for presenting the misinformation itself, may also influence how believable a correction is and whether people will comply with it.

A second process that could influence how well people disregard text is the search for coherence. If disregarding information disrupts coherence, people may attempt to repair this through selective reconstruction. If the correction includes a concrete alternative to the misinformation, people may use the alternative to regenerate key causal inferences because this would restore coherence to the account. However, they may not attempt to identify and alter inferences that are less crucial to the text structure. If a correction merely negates the misinformation, people may attempt to generate alternative hypotheses, based either on information contained in the text representation or on world knowledge. However, these would remain tentative, pending further information that confirms them. One would predict the least successful forgetting when people cannot create a coherent representation without recourse to the misinformation. This is most likely to occur when the misinformation accounts for many features in the text and no reasonable alternative is provided or comes to mind.

In conclusion, disregarding information in text is important for understanding accounts of many current events and also new scientific findings that may contradict what one learned earlier. To understand how people might accomplish this task, it is important to consider how misinformation—and corrections—become incorporated into a representation, as well as the potential forgetting processes themselves. It is hoped that this suggests further research designed to improve the successful forgetting of information individuals want to forget.

REFERENCES

Baker, L., & Wagner, J. L. (1987). Evaluating information for truthfulness: The effects of logical subordination. *Memory & Cognition, 15*, 247–255.

Basden, B. H., Basden, D. R., & Gargano, G. J. (1993). Directed forgetting in implicit and explicit memory tests: A comparison of methods. *Journal of Experimental Psychology: Learning, Memory, and Cognition, 19*, 603–616.

Bjork, R. A. (1970). Positive forgetting: The noninterference of items intentionally forgotten. *Journal of Verbal Learning and Verbal Behavior, 9*, 255–268.

Bjork, R. A. (1989). Retrieval inhibition as an adaptive mechanism in human memory. In H. L. Roediger, III & F. I. M. Craik (Eds.), *Varieties of memory and consciousness* (pp. 309–330). Hillsdale, NJ: Lawrence Erlbaum Associates.

Carpenter, P. A., Just, M. A., & Shell, P. (1990). What one intelligence test measures: A theoretical account of the processing in the Raven Progressive Matrices Test. *Psychological Review, 97*, 404–431.

Carretta, T. R., & Moreland, R. L. (1983). The direct and indirect effects of inadmissible evidence. *Journal of Applied Social Psychology, 13*, 291–309.

Casey, P. J. (1993). "That man's father is my father's son": The roles of structure, strategy, and working memory in solving convoluted verbal problems. *Memory & Cognition, 21,* 506–518.

Daneman, M., & Carpenter, P. A. (1983). Individual differences in integrating information between and within sentences. *Journal of Experimental Psychology: Learning, Memory, and Cognition, 9,* 561–584.

Epstein, W. (1969). Poststimulus output specification and differential retrieval from short-term memory. *Journal of Experimental Psychology, 82,* 168–174.

Epstein, W., & Wilder, L. (1972). Searching for to-be-forgotten material in a directed forgetting task. *Journal of Experimental Psychology, 95,* 349–357.

Fletcher, C. R. (1981). Short-term memory processes in text comprehension. *Journal of Verbal Learning and Verbal Behavior, 20,* 564–574.

Geiselman, R. E. (1974). Positive forgetting of sentence material. *Memory & Cognition, 2,* 677–682.

Geiselman, R. E. (1977). Effects of sentence ordering on thematic decisions to remember and forget prose. *Memory & Cognition, 5,* 323–330.

Geiselman, R. E., Bjork, R. A., & Fishman, D. L. (1983). Disrupted retrieval in directed forgetting: A link with posthypnotic amnesia. *Journal of Experimental Psychology: General, 112,* 58–72.

Gernsbacher, M. A. (1989). Mechanisms that improve referential access. *Cognition, 32,* 99–156.

Gernsbacher, M. A. (1990). *Language comprehension as structure building.* Hillsdale, NJ: Lawrence Erlbaum Associates.

Gernsbacher, M. A., & Faust, M. E. (1991). The mechanism of suppression: A component of general comprehension skill. *Journal of Experimental Psychology: Learning, Memory, and Cognition, 17,* 245–262.

Gernsbacher, M. A., & Hargreaves, D. J. (1988). Accessing sentence participants: The advantage of first mention. *Journal of Memory and Language, 27,* 699–717.

Gilbert, D. T., Krull, D. S., & Malone, P. S. (1990). Unbelieving the unbelievable: Some problems in the rejection of false information. *Journal of Personality and Social Psychology, 59,* 601–613.

Gilbert, D. T., Tafarodi, R. W., & Malone, P. S. (1993). You can't not believe everything you read. *Journal of Personality and Social Psychology, 65,* 221–233.

Glenberg, A. M., Wilkinson, A. C., & Epstein, W. (1982). The illusion of knowing: Failure in the self-assessment of comprehension. *Memory & Cognition, 10,* 597–602.

Golding, J. M., Fowler, S. B., Long, D. L., & Latta, H. (1990). Instructions to disregard potentially useful information: The effects of pragmatics on evaluative judgments and recall. *Journal of Memory and Language, 29,* 212–227.

Graesser, A. C., & Clark, L. F. (1985). *Structures and procedures of implicit knowledge.* Norwood, NJ: Ablex.

Graesser, A. C., Singer, M., & Trabasso, T. (1994). Constructing inferences during narrative text comprehension. *Psychological Review, 101,* 371–393.

Grice, H. P. (1987). Logic and conversation. In H. P. Grice (1989), *Studies in the way of words* (pp. 1–143). Cambridge, MA: Harvard University Press. (Original work published in 1967)

Hatvany, N., & Strack, F. (1980). The impact of a discredited key witness. *Journal of Applied Social Psychology, 10,* 490–509.

Haviland, S. E., & Clark, H. H. (1974). What's new? Acquiring new information as a process in comprehension. *Journal of Verbal Learning and Verbal Behavior, 13,* 512–521.

Johnson, H. M. (1994). Processes of successful intentional forgetting. *Psychological Bulletin, 116,* 274–292.

Johnson, H. M., & Seifert, C. M. (1994a). Sources of the continued influence effect: When misinformation in memory affects later inferences. *Journal of Experimental Psychology: Learning, Memory, and Cognition, 20,* 1420–1436.

Johnson, H. M., & Seifert, C. M. (1994b). Suppression of misinformation in memory. *Proceedings of the 16th Annual Cognitive Science Society,* 457–462.

Just, M. A., & Carpenter, P. A. (1992). A capacity theory of comprehension: Individual differences in working memory. *Psychological Review, 99,* 122–149.

Keenan, J. M., Baillet, S. D., & Brown, P. (1984). The effects of causal cohesion on comprehension and memory. *Journal of Verbal Learning and Verbal Behavior, 23,* 115–126.

Kintsch, W. (1988). The role of knowledge in discourse comprehension: A construction-integration model. *Psychological Review, 95,* 162–182.

Klin, C. M., & Myers, J. L. (1993). Reinstatement of causal information during reading. *Journal of Experimental Psychology: Learning, Memory, and Cognition, 19,* 554–560.

MacDonald, M. C., & Just, M. A. (1989). Changes in activation levels with negation. *Journal of Experimental Psychology: Learning, Memory, and Cognition, 15,* 633–642.

McKoon, G., & Ratcliff, R. (1986). Inferences about predictable events. *Journal of Experimental Psychology: Learning, Memory, and Cognition, 12,* 82–91.

Miyake, A., Just, M. A., & Carpenter, P. A. (1994). Working memory constraints on the resolution of lexical ambiguity: Maintaining multiple interpretations in neutral contexts. *Journal of Memory and Language, 33,* 175–202.

O'Brien, E. J., Duffy, S. A., & Myers, J. L. (1986). Anaphoric inference during reading. *Journal of Experimental Psychology: Learning, Memory, and Cognition, 12,* 346–352.

Otero, J., & Kintsch, W. (1992). Failures to detect contradictions in a text: What readers believe versus what they read. *Psychological Science, 3,* 229–235.

Rakover, S. S. (1975). Voluntary forgetting before and after learning has been accomplished. *Memory & Cognition. 3,* 24–28.

Reitman, W., Malin, J. T., Bjork, R. A., & Higman, B. (1973). Strategy control and directed forgetting. *Journal of Verbal Learning and Verbal Behavior, 12,* 140–149.

Roediger, H. L, & Tulving, E. (1979). Exclusion of learned material from recall as a postretrieval operation. *Journal of Verbal Learning and Verbal Behavior, 18,* 601–615.

Schul, Y., & Burnstein, E. (1985). When discounting fails: Conditions under which individuals use discredited information in making a judgment. *Journal of Personality and Social Psychology, 49,* 894–903.

Singer, M., Halldorson, M., Lear, J. C., & Andrusiak, P. (1992). Validation of causal bridging inferences. *Journal of Memory and Language, 31,* 507–524.

Swinney, D. A. (1979). Lexical access during sentence comprehension: (Re)consideration of context effects. *Journal of Verbal Learning and Verbal Behavior, 18,* 645–659.

Thompson, W. C., Fong, G. T., & Rosenhan, D. L. (1981). Inadmissible evidence and juror verdicts. *Journal of Personality and Social Psychology, 40,* 453–463.

Trabasso, T., & Suh, S. (1993). Understanding text: Achieving explanatory coherence through on-line inferences and mental operations in working memory. *Discourse Processes, 16,* 3–36.

Trabasso, T., & van den Broek, P. W. (1985). Causal thinking and the representation of narrative events. *Journal of Memory and Language, 24,* 612–630.

van Dijk, T. A., & Kintsch, W. (1983). *Strategies of discourse comprehension.* New York: Academic Press.

Wegner, D. M., Schneider, D. J., Carter, S. R., & White, T. L. (1987). Paradoxical effects of thought suppression. *Journal of Personality and Social Psychology, 53,* 5–13.

Wilkes, A. L., & Leatherbarrow, M. (1988). Editing episodic memory following the identification of error. *Quarterly Journal of Experimental Psychology, 40A,* 361–387.

Wyer, R. S., & Budesheim, T. L. (1987). Person memory and judgments: The impact of information that one is told to disregard. *Journal of Personality and Social Psychology, 53,* 14–29.

Wyer, R. S., & Unverzagt, W. H. (1985). Effects of instructions to disregard information on its subsequent recall and use in making judgments. *Journal of Personality and Social Psychology, 48,* 533–549.

Zabrucky, K. (1986). The role of factual coherence in discourse comprehension. *Discourse Processes, 9,* 197–220.

8

DIRECTED FORGETTING
IN PIGEONS

Douglas S. Grant
University of Alberta

This chapter presents a chronological treatment of how my thinking about pigeon working memory has evolved over the past 25 years. The discussion is selective in at least two senses. First, it is selective in that the issue of primary interest is whether pigeons actively postperceptually process, or rehearse, information during the retention interval in working memory tasks. Second, the treatment is selective in that research and theory development in which I was an active participant is emphasized.

EARLY RESEARCH ON WORKING MEMORY
AND THE DEVELOPMENT
OF THE TRACE DECAY MODEL

My interest in what we now call "working memory" (and what we then called "short-term memory") in animals began in the summer of 1971 when I arrived at the University of Western Ontario to pursue graduate studies in the laboratory of William Roberts. Bill was also a recent arrival at Western, having joined the faculty only the preceding summer after having spent 2 years studying human memory in Endel Tulving's laboratory at the University of Toronto. Bill obtained his PhD at Bryn Mawr College under the tutelage of two eminent comparative psychologists, M. E. Bitterman and R. C. Gonzalez, and subsequently obtained a faculty position at Vassar College. During his time at Vassar, his interest in establishing a comparative psychology of memory grew. Although Bill had acquired the methodological skills necessary to such an endeavor at Bryn Mawr, he lacked what he considered to be sufficient knowledge about theory and issues in the area of memory, hence his sojourn to Tulving's laboratory.

Bill's first study of working memory in pigeons was underway when I arrived in June, 1971 (subsequently published in Roberts, 1972). The task used in that study (and in most subsequent studies of working memory in pigeons and monkeys) was delayed matching-to-sample (DMTS). In the simplest version of DMTS, illustrated in Fig. 8.1, one of two stimuli is presented at the onset of a trial as the sample. A retention interval, which varies in duration (typically in the range of 0 to 10 sec) follows termination of the sample. The test of retention involves presenting both stimuli simultaneously for a choice. Choice of the stimulus, which is the same as the sample presented on that trial, is designated correct and is reinforced by the presentation of food (choice of the nonmatching stimulus is, of course, designated incorrect and is not reinforced). Sessions typically contain between 48 and 96 trials, with trials separated by an interval of 10 to 30 sec. The selection of the stimulus that serves as the sample is determined quasi-randomly, and the spatial position of the correct (matching) choice stimulus is equally often left and right.

The early work in Bill's lab explored the influence of sample stimulus duration and repetition, and the effect of the spacing of those repetitions, on DMTS accuracy in pigeons (Grant, 1976; Roberts, 1972; Roberts & Grant, 1974). We also explored proactive interference effects, both those arising from presentation of a distracting (interfering) sample prior to the target sample (intratrial proactive interference; Grant & Roberts, 1973) and those arising from presentation of a conflicting trial prior to the target trial (intertrial proactive interference; Grant, 1975). Guided by Morgan's canon (Morgan, 1894), we attempted to develop an account of our findings, which appealed to psychological processes that were no more complex than those necessary to provide a satisfactory explanation. The result of our theoretical efforts was the trace decay model of pigeon working memory (see Roberts & Grant, 1976, for a detailed presentation of this model). Given the data available at that time, we found it unnecessary to invoke complex psychological processes, such as rehearsal or transformational coding of information. Instead, we argued that the known facts of pigeon working memory could be adequately explained by postulating that observation of a sample established a memory trace, isomorphic with the sample, that increased in strength as a negatively accelerated function of time spent viewing the sample and that decreased in strength (i.e., decayed) as a negatively accelerated function of time spent in the absence of the sample. Quantification of the model, combined with the assumption that DMTS accuracy was a

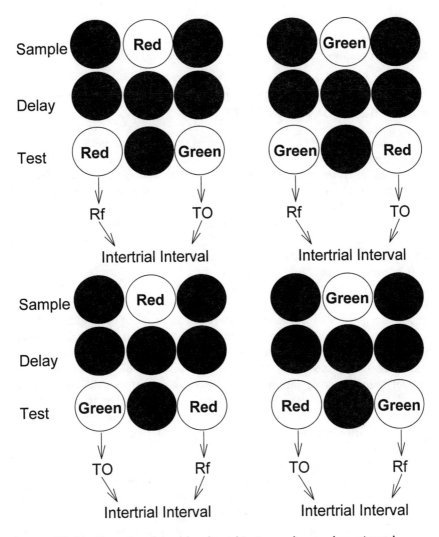

FIG. 8.1. Illustration of the delayed matching-to-sample procedure using red and green sample and test stimuli.

monotonically increasing function of trace strength, allowed us to produce an acceptable fit to our data on sample repetition and spacing effects (see Roberts & Grant, 1976). To accommodate our data on proactive interference effects, we added the assumptions that the stronger of conflicting traces controlled choice on the majority of trials and that the size of that majority was an increasing function of the absolute difference in strength between the conflicting traces. The trace decay model, as is likely clear, conceives of the pigeon as a rather passive participant in the remembering process:

Traces are established, increase and decrease in strength, compete with one another, and control behavior in ways that are rather impervious to the covert actions (i.e., cognitive processes) of the organism.

EARLY SUGGESTIONS THAT REHEARSAL MIGHT BE INVOLVED IN DMTS

While our theoretical efforts were devoted primarily to developing the trace decay theory, Bill and I directed our empirical attention to, among other issues, an analysis of retroactive interference by assessing the effects of presenting various types of stimuli during the retention interval of DMTS trials (Grant & Roberts, 1976; Roberts & Grant, 1978). Three major findings emerged from this work. First, the amount of retroactive interference was an increasing function of the physical brightness of the interpolated stimulus and was independent of other properties of that stimulus such as novelty and complexity. Second, the amount of retroactive interference was an increasing function of the duration of the interpolated stimulus. And third, presentation of an interpolated stimulus at the end of a retention interval produced greater retroactive interference than did presentation of that interpolated stimulus at the beginning of the retention interval. Although the occurrence of retroactive interference is not necessarily antithetical to the trace decay model, it does suggest the possibility that pigeons are actively remembering sample-derived information during the retention interval. On this view, attending to interpolated stimuli during the retention interval reduces the effectiveness of postperceptual processing of sample-derived information, resulting in reduced DMTS accuracy (see Grant & Roberts, 1976).

Concurrent with our investigations of retroactive interference in pigeons, the influential learning theorist Allan Wagner postulated a rehearsal process that played a critical role in classical conditioning (e.g., Terry & Wagner, 1975; Wagner, 1978; Wagner, Rudy, & Whitlow, 1973). Wagner's theorizing further encouraged me to think even more seriously about the possibility that pigeons may engage in rehearsal during the retention interval in DMTS. It later became clear, particularly so after I read Wagner's (1981) description of his *standard operating procedures* model of learning, that the type of rehearsal process that Wagner was postulating differed in some ways from the type of rehearsal process that I believed might be involved in DMTS. Wagner's rehearsal was postperceptual processing, which was initiated automatically by environmental events, and proceeded independently of cognitive control processes. In contrast, the type of rehearsal that I thought might operate in DMTS was a flexible, higher level cognitive control process that functioned to maintain information in working memory. (For more on the distinction between these two types of rehearsal see Grant, 1984b.)

THE F-CUE EFFECT

Wagner's theorizing and our work on retroactive interference in DMTS suggested that the issue of whether pigeons engage in maintenance rehearsal in DMTS was worthy of direct assessment. During my graduate years, Bill Roberts encouraged me to read extensively in the area of human memory, often by depositing large folders stuffed with reprints on my desk! One of the folders was labeled "directed forgetting," and hence, I became familiar with work on this topic using human subjects in both free recall and recognition procedures (DMTS is, of course, a recognition procedure). In the late 1970s, once established in my own laboratory at the University of Alberta, I began a project that investigated whether pigeons rehearse in DMTS. I reasoned that if pigeons do learn to engage in rehearsal in DMTS because such activity enhances the probability of remembering, thereby enhancing the probability of reinforcement, then it should be possible to bring such rehearsal under the control of postsample cues.

In my first study of directed forgetting (Grant, 1981b), red and green served as samples and choice stimuli. The successive version of the matching task, rather than the choice version described earlier, was employed in this study (see Fig. 8.2). In successive DMTS, only one test stimulus is presented following the retention interval. If the test stimulus matches the previously presented sample, the first peck after 5 sec in the presence of the stimulus is reinforced. If the test stimulus does not match the previously presented sample, the stimulus terminates in nonreinforcement after 5 sec. This technique capitalizes on the proclivity of pigeons to peck localized visual stimuli that are predictive of food and to refrain from pecking such stimuli that are not predictive of food. Matching accuracy is assessed by computing a *discrimination ratio* (DR), which is the proportion of all responses to test stimuli (excluding reinforced pecks on matching trials) that are emitted to matching stimuli.

A 1-sec vertical or horizontal white line, one serving as a remember (R) cue and the other as a forget (F) cue, was presented immediately after sample termination. Memory for the sample was tested on trials in which the R cue followed the sample, but not on trials in which the F cue followed the sample. After training, a memory test was presented on occasional F-cued trials (F-probe trials). As illustrated in Fig. 8.3, the experiment included two groups, neither of which received a memory test on F-cued trials during training. For subjects in the omission group, F-cued training trials ended immediately following termination of the F cue. For subjects in the dot-test group, the F cue was followed by a 5-sec presentation of a black dot on a white background. Responding to the dot was reinforced on a random 50% of F-cued trials, thus equating the rate of reinforcement on R- and F-cued trials in the dot-test group during training.

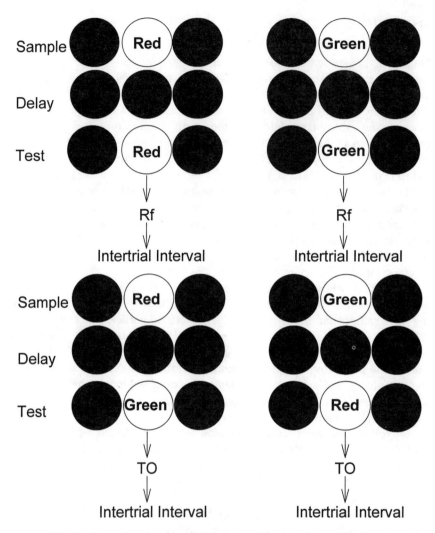

FIG. 8.2. Illustration of the successive version of the delayed matching-to-sample procedure using red and green sample and test stimuli.

As shown in Fig. 8.4, pigeons in both groups were more accurate on R-cued trials than on F-probe trials during testing, an effect referred to as the "F-cue effect." Moreover, the magnitude of the F-cue effect was approximately equivalent in the two groups, suggesting that it was the absence of memory testing during training, rather than the absence of test stimuli, that endowed the F cue with the ability to reduce matching accuracy. Notice also that the F-cue effect was larger at the longer than at the shorter retention interval, a result also obtained by Maki and Hegvik (1980) and Maki, Olson, and Rego (1981).

R-Cued Trials (Omission and Dot-Test Groups):

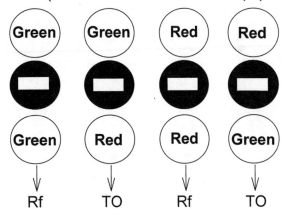

Green	Green	Red	Red
Green	Red	Red	Green
Rf	TO	Rf	TO

F-Cued Trials:

Omission Group

Dot-Test Group

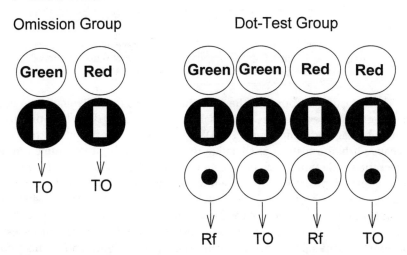

FIG. 8.3. Illustration of the training trials employed by Grant (1981b). Each pigeon was trained on the four types of R-cued trials illustrated in the upper portion of the figure. Birds in the omission group were trained on the two types of F-cued trials illustrated in the lower left-hand portion of the figure. Birds in the dot-test group were trained on the four types of F-cued trials illustrated in the lower right-hand portion of the figure. Because all stimuli were presented on the center key, the side keys are not shown.

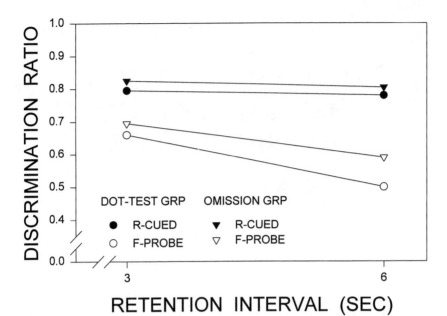

FIG. 8.4. Mean discrimination ratio on R-cued and F-probe trials in the dot-test group and the omission group as a function of length of retention interval. (The data were reported by Grant, 1981b, Experiment 3.)

These results encouraged the view that pigeons typically engage in post-perceptual processing (i.e., rehearsal) in DMTS, processing that promotes remembering and hence enhances DMTS accuracy. On this view, the F cue, because it had a history of signaling that remembering the sample did not affect the predictability of end-of-trial reinforcement, reduced or terminated the rehearsal process. The tendency for the F-cue effect to be larger at longer than at shorter retention intervals is entirely consistent with a re-hearsal-reduction account of the F-cue effect.

Thus, my view of the nature of information maintenance processes in pigeons was changing. It had evolved from a passive, automatic conception, in which traces spontaneously and inevitably lose strength, to a more active, controlled conception, in which rate of forgetting is strongly influenced by whether past training had or had not encouraged the pigeon to rehearse in those circumstances. At the same time as my view of information mainte-nance processes was changing, my view of the nature of the representation in DMTS was also changing. The trace conception implied that DMTS per-formance was mediated by retention of a representation isomorphic to the sample. By the early 1980s, however, evidence that pigeons retain a code that represents features of the correct test item had begun to accumulate (see Grant, 1981a; for a more recent discussion of coding processes in pigeons, see Grant, 1993). Thus, it now seemed appropriate to conceive of sample presentation as activating a code, rather than as establishing a memory trace.

The notion that an F cue reduces maintenance rehearsal of a sample-activated code leads to the expectation that such a cue would reduce accuracy more markedly when presented at the beginning rather than the end of a retention interval of fixed duration. Data from an experiment in which point of cue interpolation was manipulated during the F-probe testing phase are shown in Fig. 8.5. Consistent with the view that presentation of the F cue reduces maintenance rehearsal, the magnitude of the F-cue effect was considerably greater when the F cue was presented at the beginning rather than at the end of a 3-sec retention interval, a finding that was also obtained by Stonebraker and Rilling (1981).

Because the F-cue effect was as large in the dot-test group as in the omission group, the effectiveness of the F cue in reducing DMTS accuracy would appear to derive from the fact that the F cue signals the irrelevance of remembering for test responding. Although R- and F-cued training trials in the dot-test group did not differ either in terms of the presentation of stimulation during the testing phase or in terms of the probability of end-

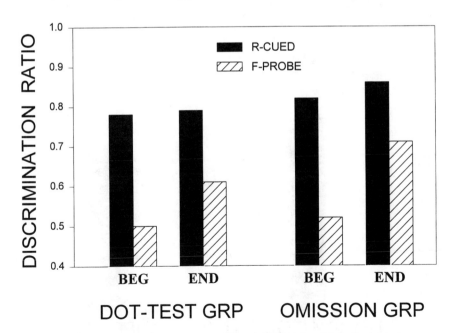

FIG. 8.5. Mean discrimination ratio on R-cued and F-probe trials in the dot-test group and the omission group as a function of whether the cue was presented during the first 1 sec (BEG) or final 1 sec (END) of a 3-sec retention interval. (The data were reported by Grant, 1981b, Experiment 2.)

of-trial reinforcement, R- and F-cued training trials did differ in one potentially important aspect. On R-cued training trials, discriminated responding was required at testing, whereas on F-cued training trials, it was not. It is therefore possible that the critical factor that endows a postsample cue with the ability to modulate DMTS performance is whether such a cue is associated with discriminated responding, rather than whether such a cue signals the relevance or irrelevance of sample memory to test responding.

Bob Barnet and I investigated this possibility (Grant & Barnet, 1991) using two groups of pigeons. F-cued training trials for both groups terminated in a choice between a circle and a triangle. In the nondifferential group, responding to either the triangle or the circle (independent of spatial position) was reinforced. In the differential group, responding to one of the stimuli was always reinforced and responding to the other stimulus was never reinforced. Thus, remembering the sample was irrelevant on F-cued training trials in both groups, but such training trials required discriminated responding in the differential group but not in the nondifferential group. If a history of signaling nondiscriminated responding is critical in producing an effective F cue, then a robust F-cue effect should be obtained in the nondifferential group but not in the differential group. Contrary to this expectation, as shown in Fig. 8.6, an F-cue effect of equivalent magnitude was obtained in both groups. This result reveals that a history of signaling nondiscriminated responding is not necessary to establishing an effective F cue and

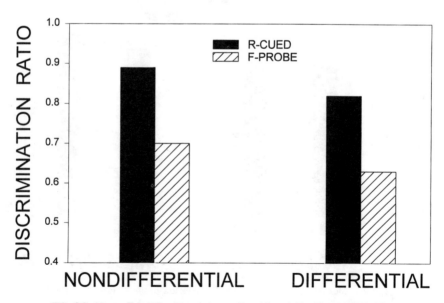

FIG. 8.6. Mean discrimination ratio on R-cued and F-probe trials in the nondifferential group and the differential group. (The data were reported by Grant & Barnet, 1991.)

thereby enhances confidence in the view that the effectiveness of an F cue in reducing memory-based performance derives from a history of signaling the irrelevance of remembering.

Research conducted in my laboratory has also used double-sample trials to assess the F-cue effect (Grant, 1984a, 1986, 1989). All three series of experiments involved the choice version of DMTS, red and green sample and choice stimuli, and vertical and horizontal R and F cues. In one series (Grant, 1984a), R and F cues were trained on single-sample trials. R-cued training trials terminated in a choice between matching and nonmatching stimuli, whereas F-cued training trials terminated in test omission (see upper portion of Table 8.1). Following extensive training, the effectiveness of R and F cues was tested on double-sample trials. Double-sample trials consisted of the sequential presentation of both samples, each of which was followed by one of the two cues. The first sample presented on a trial was a distractor or interfering sample and corresponded to the incorrect choice stimulus; the second was the target sample and corresponded to the correct choice stimulus. Three types of double-sample trials differed in terms of the cues that followed the interfering and target samples. An R-cue followed both samples on R–R trials, an F cue followed the interfering sample and an R cue followed the target sample on F–R trials, and an R cue followed the interfering sample and an F cue followed the target sample on R–F trials (see lower portion of Table 8.1).

Because double-sample trials involved presentation of an interfering sample prior to the target sample, it was anticipated that accuracy on all three types of double-sample trials would be lower than that on single-sample

TABLE 8.1
Illustration of the Training and Test Trials Employed by Grant (1984a)

Training Trials				
R-Cued			F-Cued	
Red	Green		Red	Green
R-Cue	R-Cue		F-Cue	F-Cue
Red+/Green−	Green+/Red−		Timeout	Timeout

Test Trials					
R–R		F–R		R–F	
Red	Green	Red	Green	Red	Green
R-Cue	R-Cue	F-Cue	F-Cue	R-Cue	R-Cue
Green	Red	Green	Red	Green	Red
R-Cue	R-Cue	R-Cue	R-Cue	F-Cue	F-Cue
Green+/Red−	Red+/Green−	Green+/Red−	Red+/Green−	Green+/Red−	Red+/Green−

Note. Balancing of the position of the correct test stimulus is not shown.

trials in which only a target sample, followed by an R cue, was presented (interference effect). More important, it was anticipated that if an F cue reduces rehearsal of the code activated by the immediately preceding sample, then the magnitude of the interference effect should be greater on R–R trials than on F–R trials (because the F cue should reduce processing of the interfering code) and should be less on R–R trials than on R–F trials (because the F cue should reduce processing of the target code). All three predictions were confirmed.

A final experiment in that series employed single-sample R-cued trials and double-sample R–R and F–R trials. The interval between the termination of the interfering sample and onset of the target sample (ISI) on double-sample trials was either 1, 3, or 7 sec. If presentation of an F cue reduces rehearsal of the code activated by the interfering sample, and hence accelerates the rate at which that code is forgotten, then the accuracy differential on F–R and R–R trials should increase as ISI is lengthened.

The results of this test are shown in Fig. 8.7. The interference effect was greater on R–R trials than on F–R trials at each of the three ISIs. More importantly, the discrepancy between accuracy on F–R and R–R trials increased as ISI was lengthened. Thus, the F cue was more effective in alleviating interference at longer ISI values, a finding consistent with the view that presentation of an F cue reduces rehearsal of the code activated by the preceding sample and hence accelerates the rate at which that code is forgotten.

In two subsequent series of experiments, I asked whether an effective F cue could be established in double-sample procedures. In one series (Grant, 1986), double-sample F–R trials involved the sequential presentation of an interfering sample (red or green) and a target sample (the remaining color). The interfering sample was always followed by a horizontal line (potential F cue) and the target sample was always followed by a vertical line (potential R cue). On single-sample R trials, the target sample was also followed by the vertical line. In one test to determine whether the horizontal line acquired the capacity to function as an F cue during training, performance was assessed on single-sample F-probe trials on which the target sample was followed by the horizontal rather than the vertical line. The assessment involved two identical testing phases that were separated by four consecutive training sessions.

Figure 8.8 shows performance during the two testing phases. Consider performance on baseline (training) trials, which involved single-sample R trials and double-sample F–R trials. After extensive training on these two trial types, presentation of an interfering sample no longer reduced accuracy (i.e., no interference effect was obtained). This finding suggests that the horizontal line functioned as an F cue and reduced processing of the code activated by the interfering sample and, moreover, that it did so rather

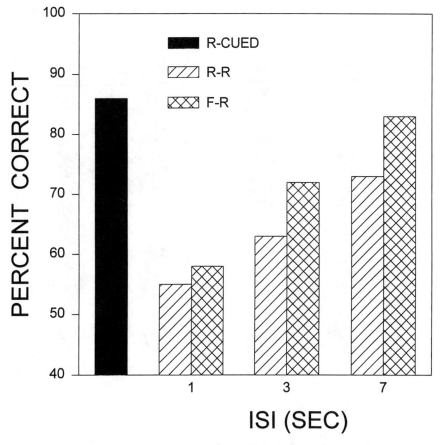

FIG. 8.7. Mean percentage of correct responses on R-cued (no interfering sample, target sample followed by an R cue), R–R (interfering and target sample each followed by an R cue), and F–R (interfering sample followed by an F cue and target sample followed by an R cue) trials. The ISI between the interfering and target samples was manipulated on R–R and F–R trials. (The data were reported by Grant, 1984a, Experiment 3.)

effectively. This view is supported by the results of probe testing in which a single sample was sometimes followed by a vertical line (R probes, identical to training trials) and other times followed by a horizontal line (F probes). As anticipated by the view that the horizontal line functioned as an effective F cue and reduced rehearsal of the code activated by the sample, accuracy was markedly lower on F-probe than on R-probe trials (see Fig. 8.8).

In a follow-up to the series of experiments just described, I asked whether an effective F cue could be established if potential R and F cues signaled the target and interfering samples, respectively, independent of the order

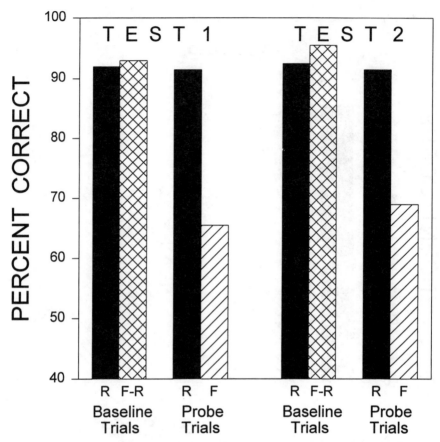

FIG. 8.8. Mean percentage of correct responses on baseline and probe trials. On baseline trials, an interfering sample was not presented and the target sample was followed by an R cue (R) or the interfering sample was followed by an F cue and the target sample was followed by an R cue (F–R). On probe trials, only the target sample was presented and was followed by either an R cue (R) or an F cue (F). Test 2 was a replication of test 1. (The data were reported by Grant, 1986, Experiment 3.)

in which the samples were presented on double-sample trials (Grant, 1989). Pigeons were first trained on choice DMTS with single-sample trials involving red and green samples and choice stimuli (no postsample cues were presented). Next, they were trained on single-sample trials and two types of double-sample trials, S1+ in which the first sample was the target (and the second was the interfering), and S2+ in which the second sample was the target (and the first was the interfering). The target sample on both single- and double-sample trials was always followed by a vertical line (potential R cue) and the interfering sample on double-sample trials was always followed by a horizontal line (potential F cue).

Combined accuracy on double-sample trials (51.1% correct) was at chance early in training, presumably because the animals had not yet learned that the cues signaled which sample was the target and which was the interfering. After extensive training (264 sessions of 96 trials each), combined accuracy on double-sample trials (73.1% correct) was well above chance, suggesting that the postsample cues were exerting control. Although above chance accuracy on double-sample trials is consistent with the possibility that the horizontal line functioned as an F cue and inhibited processing of the code activated by the preceding sample, other accounts of this result are possible (see Grant, 1989). To determine whether the horizontal line functioned as an F cue, a testing phase followed training in which the sample on single-sample trials was sometimes followed by the horizontal line (rather the vertical line as in training). As predicted by the hypothesis that the horizontal line functioned as an F cue, accuracy on these trials was 58.4% correct, considerably lower than that on single-sample trials in which the sample was followed by the vertical line (91.7%).

The data reviewed in this section appear to strongly support the contention that pigeons typically engage in an active rehearsal process during the retention interval in DMTS. The specific findings consonant with this view include the demonstration of (a) a robust F-cue effect when the F cue is associated with the same rate of reinforcement as that associated with an R cue during training; (b) a robust F-cue effect when the F cue is associated with discriminated test responding during training; (c) a stronger F-cue effect at longer than at shorter retention intervals; (d) a more robust F-cue effect when the cues occur earlier rather than later in a retention interval; and (e) a greater alleviation of interference at longer than at shorter ISIs when the interfering sample is followed by an F cue.

A NONMEMORIAL ACCOUNT
OF THE F-CUE EFFECT

Although the findings discussed in the preceding section collectively appear to constitute incontrovertible evidence for an active rehearsal process in pigeons, Roper and Zentall (1993) recently argued that they do not. Roper and Zentall identified a number of nonmemorial processes that could mediate reduced accuracy on F-probe trials (e.g., surprise-induced disruption caused by the presentation of unexpected test stimuli on F-probe trials, frustration-induced disruption caused by presentation of an F cue associated with a lower rate of reinforcement than the R cue, etc.). The operation of several nonmemorial factors (such as the two just mentioned) is precluded when the F cue is followed by test stimuli during training and is associated with the same rate of reinforcement as the R cue, as was the case in Grant's

(1981b) dot-test group, Grant and Barnet's (1991) differential and nondifferential groups, and the case where the F cue was established on double-sample trials (Grant, 1986, 1989). Even in these cases, however, Roper and Zentall argued that the F-cue effect may not provide unambiguous evidence for an active rehearsal process. Specifically, they suggested the possibility that presentation of an F cue on F-probe trials might tend to evoke the behavior pattern associated with that cue on F-cued training trials. To the extent that this does indeed happen, and to the extent that the evoked behavior pattern is incompatible with accurate DMTS performance, accuracy on F-probe trials would be reduced independent of any effect that the F cue might (or might not) have on memorial processes.

To illustrate Roper and Zentall's (1993) response-pattern incompatibility account, consider the F-cue effect in the dot-test group in Grant's (1981b) study. During training, the F cue was followed by a 5-sec presentation of a dot, to which responding was reinforced on a random 50% of presentations. As all "bird runners" would predict, the pigeons responded at a high and sustained rate to the dot stimulus. If the F cue acquires the ability to evoke this high and sustained rate of responding, and if the evocation of such a behavior pattern is independent of the identity of the test stimulus, then inaccurate DMTS performance on F-probe trials would be anticipated because the behavior pattern evoked (i.e., high rate of responding) is incompatible with the behavior pattern required for accurate DMTS (i.e., high rate of responding on matching trials and low rate of responding on nonmatching trials).

As a second illustration, consider the differential group in Grant and Barnet's (1991) study in which F-cued training trials terminated in a choice between a triangle and a circle, and choice of one stimulus was always reinforced whereas choice of the other stimulus was never reinforced. Again, Roper and Zentall (1993) argued that the F-cue effect may be attributed to the F cue evoking a behavior pattern incompatible with accurate DMTS. But, one might ask, why would a behavior pattern consisting of choosing between two stimuli necessarily interfere with a high rate of responding on matching DMTS trials and a low rate of responding on nonmatching DMTS trials? Roper and Zentall anticipated this question by postulating that the behavior of rapid choice conditioned on F-cued training trials would result in a high and sustained rate of indiscriminant responding on F-probe trials. Although unsupported, this supposition cannot be dismissed on existing empirical grounds.

It should also be noted that Roper and Zentall's (1993) response-pattern incompatibility account of the F-cue effect provides no ready account as to why the F-cue effect is larger at longer than at shorter retention intervals, and when the F cue is presented at the beginning rather than at the end of a retention interval. Nor does the behavior-incompatibility account provide an explanation for the finding that presentation of an F cue following an interfering sample alleviates interference, and does so more effectively when the ISI between interfering and target sample is long rather than when it is short. Nonetheless, Roper and Zentall's review and analysis of the research on directed forgetting in animals raises the possibility that the F-cue effect does not provide the definitive evidence for an active rehearsal process that I and others have argued (e.g., Grant, 1981a, 1984b; Maki, 1981; Rilling, Kendrick, & Stonebraker, 1984; Santi, 1989).

RECENT RESEARCH ON THE F-CUE EFFECT: THE CASE FOR A MEMORIAL ACCOUNT

Two recent studies from my laboratory strengthen the claim that the rehearsal account of the F-cue effect is the most feasible one. In one study, Alex Soldat and I ensured that the F cue during training could not become associated with a pattern of test responding that, if evoked on F-probe trials, could interfere with accurate DMTS performance (Grant & Soldat, 1995). This was accomplished by employing a training procedure highly similar to that used in Grant and Barnet's (1991) differential group, with one notable exception. In the earlier study, F-cued training trials terminated in a simple (nonconditional) simultaneous discrimination consisting of a choice between a circle and a triangle (with selecting one always reinforced and selecting the other never reinforced). As discussed previously, Roper and Zentall (1993) argued that the behavior pattern conditioned on F-cued training trials (rapid choice) might be construed as incompatible with the behavior pattern necessary to accurate performance in successive DMTS (a go/no go pattern). In Grant and Soldat's design, illustrated in Fig. 8.9, F-cued training trials also terminated in a sample-independent simple discrimination, but the discriminative stimuli were presented successively rather than simultaneously. Specifically, termination of the F cue on training trials was followed equally often by presentation of a dot *or* a circle. The first peck after 5 sec in the presence of the dot produced reinforcement whereas the circle terminated in nonreinforcement after 5 sec. Notice that on F-cued training trials (a) sample memory was irrelevant to predicting trial outcome and (b) the behavior pattern associated with the F cue on training trials was identical to the behavior pattern necessary to accurate successive DMTS performance (go/no go in both cases). Thus, a reduction in accuracy on F-probe trials (i.e., an F-cue effect) could not in this case be attributed to the evocation by the F cue of a pattern of behavior incompatible with accurate DMTS performance.

A robust F-cue effect was indeed obtained; accuracy on R-cued trials ($DR = .72$) was significantly higher than accuracy on F-probe trials ($DR = .56$). Although the F-cue effect could not be a function of response-pattern incompatibility, it is possible that the effect was mediated by processes other than

R-Cued Trials:

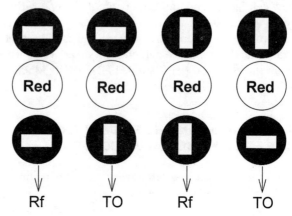

F-Cued Trials:

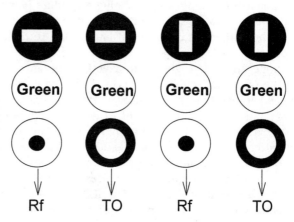

FIG. 8.9. Illustration of the training trials employed by Grant and Soldat (1995). Each pigeon was trained on the eight types of trials illustrated. Because all stimuli were presented on the center key, the side keys are not shown.

selective rehearsal (i.e., greater rehearsal on R-cued trials than on F-probe trials). Specifically, it might be suggested that during training, the F cue became a signal that the trial would terminate in presentation of either the circle or the dot. If so, performance on F-probe trials may have been disrupted by surprise induced by presentation of an unexpected line orientation (line orientations served as samples and test stimuli, and colors served as R and F cues in this study).

Two findings suggest, however, that presentation of an unexpected test stimulus produces only minor disruption of DMTS performance, and hence, that the F-cue effect obtained by Grant and Soldat (1995) was not entirely produced by surprise induced by the presentation of an unexpected test stimulus. First, Santi, Musgrave, and Bradford (1988) trained pigeons in a DMTS task in which either of two color samples was equally often followed by a choice between two colors and two lines. For both choice dimensions, the stimulus that was correct depended on which of the two samples was presented on that trial. All sample presentations were followed by presentation of a 1-sec cue (circle or triangle), which indicated which of the two choice dimensions would be presented on that trial. Notice that both cues signaled that remembering was relevant to obtaining end-of-trial reinforcement. The cues differed only in terms of which dimension of choice stimuli they signaled. After extensive training, Santi et al. conducted test trials in which the dimension of the choice stimuli was signaled incorrectly. In this case, any disruption in DMTS accuracy on incorrectly-cued test trials could reflect only surprise-induced disruption caused by the presentation of unexpected choice stimuli. Although accuracy was lower on incorrectly-cued trials than on correctly-cued trials, the magnitude of that disruption was small, 5.2% in Experiment 1 and 2.9% in Experiment 2 (see also Grant & MacDonald, 1990; Stonebraker & Rilling, 1984). Santi et al.'s results suggest that the F-cue effect obtained by Grant and Soldat (1995) was too large to be attributed solely to surprise-induced disruption on F-probe trials.

Grant and Soldat (1995) also provided evidence that the presentation of an unexpected test stimulus does not disrupt accuracy to an extent sufficient to allow the F-cue effect to be attributed exclusively to that process. The training conditions were identical to those employed in their first experiment, but the testing conditions differed from those in the first experiment in two ways. First, responding to test stimuli was recorded in 1-sec bins. Second, an additional testing condition, R-probe testing (which was the complement of F-probe testing) was employed. On R-probe trials, the R cue was followed by a circle or dot test stimulus from the simple discrimination rather than a line orientation from the conditional DMTS task. Any reduction in simple discrimination accuracy on R-probe trials relative to that on standard F-cued trials could only reflect disruption induced by the presentation of an unexpected test stimulus.

The results of this experiment are summarized in Table 8.2. Examination of the left half of the table reveals that accuracy on F-probe trials, relative to that on R-cued trials, was markedly lower in each 1-sec interval of test stimulus presentation. Examination of the right half of the table reveals that accuracy on R-probe trials, relative to that on F-cued trials, was only slightly lower and, moreover, the reduction in accuracy occurred only during the first 1 sec of the test stimulus. Thus, the F-cue effect was large in magnitude and extended throughout the 5-sec test stimulus presentation whereas the surprise-induced disruption effect was small in magnitude and was confined

TABLE 8.2
Mean Discrimination Ratio in Each 1-sec Bin
During Test Stimulus Presentation

Bin	R-Cued	F-Probe	F-Cued	R-Probe
1	0.73	0.52	0.94	0.76
2	0.88	0.56	1.00	1.00
3	0.85	0.57	1.00	1.00
4	0.84	0.50	1.00	1.00
5	0.80	0.50	1.00	1.00

Note. The task on R-cued and F-probe trials was successive DMTS. The task on F-cued and R-probe trials was a successive simple discrimination. Results come from Grant and Soldat (1995, Experiment 3).

to the first 1-sec of test stimulus presentation. The data from R-probe trials join those from Santi et al. (1988) in suggesting that surprise induced by presentation of an unexpected test item (or items) produces only a minor reduction in DMTS accuracy. It may be concluded that although surprise-induced disruption may contribute to the F-cue effect, it is not solely responsible for that effect. I believe that the primary mechanism mediating the F-cue effect is differential rehearsal on R-cued and F-probe trials.

A series of experiments by Ron Kelly and myself, although conducted for other purposes, also suggests that the nonmemorial factors specified by Roper and Zentall (1993) contribute in only minor ways to the F-cue effect in pigeons (Grant & Kelly, 1996). Pigeons were trained in a DMTS task in which the samples consisted of a short (e.g., 2-sec) and a long (e.g., 10-sec) presentation of overhead light. A postsample cue (horizontal or vertical line) indicated whether red and green choice stimuli would (R cue) or would not (F cue) be presented. On R-cued training trials, the duration of the sample determined which of the color choice stimuli was correct. On F-cued training trials, the cue signaled that the trial was over (test omission procedure). Following extensive training on R- and F-cued trials, a testing phase was conducted in which red and green choice stimuli appeared on infrequent F-probe trials.

The results of this experiment are shown in Fig. 8.10. Although accuracy was reliably lower on F-probe trials than on R-cued trials, the magnitude of that reduction was not large (approximately 6%, collapsed across retention interval). Also, in contrast to the findings of Grant (1981b), Maki and Hegvik (1980), and Maki et al. (1981), the F-cue effect was not larger at longer than at shorter retention intervals; in fact, a significant trend in the opposite direction was obtained. Before discussing the implications of these findings, consider the results of a second experiment reported by Grant and Kelly (1996). In that experiment, the cue was presented at the beginning of a 7-sec retention interval on some trials, and at the end of the retention interval on other trials. As shown in Fig. 8.11, and in contrast to the findings of Grant

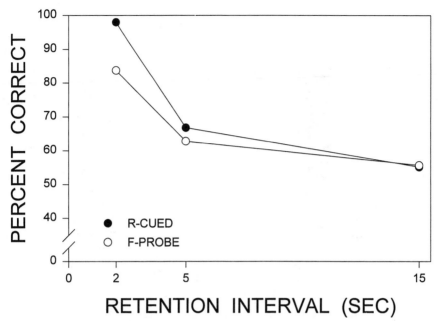

RETENTION INTERVAL (SEC)

FIG. 8.10. Mean percentage of correct responses on R-cued and F-probe trials as a function of retention interval. The samples were short and long presentations of an overhead light. (The data were reported by Grant & Kelly, 1996, Experiment 2.)

(1981b) and Stonebraker and Rilling (1981), the F-cue effect was not reliably greater when the cues were presented at the beginning rather than at the end of the retention interval.

Based on the finding that the magnitude of the F-cue effect (a) was not greater at longer than at shorter retention intervals and (b) that it was not greater when the cues were presented earlier rather than later in the retention interval, we concluded that pigeons do not postperceptually process (rehearse) in the matching-to-duration-samples task. We attributed the absence of rehearsal to the content of the representation. Considerable evidence suggests that, in the type of task employed by Grant and Kelly (1996), pigeons represent duration samples in terms of an analogical code; for example, the number of counts or pulses generated by a pacemaker during sample presentation (e.g., Grant & Spetch, 1991, 1993; Santi, Ducharme, & Bridson, 1992; Spetch, 1987; Spetch & Wilkie, 1983; Wilkie & Willson, 1990; for a recent review see Grant, Spetch, & Kelly, in press). We speculated that such a code may be inherently more difficult to rehearse than the code generated in matching tasks involving colors or lines, a code that might consist of an image of the sample or correct test stimulus (see, for example, Roitblat, 1987).

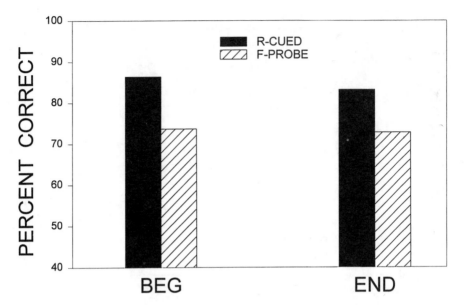

FIG. 8.11. Mean percentage of correct responses on R-cued and F-probe trials
as a function of whether the cue was presented during the first 2 sec (BEG)
or last 2 sec (END) of a 7-sec retention interval. (The data were reported by
Grant & Kelly, 1996, Experiment 4.)

Of particular relevance to the present discussion are the implications of
Grant and Kelly's (1996) findings for Roper and Zentall's (1993) suggestion
that many, and perhaps all, instances of the F-cue effect obtained at the time
of their review could be attributed to the operation of nonmemorial artifacts
rather than to active processing of a sample-activated code. Among the
nonmemorial processes that could produce the F-cue effect, they listed
frustration induced by an F cue associated with nonreinforcement during
training, inattention and/or surprise induced by the presentation of unexpected test stimuli, and evocation by the F cue of a pattern of test responding incompatible with accurate DMTS performance. Notice that the number
and potential impact of such artifacts was surely as great in Grant and Kelly's
study (recall that test omission was employed on F-cued training trials) as
in other studies employing R and F cues and color or line samples. But if
all cases of the F-cue effect are attributable solely to these artifacts, as Roper
and Zentall contend, then why did Grant and Kelly fail to obtain a stronger
F-cue effect at longer delays and when the cues were presented at the
beginning of the retention interval? And why, for that matter, did Grant and
Kelly obtain only a modest reduction in accuracy on F-probe trials (less than
8% collapsed across experiments) whereas other experiments reported decrements on F-probe trials ranging from 16% to 40% (see Kendrick, Rilling, &
Stonebraker, 1981, Figure 1, Condition B; Santi & Savich, 1985, Figure 1, NDO

condition; Zentall, Roper, & Sherburne, 1995; in the present chapter, Fig. 8.5, probe trials)? In my view, a reasonable answer to these questions involves the notion that the F-cue effect in Grant and Kelly's study was produced exclusively by nonmemorial processes because the nature of the representation precluded active rehearsal of the code. In contrast, although artifacts may, at least under some conditions, contribute to the F-cue effect in studies employing color and line samples, the primary mechanism responsible for the F-cue effect in these preparations is selective postsample processing of sample-activated codes.

CONCLUSION

The research reviewed in this chapter provides compelling evidence that pigeons typically engage in active processing (rehearsal) of sample-activated codes during the retention interval in the DMTS task. One caveat to this conclusion is that some types of samples (e.g., those differing in duration) may give rise to codes less conducive to rehearsal than other types of samples (e.g., colors, line orientations). The avian information processing system is apparently more flexible and sophisticated than we had conceded in the early 1970s. Not only are pigeons capable of learning to rehearse information, they are also capable of learning to do so selectively in situations in which such rehearsal is relevant to trial outcome.

The view that avian information maintenance processes are flexible and controlled is consistent with the view that information coding processes in avians are also flexible and controlled. Recent research (e.g., Grant, 1991; Grant & Spetch, 1991, 1993; Santi, Bridson, & Ducharme, 1993; Zentall, Sherburne, & Urcuioli, 1995) has revealed that pigeons are capable of coding the same nominal event in different ways depending on task demands (for recent reviews see, for example, Grant, 1993; Grant et al., in press; Zentall, Urcuioli, Jackson-Smith, & Steirn, 1991). Thus, the cognitive capacity to actively rehearse and code information, and the ability to exert control over those processes, may be phylogenetically far more primitive (and hence more extensive) than we had once thought.

ACKNOWLEDGMENTS

The research reported in this article and the preparation of the article was supported by grants from the Natural Sciences and Engineering Research Council of Canada. I thank Ron Kelly and Bill Roberts for commenting on an earlier draft of this chapter.

REFERENCES

Grant, D. S. (1975). Proactive interference in pigeon short-term memory. *Journal of Experimental Psychology: Animal Behavior Processes, 1,* 207–220.

Grant, D. S. (1976). Effect of sample presentation time on long-delay matching in the pigeon. *Learning and Motivation, 7,* 580–590.

Grant, D. S. (1981a). Short-term memory in the pigeon. In N. E. Spear & R. R. Miller (Eds.), *Information processing in animals: Memory mechanisms* (pp. 227–256). Hillsdale, NJ: Lawrence Erlbaum Associates.

Grant, D. S. (1981b). Stimulus control of information processing in pigeon short-term memory. *Learning and Motivation, 12,* 19–39.

Grant, D. S. (1984a). Directed forgetting and intratrial interference in pigeon delayed matching. *Canadian Journal of Psychology, 38,* 166–177.

Grant, D. S. (1984b). Rehearsal in pigeon short-term memory. In H. L. Roitblat, T. G. Bever, & H. S. Terrace (Eds.), *Animal cognition* (pp. 99–115). Hillsdale, NJ: Lawrence Erlbaum Associates.

Grant, D. S. (1986). Establishing a forget cue in pigeons using the intratrial interference procedure. *Animal Learning & Behavior, 14,* 267–275.

Grant, D. S. (1989). Use of an ambiguous-sample procedure to establish a cue to forget in pigeons. *Journal of the Experimental Analysis of Behavior, 52,* 325–334.

Grant, D. S. (1991). Symmetrical and asymmetrical coding of food and no-food samples in delayed matching in pigeons. *Journal of Experimental Psychology: Animal Behavior Processes, 17,* 186–193.

Grant, D. S. (1993). Coding processes in pigeons. In T. R. Zentall (Ed.), *Animal cognition: A tribute to Donald A. Riley* (pp. 193–216). Hillsdale, NJ: Lawrence Erlbaum Associates.

Grant, D. S., & Barnet, R. C. (1991). Irrelevance of sample stimuli and directed forgetting in pigeons. *Journal of the Experimental Analysis of Behavior, 55,* 97–108.

Grant, D. S., & Kelly, R. (1996). *Choice matching to duration samples in pigeons: Effect of postsample cues to remember and forget.* Manuscript submitted for publication.

Grant, D. S., & MacDonald, S. E. (1990). An evaluation of the role of dual coding in mediating the effect of incorrectly cuing the comparison dimension in delayed matching in pigeons. *Animal Learning & Behavior, 18,* 151–156.

Grant, D. S., & Roberts, W. A. (1973). Trace interaction in pigeon short-term memory. *Journal of Experimental Psychology, 101,* 21–29.

Grant, D. S., & Roberts, W. A. (1976). Sources of retroactive inhibition in pigeon short-term memory. *Journal of Experimental Psychology: Animal Behavior Processes, 2,* 1–16.

Grant, D. S., & Soldat, A. S. (1995). A postsample cue to forget does initiate an active forgetting process. *Journal of Experimental Psychology: Animal Behavior Processes, 21,* 218–228.

Grant, D. S., & Spetch, M. L. (1991). Pigeons' memory for event duration: Differences between choice and successive matching tasks. *Learning and Motivation, 22,* 180–190.

Grant, D. S., & Spetch, M. L. (1993). Analogical and nonanalogical coding of samples differing in duration in a choice-matching task in pigeons. *Journal of Experimental Psychology: Animal Behavior Processes, 19,* 15–25.

Grant, D. S., Spetch, M. L., & Kelly, R. (in press). Pigeons' coding of event duration in delayed matching-to-sample. In C. M. Bradshaw & E. Szabadi (Eds.), *Time and behaviour: Psychological and neuro-behavioural analyses.* Amsterdam: Elsevier.

Kendrick, D. F., Rilling, M., & Stonebraker, T. B. (1981). Stimulus control of delayed matching in pigeons: Directed forgetting. *Journal of the Experimental Analysis of Behavior, 36,* 241–251.

Maki, W. S. (1981). Directed forgetting in animals. In N. E. Spear & R. R. Miller (Eds.), *Information processing in animals: Memory mechanisms* (pp. 199–225). Hillsdale, NJ: Lawrence Erlbaum Associates.

Maki, W. S., & Hegvik, D. K. (1980). Directed forgetting in pigeons. *Animal Learning & Behavior*, *8*, 567–574.

Maki, W. S., Olson, D., & Rego, S. (1981). Directed forgetting in pigeons: Analysis of cue functions. *Animal Learning & Behavior*, *9*, 189–195.

Morgan, C. L. (1894). *An introduction to comparative psychology*. London: Scott.

Rilling, M., Kendrick, D. F., & Stonebraker, T. B. (1984). Directed forgetting in context. In G. H. Bower (Ed.), *The psychology of learning and motivation: Advances in research and theory* (Vol. 18, pp. 175–198). New York: Academic Press.

Roberts, W. A. (1972). Short-term memory in the pigeon: Effects of repetition and spacing. *Journal of Experimental Psychology*, *94*, 74–83.

Roberts, W. A., & Grant, D. S. (1974). Short-term memory in the pigeon with presentation time precisely controlled. *Learning and Motivation*, *5*, 393–409.

Roberts, W. A., & Grant, D. S. (1976). Studies of short-term memory in the pigeon using the delayed matching-to-sample procedure. In D. L. Medin, W. A. Roberts, & R. T. Davis (Eds.), *Processes of animal memory* (pp. 79–112). Hillsdale, NJ: Lawrence Erlbaum Associates.

Roberts, W. A., & Grant, D. S. (1978). An analysis of light-induced retroactive inhibition in pigeon short-term memory. *Journal of Experimental Psychology: Animal Behavior Processes*, *4*, 219–236.

Roitblat, H. L. (1987). *Introduction to comparative cognition*. New York: W. H. Freeman and Company.

Roper, K. L., & Zentall, T. R. (1993). Directed forgetting in animals. *Psychological Bulletin*, *113*, 513–532.

Santi, A. (1989). Differential outcome expectancies and directed forgetting effects in pigeons. *Animal Learning & Behavior*, *17*, 349–354.

Santi, A., Bridson, S., & Ducharme, M. J. (1993). Memory codes for temporal and nontemporal samples in many-to-one matching by pigeons. *Animal Learning & Behavior*, *21*, 120–130.

Santi, A., Ducharme, M. J., & Bridson, S. (1992). Differential outcome expectancies and memory for temporal and nontemporal stimuli in pigeons. *Learning and Motivation*, *23*, 156–169.

Santi, A., Musgrave, S., & Bradford, S. E. (1988). Utilization of cues signaling different test stimulus dimensions in delayed matching to sample by pigeons. *Learning and Motivation*, *19*, 87–98.

Santi, A., & Savich, J. (1985). Directed forgetting effects in pigeons: Remember cues initiate rehearsal. *Animal Learning & Behavior*, *13*, 365–369.

Spetch, M. L. (1987). Systematic errors in pigeons' memory for event duration: Interaction between training and test delay. *Animal Learning & Behavior*, *15*, 1–5.

Spetch, M. L., & Wilkie, D. M. (1983). Subjective shortening: A model of pigeons' memory for event duration. *Journal of Experimental Psychology: Animal Behavior Processes*, *9*, 14–30.

Stonebraker, T. B., & Rilling, M. (1981). Control of delayed matching-to-sample performance using directed forgetting techniques. *Animal Learning & Behavior*, *9*, 196–201.

Stonebraker, T. B., & Rilling, M. (1984). Retrospective versus prospective processes in delayed matching to sample. *Bulletin of the Psychonomic Society*, *22*, 372–375.

Terry, W. S., & Wagner, A. R. (1975). Short-term memory for "surprising" versus "expected" unconditioned stimuli in Pavlovian conditioning. *Journal of Experimental Psychology: Animal Behavior Processes*, *1*, 122–133.

Wagner, A. R. (1978). Expectancies and the priming of STM. In S. H. Hulse, H. Fowler, & W. K. Honig (Eds.), *Cognitive processes in animal behavior* (pp. 177–209). Hillsdale, NJ: Lawrence Erlbaum Associates.

Wagner, A. R. (1981). SOP: A model of automatic memory processing in animal behavior. In N. E. Spear & R. R. Miller (Eds.), *Information processing in animals: Memory mechanisms* (pp. 5–47). Hillsdale, NJ: Lawrence Erlbaum Associates.

Wagner, A. R., Rudy, J. W., & Whitlow, J. W. (1973). Rehearsal in animal conditioning. *Journal of Experimental Psychology*, *97*, 407–426.

Wilkie, D. M., & Willson, R. J. (1990). Discriminal distance analysis supports the hypothesis that pigeons retrospectively encode event duration. *Animal Learning & Behavior*, *18*, 124–132.

Zentall, T. R., Roper, K. L., & Sherburne, L. M. (1995). Most directed forgetting in pigeons can be attributed to the absence of reinforcement on forget trials during training or to other procedural artifacts. *Journal of the Experimental Analysis of Behavior, 63,* 127–137.

Zentall, T. R., Sherburne, L. M., & Urcuioli, P. J. (1995). Coding of hedonic and nonhedonic samples by pigeons in many-to-one delayed matching. *Animal Learning & Behavior, 23,* 189–196.

Zentall, T. R., Urcuioli, P. J., Jackson-Smith, P., & Steirn, J. N. (1991). Memory strategies in pigeons. In L. Dachowski & C. F. Flaherty (Eds.), *Current topics in animal learning: Brain, emotion, and cognition* (pp. 119–139). Hillsdale, NJ: Lawrence Erlbaum Associates.

9

A CRITICAL ANALYSIS OF DIRECTED-FORGETTING RESEARCH IN ANIMALS

Thomas R. Zentall
University of Kentucky

Karen L. Roper
University of Wisconsin–Eau Claire

Daren H. Kaiser
University of Kentucky

Lou M. Sherburne
Wabash College

Animal cognition research has focused on efforts to demonstrate and explain the active processing of information by animals. The goal often has been to look for tasks that were used to assess human cognitive behavior and to ask if analogs of these tasks can be developed to assess the cognitive behavior of animals (see e.g., Honig & Fetterman, 1992; Hulse, Fowler, & Honig, 1978; Roitblat, Bever, & Terrace, 1984; Zentall, 1993).

The cognitive approach has usually been contrasted with the more traditional associationist approach typified by Hull (1943) and Skinner (1938) in which behavior can be accounted for in simple associative terms together with simple stimulus generalization (i.e., transfer of training based on the physical similarity among trained and untrained stimuli). Thus, for those who have taken a cognitive approach, interest has focused on assessing the ability of animals to base responding on the relations between stimuli rather than on their absolute physical properties (e.g., the ability of animals to respond to stimuli according to various categorical rules). Examples of such an approach can be found in the study of learning by animals of natural polymorphous classes (Herrnstein & Loveland, 1964; Wasserman, Kiedinger, & Bhatt, 1988), natural color classes (Zentall, Jackson-Smith, & Jagielo, 1990), arbitrary stimulus classes (Urcuioli, Zentall, Jackson-Smith, & Steirn, 1989; Zentall & Urcuioli, 1993), identity concepts (Zentall, Edwards, Moore, & Hogan, 1981; Zentall & Hogan, 1978), and transitive inferences (Weaver, Steirn, & Zentall, 1995).

The role of active cognitive processing by animals has also been examined in the retention of information over time. Cognitive processing is demonstrated by the considerable flexibility shown by both rats and pigeons in their ability to remember information. In a delayed matching-to-sample task, an initial stimulus (or sample) is separated from the test stimuli (or comparisons) by a retention interval, and the initial stimulus signals which of the comparisons is correct on that trial. When pigeons are trained on this task, under some conditions they appear to represent and retain the initial stimulus (i.e., retrospective coding of the samples, Honig & Thompson, 1982; Urcuioli & Zentall, 1986; Zentall, Urcuioli, Jagielo, & Jackson-Smith, 1989), whereas under other conditions they appear to represent and retain response intentions (i.e., prospective coding of the correct comparison, Honig & Thompson, 1982; Roitblat, 1980; Zentall, Jagielo, Jackson-Smith, & Urcuioli, 1987). In other contexts (e.g., the radial-arm-maze task in which animals must respond to each of a set of locations once, and only once), pigeons and rats appear to be able to "decide" whether to code retrospectively or prospectively at the start of (or during) the retention interval (Cook, Brown, & Riley, 1985; Zentall, Steirn, & Jackson-Smith, 1990). Thus, it appears that a complete account of learning by animals requires more than simple associative-learning processes.

One of the most thoroughly examined animal memory phenomena that has been studied for its cognitive implications is directed forgetting (see Roper & Zentall, 1993, for a review). The rationale for studying directed forgetting in animals is the assumption that memory deficits resulting from presentation of a cue to forget imply that memory maintenance is an active controlled process.

DIRECTED FORGETTING IN ANIMALS

Historically, forgetting by animals was viewed as a passive process attributable to the decay of the stimulus trace (Grant & Roberts, 1973), interference, both from earlier memories (proactive interference) and from later memories (retroactive interference; Zentall & Hogan, 1977), or loss of temporal order (i.e., confusion about which memory was most recent; D'Amato, 1973). If animals can be directed to forget, however, it suggests that animals may use a more active memory maintenance process.

The typical directed-forgetting task used with animals is most analogous to a simple version of the post-item-cuing procedure used in human directed-forgetting research (see e.g., Archer & Margolin, 1970; MacLeod, 1975). In this procedure, humans are presented with a list, each item of which is followed by a cue either to remember or to forget it, and recall of items followed by a cue to forget is generally found to be worse than recall of items followed by a cue to remember.

The first evidence of a directed-forgettinglike effect in animals was reported by Maki, Gillund, Hauge, and Siders (1977). In their study, pigeons initially were trained on a matching-to-sample task and then, for some time, comparison stimuli were omitted following one of the samples. When comparisons were reinstated, performance on trials involving that sample had dropped to chance level. One interpretation of this result is that, during the comparison-omission phase, the pigeons had learned to view the sample associated with the absence of comparisons as a cue to forget. Because the absence of comparisons (and of the reinforcements associated with them) was predictable at the time of sample presentation, however, it could also be that the pigeons failed to attend to or encode those samples. Thus, a better procedure is needed to ensure that performance decrements can be attributed to true directed forgetting.

Omission Procedures

To encourage that attention to the samples is comparable on forget- and remember-cue trials and to ensure that the animals do not process the samples differentially while they are present, it is important that the forget cue not be correlated with the samples and that it be presented following sample offset. Thus, a better analog of the directed-forgetting procedure used with humans is one in which the cue to forget is presented independently of and following the sample (Maki, 1981).

The simplest of such directed-forgetting procedures involves samples that are sometimes followed by forget (F) cues and other times followed by remember (R) cues. Forget cues signal that no comparisons will follow and that the trial is over. Remember cues signal that comparisons will follow and that memory for the sample will be tested. Directed forgetting is demonstrated following such training when, on infrequently presented probe trials, comparisons are presented following an F cue and a decrement in matching accuracy is found, relative to that on R-cue trials (Grant, 1981; Maki & Hegvik, 1980; Maki, Olsen, & Rego, 1981; Roberts, Mazmanian, & Kraemer, 1984; Santi & Savich, 1985; Stonebraker & Rilling, 1981). In the animal directed-forgetting literature, a procedure such as this, in which the F cue signals that the trial is over, is referred to as a comparison-omission

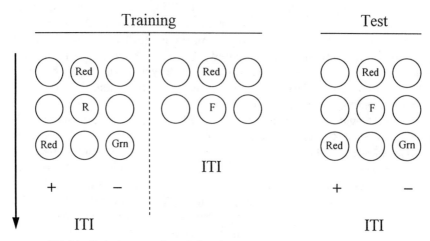

FIG. 9.1. Omission procedure: Delayed matching-to-sample with the remember cue (R) followed by comparison choice and the forget cue (F) followed by the intertrial interval (ITI). Sample hue and location (left or right) of the correct comparison are balanced over trials. On infrequently presented F-cue probe trials comparison stimuli follow the F cue. Grn = green, + = reinforced response, − = nonreinforced response.

or, more simply, an omission procedure. A schematic of the omission procedure involving delayed matching-to-sample is presented in Fig. 9.1.

Directed-forgetting experiments with animals have also been conducted with a variation of matching-to-sample known as successive matching (Grant, 1981; Kendrick, Rilling, & Stonebraker, 1981, Experiment 1; Parker & Glover, 1987; Stonebraker & Rilling, 1981; Stonebraker, Rilling, & Kendrick, 1981). With the successive matching procedure, a single test stimulus follows each sample (generally on the same response key) and if that stimulus is "correct," reinforcement is provided for the first response after some period of time. On other trials, an "incorrect" stimulus follows the sample and is turned off after some period of time, without being followed by reinforcement. In successive matching, performance is determined by a discrimination ratio (i.e., responses to correct test stimuli divided by total responses to correct and incorrect test stimuli). Once this task is acquired to a high discrimination ratio, delays are introduced between the sample and test stimuli, and delay cues typically fill the interval. Presentation of an R cue signals that a test stimulus will follow. Presentation of an F cue signals that no test stimulus will follow and that the trial will end with termination of the cue. On infrequently presented probe trials, the F cue is followed by a test stimulus, and the discrimination ratio is calculated for the probe trials. A schematic of the omission procedure involving delayed successive matching is presented in Fig. 9.2.

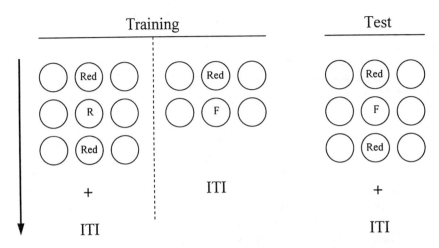

FIG. 9.2. Omission procedure: Delayed successive matching with the remember cue (R) followed by a single comparison test stimulus, and the forget cue (F) followed by the intertrial interval (ITI). Sample and comparison hue are balanced over trials. On infrequently presented F-cue probe trials, a single comparison stimulus follows the F cue. Grn = green, + = reinforced response, − = nonreinforced response.

The typical finding with this successive matching directed-forgetting task is that the discrimination ratio on F-cue probe trials is significantly lower than it is on R-cue training trials (Grant, 1988, Experiments 2 & 3; Maki & Hegvik, 1980; Maki et al., 1981; Parker & Glover, 1987; Roberts et al., 1984; Santi & Bridson, 1991, Experiment 1; Santi & Mielke, 1991; Stonebraker et al., 1981).

Although the directed-forgetting paradigm using the omission procedure appears to result in findings that are consistent with the active control of memory, delay cues may not simply function as a signal for the presence versus absence of a memory test. When the omission procedure is used, delay cues may also serve to predict the availability of reinforcement (i.e., R cues signal the opportunity to obtain reinforcement for correct responding, whereas F cues signal that reinforcement cannot be obtained). If F cues signal the absence of reinforcement, they may produce frustration (see Roper, Kaiser, & Zentall, 1995), or more technically, they may become conditioned inhibitors. As such, presentation of an F cue that signals nonreward may induce an emotional state in the animal (see Amsel, 1958) that could interfere with rehearsal of the sample, retrieval of sample memory, or correct choice of the test stimulus.

Using an omission procedure, Roper and Zentall (1994) attempted to assess the "value" of delay cues independently of matching accuracy by examining responding to the delay cues themselves, as a measure of the degree to which the delay cues were associated with reinforcement. In addition to R and F cues, Roper and Zentall included trials in which an "ambiguous" cue was presented during the delay. On one half of the ambiguous delay-cue trials, comparison stimuli were presented (i.e., memory was tested). On the remaining ambiguous-cue trials, the trial ended with the offset of the delay cue. Thus, the ambiguous cues provided no information about whether or not the trial would end with a test of sample memory.

Not surprisingly, Roper and Zentall (1994) found that a large number of delay-cue responses were made to R cues (always followed by comparison choice), very few responses were made to F cues (never followed by comparison choice), and an intermediate number of responses were made to ambiguous cues (sometimes followed by comparison choice). A somewhat different pattern of matching accuracy was found, however. Although matching accuracy on ambiguous-cue trials was clearly superior to that on F-cue probe trials, it was not inferior to that on R-cue trials. Thus, it appears that matching accuracy and delay-cue pecking may be only weakly related. This finding is especially relevant to the suggestion that delay-cue pecking is an overt reflection of an active rehearsal process (Grant, 1981) or that it serves as a retrieval cue for correct comparison choice (Kendrick et al., 1981). Rather than attributing the F-cue probe trial performance decrement to the failure to maintain memory, it seems more parsimonious to assume that differential delay-cue responding results from the differential association of delay cues with end-of-trial reinforcement. Such an account does not entail a cognitive explanation. Thus, the decrement in performance on forget-cue probe trials may result from neither reduced rehearsal nor poor retrieval (for a discussion of procedures used to distinguish between these mechanisms, see Roper & Zentall, 1993), but rather from the negative hedonic value associated with the F cues.

F-cue probe trial performance may suffer, as well, from end-of-trial behavior that is incompatible with a high level of matching performance. That is, how an animal behaves at the offset of the F cue in training (e.g., showing evidence of frustration or facing away from the response panel) may not be compatible with the behavior of choosing one of the comparison stimuli. If in training, the F cue has been followed by the intertrial interval, initially on F-cue probe trials, the pigeon may not notice the onset of the comparison stimuli, or it may flap its wings (a response often made to a signal for nonreward, see Terrace, 1972).

Finally, the deficits in matching accuracy typically seen on F-cue probe trials also may be attributable to the unexpected presentation of comparison stimuli (i.e., they may be attributable to the surprising change in conditions from those on R-cue trials experienced during training to those on F-cue probe trials in testing; what animal researchers might refer to as a generalization decrement).

Substitution Procedures

One way to separate the possible frustration associated with F cues in training from their memory-maintaining function is to use what has come to be known as a substitution procedure. In substitution procedures, the F cue still signals that comparisons (representing a test of sample memory) will not be presented. In this case, however, rather than signaling the end of the trial, the F cue is followed by a simple simultaneous discrimination (Maki & Hegvik, 1980), by a single stimulus that is either always (Kendrick & Newman, 1984) or sometimes (Grant, 1981, Experiment 1) followed by reinforcement, or directly by reinforcement (Kendrick et al., 1981, Experiment 2).

In many experiments, no evidence of directed forgetting has been found when attempts have been made to equate the motivational value of the F cue with that of the R cue (see Roper & Zentall, 1993, for a review). In particular, directed forgetting has failed to be found in experiments in which delayed matching-to-sample has served as the baseline task and substitution procedures have been used (Kendrick et al., 1981; Maki & Hegvik, 1980, Experiment 2; Maki et al., 1981, Experiment 1). On the other hand, good evidence for a directed-forgetting effect has generally been found in directed-forgetting experiments in which delayed successive matching has served as the baseline task and substitution procedures have been used (Grant, 1981, Experiment 1; Grant & Barnet, 1991; Grant & Soldat, 1995; Kendrick & Newman, 1984, Experiment 1 & Experiment 3, Test A). The difference in results on F-cue probe trials, depending on whether the baseline matching task is matching-to-sample or successive matching, may be related to the response measures used to assess matching accuracy. In the case of matching-to-sample, the response measure is a two-alternative choice response, whereas in successive matching, it is relative response rate. Response rate may not be the best measure of memory loss because it is particularly sensitive to any increase in latency of responding produced, for example, by presenting an unexpected comparison, as would occur on F-cue probe trials. In the case of delayed matching-to-sample, matching accuracy should be relatively unaffected by a small increase in latency of comparison choice (a small decrement in matching performance could result from the increase in time between sample offset and comparison response, but Maki et al., 1981, found this effect to be negligible). In the case of delayed successive matching, however, because the duration of the test stimulus is timed, any increase in the latency of response to the test stimulus is likely to have a direct effect on mean response rate, and thus, on the discrimination ratio as well (see Roper & Zentall, 1993). Alternatively, because acquisition of successive matching typically involves learning to inhibit responding on trials involving nonreward, presentation of a novel F-cue probe trial may actually result in the disinhibition of test-stimulus responding. In either case, any effect that probe-trial novelty might have should reduce the magnitude of the discrimination ratio producing an effect easily mistaken for true memory loss (see Roper & Zentall, 1993).

The failure to find effects of directed forgetting in studies where matching-to-sample was used as the baseline memory task and a substituted discrimination was following F cues in training (Kendrick et al., 1981; Maki & Hegvik, 1980, Experiment 2; Maki et al., 1981, Experiment 1; Roper & Zentall, 1994; Zentall, Roper, & Sherburne, 1995) has been attributed to one of three processes. First, it is possible that pigeons maintain sample rehearsal on all trials in which memory (of any kind) is required for accurate responding (Kendrick & Rilling, 1986). According to this theory, the mere presence of a sample-independent simultaneous discrimination on F-cue training trials is sufficient to maintain sample memory, regardless of the relevance of that memory to correct responding on that trial. It would be ironic, however, if a presumably active (cognitive) memory process like directed forgetting would be insensitive to the nature of the memory being tested. One would think that such a memory-maintaining process would not be activated when memory for the sample was unnecessary.

Second, it is possible that when substitution procedures are used in the context of delayed matching-to-sample, animals fail to learn the "meaning" of the F cue (Grant & Soldat, 1995). In other words, when substitution procedures are used, the similarity between the R-cue trials and the F-cue trials in training might result in the failure of the pigeon to discriminate the differential signaling function of the delay cues. That is, when F cues in training signal the presentation of a simple simultaneous discrimination, all delay cues are followed by similar events—stimuli presented on the left- and right-side keys and a response to one but not the other is followed by reinforcement. Unfortunately, this failure-of-discrimination hypothesis is probably not independently testable. Thus, even following extensive delay-cue training, whenever one fails to find evidence of directed forgetting, one can propose that the F cue did not become sufficiently discriminated from the R cue.

A third account of the general failure to find directed forgetting with the choice substitution procedure was proposed by Roper and Zentall (1993). According to this account, the directed-forgetting effect, as it has been generally reported, is more parsimoniously attributed to artifacts of training. These artifacts include the (already mentioned) absence of the opportunity for reinforcement at the end of F-cue trials (with omission procedures), and in experiments where reinforcement associated with R and F cues has been equated, the absence of response compatibility at the end of R- and F-cued trials in training. In some experiments, although reinforcement occurs on

F-cue trials in training, the response required following an F cue (e.g., non-differential pecking to the center response key) is quite different from the two-alternative forced choice required on R-cue trials (see e.g., Kendrick & Newman, 1984, Experiment 2). Thus, if the F cue signals that pecks to any lit response key will be reinforced, one is likely to find disrupted matching accuracy on two-alternative forced-choice probe trials because the pigeons will tend to peck at the first lit response key that they see on those test trials.

On the other hand, when one controls for both differential reinforcement associated with R and F cues and response compatibility (as one does when a simple simultaneous discrimination substitutes for the two-alternative forced-choice memory test), typically, no evidence of directed forgetting is found (Kendrick et al., 1981; Maki & Hegvik, 1980, Experiment 2; Maki et al., 1981, Experiment 1; Roper & Zentall, 1994; Zentall et al., 1995).

In a recent attempt to test the response compatibility hypothesis, Grant and Soldat (1995) used a substitution procedure in which there was high compatibility between R-cue and F-cue responding in training and F-cue probe-trial responding in test. Although evidence was found for directed forgetting under these conditions of response compatibility, Grant and Soldat used successive matching as the baseline task. And, as Roper and Zentall (1993) suggested, successive matching, with its response rate measure of matching accuracy, is particularly susceptible to the disruption of matching accuracy produced by novel stimulus sequences presented on F-cue probe trials.

Thus, there are three types of artifact, all of which must be eliminated before one can claim to have an adequate test of directed forgetting. First, the baseline matching task should involve two-alternative forced-choice matching-to-sample to avoid the novelty of F-cue probe trials from directly affecting the measure of matching accuracy (i.e., comparison response latency). Second, F-cue trials in training should end with reinforcement to avoid having the F cue associated with frustration or conditioned inhibition. And finally, the reinforced response following an F cue in training should be compatible with the reinforced response following an R cue, such that response incompatibility cannot account for disrupted matching accuracy on F-cue probe trials.

When all three types of artifact are eliminated, however, there is little evidence for directed forgetting in pigeons. On the other hand, one could argue that the procedures used with animals are not directly analogous to those used with humans. Specifically, although several items are generally presented on a trial in human directed-forgetting experiments, only a single item (the sample) is presented on a trial when directed forgetting is studied in animals. This procedural difference in the way the task is presented may have important theoretical implications. When only one item is presented per trial, and a signal indicates that memory for that item will not be tested, the incentive to forget that item may be minimal. The only advantage to the animal of forgetting the single item might be the minimal reduction in (presumed) effort needed to maintain the item in memory.

When more than one item is presented per trial, however, the termination of memory-maintaining behavior may result in enhanced memory for the remaining items. Thus, an approach to the assessment of directed forgetting in animals that comes closer to the procedures used with humans involves the presentation of two, rather than only one, sample on a trial (Grant, 1984, 1986, 1989).

Double-Sample Procedures

If two items are presented and either one may be the basis of a memory test, the presentation of an F cue, indicating that one of the items will not be tested, may have direct value. In particular, under these conditions, one might be able to reallocate one's memory-maintaining capacity to the remaining item and, by so doing, increase the probability of a correct response on that trial.

Grant (1984) trained pigeons on a standard matching-to-sample directed-forgetting task involving the omission of comparisons on F-cue trials in training. On double-sample probe trials, two samples were presented in succession on each trial and the samples were each followed by either an R or an F cue. When the comparison stimuli were then presented, a response to the comparison that matched the *second* sample was arbitrarily designated as correct and was reinforced. Although one might expect some degree of disruption in matching accuracy on all double-sample probe trials (because the two samples provided an ambiguous or confusing "instruction" as to which comparison was correct), the question was whether matching accuracy on probe trials would depend on which postsample cue was presented.

Relative to double-sample probe trials in which R cues were presented following both samples, Grant (1984) found that matching accuracy was higher when the first sample was followed by an F cue (and the second sample was followed by an R cue), and lower when the second sample was followed by an F cue (and the first sample was followed by an R cue). That the presentation of an F cue following the first (interfering) sample improved matching accuracy suggests that the function of the F cue was to instruct the pigeon to forget the preceding sample. Furthermore, Grant reasoned that if the F cue merely establishes an aversive emotional state that, under more typical conditions, interferes with the postcue processing of the test stimuli, then under these double-sample probe-trial conditions, the F cue that followed the first sample should interfere with the processing of the second sample and thus, should have resulted in *poorer* matching accuracy. Instead, matching accuracy on these probe trials was facilitated.

An alternative account is possible, however, for the improved matching accuracy on double-sample probe trials in which an F cue was presented following the first sample. Recall that double-sample probe trials might produce confusion on the part of the pigeon as to which of the two samples should serve as the basis for comparison choice. Recall, as well, that during training, presentation of an F cue always signaled that the trial was over and that the preceding sample was irrelevant to comparison choice on the following trial. Although double-sample probe trials in which R cues followed both samples are likely to be confusing to the pigeons because each signals that a different comparison response is correct, double-sample probe trials on which the first sample was followed by an F cue should signal to the pigeon that the first sample is irrelevant and only the second sample (that is followed by an R cue) should be considered at the time of memory test. Thus, with the exception that the F cue was not followed by the intertrial interval, these double-sample probe trials, with F cue following the first sample and R cue following the second, were quite similar to the presentation of two consecutive training trials—the first an F trial and the second an R trial. On the other hand, trials in which an F cue follows only the second sample are likely to be even more confusing than when both samples are followed by R cues because, for the first time, an F cue was followed by a memory test and an R cue was not.

To reduce the ambiguity that might have accompanied the pigeons' performance on the double-sample probe trials in Grant's (1984) experiments, Grant (1986) trained pigeons with double-sample trials in which the first sample was always followed by an F cue and the second sample was always followed by an R cue. In this way, the "meaning" of the F cue, with regard to the double-sample procedure, should have been well established in training. In one test, probe trials involved two samples and both were followed by R cues. Matching accuracy on these probe trials was significantly poorer than it was on double-sample training trials. Although, during training, the F cue in this experiment may have served as a signal to forget the first of two samples, it also could have served either as a signal that comparisons would not follow (i.e., as an omission cue) or as a cue to attend especially well to the next sample. Thus, the decline in matching accuracy on probe trials in which the R cue followed both samples could have resulted, at least in part, from confusion with regard to the meaning of the R cue after the first sample. Recall that in training, R cues were always followed by a memory test and never by another sample.

Grant (1986) also tested the pigeons with probe trials involving a single sample followed by an F cue and a memory test. Once again, matching accuracy was significantly poorer than on double-sample training trials. This test ruled out the possibility that the F cue that followed the first sample had its effect on matching accuracy by "instructing" the pigeon to better attend to the second sample. On the other hand, it is still unclear that the effect of the F cue was to terminate maintenance of sample memory. Recall that in training, the F cue is likely to have functioned as an omission cue, a type of cue that may result in artifactual perceptual or motivational decrements in matching accuracy on probe trials (see Roper & Zentall, 1993). A further source of disrupted matching accuracy in Grant's single-sample F-cue probe trials, which cannot be attributed to memory loss, may be response incompatibility. In training, the F cue was always followed by a second sample, a stimulus likely to produce responding. However, on single-sample F-cue probe trials, the F cue is followed by a choice between the two comparisons. As mentioned earlier, when the F cue in training is followed by a response (in this case, to the second sample) that is incompatible with the comparison choice on probe trials, an artifactual disruption of matching accuracy may be found (see Roper & Zentall, 1993).

One way to avoid the problem of always following F cues in training with a second sample but then testing with comparison choice following the F cue on probe trials, is to train the pigeon with double-sample trials in which either the first or the second sample can be the target of a memory test. Grant (1989, Experiment 1) trained pigeons with single-sample trials in which the sample was always followed by an R cue, and with double-sample trials in which the target sample (that signaled which comparison was correct— either the first or the second) was always followed by an R cue, whereas the other sample was always followed by an F cue. That pigeons could acquire this task indicates that the R and F cues were effective in controlling comparison choice. It does not address the question of sample memory, however. One possibility, suggested by Grant, is that on double-sample trials the pigeons learned to use the four-stimulus sample sequence (sample-cue-sample-cue) as a serial-compound sample. Each of the four sample sequences in training could have been associated with a particular comparison choice response. More importantly, because each of the two samples instructed the pigeon to respond to a different comparison, the task could be acquired by using the second postsample cue alone. When an R cue followed the second sample, it could have served as a cue to *match* it, and when an F cue followed the second sample, it could have served as a cue to *mismatch* it (i.e., if the second sample is red, respond to the green comparison). Finally, it is possible that the R cue following the first sample in training could have signaled that the second sample should be ignored, and the F cue could have signaled that the second sample should be better attended to.

Grant (1989, Experiment 2) attempted to rule out these possibilities by presenting single-sample probe trials with R and F cues. Although matching accuracy was significantly disrupted on single-sample F-cue probe trials, matching accuracy did not drop below chance, as would be expected if the

F cue had served as a cue to mismatch. In contrast, Grant found a high level of matching accuracy on single-sample R-cue probe trials. This finding rules out the possibility that, in training, the pigeons learned to use the four-stimulus sample sequence as a serial-compound sample.

It is possible, however, that presentation of an F or an R cue following the first sample does not affect the pigeon's memory for the first sample, but instead, affects the pigeons processing of the second cue. Thus, Grant's (1989) single-sample probe-trial data do not address the possibility that in training, an F cue following the first sample served as a cue to attend to the second sample, and an R cue following the first sample served as a cue to ignore the second sample. If this were the case, matching accuracy on single-sample R-cue probe trials would be expected to be high because the R cue would instruct the pigeon to ignore the second sample, and it should be easy to ignore a stimulus if it is not presented. On the other hand, matching accuracy on single-sample F-cue probe trials would be expected to be poor because the F cue would instruct the pigeon to attend to the second sample, but no second sample would appear. That is exactly what Grant found.

A general problem with the double-sample procedures used by Grant is that it is difficult to determine whether the disruption in matching accuracy is produced by a decrease in memorability of the target sample or by an increase in memorability of the nontarget sample. This symmetry of effect on matching accuracy is especially problematic given the number of possible nonmemorial artifacts that have been identified following F-cue training (e.g., nonreinforcement, response incompatibility, postcue attention, serial compounds). Roper and Zentall (1993) suggested that this problem could be avoided by using a variant of the double-sample procedure in which each of the two successively presented samples is associated with one member of a different pair of comparisons (e.g., the first sample may be red or green and the second sample either vertical or horizontal lines). Then one could test for first-sample memory by presenting red and green comparisons or for second-sample memory by presenting vertical- and horizontal-line comparisons. Furthermore, one could also signal, by means of a cue following the first sample, the second sample, or both, which comparison dimension would be tested. This procedure would be analogous to telling a human subject that he or she will be tested on the first list or the second list. In this way, one should be able to avoid effects of interference produced by confusion or by an instructional failure (i.e., ambiguity of meaning of the R or F cue), when probe trials are presented, and decrements in matching accuracy could be more certainly attributed to memory loss.

Recently, an experiment of this type was reported by Roper et al. (1995). On half of the trials in training, a sample stimulus (e.g., red) was followed by an R cue and a test of sample memory (red vs. green comparisons). On the remaining trials in training, a sample stimulus was followed by one of two F cues, each of which also served as a sample for a second matching task. F cues were followed by a different set of comparisons (vertical and horizontal lines), and which comparison was correct depended on which of the two F cues had been presented. The design of this experiment is presented in Fig. 9.3. This design allows the pigeon, when presented with an F cue, to reallocate its memory-maintaining capacity from the initial sample to the second sample (i.e., in this case, the F cue). In addition, with this design, unlike with Grant's (1984, 1986, 1989) procedures, any confusion on F-cue probe trials produced by presentation of the hue comparison stimuli should not lead specifically to the choice of the incorrect comparison. Furthermore, in the Roper et al. (1995) experiment, F cues were followed by comparison choice in training. Thus, not only were R and F cues followed by approximately the same probability of reinforcement but, in addition, there was a high degree of response compatibility following R and F cues. Roper et al. found significantly poorer matching accuracy on F-cue probe trials than on R-cue trials. Under these conditions, the deficit in matching accuracy found on F-cue probe trials is consistent with a shift in active memory maintenance from the sample to the F cue on F-cue trials in training.

Grant (personal communication, August 17, 1995) pointed out, however, that there may be a difference in the degree to which R and F cues are processed when such a reallocation procedure is used. Specifically, an R cue need only be identified as not an F cue and then it can be ignored. An F cue, however, must first be identified as an F cue and then must be maintained in memory so that it can serve as the basis for comparison choice. Thus, the extra processing of F cues can account for the loss in matching accuracy on F-cue-probe trials.

One way to equate the need to process F and R cues would be to train animals with two R cues and, on some trials, require that they match the R cues, just as on other trials, they must do with the F cues. Thus, there would be two kinds of trials involving R cues; trials in which the R cue signals a test of sample memory and trials in which memory for the R cue itself is tested. Of course, one could argue that with such a procedure, R cues would not consistently signal a test of sample memory and thus, might not yield a level of matching accuracy comparable to that typically obtained with R cues. But, as already noted, Roper and Zentall (1994) reported that matching accuracy on such ambiguous-cue trials is not inferior to matching accuracy on standard R-cue trials. Finally, to equate the R and F cues for the degree to which they predict the comparison stimuli that follow them, F cues should be followed by a test of memory for the F cue on half of the F-cue trials, and by a simple simultaneous discrimination on the remaining F-cue trials. A schematic of the design of this experiment is presented in Fig. 9.4.

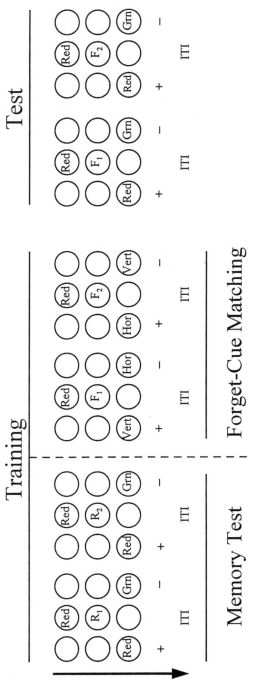

FIG. 9.3. Reallocation substitution procedure involving matching-to-sample as the baseline memory task. The remember cue (R) is followed by a test of memory for the sample. In training, the forget cue (F) on each trial is followed by a test of memory for that F cue. On F-cue probe trials, the F cue is followed by a test of memory for the sample. Grn = green, + = reinforced response, − = nonreinforced response.

279

Training: Ambiguous/Remember Task

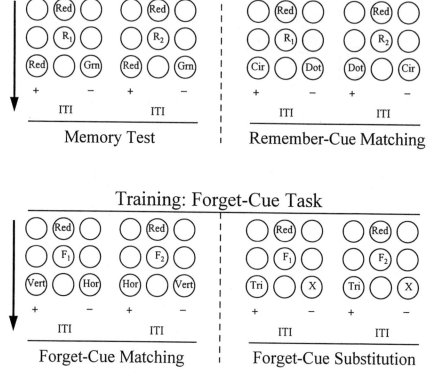

FIG. 9.4. Reallocation substitution procedure involving matching-to-sample with control for the need to attend to all delay cues. On some remember-cue (R) trials the remember cue is followed by a test of memory for the sample. On other remember-cue trials the remember cue is followed by a test of memory for the remember cue. On some forget-cue (F) trials the forget cue is followed by a test of memory for the forget cue. On other forget-cue trials the forget cue is followed by a simple simultaneous discrimination. On forget-cue probe trials the forget cue is followed by a test of sample memory. Grn = green, vert = vertical lines, hor = horizontal lines, cir = circle, tri = triangle, + = reinforced response, − = nonreinforced response.

Pigeons were trained to a high level of performance on all four tasks: The sample memory task, the R-cue memory task, the F-cue memory task, and the simple simultaneous discrimination. Matching accuracy on F-cue probe trials was then assessed, testing sample memory following F cues. If matching accuracy on F-cue probe trials is significantly poorer than on R-cue trials, it suggests the presence of true directed forgetting. Alternatively, if matching accuracy on F-cue probe trials is comparable to that on R-cue trials, suggests that previous evidence of directed forgetting may be attributable to one or more nonmemorial factors.

To verify that a decrement in matching accuracy on F-cue probe trials, if found, is attributable to the reallocation of memory-maintaining capacity, the decrement in matching accuracy was compared to that of a control group. For the control group, all trials involving R cues were the same as for the experimental group but all F cues in training were followed by a "no-memory-load" simple simultaneous discrimination. To control for the possible effects of comparison unpredictability on F-cue trials, both pairs of comparisons presented to pigeons in the experimental group were also presented to control pigeons. Thus, on F-cue trials, control pigeons experienced two simultaneous discriminations on randomly alternating trials. The results indicated that for the experimental group, matching accuracy on F-cue probe trials was significantly worse than that on R-cue trials (13.0%). Furthermore, the comparable difference between matching accuracy on F-cue probe trials and R-cue trials for the substitution control group (3.4%) was significantly less for the experimental group and it was not significantly different from zero (Kaiser, Sherburne, & Zentall, in press).

Memory Loss or Retrieval Failure

Whereas researchers in animal directed forgetting have attempted to demonstrate the presence of an active memory-maintaining process, those working with humans have focused on alternative accounts. For example, the fact that directed-forgetting effects can be readily found using recall measures but not using recognition measures (Block, 1971; Elmes, Adams, & Roediger, 1970, Experiment 4; Epstein, Massaro, & Wilder, 1972; Geiselman, Bjork, & Fishman, 1983; but see also Archer & Margolin, 1970; Davis & Okada, 1971; MacLeod, 1975) has been taken as evidence that directed-forgetting performance deficits may represent a failure of retrieval rather than a failure of encoding or storage (Bjork, 1972, 1989; Epstein, 1972). Epstein suggested that to-be-forgotten items are stored separately from to-be-remembered items and for this reason are less accessible without the aid of retrieval cues. But recognition tests are clearly involved in directed-forgetting experiments with animals (e.g., a choice between two comparison stimuli). If similar segregation of remember and forget items occurs in directed-forgetting experiments with animals, then the retrieval cues needed for recovery of the F-cue items should be present at the time of testing, and little evidence of directed forgetting should be found. Thus, it may be that different mechanisms underlie the directed-forgetting effects reported for humans and pigeons.

The Problem of Instructions
in Animal Memory Research

Problems associated with the unambiguous assessment of directed forgetting in animals suggest that there are important differences between the way research is carried out with humans and with other animals. First, in most directed-forgetting research with humans, the assessment of memory is conducted with tests of item *recall* (e.g., Epstein, 1969; Woodward & Bjork, 1971). Given the limited response repertoire that animals possess, it would be difficult to devise appropriate recall tests. On the other hand, as already noted, in some directed-forgetting research with humans, memory has been assessed using *recognition* procedures (e.g., Block, 1971; Davis & Okada, 1971; Elmes et al., 1970). Thus, the nature of the assessment measure should not limit interspecies comparisons. Second, humans can be instructed not only to indicate whether an item was presented, but also to indicate whether it was presented as an item to-be-remembered or to-be-forgotten. When studying humans, an experimenter can capitalize on their extensive language training to eliminate ambiguity in what is being requested on memory tests. This cannot be done with animals. Furthermore, memory tests used with animals often encourage ambiguity because in many cases (e.g., double-sample test trials), a response to the "distractor" on test trials could be considered a correct matching response for the first sample presented on that trial.

In the assessment of animal memory, the pervasive problem of separating the effects of memory loss from those of a failure of instructions has been acknowledged for some time (see e.g., Chizar & Spear, 1969; Zentall, 1970). Even in a simple delayed-matching task, in which pigeons are trained with no delay between sample and comparison stimuli and they are then tested with delays, the isolation of true memory deficits from instructional failure, contextual change, or generalization decrement may be very difficult. For example, if pigeons acquire a zero-delay matching task by "judging" which previous sample was presented following the last intertrial interval, and on delay trials, they "mistake" the delay for an intertrial interval, then the pigeons may "decide" that no sample was presented, even if memory for the sample on that trial was perfect. One way to reduce confusion between the intertrial interval and the delay is to make one highly distinctive from the other. For example, during the intertrial interval, the house light could be illuminated, and during the delay interval, the house light could be turned off. A second possible source of decrement in matching accuracy can result from confusion between the sample on the present trial and the sample from the preceding trial. A pigeon might remember both samples perfectly, but forget their temporal order (i.e., forget which was presented last). Such intertrial interference could be reduced by using intertrial intervals that are long, relative to the longest delays.

The problem of instructional deficits in animal research has not been adequately addressed because it appears to imply that animals have cognitive abilities beyond what is normally considered to be their capacity. But one does not have to use cognitive terminology to acknowledge the problem (it only makes it easier for humans to understand). To some extent, the longstanding controversy over the meaning of the gradient of stimulus generalization following single stimulus training is an example of a similar issue. Some researchers argue that responding to stimuli that are similar to a stimulus experienced in training represents instances of a failure to discriminate the differences among the stimuli (Lashley & Wade, 1946), whereas others interpret the generalization gradient as the spread of excitatory strength (Hull, 1943). In spite of the mechanistic (behaviorist) basis of excitation and inhibition, one can easily translate this latter theory into more cognitive terms by replacing the animal with a human. It is not that the human fails to discriminate, for example, a red training stimulus from an orange test stimulus, but rather that, in the absence of instructions about how to deal with new stimuli, a human may try to predict the likelihood that responses in the presence of each new stimulus will be reinforced. Simple instructions that one could not easily give to an animal, such as, "Respond only to the training stimulus and to no other value, no matter how similar," would result in a very steep gradient, whereas other instructions, such as, "Respond similarly to any color," would result in a very flat gradient.

The reason for asking whether a change in performance might be attributable to confusion or to an instructional failure rather than to a failure of memory lies in its heuristic value. One does not have to accept the cognitive implications of the word instructions to recognize that nonmemorial processes can affect the performance of an animal. However, by using cognitive terminology, one may be better able to identify confounds that could be ruled out or isolated through the appropriate design of experiments.

SUMMARY

Researchers who study directed forgetting in animals have attempted to demonstrate that animals can develop control over memory maintenance. Unfortunately, the analog tasks that have been used with animals do not always allow for control over nonmemorial processes that may affect probe-trial accuracy, such as differential reinforcement history and response incompatibility. Furthermore, simple delayed-matching tasks may not encourage the animal to forget because they may not allow the animal to benefit from the termination of memory on F-cue trials, as they do for humans. We suggest that an unambiguous multiple-item task, more analogous to that used with humans, is one in which an F cue not only signals that memory for the preceding sample will not be tested, but also allows the animal to reallocate its memory maintenance capacity. When efforts are made to draw more accurate parallels between procedures used with animals and humans, not only can better comparisons be made, but it can help us to better understand the mechanisms underlying directed forgetting, as well as the demands of the directed-forgetting task.

Concerns in the human directed-forgetting literature about the relative roles of memory loss and retrieval failure in the directed-forgetting phenomenon (Bjork, 1972, 1989; Epstein, 1972) suggest that there may be further analogies that should be explored. The memory-loss versus retrieval distinction has been used effectively to clarify the animal memory literature (Lewis, 1979; Miller & Springer, 1973; Riccio & Richardson, 1984; Spear, 1973). It has not been applied specifically to directed forgetting, but perhaps it should be.

Finally, the present analysis raises the broader question of how to make appropriate comparisons between humans and other animals given the problems associated with instructing animals about the "rules" of the task. This issue must be adequately addressed before such comparisons are meaningful (see e.g., Zentall, 1997).

ACKNOWLEDGMENTS

The research described in this chapter was conducted with support from the National Institute of Mental Health (Grant 1 RO1 MH45979) and the National Science Foundation (Grants BNS 9019080 and IBN 9414589). Karen Roper is now at the Department of Psychology, University of Wisconsin–Eau Claire, Eau Claire, WI. Lou Sherburne is now at the Department of Psychology, Wabash College, Crawfordsville, IN.

REFERENCES

Amsel, A. (1958). The role of frustrative nonreward in noncontinuous reward situations. *Psychological Bulletin, 55,* 102–119.

Archer, B. U., & Margolin, R. R. (1970). Arousal effects in intentional recall and forgetting. *Journal of Experimental Psychology, 86,* 8–12.

Bjork, R. A. (1972). Theoretical implications of directed forgetting. In A. W. Melton & E. Martin (Eds.), *Coding processes in human memory* (pp. 217–235). New York: Winston.

Bjork, R. A. (1989). Retrieval inhibition as an adaptive mechanism in human memory. In H. L. Roediger & F. I. M. Craik (Eds.), *Varieties of memory and consciousness* (pp. 309–330). Hillsdale, NJ: Lawrence Erlbaum Associates.

Block, R. A. (1971). The effects of instructions to forget in short-term memory. *Journal of Experimental Psychology, 89,* 1–9.

Chizar, D. E., & Spear, N. E. (1969). Stimulus change, reversal learning, and retention in the rat. *Journal of Physiological and Comparative Psychology, 69,* 190–195.

Cook, R. G., Brown, M. F., & Riley, D. A. (1985). Flexible memory processing by rats: Use of prospective and retrospective information in the radial maze. *Journal of Experimental Psychology: Animal Behavior Processes, 11,* 453–469.

D'Amato, M. R. (1973). Delayed matching and short-term memory in monkeys. In G. H. Bower (Ed.), *The psychology of learning and motivation: Advances in theory and research* (Vol. 7, pp. 227–269). New York: Academic Press.

Davis, J. C., & Okada, R. (1971). Recognition and recall of positively forgotten items. *Journal of Experimental Psychology, 89,* 181–186.

Elmes, D. G., Adams, C., & Roediger, H. (1970). Cued forgetting in short-term memory: Response selection. *Journal of Experimental Psychology, 86,* 103–107.

Epstein, W. (1969). Poststimulus output specification and differential retrieval from short-term memory. *Journal of Experimental Psychology, 82,* 168–174.

Epstein, W. (1972). Mechanisms of directed forgetting. In G. H. Bower (Ed.), *The psychology of learning and motivation* (Vol. 6, pp. 147–191). San Diego, CA: Academic Press.

Epstein, W., Massaro, D. W., & Wilder, L. (1972). Selective search in directed forgetting. *Journal of Experimental Psychology, 94,* 18–24.

Geiselman, R. E., Bjork, R. A., & Fishman, D. (1983). Disrupted retrieval in directed forgetting: A link with posthypnotic retrieval. *Journal of Experimental Psychology: General, 112,* 58–72.

Grant, D. S. (1981). Stimulus control of information processing in pigeon short-term memory. *Learning and Motivation, 12,* 19–39.

Grant, D. S. (1984). Directed forgetting and intratrial interference in pigeon delayed matching. *Canadian Journal of Psychology, 38,* 166–177.

Grant, D. S. (1986). Establishing a forget cue in pigeons using the intratrial interference procedure. *Animal Learning and Behavior, 14,* 267–275.

Grant, D. S. (1988). Directed forgetting in pigeons: Tests of transfer of cue effectiveness across samples from different dimensions. *Learning and Motivation, 19,* 122–141.

Grant, D. S. (1989). Use of an ambiguous sample procedure to establish a cue to forget in pigeons. *Journal of the Experimental Analysis of Behavior, 52,* 325–334.

Grant, D. S., & Barnet, R. C. (1991). Irrelevance of sample stimuli and directed forgetting in pigeons. *Journal of the Experimental Analysis of Behavior, 55,* 97–108.

Grant, D. S., & Roberts, W. A. (1973). Trace interaction in pigeon short-term memory. *Journal of Experimental Psychology, 101,* 21–29.

Grant, D. S., & Soldat, A. S. (1995). A postsample cue to forget does initiate an active forgetting process in pigeons. *Journal of Experimental Psychology: Animal Behavior Processes, 21,* 218–228.

Herrnstein, R. J., & Loveland, D. H. (1964). Complex visual concept in the pigeon. *Science, 146,* 549–551.

Honig, W. K., & Fetterman, J. G. (Eds.). (1992). *Cognitive aspects of stimulus control.* Hillsdale, NJ: Lawrence Erlbaum Associates.

Honig, W. K., & Thompson, R. K. R. (1982). Retrospective and prospective processing in animal working memory. In G. H. Bower (Ed.), *The psychology of learning and motivation* (Vol. 16, pp. 239–283). Orlando, FL: Academic Press.

Hull, C. L. (1943). *Principles of behavior.* New York: Appleton-Century-Crofts.

Hulse, S. H., Fowler, H., & Honig, W. K. (Eds.). (1978). *Cognitive processes in animal behavior.* Hillsdale, NJ: Lawrence Erlbaum Associates.

Kaiser, D. H., Sherburne, L. M., & Zentall, T. R. (in press). Directed forgetting in pigeons resulting from the reallocation of memory-maintaining processes on forget-cue trials. *Psychonomic Bulletin & Review.*

Kendrick, D. F., & Newman, D. R. (1984). *Procedural factors influencing directed forgetting in pigeon short-term memory.* Unpublished manuscript.

Kendrick, D. F., & Rilling, M. E. (1986). AIM: A theory of active and inactive memory. In D. F. Kendrick, M. E. Rilling, & M. R. Denny (Eds.), *Theories of animal memory* (pp. 129–152). Hillsdale, NJ: Lawrence Erlbaum Associates.

Kendrick, D. F., Rilling, M. E., & Stonebraker, T. B. (1981). Stimulus control of delayed matching in pigeons: Directed forgetting. *Journal of the Experimental Analysis of Behavior, 36,* 241–251.

Lashley, K. S., & Wade, M. (1946). The Pavlovian theory of generalization. *Psychological Review, 53,* 72–87.

Lewis, D. J. (1979). Psychology of active and inactive memory. *Psychological Bulletin, 86,* 1054–1083.

MacLeod, C. M. (1975). Long-term recognition and recall following directed forgetting. *Journal of Experimental Psychology: Human Learning and Memory, 104*, 271–279.

Maki, W. S. (1981). Directed forgetting in animals. In N. E. Spear & R. R. Miller (Eds.), *Information processing in animals: Memory mechanisms* (pp. 199–226). Hillsdale, NJ: Lawrence Erlbaum Associates.

Maki, W. S., Gillund, G., Hauge, G., & Siders, W. A. (1977). Matching-to-sample after extinction of observing responses. *Journal of Experimental Psychology: Animal Behavior Processes, 3*, 285–296.

Maki, W. S., & Hegvik, D. K. (1980). Directed forgetting in pigeons. *Animal Learning and Behavior, 8*, 567–574.

Maki, W. S., Olson, D., & Rego, S. (1981). Directed forgetting in pigeons: Analysis of cue functions. *Animal Learning and Behavior, 9*, 189–195.

Miller, R. R., & Springer, A. D. (1973). Amnesia, consolidation, and retrieval. *Psychological Review, 80*, 69–79.

Parker, B. K., & Glover, R. L. (1987). Event duration memory: The effect of delay-interval illumination and instructional cuing. *Animal Learning and Behavior, 15*, 241–248.

Riccio, D. C., & Richardson, R. (1984). The status of memory following experimentally induced amnesia: Gone but not forgotten. *Physiological Psychology, 12*, 59–72.

Roberts, W. A., Mazmanian, D. S., & Kraemer, P. J. (1984). Directed forgetting in monkeys. *Animal Learning and Behavior, 12*, 29–40.

Roitblat, H. L. (1980). Codes and coding processes in pigeon short-term memory. *Animal Learning and Behavior, 8*, 341–351.

Roitblat, H. L., Bever, T. G., & Terrace, H. S. (Eds.). (1984). *Animal cognition*. Hillsdale, NJ: Lawrence Erlbaum Associates.

Roper, K. L., Kaiser, D. H., & Zentall, T. R. (1995). True directed forgetting in pigeons may occur only when alternative working memory is required on forget-cue trials. *Animal Learning and Behavior, 23*, 280–285.

Roper, K. L., & Zentall, T. R. (1993). Directed forgetting in animals. *Psychological Bulletin, 113*, 513–532.

Roper, K. L., & Zentall, T. R. (1994). Directed forgetting in pigeons: The role of retention interval keypecking on delayed matching accuracy. *Learning and Motivation, 25*, 26–44.

Santi, A., & Bridson, S. (1991). The effects of scopolamine and cues to forget on pigeons' memory for time. *Pharmacology, Biochemistry and Behavior, 39*, 935–940.

Santi, A., & Mielke, M. (1991). Flexible coding of temporal information by pigeons: Event durations as remember and forget cues for temporal samples. *Animal Learning and Behavior, 19*, 171–176.

Santi, A., & Savich, J. (1985). Directed forgetting effects in pigeons: Remember cues initiate rehearsal. *Animal Learning and Behavior, 13*, 365–369.

Skinner, B. F. (1938). *The behavior of organisms: An experimental analysis*. New York: Appleton-Century-Crofts.

Spear, N. E. (1973). Retrieval of memory in animals. *Psychological Review, 80*, 163–194.

Stonebraker, T. B., & Rilling, M. E. (1981). Control of delayed matching-to-sample performance using directed forgetting techniques. *Animal Learning and Behavior, 9*, 196–201.

Stonebraker, T. B., Rilling, M., & Kendrick, D. F. (1981). Time dependent effects of double cuing in directed forgetting. *Animal Learning and Behavior, 9*, 385–394.

Terrace, H. S. (1972). By-products of discrimination learning. In G. H. Bower (Ed.), *The psychology of learning and motivation* (Vol. 5). New York: Academic Press.

Urcuioli, P. J., & Zentall, T. R. (1986). Retrospective memory in pigeons' delayed matching-to-sample. *Journal of Experimental Psychology: Animal Behavior Processes, 12*, 69–77.

Urcuioli, P. J., Zentall, T. R., Jackson-Smith, P., & Steirn, J. N. (1989). Evidence for common coding in many-to-one matching: Retention, intertrial interference, and transfer. *Journal of Experimental Psychology: Animal Behavior Processes, 15*, 264–273.

Wasserman, E. A., Kiedinger, R. E., & Bhatt, R. S. (1988). Conceptual behavior in pigeons: Categories, subcategories, and pseudocategories. *Journal of Experimental Psychology: Animal Behavior Processes, 14*, 235–246.

Weaver, J. E., Steirn, J. N., & Zentall, T. R. (1997). Transitive inference in pigeons: Control for differential value transfer. *Psychonomic Bulletin and Review, 4*, 113–117.

Woodward, A. E., Jr., & Bjork, R. A. (1971). The effect of forget instructions on recall of forget items. *Journal of Experimental Psychology, 89*, 109–116.

Zentall, T. R. (1970). Effects of context change on forgetting in rats. *Journal of Experimental Psychology, 86*, 440–448.

Zentall, T. R. (Ed.). (1993). *Animal cognition: A tribute to Donald A. Riley.* Hillsdale, NJ: Lawrence Erlbaum Associates.

Zentall, T. R. (1997). Animal memory: The role of instructions. *Learning and Motivation, 28*, 248–267.

Zentall, T. R., Edwards, C. A., Moore, B. S., & Hogan, D. E. (1981). Identity: The basis for both matching and oddity learning in pigeons. *Journal of Experimental Psychology: Animal Behavior Processes, 7*, 70–86.

Zentall, T. R., & Hogan, D. E. (1977). Short-term proactive inhibition in the pigeon. *Learning and Motivation, 8*, 367–386.

Zentall, T. R., & Hogan, D. E. (1978). Same/different concept learning in the pigeon: The effect of negative instances and prior adaptation to the transfer stimuli. *Journal of the Experimental Analysis of Behavior, 30*, 177–186.

Zentall, T. R., Jackson-Smith, P., & Jagielo, J. A. (1990). Categorical color and shape coding by pigeons. In M. L. Commons, R. J. Herrnstein, & S. Kosslyn (Eds.), *The quantitative analyses of behavior: Vol. 8. Pattern recognition and concepts in animals, people, and machines* (pp. 3–21). Hillsdale, NJ: Lawrence Erlbaum Associates.

Zentall, T. R., Jagielo, J. A., Jackson-Smith, P., & Urcuioli, P. J. (1987). Memory codes in pigeon short-term memory: Effect of varying number of sample and comparison stimuli. *Learning and Motivation, 18*, 21–33.

Zentall, T. R., Roper, K. L., & Sherburne, L. M. (1995). Most directed forgetting in pigeons can be attributed to the absence of reinforcement on forget cue trials during training or to other procedural artifacts. *Journal of the Experimental Analysis of Behavior, 63*, 127–137.

Zentall, T. R., Steirn, J. N., & Jackson-Smith, P. (1990). Memory strategies in pigeons' performance of a radial-arm-maze analog task. *Journal of Experimental Psychology: Animal Behavior Processes, 16*, 358–371.

Zentall, T. R., & Urcuioli, P. J. (1993). Emergent relations in the formation of stimulus classes by pigeons. *Psychological Record, 43*, 795–810.

Zentall, T. R., Urcuioli, P. J., Jagielo, J. A., & Jackson-Smith, P. (1989). Interaction of sample dimension and sample-comparison mapping on pigeons' performance of delayed conditional discriminations. *Animal Learning and Behavior, 17*, 172–178.

10

CONSEQUENCES OF ATTEMPTS TO DISREGARD SOCIAL INFORMATION

Linda M. Isbell
Heidi L. Smith
Robert S. Wyer, Jr.
University of Illinois at Urbana-Champaign

People often make conscious efforts to avoid being influenced by experiences they have had. In some cases, they attempt to forget the experiences, or, at least, try not to think about them. When this is impossible, they try to compensate for biases in judgment and behavior that their experience-related knowledge might have produced. However, people are not always successful in these attempts. For one thing, they are often unaware of the factors that affect their behavior (Bargh, 1984, 1994, in press; Nisbett & Wilson, 1977; Wilson & Brekke, 1994). And even when conscious of these factors, people cannot always estimate accurately the magnitude of their influence.

This chapter examines the ways in which people attempt to avoid being influenced by information they have received and how successful they are in these attempts. We focus primarily on conditions that can arise in a social context. At least three factors are particularly important to consider; (a) the ease with which the implications of to-be-disregarded information can be dissociated from those of other knowledge about its referents, (b) whether people attempt to disregard information in response to external demands or whether these attempts occur spontaneously in an effort to avoid unpleasant thoughts and emotions that the information elicits, and (c) the purpose for which the information is acquired. The mental representations that are formed, and the extent to which the implications of to-be-forgotten information can later be purged from these representations, can depend to a great degree on recipients' expectations for how the information will be used (Hamilton, Katz, & Leirer, 1980; Srull, 1981; Wyer & Gordon, 1982).

The situations considered in this and other chapters of this volume can be distinguished in terms of these factors. In the directed-forgetting paradigm employed by Bjork (1972), for example, participants are often given a list of unrelated words with instructions either to remember or to forget each word, depending on a cue that immediately follows its presentation. In contrast, most of the issues we address in this chapter concern conditions in which people's objective at the time they receive information is to construe its implications for a judgment or behavioral decision. Moreover, the information they wish to disregard is often related to other knowledge they have acquired either in the same situation or previously. We consider conditions in which people's motivation to avoid thinking about or using information is internally generated as well as externally imposed. Our general concern throughout the chapter is not only with whether information is actually forgotten, but also with whether people are wittingly or unwittingly *influenced* by information despite their attempts to ignore its implications. In this context, we focus on the influence of both the descriptive aspects of information and the emotional reactions that the information elicits.

THEORETICAL FRAMEWORK

A formulation proposed by Wyer and Srull (1986, 1989) is particularly useful in conceptualizing the phenomena to be discussed in this chapter (for other general theories of social information processing, see Carlston, 1994; Smith, 1990; Wyer & Carlston, 1979). This theory specifies the storage and retrieval processes that occur in the course of responding to information with a particular goal in mind, and defines the conditions in which information is likely to influence judgments and behavior. Thus, the model potentially specifies the processes that are likely to occur when people attempt to "forget" information they have received, and also when they are later called on to recall and use this information.

Because the model is described in detail elsewhere (Wyer & Srull, 1986, 1989), we restrict our present discussion to those features of particular relevance to the issues at hand. The overall model consists metaphorically of a number of information storage and processing units. Two memory stores are of particular importance. One, the *Work Space*, is somewhat analogous to working memory (Baddeley, 1976) but is assumed to have larger capacity and to function somewhat differently. It is a temporary repository of stimulus input information, previously formed knowledge representations that have been involved in the processing of this information, and the output of this processing. This material can be retained in the Work

Space indefinitely as long as it is necessary to pursue the processing objectives to which it is relevant, and often remains there for a short time after these objectives have been attained. Ultimately, however, the Work Space is cleared to make room for more immediate goal-relevant material.

In contrast, *Permanent Storage* is a permanent repository of the output of goal-directed processing. It consists of a number of content-addressable storage bins. One, the *semantic* bin, serves as a cognitive dictionary of noun, attribute, and action concepts that are used to encode information at a low level of processing. *Referent* bins pertain to either a specific referent (person, object, or event) or a general class (e.g., "African Americans," "war," "baseball games"). (Note that the distinction between semantic and referent bins is not quite analogous to that between semantic and episodic memory [Tulving, 1983]. Although the semantic bin contains purely semantic knowledge, the contents of referent bins can be either semantic or episodic.) Each referent bin is denoted by a *header*, or set of features that includes the name of the referent and other attributes that can be used to identify it.

Bins can pertain to referents at several different levels of generality. For example, one might have a bin pertaining to "football games" and a bin concerning the "1994 Illinois–Michigan game." Knowledge about a referent can be stored in several different bins, each pertaining to a different time or social context ("Mary at the office," "Mary on a date," etc.). In this regard, the bin in which knowledge is stored depends on one's processing objectives at the time it is acquired. Thus, information that Mary kissed John could be stored in either a bin referring to Mary or a bin referring to John, depending on which person is the focus of one's attention.

The mental representations that are stored in a referent bin can be of many types. For example, a representation could consist of a mental image, a single trait description or evaluative judgment, or a configuration of associated traits and behaviors (Srull & Wyer, 1989). It might also be a sequence of thematically related events in which the referent was involved (Schank & Abelson, 1995). The features of these mental representations can be coded in many sense modalities, and can include affective reactions as well as visual or auditory "maps." Regardless of form, each representation constitutes a separate unit of knowledge that is deposited in the bin and can be retrieved as a whole, independent of other knowledge units.

Retrieval Processes

The Work Space is theoretically searched first for goal-relevant information. If this search is unsuccessful, the Executor compiles a set of "probe cues" composed largely of goal-relevant features and identifies a bin in Permanent Storage whose header contains these features. In some cases, other features of the bin header provide sufficient information to permit the goal to be attained. In these instances, the content of the bin itself may not be consulted.

Several other assumptions concerning retrieval processes are important. These assumptions, several of which are analogous to those made by other theories of memory, are conveyed as postulates.

Postulate 1. The bin that is identified by a given set of probe cues is the one whose header contains all of these cues but the smallest number of additional features that are not included in the probe set. (If no bin header contains all of the probe cues in the set, a subset of the original cues is compiled and the search is repeated.)

Postulate 2. The probe cues are compiled from a random subset of features contained in the first compartment of the Work Space. Because the goal specification is typically in this compartment (see Wyer & Srull, 1989), the probe set is likely to include goal-relevant features. However, other extraneous features that are not relevant to the goal can sometimes fortuitously be selected and can therefore influence which bin is identified.

Postulate 3. Once information is stored in a bin, it is never removed. Whenever a knowledge unit is necessary for attaining a processing objective, a copy of the unit is retrieved and used. Then, when processing is complete, this copy is returned to the top of the bin. Thus, a bin can contain several copies of a given knowledge unit, depending on how often the unit was involved in information processing.

Postulate 4. The goal-relevant knowledge contained in a bin is retrieved by means of a probabilistic top-down search. Thus, knowledge units near the top of the bin are most likely to be identified. However, because the search is imperfect, knowledge units at the top of the bin can often be missed. Consequently, the likelihood of retrieving a given unit is a function of not only the recency with which it was deposited (and, therefore, its proximity to the top of the bin) but also the frequency with which the unit was used in the past (e.g., the number of copies that have been formed of it).

Postulate 5. Once information sufficient to attain an immediate processing objective has been identified, the search of memory terminates. This means that the most recently and frequently used knowledge units are most likely to be identified and used again in processing information to which they are relevant, whereas other, equally applicable knowledge units are often ignored.

Postulate 6. The consciousness of the system resides in the Executor. Thus, individuals are aware of the information that is retrieved from Permanent Storage for use in goal-directed processing, and also of the results of this processing. However, the processes themselves, which take place in various processing units, are not subject to awareness.

Operation of the Model

New information that enters the processing system is first encoded by the Comprehender in terms of concepts drawn from the semantic bin. Copies of the concepts that are used at this stage are returned to the top of the bin, thus becoming more likely to be retrieved and used again. These initial comprehension processes are assumed to occur spontaneously and independently of more specific goal-directed processing, and are not monitored by the Executor. Thus, they typically occur without awareness.

The Executor continuously scans the first compartment of the Work Space, which typically contains both the material transmitted by the Comprehender and previously acquired knowledge that may have been recently retrieved from Permanent Storage. If this cognitive material contains a goal specification (either internally generated or externally imposed), the Executor retrieves a goal schema from Permanent Storage and uses it to direct subsequent processing in pursuit of these objectives. In the course of this processing, the Executor often retrieves knowledge from a goal-relevant referent bin and transmits it along with new information to a special-purpose processing unit with instructions to perform operations that fall within its purview.

Before discussing the specific issues of concern in this chapter, some more general implications of the proposed formulation are worth noting. These implications concern the conditions in which people do not recall information that is actually relevant to a goal being pursued, and the factors that determine the accessibility of concepts and knowledge that people try to ignore.

When Is Goal-Relevant Information Not Recalled and Used?

Postulates 1–6 have implications for the conditions in which information will not be recalled and used despite its relevance to one's processing objectives.

Goal-relevant knowledge will not be retrieved if probe cues fail to identify the bin in which the knowledge is stored. For example, if a representation of Mary's slapping John at a dinner party is stored in a referent bin pertaining to "John," it will not be recalled later when one is asked for information about "Mary" and searches for this information in a "Mary" bin.

In some cases, knowledge is not retrieved because too many probe cues are selected, some of which are irrelevant. In other cases, the knowledge retrieved may be biased. An example is suggested by a study of mood and memory reported by Bower (1981). People who are feeling happy might have concepts in the Work Space that are associated with this mood. Suppose they are asked to recall "childhood experiences." A mood-congruent concept (e.g., "happy") might sometimes be fortuitously included in the probe set along with goal-relevant features. If this occurs, it will lead information to be retrieved from a "happy childhood experiences" bin, and a more representative body of knowledge about one's childhood will not be identified.

Goal-relevant knowledge contained in a referent bin will not be retrieved if features of the bin's header are sufficient to attain the goal at hand. In this case, the header information is used and the contents of the bin itself are not consulted. Thus, suppose the header of a "Richard Nixon" bin contains the feature "dishonest" as well as the name of the referent. Then, this feature will be used as a basis for judging Nixon's honesty, and knowledge units that concern particular incidents involving Nixon (some of which might imply honesty) will not be recalled.

Goal-relevant knowledge will not be retrieved if it is buried beneath other units of knowledge that are sufficient for attaining the objective being pursued, and thus is unlikely to be identified in a top-down search of the bin in which it is stored. Note that when goal-relevant knowledge units have recently or frequently been used, copies of these units are theoretically redeposited on top of the bin pertaining to their referent. Consequently, other goal-relevant knowledge becomes less likely to be identified in the future. Thus, for example, an individual who has retrieved and used an ethnic stereotype as a basis for judgments at one point in time will be likely to do so again despite other judgment-relevant information the person might have acquired.

Determinants of the Accessibility
of Unwanted Concepts and Knowledge

The processes that underlie the failure to recall goal-relevant information are obviously related to those that underlie the tendency to recall information one is actively trying to forget. However, several additional considerations discussed in detail later in this chapter may be worth summarizing.

The information one is told to forget or to disregard is typically interpreted by the Comprehender in terms of concepts stored in the semantic bin before the instructions to disregard it are given. As a result, these concepts, copies of which are redeposited in the bins from which they are drawn, become more accessible in memory and are more likely to be used to attain future objectives to which they are relevant. Somewhat analogously, the process of trying to suppress preexisting knowledge may itself cause copies of the to-be-suppressed knowledge to be activated and redeposited in a relevant referent bin, thus increasing the accessibility of this knowledge, or concepts associated with it, relative to conditions in which no attempt at suppression was made.

Attempts to disregard new information are likely to cause the information to be stored in a referent bin whose header contains features that denote the information as "to be disregarded." If this bin is later encountered in the search for goal-referent information, it will presumably be identified as one whose contents are to be avoided, and the retrieval of these contents will therefore be inhibited.

Moreover, the addition of "to be forgotten" to the features contained in a bin header is often sufficient to prevent the bin from being spontaneously identified in a search for information about its referent. For example, suppose two bins exist pertaining to a referent, one whose header specifies the referent's name alone and the other whose header also contains the feature "to be forgotten." Then, probe cues containing the referent's name alone will lead the former bin to be identified but not the latter (see Postulate 1). Nevertheless, explicit requests to recall the to-be-forgotten information (which presumably would lead "to be forgotten" to be included among the probe cues) might lead this information to be retrieved rather easily.

New representations of an experience are often constructed in the course of thinking about it or in describing it to others. These new representations can differ from the original in a number of ways. For example, features can be added that are necessary to adequately convey the overall sequence of events that occurred. By the same token, certain features of the original representation might be deleted. Because the newly formed representation is stored in memory on top of the original, it is relatively more likely to be retrieved and used to attain goals to which it is relevant. Thus, for example, a person who has experienced a traumatic event may initially have a representation of the event containing a number of emotion-eliciting features. In describing the event to others, however, the person might try to avoid mentioning these features and, in doing so, avoid the embarrassment or continued emotional distress of expressing the emotions elicited by them. After several such communications, a number of relatively emotion-free copies of the experience would theoretically be formed and stored on top of the original. As a result, the emotion-eliciting event representation becomes unlikely to be identified, and the person can recall the event without experiencing the emotions that occurred at first.

UNCONSCIOUS INFLUENCE OF KNOWLEDGE ON JUDGMENTS AND BEHAVIORS

People are often unaware of the effects of information they have acquired. This is true whether or not they have tried to disregard the information. The conditions that surround the unconscious influence of information on judgments and behaviors have been reviewed in detail elsewhere (Bargh, in press; Jacoby & Kelley, 1987; Wilson & Brekke, 1994). A few examples of this influence suffice in the present context.

First, semantic concepts that have been activated for use in one context can often affect judgments and behaviors in other, unrelated contexts (Bargh, in press; Wyer & Srull, 1989). This influence can occur even when people cannot recall the conditions in which these concepts were activated. In a study by Tulving, Schacter, and Stark (1982), participants were first asked to learn a list of fairly uncommon words. Then, either a few minutes or several days later, they were either given a recognition memory test on a subset of the words they had learned or were asked to complete a number of word fragments (e.g., _SS_SS_N), some answers to which were contained on the original word list. Not surprisingly, recognition memory for words on the list decreased over time. However, performance on the word-fragment completion test, which was facilitated by exposure to words on the original list, was maintained over time.

These results are interpretable in terms of the Wyer and Srull model. Participants who tried to learn the word list presumably formed a representation of the words to be learned and stored them in a referent bin pertaining to "word list." However, learning was imperfect, and not all of the words to be learned were included in these representations. After a short delay, many of the to-be-learned words were still in the Work Space as well as in Permanent Storage, and so memory for the words was relatively high. After a long delay, however, the Work Space had been cleared, and so performance deteriorated. Note, however, that the initial comprehension of words in the word list presumably required the use of concepts in the semantic bin. Once copies of these relatively unfamiliar concepts were retrieved and used, these copies were redeposited on the top of this bin. Because performance on the word-fragment completion task also required access to concepts in the semantic bin, it was facilitated when these concepts were easily accessible, and this facilitation was evident even after a long delay.

The activation of semantic concepts can also unconsciously influence overt behavior. In an experiment by Bargh and Chen (1995; see also Bargh, in press), participants were first asked to construct sentences from sets of words, some of which activated concepts associated with either politeness or rudeness. After completing the task, they reported to an experimenter who was waiting in a room down the hall. However, they found the experimenter engaged in a conversation with another student (a confederate). Participants who had been primed with rudeness-related concepts interrupted the conversation more quickly than did those who had been primed with politeness-related concepts. This was true despite the fact that participants later reported no insight into the fact that the behavior-relevant concepts had been primed. Apparently, the traits that were primed activated concepts in the semantic bin that, once accessible, affected participants' interpretation of the experimenter's behavior. This interpretation, in turn, mediated their own behavior. (But see Bargh, in press, for an alternative explanation of this finding.)

Thus, both Bargh and Chen's (1995) and Tulving et al.'s (1982) studies converge on the conclusion that semantic concepts that are activated in one context can affect behavior and judgments in an unrelated context even when participants have forgotten the stimuli that led the concepts to be activated. Knowledge retrieved from referent bins can presumably have similar effects. For example, participants in a study by Ross, Lepper, and Hubbard (1975) were given a series of suicide notes with instructions to indicate whether each note was either a true suicide note or bogus. After judging each note, they were given feedback that they were either correct or incorrect. Some participants were led to believe they were correct on a large majority of the trials, whereas others were told they were incorrect. After performing the task, however, participants were debriefed, being told that the feedback they had received was predetermined. The debriefing was very compelling, eliminating any possibility that participants still believed that the feedback actually reflected their true performance. Nevertheless, persons who were told they had done well predicted they would do better on a subsequent task requiring similar skills than did those who were told they had done poorly.

One interpretation of this finding is that persons who were led to believe they were doing much better (or worse) than they expected spontaneously attempted to explain their performance. In doing do, they retrieved knowledge about themselves from a "self" bin with implications consistent with the feedback. This selective subset of self-knowledge, copies of which were redeposited on top of the relevant self bin, was later used as a basis for predicting future performance despite the fact that participants knew the feedback they had been given was false.

EFFECTS OF EXPLICIT DEMANDS TO DISREGARD INFORMATION ON CONCEPT ACCESSIBILITY

Effects of Instructions to Forget Information

As the studies described in the previous section indicate, the unconscious influence of concepts and knowledge on judgments and behaviors often occurs because these concepts, once activated in the course of comprehending and reacting to one experience, remain accessible in memory after the experience itself is no longer thought about. Therefore, these cognitions are likely to influence responses to subsequent situations, independent of the experiences that initially activated them. Similar effects can often occur even when subjects intentionally try to ignore experiences they have had, or thoughts associated with these experiences. Two quite different series of studies support this possibility.

In an experiment by Basden, Basden, and Gargano (1993, Experiment 2), participants were given a series of words to learn. Immediately after each word was presented, participants in some conditions were told either to remember it or to forget it. Persons presumably thought more extensively about the words they were told to remember than those they were told to forget, and therefore were more likely to retain these words in a "word list" bin in permanent storage. Therefore, these words should be recalled better later when the bin was searched for task-relevant information. However, the initial encoding of *both* types of words presumably required the use of concepts in the semantic bin, consequently making these concepts more accessible. Consistent with the implications of this reasoning, participants had better recall of words they were told to remember than those they were told to forget. However, both sets of words equivalently facilitated perform-ance on a word-fragment completion task containing items corresponding to the words in question.

Kihlstrom's (1980) investigations of the effects of posthypnotic amnesia are also of interest in this context. In these studies, hypnotized participants were first given a word list to learn, followed by a posthypnotic suggestion that when they awakened, they would be unable to remember the words. This instruction presumably led subjects to designate the bin containing the word list as "to be forgotten," and this retrieval cue prevented them from identifying and searching the bin for words they had learned until they were released from their posthypnotic state (for alternative interpretations of this effect, see Kihlstrom, 1980). Nevertheless, the initial exposure to the words presumably activated concepts in the semantic bin, and the increased ac-cessibility of these concepts facilitated participants' performance on a sub-sequent word-fragment completion task despite their inability to recall the words.

The effects of to-be-disregarded information on the performance of word-fragment completion tasks might not appear to have many implications for social judgment and behavior. However, it seems likely that the concepts and knowledge activated by such information would have effects analogous to those observed by Bargh and others cited earlier. That is, knowledge that has become more accessible in memory in the course of processing infor-mation one is later told to disregard will influence judgments and behavior independent of the "to be disregarded" information per se.

Effects of Thought Suppression

In many situations that arise outside the laboratory, people often have difficulty suppressing thoughts about the information they have acquired. Wegner, Schneider, Carter, and White (1987) noted that people typically try to suppress a concept by distracting themselves from thinking about it. However, these efforts are likely to strengthen the association of this concept with other thoughts that serve as distractors, and also with stimuli in the immediate environment in which the cognitive activity occurs. Therefore, the presence of these distracting thoughts and stimuli in a later situation can cue the recall of the to-be-suppressed concept, increasing its accessibility in memory rather than decreasing it. In this regard, one cannot intentionally avoid thinking about a referent without activating a concept of the referent that one is attempting to suppress. Moreover, the more times one engages in this avoidance activity, the more times the concept is activated, and the more copies of it are redeposited on top of the bin from which it was drawn. Consequently, the likelihood that the concept will be reactivated in the future is increased.

Evidence that instructions to avoid thinking about an object can have the opposite effect to that intended was reported by Lavy and van den Hout (1990; see also Muris, Merckelbach, van den Hout, & De Jong, 1992; Salkovskis & Campbell, 1994). Specifically, persons who were told to think about "anything except vehicles" reported more instances of vehicles in a think-aloud protocol than did persons who were told to think about "anything including vehicles." These data confirm the fact that the cognitive activity associated with intentional suppression of a concept increases rather than decreases the concept's accessibility in memory.

More direct support for the interpretation proposed by Wegner was obtained by Howell and Conway (1992, Experiment 1). Participants were asked to suppress either a positive or a negative personal life experience while in an experimentally manipulated mood state. Their think-aloud protocols showed more intrusive thoughts about the to-be-suppressed experience when their mood was affectively congruent with the experience than when it was not. Chronic affective states appear to have analogous effects (Howell & Conway, 1992, Experiment 2).

In combination, the data confirm the hypothesis that conscious attempts to suppress thoughts about an event can actually increase the frequency with which these thoughts occur. Note that in the course of this thinking, copies of concepts to which the thoughts refer should be redeposited on top of bins to which they are relevant (either referent bins or the semantic bin). To this extent, these concepts are more likely to be called upon for use in the future.

Research by Wegner and his colleagues provided evidence of this. For example, Wegner et al. (1987) found that people were more likely to report thinking about a white bear in a think-aloud protocol if they had been told explicitly to suppress thoughts about it earlier in the experiment than if they had previously been told to think about it. Subsequent studies (Wegner, Schneider, Knutson, & McMahon, 1991; Wenzlaff, Wegner, & Klein, 1991) demonstrated that these effects are enhanced when external or internal stimulus cues (e.g., mood) that existed at the time of thought suppression are also present during the subsequent think-aloud task. Thus, the cognitive activity involved in the intentional suppression of thoughts about the object can increase the number of times the object is actually thought about and, therefore, can strengthen its association with situational factors that cue its later retrieval. (For an alternative interpretation, see Wegner, 1994.)

There is an important contingency in this phenomenon, however. That is, it is unlikely to occur when people are asked to suppress thoughts about an affect-eliciting, personally relevant experience. Kelly and Kahn (1994), for example, found that instructions to suppress intrusive thoughts about a recent happy or unhappy experience decreased the likelihood of spontaneously generating these thoughts in a later situation. Analogously, Wegner and Gold (1995) reported that men's attempts to suppress thoughts about an old flame only increased their subsequent thoughts about her when they no longer felt emotionally attached to her.

Perhaps an increase in spontaneous thoughts about an object following explicit instructions to suppress them occurs only when people would not normally think about the object in the absence of these instructions. People who are asked to suppress an experience that spontaneously intruded on their thoughts in the past may have already developed effective mechanisms for avoiding these thoughts. In terms of the model we propose, this could be done by adding the feature "to be avoided" to the header of the bin that contains the knowledge to be suppressed. Then, when the bin is identified, this feature can serve as a warning not to peruse the bin's contents, preventing a detailed depiction of the events contained in it from being retrieved and called into consciousness. Under these circumstances, explicit instructions to suppress thinking about the object or event may simply reinforce the mechanisms that have already been established for doing so, and so they may have little influence. In contrast, suppose no inhibitory mechanisms exist at the time participants are asked explicitly to suppress thoughts about an object. Then, the processes postulated by Wegner and others are more likely to occur.

Effects of Suppressing Stereotypes on Their Accessibility and Use

If attempts to suppress thoughts about a target increase the accessibility of concepts to which these thoughts pertain, they should increase the likelihood of employing these concepts spontaneously in a subsequent situation. This possibility was evaluated in research by Macrae and Bodenhausen on the determinants of stereotype use. In one series of studies (Macrae, Boden-hausen, Milne, & Jetten, 1994), people were asked to write about an individual based on a picture of a skinhead and a series of attributes describing him. In doing so, some participants were asked to avoid thinking about the target in a "category-based manner." Their efforts to suppress these thoughts were apparently successful. In a later judgment situation, however, suppressors were *more* inclined to use the stereotype to describe a different target person than were participants who had not previously been told to suppress its use. Moreover, they responded more quickly to stereotype-related words in a lexical decision task. Finally, under conditions in which participants actually expected to meet the person they had judged, suppressors chose to sit further away from the seat ostensibly occupied by this person than did control participants.

In combination, these results indicate that instructions to avoid thinking about the target person activate a "suppression" mechanism that requires activation of the to-be-suppressed concepts in order to operate. Copies of these concepts are redeposited on top of the bin from which they were drawn (e.g., the semantic bin). As a result, the likelihood that the concepts will be brought to bear on the processing of information in the future is increased.

This conceptualization also has implications for conditions in which the use of the stereotype-related concepts can be decreased. This decrease should occur when other goal-relevant concepts are deposited on top of the stereotype-relevant ones, thus decreasing their accessibility in memory. A study by Macrae, Bodenhausen, and Milne (1995) found support for this possibility. Subjects observed a videotape of a Chinese woman either eating with chopsticks or applying makeup. The first videotape presumably disposed viewers to categorize the target as Chinese, whereas the second disposed them to classify her as female. After watching the tape, participants performed a lexical decision task containing several words associated with each stereotype. Relative to control conditions, watching the videotape decreased the time required to identify words that were consistent with the stereotype activated by the tape. However, it increased the time to identify words associated with the alternative stereotype. In other words, activating a stereotype not only increased the accessibility of concepts contained in this stereotype but correspondingly decreased the accessibility of concepts contained in others.

EFFECTS OF DEMANDS TO DISREGARD JUDGMENT-RELEVANT KNOWLEDGE

Macrae and Bodenhausen's research suggests that concepts activated by to-be-disregarded information can influence judgments and behavior to which the information itself is objectively irrelevant. Additional considerations arise, however, when the information to be disregarded concerns the same people and events to which one's processing goals refer. The most obvious examples of such situations occur in the courtroom, where jurors are often instructed that certain pieces of evidence they have heard are inadmissible. But other circumstances arise as well. For example, a job recruiter may believe (s)he should disregard a candidate's race or sex when evaluating the person's qualifications. Or, a professor may attempt to ignore his or her personal feelings about a colleague when evaluating the colleague's eligibility for promotion.

The success of such attempts can depend on several factors. Of these, perhaps the most important is the extent to which the to-be-disregarded information has already become integrated into a mental representation of the referent by the time one is told to disregard it, and the ease with which its implications can be extracted from this representation. The importance of this factor was demonstrated in a series of studies by Wyer and his colleagues (Wyer & Budesheim, 1987; Wyer & Unverzagt, 1985) in the area of impression formation. The research paradigm they employed was stimulated by a theoretical formulation of impression formation that allowed the mental representations formed to be specified a priori and the use of these representations in both recall and judgment to be predicted. Although the specific findings obtained may have limited generalizability, they call attention to the need to specify the nature of the representations that are formed to predict the effects of to-be-disregarded information.

Participants were asked to form an impression of a target person on the basis of a series of behaviors. In Wyer and Unverzagt's (1985) study, the first set of behaviors presented in some conditions conveyed a favorable trait (e.g., "kind") and the last set of behaviors conveyed an unfavorable one (e.g., "dishonest"). In other cases, the sequence of behaviors was reversed. Some participants received the entire sequence of behaviors without interruption. Others, however, were told after reading the first set that a mistake had been made, that these behaviors pertained to a totally different person than the one they were supposed to judge, and to disregard them. Still other subjects were not told to disregard these behaviors until all of the remaining ones had been presented. Finally, some subjects were told to disregard the last set of behaviors in the series. In a fourth condition, a control condition, the to-be-disregarded behaviors were not presented at all. After receiving the information, participants in all conditions judged the target person along the trait dimensions to which the behaviors were relevant and estimated their liking for the person. Finally, they were asked to recall all the behaviors they had read, regardless of whether they had been told to disregard them or not.

Predictions were based on a theory of the mental representations that people construct when they form an impression of someone on the basis of the person's behaviors (Wyer & Srull, 1989; see also Srull & Wyer, 1989). First, they form "trait-behavior clusters" as a result of encoding several different behaviors in terms of a given trait concept. Second, they form a concept of the target person as likeable or dislikeable on the basis of the initial behaviors in the sequence. Finally, they organize these and other behaviors around the concept, forming an evaluative person representation. Thus, each behavior presented can be represented twice; once in a trait-behavior cluster and once in the evaluative person representation. These representations are stored independently in a referent bin pertaining to the target.

Subsequent evaluative and trait judgments of the target person are theoretically based on the central concept defining the evaluative person representation and relevant trait-behavior clusters, respectively. Suppose, however, that a judgment-relevant trait-behavior cluster does not exist. Then, trait judgments are based on the evaluative implications of the central concept defining the person representation and the descriptive implications of a random subset of the behaviors associated with it. Note that once behaviors have become associated with a person concept and are integrated into a representation of this person, they cannot be "erased" (see Postulate 3). Therefore, these behaviors can potentially influence judgments of the trait they exemplify even though people are later told to disregard them.

To see this, first assume that people are given a series of kind behaviors followed by a series of dishonest ones with instructions to form an impression of the person they describe. They should form trait-behavior clusters around the concepts "kind" and "dishonest." They should also form a favorable concept of the person on the basis of the initial (kind) behaviors, and construct a person representation around this concept. These representations are shown metaphorically in Fig. 10.1, where pathways denote associations between behaviors and concepts that result from thinking about the behaviors in relation to these concepts. Thus, recipients should judge the target to be kind, dishonest, and likeable.

Now, however, suppose that immediately after the initial, kind behaviors are presented, recipients are told to disregard them. In this case, recipients could easily segregate the representations containing these behaviors from the remaining information they receive. This is presumably done by designating the bin containing these representations as "to be disregarded" and storing the representations formed from the remaining behaviors in a new, judgment-relevant bin. Therefore, recipients should judge the target to be dishonest (based on the trait concept defining the "dishonest" trait-behavior cluster) and dislikeable (based on a person concept formed from the dishonest behaviors). They should also judge him to be "unkind," because (a) a judgment-relevant trait-behavior cluster does not exist in the judgment-relevant bin, (b) the evaluative implications of the person concept are unfavorable, and (c) the behaviors associated with this concept have no

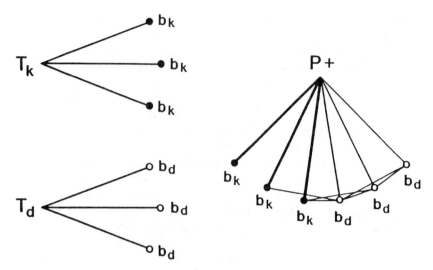

FIG. 10.1. Metaphorical representation of the cognitive representations formed from three kind behaviors (b_k) followed by three dishonest behaviors (b_d) under instructions to form an impression of the person they describe. P+ is a favorable person concept formed from the initial behaviors, and T_k and T_d are trait concepts. Pathways denote associations formed as a result of thinking about the behaviors and concepts in relation to one another.

descriptive implications for the trait being judged. In short, the to-be-disregarded behaviors should have no impact on judgments in this case.

In contrast, suppose the kind behaviors that recipients are told to disregard were presented last, after the dishonest behaviors. In this case, both trait-behavior clusters have been formed by the time instructions to disregard the kind behaviors are given. Moreover, the kind behaviors have already been integrated into the evaluative person representation. To segregate the implications of the to-be-disregarded information from the information they are supposed to consider, recipients must designate the bin containing the existing representations as "to be disregarded" and copy the two relevant representations (the "dishonest" trait-behavior cluster and the evaluative person representation) into a new judgment-relevant bin. Therefore, these recipients should later judge the target to be dishonest, and also as dislikeable (because the central concept of the evaluative person representation, based on the initial, dishonest behaviors, is unfavorable). However, suppose recipients are asked to judge the target's kindness. In this case, they are likely to identify some of the to-be-disregarded behaviors in the course of scanning the evaluative person representation for descriptively relevant information. As a result, recipients are more likely to judge the target as kind than if the kind behaviors had not been presented at all.

Suppose these participants are now asked to recall the behaviors they have been told to disregard. They do this by perusing the contents of the "to be disregarded" bin. When the behaviors to be disregarded are at the beginning of the series, they are the only ones contained in this bin, and so they should be recalled easily. When the to-be-disregarded behaviors are last, however, judgment-relevant behaviors are also contained in the representations stored in the "to be disregarded" bin, and these behaviors are likely to interfere with recall of the "to be disregarded" ones. Therefore, the latter behaviors should be recalled relatively poorly.

These predictions, considered in combination, imply that behaviors at the beginning of a series that recipients are told to disregard should have little impact on judgments although recipients can recall these behaviors very well. In contrast, behaviors at the end of the series that recipients are told to disregard should have an influence on judgments of the trait to which they are relevant although recipients can recall them relatively poorly. The studies by Wyer and his colleagues supported these predictions. However, a number of contingencies in these effects exist.

Effects of Task Objectives. In the studies by Wyer and colleagues, recipients were told to use the information to form an impression of the person described. If people read the information for the purpose of remembering it, or simply wish to comprehend the information, the sorts of representations shown in Fig. 10.1 would undoubtedly not be formed (Hamilton et al., 1980; Srull, 1981; Wyer & Gordon, 1982). Consequently, the recall of the to-be-disregarded behaviors, and the effects of these behaviors on judgments, would be likely to differ appreciably.

Instructions to Disregard Information. The effect of to-be-disregarded information also depends on the reason it should ostensibly be ignored. In the paradigm employed by Wyer and colleagues, recipients were more strongly influenced by the to-be-disregarded information when it ostensibly referred to the person they were told to evaluate than when it referred to someone completely different (Wyer & Unverzagt, 1985). In the former condition, participants often tended to ignore the instructions to disregard the behaviors in an effort to make accurate judgments. This tendency contributed to the effects of to-be-disregarded behaviors over and above the effects predicted on the basis of the theoretical analysis outlined earlier.

Similarity of the To-Be-Disregarded Information to the Remaining Information. When the to-be-disregarded behaviors are along the same trait dimension as those to be considered, the mental representations formed are theoretically dissimilar to those described in Fig. 10.1, and so the predicted effects of to-be-disregarded behaviors also differ (for details, see Wyer & Budesheim, 1987; Wyer & Srull, 1989). Specifically:

1. When the behaviors to be disregarded are descriptively unrelated to the other behaviors presented (as in Wyer and Unverzagt's study and the example shown in Fig. 10.1), they influence trait judgments only when they are presented last, after the behaviors to be considered.

2. When the behaviors to be disregarded are both descriptively and evaluatively inconsistent with the remaining ones (e.g., they imply dishonesty, whereas the behaviors to be considered imply honesty), they influence trait judgments only when they are presented first and recipients are not told to ignore them until after the remaining behaviors have been presented.

3. When the behaviors to be disregarded are both descriptively and evaluatively consistent with the remaining ones (e.g., when both sets of behaviors imply honesty), they influence trait judgments under both of the above conditions.

Effects of Inadmissible Evidence

The contingencies summarized earlier call attention to the difficulty of drawing general conclusions concerning the effects of information that people attempt to disregard. The mental representations constructed on the basis of information presented in a criminal trial, for example, are likely to bear little resemblance to those constructed by participants in Wyer and colleagues' research. Rather, recipients of courtroom testimony may attempt to construct a "story" or narrative of the sequence of events surrounding the crime, and may base their judgments on the plausibility of this sequence (Pennington & Hastie, 1988, 1992). The effects of inadmissible evidence in these circumstances are likely to differ considerably from those reported by Wyer and colleagues.

Striking evidence of this difference was obtained by Budesheim (1988). Participants read excerpts from the summary statements made by opposing lawyers in a fictitious murder trial. In some conditions, a prosecution statement referred to evidence that a knife found in a defendant's house was likely to be the murder weapon. This evidence, which was conveyed either near the beginning or near the end of the transcript, was sometimes followed by a statement from the judge that it was inadmissible. After reading the transcript, participants reported their beliefs that the defendant was guilty and indicated whether they would vote to convict him.

The incriminating evidence had an overall effect on judgments regardless of whether or not it was declared inadmissible. However, its influence was greatest when it was presented early in the transcript and was declared inadmissible immediately afterwards. In fact, judgments were more extreme in this condition than they were when the incriminating evidence was not disparaged at all. They were also more extreme than judgments made when either the incriminating evidence was not presented until the end of the transcript, or the evidence was conveyed at the outset but not declared inadmissible until later. When participants learned that the incriminating evidence was inadmissible early in the transcript, they appeared to pay selective attention to aspects of the remaining information that confirmed its implications. Consequently, they judged the defendant even more likely to be guilty than they would have if the instructions to disregard the incriminating evidence had not been given. When they did not learn that the incriminating evidence should be disregarded until all of the information had been received, however, this selective processing was not possible, and so instructions to disregard the evidence were more effective.

Note that the effects observed in Budesheim's study are almost diametrically opposite to those obtained by Wyer and his colleagues in the impression formation research we described earlier. In this latter research, behaviors at the beginning of the information sequence that people were told to disregard immediately had no effect at all on judgments. This difference underscores the importance of taking into account not only the type of information presented but persons' processing goals when predicting the impact of to-be-disregarded information.

ADJUSTMENTS FOR BIAS

In many instances where people have acquired information they believe they should disregard, they consciously adjust for its potential influence on their judgments and decisions. However, they often do not have a clear perception of how much they need to adjust. If they do not adjust enough, the information will still have an impact. If they adjust too much, the information could have a "boomerang" effect, biasing judgments in a direction opposite to that implied by the information they are trying to ignore. Two questions are raised by these observations. First, when are people motivated and able to adjust for the biases they perceive to exist? Second, what factors determine how much they believe they should adjust?

Motivation and Ability to Compensate for Bias

People often believe they are expected to be as accurate as possible in reporting judgments and to communicate the truth as they see it (Grice, 1975; Higgins, 1981). They may therefore attempt to comply with this expectation (Schwarz, 1990; Strack, 1991). One implication of this is that if persons perceive that a judgment might be influenced by extraneous factors, they will actively attempt to compensate for this bias. This of course assumes that they have the time, ability, and motivation to do so.

A series of studies by Martin and his colleagues (Martin, 1986; Martin, Seta, & Crelia, 1990) supported this possibility. Participants first performed a task that required a set of either favorable trait concepts ("adventurous," "self-confident," etc.) or unfavorable ones ("reckless," "conceited," etc.). Then, they were asked to form an impression of someone described by behaviors that could alternatively be interpreted in terms of either set of traits (e.g., "plans to go sky-diving, and to cross the Atlantic in a sailboat," "is well aware of his ability to do things well," etc.). Participants were presumably aware that the concepts activated by the initial task might influence their interpretation of the target's behaviors. In some conditions of the study, however, they were asked to perform a secondary task while they read information about the target. Consequently, they were unable to search extensively for alternative concepts to apply, and used the primed concepts despite the bias they introduced. As a result, these participants' evaluations of the target person increased with the favorableness of these concepts. In the absence of distraction, however, participants were able to identify alternative concepts that often had different evaluative implications from the ones that had been primed. Consequently, the primed concepts in this condition had a *contrast* effect on evaluations of the target.

These results indicate that persons' attempts to avoid the biasing influence of past experiences on their interpretation of information can often lead them to use concepts less often than they would if the experience had never occurred. As a result, the experiences have a "boomerang" effect. This effect, of course, should only occur when persons are actually motivated to identify alternative concepts. Both individual differences and situational factors can affect this motivation, as Martin et al. (1990) demonstrated in other experiments.

Martin et al.'s work has obvious implications for judgment situations outside the laboratory. For example, information about job candidates often provides an indication of their sex and ethnicity. This information might activate stereotypic concepts that could affect the interpretation of more job-relevant material, and therefore could bias the evaluations that are based on it. On the other hand, suppose the evaluator is aware of this possibility and attempts to compensate for the biasing effect of these concepts by adjusting the evaluation (s)he ultimately reports. If this adjustment is too great, it could produce an evaluation that is opposite in direction to that implied by the stereotype.

A recent study by Radhakrishnan (1996) suggested this possibility. Participants were given information about six job candidates, three Black and three White. Before receiving this information, some participants were told that they could hire up to six candidates, and others were told they could hire only three. Still others were given no information at all about the number they could hire. Participants in the latter (no information) condition rated Black and White candidates equally favorably. In contrast, participants who were told they could hire a given number of candidates (regardless of whether this number was three or six) rated Blacks more favorably than Whites. Apparently, mentioning the amount of resources available called participants' attention to affirmative action considerations, and this in turn made salient the possibility that their decisions might be contaminated by ethnic biases. Consequently, they adjusted (in fact, overadjusted) for these biases in making their ratings.

A conceptually related phenomenon was captured by Sherman and Gorkin (1980). Male participants were asked to decide the amount of damages that should be awarded to a woman in a fair employment case. Before being exposed to the case, some participants were asked to solve a riddle that was such that a failure to solve it could be construed as evidence of sexist attitudes. Those participants who failed to solve the riddle subsequently awarded higher damages to the woman than did control participants. Sherman and Gorkin interpreted their results as evidence that participants did not want to think of themselves as sexist, and that the damages they awarded reflected a desire to maintain their self-perceptions. However, an unwillingness to appear sexist in the eyes of others could also have contributed to these results.

Determinants of the Amount of Adjustment

Wegener and Petty (1995; Petty & Wegener, 1993) proposed that when individuals wish to correct for a potential bias in their judgments, they infer the amount they should correct from their naive theories about social reality. This implies that people are likely to correct more if their uncorrected judgment is inconsistent with their theory-based expectations than if it is consistent with these expectations (and therefore appears less biased).

As an example, people are generally expected to be likeable and to have favorable attributes (Kanouse & Hanson, 1971; Wyer, 1970). If this is so, participants in Wyer and Budesheim's (1987) study should have perceived their judgments to be less contaminated by the information they were told to disregard, and therefore, should have adjusted less for its influence when the implications of the information were favorable than when they were unfavorable. This was in fact the case. That is, in all conditions in which to-be-disregarded behaviors were theoretically expected to have an influence, this influence was greater when the information was favorable than when it was unfavorable. In fact, the to-be-disregarded information typically had a contrast effect in these latter conditions, suggesting that participants adjusted too much to compensate for the bias it produced.

Biasing Effects of Affect and Emotion

Our discussion thus far has been limited to the biasing effects of descriptive implications of information and knowledge. However, similar considerations arise in construing the impact of affect and emotion. Many judgments and decisions are based on one's subjective, affective reactions to the object being judged (for a summary of research on the informational influences of affect on judgment, see Clore, Schwarz, & Conway, 1994). However, it is often very difficult to separate one's affective reactions to a particular person or object from the affect one is experiencing for other reasons. Consequently, this latter, extraneous affect can often have an impact on the judgments one makes (Schwarz & Clore, 1983).

A particularly interesting situation in which affective reactions are often used as a basis for judgment occurs when evaluating political candidates. People's feelings about a candidate may be elicited both by his or her issue stands and by more general personal qualities (e.g., the candidate's "image"). However, the affect they happen to be experiencing for other reasons can often become confused with the feelings elicited by the candidate's attributes, and therefore, can also influence judgments. Ottati and Isbell (1996) obtained evidence of this influence, and also showed that people's tendency to adjust for it often depends on their processing efficiency. In each of three experiments, participants were induced to be in a good or bad mood before learning about a political candidate's stands on a number of social issues. Mood was manipulated by either giving participants feedback about their performance on a midterm exam, by asking them to write about a happy or unhappy personal experience, or by viewing films designed to elicit a positive or negative affective state. Participants who were classified as inefficient political information processors reported more favorable reactions to the candidate when they were in a good mood than when they were in a bad mood. However, mood had a negative, contrast effect on judgments by participants who were high in processing efficiency. The latter participants were apparently either better able or more motivated to distinguish between the two sources of affect, and therefore, were more inclined to adjust for the bias produced by their general mood state. However, they *over*adjusted, producing a contrast effect of their mood on evaluations.

SPONTANEOUS ATTEMPTS TO DISREGARD SOCIAL KNOWLEDGE

In most of the conditions we have considered thus far, attempts to disregard information and knowledge have been in response to implicit or explicit situational demands. Thus, our discussion has ignored a very large and obviously important number of circumstances in which people are *intrinsi-*

cally motivated to forget or otherwise avoid thinking about knowledge they have acquired. This is most often knowledge that elicits unpleasant affective reactions (Roemer & Borkovec, 1993).

Many consequences of unwanted thoughts are undoubtedly similar to those described in previous sections. That is, the concepts to which these thoughts pertain can affect the interpretation of new information about the same or different referents. Moreover, they can potentially influence behavior and decisions in ways one is not aware (Bargh & Chen, 1995). Finally, unwanted thoughts that intrude on immediate goal-directed cognitive activity can disrupt this activity and, therefore, can interfere with goal attainment.

The major question left unanswered by our previous discussion surrounds the factors that govern the extent to which intrusive thoughts occur despite the desire to suppress them. A complete analysis of these factors is beyond the scope of this chapter. We therefore restrict our remarks to two topics that potentially fall within the purview of the information processing model we propose. These topics concern the effects of goal blocking on the spontaneous intrusion of thoughts about goal-relevant knowledge and experiences, and individual differences in the tendency and ability to suppress emotion-eliciting events.

Effects of Goal Blocking on Rumination

One of the best known conceptualizations of the intrusive effects of unwanted thoughts was proposed by Klinger (1975). The central construct of this theory, denoted *current concerns*, is conceptualized as "a nonconscious directive (brain) process that persists from the time of commitment to a particular goal to the termination of the pursuit" (Klinger, 1996, p. 110). This goal-directed cognitive activity can lead to the spontaneous activation of goal-relevant concepts and knowledge that, in turn, affects not only the incidence of goal-relevant thoughts and behaviors but the interpretation of new experiences in terms of goal-related constructs. The cognitive biases produced by these effects are likely to persist until the goal in question is attained.

A conceptualization of rumination by Martin and Tesser (1996) has similar implications (but see Klinger, 1996). Like Klinger, these authors assumed that people are most often stimulated to ruminate about unpleasant experiences or states of affairs when they perceive these experiences or states to be relevant to long-range, higher order goal attainment. Thus, failure on a midterm exam is more likely to stimulate rumination if it is believed to have adverse consequences for graduating from college than if it is not.

Individuals differ in the extent to which they form cognitive linkages between immediate and long-range goals and, therefore, in the extent to which they ruminate. McIntosh and Martin (1992) identified both "linkers" (persons who typically perceive their current life situation to have implications for their long-range goal attainment) and "nonlinkers" on the basis of a general questionnaire measure. These participants were later exposed to a word-identification task in which some of the words were relevant to romantic relationships. Linkers identified relationship-relevant words more quickly if they were not currently involved in a relationship (but wanted one) than if they were. In contrast, nonlinkers' response times to the words did not depend on whether or not they were currently involved in a relationship. It seems reasonable to suppose that both linkers and nonlinkers considered romantic involvements to be intrinsically desirable. However, linkers were likely to perceive such involvements to be relevant to long-range goal attainment (e.g., marriage or having a family). Consequently, those who were not in a current relationship tended to ruminate about it, making relationship-relevant concepts more generally accessible in memory. In contrast, nonlinkers did not consider a current relationship to have implications for their long-range goal attainment. Therefore, they did not ruminate about the absence of such a relationship, and so the accessibility of relationship-relevant concepts did not depend on whether they were currently involved or not.

Individual Differences in the Ability to Repress Unwanted Thoughts

Individual differences also exist in the effectiveness with which people avoid thinking about unpleasant experiences that are independent of the relevance of these experiences to goal attainment. These differences have long been a focus of research on emotional repression (e.g., Dollard & Miller, 1950; Erdelyi, 1985; Greenwald, 1992; Singer, 1990). Repressors differ from nonrepressors in terms of their ability to keep unpleasant thoughts and concepts out of consciousness.[1] The mechanisms that underlie these effects are somewhat controversial. Repressors could differ from nonrepressors in their initial attention to unpleasant events, in their interpretation of the events as emotional at the time they are encountered, or in the later recall of the events once they are stored in memory. Of course, these possibilities are not mutually exclusive.

---

[1]Repression is often operationalized in terms of responses to the Taylor (1953) Manifest Anxiety Scale and the Social Desirability Scale (Crowne & Marlowe, 1960). Specifically, repressors are defined as persons who score low in manifest anxiety but high in defensiveness (Weinberger, 1990; Weinberger, Schwartz, & Davidson, 1979). Although this operationalization seems remote from the conceptual definition, individuals identified as repressors on the basis of this criterion do, in fact, appear to exhibit behavior that is consistent with the conceptual definition.

Attentional Processes

One way in which repressors can avoid negative emotional information is by selectively excluding that information from their focus of attention. Baumeister and Cairns (1992) provided repressors and nonrepressors with bogus personality feedback that contained both positive and negative information. Repressors spent less time looking at the negative feedback than nonrepressors when this feedback was given in private, but spent more time than nonrepressors when the feedback was given in a public disclosure situation. Debriefing suggested that the additional time taken by repressors in the public condition was spent worrying about what others would think of them and generating counterexamples of the negative traits. To conclude, the first line of defense against threatening emotional material may be decreased attention. However, when other goals (e.g., impression management) become relevant, repressors use different strategies to discount or forget threatening information.

Encoding Processes

People who encounter a complex stimulus event are unlikely to identify and encode all of its features simultaneously. Rather, encoding proceeds through a series of stages. Lazarus (1982) postulated that people's detailed encoding of a stimulus event is preceded by an undifferentiated cognitive appraisal of the event that can lead it to be identified as potentially pleasant or unpleasant. This initial representation of the event is "schematic," and does not require conscious awareness of the individual features that compose the situation.

Subsequent to this initial appraisal, more specific details of the event are usually identified and cognitively elaborated. If the event is affect eliciting, this more detailed analysis is likely to elicit stronger emotional reactions than did the initial appraisal. More generally, reactions to an emotion-eliciting event are likely to become more intense as the event is encoded and elaborated more fully. If these reactions are aversive, however, the intensity of the reactions may ultimately exceed the level one is willing and able to tolerate, and at this point, cognitive processing will cease. The event will then be stored in memory at whatever level of detail existed at the time this processing was terminated.

Note that individual differences in tolerance of negative affect should produce corresponding differences in the intensity of negative emotions that are associated with the events that are encoded and stored in memory, and correspondingly in the detail with which these events are represented. Thus, relative to people with high tolerance thresholds, people with low tolerance thresholds not only should be less likely to remember any given event as intensely emotional, but also should report fewer events as eliciting intense emotions. Moreover, people with low tolerance thresholds should recall unpleasant events in relatively less detail.

Therefore, suppose repressors typically have lower tolerance thresholds than nonrepressors. Then they should encode events as less emotional and should report having less frequent emotional experiences than nonrepressors. Two studies by Schimmack and Hartmann (1996) confirmed this prediction. In one experiment, participants were asked to read 30 vignettes describing emotion-eliciting situations. In each case, they were told to imagine that they were the protagonist, and to rate the emotional reactions they would have to the situation. As expected, repressors reported less intense negative emotional reactions to the situations than did nonrepressors. Moreover, they later estimated that fewer vignettes had elicited negative emotional reactions. In contrast, repressors' and nonrepressors' reactions to and memory for positive events did not differ. In a second study, participants kept a daily diary of the frequency with which they actually experienced emotion-eliciting events over a 2-week period. As in the first study, repressors both reported fewer negative emotional experiences on a daily basis, and retrospectively recalled having fewer such experiences than did nonrepressors.

A study by Hansen and Hansen (1988) suggests an additional way in which repressors' encodings of emotional events can differ from nonrepressors'. Participants were asked to recall experiences associated with feelings of anger, sadness, fear, and embarrassment. Participants rated both the dominant and nondominant emotions associated with each memory. Repressors and nonrepressors did not differ in the rated intensity of the dominant emotion evoked by the memories. However, repressors described the nondominant emotions evoked by the memory as less intense than did nonrepressors. For example, when participants were asked to recall an experience that made them angry, repressors reported the same amount of anger as nonrepressors, but reported less intense emotions of other types (fear, sadness, or embarrassment).

Retrieval Processes

Repressors have more difficulty retrieving negative emotional memories than do nonrepressors, especially memories associated with anger and fear (Davis, 1987; Davis & Schwartz, 1987). Schimmack and Hartmann's (1996) findings suggest that these retrieval differences are due at least in part to the frequency with which the events were encoded as eliciting strong emotions at the time they occurred. Another reason why repressors might successfully avoid the retrieval of threatening memories is suggested by the discrete appraisals they make of their emotional experiences at the time of encoding (Hansen & Hansen, 1988; Hansen, Hansen, & Shantz, 1992). That is, because repressors associate relatively few emotions with an event at the time it occurs, their subsequent thoughts about the event are less likely to cue the retrieval of other emotional memories.

A third way in which the recall of emotion-eliciting experiences might be avoided was noted earlier. That is, people who wish to avoid specific knowledge they have about a referent might spontaneously deposit this knowledge along with the referent's name in a bin that they label "to be avoided." Other knowledge about the referent might be stored in a bin denoted by the referent's name alone. Under these conditions, a subsequent search for information about the referent should theoretically lead the second bin to be identified but not the first (Postulate 1). Thus, individuals can later retrieve information about the referent without accessing the specific emotion-eliciting knowledge they wish to avoid. Perhaps repressors are more inclined than nonrepressors to denote bodies of knowledge as "to be avoided" and, therefore, are better able to avoid the identification and use of this knowledge in the course of subsequent goal-directed processing.

Three studies by Davis (1989) are worth considering in this context. In these studies, people were asked to recall childhood experiences. Repressors' initial recall of childhood fear and anger experiences was quite low relative to that of nonrepressors. Across time and with repeated cuing, however, repressors showed a 53% increase in the number of such experiences they were able to remember. Furthermore, their final recall level equalled that of the nonrepressor controls. Davis suggested that repressors' threatening memories were not unavailable but were simply inaccessible. The sort of tagging of these memories suggested in the preceding paragraph might potentially account for these findings.

FINAL COMMENTS

This chapter covered a number of topics surrounding the conditions in which people are and are not likely to avoid being influenced by social information. We considered the effects of to-be-disregarded information and knowledge on both the interpretation of new information to which the prior knowledge is irrelevant and judgments to which the information objectively pertains. Moreover, we considered both conditions in which people disregarded information in response to external demands and conditions in which they were intrinsically motivated to do so.

We generally interpreted the research bearing on these issues in terms of a more general model of social information processing that permits it to be conceptually integrated (see Wyer & Srull, 1986, 1989). This formulation is undoubtedly not the only conceptualization that might be brought to bear on the issues at hand. Nevertheless, the model provides a set of conceptual tools that can be used to develop hypotheses concerning the determinants and consequences of intentionally suppressing information in a social context.

Attempts to avoid being influenced by knowledge and experiences we have acquired are pervasive aspects of information processing in our daily lives. We must be able to guard against the influence of unwanted thoughts and emotions if we are to function effectively in a social environment. The present chapter hopefully provided insights into some of the ways in which this might be done.

ACKNOWLEDGMENTS

This chapter was written with partial support of a National Science Foundation grant to the third author. Appreciation is extended to the University of Illinois Social Cognition Group for insightful comments and feedback concerning the ideas expressed.

REFERENCES

Baddeley, A. D. (1976). *The psychology of memory*. New York: Basic Books.

Bargh, J. A. (1984). Automatic and conscious processing of social information. In R. S. Wyer & T. K. Srull (Eds.), *Handbook of social cognition* (Vol. 3, pp. 1–43). Hillsdale, NJ: Lawrence Erlbaum Associates.

Bargh, J. A. (1994). The four horsemen of automaticity: Awareness, intention, efficiency, and control in social cognition. In R. S. Wyer & T. S. Srull (Eds.), *Handbook of social cognition* (2nd ed., Vol. 1, pp. 1–40). Hillsdale, NJ: Lawrence Erlbaum Associates.

Bargh, J. A. (in press). The automaticity of everyday life. In R. S. Wyer (Ed.), *Advances in social cognition* (Vol. 10). Hillsdale, NJ: Lawrence Erlbaum Associates.

Bargh, J. A., & Chen, M. (1995). *The chameleon effect: Automatic social perception provides automatic social behavior*. Unpublished manuscript, New York University.

Basden, B. H., Basden, D. R., & Gargano, G. J. (1993). Directed forgetting in implicit and explicit memory tests: A comparison of methods. *Journal of Experimental Psychology: Learning, Memory, and Cognition, 19*, 603–616.

Baumeister, R. F., & Cairns, K. J. (1992). Repression and self-presentation: When audiences interfere with self-deceptive strategies. *Journal of Personality and Social Psychology, 62*, 851–862.

Bjork, R. A. (1972). Theoretical implications of directed forgetting. In A. W. Melton & E. Martin (Eds.), *Coding processes in human memory* (pp. 217–235). Washington, DC: Winston.

Bower, G. H. (1981). Mood and memory. *American Psychologist, 36*, 129–148.

Budesheim, T. L. (1988). *The effects of inadmissible and discredited evidence in a mock juror paradigm*. Unpublished master's thesis, University of Illinois, Champaign, IL.

Carlston, D. H. (1994). Associated systems theory: A systematic approach to cognitive representations of persons. In R. S. Wyer (Ed.), *Advances in social cognition* (Vol. 7, pp. 1–78). Hillsdale, NJ: Lawrence Erlbaum Associates.

Clore, G. L., Schwarz, N., & Conway, M. (1994). Affective causes and consequences of social information processing. In R. S. Wyer & T. K. Srull (Eds.), *Handbook of social cognition* (2nd ed., Vol. 1, pp. 323–417). Hillsdale, NJ: Lawrence Erlbaum Associates.

Crowne, D. P., & Marlowe, D. A. (1960). A new scale of social desirability independent of psychopathology. *Journal of Consulting Psychology, 24,* 349–354.

Davis, P. J. (1987). Repression and the inaccessibility of affective memories. *Journal of Personality and Social Psychology, 53,* 585–593.

Davis, P. J. (1989). Repression and the inaccessibility of emotional memories. In A. F. Bennett & K. M. McConkey (Eds.), *Cognition in individual and social contexts* (pp. 399–406). Amsterdam: North-Holland.

Davis, P. J., & Schwartz, G. E. (1987). Repression and the inaccessibility of affective memories. *Journal of Personality and Social Psychology, 52,* 155–163.

Dollard, J., & Miller, N. (1950). *Personality and psychotherapy.* New York: McGraw-Hill.

Erdelyi, M. H. (1985). *Psychoanalysis: Freud's cognitive psychology.* New York: Freeman.

Greenwald, A. G. (1992). New Look 3: Unconscious cognition reclaimed. *American Psychologist, 47,* 766–779.

Grice, H. P. (1975). Logic and conversation. In P. Cole & J. Morgan (Eds.), *Syntax and semantics: Vol. 3. Speech acts* (pp. 68–134). New York: Academic Press.

Hamilton, D. L., Katz, L. B., & Leirer, V. O. (1980). Organizational processes in impression formation. In R. Hastie, T. Ostrom, E. Ebbesen, D. Hamilton, & D. Carlston (Eds.), *Person memory: The cognitive basis of social perception* (pp. 121–154). Hillsdale, NJ: Lawrence Erlbaum Associates.

Hansen, R. D., & Hansen, C. H. (1988). Repression of emotionally tagged memories: The architecture of less complex emotions. *Journal of Personality and Social Psychology, 55,* 811–818.

Hansen, C. H., Hansen, R. D., & Shantz, D. W. (1992). Repression at encoding: Discrete appraisals of emotional stimuli. *Journal of Personality and Social Psychology, 63,* 1026–1035.

Higgins, E. T. (1981). The "communication game": Implications for social cognition and persuasion. In E. T. Higgins, C. P. Herman, & M. P. Zanna (Eds.), *Social cognition: The Ontario Symposium* (Vol. 1, pp. 343–392). Hillsdale, NJ: Lawrence Erlbaum Associates.

Howell, A., & Conway, M. (1992). Mood and the suppression of positive and negative self-referent thoughts. *Cognitive Therapy and Research, 16,* 535–555.

Jacoby, L., & Kelley, C. M. (1987). Unconscious influences of memory for a prior event. *Personality and Social Psychology Bulletin, 13,* 314–336.

Johnson, H. M. (1994). Processes of successful intentional forgetting. *Psychological Bulletin, 116,* 274–292.

Kanouse, D. E., & Hanson, L. R. (1971). Negativity in evaluations. In E. E. Jones, D. E. Kanouse, H. H. Kelly, R. E. Nisbett, S. Valins, & B. Weiner (Eds.), *Attribution: Perceiving the causes of behavior* (pp. 47–62). Morristown, NJ: General Learning Press.

Kelly, A. E., & Kahn, J. H. (1994). Effects of suppression of personal intrusive thoughts. *Journal of Personality and Social Psychology, 66,* 998–1006.

Kihlstrom, J. F. (1980). Posthypnotic amnesia for recently learned material: Interactions with "episodic" and "semantic" memory. *Cognitive Psychology, 12,* 227–251.

Klinger, E. (1975). Consequences of commitment to and disengagement from incentives. *Psychological Review, 82,* 1–25.

Klinger, E. (1996). Theories of thought flow: Points of kinship and fertile contrasts. In R. S. Wyer (Ed.), *Advances in social cognition* (Vol. 9, pp. 107–120). Hillsdale, NJ: Lawrence Erlbaum Associates.

Lavy, E. H., & van den Hout, M. A. (1990). Thought suppression induces intrusions. *Behavioral Psychotherapy, 18,* 251–258.

Lazarus, R. S. (1982). Thoughts on the relations between emotion and cognition. *American Psychologist, 37,* 1019–1024.

Macrae, C. M., Bodenhausen, G. V., & Milne, A. B. (1995). The dissection of selection in person perception: Inhibitory processes in social stereotyping. *Journal of Personality and Social Psychology, 69*, 397–407.

Macrae, C. M., Bodenhausen, G. V., Milne, A. B., & Jetten, J. (1994). Out of mind but back in sight: Stereotypes on the rebound. *Journal of Personality and Social Psychology, 67*, 805–817.

Martin, L. L. (1986). Set/reset: Use and disuse of concepts in impression formation. *Journal of Personality and Social Psychology, 51*, 493–504.

Martin, L. L., Seta, J. J., & Crelia, R. A. (1990). Assimilation and contrast as a function of people's willingness and ability to expend effort in forming an impression. *Journal of Personality and Social Psychology, 59*, 27–37.

Martin, L. L., & Tesser, A. (1996). Some ruminative thoughts. In R. S. Wyer (Ed.), *Advances in social cognition* (Vol. 9, pp. 1–47). Hillsdale, NJ: Lawrence Erlbaum Associates.

McIntosh, W. D., & Martin, L. L. (1992). The cybernetics of happiness: The relation between goal attainment, rumination, and affect. In M. S. Clark (Ed.), *Review of personality and social psychology* (Vol. 14, pp. 222–246). Newbury Park, CA: Sage.

Muris, P., Merckelbach, H., van den Hout, M., & de Jong, P. (1992). Suppression of emotional and neutral material. *Behavioral Research and Therapy, 30*, 639–642.

Nisbett, R. E., & Wilson, T. D. (1977). Telling more than we know: Verbal reports on mental processes. *Psychological Review, 84*, 231–259.

Ottati, V. C., & Isbell, L. M. (1996). Effects of mood during exposure to target information on subsequently reported judgments: An on-line model of assimilation and contrast. *Journal of Personality and Social Psychology, 71*, 39–53.

Pennington, N., & Hastie, R. (1988). Explanation-based decision making: Effects of memory structure on judgment. *Journal of Experimental Psychology: Learning, Memory, and Cognition, 14*, 52–533.

Pennington, N., & Hastie, R. (1992). Explaining the evidence: Tests of the story model for juror decision making. *Journal of Personality and Social Psychology, 62*, 189–206.

Petty, R. E., & Cacioppo, J. T. (1986). *Communication and persuasion: Central and peripheral routes to attitude change.* New York: Springer-Verlag.

Petty, R. E., & Wegener, D. T. (1993). Flexible correction processes in social judgment: Correcting for context-induced contrast. *Journal of Experimental Social Psychology, 29*, 137–165.

Radhakrishnan, P. (1996). *Perceptions of ability and decisions to hire: The role of race and limited hiring resources.* Unpublished doctoral dissertation, University of Illinois at Urbana-Champaign.

Roemer, L., & Borkovec, T. D. (1993). Worry: Unwanted cognitive activity that controls unwanted somatic experience. In D. M. Wegner & J. M. Pennebaker (Eds.), *Handbook of mental control* (pp. 220–238). Englewood Cliffs, NJ: Prentice-Hall.

Ross, L., Lepper, M., & Hubbard, M. (1975). Perseverance in self-perception and social perception: Biased attributional processes in the debriefing paradigm. *Journal of Personality and Social Psychology, 32*, 880–892.

Salkovskis, P. M., & Campbell, P. (1994). Thought suppression induces intrusion in naturally occurring negative intrusive thoughts. *Behavioral Research and Therapy, 32*, 1–8.

Schank, R. C., & Abelson, R. P. (1995). Knowledge and memory: The real story. In R. S. Wyer (Ed.), *Advances in social cognition* (Vol. 8, pp. 1–85). Hillsdale, NJ: Lawrence Erlbaum Associates.

Schimmack, U., & Hartmann, K. (1996). *Interindividual differences in the memory representation of emotional episodes: Exploring the cognitive processes in repression.* Unpublished manuscript, Free University, Berlin, Germany.

Schwarz, N. (1990). Assessing frequency reports of mundane behaviors: Contributions of cognitive psychology to questionnaire construction. In C. Hendrick & M. Clark (Eds.), *Review of personality and social psychology* (Vol. 11, pp. 98–119). Beverly Hills, CA: Sage.

Schwarz, N., & Clore, G. L. (1983). Mood, misattribution, and judgments of well-being: Informative and directive functions of affective states. *Journal of Personality and Social Psychology, 45,* 513–523.

Sherman, S. J., & Gorkin, L. (1980). Attitude bolstering when behavior is inconsistent with central attitudes. *Journal of Experimental Social Psychology, 16,* 388–403.

Singer, J. L. (1990). *Repression and dissociation: Implications for personality theory, psychopathology, and health.* Chicago: University of Chicago Press.

Smith, E. R. (1990). Content and process specificity in the effects of prior experiences. In T. K. Srull & R. S. Wyer (Eds.), *Advances in social cognition* (Vol. 3, pp. 1–59). Hillsdale, NJ: Lawrence Erlbaum Associates.

Srull, T. K. (1981). Person memory: Some tests of associative storage and retrieval models. *Journal of Experimental Psychology: Human Learning and Memory, 7,* 440–463.

Srull, T. K., & Wyer, R. S. (1989). Person memory and judgment. *Psychological Review, 96,* 58–83.

Strack, F. (1994). *Handbook of social cognition* (2nd ed., Vol. 1, pp. 287–322). Hillsdale, NJ: Lawrence Erlbaum Associates.

Taylor, J. A. (1953). A personality scale of manifest anxiety. *Journal of Abnormal and Social Psychology, 48,* 285–290.

Tulving, E. (1983). *Elements of episodic memory.* Oxford: Clarendon Press.

Tulving, E., Schacter, D. L., & Stark, H. A. (1982). Priming effects in word-fragment completion are independent of recognition memory. *Journal of Experimental Psychology: Learning, Memory, and Cognition, 8,* 336–342.

Wegener, D. T., & Petty, R. E. (1995). Flexible correction processes in social judgment: The role of naive theories in corrections for perceived bias. *Journal of Personality and Social Psychology, 68,* 36–51.

Wegner, D. M. (1989). *White bears and other unwanted thoughts.* New York: Viking.

Wegner, D. M. (1994). Ironic processes of mental control. *Psychological Review, 101,* 34–52.

Wegner, D. M., & Gold, D. B. (1995). Fanning old flames: Emotional and cognitive effects of suppressing thoughts of a past relationship. *Journal of Personality and Social Psychology, 68,* 782–792.

Wegner, D. M., Schneider, D. J., Carter, S. R., III, & White, T. L. (1987). Paradoxical effects of thought suppression. *Journal of Personality and Social Psychology, 58,* 409–418.

Wegner, D. M., Schneider, D. J., Knutson, B., & McMahon, S. R. (1991). Polluting the stream of consciousness: The effect of thought suppression on the mind's environment. *Cognitive Therapy and Research, 15,* 141–152.

Weinberger, D. A. (1990). The construct validity of the repressive coping style. In J. L. Singer (Ed.), *Repression and dissociation* (pp. 337–386). Chicago: University of Chicago Press.

Weinberger, D. A., Schwartz, G. E., & Davidson, R. (1979). Low-anxious, high-anxious, and repressive coping styles: Psychometric patterns and behavioral and physiological responses to stress. *Journal of Abnormal Psychology, 88,* 369–380.

Wenzlaff, R. M., Wegner, D. M., & Klein, S. B. (1991). The role of thought suppression in the bonding of thought and mood. *Journal of Personality and Social Psychology, 60,* 500–508.

Wilson, T. D., & Brekke, N. (1994). Mental contamination and mental correction: Unwanted influences on judgments and evaluations. *Psychological Bulletin, 116,* 117–142.

Wyer, R. S. (1970). Information redundancy, inconsistency and novelty and their role in impression formation. *Journal of Experimental Social Psychology, 6,* 111–127.

Wyer, R. S., & Budesheim, T. L. (1987). Person memory and judgments: The impact of information that one is told to disregard. *Journal of Personality and Social Psychology, 53,* 14–29.

Wyer, R. S., & Carlston, D. E. (1979). *Social cognition, inference, and attribution.* Hillsdale, NJ: Lawrence Erlbaum Associates.

Wyer, R. S., & Gordon, S. E. (1982). The recall of information about persons and groups. *Journal of Experimental Social Psychology, 18,* 128–164.

Wyer, R. S., & Srull, T. K. (1986). Human cognition in its social context. *Psychological Review, 93,* 322–359.

Wyer, R. S., & Srull, T. K. (1989). *Memory and cognition in its social context.* Hillsdale, NJ: Lawrence Erlbaum Associates.

Wyer, R. S., & Unverzagt, W. H. (1985). The effects of instructions to disregard information on its subsequent recall and use in making judgments. *Journal of Personality and Social Psychology, 48,* 533–549.

11

Suspicion and Discounting: Ignoring Invalid Information in an Uncertain Environment

Yaacov Schul
Hebrew University

Eugene Burnstein
University of Michigan

Suspicion is a fact of life. Of the many people with whom we communicate daily, some, unbeknownst to us (or to them), are very likely to be telling us an untruth. Moreover, it is a recognized fact of life: When a convenient sample of students at the University of Michigan was asked to recall the various people with whom they had spoken over the past several days and to estimate the probability that one or more of these people had either intentionally or accidentally told the respondents something that was mistaken, untrue, or invalid, the average estimate was well over .50. This may not be surprising in light of the fact that these same individuals described about a quarter of their conversations as involving some gossip or rumor. Furthermore, over 20% of the conversations were reported to contain irony, hyperbole, sarcasm, metaphor, or other conversational devices that assume a wary listener, one who automatically recognizes and recodes the "error" in explicit statements to grasp the "underlying (and intended) truth." The threat of receiving invalid information is sufficiently pervasive in social life that some argue that people have evolved an "early warning" system that comes into play when an action on the basis of erroneous knowledge has significant costs (e.g., Cosmides, 1989; Cosmides & Tooby, 1989; Kraut, 1978). In this chapter, we discuss how people attempt to cope in such an uncertain environment. In particular, we focus on how people prepare for falsehoods while receiving information, and how they ignore them once they are discovered.

SENSITIVITY TO FALSEHOOD

In his provocative model, Gilbert (1991; Gilbert, Tafarodi, & Malone, 1993) suggested that receivers of communications are initially trusting. Contrary to the evolutionists (discussed later), he argued that the default value of a new message is *true* so that information is accepted uncritically as correct following its initial encoding. Only after reflection and elaboration can perceivers reject information as false. Although the evidence marshaled by Gilbert for this hypothesis is impressive, on reflection one might remain skeptical about its validity. In addition to our ability to readily understand messages that use irony or other rhetorical devices that recast their meaning, it seems intuitively wrong to assume either that individuals are insensitive to the context of communication or that context cannot influence the default truth value of a communication early in its processing.

Darwinian models are particularly interesting in this respect. They predict the development of a built-in discounting mechanism. According to this reasoning, we live in groups and can gain from communication to the extent that we are not misled. At the same time, again on theoretical grounds, attempts to mislead are common; "the conflict of interests that exist because of the histories of genetic difference imply . . . that nearly all communicative signals, human or otherwise, should . . . involve significant deceit" (Alexander, 1987, p. 73). Hence, the predisposition to communicate assumes an adaptation whereby the receiver can detect and ignore invalid information transmitted by the source. Generally speaking, discounting is increasingly likely to evolve as the cost–benefit ratio for rejecting a communication when it is valid (incorrect rejection) declines relative to that for accepting the communication when it is invalid (false alarm).

In his classic analysis of kin selection and the evolution of altruism, Hamilton (1964; Dawkins, 1976) demonstrated that although helping is by definition costly to the altruist and, thus, tendencies to engage in such behavior should be selected against, this does not hold when the recipient of help is kin. In these circumstances, altruist and recipient are likely to share the genetic structures that give rise to cooperation and helping. However, this implies that helping, or other kinds of cooperative relations such as reciprocity, are inherently vulnerable to "free riders" in that it is always in members' self-interest to take advantage of the altruist in the group (Bornstein, 1992). By convincing the altruist that they are deserving of help (e.g., that they are kin or kin-like, say, allies) when they are not, or that they will reciprocate when they have no intention of doing so, "free riders" benefit and the altruist suffers a cost. The upshot is that because group living creates egoistic incentives to communicate false information, those who are inclined to share resources will be selected against *unless* they are capable of suspicion and discounting.

According to this rudimentary evolutionary analysis, humans have evolved so that they are sensitive to the context of communication, particularly information about the utility of accepting or rejecting a message, and they use this information in evaluating the source. It is reasonable to assume, therefore, that the costs and benefits to both parties usually are such that the judgment of whether the source is trustworthy affects the receiver's interpretation of the message, namely, whether the message is deemed valid or invalid. This suggests that characteristics of the source are encoded prior to or, at a minimum, in parallel with the message, and that they influence its encoding at the very earliest stages. It follows then that messages are not privileged; the cognitive system does not automatically and ubiquitously confer validity on them without consulting context. To the contrary, the context of communication, in particular the foreseeable consequences to source and receiver, determines the default truth value of a message. Note that the issue is not whether the source can affect how receivers use information in making judgments. Much research over the past 30 years indicates that when receivers know the characteristics of the source (e.g., his or her credibility), this knowledge can indeed alter the impact of a communication on the judgments they will make at some later point (see Eagly & Chaiken, 1993, for a recent review). Our concern, however, is whether the source influences how messages are encoded *from the very beginning* of their processing and *prior to judgment.*

Recently, we (Knafo & Schul, 1995; Mayo & Schul, 1995) examined the conditions under which receivers attend to attributes of the source by comparing the inferences drawn from a message when the source is trustworthy with those drawn when the source is untrustworthy. In one study, the manipulation of trustworthiness involved exposure to several "journalists" who varied in the reliability of their reports: One was extremely reliable (all his reports proved to be true), another was extremely unreliable (only one out of six reports was found to be true). In a second study, source trustworthiness was manipulated via schematic knowledge subjects have about various occupations: The source was either a family doctor (high trustworthiness) or an actress in a commercial (low trustworthiness). Encoding and inferential processing occurred under either high or low cognitive load. As cognitive load increases, it interferes with the person's ability to elaborate upon and to assess a communication critically (e.g., Bargh, 1989; Gilbert, 1991). Therefore, if characteristics of the source have priority in processing over those of the message, then receivers under high load should believe a message from an untrustworthy source *less*, and should believe a message from a trustworthy source *more* (relative to receivers under low load). If, however, the content of the message has priority and processing of the source and context is only performed during a late stage (e.g., after the initial encoding of the message has been completed), then source trustworthiness ought to have little or no impact under conditions of high cognitive load—if anything, communication from an untrustworthy source should be seen as more believable under conditions of high cognitive load than under conditions of low load. Preliminary results suggest that people are appreciably more sensitive to the trustworthiness of the source under high cognitive load than under low cognitive load. In particular, when messages provided by untrustworthy sources were processed under high cognitive load, they were seen as less valid and less persuasive than messages provided by trustworthy sources. Moreover, the difference in impact between trustworthy and untrustworthy sources was more pronounced when the person's processing resources were limited than when they were abundant.

At a minimum, these results suggest that in social communication, receivers give contextual information a high priority in encoding, especially if it has to do with source trustworthiness. Furthermore, evaluation of the message is influenced by the characteristics of the source to a larger extent when cognitive resources are limited. It could be that, lacking sufficient resources, receivers decide on their position heuristically (Cacioppo & Petty, 1987; Chaiken, 1987): Messages typically are long and complex compared to descriptions of the source. Therefore, using a source-activated heuristic, say, "if trustworthy, then true—if untrustworthy, then untrue" would allow receivers to forego the relatively effortful processing demanded by the message. Alternatively, these findings could mean that as their cognitive resources diminish, receivers' representations of the message become increasingly dependent on context, so that the default truth value accorded to information gleaned from a trustworthy source is more likely to be "truth," whereas that accorded to information from an untrustworthy source is more likely to be "false." In the former case, the context changes the way the decision is made; in the latter case, it changes the encoding of the message.

Reasons for Mistrust

Psychologically, not all kinds of untrustworthiness are equal. Research suggests that the inferences people draw from a communication vary markedly with the perceived cause of distrust. Eagly, Wood, and Chaiken (1978) distinguished between two types of biases receivers attribute to a source of information; knowledge bias and reporting bias. The former is an unmotivated bias and the latter is a motivated one. By definition, sources with an unmotivated bias do not have a desire to deceive the receiver. Nonetheless, their testimony should be ignored because they fail to provide a valid message. In the case of sources with motivated bias, the testimony is doubted because the interests of the source are in conflict with those of the receiver, so that the source benefits at the cost of a receiver who is gullible. Indeed, receivers probably are often wary and believe that although they are motivated by accuracy or truth, the source may have a vested interest. And to the extent that the source's motivation is not considered to be a quest for accuracy, receivers infer that the source might deceive or, at least, that his or her credibility is uncertain.

Paranoid or Pollyanna, the receiver's analysis of the source's motivation is important because such analysis allows further inferences regarding the message. When the source is seen as incompetent (falsehoods are unmotivated), the assertion that x is true merely allows the receiver to doubt its validity (i.e., to suspect that x may not be true), but not to infer what is in fact true. However, when the source is seen as having a vested interest in persuading (falsehoods are motivated), the assertion that x is true can lead to a chain of inferences about what is actually true. For example, a receiver might reason that by asserting x, the source wants the receiver not to believe y. Therefore, receivers in this case can infer not only that x is untrue but also that y is true. The chain of inference could become quite convoluted if the source's theories about receivers' reasoning strategies are introduced into the game. The main point is that, unlike the case of an unmotivated source, when untrustworthiness is attributed to a source who has a vested interest, an invalid message carries information.

Research on misleading advertisements provides some evidence for the importance of the distinction between motivated and unmotivated sources. In these studies, consumers might be informed after viewing a TV commercial that a claim attributing a particular quality to a product was invalid (e.g., "Research has not established that consuming sugar before meals will contribute to weight reduction or even keep you from gaining weight"; see Wilkie, McNeill, & Mazis, 1984, for additional examples). Note that the discounting cue in this case describes what is untrue without specifying what is true (i.e., the receiver does not know whether sugar before meals in fact contributes to weight reduction). Thus, the kind of inferences receivers draw from the discounting cue are similar to the ones they can draw from an invalid testimony attributed to an unmotivated source.

There are cases, however, when consumers are explicitly told what is true (e.g., "Research has established that Listerine *will not* help prevent colds or sore throats or lessen their severity"; see Wilkie et al., 1984, for more examples). Here, receivers are not only informed that the original claim is untrue, but they also learn what is actually true. In this respect, the inferences receivers make about the challenged claim are comparable to those made by receivers who are told that a source is biased and the bias is motivated; hence, receivers are likely to perceive that the source intends to deceive. Our analysis suggests, therefore, that discounting should be more successful in this case.

To explore differences between the two types of discounting cues, we (Schul & Mazursky, 1990) provided individuals with advertising leaflets making a series of claims about a product. After reading the claims, receivers were given a discounting cue attributed to a well-known and highly reliable consumer protection agency. In one condition, the agency advised consumers to ignore a particular claim about the product because it was based on tests that were done in a different country and therefore, the findings could not be applied to the usage conditions in Israel, where the participants lived. In the other condition, participants were told not only that the tests were invalid in Israel, but that similar tests performed in Israel showed the opposite results. Participants who were told to ignore a claim without being told what was actually true failed to discount, especially when they had integrated the information in the advertisement prior to receiving the discounting cue. In contrast, receivers who were given the additional information about what was actually true readily discounted the information. More importantly, these participants were not hampered by integrative encoding. In fact, under these conditions, there was a hint of a "boomerang effect," a nonsignificant trend suggesting that receivers who had integrated the information subsequently responded in the opposite direction, as if they wanted to "punish" the source for communicating invalid information. We return to the influence of integrative encoding on the success of discounting in the next section.

The Case of Multiple Sources

Our research on the trustworthiness of sources, as well as virtually all of the past research on source credibility and deceptive communication, dealt with situations in which there was a single sender who had good reason to transmit biased information (e.g., Eagly, Wood, & Chaiken, 1978; Papageorgis, 1968; Petty & Cacioppo, 1977). Under these conditions, suspicion is focused: Receivers know ahead of time that a particular source may have the intention to mislead. Hence, they can prepare for discounting prior to or during the encoding of the message without worrying about whether they are being suspicious of the wrong person. In the case of focused suspicion, preparation can take one of two forms: Receivers can restrict (or avoid altogether) their exposure to suspect messages, or they can counterargue at the time they encode the message (see Frey, 1986, for a summary of research on selective exposure; see also Wilson & Brekke, 1994).

There are many social situations, however, when suspicion is unfocused. Under unfocused suspicion, receivers not only know that invalid information is likely to be communicated, but they also know that during encoding, they will have no sure grounds for distinguishing the valid from the invalid. As a result, they foresee that they will be incapable of discounting during encoding except by guessing. For example, consider a single source who communicates messages about many different subjects. Receivers suspect that on occasion the source is wrong, but they have no way of telling in advance when. Unlike the case in which a single source delivers a single message, it would be costly to discount the source altogether because not every message is incorrect; some in fact are correct. The problem, of course, is that the receiver is unsure which is which.

Unfocused suspicion can also be evoked when more than one source transmits messages regarding the same object. Suppose several witnesses testify in a trial, and the jurors suspect that some of them are unreliable so their testimony should be ignored. However, the jurors have no sure way of distinguishing between either reliable and unreliable witnesses or valid and invalid testimony. Needless to say, they cannot do what they would do under focused suspicion, namely, discount their testimony as a whole. To cope with unfocused suspicion, the receiver must resort to different discounting strategies. In our analysis, we assume that unfocused suspicion, whether due to multiple messages or to multiple sources, motivates receivers to prepare to encode a communication so that afterward, once the invalid information is identified, they can correct for its impact.

PREPARING TO DISCOUNT IN CASE OF UNFOCUSED SUSPICION

The Role of Integrative Encoding in Failure to Discount

How should receivers prepare to encode potentially invalid information? To answer this question, let us discuss in more detail mechanisms that facilitate or impair successful discounting. One of the early studies of belief perseverance (Ross, Lepper, Strack, & Steinmetz, 1977) demonstrated that people fail in discounting when they construct causal explanations that link the to-be-ignored information to the to-be-used information. In other words, integration of information during encoding hinders successful discounting. Later research clarified this effect by suggesting that, because the to-be-used information is elaborated in the context of the to-be-ignored information, it contains meanings and implications that are consistent with the to-be-ignored information (Anderson, Lepper, & Ross, 1980; Schul & Burnstein, 1985; Schul & Mazursky, 1990; Wyer & Budesheim, 1987). For example, imagine thinking about two boys, Bill and Tom. Initially each is characterized by two pieces of information. You learn that Bill is (a) smart and (b) seems bored in class. You learn that Tom is (a) stupid and (b) seems bored in class. Next, you are told that the testimony about their smartness or stupidity is based on an unfair test, and therefore should be ignored in any future consideration of Tom and Bill. Nonetheless, you are to do the best you can to predict their success in school.

Whether one can actually ignore information gleaned from the unfair test depends on the degree of elaborative encoding of the original information. If receivers encode the two pieces of information integratively, the behavioral description "seems bored in class" will come to mean different things as a function of the information about intelligence. In the case of Bill, the concept of boredom is elaborated in a schema that causally links it with being overly knowledgeable and competent; in the case of Tom, the concept is elaborated upon in a schema that implies a kind of boredom that reflects numbing ignorance and incompetence. Consequently, people make different predictions regarding school success for the two, even though after receiving the discounting cue, they seemingly possess the "identical" valid information about the two boys. Generally, then, even if individuals succeed in blocking the direct meaning of the to-be-ignored testimony (Bjork, 1989; MacLeod, 1989), they often fail to undo its residual meanings, nuances that were associatively imported to the to-be-used sections of the message during elaboration and integration (Schul & Burnstein, 1985). It is in these circumstances that discounting fails.

Evidence to support our hypothesis that integrative encoding impairs discounting comes from two lines of research (see Johnson, 1994, for a more detailed review). First, discounting is more successful when receivers are prevented from elaborating on the message than when they are not prevented from doing so (Fleming & Arrowood, 1979; Schul & Burnstein, 1985), and is less successful when receivers are induced to encode the to-be-used and to-be-ignored messages integratively (Anderson et al., 1980; Schul & Mazursky, 1990). Fleming and Arrowood, for example, inhibited the integration of the to-be-ignored and to-be-used information by having subjects perform an additional task that interfered with such processing. In contrast to noninterference controls, who showed the typical belief-perseverance effect, judgments by subjects whose integrative activity had been prevented were not biased by the to-be-ignored information and, hence, did not show the typical belief-perseverance effect. Additional support for the notion that integrative encoding tends to hinder successful discounting was obtained by Wyer and Budesheim (1987). These authors showed that discounting is facilitated when the to-be-used and to-be-ignored messages refer to unrelated issues; discounting is impaired when they refer to the same issue. In the latter case, it is likely that receivers integrate the information even without being explicitly instructed to do so.

A second line of research on the difficulty of discounting concerns the malleability of both kinds of information. When can the to-be-ignored information influence the interpretation of the to-be-used information and, when can the to-be-used information influence the interpretation of the to-be-ignored information? In our earlier example, information about Bill's smartness can influence the inferences one makes from the testimony about Bill's boredom in class, and the information about boredom can influence the inferences one makes from the testimony about smartness. The extent of influence depends on the ambiguity of the information (e.g., Trope, 1986). The to-be-ignored testimony has its maximal impact on the interpretation of the to-be-used information when the to-be-ignored information is unambiguous with respect to the judgment, and the to-be-used information, ambiguous. Under these conditions, discounting should be particularly difficult.

An interesting example is found in Darley and Gross (1983). The basic finding in this research is that subjects told to ignore stereotypic information did so successfully when the message contained only this kind of information; however, they failed to ignore it when it was coupled with additional information that was nondiagnostic and ambiguous. Specifically, all subjects were given information about the socioeconomic status (SES) of a protagonist. In addition, half of them were also given nondiagnostic information regarding the protagonist's ability. It was found that the inferences of those given the additional nondiagnostic information were influenced by the SES information, whereas the inferences of those without the additional nondiagnostic information were not influenced by SES. It seems, therefore, that individuals can ignore stereotypic knowledge to the extent that it has not already been integrated with other to-be-used (nondiagnostic) information. Similarly, we found that failure in discounting occurs primarily when the to-be-used information includes features that are either ambiguous or conflictual with respect to the dimension of judgment (see descriptions of the stimulus persons in Schul & Burnstein, 1985; Schul, Bernstein, & Bardi, 1996; see also Golding, Fowler, Long, & Latta, 1990; Wyer & Unverzagt, 1985).

Combating the Effect of Integrative Encoding

The preceding discussion highlights the fact that although integrative encoding is a pervasive form of information processing, if unrestricted, it hinders the person's ability to discount a suspect communication. Because discounting is highly adaptive, the cognitive system is likely to develop procedures for circumventing or at least mitigating the deleterious effects of integration under conditions of unfocused suspicion. The most likely procedure in such circumstances is to give discounting priority over integration. In short, an adaptive mechanism is hypothesized that forestalls the integration of a communication when the source is untrustworthy. Recently we suggested (Schul, 1993; Schul et al., 1996) two strategies that might have this effect. In one, the receivers simply reduce the amount of processing per message. Hence, invalid as well as valid messages receive only minimal elaboration and, as a result, are represented as relatively distinct pieces of knowledge rather than in an integrated fashion (see the discussion of maintenance rehearsal in Johnson, 1994). As an everyday illustration of this strategy, suppose that while reading a newspaper story you come to doubt its truthfulness and decide simply to scan the story, trying not to spend too much time thinking about the facts or their interrelations, at least until you can establish the story's accuracy. According to this line of reasoning, a reduction in elaborative processing would allow receivers to minimize the impact of the to-be-ignored information on the to-be-used information. Therefore, once the to-be-ignored information is identified, it can readily be set aside or discounted because it has little direct or residual impact on the representation of the to-be-used information. There is little support for the existence of this suspension of integration or scanning strategy, however. The reasons for this are considered shortly.

The bulk of experimental evidence is consistent with the suggestion that while anticipating invalid information, people increase rather than decrease elaborative processing. In Schul (1993), suspicion was induced explicitly by warning subjects just prior to the communication that parts of it might not be valid and by reminding them of this while they were processing the information. Compared to unsuspicious individuals, those who were warned about the possibility of invalid messages needed more time to read and integrate the information. Schul et al. (1996) extended these findings by showing that subjects who were led to believe they might be deceived generated more inferences from a message than those who were not made distrustful. Equally important, we found that whereas there was no difference as a function of the manipulated suspicion in the time to process the initial message in a series, suspicious individuals required more time than did unsuspicious individuals to process the later messages. This tallies nicely with our model that argues (a) elaborative encoding uses resources; (b) the amount of resources used in elaborative encoding increases with the number of messages in working memory; hence, (c) suspicious receivers need no more time than do trusting receivers to process messages early in a series when working memory is empty; but (d) suspicious receivers need more time than do trusting receivers to process messages late in a series when working memory is full and elaboration has to be performed in the context of many other messages.

These findings are consistent with results reported by Kruglanski and coworkers (Kruglanski, 1989; Kruglanski & Freund, 1983), who concluded that when people fear that a belief is mistaken, they delay the "freezing" of the belief and continue to look for alternatives. Moreover, as the cost of the mistaken belief increases, people seek additional information and examine it carefully. Hilton and coworkers (Fein, Hilton, & Miller, 1990; Hilton, Fein, & Miller, 1993) also found that suspicion regarding a source leads to increased processing of the communication. In their research, people who discovered a possible hidden motive for the source's statement engaged in more elaborative encoding than did those who did not suspect a hidden motive. These researchers suggested that the suspicious subjects behaved as if they were examining the communication within two scenarios, one consistent with the source's explicit motive, and the other consistent with the hidden motive.

Counterscenarios

At first glance, a preparatory strategy in which suspicious individuals increasingly elaborate upon the message may seem counterproductive. After all, we noted earlier that, in general, elaborative encoding impairs discounting (Anderson et al., 1980; Ross et al., 1977; Schul & Burnstein, 1985; Schul & Manzury, 1990; Schul & Mazursky, 1990). If so, why would an increase in elaboration facilitate discounting here? Usually, when the receiver is not particularly wary and the source is not particularly distrusted, elaboration is performed within a single common interpretive frame that is established by the early sections of the communication. Under these conditions, the pieces of information making up the message become densely linked to each other to form a coherent knowledge structure—that is, they are integrated (Burnstein & Schul, 1982, 1983). For example, upon receiving two messages, one describing the protagonist positively (e.g., Miriam is a good mother), the other describing her as bad (e.g., Miriam stole some money), receivers may integrate the messages by inventing a plausible story that explains away the inconsistencies (e.g., to feed her starving children). As a result, apparently inconsistent messages can become well integrated (Hastie & Kumar, 1979; Schul, Burnstein, & Martinez, 1983; Wyer & Srull, 1989).

Because receivers typically activate a single interpretive frame, increasing elaboration normally produces increasing integration. However, this is not what individuals do in the case of preparing to receive invalid information. When receivers distrust their sources, instead of imposing a single interpretive frame, we assume they entertain multiple interpretations of the messages. Further, if parts of a communication are elaborated within different interpretive frames, integration is hindered. In other words, when individuals are suspicious and are denied cues to invalidity (e.g., information about the motivation or competence of a source), they behave as if they consider each message in turn. To the extent that a given message elicits wariness, they think whether the already encoded messages could be interpreted in a sensible, coherent fashion if the current message were untrue. We call this interpretation, namely, a more or less plausible representation of the information under the assumption that the current message is untrue, a *counterscenario* (Schul et al., 1996).

It seemed to us that an interesting test of the hypothesized counterscenario mechanism might be performed by observing whether suspicious individuals exhibit less (or more) primacy bias than do trusting individuals.

Past research has shown that when receivers process a series of messages, the early ones activate a frame that controls the interpretation of later messages (Asch, 1946; see Hogarth & Einhorn, 1992, for a recent review). This phenomenon of sticking to the initial interpretive frame enhances the impact of early information on judgments and has, therefore, been called the *primacy bias*. It follows, then, that if suspicious receivers elaborate on the information more than unsuspicious receivers, and do it within the single frame established by messages transmitted early in the series, they should be more susceptible to a primacy bias than those who are unsuspicious. On the other hand, suppose suspicious receivers elaborate on each message in the series by means of counterscenarios whereas unsuspicious receivers do not. Note, first, that in counterscenario processing, both the message *and* its obverse are interpreted in light of earlier messages; and, second, that the frame for interpreting and integrating the obverse with the other information diminishes the interpretive and integrative effects of the message frame. If this is indeed the case, then the meaning of a message ought to be less influenced by the already encoded messages (e.g., Janoff-Bulman, Timko, & Carli, 1985; Koehler, 1991; Koriat, Lichtenstein, & Fischhoff, 1980). This implies a weaker primacy bias when receivers are suspicious than when they are unsuspicious. In fact, our findings show that suspicion virtually eliminates the primacy bias (Schul et al., 1996).

As we noted earlier, the current literature indicates that receivers who are wary of falsehoods increase their encoding effort. If receivers ever use the seemingly quite reasonable alternative strategy of discounting by suspending processing, they do so infrequently. Nevertheless, we believe that suspension of processing is quite a useful strategy in the real world, even though it appears not to be functional in the laboratory, or more precisely, within the experimental paradigms characteristic of research on discounting. In these paradigms, the receiver is induced to focus primarily on the messages; usually the communication concerns a single protagonist; receivers are either forewarned that some of the information might be invalid or they discover the potential for invalidity while processing the information; and the messages themselves do not contain cues that allow receivers to separate those that are true from those that are false.

There are several reasons why procedures of this kind lead individuals who distrust the source to elaborate more extensively on the message rather than to suspend processing. First, in nature, there are always other processing tasks awaiting the person's attention. It is easy to think of occasions in which this is the case: While we are watching the second half of the Michigan–Ohio State game, a task of primary importance, we also want to know what is in the newspaper, a task of secondary importance. Hence, with one eye on the TV in case of an interesting play, we quickly skim the dubious or uncertain stories and read only those that seem sound. Unlike in this example, in the typical discounting study, there is very little demand on processing capacity from other tasks. Our conjecture is that, when demands on processing capacity increase, other things being equal, individuals shift attention away from tasks that involve uncertainty. Therefore, we speculate that it is when cognitive resources are scarce that suspicious receivers are more likely than trusting ones to adopt a suspend-processing strategy.

Moreover, we noted that in the typical discounting experiment, cues to invalidity are either absent or merely probabilistic (e.g., sources may have ulterior motives for saying something but they may also say it because they believe it is true). Therefore, although receivers can try to identify the invalid information, they can never be sure that they have succeeded. However, as the cues for invalidity become more diagnostic, receivers are more certain they can detect which messages to discount—on learning which descriptions of the Gulag are by Stalin and which by Solzhenitsyn, deciding what needs discounting would, for most people, be effortless. In these circumstances, receivers have no incentive to engage in counterscenario processing and are unlikely to do so. Instead they would probably reduce processing and even suspend integration until all the invalid information has been segregated and discounted.

Finally, elaboration is functional to the extent that it is undemanding and the information gained thereby is useful. However, its costs grow as the number of suspect messages (or sources) increases. To illustrate, participants in the Schul et al. (1996) experiments knew that just one of the messages they received might be invalid, which meant that most of them were valid. But imagine that as many as half of the messages were invalid. In these circumstances, a comparison of the nonsuspicious messages with each of the suspicious messages and their obverse would be quite effortful. Indeed, we hypothesize that the cost of elaboration and reinterpretation within multiple counterscenarios is excessive when there is more than just a relatively small number of potentially invalid messages. Therefore, in such cases, receivers may decide to merely scan the communication and suspend further processing or even to ignore the messages altogether until they learn which are valid and which are invalid.

In summary, elaborative encoding may increase with suspicion either as a by-product of the search for invalid messages or because of a deliberate attempt by receivers to construct and test alternative interpretations of the information. Each of these processes requires that the receiver have both the ability and motivation to carry it out. If cognitive resources are limited relative to the demands associated with the search task or the reinterpretation task, or if receivers do not anticipate that these efforts will pay off, then suspicion may well elicit a suspension-processing strategy.

DISCOUNTING INVALID MESSAGES

During or after encoding of the original message, receivers may identify which information is invalid. Sometimes the discovery is triggered by the information itself. For example, jurors may recognize that a witness is untrustworthy based on cues that are internal to the testimony, such as "convenient" lapses of memory. On many other occasions, however, the cue for invalidity is external to the message and is available only afterward, as is the case when earlier testimony is later corrected by an expert witness (see Wilkie et al., 1984, for examples of such corrections in advertising). In this case, the impact of the invalidity cue depends on its being appropriately linked in memory with the already encoded message so that later, when receivers have to evaluate the protagonist on a particular judgmental dimension (e.g., whether the defendant is guilty or not guilty, whether the candidate is pro- or anti-abortion), they use only the knowledge previously shown to be valid, while discounting the knowledge previously shown to be invalid. Under these conditions, success of discounting depends on two types of processes; retrieval and correction. The retrieval process determines what information is brought into working memory to make the judgment. The correction process determines how the information is used in the service of accuracy.

Retrieval Processes

Research on directed forgetting (see Johnson, 1994, for a recent review) identified several mechanisms by which people could intentionally forget invalid messages. A cue to forget helps receivers to segregate or dissociate the memory codes of the to-be-remembered (TBR) and to-be-forgotten (TBF) information, to actively inhibit the TBF information, and also to tag the two types of information as TBF and TBR. As a result, instructions to forget seem to work within the intentional-forgetting paradigm. It appears, however, that these mechanisms cannot explain success and failure in tasks that involve ignoring a message.

In part, the dissimilarity stems from the role of integrative encoding in the two paradigms. The stimulus material and the contextual information in the intentional-forgetting paradigm do not encourage links between the TBF and TBR information. However, in discounting research, the stimulus information usually is about one person; receivers encode it by associating the different messages because they are explicitly instructed to do so or because this is an habitual mode of processing information about persons and occurs automatically (Burnstein & Schul, 1982; Wyer & Srull, 1989).[1] For

---

[1]Indeed, Golding, Long, and MacLeod (1994) showed that it is essentially impossible to forget information closely related to the to-be-recalled information.

these reasons, we think, the mechanisms that are useful in intentional for-getting are ineffective in the discounting paradigm. This is illustrated nicely in the following example: If failure to discount was equivalent to failure of retrieval of the to-be-used information, then discounting should be success-ful in conditions where the to-be-used but not the to-be-ignored information was made salient prior to judgment. In fact, when the to-be-used messages were highlighted to receivers just before they were to judge, discounting typically failed (Schul, 1993; Schul & Burnstein, 1985). It was when the to-be-ignored rather than the to-be-used information was made salient that receiv-ers discounted successfully (Schul & Burnstein, 1985). This is not consistent with the segregation mechanism discussed earlier (Johnson, 1994).

Several studies (Golding & Hauselt, 1994; Golding et al., 1990; Schul & Burnstein, 1985; Wyer & Unverzagt, 1985) assessed people's memory for the to-be-used and to-be-ignored messages directly by recall measures collected following the judgment responses (note that such a sequence of measure-ments makes the interpretation of the recall-judgment relation somewhat problematic because judgments always precede recall and can influence it). Overall, the results indicated that failure in discounting does not represent retrieval failure (see also Johnson, 1994). For example, Wyer and Unverzagt (1985) found that discounting succeeds under conditions that promote suc-cessful retrieval of the to-be-ignored information. Golding and Hauselt (1994) reported zero correlation between recall of the to-be-used and the to-be-ig-nored information and evaluations based on this information. They further showed that receivers recall the messages as accurately when they are instructed to use them in an upcoming judgment as when they have to ignore them in such a judgment. To the best of our knowledge, Schul and Burnstein (1985) provided the only evidence linking judgments and recall. They found that receivers who confuse the to-be-ignored information and recall it as to-be-used information are more likely to fail in discounting than those who do not confuse the two types of information.

Interestingly, the segregation mechanism does account for failure of dis-counting in research on the *sleeper effect* (Cook & Flay, 1978; Mazursky & Schul, 1988). In this paradigm, messages are attributed to an untrustworthy source (e.g., a source who is proven to be unreliable) and their immediate impact is compared to their impact at some later point in time. The typical finding is that the testimony of the untrustworthy source is discounted in the immediate judgment condition but not in the delayed judgment condi-tion. The failure to discount is attributed to a dissociation of the message from the discounting cue when there is a delay in measurement. Mazursky and Schul (1988) showed that, when receivers were encouraged to elaborate on the message by imagining themselves using the product described by the message, they were more susceptible to sleeper effects than were re-ceivers who did not elaborate on the information. Analyses of receivers' memory for the message and the discounting cue indicated that at the time of the delayed measurement (10 days after receivers viewed the original information), those receivers who had elaborated on the message at encoding remembered the message better and remembered the discounting cue worse than did those who had not elaborated on the message. This is consistent with the suggestion that in the sleeper effect, receivers do not discount at a later point because the cue for discounting becomes dissociated from the message, and hence fails to inhibit the impact of the message.

Correction Processes

The bulk of the evidence in the discounting literature suggests that success in discounting depends on the correction procedures people utilize. Because models of correction have been discussed extensively in recent years (e.g., Martin, Seta, & Crelia, 1990; Schwarz & Bless, 1992; Strack & Hannover, in press; Wegener & Petty, 1995), and because the models make similar predictions for success of discounting, we shall not review this literature here. However, it is important to keep in mind the conditions these models specify as necessary and sufficient for successful correction in the general case: To undo a bias, one must (a) be aware that a bias exists; (b) know its direction and magnitude; (c) be motivated to eliminate the bias; and (d) have the cognitive resources to do so. In the following sections, we show how these conditions apply when a message is supposed to be ignored.

Awareness of Bias

Schul and Burnstein (1985) distinguished between two ways people might be instructed to discount: Receivers may be informed of the subset of to-be-used messages and told to ignore all the messages that are not members of the subset, or receivers may be informed of the subset of to-be-ignored messages and told to use only the messages that are not members of the subset. We found that discounting was more successful when subjects were given the to-be-ignored information. At first glance, this may seem counterintuitive: Why can't the receivers who are given the to-be-used information use it to compute judgments as if they have just received a new communication? Note, however, that the to-be-used information has already been interpreted in light of the to-be-ignored information. Therefore, to effectively ignore the to-be-ignored information, receivers must not only consider the to-be-used information, they must also try to undo the effect of the to-be-ignored on the to-be-used information. At a minimum, this requires some recognition of how the former biases the latter. Our findings indicate that receivers who are given only the to-be-used messages are less aware of the bias than are those given the to-be-ignored. Therefore, they are more likely to fail in discounting.

Awareness of the bias may also play an important role in situations in which the instructions to ignore information are not given explicitly. A case in point is research on judgments that can be influenced by a stereotype (Strack & Hannover, in press). When the only information receivers have is the social category of a protagonist (gender, race, age), they can easily resist using it in evaluating the person. If, however, the person is characterized by additional information, some attention is directed away from the stereotype. As a result, receivers are less aware of the potentially biasing impact of the stereotype, and are less likely to correct for it (e.g., Darley & Gross, 1983).

Our research suggests that awareness of bias may also account for the relative success of jurors in ignoring invalid evidence during a simulated trial. Subjects in Schul and Manzury (1990) role played jurors in an assault case where testimony was given by several different witnesses. The judge ruled one of the testimonies for the prosecution invalid because the witness was said to have been drunk at the time of the incident. Subjects were asked to make judgments of guilt or innocence as well as to rate the defendant for aggressiveness and likeability. When it was a matter of deciding guilt or innocence, successful discounting occurred when testimony by the prosecution's witness was invalidated without further evidence supportive of drunkenness (i.e., weak discounting cue), as well as when supportive evidence was provided by a key defense witness who testified that the prosecution's witness was drunk at the time (i.e., strong discounting cue). That is to say, in both of these experimental conditions, the guilt judgments were no more or less extreme that those of control subjects who received neither the testimony of the key prosecution witness nor that of the key defense witness. However, the two groups of experimental subjects did fail to discount in judging the defendant's aggressiveness and likeability.

One way to interpret these findings (but see also the issue of motivation discussed later) is that the jurors' decision frame itself prepares receivers to discount: Not only does it make salient the costliness of an error in judgment and, thereby, brings to mind an obligation to avoid bias, but it also facilitates the recall of to-be-ignored information by providing ready-made (and readily available) encoding categories that mark testimony as "inadmissible" or "admissible." Personality judgments (e.g., likeability), however, operate within quite a different frame, one in which such concepts as the cost of an error, the inadmissibility of information, and the obligation to correct are at best only weakly represented and have virtually no associative connections.

Awareness of the Direction and Magnitude of the Bias

Although instructions to ignore may alert a receiver to the need to correct, they often do not specify the magnitude and direction of the required correction. Direction is typically not a problem because receivers can assess the message's overall bias and simply alter the interpretation (or the judgment) in the opposite direction (i.e., if the suspect witness' testimony is pro-guilt, the correction must be in the direction of innocence). Determining the amount of correction needed is much more problematic, however. To discount for magnitude of bias, receivers not only have to gauge the direct impact of the to-be-ignored information, say, shifting to a more anti-x position when a source that made a pro-x assertion turns out to be untrustworthy, but they must also take into account its indirect impact (via the to-be-used information). It is not too surprising, therefore, that research has found cases of undercorrection, overcorrection, and appropriate correction.

One feature of messages that seems to be related to the tendency to over- or undercorrect is the valence of the to-be-ignored messages. Hatvany and Strack (1980), Thompson, Fong, and Rosenhan (1981), and Wyer and Budesheim (1987) observed that judges ignore negative messages successfully but fail to ignore positive messages. This finding was interpreted (e.g., Wyer & Budesheim, 1987) as reflecting commonly held beliefs about a "negativity bias" whereby people think that negative information exerts greater influence on judgment than positive information. It follows, therefore, that they correct more when discounting a negative message than a positive one.

Schul and Goren (in press) manipulated the potential impact of the to-be-ignored information directly to explore how it influences the success of discounting. We assumed that strong messages are seen as more capable of biasing judgments than weak ones. Therefore, we predicted that receivers would correct more when they were instructed to ignore a strong message than a weak one. Again, the experiments were framed as a simulated trial. Subjects received a series of testimonies, one of which was later found to be invalid. In one experiment, we manipulated the strength of the to-be-ignored testimony through its typicality. The "weak" testimony indicated that the defendant's behavior was typical of his behavior in the past, whereas the "strong" testimony indicated that his behavior on the day of the incident was different from the past. Previous research indicates that atypical behavior is seen as more extreme than typical behavior and protagonists who perform atypical acts are perceived as more responsible for their actions than those who perform typical ones (Kahneman & Miller, 1986; Macrea, 1992; Miller & McFarland, 1986). Therefore, it was expected that the defendant would be seen as more guilty when described by the atypical (strong) testimony than by the typical (weak) testimony. However, because subjects have good cues for the potency of the strong testimony, we predicted that the subjects would correct more if instructed to ignore it. Indeed, the defendant was seen as less guilty when subjects ignored the strong testimony than when they ignored the weak testimony. In a second experiment, we manipulated the strength of the to-be-ignored testimony by varying the confidence expressed by the witness. As in the first experiment, subjects discounted the strong testimony (high confidence) more effectively than the weak testimony (low confidence), suggesting that the magnitude of perceived bias was inferred from the strength of the to-be-ignored testimony.

The research of Ross, Lepper, and Hubbard (1975) demonstrated the importance of receivers' theories about the magnitude of required correction in a different way. In their study, subjects received false feedback about their performance, then were debriefed about the invalidity of the feedback and were requested to ignore it while evaluating some of their abilities that were relevant to the performance. The request to ignore the feedback was made in two ways: Subjects in the outcome-request condition were told that the feedback was completely false and should therefore be ignored in making inferences about their ability; subjects in the process-request condition were told not only that the feedback was false and should be ignored, but also that such feedback induces belief perseverance, which is the phrase Ross et al. (1975) coined to indicate an inability to discount invalid information that has already been encoded. The fact that subjects who received the outcome request failed in discounting, whereas those who received the process request succeeded, suggests that knowledge about the magnitude of the bias can, by itself, enhance discounting. That is, according to Ross et al., the process request served to inform subjects that the bias produced by the invalid feedback is stronger than they would otherwise have thought. Thus, not surprisingly, they made a larger correction in judgment than did those in the outcome-request condition who did not have this knowledge.

Motivation to Correct

The motivation to correct depends on factors that make correction a useful or appropriate course of action. Golding and his associates (Golding et al., 1990; Golding & Hauselt, 1994) offer a good example of this. Their research compared two types of discounting requests: One stressed procedural concerns in that subjects were asked to ignore a message describing a person because, according to the rules of the game, they shouldn't have heard it. The other request to ignore emphasized that the message and the protagonist were paired by mistake. That is to say, the message did not actually describe the protagonist and should therefore be ignored. Golding and his colleagues observed that individuals discount successfully when the request is based on an error in pairing so that the information is incorrect, but not when it is based on a procedural violation. Although those receiving the procedural request may be aware of the magnitude as well as the direction of the bias associated with the to-be-ignored description, they seem to reason that if the cost of failing to discount is minimal, it would be wasteful to ignore factually correct, albeit procedurally invalid, information.

Conceptually similar explanations may account for the discounting of forced confessions. Kassin and Wrightsman (1980, 1981) found that mock jurors successfully discounted confessions that were elicited by threats of punishment, whereas they failed to discount confessions elicited by promises of reward, such as an offer of leniency. Although Kassin and Wrightsman had no direct evidence that benefit-induced confessions are perceived as more voluntary than cost-induced ones, they speculated that promises of reward, other things being equal, are considered a weaker incentive to confess than threats of punishment. It follows from this line of reasoning that confessions obtained by promises were seen as more likely to be true and, therefore, aroused less motivation to correct for their impact on judgment than did confessions obtained by threats.

It should be noted that requests to ignore valid information on purely procedural grounds are unusual in most contexts and hence difficult for receivers to interpret. However, there are circumstances in which requests of this kind are natural and readily understood. In such situations, procedural requests are perceived as appropriate and they may cause receivers to discount the inadmissible information successfully. For instance, Lenehan and O'Neill (1981) found that when jurors were asked to ignore testimony because it was obtained by means of an illegal wiretap, they were able to discount successfully. It is interesting to note at this point that Golding and associates (discussed earlier) observed failure in discounting of procedurally invalid information in a social judgment context, so that the Lenehan and O'Neill results can be taken as further evidence that an obligation-to-correct rule is more appropriate within the jury frame than within other contexts. Their study also suggests that the success of discounting is not a linear function of the directness and strength of the request to discount. Rather, the effect was observed most clearly when the judge made the procedural request in a neutral tone (as compared to a forceful admonition). This suggests that if the request to ignore information is put too strongly, subjects may perceive it as an attack on their freedom of decision and react against it (see also Wolf & Montgomery, 1977).

Finally, the framing of the request as appropriate or expected may influence the receiver's motivation to discount. This may explain why most studies in the belief-perseverance paradigm—where the request to discount is made under highly peculiar circumstances—show that people fail at discounting, whereas a majority of studies done in the simulated-trial paradigm—where the context of the request makes it readily understood—show that people succeed in it (see review in Schul & Manzury, 1990).

Ability to Correct

Research suggests that correction is an effortful process (e.g., Gilbert & Hixon, 1991; Martin et al., 1990). Therefore, if receivers lack sufficient cognitive resources to correct, discounting should fail. Moreover, Wegner (1994) recently postulated that correction involves two processes; a search for the invalid or to-be-corrected idea, and attempts to correct for it once it is found. According to Wegner, searching is relatively effortless compared to correcting. Therefore, when cognitive resources become scarce, the correction process is terminated, whereas the search process, being relatively cost-free, is likely to continue. This is assumed to leave a residue, namely, the representation of the mental state it seeks (i.e., the to-be-corrected idea), which is activated to guide the search. As a result, individuals who are concerned about correcting a particular bias but have insufficient cognitive resources to do so actually may be more likely to fail in discounting and, therefore, display an even greater bias in judgment than do those who are unconcerned about the matter.

Suspicion and Success of Discounting

We discussed earlier two lines of evidence suggesting that suspicion may facilitate successful discounting. The first line of evidence is indirect. A comparison of discounting in experiments done in the simulated-trial paradigm with discounting in experiments using the belief-perseverance paradigm shows that receivers discount better in the former than in the latter (Schul & Manzury, 1990). An important difference between the two paradigms has to do with the way messages are framed: In a court, but not in a laboratory, the sources as well as the information they communicate are inherently suspect. Cultural knowledge automatically makes members of a jury aware that witnesses often are unreliable, either because they are motivated to deceive or because of nonmotivational factors such as a faulty memory. Similarly, when asked to role play a juror, subjects are likely to be put on alert. In contrast, the typical belief perseverance study attempts to allay any suspicion during the initial communication—it is critical for the research that this be done successfully. Considerable stress is put on the fact that the source (the experimenter) is not only highly reliable but also motivated to provide the receiver (the subject) with correct information. Still, the evidence from such comparisons is quite indirect and far from conclusive; the two sets of studies differ in many ways besides the fact that in one case the message is automatically interpreted within a suspicion frame and in the other case, it is not.

More recently, we (Schul, 1993; Schul et al., 1996) manipulated suspicion directly. Earlier, an analysis was made of how suspicion helps receivers' judgments by preparing them to discount invalid information during encoding. Now we discuss how suspicion helps receivers make more accurate judgments, above and beyond its influence during encoding. To begin with, suspicion can influence retrieval by increasing receivers' concern for judgmental accuracy and by making them try harder to retrieve detailed information about the target of the communication or about the source, information that might not have come to mind otherwise (Chaiken, Liberman, & Eagly, 1989; Kruglanski, 1989; Neuberg, 1994; Thompson, Roman, Moskowitz, Chaiken, & Bargh, 1994).

In addition, suspicion may influence how the receiver gauges the magnitude of correction that is needed. Our hypothesis is that the latter effect depends on whether the presence of a to-be-ignored message is expected: If receivers are very surprised to learn that a communication contained to-be-ignored information, this in large part reflects a sudden recognition that they did not take this into account during encoding, which, in turn, leads them to overestimate the impact of the to-be-ignored information on their judgment. Suppose, however, they are aware ahead of time that errors in communication were quite likely (e.g., the source was famous for being incompetent or deceptive). In these circumstances, when receivers are told about the specific to-be-ignored message, there is no surprise. Instead, they feel that they already knew it, have taken it into account, and, hence, when required to correct, are likely to underestimate its impact on judgment. The upshot, according to this hypothesis, is that upon learning that an earlier communication contained to-be-ignored information, trusting receivers tend to correct more than do suspicious receivers. Indeed, according to folk knowledge, when they learn of being mislead, naive lovers experience a larger shock, estimate the betrayal to be of greater magnitude, and are less forgiving in their judgment of the partner than worldly lovers. Of course, whether the tendency to correct a lot leads to more successful discounting than the tendency to correct a little depends on the actual influence of the to-be-ignored message. A highly surprising to-be-ignored message may lead to overcorrection, whereas a to-be-ignored message that is totally expected may lead to undercorrection.

Finally, suspicion can strengthen the motivation to correct for a bias by increasing concerns for accuracy. We think that the findings reported in Schul and Manzury (1990), namely, that receivers' relative success in discounting when making guilt judgments and their relative failure when making judgments of aggressiveness, are related to a greater concern for accuracy in the former than in the latter case.

SUMMARY AND CONCLUSIONS

We argue that wariness about communication is natural and endemic because false information from others is costly, pervasive, and inherent to social life. It follows that the ability to discount is a vital adaptation and must have been so almost from the very beginning of human history. In this chapter, we describe what is known about this adaptation at the psychological level. From this perspective, it is important to remember that the discounting mechanism evolved to deal with the problem of invalidity and deception in social communication, and in all likelihood, has little in common with the recognition and correction of errors in physical perception. So it may well be that information that is not associated with another person (or group) is automatically coded as true regardless of context. But this is not the case in social communication. Rather, receivers give contextual information, particularly cues to a source's trustworthiness, at least as high a priority in encoding as the message. Not surprisingly, then, we find that as attentional resources decrease and receivers are less able to critically analyze the message, its truth value comes to depend on whether contextual information makes the source suspect.

Moreover, the receiver's reason for being suspicious is important. Recognition that the source is ignorant of the facts of the case does not help the receiver to know what these facts are. However, when the potential bias is motivated so that it reflects self-interest, receivers not only recognize which message ought to be set aside, but they can also infer that its opposite is likely to be closer to the truth and use the inference as a replacement for the suspect information. Consequently, when the source's bias is perceived as motivated, discounting is more successful than when it is perceived as unmotivated.

Once receivers are made wary about being deceived, successful discounting depends in large part on how they prepare to process the suspect communication. It is clear that encoding that integrates to-be-ignored information (marked as invalid only after encoding) and to-be-used information (marked as valid only after encoding) hinders discounting. We suggest that even though receivers can segregate the to-be-ignored from the to-be-used messages once they learn which is which, at that point they will have already elaborated on the to-be-used messages in the context of the to-be-ignored messages. Under these conditions, therefore, to-be-used information inevitably contains associations and implications that are consistent with the to-be-ignored information and that influence judgment even after the to-be-ignored messages have been set aside and ignored.

To overcome this problem, receivers must evolve a strategy that allows minimally sufficient encoding but forestalls integration. Two such strategies can be identified. One would have receivers simply scan the information. By decreasing the amount of elaboration per chunk, receivers represent the series of messages as relatively distinct pieces of information rather than as an integrated communication or gist. This reduces the residual impact of to-be-ignored information on to-be-used information so that once the former is identified, it can be fully discounted. The research literature suggests, however, that this strategy is rarely used. Instead, suspicion usually increases rather than decreases the amount of elaboration performed on a message. We hypothesize that this increase reflects a counterscenario processing strategy whereby receivers test the obverse of the message currently

SCHUL AND BURNSTEIN

being encoded for plausibility in light of messages that were encoded earlier. If counterscenario processing is successful, it allows receivers to identify and to segregate the to-be-ignored information early on before it is integrated with the to-be-used information.

Often, the cues telling receivers which sections of a communication are untrue become available only after the communication is encoded and a judgment has to be made. In these circumstances, one would think that discounting must depend in large part on what messages receivers retrieve. However, it seems clear that unsuccessful discounting does not reflect retrieval failure. Indeed, when receivers are reminded only of the to-be-used messages, discounting is worse than when they are reminded only of the to-be-ignored messages. If ability to remember the communication and to segregate to-be-used and to-be-ignored information is not critical for successful discounting, what is? The best evidence is that when receivers learn which pieces of information are invalid only after the communication had been encoded, discounting is primarily influenced by how they correct for the biasing effects of the invalid material. Generally speaking, we know that to undo a bias, receivers must be aware of its existence, know its direction and magnitude, be motivated to eliminate the bias, and have the attentional resources to do so. The observation that reinstating only the to-be-used messages immediately prior to judgment hinders discounting, whereas reinstating only the to-be-ignored messages facilitates it, is perhaps the clearest demonstration that awareness of bias is critical. Similar conclusions follow from the fact that discounting of already encoded information is more readily obtained in studies in which the experimental frame serves to highlight the inherent biases in communication, their costs, and the receiver's accountability (e.g., juror decision tasks) than in studies in which it does not (e.g., person impression tasks).

Finally, knowledge or beliefs that allow receivers to infer the magnitude of the bias or the difficulty in correcting increase the likelihood of successful discounting. Thus, for example, receivers who believe the behavior described is atypical perceive it to be relatively extreme and correct for it in their judgments more than do receivers who believe it to be typical. Although the importance of the receivers' estimates of the magnitude of their bias was discovered quite early in the research on belief perseverance, important questions about the types of correction strategies available to receivers and the conditions under which a strategy is automatically versus deliberately engaged remain open.

ACKNOWLEDGMENT

Preparation of this manuscript was supported by a grant from the United States-Israel Binational Science Foundation.

REFERENCES

Alexander, R. D. (1987). *The biology of moral systems.* New York: Aldine De Gruyter.

Anderson, C. A., Lepper, M. R., & Ross, L. (1980). Perseverance of social theories: The role of explanation in the persistence of discredited information. *Journal of Personality and Social Psychology, 39,* 1037–1049.

Asch, S. E. (1946). Forming impressions of personality. *Journal of Abnormal and Social Psychology, 41,* 258–290.

Bargh, J. A. (1989). Conditional automaticity: Variety of automatic influence in social perception and cognition. In J. S. Uleman & J. A. Bargh (Eds.), *Unintended thoughts* (pp. 3–51). New York: Guilford.

Bjork, R. A. (1989). Retrieval inhibition as an adaptive mechanism in human memory. In H. L. Roediger & F. I. M. Craik (Eds.), *Varieties of memory and consciousness* (pp. 309–330). Hillsdale, NJ: Lawrence Erlbaum.

Bornstein, G. (1992). The "free rider" problem in intergroup conflicts over step-level and continuous public goods. *Journal of Personality and Social Psychology, 4,* 597–606.

Burnstein, E., & Schul, Y. (1982). The informational basis of social judgments: Operations in forming an impression of another person. *Journal of Experimental Social Psychology, 18,* 217–234.

Burnstein, E., & Schul, Y. (1983). The informational basis of social judgments: Memory for integrated and non-integrated trait descriptions. *Journal of Experimental Social Psychology, 19,* 49–57.

Cacioppo, J. T., & Petty, R. E. (1987). Stalking rudimentary processes of social influence: A psychophysiological approach. In M. P. Zanna, J. M. Olson, & C. P. Herman (Eds.), *Social influence: The Ontario symposium* (Vol. 5, pp. 41–74). Hillsdale, NJ: Lawrence Erlbaum Associates.

Chaiken, S. (1987). The heuristic model of persuasion. In M. P. Zanna, J. M. Olson, & C. P. Herman (Eds.), *Social influence: The Ontario symposium* (Vol. 5, pp. 3–39). Hillsdale, NJ: Lawrence Erlbaum Associates.

Chaiken, S., Liberman, A., & Eagly, A. H. (1989). Heuristic and systematic processing within and beyond the persuasion context. In J. S. Uleman & J. A. Bargh (Eds.), *Unintended thought* (pp. 212–252). New York: Guilford.

Cook, T. D., & Flay, B. R. (1978). The persistence of experimentally induced attitude change. In L. Berkowitz (Ed.), *Advances in experimental social psychology* (Vol. 11, pp. 1–57). New York: Academic Press.

Cosmides, L. (1989). The logic of social exchange: Has natural selection shaped how humans reason? Studies with the Wason selection task. *Cognition, 31,* 187–276.

Cosmides, L., & Tooby, J. (1989). Evolutionary psychology and the generation of culture. Part II. Case study: A computation theory of social exchange. *Ethology and Sociobiology, 10,* 51–91.

Darley, J. M., & Gross, P. H. (1983). A hypothesis-confirming bias in labeling effects. *Journal of Personality and Social Psychology, 44,* 20–33.

Dawkins, R. (1976). *The selfish gene.* New York: Oxford University Press.

Eagly, A. H., & Chaiken, S. (1993). *The psychology of attitudes.* New York: Harcourt Brace.

Eagly, A. H., Wood, W., & Chaiken, S. (1978). Causal inferences about communicators and their effect on opinion change. *Journal of Personality and Social Psychology, 36,* 424–435.

Fein, S., Hilton, J. L., & Miller, D. T. (1990). Suspicion of ulterior motivation and correspondence bias. *Journal of Personality and Social Psychology, 58,* 753–764.

Fleming, I., & Arrowood, J. (1979). Information processing and the perseverance of discredited self-perceptions. *Personality and Social Psychology Bulletin, 5,* 201–205.

Frey, D. (1986). Recent research on selective exposure to information. In L. Berkowitz (Ed.), *Advances in experimental social psychology* (Vol. 19, pp. 41–80). New York: Academic Press.

Gilbert, D. T. (1991). How mental systems think. *American Psychologist, 46,* 107–119.

Gilbert, D. T., & Hixon, J. G. (1991). The trouble of thinking: Activation and application of stereotypic beliefs. *Journal of Personality and Social Psychology, 60,* 509–517.

Gilbert, D. T., Tafarodi, R. W., & Malone, P. S. (1993). You can't not believe everything you read. *Journal of Personality and Social Psychology, 65,* 221–233.

Golding, J. M., Fowler, S. B., Long, D. L., & Latta, H. (1990). Instructions to disregard potentially useful information: The effects of pragmatics on evaluative judgments and recall. *Journal of Memory and Language, 29,* 212–227.

Golding, J. M., & Hauselt, J. (1994). When instructions to forget become instructions to remember. *Personality and Social Psychology Bulletin, 20,* 178–183.

Golding, J. M., Long, D. L., & MacLeod, C. M. (1994). You can't always forget what you want: Directed forgetting of related pairs. *Journal of Memory and Language, 33,* 493–510.

Hamilton, W. D. (1964). The genetical evolution of social behavior. Parts I and II. *Journal of Theoretical Biology, 7,* 1–52.

Hastie, R., & Kumar, P. A. (1979). Person memory: Personality traits as organizing principles in memory for behavior. *Journal of Personality and Social Psychology, 37,* 25–38.

Hatvany, N., & Strack, F. (1980). The impact of a discredited key witness. *Journal of Applied Social Psychology, 10,* 490–509.

Hilton J. L., Fein, S., & Miller, D. T. (1993). Suspicion and dispositional inference. *Personality and Social Psychology Bulletin, 19,* 501–512.

Hogarth, R. M., & Einhorn, H. J. (1992). Order effect in belief updating: The belief-adjustment model. *Cognitive Psychology, 24,* 1–55.

Janoff-Bulman, R., Timko, C., & Carli, L. L. (1985). Cognitive biases in blaming the victim. *Journal of Experimental Social Psychology, 21,* 161–177.

Johnson, M. (1994). Processes of successful intentional forgetting. *Psychological Bulletin, 116,* 274–292.

Kahneman D., & Miller, D. T. (1986). Norm theory: Comparing reality to its alternatives. *Psychological Review, 93,* 136–153.

Kassin, S. M., & Wrightsman, L. S. (1980). Prior confessions and mock-jury verdicts. *Journal of Applied Social Psychology, 10,* 133–146.

Kassin, S. M., & Wrightsman, L. S. (1981). Coerced confessions, judicial instruction, and mock juror verdicts. *Journal of Applied Social Psychology, 11,* 489–506.

Knafo, A., & Schul, Y. (1995). *The effects of source trustworthiness and cognitive load on judgments.* Unpublished manuscript.

Koehler, D. J. (1991). Explanation, imagination, and confidence in judgment. *Psychological Bulletin, 110,* 499–519.

Koriat, A., Lichtenstein, S., & Fischhoff, B. (1980). Reasons for confidence. *Journal of Experimental Psychology: Human Learning and Memory, 6,* 107–118.

Kraut, R. E. (1978). Verbal and non-verbal cues in the perception of lying. *Journal of Personality and Social Psychology, 36,* 380–391.

Kruglanski, A. W. (1989). *Lay epistemics and human knowledge.* New York: Plenum Press.

Kruglanski, A. W., & Freund, T. (1983). The freezing of lay inferences effects of impressional primacy, ethnic stereotyping and numerical anchoring. *Journal of Experimental Social Psychology, 19,* 448–468.

Lenehan, G. E., & O'Neill, P. (1981). Reactance and conflict as determinants of judgments in a mock jury trial. *Journal of Applied Social Psychology, 11,* 231–239.

MacLeod, C. M. (1989). Directed forgetting affects both direct and indirect tests of memory. *Journal of Experimental Psychology: Learning, Memory, and Cognition, 15,* 13–21.

Macrea, C. N. (1992). A tale of two curries: Counterfactual thinking and accident-related judgments. *Personality and Social Psychology Bulletin, 18,* 84–87.

Martin, L. L., Seta, J. J., & Crelia, R. A. (1990). Assimilation and contrast as a function of people's willingness and ability to expand effort in forming an impression. *Journal of Personality and Social Psychology, 59,* 27–37.

Mayo, R., & Schul, Y. (1995). *Source information versus message information in conditions of limited cognitive resources.* Unpublished manuscript.

Mazursky, D., & Schul, Y. (1988). The effects of advertisement encoding on the failure to discount information: Implications for the sleeper effect. *Journal of Consumer Research, 15,* 24–36.

Miller, D. T., & McFarland, C. (1986). Counterfactual thinking and victim compensation: A test of norm theory. *Personality and Social Psychology Bulletin, 12,* 513–519.

Neuberg, S. L. (1994). Expectancy-confirmation processes in stereotype-tinged social encounters: The moderating role of social goals. In M. P. Zanna & J. M. Olson (Eds.), *The psychology of prejudice: The Ontario symposium* (Vol. 7, pp. 103–130). Hillsdale, NJ: Lawrence Erlbaum Associates.

Papageorgis, D. (1968). Warning and persuasion. *Psychological Bulletin, 70,* 271–282.

Petty, R. E., & Cacioppo, J. T. (1977). Forewarning, cognitive responding, and resistance to persuasion. *Journal of Personality and Social Psychology, 35,* 645–655.

Ross, L., Lepper, M. R., & Hubbard, M. (1975). Perseverance in self-perception and social perception: Biased attributional processes in the debriefing paradigm. *Journal of Personality and Social Psychology, 32*(5), 880–892.

Ross, L., Lepper, M. R., Strack, F., & Steinmetz, J. (1977). Social explanations and social expectations: Effects of real and hypothetical explanations on subjective likelihood. *Journal of Personality and Social Psychology, 35,* 817–829.

Schul, Y. (1993). When warning succeeds: The effect of warning on success of ignoring invalid information. *Journal of Experimental Social Psychology, 29,* 42–62.

Schul, Y., & Burnstein, E. (1985). When discounting fails: Conditions under which individuals use discredited information in making a judgment. *Journal of Personality and Social Psychology, 49,* 894–903.

Schul, Y., Burnstein, E., & Bardi, A. (1996). Dealing with deceptions that are difficult to detect: Encoding and judgment as a function of preparing to receive invalid information. *Journal of Experimental Social Psychology, 32,* 228–253.

Schul, Y., Burnstein, E., & Martinez, J. (1983). The informational basis of social judgments: Under what conditions are inconsistent trait descriptions processed as easily as consistent ones? *European Journal of Social Psychology, 13,* 143–151.

Schul, Y., & Goren, H. (in press). When strong evidence has less impact than weak evidence: Bias, adjustment, and instructions to ignore. *Social Cognition.*

Schul, Y., & Manzury, F. (1990). The effect of type of encoding and strength of discounting appeal on the success of ignoring an invalid testimony. *European Journal of Social Psychology, 20,* 337–349.

Schul, Y., & Mazursky, D. (1990). Conditions facilitating successful discounting in consumer decision making: Type of discounting cue, message encoding, and kind of judgment. *Journal of Consumer Research, 16,* 442–451.

Schwarz, N., & Bless, H. (1992). Scandals and the public trust in politicians: Assimilation and contrast effects. *Personality and Social Psychology Bulletin, 18,* 574–579.

Strack, F., & Hannover, B. (in press). Awareness of influence as a precondition for implementing correctional goals. In P. M. Gollwitzer & J. A. Bargh (Eds.), *The psychology of action: Linking motivation and cognition to behavior* (pp. 579–595). New York: Guilford.

Thompson, E. P., Roman, R. J., Moskowitz, G. B., Chaiken, S., & Bargh, J. A. (1994). Accuracy motivation attenuates covert priming: The systematic reprocessing of social information. *Journal of Personality and Social Psychology, 66,* 474–489.

Thompson, W. C., Fong, G. T., & Rosenhan, D. L. (1981). Inadmissible evidence and juror verdicts. *Journal of Personality and Social Psychology, 40,* 453–463.

348   SCHUL AND BURNSTEIN

Trope, Y. (1986). Identification and inferential processes in dispositional attribution. *Psychological Review, 93*, 239–257.

Wegener, D. T., & Petty, R. E. (1995). Flexible correction processes in social judgment: The role of naive theories in corrections for perceived bias. *Journal of Personality and Social Psychology, 68*, 36–51.

Wegner, D. M. (1994). Ironic processes of mental control. *Psychological Review, 101*, 34–52.

Wilkie, W. L., McNeill, D. L., & Mazis, M. B. (1983). Marketing's "Scarlet letter": The theory and practice of corrective advertising. *Journal of Marketing, 48*, 11–31.

Wilson, T. D., & Brekke, N. (1994). Mental contamination and mental correction: Unwanted influences on judgments and evaluations. *Psychological Bulletin, 116*, 117–142.

Wolf, S., & Montgomery, D. A. (1977). Effects of inadmissible evidence and level of judicial admonishment to disregard on the judgment of mock jurors. *Journal of Applied Social Psychology, 7*, 205–219.

Wyer, R. S., & Budesheim, T. L. (1987). Person memory and judgments: The impact of information that one is told to disregard. *Journal of Personality and Social Psychology, 53*, 14–29.

Wyer, R. S., & Srull, T. K. (1989). *Memory and cognition in its social context.* Hillsdale, NJ: Lawrence Erlbaum Associates.

Wyer, R. S., & Unverzagt, W. H. (1985). Effects of instructions to disregard information on its subsequent recall and use in making judgments. *Journal of Personality and Social Psychology, 48*, 533–549.

12

DISREGARDING SOCIAL STEREOTYPES: IMPLICATIONS FOR MEMORY, JUDGMENT, AND BEHAVIOR

Galen V. Bodenhausen
Northwestern University

C. Neil Macrae
University of St. Andrews

Alan B. Milne
University of Aberdeen

One of the hallmarks of successful development in childhood is the acquisition of the ability to control one's impulses, sacrificing the immediate gratification that might come from impulsive action in pursuit of higher order goals. For instance, the desire to kick a sibling who has made a teasing remark must be inhibited to appease parental authority, even though an aggressive response might seem to be a terribly appealing option. Although undoubtedly frustrating to those who are in the process of mastering it, skilled self-regulation is central to successful functioning in all of life's domains (e.g., Carver & Scheier, 1981; Miller, Galanter, & Pribram, 1960). For example, the common impulse to eat rich and sugary foods may have strong evolutionary roots (e.g., Harris & Ross, 1987), but in the contemporary environments of industrialized nations, with their abundant supply of "junk food," failure to rein in this impulse can lead to a host of maladaptive outcomes. Personal well-being, it would seem, is intimately tied to self-regulatory skill.

Impulse control also operates in the service of broader social goals. To function smoothly, societies require their individual members to restrain themselves from performing a variety of socially undesirable behaviors, even if these acts have strong motivational underpinnings. Selfish overconsumption of shared public goods, for instance, may seem very enticing to the individual who stands to benefit personally from it, yet it can lead to disastrous outcomes for the community as a whole. Consider as an example the "tragedy of the commons," in which selfish overgrazing of a shared pasture resource led to its depletion (Hardin, 1968; see Komorita & Parks, 1994). The tragedy of the situation lies in the fact that, with appropriate restraint, the resource could have remained sufficient for the basic needs of all users, but individual selfishness ruined the resource for everyone. Social harmony and well-being may thus depend on the successful operation of socialization pressures and other normative influences that encourage the inhibition of selfish, disruptive, and destructive impulses on the part of individuals (cf. Freud, 1933; Hobbes, 1651/1968).

Stereotypes and prejudice, we argue, constitute another form of undesirable, impulsive response that societies, and individuals, need to regulate effectively if a harmonious and sustainable multicultural environment is to be created. In the distant evolutionary past of our species, living arrangements were highly group segregated, and the tendency to develop negative and rigid views of the members of other groups might have had relatively few costs in terms of social harmony and might even have been adaptive in the context of intergroup competition for scarce resources (see Fox, 1992; Reynolds, Falger, & Vine, 1987). In the modern world, however, contact with members of many different social groups is a commonplace occurrence, and reliance on prejudice and stereotypes in responding to these groups has been associated with seemingly countless tragedies and injustices, ranging from random acts of harassment targeting the members of minority groups to institutionalized forms of discrimination and even organized genocidal movements. This toxic impact of prejudice and stereotypes has been increasingly recognized in recent decades. Correspondingly, formal laws and informal norms have taken shape dictating that the discriminatory influence of stereotypes and prejudice should be avoided in a variety of contexts, such as personnel decision making, legal judgment, and educational opportunity. The focus of the present chapter is the nature and consequences of such efforts to disregard stereotypic preconceptions when evaluating and reacting to the members of social groups.

COUNTERACTING THE STEREOTYPIC IMPULSE

A variety of motivations seem to underlie the social perceiver's tendency to rely on social stereotypes in judging others. Stereotyping confers an efficiency on social perception processes that permits rapid assessments with minimal investment of cognitive resources, which can instead be allocated to the performance of other pressing tasks (Macrae, Milne, & Bodenhausen, 1994). Emphasizing stereotypic qualities in others also produces a feeling of orderliness in complex social stimuli, giving the perceiver a reassuring sense of the predictability of the social world. Moreover, because stereotypes so often emphasize negative attributes in the members of other groups, stereotyping can promote a sense of superiority, addressing the perceiver's ego needs (Tajfel & Turner, 1986). For these and other reasons (for reviews, see Bodenhausen & Macrae, 1996; Hamilton & Sherman, 1994), stereotyping others may come to be a dominant impulse in social perception. Indeed, Devine (1989) argued that stereotype activation is aptly viewed as a habit of mind that occurs automatically in the presence of members of stereotyped groups, irrespective of the intentions of the perceiver (see also Banaji & Greenwald, 1995; Bargh, 1997; Gilbert & Hixon, 1991). In line with this view, numerous studies now show that stereotypes about racial minorities, the elderly, women, and various other social groups are mentally activated merely by exposure to members of these groups (for recent reviews, see Bodenhausen, Macrae, & Garst, in press; Hilton & von Hippel, 1996).

At the same time, historical and political forces (e.g., the Civil Rights movement in the United States; the holocaust in Nazi Germany) have led many people to feel an aversion to stereotyping others, or at least to worry about the social disapproval that might result from public expressions of prejudice. Thus, as Devine (1989) emphasized, there is a tension between the automatic tendency toward stereotyping the members of other groups and the frequent desire on the part of perceivers to avoid the influence or expression of this tendency. Given that stereotypic impulses are highly likely to arise spontaneously in intergroup situations, how easily can they be disregarded? This question has guided a number of our empirical investigations in recent years. In what follows, we describe the results of several studies designed to examine the process and consequences of attempting to eradicate stereotypic influences on interpersonal assessments.

Forgetting Stereotypic Data: Memorial Consequences of Stereotype Suppression

Occasionally, we learn information that we later discover to be biased, mistaken, or irrelevant. In such cases, it would of course be adaptive not to use this information in making subsequent decisions. In the present context, consider a police officer who is called to testify in a criminal trial. Later, it is discovered that the officer has espoused racist views. The defendant in the trial is a member of an ethnic minority, so people following the trial (including the jurors, presumably) may want, retrospectively, to disregard aspects of the officer's testimony that may simply reflect his stereotypic preconceptions of the defendant. In essence, the stereotypic information becomes "inadmissible evidence," which the juror may seek to ignore, focusing instead on the remaining case information. Previous research does not offer much basis for optimism in assessing the prospects for success in disregarding discredited information (e.g., Golding & Hauselt, 1994; Hatvany & Strack, 1980; Wyer & Budesheim, 1987). However, perhaps given the motivation many perceivers possess to avoid the compunction and stigma associated with prejudice and stereotyping (Devine, Monteith, Zuwerink, & Elliott, 1991), they might be able to effectively ignore stereotypic evidence in forming social judgments.

Research and theory suggest that, although stereotype activation occurs relatively automatically, stereotype suppression is an effortful process. Devine's (1989) research suggested that the avoidance of stereotyping requires the deployment of deliberative, controlled processing strategies (see also Fiske, 1989). More generally, research on mental control points to the considerable amount of effort it can take to banish unwanted thoughts from mind (Wegner, 1994; Wegner & Pennebaker, 1993). If stereotype suppression is indeed effortful, this creates the potential for an ironic dilemma. If one assumes that the perceiver's pool of attentional resources is finite (e.g., Johnston & Heinz, 1978), it may be the case that the demands made by effortful processes on the perceiver's limited information-processing resources will leave less available capacity to be devoted to other mental tasks. Thus, working hard to put stereotypes out of mind, perceivers may actually be spending both less time and less mental energy attending to other, nonstereotypic information. To return to our previous analogy, they may be expending so much effort to avoid the influence of "inadmissible" evidence that they fail to make full use of the "admissible" evidence. In a recent pair of studies, we sought to test this possibility by directly examining the resource demands of stereotype suppression, and the consequences of suppression activity for memory of stereotypic and nonstereotypic information.

In an initial study (Macrae, Bodenhausen, Milne, & Wheeler, 1996, Experiment 1), we employed a dual-task paradigm. In the primary task, undergraduates were shown a picture of a target person and asked to form an impression of the individual while listening to an audiotaped description of him that was presented on headphones. The picture made it clear that the person was a skinhead, a social category with many strongly associated stereotypes. The taped description contained a core set of information that was irrelevant to stereotypes about skinheads and that was constant across all conditions. In "low stereotype" conditions, a single piece of stereotypic information was added to the profile; in "high stereotype" conditions, five pieces of stereotypic information were interspersed into the description. The control condition contained only the nonstereotypic data. Cross-cutting this manipulation was an instructional manipulation. Before listening to the tape, half of the participants were told that previous research indicated that our impressions of others are often influenced by stereotypic beliefs that are based on people's appearance, and they were asked to try to ignore this sort of information in forming their impressions of the target. The remaining (control) participants were given no particular instructions in this regard. Thus, the experiment had a 3 (stereotypic content; none, low, or high) × 2 (instruction; suppress or control) between-subjects design.

While completing the impression formation task, participants also were asked to do a probe reaction task. In this task, the participants monitored a computer screen. When a randomly initiated visual stimulus appeared on the screen, they hit a key to turn the stimulus "off" as quickly as possible. Several probe trials occurred unpredictably for each participant. Mean speed of performance on this secondary task was taken as an indicator of the availability of attentional capacity; if the primary task was using a lot of the perceivers' attentional resources, then their probe reaction times (RTs) should be noticeably slower (cf. Brown, 1964; Johnston & Heinz, 1978). Thus, if stereotype suppression is an effortful process, as we hypothesized, we should observe longer probe RTs among stereotype suppressors, especially to the extent that there is more to-be-suppressed material for them to deal with.

Our results, shown in Fig. 12.1, supported this prediction. Nonsuppressors' RTs were relatively fast and were equivalent, regardless of the stereotypicality of the description they heard. In the no stereotypic information condition, the suppressors' RTs were similarly fast. However, when they had stereotypic information to contend with, probe RTs for the suppressors became markedly slower. In the high stereotypic conditions, suppressors'

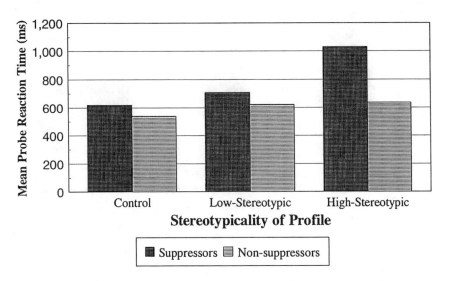

FIG. 12.1. Mean probe reaction time as a function of suppression instruction and stereotypicality of self-description profile. (Data from Macrae, Bodenhausen, Milne, & Wheeler, 1996, Experiment 1.)

probe RTs were nearly 400 ms longer than those of the nonsuppressors, a highly significant difference. The low stereotypic condition showed an intermediate pattern, as seen in the figure.

These results confirm that stereotype suppression is a resource-consuming affair. Given that attentional resources are being consumed by this suppression activity, our central hypothesis gains plausibility. To investigate whether stereotype suppression might ironically reduce the processing of nonstereotypic information, we used an incidental learning task. Upon completion of the impression formation task, participants were given a 5-minute distractor task, followed by a memory test for the nonstereotypic information in the target description they had heard previously. Our main prediction was that the same conditions where we observed diminished processing resources due to the demands of stereotype suppression would also show evidence of impaired memory for the nonstereotypic information. This was in fact the case (see Fig. 12.2). Nonsuppressors' memory for the nonstereotypic information was equivalent across informational conditions, but suppressors' memory for this information diminished as the amount of stereotypic information increased. When no stereotypic information was presented, suppressors and nonsuppressors recalled equivalent amounts of nonstereotypic information. However, in the high stereotypic conditions, suppressors correctly recalled 37% less information than the nonsuppressors, again a highly significant difference. Together, these results suggest that the effort requirements of stereotype suppression can result in some

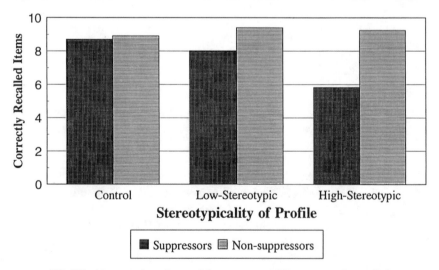

FIG. 12.2. Mean number of neutral (nonstereotypic) items correctly recalled as a function of suppression instruction and stereotypicality of self-description profile. (Data from Macrae, Bodenhausen, Milne, & Wheeler, 1996, Experiment 1.)

quite unintended consequences for memory. Specifically, trying not to rely on stereotypes can result in the neglect of nonstereotypic information, the very information that should be the focus of processing.

The probe reaction data clearly indicate that stereotype suppression is an effortful activity, but they do not specify exactly what type of effort is involved. Wegner's (1994) model of mental control suggests that one standard component of thought suppression is an "operating process" that works to move attention away from unwanted thoughts whenever they are detected. This process typically involves the identification of a suitable distractor thought that is free of unwanted content. Other effortful processes may be at work in the present context as well. For instance, participants may be consciously attempting to formulate strategies for the avoidance of stereotypes, or they may be devoting a fair amount of processing resources to the process of deciding whether or not a given thought is indeed stereotypic. Whatever the stereotype suppressors are doing, it appears to be a process that places constraints on their ability to respond quickly to a probe stimulus because of the resource demands involved, and it interferes with their processing of nonstereotypic material.

In a second study (Macrae et al., 1996, Experiment 2), we sought to extend upon these initial findings by assessing memory for stereotypic as well as for nonstereotypic information. In this study, participants completed only the impression formation task. In this case, they saw a photograph of an elderly man. Half were instructed to disregard age-related stereotypes, whereas the others were given no suppression instructions. The taped description they heard contained 12 stereotypic items (e.g., "likes to think about the good old days") and 18 nonstereotypic items (e.g., "likes to cook"). One week later, participants returned to the laboratory and were asked to complete a free recall task. The proportion of stereotypic and nonstereotypic information recalled was examined as a function of instructional condition. Replicating our first study, we found that stereotype suppressors recalled less of the nonstereotypic information than did nonsuppressors (mean proportions = .22 vs. .33, respectively). Adding to the irony, suppressors also recalled significantly more of the stereotypic information than did nonsuppressors (mean proportions = .48 vs. .34, respectively). Thus, although they were trying to disregard stereotypes, the suppressors ended up with memories of the target that consisted of more of the stereotypic information and less of the nonstereotypic information. The troubling implication of these findings is that even well-intentioned perceivers who want to put stereotypes aside may be prone to unintended memorial biases.

In the previously described experiments, explicit instructions were given to suppress stereotypes. It is conceivable that, in addition to imposing a cognitive goal, such instructions create some degree of social anxiety. Prejudice and bigotry are not appealing labels to most people, so perceivers may have concerns about their own reputations, should they not be able to comply with the experimental instructions to disregard stereotypic data. Because anxiety is known to have disruptive effects on performance (e.g., Darke, 1988), perhaps our participants' failure to comply with the disregard instructions was due largely to these sorts of anxieties. Such anxieties are also a part of the everyday world, so their operation would not trivialize the findings we reported. But another possibility may be that stereotypes are simply perversely potent and exert effects on information processing that are hard to resist, whether or not anxiety is involved. To examine this issue, we employed a standard directed-forgetting paradigm (e.g., Bjork, 1989; MacLeod, 1989). In this paradigm, participants study various stimuli, some of which they are subsequently instructed to forget. For example, they may be told that they were given some information in error, and they should ignore it (e.g., Golding & Hauselt, 1994). By adapting this kind of paradigm, we were able to create conditions in which participants are not told to disregard stereotypes per se, but rather are asked to disregard some information that is not relevant. In this procedure, the specter of stereotyping and bigotry is never raised, so anxieties about the reputational consequences of failing to inhibit stereotypic thoughts should not be an issue.

There are two standard versions of the directed-forgetting procedure— the item method and the list method (see Basden & Basden, this volume). We used the list method, in which participants are presented with two lists of stimuli. After the first list is presented, half the participants are told to disregard it and to focus only on the second list. The remaining participants are expected to learn both lists, receiving no instruction to disregard the first section. Some straightforward effects emerge in this situation (Basden & Basden, this volume; Bjork, 1989). First, participants who are told to disregard the first list tend to recall *less* of the material from that list than do participants who are asked to remember it. Second, participants who are told to disregard the first list tend to recall *more* of the material from the second list than do the people who are trying to remember both lists. Being able to forget about the first list, these participants are able to bring more resources to bear on the task of remembering the second list. What would happen, however, if the first list fortuitously consisted of stereotypic information? Would it be harder to put it out of mind?

A number of studies suggest that when stereotypes are activated, they tend to facilitate the encoding and storage of stereotype-consistent information (Fyock & Stangor, 1994; Macrae, Hewstone, & Griffiths, 1993), even if the stereotype activation occurs subliminally (Macrae et al., 1994b). Stereotypes appear to provide a framework for organizing judgment-relevant information (Bodenhausen, 1988; Bodenhausen & Wyer, 1985), and this function can occur in largely automatic, unintended ways. Thus, the instruction to forget stereotypic information could be more difficult to comply with, compared to cases where no stereotype was activated, simply because this information may be encoded and organized more coherently.

In one experiment (Macrae, Bodenhausen, Milne, & Ford, 1997), undergraduates were brought into the laboratory under the guise of pilot testing a number of tasks. The first task was allegedly a prose comprehension task in which each student was asked to read a brief newspaper article. Half of the students read about a child abuser (stereotype activation condition); the remainder read about driving laws in Ireland (control condition). Participants believed that they would be answering some questions about the passages later in the session. In the meantime, they were asked to complete an ostensibly unrelated list-learning task. In this task, students were asked to memorize a list of words to be presented via computer. The first 10 words ("list 1") consisted exclusively of words that had been shown by pretesting to be stereotypically associated with child abusers (e.g., "compulsive," "sordid"). The second 10 words ("list 2") consisted exclusively of words that, although matched in length, valence, and frequency of use, were not associated with child abusers (e.g., "insolent," "prejudiced").

Of critical interest was the question of whether participants would be able to disregard the stereotypic words after a relevant stereotype had been activated. If stereotypes automatically exert an organizing influence on information acquisition, it may be relatively more difficult to forget this information when a stereotype has been activated. To examine this issue empirically, an additional manipulation was introduced. For half of the participants, the experimenter apologetically explained, after the presentation of list 1, that participants had been given the wrong list, and that they should disregard all of these items and focus only on the next set of 10 items (i.e., list 2). Other participants were given no such instruction; therefore, they were attempting to remember all 20 items from both lists. After the study period, all participants spent 3 minutes on a distractor task (counting backward from 1000 by 3s) and then completed a memory test in which they were asked to recall as many items from *both* lists as possible.

When no stereotype was activated prior to the list-learning task, we expected to observe the standard findings seen in previous directed-forgetting studies of this sort (e.g., Bjork, 1989; Zacks & Hasher, 1994). That is, compared to participants who were attempting to remember both lists, participants who were told to disregard list 1 should show poorer memory for list 1 items, but enhanced memory for list 2 items. Proportional recall measures showed exactly this pattern, as illustrated in Fig. 12.3. But what about the cases where a relevant stereotype was activated? We hypothesized that disregarding stereotypic information would be more difficult because such information is relatively insistent, given the automatic processes that promote efficient encoding and organization of information with reference to stereotypic expectations. Thus, disregarding the stereotypic list 1

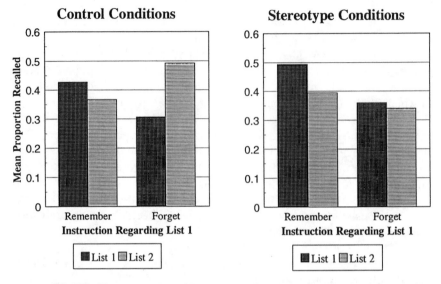

FIG. 12.3. Mean proportion of list 1 and list 2 items recalled as function of experimental instruction and the absence (left panel) or presence (right panel) of a previously activated stereotype. (Data from Macrae, Bodenhausen, Milne, & Ford, 1996, Experiment 1.)

may be harder to accomplish, disrupting the usual benefits that accrue to the processing of list 2. And indeed, this is what we found. When a stereotype was activated, participants in the disregard condition did seem to be able to forget the stereotypic list 1 words, in that they recalled proportionally fewer of these words than did the participants who were trying to remember list 1 (*Ms* = .36 vs. .49, respectively). However, when the to-be-forgotten material was rendered stereotypic (by the prior activation of a relevant stereotype), the forget instruction failed to facilitate the memorability of the list 2 information (*Ms* = .34 and .39 for the forget and remember instructions, respectively), as it had in the control condition. Normally, forgetting list 1 means that more attention and effort can be devoted to remembering list 2, but apparently when list 1 consisted of stereotype-relevant content, disregarding it was more difficult, and consequently, no benefits in list 2 processing were evident following the forget instruction. Instead, the forget instruction was associated with impaired performance on both lists.

Our interpretation of these data rests on the assumption that participants were eventually able to put the stereotypic concepts out of mind, but because of the relatively greater effort required to do so, their processing of the second list did not benefit from the forget instruction. This explanation implies that if people lack sufficient resources to work on pushing stereotypic notions out of mind, not only would the forget instruction fail to produce benefits in learning list 2, it might also fail entirely, producing superior memory for the to-be-disregarded list 1 (and thereby effectively reversing the typical pattern seen in directed-forgetting studies in the absence of any stereotypic expectations). To investigate this possibility, Macrae et al. (1997, Experiment 2) again investigated the impact of a "forget" instruction on memory performance, but we also included a manipulation of resource availability. Specifically, some participants completed the list-learning task under conditions of cognitive busyness created by an additional task. We assumed that this task would be especially disruptive to those participants striving to forget stereotypic stimuli, perhaps resulting in the precisely counterintentional outcome of greater recall of the to-be-forgotten words.

In this study, we again primed half of the participants with a particular stereotype ("child abuser") via an apparently unrelated prior task, then presented them with two 10-word lists to learn. As before, the first list consisted of 10 words that are stereotypic with respect to child abusers, and the second list consisted of 10 words that are irrelevant to such stereotypes. In this study, all students received the "forget" instructions immediately after the presentation of list 1. Thus, their conscious goal was always to forget list 1 and learn list 2. In addition, we introduced a new manipulation in this study. Half of the participants completed the list-learning task just as in the previous study (control, nonbusy condition), whereas the other half were given a concurrent task to perform (busy condition). Specifically, while learning the list 2 items, participants in this condition were required to keep a running count of the number of vowels that occurred in the stimulus list. Thus, these participants were trying simultaneously to forget list 1, learn list 2, and count vowels. This collection of tasks is probably challenging in general, but we expected it to be especially so in the condition where a stereotype had been activated, making the forget instruction more difficult to comply with.

Results are displayed in Fig. 12.4. Because the "nonbusy" conditions constituted an exact replication of the "forget" conditions from the previous experiment, we expected to find the same pattern of results. That was the case. In the absence of a stereotype, the forget instruction produced the expected result; list 2 was better recalled than list 1, suggesting that participants were able to forget list 1 and focus on list 2, as instructed. When a stereotype was activated, however, the enhanced memory for list 2 disappeared entirely. Of greater interest are the findings in the "busy" conditions. Once again, we see an ironically counterintentional pattern of memory. Specifically, when a stereotype was activated, those who were trying to forget list 1 and learn list 2 actually remembered more list 1 than list 2 items. In the absence of a stereotype, memory performance was similar for both lists, suggesting that the vowel counting task was sufficient to wipe out the usual benefit to list 2 processing that follows from an instruction to forget list 1.

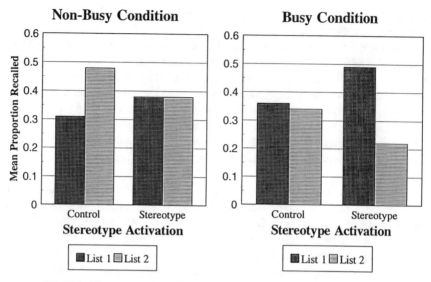

FIG. 12.4. Mean proportion of list 1 and list 2 items recalled as a function of stereotype activation and cognitive busyness. Note that all participants were instructed to forget list 1. (Data from Macrae, Bodenhausen, Milne, & Ford, 1996, Experiment 2.)

The fact that the pattern actually reverses under conditions of stereotype activation is of key importance. Once again, we see evidence that forgetting stereotypic material is a goal that is easily thwarted. And in these studies, the stereotypic material is not even explicitly linked to a stereotyped target (because the material seems to be just a list of disembodied trait terms), so anxieties about social desirability and reputation are irrelevant here. But such is the potency of stereotypic knowledge structures that they seem to capture relevant stimuli in a manner that renders them relatively difficult to forget. If sufficient resources are lacking to accomplish the effortful work of disregarding the stereotypic material, that material may actually end up being especially well remembered.

Inhibiting Stereotypic Inferences: Judgmental Consequences of Stereotype Suppression

Often it is our judgments and decisions about others that are of the greatest significance, rather than our memories pertaining to them. For instance, biased decisions about social targets in employment or legal settings would seem to be far more serious than biased memories about them per se. At the same time, memory and judgment are obviously intimately interconnected phenomena, and decisions and judgments may be heavily influenced by memorial representations and inferences drawn from them. Consider a juror who is trying hard to disregard stereotypic information in a trial. Given the memory data that we just reviewed, our hypothetical juror may ironically end up with enhanced memory for stereotypic evidence, while showing an impoverished memory for other kinds of testimony. When the time comes for the juror to render a verdict, there seems to be a real danger that judgments could be dominated by the unwanted but well-remembered stereotypic data, especially because the other, less well-learned material may not be available as input for deliberations.

More generally, people may want to avoid generating stereotypic inferences themselves. As an example, consider a faculty committee that is screening candidates for admission to graduate school. The ethnicity, sex, and age of such candidates is not considered an acceptable basis for admissions decisions, yet stereotypes exist suggesting that these demographic characteristics may be associated with performance-related attributes. For example, women may be stereotypically viewed as less mathematically sophisticated, or an older candidate may be seen as less flexible or slower in the acquisition of new career-related skills. Such assumptions may be totally invalid; indeed, even if there are "real" between-group differences lending credence to them, whether they apply in a particular individual's case is another matter entirely. Thus, committee members often want to avoid thinking these kinds of stereotypic thoughts, to be fair and unprejudiced to the candidates. Here, the challenge is no longer ignoring stereotypic information available in the social environment; rather, it is to inhibit self-generated stereotypic inferences. As previously noted, there is an impulse to stereotype that must be effortfully controlled.

To understand the prospects for successful self-regulation of inference and judgment processes, it is useful to turn to the growing literature on mental control (e.g., Baumeister & Newman, 1994; Wegner, 1994; Wegner & Pennebaker, 1993). Inspection of research on thought control in many different domains does not leave one feeling sanguine about the probable outcome of attempts to avoid stereotypic inferences and judgments. For example, Wegner (1994) reviewed evidence related to the control of negative moods, jealousy, thoughts about high-fat snack foods, and many other kinds of unwanted thoughts. Although controlling such thoughts does appear to be possible, it is also an objective fraught with peril, because time and again, the attempt to control unwanted thoughts has been shown to backfire. Dieters working hard not to think of junk food often end up bingeing on it, for instance.

Wegner and Erber (1992) provided an integrated explanation for the frequent failure of efforts at mental control. The key to their view is the notion of hyperaccessibility. In their view, the act of trying to suppress a given thought actually renders it more accessible in mind. Logically, if one is trying to avoid a particular thought, it must necessarily be the case that, at some level, they are keeping the unwanted thought in mind, as a criterion of what they are trying to avoid. We can only test whether a thought is wanted or unwanted by keeping in mind, even only at low levels of activation, some representation of what it is that we are trying to avoid. When we are actively trying not to stereotype a candidate for admission to graduate school, that means at some level we must check each of our thoughts about the candidate against a criterion of stereotypicality, and this must involve the frequent activation of stereotypic concepts. It is for this reason that the stereotype is rendered hyperaccessible. Wegner and Erber proposed that, as long as the perceiver has abundant processing resources available, attempts to avoid unwanted thoughts can work because the effortful attempt to distract oneself from any stereotypic thoughts that do emerge can be successful. However, if resources are constrained in some way, effortfully overriding the unwanted thought becomes problematic, and the hyperaccessibility of the unwanted thought can then result in its being even more intrusive on consciousness and judgment than if the perceiver had not tried to suppress it in the first place. This phenomenon is termed the "rebound effect."

An initial demonstration of the relevance of these processes to social stereotyping was provided by Wegner, Erber, and Bowman (as cited in Wegner, 1994). In their study, participants were asked to furnish completions of sentence stems pertaining to women (e.g., "Mary is popular because . . ."). Half of the participants were told to avoid sexist completions, whereas the remainder received no particular instructions in this regard. Crossed with this manipulation, half of the participants were required to respond immediately (i.e., high time pressure) whereas the others could respond at their leisure. All completions were coded in terms of how sexist they were, and comparisons were made across conditions. Wegner et al. reasoned that, with ample time to respond, participants could successfully avoid making stereotypic statements. However, with the imposition of a strict response deadline, effortful processes to censor stereotypic remarks might not be able to be executed. Under such conditions, the relatively automatic hyperaccessibility of the sexist concepts would go unchecked by effortful processes of self-censorship, so sexist remarks may actually be higher under this condition than if no suppression goal was being pursued. As expected, when time pressure was applied, those participants who had been instructed not to be sexist produced significantly more sexist sentences than those who had received no instructions vis-à-vis sexism.

The consequences of attempting to avoid stereotypic inferences were examined further in a series of studies conducted by Macrae, Bodenhausen, Milne, and Jetten (1994a). In one study, for example, we presented undergraduates with a photograph of a skinhead and asked them to write a projective passage about the person. Half of the students were instructed to avoid stereotypic inferences, whereas the remainder were given no special instructions about the content of their descriptions. No time pressure was imposed. Passages were subsequently coded for stereotypicality. As instructed, the stereotype suppressors produced significantly less stereotypic passages than the control group. Of key interest, however, was the possibility that the act of suppression, although ostensibly successful, may have resulted in heightened accessibility of stereotypic concepts that might carry over to subsequent tasks. To investigate this possibility, our participants were later asked to write another projective passage about a different skinhead. In this case, however, no suppression instructions were imposed. Examination of these second passages revealed an interesting reversal: The students who had previously been suppressing their skinhead stereotypes now wrote significantly *more* stereotypic passages than the nonsuppressors. Apparently, our participants were quite able to suppress stereotypic content in their passages while they were actively pursuing this goal. However, the suppression rendered the stereotypic concepts hyperaccessible, and when the suppression motivation dissipated, the hyperaccessibility of stereotypic concepts was not checked by any effortful self-censorship. Ironically, this hyperaccessibility led to even greater subsequent stereotyping than was observed among the nonsuppressors, who were free to stereotype to their hearts' content. Successful short-term suppression, then, may come at the cost of enhanced stereotype accessibility in the longer term, and this hyperaccessibility can have some rather unintended consequences.

To provide more direct evidence for the hyperaccessibility mechanism postulated to account for this rebound effect, Macrae et al. (1994a, Experiment 3) directly examined the consequences of stereotype suppression for the cognitive accessibility of stereotype contents. We had a new group of students complete the same projective passage task, either with or without instructions to suppress stereotypes about the target's social group. As before, suppression instructions did result in less stereotypic passages. Afterward, the students were asked to complete an apparently unrelated word verification task. In a standard lexical decision paradigm, participants were presented with a string of characters on a computer screen and simply asked for a decision as to whether the string was a word (e.g., "violent") or not a word (e.g., "loviten"). Of the strings that were actually words, half were words that were stereotypically associated with skinheads, whereas the others were nonstereotypic words that were matched in terms of length, valence, and frequency. If the stereotype activation occurred, one would expect heightened accessibility of stereotypic concepts. This would be reflected in faster lexical decision times. As expected, among baseline participants who did not complete the projective passage test but who simply did the lexical decision task, there was no difference in lexical decision times as a function of stereotypicality of the words. Among participants who completed the projective passage without any suppression instruction, lexical decision times for the stereotypic terms were significantly faster than for the nonstereotypic terms. Because these participants were free to use stereotypes in their passages (and did so), it was not surprising that stereotypic concepts showed evidence of heightened accessibility. Of greatest interest, however, is the fact that among the stereotype suppressors who actively strove not think stereotypic thoughts about the target, lexical decision times for the stereotypic terms were significantly faster even than in the nonsuppression condition. The act of suppression did indeed seem to make stereotypic concepts hyperaccessible, and this can explain why subsequent information processing is ironically colored by stereotypic notions to a greater degree among suppressors than among nonsuppressors.

Preventing Discriminatory Actions: Behavioral Consequences of Stereotype Suppression

The desire to inhibit stereotypic reactions is perhaps most pressing in conditions of intergroup contact. When we are actively interacting with a member of a stereotyped social group, such as an ethnic minority group, we may be keenly aware of the possibility of biased or prejudicial responses, and we may seek very actively to avoid doing anything that may look like a manifestation of prejudice or bias. Assuming that we have a clear goal of stereotype suppression in place *and* ample processing resources to pursue it, there is no reason why such laudable goals cannot meet with success. However, the demands of ongoing social interaction are often considerable, and if they consume too large a portion of cognitive resources, unwanted rebound effects may be a very real danger.

As a first step toward examining the possible behavioral consequences of stereotype suppression, Macrae et al. (1994a, Experiment 2) again asked participants to construct a projective passage about a skinhead depicted in a photograph, either with or without suppression instructions. In line with the previously described findings, it was expected that suppressors would be able to produce less stereotypic passages (and they were), but the suppression activity was also expected to render skinhead stereotypes hyperaccessible and thus more likely to influence subsequent interactions with members of this group. One of the most commonly used behavioral indices of intergroup attitudes is social distance (e.g., Triandis, 1977). In general, the preference for greater distance is typical with groups to whom negative characteristics are attributed. Segregation, in turn, plays a major and insidious role in the perpetuation of negative intergroup climates (e.g., Massey & Denton, 1993). In this study, we used social distance as a simple but potentially important behavioral index.

Upon completion of the projective passage, participants were told that they would next be engaging in a "get acquainted" interaction with the person whom they had been writing about in the previous task (i.e., the skinhead). To this end, they were ushered to a different lab room where the interaction was to take place. Upon arrival there, it was discovered that the room was empty, but on one chair there were various items of skinhead paraphernalia presumably belonging to the target person. At this point, the experimenter indicated that the other person would be right back and asked the participant to take a seat and wait for him to return. Several different seats were available; of key interest was the distance between the skinhead's seat and the one selected by the participant. If stereotype suppression does indeed render negative stereotypes about skinheads highly accessibility, it may have the consequence of leading suppressors to prefer a greater social distance than nonsuppressors. This was indeed the case. There was a significant tendency for the stereotype suppressors to sit further away from the skinhead than the nonsuppressors.

Obviously, this study is only an initial and fairly preliminary foray into the question of how stereotype suppression plays out in the complex domain of intergroup contact. However, it does clearly indicate that the kinds of ironic and unintended consequences that we observed with respect to memory and inference can also be manifested in behavior.

SUMMARY AND CONCLUSIONS

The use of stereotypes and other mental short cuts has both costs and benefits for the social perceiver (see Sherman & Corty, 1984, for an extensive summary). Noteworthy among the benefits of stereotype use is the streamlined efficiency they can confer on processes of social perception and the satisfying sense of orderliness and predictability they can confer on the complex social environment in which we live. However, for a variety of reasons, reliance upon many forms of stereotyping has become increasingly unpalatable in the modern world and can impose costs in the form of social disapproval and scorn as well as feelings of guilt and compunction (Devine et al., 1991). To avoid such costs, perceivers may adopt the laudable goal of avoiding stereotypic influences, but it seems that such influences are tenacious and often resistant to the perceiver's self-regulatory efforts. To be sure, these efforts can succeed, at least in the short-term, when sufficient processing resources are available for their execution. But as we have seen, memory, inference, and behavior can be affected in a precisely counterintentional fashion when processing resources are compromised, or when suppression motivation dissipates over time. These findings suggest that a full functional analysis of the costs and benefits of stereotype use will also require a consideration of the costs and benefits of their attempted disuse.

It is clearly premature to be entirely pessimistic about the social perceiver's ability to disregard stereotypic impulses and operate on the basis of other, more evidence-driven kinds of interpersonal assessments. Devine's (1989) model suggests that practice is a key element of success in breaking the prejudice habit. Low-prejudice persons who consistently strive to inhibit their stereotypes about women and minorities may gain skill that allows them to circumvent the negative consequences of hyperaccessibility evident in our studies (cf. Monteith, 1993). And many important questions remain to be addressed, such as the duration of hyperaccessibility effects. What is now abundantly clear, however, is that disregarding social stereotypes is no simple matter, and much remains to be learned about the factors that determine whether the pursuit of this goal will be met with success or failure.

REFERENCES

Banaji, M. R., & Greenwald, A. G. (1995). Implicit gender stereotyping in judgments of fame. *Journal of Personality and Social Psychology, 68*, 181–198.

Bargh, J. A. (1997). The automaticity of everyday life. In R. S. Wyer, Jr. (Ed.), *Advances in social cognition* (Vol. 10, pp. 1–61). Mahwah, NJ: Lawrence Erlbaum Associates.

Baumeister, R. F., & Newman, L. S. (1994). Self-regulation of cognitive inference and decision processes. *Personality and Social Psychology Bulletin, 20*, 3–19.

Bjork, R. A. (1989). Retrieval inhibition as an adaptive mechanism in human memory. In H. L. Roediger, III, & F. I. M. Craik (Eds.), *Varieties of memory and consciousness: Essays in honor of Endel Tulving* (pp. 309–330). Hillsdale, NJ: Lawrence Erlbaum Associates.

Bodenhausen, G. V. (1988). Stereotypic biases in social decision making and memory: Testing process models of stereotype use. *Journal of Personality and Social Psychology, 55*, 726–737.

Bodenhausen, G. V., & Macrae, C. N. (1996). The self-regulation of intergroup perception: Mechanisms and consequences of stereotype suppression. In C. N. Macrae, M. Hewstone, & C. Stangor (Eds.), *Foundations of stereotypes and stereotyping* (pp. 227–253). New York: Guilford.

Bodenhausen, G. V., Macrae, C. N., & Garst, J. (in press). Stereotypes in thought and deed: Social-cognitive origins of intergroup discrimination. In C. Sedikides, C. Insko, & J. Schopler (Eds.), *Intergroup cognition and intergroup behavior*. Mahwah, NJ: Lawrence Erlbaum Associates.

Bodenhausen, G. V., & Wyer, R. S., Jr. (1985). Effects of stereotypes on decision making and information-processing strategies. *Journal of Personality and Social Psychology, 48*, 267–282.

Brown, I. D. (1964). The measurement of perceptual load and reserve capacity. *Transactions of the Association of Industrial Medical Officers, 14*, 44–49.

Carver, C. S., & Scheier, M. F. (1981). *Attention and self-regulation: A control-theory approach to human behavior*. New York: Springer-Verlag.

Darke, S. (1988). Anxiety and working memory capacity. *Cognition & Emotion, 2*, 145–154.

Devine, P. G. (1989). Stereotypes and prejudice: Their automatic and controlled components. *Journal of Personality and Social Psychology, 56*, 5–18.

Devine, P. G., Monteith, M. J., Zuwerink, J. R., & Elliot, A. J. (1991). Prejudice with and without compunction. *Journal of Personality and Social Psychology, 60*, 817–830.

Fiske, S. T. (1989). Examining the role of intent: Toward understanding its role in stereotyping and prejudice. In J. S. Uleman & J. A. Bargh (Eds.), *Unintended thought* (pp. 253–286). New York: Guilford.

Fox, R. (1992). Prejudice and the unfinished mind: A new look at an old failing. *Psychological Inquiry, 3*, 137–152.

Freud, S. (1933). *New introductory lectures on psychoanalysis*. New York: Norton.

Fyock, J., & Stangor, C. (1994). The role of memory biases in stereotype maintenance. *British Journal of Social Psychology, 33*, 331–343.

Gilbert, D. T., & Hixon, J. G. (1991). The trouble of thinking: Activation and application of stereotypic beliefs. *Journal of Personality and Social Psychology, 60*, 509–517.

Golding, J. M., & Hauselt, J. (1994). When instructions to forget become instructions to remember. *Personality and Social Psychology Bulletin, 20*, 178–183.

Hamilton, D. L., & Sherman, J. W. (1994). Stereotypes. In R. S. Wyer, Jr., & T. K. Srull (Eds.), *Handbook of social cognition* (2nd ed., Vol. 2, pp. 1–68). Hillsdale, NJ: Lawrence Erlbaum Associates.

Hardin, G. (1968). The tragedy of the commons. *Science, 162*, 1243–1248.

Harris, M., & Ross, E. B. (1987). *Food and evolution: Toward a theory of human food habits*. Philadelphia: Temple University Press.

Hatvany, N., & Strack, F. (1980). The impact of a discredited key witness. *Journal of Applied Social Psychology, 10*, 490–509.

Hilton, J. L., & von Hippel, W. (1996). Stereotypes. *Annual Review of Psychology, 47*, 237–271.

Hobbes, T. (1968). *Leviathan*. Baltimore, MD: Penguin Books. (Original work published 1651)

Johnston, W. A., & Heinz, S. P. (1978). Flexibility and capacity demands of attention. *Journal of Experimental Psychology: General, 107*, 420–435.

Komorita, S. S., & Parks, C. D. (1994). *Social dilemmas*. Madison, WI: Brown & Benchmark.

MacLeod, C. M. (1989). Directed forgetting affects both direct and indirect tests of memory. *Journal of Experimental Psychology: Learning, Memory, and Cognition, 15*, 13–21.

Macrae, C. N., Bodenhausen, G. V., Milne, A. B., & Ford, R. L. (1997). On the regulation of recollection: The intentional forgetting of stereotypical memories. *Journal of Personality and Social Psychology, 72*, 709–719.

Macrae, C. N., Bodenhausen, G. V., Milne, A. B., & Jetten, J. (1994a). Out of mind but back in sight: Stereotypes on the rebound. *Journal of Personality and Social Psychology, 67*, 808–817.

Macrae, C. N., Bodenhausen, G. V., Milne, A. B., & Wheeler, V. (1996). On resisting the temptation for simplification: Counterintentional effects of stereotype suppression on social memory. *Social Cognition, 14*, 1–20.

Macrae, C. N., Hewstone, M., & Griffiths, R. J. (1993). Processing load and memory for stereotype-based information. *European Journal of Social Psychology, 23*, 77–87.

Macrae, C. N., Milne, A. B., & Bodenhausen, G. V. (1994b). Stereotypes as energy-saving devices: A peek inside the cognitive toolbox. *Journal of Personality and Social Psychology, 66*, 37–47.

Massey, D., & Denton, N. (1993). *American apartheid: Segregation and the making of the underclass*. Cambridge, MA: Harvard University Press.

Miller, G. A., Galanter, E., & Pribram, K. H. (1960). *Plans and the structure of behavior*. New York: Holt, Rinehart & Winston.

Monteith, M. J. (1993). Self-regulation of prejudiced responses: Implications for progress in prejudice-reduction efforts. *Journal of Personality and Social Psychology, 65*, 469–485.

Reynolds, V., Falger, V. S. E., & Vine, I. (Eds.). (1987). *The sociobiology of ethnocentrism: Evolutionary dimensions of xenophobia, discrimination, racism, and nationalism*. London: Croom Helm.

Sherman, S. J., & Corty, E. (1984). Cognitive heuristics. In R. S. Wyer, Jr., & T. K. Srull (Eds.), *Handbook of social cognition* (1st ed., Vol. 1, pp. 189–286). Hillsdale, NJ: Lawrence Erlbaum Associates.

Tajfel, H., & Turner, J. C. (1986). The social identity theory of intergroup behavior. In S. Worchel & W. G. Austin (Eds.), *Psychology of intergroup relations* (2nd ed., pp. 7–24). Chicago: Nelson-Hall.

Triandis, H. C. (1977). *Interpersonal behavior*. Monterey, CA: Brooks/Cole.

Wegner, D. M. (1994). Ironic processes of mental control. *Psychological Review, 101*, 34–52.

Wegner, D. M., & Erber, R. (1992). The hyperaccessibility of suppressed thoughts. *Journal of Personality and Social Psychology, 63*, 903–912.

Wegner, D. M., & Pennebaker, J. W. (Eds.). (1993). *Handbook of mental control*. Englewood Cliffs, NJ: Prentice-Hall.

Wyer, R. S., & Budesheim, T. L. (1987). Person memory and judgment: The impact of information that one is told to disregard. *Journal of Personality and Social Psychology, 53,* 14–29.

Zacks, R. T., & Hasher, L. (1994). Directed ignoring: Inhibitory regulation of working memory. In D. Dagenbach & T. Carr (Eds.), *Inhibitory mechanisms in attention, memory, and language* (pp. 241–264). San Diego, CA: Academic Press.

13

INSTRUCTIONS TO DISREGARD POTENTIALLY USEFUL UNSHARED INFORMATION IN A GROUP CONTEXT

Jonathan M. Golding
University of Kentucky

Alan L. Ellis
San Francisco State University

Jerry Hauselt
Southern Connecticut State University

Sandra A. Sego
University of Kentucky

Individuals are often asked to form impressions about others and about actions that will affect them. Often, these impressions are developed with input from other individuals. For example, imagine a situation in which two colleagues meet to discuss a job applicant for a position in their organization. The task focuses on each individual sharing information about their impressions of the individual being considered. How is this information presented and how does it influence their mutual impression? Of particular interest in the current study is how information that is shared by all members of a group influences their mutual impression as compared to information that only some of the group possess (i.e., unshared information). The importance of this issue is evidenced by the increasing attention being paid to how groups sample shared and unshared information (e.g., Larson, Foster-Fishman, & Keys, 1994; Stasser, 1992; Stasser & Stewart, 1992; Stasser, Taylor, & Hanna, 1989; Stasser & Titus, 1985, 1987).

Most likely, each individual will possess some combination of shared and unshared information. For example, both might know that the job applicant completed his degree in less than 4 years, but only one knows that he is often perceived as argumentative. In general, it has been found that tasks requiring a group decision[1] lead to greater dissemination of shared information than of unshared information (e.g., Larson et al., 1994; Laughlin & Ellis, 1986; Stasser & Titus, 1985, 1987). As an illustration, Stasser et al. (1989) found that, on average, group discussions contained 46% of the shared information and only 18% of the unshared information. Stasser et al. (1989) also found that the ratio of shared to unshared information had little effect on the final group decision and that prediscussion preferences using a majority or plurality decision scheme (Davis, 1973; Laughlin & Ellis, 1986) predicted 84% of the group decisions.

The failure to disseminate unshared information in groups leads to a "hidden profile" (Stasser, 1988), a superior alternative that exists but is hidden from the individual group members because they each have only a portion of the information that supports the alternative. In general, the hidden profile has not manifested itself in studies involving judgments, but recent research suggested that this may not always be the case. Stasser and Stewart (1992) found that unshared information dealing with solving a murder mystery will be disseminated in an intellective task (i.e., determining a correct solution to a problem) compared to a judgment task (i.e., determining a likely answer to the problem) in which participants were told that there may not have been enough information to determine what was the correct answer (see also Laughlin & Ellis, 1986, for a discussion of the differences between intellective and judgment tasks). It would appear that if a group believes that there is a correct answer, they are particularly receptive to new information, and may be willing to enhance the apparent relevance of the unshared information (Stasser & Stewart, 1992).

One might expect that, in addition to the nature of the task (intellective vs. judgmental), the nature of the information presented could influence the apparent relevance of unshared information, and the likelihood that such information will be presented to the group. For example, Stasser (1992) conducted a computer simulation of 100 groups and found that the saliency of the unshared information had relatively little impact on the group judgments, except in the case of smaller groups (in this case, four-person groups). This finding suggests that even when unshared information is salient, it is unlikely to affect most group judgments.

Even so, it seems likely that certain characteristics of unshared information may influence its relevance and dissemination in the group. The importance of judging relevance is to prevent irrelevant information from inter-

---

[1]The term *decision* is, at times, used interchangeably with *impression* and *judgment* to indicate that a group of individuals have come to a collective agreement about either another person (Experiments 1A, 2A, and 3) or a company contract (Experiments 1B and 2B).

fering with individual performance (Bjork, 1972), thereby facilitating effective integration of information in group settings (Kaplan & Miller, 1983). The ability to differentiate relevant and irrelevant information is usually based on implicit cues. For example, in a given conversation, the topic of the conversation is relevant, whereas "side comments" are often irrelevant. There are instances, however, in which explicit cues are used to distinguish the two. In the initial example, the person who heard that the applicant is argumentative (i.e., unshared information) may have been told to "disregard" this information because it was "confidential." In this case, the to-be-disregarded information was explicitly designated "irrelevant." In discussing the job candidate, the individual is faced with whether or not to disseminate the confidential information, which is likely to be a critical determinant in the mutual impression that is reached.

Although the use of explicit cues may be important to the dissemination of information in a group context, no research has specifically investigated this issue. There has been, however, a great deal of research on the effectiveness of explicit cues to differentiate relevant and irrelevant information at the individual level. This research investigated directed forgetting (see Bjork, 1972 for an early review; Johnson, 1994). Specifically, explicit cues (e.g., the letters "RRRR" for remember vs. "FFFF" for forget) are presented during study to designate unrelated words as either "to be forgotten" or "to be remembered." Following the presentation of the items, memory is typically tested for both types of information. The results indicated a decrease in recall of the to-be-forgotten words coupled with an increase in recall of the to-be-remembered words; the "directed-forgetting effect."

The primary purpose of the current set of experiments was to investigate what characteristics might increase the likelihood that unshared information would be presented in smaller (two-person) and larger (six-person) groups and would therefore affect their mutual decision. Specifically, the current study sought to address the question of whether unshared information might be disseminated as a function of the situational context (i.e., pragmatics) in which the unshared information was presented. The term pragmatics refers to information that guides the use of language in context, such as knowledge about the speaker (e.g., his or her intentions, beliefs, and knowledge of and attitude toward the listener), and information about the relationship between the speaker and the listener (Keenan, MacWhinney, & Mayhew, 1977; van Dijk, 1980).

The likelihood that pragmatics will influence the dissemination of unshared information is based on findings from a number of areas in group research. For example, although not dealing with unshared information, studies investigating mock jurors' use of inadmissible evidence shows how the situational context (i.e., an instruction to disregard inadmissible evidence) associated with a particular piece of evidence influences the use of that evidence. The results from these studies found that the instruction to disregard is extremely *ineffective* in keeping jurors from using this evidence when making individual judgments (e.g., Sue, Smith, & Caldwell, 1973; Thompson, Fong, & Rosenhan, 1981), or disseminating this evidence during deliberations (e.g., Caretta & Moreland, 1983). It is likely that jurors perceive the to-be-disregarded information as relevant to the verdict to be rendered (see also Devine & Ostrom, 1985), perhaps even more so because it has been explicitly "flagged."

In the present study, the question of the conditions under which participants would consider the unshared information to be relevant based on pragmatics is addressed. In the five experiments, each participant was a member of a relatively small group. In Experiments 1A, 1B, 2A, and 2B, the group size was two, so that the unshared information would not be heard by a majority or minority within the group. In Experiment 3, the group size was six, so that the unshared information would be heard by a clear minority (one or two group members) in all cases. The participants received information about a fictitious target person (Experiments 1A, 2A, and 3) or a company contract (Experiments 1B and 2B) and were asked to form an impression of the target person or contract. The presentation of the information was similar to other research on directed forgetting (see Basden, Basden, & Gargano, 1993), which used a list method of presentation. In the two-person groups (dyads), one participant in the dyad was in a no-presentation condition and received a set of positive and neutral items (i.e., the shared set). The other dyad member was either in the same no-presentation condition or was in one of three other experimental conditions that received the shared set plus an unshared set of negative items. These experimental conditions reflected whether a group member was given the unshared information and told nothing about it (no-disregard) or was told to disregard the unshared information. The relevance of the information in the disregard conditions was manipulated as a function of whether the unshared information was true but confidential, or was incorrect. In other words, unshared information was still relevant when deemed confidential, but should not be perceived as relevant when presented as incorrect. For the six-person groups, one or two group members were in an experimental condition, whereas the remaining group members were in the no-presentation condition.

The use of negative information in the unshared set of items served to make the evaluative nature of the unshared information distinct from the shared information. As a result, participants who received unshared information that was relevant (i.e., the confidential and no-disregard participants) should perceive the target person or contract more negatively than those who either perceived the same negative information as irrelevant (i.e., the incorrect participants) or did not receive the unshared information (no-presentation participants). This pattern of evaluation was used in previous research investigating instructions to disregard behaviors during an impression formation task (e.g., Golding, Fowler, Long, & Latta, 1990; Golding & Hauselt, 1994; Golding, Sego, Hauselt, & Long, 1994). The dependent measures of interest included (a) how often the unshared items were introduced during group discussion, (b) how often self-generated statements related to or consistent with the unshared information were introduced during group discussion, and (c) group ratings involving evaluative judgments (e.g., person impression judgments).

Previous findings (e.g., Stasser, 1992) suggest that little of the unshared information would be disseminated during group discussion involving judgments. As a result, the unshared information would have little impact on the final impressions of the group. However, the same research does indicate that, for smaller groups (e.g., four members), unshared information may be disseminated and consequently may impact the final judgment when it is relatively salient or highlighted. Although the present study investigated the dissemination of unshared information in relatively small groups, the change of context from Stasser's previous studies limits the absolute comparability between his paradigm and that of the present study. For example, unlike Stasser et al. (1989) and Stasser and Stewart (1992), the shared and unshared information in the present study were not approximately equal in average desirability. In fact, in the present study, the shared information was always positive (or neutral) and the unshared information was always negative. The oppositional nature of the unshared information may lead participants who perceive the unshared information as relevant (confidential and no-disregard group members) to disseminate it, leading to the group's use of the unshared information in reaching a decision. Therefore, the current study suggests that the evaluative nature of the unshared information is important in affecting its dissemination along with its perceived relevancy (as determined by pragmatics).

EXPERIMENTS IA AND IB

Two experiments are presented simultaneously because of the similarity in method and results. Experiment 1A investigated the question of interest in a person-impression context; Experiment 1B used an object-impression context (i.e., a company contract). The results of the two studies should provide convergence and replication, in that they were highly similar procedurally.

The stimulus materials for Experiment 1A were a subset of behaviors used in Wyer and Unverzagt (1985). The 18 behaviors were divided into three sets: (a) The honest set included 4 honest behaviors (e.g., Returned a wallet containing $50 to the lost and found), (b) the neutral set included 10 behaviors rated as neutral with regard to honesty and unkindness (e.g.,

Exercised daily), and (c) the unkind set included 4 unkind behaviors (e.g., Made fun of a disabled person). The honest and neutral sets together are the "shared" set of behaviors; the unkind set is the "unshared" set of behaviors. When both unshared and shared information were presented, the order of behavior sets was unkind–neutral–honest. When only shared information was presented, the neutral set preceded the honest set.

For Experiment 1B, the materials were those used in Experiment 2 of Golding et al. (1990). The 15 statements were divided into three sets of 5 behaviors each. The assembly line workers set included statements rated "good" for assembly line workers (e.g., An increase in paid vacation time from 2 to 3 weeks for assembly line workers). The board of directors set included statements rated "good" for a board of directors (e.g., An increase in paid lunch period from 45 minutes to an hour for those on the board of directors). The neutral set consisted of statements rated good for both assembly line workers and the board of directors (e.g., Company participation in the Special Olympics). The assembly line workers and neutral sets together are the "shared" statements, and the board of directors set is the "unshared" set. When both unshared and shared information were presented, the order of sets was board of directors–neutral–assembly line workers. When only shared information was presented, the neutral set preceded the assembly line workers set.

These two experiments used two-person groups, or dyads. For each dyad, one participant was always presented information in the no-presentation condition, whereas the other participant was presented information in one of the three experimental conditions (i.e., confidential, incorrect, no-disregard) or was also presented information in the no-presentation condition (i.e., control condition). There were nine dyads in each of the experimental and control conditions. Table 13.1 presents the four experimental conditions.

On entering the laboratory, the participants were separated. Each participant was brought into a small room by one of the experimenters. Par-

TABLE 13.1
Order (From Left to Right) of Information Presented to Participants

Condition	Information			
Conf	Unkind behaviors	Forget instruction and justification	Neutral behaviors	Honest behaviors
Inc	Unkind behaviors	Forget instruction and justification	Neutral behaviors	Honest behaviors
No-Dis	Unkind behaviors	-----------------	Neutral behaviors	Honest behaviors
No-Pres	------------	-----------------	Neutral behaviors	Honest behaviors

Note. Conf = confidential condition; Inc = incorrect condition; No-Dis = no-disregard condition; and No-Pres = no-presentation condition.

ticipants in Experiment 1A were told that the experiment involved role playing, and that they were to put themselves in the position of a person who was to meet a man named "John Pennebaker" for the first time. The experimenter said she was going to tell them things about Pennebaker and that the participants were to form an impression of Pennebaker because later they would discuss Pennebaker with their partner and then together answer a few questions about him. The experimenter then read behaviors about Pennebaker, at a rate of one every 6 seconds.

Participants in Experiment 1B were also involved in a role-playing task. They were told, however, that the study concerned how small groups make judgments about company contracts. The participants were told to pretend to be assembly line workers, while the experimenter said she was a lawyer for the board of directors of the company. The participants were told to evaluate each issue and its implication for their vote on the contract, and to form an impression of what it would be like to work for this company. They were told that later they would discuss the contract with their partner, and then together answer a few questions about the contract.

At this point, for both experiments, the procedure varied depending on the specific condition. For participants in the no-disregard and no-presentation conditions, the experimenter read through the appropriate sets of items. For participants in the confidential and incorrect conditions, the experimenter stopped after reading the unshared set of items. Participants in the confidential condition were instructed that the items just read were not supposed to have been read because they were confidential. Moreover, the participants were instructed to disregard the items just read. The experimenter then started reading the shared set of items. Participants in the incorrect condition were told that the items just read were not supposed to have been read because they were incorrect (e.g., about someone other than Pennebaker). They too were instructed to disregard the items just read, and then the experimenter started reading the shared set of items.

After hearing the appropriate sets of items (depending on condition), participants were given a 5-minute distractor task. During this time, they were given a sheet of paper and asked to draw a map of the United States, and to label the states on the map. Following the intervening task, the participants made seven prediscussion judgments. For Experiment 1A, these judgments concerned how much they would like Pennebaker. In addition, the judgments included two adjectives (honest and untrustworthy) that dealt with the trait of honesty, two adjectives (unkind and friendly) that dealt with the trait of kindness, and two adjectives (intelligence and hard-working nature) that were filler items describing traits unrelated to the behaviors presented to the participants. Participants rated the target person on these adjectives, which were always presented in the same random order, using a scale from 1 (not at all) to 10 (extremely). For Experiment 1B, participants rated how likely it was that they would vote for the contract on a 1 (extremely unlikely) to 10 (extremely likely) scale. Then they rated the contract with respect to three other questions, presented in a single random order. The first question dealt with rating the contract on whether it was "good" for assembly line workers, and a second question dealt with rating the contract on whether it was "good" for the board of directors; both questions were rated on a 1 (extremely bad) to 10 (extremely good) scale. The final question asked whether they would recommend this company to someone looking for work using a 1 (definitely would not recommend) to 10 (definitely would recommend) scale.

Upon completion of the rating task, one of the participants was taken to the room where their partner was located. This room was equipped with a one-way mirror, behind which was a video camera. Participants were not informed that they were being videotaped. The pair of participants was given a sheet of paper that contained the prediscussion questions with no rating scales. They were told to discuss these questions, and that after their discussion, they would be asked to answer each question with a single dyad score. The experimenter left the room and the participants were given either 3 minutes (Experiment 1A) or 2 minutes (Experiment 1B) to discuss the questions. After the discussion period, the experimenter returned, gave the participants the rating scale, and told the participants to answer each question with a single score. The experimenter left the room while the participants answered the questions. After answering these questions as a dyad, the participants were again separated and asked to answer the questions once more individually (i.e., postdiscussion judgments; the pre- and postdiscussion judgments were not analyzed). Finally, participants were informed about the videotaping, given the opportunity to have the tape erased immediately, and a video consent sheet was presented to participants to obtain their permission to use the videotapes as data. All participants consented to the use of the videotape data. Informal discussions with all participants indicated that participants had no difficulty taking part in the role playing, including (for the participants told to disregard information) the portion of the role playing in which they were instructed to disregard information.

For Experiment 1A, three scores were averaged to yield a composite evaluation score ranging from 1 (negative) to 10 (positive). These scores were the likeability score, the average of the honesty and (after reverse scoring) untrustworthiness scores, and the average of the friendliness and (after reverse scoring) unkindness scores. The reliability (Cronbach's alpha) of the three dyad scores was .82. The filler judgments were not scored.

For Experiment 1B, the scores for voting for the contact, good for Assembly Line Workers, (after reverse scoring) good for Board of Directors, and recommend the company, were averaged to yield a composite evaluation score ranging from 1 (negative) to 10 (positive). The reliability (Cronbach's alpha) of these four dyad scores was .77.

The videotapes of the dyad interactions were scored in two ways.[2] First, the number of times a presented statement was introduced by each dyad member was coded. Two individuals naive to the experimental hypotheses scored each tape. For Experiment 1A using the unkind set of statements, the correlation between the scorers was .93; for Experiment 1B using the board of directors set of statements, the correlation between scorers was .97.

Second, the scoring included a count of the self-generated statements that were consistent with the unshared information. In Experiment 1A, such a statement as "He wasn't very nice" would be negative. To assess reliability (Rosenthal, 1982), two individuals naive to the experimental hypotheses watched each tape separately and wrote down all the evaluative statements they heard, without categorizing them as negative or positive. Two other individuals scored each of the evaluative statements as either negative or positive, and the correlation between these two scorers for negative statements was .99. Using the scoring of these latter individuals, we were able to calculate the correlations for the individuals who wrote down the evaluative statements from the videotapes. The correlations were .92 for the negative statements.

In Experiment 1B, the self-generated statements that were consistent with the unshared information were categorized as being anticontract from the worker's perspective. Anticontract statements included statements specifically against the contract or in favor of the board of directors (e.g., "The contract was bad."). Two individuals naive to the experimental hypotheses watched each tape and wrote down (in a single list) all the anticontract and procontract statements they heard. Two other individuals scored each of these statements for whether they were anticontract. The correlation between the latter scorers for anticontract statements was .93. Using the scoring of these latter individuals, the correlation for the individuals who wrote down the statements from the videotapes was .85 for the anticontract statements.

Introduction of Presented Unshared Items

The number of presented unshared items introduced during the dyad discussion by the experimental dyad member who heard the unshared information (averaged across scorers) is presented in Table 13.2. It should be noted that because only one participant per dyad who was presented the

---

[2]For all experiments, the dissemination data were scored and analyzed for the number of shared presented items introduced by the experimental group members and for the number of positive self-generated items introduced by the experimental and no-presentation group members. In general, these analyses found no reliable effects of pragmatics.

TABLE 13.2
Mean Number of Items and Standard Deviations (in Parentheses)
Introduced by the Experimental Group Member During the
Group Discussion in Experiments 1A and 1B

	Confidential		Incorrect		No-Disregard	
Experiment 1A						
Unshared Presented Behaviors	2.00	(2.15)	0.17	(0.35)	3.44	(1.93)
Negative Self-Generated Behaviors	4.89	(3.27)	0.42	(0.70)	5.03	(3.64)
Experiment 1B						
Board of Directors Presented Statements	1.28	(1.66)	0.00	(0.00)	1.28	(1.34)
Anticontract Self-Generated Statements (Positive Board of Directors/Negative Contract)	3.06	(2.56)	0.72	(0.67)	2.31	(1.78)

unshared information was analyzed (thus, making dyad the unit of analysis),
the assumption of independence for this analysis was not violated. In Experiment 1A (the top half of Table 13.2), more unshared items were introduced in confidential than in incorrect dyads. The same result was shown
in Experiment 1B (the bottom half of Table 13.2). In addition, the number of
unshared items disseminated in no-disregard dyads was greater than that
introduced in the confidential condition in Experiment 1A, and greater than
that introduced by the incorrect dyads in both experiments.

These results offer strong support for the view that perceiving unshared
information as relevant affects whether this information will be introduced
during dyad discussion. Unshared information perceived as relevant to the task
at hand (e.g., confidential information) was introduced during the dyad discussion. Conversely, when the unshared information was perceived as irrelevant
to the task at hand (i.e., incorrect information), it was rarely introduced.

Introduction of Self-Generated Items

The results for the number of self-generated items introduced during the
dyad discussion by only the experimental dyad members who heard the
unshared information (averaged across scorers) are also presented in Table
13.2. More negative self-generated items were presented in confidential dyads than in incorrect dyads in both Experiment 1A and Experiment 1B. Once
again, it was also the case that the no-disregard dyads generated more of
these items than did incorrect dyads in both experiments. This result indicates that in confidential condition dyads, not only were unshared presented
items introduced during dyad discussion, but the unshared information was
used to introduce self-generated items related to the unshared information.
Unlike presented items, the results for self-generated items indicated no
difference between the confidential and no-disregard conditions in either
experiment.

Dyad Judgments

Planned contrasts found strong support for the impact of pragmatics. That is, the unshared information only affected dyad ratings when one member received unshared information that was perceived as relevant to the dyad's goal. In Experiment 1A, the incorrect ($M = 8.33$, $SD = 1.26$) and no-presentation ($M = 8.02$, $SD = 0.86$) dyads rated Pennebaker more favorably than did the confidential dyads ($M = 6.18$, $SD = 1.48$). In addition, the incorrect and no-presentation dyads rated Pennebaker more favorably than did the no-disregard dyads ($M = 6.00$, $SD = 1.08$). Neither the confidential and no-disregard dyads, nor the incorrect and no-presentation dyads, differed reliably.

The same general pattern of results was found in Experiment 1B. The confidential dyads ($M = 5.44$, $SD = 1.33$) differed in the predicted direction from both the incorrect ($M = 8.14$, $SD = .49$) and no-presentation dyads ($M = 7.92$, $SD = .39$). The incorrect and no-presentation dyads also differed from the no-disregard dyads ($M = 6.58$, $SD = .73$). Unlike Experiment 1A, however, the confidential dyads differed reliably from the no-disregard dyads, but the incorrect and no-presentation dyads did not differ reliably in their judgments.

These results support the view that designating unshared information as to-be-disregarded can affect the use and dissemination of unshared information, particularly when that information is evaluatively distinct from the shared information. When the unshared information was perceived as relevant (confidential or no-disregard conditions), it was in fact introduced during dyad discussion. Furthermore, self-generated items consistent with the unshared information were presented, and the dyad judgments were affected by the unshared information.

These findings are consistent with Stasser's (1992) computer simulation results: Unshared information may be disseminated in smaller groups. In addition, Stasser (1992) found that saliency of the unshared information had its greatest effect when it occurred prior to the group discussion. This finding was supported by the results of the present experiment to the degree that our participants received the unshared information prior to the dyad discussion, and disseminated this information when it was deemed relevant to the discussion (although no direct comparison of unshared information presentation was made in the present study).

In conjunction with Stasser and his associates' work, our results suggest the possibility that dissemination of unshared information may be a function of the evaluative nature of the unshared information. This possibility is further explored at the end of the chapter. For the present, we consider whether the results found in these initial experiments will be found when the "confidential" information is paired with a potentially negative conse-quence for disseminating this information. If individuals simply determine whether the to-be-disregarded information is relevant or not based on prag-matic considerations, then information designated "confidential" should always be used, regardless of the consequences. It may be the case, however, that an explicit warning against using the confidential information may cause individuals to not focus on the pragmatic implication of this information. This would then lead participants to heed the disregard instruction. This question was investigated in the next pair of experiments.

EXPERIMENTS 2A AND 2B

Experiment 2A used the person-impression context used in Experiment 1A, and Experiment 2B used the object-impression context used in Experiment 1B. These experiments were designed to investigate whether the dissemination of unshared information in a group context and its subsequent impact on group judgments would be attenuated when there was a potentially negative consequence for introducing "confidential" information. The explicit mention of a negative consequence may prevent participants from disseminating either the explicitly presented confidential information or self-generated negative statements in both experiments. It is possible, however, that participants will not be prevented from introducing either of these statements in Experiment 2B. For example, because the evaluation of the contract for each of the participants is more relevant (i.e., would have a greater impact) than the evaluation of Pennebaker, an explicit consequence for using the confidential information may simply not matter to these "workers."

The materials and procedure were generally the same as in Experiments 1A and 1B. The same confidential and incorrect conditions were used, but there was also an experimental condition in which a subject was explicitly told of a potential negative consequence (i.e., the speaker would get in trouble) if the unshared confidential information was disseminated. This latter condition will be referred to as the "confidential-consequence" condition. Ten dyads were tested in each of the three experimental conditions (30 experimental and 30 no-presentation participants) in both experiments.[3]

The same scoring procedure was used as in Experiment 1. For Experiment 2A, the reliability for the composite scores was .63 for group scores. For the dissemination data, the correlation between the scorers was .93 for the unkind presented set of statements. For the self-generated statements, the correlation between the scorers who rated the statements was .97 for negative statements. Based on the preceding scorers, the correlation for the original scorers was .85 for negative statements.

For Experiment 2B, the reliability for the composite scores was .83 for group scores. For the dissemination data, the correlation between scorers

---

[3]The data from all groups were included in the dyad judgment analyses of the ratings, but in Experiment 2A, because of equipment malfunctions, only nine groups for the confidential and confidential-consequence conditions had videotape data included in the dissemination analyses.

was .90 for the board of directors set of statements. For the self-generated statements, the correlation between the scorers who rated the statements was .86 for negative statements. Based on the preceding scorers, the correlation for the scorers who originally wrote down the positive and negative statements from the videotapes was .80 for negative statements.

Introduction of Presented Statements

These results are presented in Table 13.3. In Experiment 2A, participants in the confidential dyads introduced more unshared statements than did group members from incorrect dyads or confidential-consequence dyads. Therefore, although pragmatics affected whether unshared information was introduced during group discussion, this dissemination decreased when unshared information was paired with a potential negative consequence. The difference between the incorrect and confidential-consequence conditions was not reliable.

In Experiment 2B, however, the pattern of results was somewhat different. Experimental group members in confidential dyads did not introduce more unshared statements than did group members from the confidential-consequence dyads, but did introduce more than participants in incorrect dyads. There also was an almost reliable difference between the incorrect and confidential-consequence conditions. Possible reasons for the lack of consistency across experiments are discussed later in the chapter.

Introduction of Self-Generated Statements

These results are also presented in Table 13.3, and were analyzed as in the initial experiments. Experimental group members from confidential and confidential-consequence dyads did not differ reliably in the introduction of self-generated statements in Experiment 2A. In Experiment 2B, experimental

TABLE 13.3
Mean Number of Items and Standard Deviations (in Parentheses)
Introduced by the Experimental Group Member
During the Group Discussion in Experiments 2A and 2B

	Confidential		Confidential-Consequence		Incorrect	
Experiment 2A						
Unshared Presented Behaviors	2.67	(2.19)	0.17	(0.35)	0.05	(0.16)
Negative Self-Generated Behaviors	2.14	(2.44)	2.56	(2.39)	0.65	(0.75)
Experiment 2B						
Board of Directors Presented Statements	1.56	(1.31)	1.06	(1.49)	0.00	(0.00)
Anticontract Self-Generated Statements (Positive Board of Directors/Negative Contract)	0.72	(0.89)	1.67	(1.25)	0.28	(0.26)

group members from confidential-consequence dyads generated *more* anti-contract statements than did those from confidential dyads. In addition, confidential-consequence group members introduced more of these statements than did group members from incorrect dyads in both experiments. Thus, although the confidential-consequence participants did not introduce the unshared information itself (as per the disregard instruction), they instead disseminated related negative information that indicated their individual impression to their fellow group member. Essentially, they delivered the message indirectly. The introduction of self-generated negative statements was also somewhat higher for the confidential group members than for the incorrect group members, though not reliably so in either experiment.

Dyad Judgments

In both experiments, the incorrect groups (Experiment 2A: $M = 8.20$, $SD = .57$; Experiment 2B: $M = 7.86$, $SD = .66$) rated Pennebaker and the contract more favorably than did the confidential groups (Experiment 2A: $M = 5.85$, $SD = .90$; Experiment 2B: $M = 6.14$, $SD = 1.37$). Also, the incorrect groups rated Pennebaker and the contract more favorably than did the confidential-consequence groups (Experiment 2A: $M = 6.58$, $SD = .77$; Experiment 2B: $M = 5.86$, $SD = 1.87$). Finally, the confidential and confidential-consequence groups differed reliably in Experiment 2A, but not in Experiment 2B. The different pattern of results for the confidential-consequence and confidential groups across the two experiments may reflect participants perceiving the to-be-disregarded information as having a greater impact in Experiment 2B than in Experiment 2A. This greater impact in turn led participants in Experiment 2B not to concern themselves with the explicit consequence for using the confidential information.

The results from the present experiment again support the view that pragmatics affect the use and dissemination of unshared information. Participants continued to use the to-be-disregarded information when it was confidential, but not when it was incorrect. These results, however, also indicate that the effect of pragmatics may be attenuated in certain contexts if there is a potential negative consequence for not heeding the instruction to disregard specific information. Thus, it is not the case that to-be-disregarded information perceived as relevant is always disseminated and used; relevance may vary in different contexts, thereby affecting the degree to which the to-be-disregarded information is disseminated and used.

EXPERIMENT 3

Experiment 3 was designed to extend the findings from the earlier sets of experiments by investigating the effect of pragmatics on minority influence in a group context, and the sources of anxiety in a group context and the impact of anxiety on a group decision. In the present experiment, the same four conditions used in Experiment 1A involving the presentation of behaviors about John Pennebaker were used. In addition, each group had one or two members who were presented with the unshared behaviors. With regard to the impact of one- versus two-person minorities' influence on the group decision, past research suggests one of two possibilities. Moscovici and Faucheux (1972) noted that the "testimony of a single subject who is perforce more consistent with himself is more influential than the testimony of a theoretically less consistent subgroup" (pp. 179–180). As noted by Latane and Wolf (1981), "increasing the size of a minority beyond one almost inevitably implies a reduction in consistency and consequently in influence" (p. 440). From these two statements, it might be expected that a single naive subject would have a greater impact on the group decision than two naive subjects whose joint presentation may be seen as less consistent than the presentation of the single subject. In addition, one would expect that the pragmatic implication of the instruction to disregard might affect the influence of the minority on the group decision. But another perspective results in the opposite prediction. Research on social combination processes (e.g., Davis, 1973; Laughlin, 1980) and research looking at social impact theory (Latane & Wolf, 1981) suggests that an individual receiving support from another would have a greater impact on the group decision than an individual without such support (e.g., Laughlin & Ellis, 1986).

With regard to better understanding sources of anxiety in a group context and the impact of anxiety on a group decision, the knowledge gained from this research will also enhance our understanding of how individuals deal with information that is relevant but that should not be brought up in group discussions, and how such information affects the individual's perception of the group experience. For example, group members who are aware of confidential information may perceive the group experience as more anxiety inducing than do those for whom the information was relevant but not described as confidential (i.e., no-disregard participants). The level of anxiety experienced by a group member may affect the manner in which he or she presents the information and the subsequent impact of this information on group judgments.

The same materials and procedure were used as in Experiment 1A, except for the following aspects of the procedure. First, there were 10 groups in each of the experimental and control conditions (5 groups of females and 5 groups of males), and each group had six members, not two. Second, each participant completed the state portion of the State–Trait Anxiety Inventory (Spielberger, 1977) before the behaviors were read and after the group discussion. Third, for one-person minority groups, only one participant was presented with the unshared behaviors; for two-person minority groups, two participants were presented with the unshared information. Fourth, all subjects knew they were being videotaped during the group discussion, which lasted 10 minutes. Finally, after the group discussion, each participant was asked to indicate their perception of how confidently and persistently the group presented negative information about Pennebaker on two 11-point scales (0–not at all to 10–extremely) and their perception of support for their own position within the group on an 11-point scale (0–extremely low to 10–extremely high). (The judgments about the group discussion were not analyzed.)

For this experiment, the videotapes of the group interactions were transcribed. Then, one individual naive to the experimental hypothesis, scored the tapes. This scoring included a count of the number of times a presented statement was introduced by each group member, and a count of the self-generated statements that were of a negative or positive evaluative nature about Pennebaker. A second scorer, also naive to the experimental hypotheses, scored 25% of the tapes from the study. Interrater reliability between the two scorers was 87% for presented unkind statements and 95% for negative self-generated statements.

Introduction of Presented Unshared Items

Consistent with the previous experiments, minority group members who possessed unshared negative information that was perceived as relevant to the target person disseminated the unshared information more than did other minority group members (see the top row of Table 13.4). More unshared items were introduced in confidential groups than in incorrect groups. In addition, the number of unshared items disseminated in no-disregard groups was greater than in incorrect groups or in confidential groups.

Introduction of Self-Generated Statements

The results for self-generated statements followed the same pattern as presented statements. Fewer self-generated items were introduced in the incorrect groups compared to the confidential groups and no-disregard groups. The difference between the confidential and no-disregard groups was not reliable.

TABLE 13.4
Mean Number of Items and Standard Deviations (in Parentheses)
Introduced by the Experimental Group Members
During the Group Discussion in Experiment 3

	Confidential	Incorrect	No-Disregard
Unshared Presented Behaviors	1.12 (1.56)	0.00 (0.00)	2.00 (1.55)
Negative Self-Generated Behaviors	4.45 (3.63)	2.25 (1.98)	5.67 (3.87)

Group Judgments

Based on the predictions, the impact of the unshared negative information on a group would be greater for the two-person minority groups (due to greater support and consistency) than for one-person minority groups (i.e., social comparison). These were compared for each experimental condition. It should be noted that this prediction would mean more positive ratings of Pennebaker for two-person incorrect groups than for one-person incorrect groups, and less positive ratings of Pennebaker for two-person no-disregard and confidential groups than for one-person no-disregard and confidential groups.

For groups containing incorrect group members, this prediction was supported. Two-person minority groups ($M = 8.37$, $SD = .56$) rated Pennbaker more positive than did one-person minority groups ($M = 7.83$, $SD = .72$). This prediction was also correct for groups containing no-disregard group members. Two-person minority groups ($M = 5.57$, $SD = .94$) rated Pennebaker more negative than did one-person minority groups ($M = 6.65$, $SD = 1.53$). The difference between the one-person minority groups ($M = 6.30$, $SD = 1.53$) and the two-person minority groups ($M = 5.87$, $SD = 1.09$) was not reliable for the confidential groups. Therefore, the introduction of confidential to-be-disregarded information did not lead to minority-size differences. This may reflect participants perceiving confidential information as critical (i.e., high impact) to the group judgment, regardless of the number of group members who knew this information.

Anxiety

With regard to anxiety, it was predicted that the confidential group members would experience a greater increase in levels of anxiety from pregroup discussion to postgroup discussion than the no-disregard group members. This would likely be the result of the designation of the unshared information as "confidential." However, if support leads to greater minority influence, it might be expected that the anxiety level experienced by minority subjects in the two-person condition would be less than that experienced by minority subjects in the one-person condition.

Based on the foregoing predictions, we compared the confidential and no-disregard participants in the one- and two-person minority conditions, and found a reliable difference for participants in the one-person minority condition. Participants in the confidential groups ($M = -2.50$, $SD = 9.36$) had a greater increase in anxiety from pre- to postgroup than did participants in the no-disregard groups ($M = 6.40$, $SD = 5.80$). With regard to the two-person minority condition, however, the difference between participants in confidential groups ($M = 1.70$, $SD = 4.06$) and no-disregard groups ($M = 3.35$,

$SD = 5.37$) was not reliable. Thus, when a group member was the only person who was aware of confidential information, he or she disseminated the information, while perceiving the group experience as more anxiety inducing than those for whom the information was not described as confidential (i.e., no-disregard group members).

Once again, pragmatics affected the use and dissemination of unshared information. Even though the group members who had heard the unshared information were in the minority, they still disseminated this information, and this information affected the group judgments. Moreover, the dissemination and use of the unshared information occurred even for those participants who experienced the highest level of anxiety from being privy to the unshared information (i.e., participants in the one-person minority confidential condition).

INTERPRETATION AND CONCLUSIONS

The results of this study suggest that certain characteristics can enhance the likelihood that unshared information will be disseminated in groups. These characteristics include the perceived relevancy of the information, and (possibly) its evaluative nature. In all experiments, unshared information perceived as relevant—or other related information—was disseminated during the group discussions, and the dissemination of this information influenced the group judgments. Moreover, these results were found in smaller (two-person) and larger (six-person) groups, and were found even when the unshared information was known by only a minority of the group, and when the knowledge of the unshared information led to relatively high levels of anxiety.

The Importance of Pragmatics

With regard to explicit instructions to disregard unshared information, these results illustrate the importance of pragmatics. Participants willingly disseminated information they had been instructed to disregard if it was designated "confidential," but chose not to disseminate that same information if it was designated "incorrect." Clearly, participants were using their knowledge of the use of language in context to determine whether the to-be-disregarded information was relevant, and should or should not be transmitted. In this way, the hidden profile (i.e., the superior alternative that exists but is hidden from the individual group members because they each have only a portion of the information that supports the alternative) manifested itself in all experiments, but only when pragmatics dictated the dissemination of the unshared information.

Although these results indicate the important role of pragmatics in assessing the relevancy of the unshared information, they also show that the effect of pragmatics can be attenuated to some degree. This was clear from Experiment 2A, when "confidential" information was not disseminated in a case where the potential consequence for introducing this information was negative. These confidential-consequence participants, however, still found the opportunity to disseminate negative information but did so by introducing *related* negative information that had not been explicitly presented.

The lack of a similar effect of potential negative consequences for disseminating confidential information in Experiment 2B may be due to the relevance of the to-be-disregarded information in the different contexts we used. In the person-impression task about Pennebaker, participants simply indicated their favorableness toward another person. In the object-impression task about the contract, participants were asked to play the role of a worker who indicates her like or dislike of a contract that would affect her job security, wages, and working conditions. The evaluation of the contract for each of the participants, therefore, is more relevant than the evaluation of Pennebaker. This greater relevance may have caused participants in the confidential-consequence condition of Experiment 2B to disseminate the confidential information despite the potential negative consequence. This would be consistent with a large body of research that suggests self-relevant information is processed somewhat differently from information that is not self-relevant (e.g., Greenwald & Pratkanis, 1984). In particular, self-relevant information is encoded more elaboratively and creates more associations than information that is not self-relevant.

In addition, the differential effects of the potential negative consequence may be tied to differences in person versus object perception (i.e., impression formation). Fiske and Taylor (1991) noted that the principles that explain how people think about objects and people are often remarkably similar. In addition, however, they noted that some important differences exist between person and object perception. These differences include the fact that only people have intentions, abilities, desires, and feelings. They also pointed out that when an individual observes the actions of another human being, quite often the person who is observed perceives the observer, causing the observer to become more aware of him- or herself. As a result, person perception is often described as more complex than object perception, in part due to the many ambiguities associated with individual behavior (Fiske & Taylor, 1991). It is possible that the differences between person and object perception led to the differences in dissemination when there were potential negative consequences. Future research should attempt to determine the extent to which self-relevant information influences dissemination, as well as the extent to which differences in person and object perception influence the introduction of information in a group context.

The Evaluation of Information

As for the possible influence of the evaluative nature of the unshared information, the use of evaluatively negative information may have increased its likelihood of dissemination. Earlier research considering the use of unshared information avoided the use of clearly undesirable items in the unshared set of items (e.g., Stasser et al., 1989). As a result, both shared and unshared information consisted of items ranging from slightly undesirable to very desirable and, prior to group discussion, each group member received equally attractive descriptions of the target individual. In other words, all group members in Stasser et al. (1989) received information that probably led to the creation of similar impressions of the target individual prior to group discussion. With this being the case, it seems unlikely that a particular member would hear information in the group discussion that strongly contradicted the impression that he or she had already formed of the target. This presents the possibility that in group settings in which the impressions held by the group members are similar, the likelihood is relatively low that unshared information, even if perceived as relevant, would be introduced. When group members hold similar impressions, it is probable that as the group process unfolds, group members experience relatively little conflict between their own and the group's impression, so that the need to disseminate unshared information is low. This is consistent with a number of previous studies (e.g., Stasser et al., 1989; Stasser & Stewart, 1992).

In the present study, however, the unshared and shared information were in opposition. Therefore, negative unshared information that was perceived as relevant by a participant in the confidential and no-disregard conditions led to a contradictory impression compared to a no-presentation participant in the same group. Given that both the confidential and no-disregard participants then disseminated the unshared (and/or related) information, it appears that the relation between the shared and unshared information was also an important determinant for the dissemination of the unshared information in groups.

A final point should be made with regard to the evaluative nature of the unshared behavior set: Only negative unshared behaviors were included in the to-be-disregarded set. This was done because it was felt that such information is much more likely to be labeled as "confidential" in a social interaction. It is possible, therefore, that information with a more favorable evaluative implication would lead to a different pattern of results. For example, Wyer and Budesheim (1987) postulated that individual participants compensate for the effect of incorrect to-be-disregarded information by adjusting their evaluative judgments according to the amount of bias they perceive to exist. Favorable incorrect to-be-disregarded behaviors would be consistent with normative expectations for people to be likeable. Therefore, little bias would be perceived from these behaviors, and the corresponding adjustment would be small. When the incorrect to-be-disregarded behaviors are unfavorable, however, the perceived bias—and the corresponding adjustment—is large. Taken together, these ideas lead to the expectation that less correction will be made when the incorrect behaviors are favorable, thereby allowing these behaviors to affect evaluative judgments. Wyer and Budesheim (1987) found support for this postulate, with favorable incorrect to-be-disregarded behaviors having more impact on evaluative judgments than unfavorable incorrect to-be-disregarded behaviors. Future research is necessary to determine the impact of favorable to-be-disregarded behaviors within the present group paradigm.

It should be emphasized that this study does not imply that the dissemination of unshared information occurs more than previously thought. Indeed, the present study differs in important ways (e.g., group size, type of group task, evaluative nature of materials, use of role playing) from that of previous research that has not found dissemination of unshared information in group-judgment tasks. The value of the current study is that it suggests that there may be characteristics such as pragmatics and consideration of the evaluative nature of the unshared information that influence the dissemination of unshared information. As such, this study represents another step in understanding the characteristics and situations that might increase the likelihood that unshared information is disseminated. As Stasser (1992) suggested, groups seemingly have an advantage over individuals, yet in many cases this advantage is not realized, and can even turn out to be a disadvantage.

Methodological Issues

With regard to the use of role playing in the present study, although there are potential problems associated with role-playing scenarios, there is a long history of the use of such simulations in group research (e.g., Deutsch & Krauss, 1960; also, see McGrath, 1984, for a review of the various paradigms used in the study of groups), and many view role playing as a preferred alternative to studies that rely almost exclusively on deception (see Kelman, 1968). The use of role playing has increased our knowledge about group processes in areas where it may have been difficult to use a more realistic context. For example, in the present experiment, role playing was used to present confidential information about another person because of concerns about whether participants would believe an experimenter would mention, let alone know, confidential information. In addition, the ethical concerns of presenting confidential information about another person argued in favor of using a role-playing scenario.

Related to the use of role playing is the issue of external validity. As discussed above in relation to the use of role playing, the critical issue is that the present paradigm was used to investigate specific processes that are predicted by certain theoretical models of group behavior. In this regard, the present paradigm gives the theoretical views in question a "fair hearing" (see Mook, 1983). Of course, it could always be argued that there are more ecologically valid contexts in which to investigate the effect of the dissemination of unshared information. However, like the contexts used in the present study, there are many instances in which individuals are presented with shared and unshared information about a target and must together determine their impression of the target, as anyone who has ever been involved in a hiring decision can attest. This is not to say that more realistic paradigms should be avoided when investigating the issue in question, but that both laboratory and more naturalistic research can both be used effectively to test theoretical positions (see Ceci & Bronfenbrenner, 1991). As always, the two approaches are complementary.

Clearly, understanding the conditions under which relevant and beneficial unshared information is disseminated is of considerable value to group researchers and those who apply their findings. There are a number of lines of research that could follow from this study and the work of Stasser and his colleagues. These might include varying the status of the individual who possesses the unshared information as well as his or her social or cultural relationship to the other group member(s). Indeed, much of what we have learned about group judgments over the past 40 years could be applied specifically to understanding the conditions under which unshared information will be disseminated in the group process (see Davis, 1992, for an excellent review of the history of group research from 1950 to 1990). The desire to understand and facilitate increased group productivity has long been a primary goal of group researchers. A better understanding of when and how unshared information is disseminated provides an important step toward reaching that goal.

Instructions to Disregard and Directed Forgetting

The present study, involving instructions to disregard during impression formation, shares a great deal with research on directed forgetting. First, the methodologies are very similar. Both types of studies involve the use of explicit cues to segregate relevant and irrelevant information, and the list-method presentation (see Basden et al., 1993) is common to both types of studies. It is also the case that the use of related items in the present study is found in some directed-forgetting studies (e.g., Golding, Long, & MacLeod, 1994).

Second, both types of studies show that the explicit cues are effective to the extent that the information designated irrelevant is actually perceived as irrelevant. In the present study, only to-be-disregarded information that was designated "incorrect" was not used by the groups. The pragmatic implication of this designation indicated to participants that the to-be-disregarded information had no relevance to the impression task. In directed-forgetting studies, the to-be-forgotten words are forgotten, because there is no reason to keep trying to remember them.

Finally, both types of research are concerned with similar aspects of information processing. That is, both are concerned with how individuals use explicit cues to encode and represent irrelevant and relevant information, and how this representation affects the later retrieval of information. Although the ultimate processing goal for using the stored information may vary (e.g., forming an impression vs. remembering the information), researchers in both domains investigate the impact of the irrelevant information on the relevant information, and whether the former information can even be accessed. Thus, researchers investigating intentional forgetting, be it with behaviors or unrelated words, are pursuing many of the same goals, and should not (as might be perceived from a review of most of the literature) be viewed as being on divergent paths. Quite simply, each area of research has a unique vantage point, and each has a great deal to offer to the other.

ACKNOWLEDGMENTS

Portions of this research were presented as part of a symposium on directed forgetting at the meeting of the American Psychological Association, San Francisco, August 1991. Experiment 3 was supported by a grant from the National Institute of Mental Health (MH49410).

We would like to thank Rebecca Bertram, Lorie Casey, Sidney Fooshee, Susan Fowler, Luci Guttermuth, Amie Hedges, Alison Lang, Terri Lee, Karin Levitt, Kerri Moriarty, Kelli Osborn, Karen Rollefson, Stacey Routon, Michalle Strange, Emily Stromberg, Tracey Tipton, and Chris Wright for their assistance in collecting and scoring the data.

REFERENCES

Basden, B. H., Basden, D. R., & Gargano, G. J. (1993). Directed forgetting in implicit and explicit memory tests: A comparison of methods. *Journal of Experimental Psychology: Learning, Memory, and Cognition, 19*, 603–616.

Bjork, R. A. (1972). Theoretical implications of directed forgetting. In A. W. Melton & E. Martin (Eds.), *Coding processes in human memory* (pp. 217–235). Washington, DC: Winston.

Caretta, T. R., & Moreland, R. L. (1983). The direct and indirect effects of inadmissible evidence. *Journal of Applied Social Psychology, 13*, 291–309.

392

Ceci, S. J., & Bronfenbrenner, U. (1991). On the demise of everyday memory. *American Psychologist, 46,* 27–31.

Davis, J. H. (1973). Dyad decision and social interaction: A theory of social decision schemes. *Psychological Review, 80,* 97–125.

Davis, J. H. (1992). Some compelling intuitions about group consensus decisions, theoretical and empirical research, and interpersonal aggregation phenomena: Selected examples, 1950–1990. *Organizational Behavior and Human Decision Processes, 52,* 3–38.

Deutsch, M., & Krauss, R. M. (1960). The effect of threat upon interpersonal bargaining. *Journal of Abnormal and Social Psychology, 61,* 181–189.

Devine, P. G., & Ostrom, T. M. (1985). Cognitive mediation in inconsistency discounting. *Journal of Personality and Social Psychology, 49,* 5–21.

Fiske, S. T., & Taylor, S. E. (1991). *Social cognition.* New York: McGraw-Hill.

Golding, J. M., Fowler, S. B., Long, D. L., & Latta, H. (1990). Instructions to disregard potentially useful information: The effects of pragmatics on evaluative judgments and recall. *Journal of Memory and Language, 29,* 212–227.

Golding, J. M., & Hauselt, J. (1994). When instructions to forget become instructions to remember. *Personality and Social Psychology Bulletin, 20,* 178–183.

Golding, J. M., Long, D. L., & MacLeod, C. M. (1994). You can't always forget what you want: Directed forgetting of related words. *Journal of Memory and Language, 33,* 493–510.

Golding, J. M., Sego, S. A., Hauselt, J., & Long, D. L. (1994). Pragmatics and the effect of instructions to forget information that varies in the magnitude of a trait. *The American Journal of Psychology, 107,* 223–243.

Greenwald, A. G., & Pratkanis, A. R. (1984). The self. In R. S. Wyer, Jr., & T. R. Srull (Eds.), *Handbook of social cognition* (Vol. 3, pp. 129–178). Hillsdale, NJ: Lawrence Erlbaum Associates.

Johnson, H. (1994). Processes of successful intentional forgetting. *Psychological Bulletin, 116,* 274–292.

Kaplan, M. F., & Miller, C. E. (1983). Group discussion and judgment. In P. B. Panlus (Ed.), *Basic group processes* (pp. 65–94). New York: Springer-Verlag.

Keenan, J. M., MacWhinney, B., & Mayhew, D. (1977). Pragmatics in memory: A study of natural conversation. *Journal of Verbal Learning and Verbal Behavior, 16,* 549–560.

Kelman, H. C. (1968). *A time to speak.* San Francisco: Jossey-Bass.

Larson, J. R., Foster-Fishman, P. G., & Keys, C. B. (1994). Discussion of shared and unshared information in decision-making groups. *Journal of Personality and Social Psychology, 67,* 446–461.

Latane, H. C., & Wolf, S. (1981). The social impact of majorities and minorities. *Psychological Review, 88,* 438–453.

Laughlin, P. R. (1980). Social combination processes and individual learning for six-person cooperative groups on an intellective task. *Journal of Personality and Social Psychology, 38,* 941–947.

Laughlin, P. R., & Ellis, A. L. (1986). Demonstrability and social combination processes on mathematical intellective tasks. *Journal of Experimental Social Psychology, 22,* 177–189.

McGrath, J. E. (1984). *Groups: Interaction and performance.* Englewood Cliffs, NJ: Prentice-Hall.

Mook, D. G. (1983). In defense of external validity. *American Psychologist, 38,* 379–387.

Moscovici, S., & Faucheux, C. (1972). Social influence, conforming bias, and the study of active minorities. In L. Berkowitz (Ed.), *Advances in experimental social psychology* (Vol. 6, pp. 149–202). New York: Academic Press.

Rosenthal, R. (1982). Conducting judgment studies. In K. R. Scherer & P. Ekman (Eds.), *Handbook of methods in nonverbal behavior research* (pp. 287–361). Cambridge, MA: Cambridge University Press.

Spielberger, C. D. (1977). *Manual for State–Trait Anxiety Inventory (Self-Evaluation Questionnaire).* Palo Alto, CA: Consulting Psychologists Press.

Stasser, G. (1988). Computer simulation as a research tool: The DISCUSS model of group decision making. *Journal of Experimental Social Psychology, 24,* 393–422.

Stasser, G. (1992). Information salience and the discovery of hidden profiles by decision-making groups: A "thought" experiment. *Organizational Behavior and Human Decision Processes, 52,* 156–181.

Stasser, G., & Stewart, D. (1992). Discovery of hidden profiles by decision-making groups: Solving a problem versus making a judgment. *Journal of Personality and Social Psychology, 63,* 426–434.

Stasser, G., Taylor, L. A., & Hanna, C. (1989). Information sampling in structured and unstructured discussions of three- and six-person groups. *Journal of Personality and Social Psychology, 57,* 67–78.

Stasser, G., & Titus, W. (1985). Pooling of unshared information in group decision making: Biased information sampling during discussion. *Journal of Personality and Social Psychology, 48,* 1467–1478.

Stasser, G., & Titus, W. (1987). Effects of information load and percentage of shared information on the dissemination of unshared information during group discussion. *Journal of Personality and Social Psychology, 53,* 81–93.

Sue, S., Smith, R. E., & Caldwell, C. (1973). Effects of inadmissible evidence on the decisions of simulated jurors: A moral dilemma. *Journal of Applied Social Psychology, 3,* 345–353.

Thompson, W. C., Fong, G. T., & Rosenhan, D. L. (1981). Inadmissible evidence and juror verdicts. *Journal of Personality and Social Psychology, 40,* 453–463.

van Dijk, T. A. (1980). *Macrostructures.* Hillsdale, NJ: Lawrence Erlbaum Associates.

Wyer, R. S., & Budesheim, T. L. (1987). Person memory and judgments: The impact of information that one is told to forget. *Journal of Personality and Social Psychology, 53,* 14–29.

Wyer, R. S., & Unverzagt, W. H. (1985). Effects of instructions to disregard information on its subsequent recall and use in making judgments. *Journal of Personality and Social Psychology, 48,* 533–549.

INTENTIONAL FORGETTING AND CLINICAL DISORDERS

Marylene Cloitre
New York Hospital–Cornell Medical Center

Clinical research has typically identified two distinct types of unusual cognitive activities in clinical samples (Christianson, 1992; Stein & Young, 1992). One concerns the presence of intrusive thoughts and memories where processing resources are disproportionally allotted to threatening or negative information (Mathews & MacLeod, 1994). The other concerns impoverished memory for information that derives from diminished encoding or impaired retrieval abilities (Cloitre, 1992). The "excessive" remembering and "excessive" forgetting observed in clinical samples represent the extreme ends of the continuum of human memory and as such warrant systematic investigation. Because the directed-forgetting paradigm demands engagement in enhanced or excessive remembering and forgetting, it has the potential to elicit processing biases that, under other conditions, would remain latent. Thus, the directed-forgetting paradigm not only identifies the balance of remembering and forgetting that occurs among healthy individuals, it can also help us identify the outer limits of remembering and forgetting among humans through the study of clinical populations.

The application of experimental paradigms to clinical samples allows us to test hypotheses about the cognitive characteristics of individuals with clinical disorders relative to healthy individuals in a systematic and controlled way. Such activity serves at least two distinct purposes. From the perspective of pure science, the inclusion of clinical populations presents challenging "test cases" in which competing models of memory functioning can be compared with respect to their success in accounting for the range of memory phenomena. The better models are those whose working principles are flexible enough to account for both normal and abnormal functioning. The clinical value of drawing out the memory characteristics of clinical disorders, especially as they contrast with healthy functioning, is the specification of the "lesions" or problem areas in functioning. This, in turn, can shape the development of effective clinical interventions.

Thus far, only five studies have applied the directed-forgetting paradigm to clinical samples. In each case, the hypotheses assessed the presence of either intrusive memories and/or reduced ability to recollect information on demand (see Table 14.1). People who report suffering from intrusive memory, such as individuals with obsessive-compulsive disorder (OCD), would be expected to reveal diminished capacity to follow "forget" instructions and perhaps show increased capacity to recollect information designated for remembering, especially if it is of personal significance (Barlow, 1988). In contrast, there are populations such as those with early life trauma who are expected to have impaired autobiographical memory and an uncanny ability to "forget" information at will, especially information associated with negative personal valence. These individuals would be expected to reveal difficulties remembering information designated for recall and perhaps, in addition, enhanced capacity to follow "forget" instructions, especially if the material is personally disturbing (Cloitre, 1992).

Other populations, such as individuals with Post Traumatic Stress Disorder (PTSD) represent an interesting test case of a potential blend of alternating intrusive memories with lapses or loss of memory (van der Kolk, 1988a). PTSD is a disorder that is diagnosed only when someone has suffered a significant life trauma (such as rape, child abuse, war combat) and, as a result, has several psychological disturbances, among which impaired memory functioning is salient (American Psychiatric Association, *Diagnostic and Statistical Manual of Mental Disorders* [DSM-IV], 4th ed., 1994). The individual with PTSD can experience alternating or nearly simultaneous difficulties with repeating intrusive memories as well as loss of memory for certain aspects of their trauma. It remains to be determined whether, within the directed-forgetting paradigm, predictions of either excessive remembering or excessive forgetting—or some combination—would be associated with this population.

In the following review, the reader will note that results do not always confirm the above generated hypotheses. In these failures, some of the characteristics of the directed-forgetting task emerge clearly and provide converging evidence to support hypotheses concerning the mechanisms postulated to underlie the directed-forgetting effect. The studies also reveal unexpected memory characteristics among the clinical samples, which have forced clinicians to rework descriptions of certain syndromes, but in the process have provided more information about clinical syndromes than would have otherwise been obtained. It is "early days" in clinical research using directed forgetting, yet the technique shows considerable promise.

TABLE 14.1
Directed Forgetting Studies Among Clinical Populations

Study	Participants	Type of Instruction	Type of Memory Task	Type of Word Stimuli	Results
Cloitre, Cancienne, Brodsky, Dulit, & Perry (1996)	24 women with BPD and child abuse history 24 women with BPD 24 women healthy controls	item cued	cued recall word-stem completion	positive negative neutral	BPD with abuse group showed enhanced DF compared to BPD alone and healthy control group.
Cloitre & MacLeod (1996)	15 women with rape-related PTSD 19 women with rape but no PTSD 24 women healthy controls	item cued	cued recall word-stem completion	rape-related general threat positive neutral	PTSD group showed diminished DF specific to rape-related and general threat words. Both rape groups showed better memory for rape words than for other word types.
McNally, Metzger, Lasko, & Pitman (1996)	14 women with child abuse and PTSD 12 women with child abuse and no PTSD	item cued	free recall cued recall recognition	trauma-related positive neutral	PTSD group did not show DF effect; no-PTSD group showed DF effect. PTSD group remembered trauma words better than other types of words.
McNally, Otto, Yap, Pollack, & Hornig (1996)	17 men and women with Panic Disorder 18 men and women with no disorder	item cued	free recall recognition	threat positive neutral	Panic Disorder and healthy controls showed equivalent DF effect. Panic group did not respond differentially to threat words. Some hemispheric differences were obtained in DF responding in both groups.
Wilhelm, McNally, Baer, & Florin (in press)	36 men and women with OCD 24 men and women with no disorder	item cued	free recall recognition	negative positive neutral	OCD patients showed difficulty in forgetting negative material relative to positive and neutral material, whereas control subjects did not.

REVIEW OF STUDIES

Directed Forgetting in Obsessive-Compulsive Disorder

Individuals with Obsessive-Compulsive Disorder (OCD) suffer from recurrent intrusive thoughts. The thoughts usually involve concerns about being contaminated by germs or dirt, or notions that they might hurt someone even though they do not want to (*DSM-IV*). People with OCD view the thoughts as irrational but feel powerless to stop or suppress them. Wilhelm, McNally, Baer, and Florin (in press) suggested that difficulties dispelling such thoughts might derive from an inability to forget unwanted information. The authors tested the directed-forgetting skills of 36 OCD patients compared to 24 healthy control participants, all of whom were presented with negative, positive, and neutral words for study. The negative words were weighted toward typical OCD concerns (e.g., violence, filthy, dirty, disease). The words were organized into sets of an equal number of positive, negative, and neutral words, and, within each set, the mean frequency did not vary by valence. Each word was followed by an instruction to remember or to forget. The pairings were random, except that half of the items of each valence was followed by remember instructions and the remaining half was followed by forget instructions. Subjects were tested with a free recall task followed by a recognition task.

A directed-forgetting effect was obtained across both groups and all types of word stimuli. Wilhelm et al. (in press) hypothesized that if OCD patients are characterized by an inability to forget disturbing material, they ought to recall and recognize more negative-forget words than positive-forget or neutral-forget words. Results were in line with this hypothesis. Planned contrasts showed that OCD participants recalled more negative-forget words than positive-forget or neutral-forget words whereas the control participants did not. The same pattern of findings was obtained on both tests.

After the recognition test, participants were asked to rate the personal significance of each of the experimental words on a 7-point scale ranging from −3 (very negative) to +3 (very positive). Consistent with the main findings, OCD patients rated "forget" words that they had recalled as significantly more negative than either "forget" words or "remember" words that they had forgotten on the tests. In contrast, control participants did not show any differences in emotionality ratings across word type or instruction categories. Based on these data, Wilhelm et al. (in press) suggested that when OCD patients fail to forget words, those words tend to be characterized by negative personal emotional significance.

Wilhelm et al. (in press) also wished to determine whether the difficulty forgetting negative material was related to elaborate encoding of negative material (i.e., selective rehearsal) or to problems in inhibiting retrieval of such information. The authors argued that if the directed-forgetting effect is attributable to retrieval inhibition, then the effect should disappear on a recognition test, as this type of test releases the subject from inhibition. The presence of a directed-forgetting effect in both the free recall and recognition tasks was interpreted to mean that the differential memory for the negative material was related to preferential encoding of the negative material and not to retrieval inhibition.

Comparing the magnitude of the effect in recall and recognition suggests that this conclusion is too strong. In the recognition task, the proportion of words remembered with the "forget" instruction is about 20% to 30% less than that with the "remember" instruction. In the recall task, participants recalled approximately 45% fewer words following the "forget" as opposed to the "remember" instruction. Assuming that recognition performance involves less retrieval activity, the directed-forgetting effect must be driven by differential encoding. However, free recall is typically subject to both encoding and retrieval processes. The increased size of the directed-forgetting effect in the free recall task relative to the recognition task suggests that both differential encoding and some form of retrieval dysfunction may be cumulatively contributing to the increased forgetting of negative material.

Directed Forgetting in Panic Disorder

Studies of attention and memory in panic disorder patients found that these individuals tend to show attentional and memory biases toward threat information, specifically that related to potential bodily harm (Cloitre & Liebowitz, 1991; Cloitre, Shear, Cancienne, & Zeitlin, 1994; McNally, Foa, & Donnell, 1989). Individuals with panic disorder experience sudden and unexpected attacks of excruciating anxiety where in a matter of minutes, there is a dramatic increase in the arousal system, often marked by palpitations, increased heart rate, chest pains, dizziness, sweating, nausea, and depersonalization or derealization (DSM-IV). People who experience these attacks often think they are having a heart attack, dying, or going crazy.

Clinical assessment and treatment of these patients indicate that one trigger for these attacks is hypervigilance to and awareness of bodily sensations associated with panic attacks. These individuals monitor their bodies for sensations associated with attacks such as increased heart rate or breathlessness. Although these sensations may have an innocuous source (e.g., a jog through the park or walk up a flight of stairs), they trigger a series of catastrophic thoughts such as "I am dying" or "I am having another panic attack and I won't survive." These thoughts are critical in the generation of the attack itself. The thoughts produce the physical arousal that leads to the crescendo of symptoms that constitute the panic attack. The findings from the cognitive studies support this interpretation of the onset and maintenance of panic attacks. It has been found that panic patients show biased explicit and implicit memory for bodily sensation words (e.g., palpitations) compared to positive and neutral words, whereas normal controls do not (Cloitre & Liebowitz, 1991; Cloitre et al., 1994). This memory bias, whether with or without consciousness, supports the notion that panic patients are preoccupied with negative bodily sensation information.

McNally et al. (1996b) conducted a directed-forgetting study in which panic patients ($n = 17$) and normal controls ($n = 18$) were presented with threatening (e.g., suffocate), positive (e.g., healthy), and neutral (e.g., curtain) stimuli. Both groups exhibited the expected directed-forgetting effect. However, the panic disorder group did not show preferential recall or recognition of threat words in either the remember or forget instruction conditions. Yet, it seems that both panic patients and normal controls recognized significantly fewer threat-remember than positive-threat or neutral-threat words. Perhaps everyone spontaneously tends to reduce engagement in elaborated encoding of threat material, whereas instructions to remember other forms of material are much more easily complied with. Still, these results are inconsistent with previous memory studies, because directed remembering instructions would be expected to enhance the predisposition toward recollection of bodily threat information as established in previous studies.

Interestingly, the investigators found a relationship between auditory hemispheric bias and memory for threat information. A measure of right ear (left hemispheric) advantage was calculated and taken to reflect the tendency to engage in processing of negative verbal material. Multiple regressions were used to examine the contribution of laterality bias, group status (panic vs. normal controls), and their interaction in explaining potential recall bias for threat. Two indices were calculated; the difference between memory for threat and neutral words and between memory for threat and positive words. These two indices were calculated separately for remember-cued words and forget-cued words. The only finding of significance was the presence of an interaction effect for the threat bias indices under the forget instruction. The interaction derived from the presence of a positive association between right-hemispheric bias and memory for threat information among panic patients, but a negative association between auditory laterality and threat memory among the control participants. Among panic patients, there was a tendency to show a bias toward the processing of threat information as right-hemisphere bias increased; there was also a tendency to *avoid* the processing of threat information as right-hemisphere bias diminished. Healthy controls revealed the reverse association, showing a bias toward positive or neutral material as right-hemisphere bias increased and processing threat information more as right-hemisphere bias decreased. Thus, the apparent processing bias for threat material among panic patients is mediated by laterality differences, indicating unusual tendencies in both attending to and avoiding threat information.

DIRECTED FORGETTING IN TRAUMA POPULATIONS

Childhood Trauma

The greatest interest in the application of the directed-forgetting effect has been concentrated on the memory functioning of individuals who experienced a significant personal trauma. Individuals with a history of trauma during childhood have been of greatest scientific interest because childhood represents a developmentally sensitive period in which skills in memory and other cognitive tasks are crystallizing. From a clinical perspective, two psychiatric disorders among adults believed to be commonly associated with a history of childhood trauma are Borderline Personality Disorder (BPD) and Post Traumatic Stress Disorder (PTSD; Foy, 1992; Herman & van der Kolk, 1988). Although there is some debate about the extent to which these two disorders may be related, they have been studied independently and the memory characteristics associated with each disorder are believed to be somewhat different (*DSM-IV*; Herman & van der Kolk, 1988).

Nevertheless, the hypotheses generated in regard to the memory characteristics of these two disorders share similar rationales. Generally, the notion is that children who are abused may use (and thus become proficient at) attentional and/or memory strategies to attenuate the impact of the abuse and that these strategies may be revealed in performance of the directed-forgetting task.

The most common hypothesis in the clinical literature is that adults with a history of childhood abuse may cope with the trauma by engaging in selective forgetting of information associated with their abuse experiences. Adults with traumatic histories seem to shift in and out of awareness of certain aspects of their experience (van der Kolk, 1988a) or may fail to recall entire episodes of documented abuse (Williams, 1994). This coping strategy may have its roots in childhood during the time of the abuse when there is heightened motivation to cognitively disengage from the abuse event. Children who are being either physically or sexually abused by their caretakers have limited resources with which to avoid the abuse or to find alternative sources of care. They are, according to McNally et al. (1996a) "trapped in uniquely traumatic circumstances. Not only are they smaller and weaker than their victimizers, they depend on them for food, shelter and clothing" (p. 3, ms). Thus, the child may rely on psychological resources such as temporarily "forgetting" or putting away memories of the parent as abuser to maximally relate to the parent as a source of care.

It has also been suggested that abusing carefigures command or prompt young children to disregard episodes of abuse (Finklehor & Browne, 1985; Herman, 1981; Russell, 1986). This would seem to create further incentive for the child to engage in, and become expert at, activities directing memory toward some experiences (positive events) and away from others (abusive events). Thus, it has been postulated that an abused population would perform well on a task such as directed forgetting by virtue of having engaged in and become proficient at similar activities as part of their cognitive repertoire for coping with abuse (Cloitre, 1992, 1996).

Interestingly, either differential encoding or retrieval inhibition are reasonable explanations for the enhanced directed-forgetting effect predicted among individuals with child abuse histories. For example, abused children may learn to stop encoding information that is frightening or disturbing and thus develop proficiency at discontinuing on demand the elaboration of information. Alternatively, abusive episodes may be well encoded or better encoded than other information, but the child may become skilled at inhibiting or disabling retrieval activities to protect himself or herself from painful memories.

Directed Forgetting Among Women With Childhood Abuse and Borderline Personality Disorder

A recently published study investigated the basic hypothesis that a history of childhood abuse would be associated with enhanced skills at directed forgetting (Cloitre, Cancienne, Brodsky, Dulit, & Perry, 1996). Several controls were introduced into the study. First, it is well known that child abuse is associated with a range of personality features and disorders (Cole & Putnam, 1992) and that directed-forgetting effects are influenced by personality characteristics (Geiselman & Panting, 1985). Thus, it was important to control for the personality characteristics of the study sample. Borderline personality disorder (BPD) has been consistently found to be associated with child abuse (Herman, Perry, & van der Kolk, 1989; Ogata et al., 1990) and can be reliably diagnosed (Spitzer, Williams, Gibbon, & First, 1989). The study included three groups: women with BPD and a history of abuse ($n = 24$), women with BPD and no history of abuse ($n = 24$), and women with no personality or other type of psychiatric disorder and no history of abuse ($n = 24$). Comparisons across these three groups allowed determination of whether any differences in directed-forgetting effects were specifically associated with childhood abuse as opposed to the more general psychopathology associated with BPD.

Second, it was important to have the predictions of directed forgetting be quite specific. Research with nonclinical college samples indicated that directed-forgetting effects are obtained for explicit tests (e.g., cued recall) but are less common on implicit tests (e.g., word-stem completion task) (see MacLeod, this volume). Thus, it was hypothesized that directed-forgetting effects would be obtained primarily on an explicit test, with greater effects obtained among the abused group, and that performance on an implicit memory task would remain unaffected by directed-forgetting instructions, with the abused and nonabused groups performing similarly. Lastly, the affective valence of the stimuli was manipulated (positive, negative, and neutral) to determine whether a directed-forgetting effect would be stronger for negatively valenced words either across all three groups or for the abused group alone. Each word was followed by directions to either remember or forget that word.

Results for explicit memory condition revealed that individuals with abuse histories showed greater differential recall of "to-be-remembered" versus "to-be-forgotten" material compared to the two comparison groups. Implicit memory performance, as measured by a word-stem completion task, was equivalent for all three groups. Unfortunately, the affective valence variable was dropped from the analyses because too few words within each affective category were remembered to allow for appropriate statistical analysis. Of note, however, was the observation that the enhanced selective memory in the abused group was the result of better recall for "remember" and not poorer recall for "forget" information.

These results have implications for our views on the cognitive aspects of coping strategies of abuse survivors and more generally on our understanding of the mechanisms underlying the directed-forgetting effect. If the abused group's enhanced skill at the directed-forgetting task had derived from decreased recall of the "forget" information, the hypothesis about "forgetting" skills of abuse survivors would have been supported, with the effect presumably deriving from the abused group's enhanced ability to either discontinue elaboration on command and/or engage in retrieval inhibition of information targeted for forgetting. However, the presence of equivalent recall of forget words and enhanced recall of remember words suggests that the abused group differed from the other two groups in their ability to engage in relatively increased elaboration and thus preferential retrieval of remember words.

From a clinical perspective, these results suggest that coping strategies other than inhibition of memories may be at work. An enhanced ability to focus attention toward and engage in increased elaboration of designated information is consistent with some reports of abuse victims attempting to distract themselves from the event (Terr, 1994). These victims recall engaging in conscious and effortful attention to "neutral" material as represented in activities such as counting spots on a ceiling or slats in a venetian blind during abuse episodes. A broader interpretation, consistent with the attachment model (Bowlby, 1977) rationale for the study, might be that abused individuals do not necessarily forget their abuse experiences but that other more positive material may be highly elaborated; in turn, this would make the to-be-forgotten material relatively less salient. This interpretation is consistent with the perplexing phenomenon, anecdotally reported by clinicians and potentially exploited in courtrooms, that some abused individuals seem to have heightened memories of positive experiences with their caretakers even though they have acknowledged them as abusive (Terr, 1994).

The implications of the study from a scientific perspective are of interest. The study's unexpected finding of enhanced recall of to-be-remembered information is consistent with arguments that the cognitive processes underlying directed-forgetting effects differ depending on the way the task is presented. Basden, Basden, and Gargano (1993) convincingly showed that when words were cued as to-be-remembered or to-be-forgotten on an item-by-item basis, as in the Cloitre et al. (1996) study, participants engaged in preferential encoding of the R words. In contrast, when the instructions to remember or forget were given once in the middle of the list, retrieval inhibition of F words occurred. The authors suggested that it is relatively easy to use differential encoding in word but not list presentation. Conversely, it is easier for participants to inhibit retrieval of an entire list than of a random subset of individual words. The Basden et al. (1993) explanation is of significance because it indicates that differential recall of designated information can be achieved in different ways depending on even slight shifts in task demands.

The Cloitre et al. (1996) study used an item-by-item presentation procedure, and the results were consistent with the Basden et al. (1993) account and findings. Whereas the current study documented that differential recall of designated information is enhanced among abuse survivors through differential encoding, it leaves unstudied the question of the ease with which abuse survivors may engage in retrieval inhibition.

Directed Forgetting in Post-Traumatic Stress Disorder Related to Childhood Sexual Assault

In the Cloitre et al. (1996) study described earlier, the results indicated that women with abuse histories showed an enhanced directed-forgetting effect and that this effect was directly related to a history of abuse, because women without abuse but with the same type of personality disorder performed quite similarly to the normal control (no abuse and no personality disorder) group. In a recently completed study, McNally and colleagues (McNally, Metzger, Lasko, & Pitman, 1996a) focused on the effect that post-traumatic stress disorder (PTSD) might have on performance on a directed-forgetting task. Although the PTSD was related to the trauma of having been sexually abused as a child, the control group was comprised of women who had been abused but who did not have PTSD. Thus, the goal of this investigation was to investigate memory effects deriving from PTSD rather than from an abuse history.

The focus on PTSD is of interest because one of the hallmark characteristics of the disorder is disturbed memory functioning. Individuals with PTSD suffer memory deficits or intrusive memories, usually specific to the traumatic event (*DSM-IV*; Davidson & Foa, 1993). McNally et al. (1996a) presented two competing hypotheses for the PTSD patients, a "dissociation model" and an "intrusion model." The dissociation model has a logic similar to that put forward about the attentional and memory style of child abuse victims in general. Based on the reports that children tend to disengage from abuse episodes by turning attention elsewhere, it was hypothesized that adults with such a history might become expert at a dissociative encoding style. Although this strategy is believed to be adaptive in the context of an inescapable traumatic environment, McNally et al. (1996a) suggested that in adulthood it may lead to a tendency toward cognitive avoidance, and thus, lack of resolution of disturbing memories. Alternatively, the "intrusion model" derives from reports of some trauma survivors that they have quite the opposite memory problems, namely unbidden recollections of the trauma from which they have difficulty disengaging.

The study assessed directed-forgetting performance using an item method of presentation in two groups of women with a history of child abuse, one with PTSD ($n = 14$) and the other without PTSD ($n = 12$). Study participants were exposed to a series of three types of words matched for word frequency and length; trauma words (molested, abused, scream), positive words (carefree, healthy, secure), and neutral words (cabinet, doorknob, stairs). The authors hypothesized that if a dissociative encoding style characterized the PTSD group, they should, relative to the no-PTSD group, exhibit diminished memory for trauma words, especially following "forget" instructions. In addition, they should remember nontrauma words better than trauma words. In contrast, if an intrusion model more accurately characterized the PTSD group, they should show superior memory for the trauma words relative to other words, even under "forget" instructions. Memory was assessed using free recall, cued recall, and recognition tasks.

Perhaps the most dramatic finding of the study was that the PTSD group did not show a directed-forgetting effect in any of the three memory tests. In contrast, the no-PTSD group showed the expected directed-forgetting effect in all tasks. The two groups also differed in their memory for material depending on the word content. In the free recall task, the PTSD group showed better memory for trauma words relative to positive and neutral words in both the remember and forget instruction categories; the no-PTSD group performed equivalently across all word categories. The authors interpreted the findings to mean that the PTSD group failed to recall non-trauma words and recalled trauma words, even under conditions where they were told to forget such words, indicating support for an intrusion rather than a dissociation model of cognitive functioning in PTSD.

This interpretation of the data may be the best fit of data to the competing explanatory models. However, it should be noted that although the PTSD participants recalled more trauma words than positive or neutral words, their recall of trauma words was equal to that of the no-PTSD group, suggesting that the PTSD group had reasonably good but not excessive recall of trauma words. Rather, it appears that the locus of deviant responding occurred with the positive and neutral words in which performance was quite inferior to the no-PTSD group.

This pattern of results was essentially repeated in the cued recall and recognition tasks. In the cued recall task, the PTSD group showed no directed-forgetting effect but the same recall performance for threat words as the no-PTSD group. Both groups showed better cued recall for trauma words than for other types of words. The PTSD group showed better memory for trauma words than for positive and neutral words. The no-PTSD group showed better and equivalent memory for trauma and neutral words, and poorer memory for positive words. In the recognition task, there were no word effects in either group; the only effect obtained was the presence of directed forgetting in the no-PTSD group.

There are several aspects of the study that are unexpected and require further examination. First, it should be noted that a dissociation model for trauma information among individuals with PTSD was not supported. Memory for trauma information in the PTSD group was not diminished. Rather, it was the best recalled type of information in both groups. Unfortunately, it is difficult to assess whether memory for trauma information is enhanced in the PTSD group and thus represents "intrusive" memory or whether PTSD is characterized by a general memory deficit with the exception of trauma-related material. Certainly, relative to the PTSD group's performance on other types of information, the trauma information is significantly better remembered. However, compared to the performance of individuals without PTSD, it is about the same.

McNally and colleagues began with two competing models of trauma-related processing; a "dissociation" model and an "intrusion" model. The results suggest that the compelling comparison models are actually a "trauma-related intrusion" model versus a "general deficit" model. A deficit model was not hypothesized in this study, however, there is some independent data that suggest this as a reasonable possibility. Specifically, Yehuda et al. (1995) recently found that combat veterans with PTSD show long-term memory deficits following interference tasks. The effect is a general memory phenomenon and not specific to trauma-related information.

Thus, perhaps PTSD, regardless of its source, is associated with content-nonspecific long-term memory deficits that derive from an inability to keep information ordered and categorized.

It is critical to assess the memory performance of a nonclinical/nontraumatized (i.e., "healthy") control group to test the above competing models. For example, it is possible that, compared to a healthy comparison group, both trauma groups, with and without PTSD, would show enhanced memory for trauma materials, giving support to an "intrusion model," for those who have experienced a trauma, regardless of their diagnostic status. Following the same reasoning, healthy controls would provide baseline data for non-trauma words in a test of the "deficit model," and allow a determination of whether both, one, or neither of the trauma groups show generally poor memory for nontrauma information.

Directed Forgetting in Post-Traumatic Stress Disorder Among Adult Rape Victims

In this study (Cloitre & MacLeod, 1996), item-cued directed-forgetting instructions were given to three participant groups; women who had been raped in adulthood and suffered PTSD ($n = 15$), women who had been raped in adulthood and did *not* suffer PTSD ($n = 19$), and women had never been assaulted and were psychiatrically healthy ($n = 24$). All three groups were exposed to four different types of words; rape-related (e.g., sodomy, assault), general threat (e.g., illness, coffin), positive (e.g., entertainment, sunshine), and neutral (e.g., envelope, literature), and then given a cued-recall (explicit memory) task followed by a word-stem completion (implicit memory) task. The four word groups were matched on length and frequency and the rape and general threat words had equivalent threat value.

Given the results of the PTSD study by McNally et al. (1996a), one purpose of this study was to determine whether the PTSD-related pattern of results found among women with childhood sexual assault would be replicated among women with adult sexual assault. Second, the presence of a control group with no assault history allowed us to test an "intrusion" model versus a "general deficit" model by comparing the performance of the trauma groups to the baseline memory performance provided by the no-trauma group. Preliminary analyses indicated that all three groups showed equivalent cued-recall performance, suggesting that memory functioning for the rape groups—both with and without PTSD status—was not globally impaired. All three groups showed enhanced cued recall for rape-remember words relative to general threat, positive, and neutral words. In addition, rape victims both with and without PTSD showed diminished directed-forgetting effects. This phenomenon was moderated by the affective content of the words. Both rape groups showed *no* directed-forgetting effect for rape words compared to other types of words. In contrast, the no assault control group showed large and equivalent directed forgetting across all words types. The absence of a directed-forgetting effect for the rape words among the two rape groups derived from difficulty that the rape groups had in forgetting rape-forget words.

The finding that the rape groups experienced difficulty in "forgetting" rape words supports an "intrusion model" of impaired cognition in sexual trauma. In addition, the rape groups did not show impaired recall for other types of words and thus did not lend support to a "general deficit" model. It should be emphasized that difficulty forgetting rape words was observed among rape victims with and without the diagnosis of PTSD. Clinical observation suggests that all the women who had been raped suffered some post traumatic stress symptoms and that the PTSD group was distinguished by the greater intensity and frequency of these symptoms. Thus, obtained effects may be related to the intensity and frequency of post traumatic stress symptoms, rather than to the absence or presence of a diagnosis per se. Further analyses will be conducted to test this hypothesis. It will be of interest to assess whether particular sets of post traumatic stress symptoms, such as self-reported intrusive thoughts, are more highly correlated with directed-forgetting difficulties than reports of hyperarousal and emotional numbing.

Lastly, it should be noted that all three groups showed enhanced recall of to-be-remembered rape words relative to threat, positive, and neutral words, suggesting that there may be something salient or intrinsically noteworthy about sexual assault terms to women regardless of their assault history or PTSD status.

CONCLUSION

Summary of Studies

The assessment of OCD patients is the only study in which the findings map directly onto a specified clinical profile (Wilhelm et al., in press). OCD patients showed difficulty in forgetting words related to their obsessions and compulsions but performed similarly to the healthy comparison group in every other respect. This finding gives empirical support to the clinical observation that OCD patients essentially suffer from intrusive thoughts deriving from an inability to put away information designated for "forgetting," a facility that is commonplace among individuals without the disorder.

The study with panic disorder patients provided partial support for this "inability to forget" hypothesis (McNally, Otto, Yap, Pollack, & Hornig, 1996b). Whereas panic patients did not show preferential memory for threat-related information under either remember or forget instructions, hemispheric differences emerged suggesting that panic patients show quite distinctive preferential processing of emotional material compared to the healthy control group. The findings suggest that patients show biased processing toward and away from threat material. The study is perhaps most interesting in its contribution to the longstanding investigation concerning the extent to which hemispheric laterality differences may play a role in the processing of verbal emotional material. It would be interesting to assess hemispheric laterality differences in other populations, particularly individuals with post traumatic stress symptoms given that difficulty processing emotional material is believed to be a critical roadblock in recovery from trauma.

The first published study on directed-forgetting effects in a trauma population focused on individuals abused in childhood who also suffered from BPD (Cloitre, 1996). The results indicated that these individuals have enhanced directed-forgetting skills that derive not so much from the ability to "forget" information on command, but rather, from an enhanced ability to focus attention on information designated for remembering. The finding contrasts with those obtained in the two PTSD studies in which traumatized individuals showed diminished directed-forgetting skills (Cloitre & MacLeod, 1996; McNally et al., 1996a). One possible reason for this discrepancy is that the diminished directed-forgetting effect associated with the trauma groups derives primarily from responses to trauma-related information, and that such material was not successfully evaluated in the BPD study.

Secondly and more importantly, differences in memory performance may reflect differences in the character of the disorders. Whereas PTSD is always and BPD is frequently associated with a traumatic history, the cognitive-affective components associated with each disorder differ. In particular, in both clinical papers (Kernberg, 1975; Marmer & Horowitz, 1986) and experimental studies (Cancienne, 1995), BPD has been associated with a tendency to compartmentalize information into distinct sets along affective lines. A person with BPD is expected to categorize information with sets of both "good" events and persons, and "bad" events and persons. This type of activity is believed to function as a coping strategy in which good events in the individual's life are protected from being overwhelmed by negative events, such as chronic assaults, and their associated negative affective valence. The engagement of this type of coping strategy is hypothetically associated with an early life developmental period in which the skill of integration of information across time and space has not yet been solidly achieved.

In contrast, formulation of the cognitive-affective characteristics of PTSD are less well developed. The data thus far seem to suggest that unlike BPD, PTSD may be associated with a tendency to blur categories of information (e.g., things to remember vs. things to forget). This may be related to the high arousal state that many PTSD victims recall experiencing during their traumatic events and which, after the trauma has ended, appears to be quite easily triggered in relatively low stress situations (van der Kolk, 1988b).

The Cloitre and MacLeod (1996) study on PTSD patients, which included a healthy nontraumatized group, supported an intrusion rather than dissociative or deficit model of PTSD. A further refinement of the previous studies was that enhanced recall of trauma words was not associated with the diagnosis of PTSD per se but seemed to be related to the severity and frequency of post traumatic stress symptoms.

Future Directions

The most obvious limitation in all of the studies completed thus far is methodological, namely, the reliance on an item-cued rather than list-cued presentation of the stimuli. Basden et al. (1993) found that, at least among nonclinical samples, item-cued presentation elicited elaboration of to-be-remembered items as the strategy of choice in accomplishing the directed-forgetting task, whereas list presentation elicited inhibition of the to-be-forgotten information. The fact that differences in processing strategies can be created through minor changes in task demands reflects the efficiency and flexibility of the human processing system. However, such findings strongly suggest that we have uncovered only a partial picture of the deviations in cognitive-affective processing in clinical populations.

The item-cued method has revealed ways in which clinical populations deviate in the encoding and elaboration of information. The examination of list presentation formats is necessary to assess potential differences in inhibitory and other retrieval mechanisms. There is some irony in the current state of affairs as clinical researchers have been more interested in inhibition than in encoding mechanisms in clinical populations (Herman & Schatzow, 1987; Williams, 1994). Future studies should apply both item-cued and list-cued stimuli presentations to trauma victims and comparison groups. It may be that under relevant testing conditions, trauma populations will show enhanced forgetting as well as enhanced (or intrusive) remembering. Clearly these two phenomena need not be mutually exclusive.

Lastly, the debate about the merits of using different types of memory tasks following directed-forgetting instructions needs to be resolved by experimental psychologists before clinical researchers can meaningfully compare and interpret performances on these tasks in clinical populations. The extent to which encoding and retrieval activities differentially contribute to tasks such as free recall and recognition, not to mention other memory tests, remains unclear (see MacLeod, this volume). In general, methodological advances in cognitive science can be accomplished better by experimentalists who have relatively large numbers of healthy study participants readily available. Once techniques and methods have been refined, they can be applied to clinical populations that are smaller in number and less accessible. The value in assessing clinical populations lies in the fact that such assessments test the theoretical principles that have been constructed during the method development and initial data collection phases of research spearheaded by the cognitive scientists.

The few studies completed in directed forgetting among clinical samples have identified the durability of the phenomenon and the affective variables under which the effect can be enhanced or diminished. They have also provided converging evidence that encoding as well as retrieval mechanisms contribute to the effect. Future studies with clinical populations can test the boundaries of enhancing and diminishing the directed-forgetting effect in both its encoding and retrieval components. More broadly, research with clinical populations helps facilitate the incorporation of affective variables into models of attention and memory. The linking of emotion and cognition is a worthwhile goal if we are to understand the richness of psychological processes.

REFERENCES

American Psychiatric Association. (1994). *Diagnostic and statistical manual of mental disorders* (4th ed.). Washington, DC: Author.

Barlow, D. H. (1988). Anxiety and its disorders. New York: Guilford.

Basden, B. H., Basden, D. R., & Gargano, G. J. (1993). Directed forgetting in implicit and explicit memory tests: A comparison of methods. *Journal of Experimental Psychology: Learning, Memory and Cognition, 19*, 603–616.

Bowlby, J. (1977). The making and breaking of affectional bonds, II: Aetiology and psychopathology in the light of attachment theory. *British Journal of Psychiatry, 130*, 201–210.

Cancienne, J. C. (1995). *An examination of splitting as found in borderline patients: A cognitive viewpoint in terms of the processing of information about important relationship experiences.* Unpublished dissertation. New School for Social Research, New York.

Christianson, S-A. (1992). *The handbook of emotion and memory: Research and theory.* Hillsdale, NJ: Lawrence Erlbaum Associates.

Cloitre, M. (1992). The avoidance of emotional processing: A cognitive science perspective. In D. J. Stein & J. E. Young (Eds.), *Cognitive science and clinical disorders* (pp. 20–40). Orlando, FL: Academic Press.

Cloitre, M. (1996, November). Directed forgetting in rape victims. Paper to be presented in symposium "Memory in survivors of sexual violence" (Chair: R. J. McNally). *Association for the Advancement of Behavior Therapy*, New York, NY.

Cloitre, M., Cancienne, J., Brodsky, B., Dulit, R., & Perry, S. (1996). Memory performance among women with parental abuse histories: Enhanced directed forgetting or directed remembering? *Journal of Abnormal Psychology, 105*, 204–211.

Cloitre, M., & Liebowitz, M. (1991). Memory bias in panic disorder: An investigation of the cognitive avoidance hypothesis. *Cognitive Therapy and Research, 15*, 371–386.

Cloitre, M., & MacLeod, C. M. (1996). *Directed forgetting in rape victims: The relative contributions of childhood abuse and current PTSD.* Manuscript in preparation.

Cloitre, M., Shear, M. K., Cancienne, J., & Zeitlin, S. (1994). Explicit and implicit memory for catastrophic associations to bodily sensation words in panic disorder. *Cognitive Therapy and Research, 18*, 225–240.

Cole, P. M., & Putnam, F. W. (1992). Effect of incest on self and social functioning: A developmental psychopathology perspective. *Journal of Consulting and Clinical Psychology, 60*, 174–184.

Davidson, J. R. T., & Foa, E. B. (1993). *Posttraumatic stress disorder: DSM-IV and beyond.* Washington, DC: American Psychiatric Press.

Finkelhor, D., & Browne, A. (1985). The traumatic impact of child sexual abuse: A conceptualization. *American Journal of Orthopsychiatry, 55*, 530–541.

Foy, D. W. (1992). *Treating PTSD: Cognitive-behavioral strategies.* New York: Guilford.

Geiselman, R. E., & Panting, T. M. (1985). Personality correlates of retrieval processes in intentional and unintentional forgetting. *Personality and Individual Differences, 6*, 685–691.

Herman, J. L. (1981). *Father-daughter incest.* Cambridge, MA: Harvard University Press.

Herman, J. L., Perry, J. C., & van der Kolk, B. A. (1989). Childhood trauma in borderline personality disorder. *American Journal of Psychiatry, 146*, 490–495.

Herman, J. L., & Schatzow, E. (1987). Recovery and verification of memories of childhood sexual trauma. *Psychoanalytic Psychology, 4*, 1–14.

Herman, J. L., & van der Kolk, B. A. (1988). Traumatic antecedents of borderline personality disorder. In B. A. van der Kolk (Ed.), *Psychological trauma* (pp. 111–126). Washington, DC: American Psychiatric Press.

Kernberg, O. F. (1975). *Borderline conditions and pathological narcissism.* New York: Aronson.

Marmer, C. R., & Horowitz, M. J. (1986). Phenomenological analysis of splitting. *Psychotherapy, 23*, 21–29.

Mathews, A., & MacLeod, C. (1994). Cognitive approaches to emotional disorders. *Annual Review of Psychology, 45*, 25–50.

McNally, R. J., Foa, E. B., & Donnell, C. D. (1989). Memory bias for anxiety information in patients with panic disorder. *Cognition and Emotion, 3*, 27–44.

McNally, R. J., Metzger, L. J., Lasko, N. B., & Pitman, R. K. (1996a). *Directed forgetting of trauma cues in women with histories of childhood sexual abuse.* Manuscript under review.

McNally, R. J., Otto, M. W., Yap, L., Pollack, M. H., & Hornig, C. D. (1996b). *Is panic disorder linked to cognitive avoidance of threatening information?* Manuscript in preparation.

Ogata, S. N., Silk, K. R., Goodrich, S., Lohr, N. E., Westen, D., & Hill, E. M. (1990). Childhood sexual and physical abuse in adult populations with borderline personality disorder. *American Journal of Psychiatry, 147*, 1008–1013.

Russell, D. E. H. (1986). *The secret trauma: Incest in the lives of girls and women.* New York: Basic Books.

Spitzer, R. L., Williams, J. B., Gibbon, M., & First, M. (1989). *Structured clinical interview for DSM-III-R Axis II disorders.* New York: Biometrics Research Department, New York State Psychiatric Institute.

Stein, D. J., & Young, J. E. (1992). *Cognitive science and clinical disorders.* San Diego, CA: Academic Press.

Terr, L. (1994). *Unchained memories: True stories of traumatic memories lost and found.* New York: Basic Books.

van der Kolk, B. (1988a). *Psychological trauma.* Washington, DC: American Psychiatric Press.

van der Kolk, B. A. (Ed.). (1988b). *Psychological trauma.* Washington, DC: American Psychiatric Press.

Wilhelm, S., McNally, R. J., Baer, L., & Florin, I. (in press). Directed forgetting in obsessive-compulsive disorder. *Behaviour Research and Therapy.*

Williams, L. M. (1994). Recall of childhood trauma: A prospective study of women's memories of childhood sexual abuse. *Journal of Consulting and Clinical Psychology, 62*, 1167–1176.

Yehuda, R., Keefe, R. S. E., Harvey, P. D., Levengood, R. A., Gerber, D. K., Geni, J., & Siever, L. J. (1995). Learning and memory in combat veterans with post traumatic stress disorder. *American Journal of Psychiatry, 152*, 137–139.

15

Instructions to Disregard and the Jury: Curative and Paradoxical Effects

Saul M. Kassin
Williams College

Christina A. Studebaker
University of Nebraska

It was called the "trial of the century." As in live theater, the O. J. Simpson trial was packed with drama—and much of it was created by information that was not in evidence. In his opening statement, defense lawyer Johnnie Cochran repeatedly made reference to witnesses who would not later testify, eliciting a series of objections from prosecuting attorney Marcia Clark. Eventually, the trial judge ordered the jury to disregard these references. A few days later, Denise Brown, Nicole's sister, broke down and cried on the witness stand as gruesome crime photos triggered a gasp in the courtroom. Also during the trial, Simpson published his story in a book, Marcia Clark became embroiled in a child custody suit, and defense lawyers were caught withholding key evidence. As in other cases, the jury was shielded from some of these events, but it was instructed to disregard the rest. The question is, are juries influenced by information not in evidence? And to what extent do they, or can they, comply with the all-too-familiar admonishment to disregard?

During the course of every trial, the jury is instructed to render a verdict based solely on evidence presented through the sworn testimony of witnesses, exhibits, and facts stipulated to by the opposing attorneys, and to ignore all facts not formally admitted into evidence. Over the years, the courts have developed elaborate rules of evidence and trial procedure designed to regulate the traffic of information in the courtroom and to help ensure that these goals are achieved. These rules dictate who may serve as a witness, the kind of testimony that may be given, the content and format of direct- and cross-examination questions, the scope of opening and closing statements, and the phrasing of the judge's instructions (for a comprehensive review, see Mueller & Kirkpatrick, 1995).

Although the trial is a well-orchestrated event, juries are often exposed to information that is not admissible as evidence. To the extent that such extralegal factors increase or decrease perceptions of a defendant's guilt or liability, or precipitate a raising or lowering of the standard of proof seen as necessary for conviction, they will have a prejudicial effect on jury decision making. Indeed, mock jury research has shown that verdicts can be influenced by a wide range of nonevidentiary factors presented both inside and outside the courtroom. Such factors include pretrial publicity about the defendant (Kramer, Kerr, & Carroll, 1990; Moran & Cutler, 1991; Ogloff & Vidmar, 1994; Otto, Penrod, & Dexter, 1994; Padawer-Singer & Barton, 1975), disclosure of his or her prior record (Greene & Dodge, 1995), trial-relevant events in the news (Greene & Loftus, 1984), testimony ruled inadmissible by the judge (Carretta & Moreland, 1983; Pickel, 1995; Sue, Smith, & Caldwell, 1973; Thompson, Fong, & Rosenhan, 1981; Wissler & Saks, 1985), hideous crime-scene images (Kassin & Garfield, 1991), coerced confessions (Kassin & McNall, 1981; Kassin & Sukel, 1997; Kassin & Wrightsman, 1980), a presumptuous death qualification voir dire (Haney, 1984), conjectural cross-examination questions (Kassin, Williams, & Saunders, 1990), the "dynamite charge," an instruction used to prod deadlocked juries into unanimous verdicts (Kassin, Smith, & Tulloch, 1990; Smith & Kassin, 1993), and hearsay, as communicated by an expert witness (Schuller, 1995).

It is often said that the biases exhibited by the individual jurors are attenuated by deliberation, the process by which the group comes together to discuss the facts, arguments, and law in an effort to reach a unanimous verdict. To the contrary, however, research has shown that jury verdicts are highly predictable from the predeliberation distribution of the initial votes (Kalven & Zeisel, 1966; Kerr, 1981; Sandys & Dillehay, 1995; Stasser & Davis, 1981). Indeed, illustrating the phenomenon of group polarization, the biasing effects of pretrial publicity, inadmissible testimony, and other objectionable material appear to persist—and are often exacerbated by—the process of jury deliberation (Carretta & Moreland, 1983; Kramer et al., 1990; Padawer-Singer & Barton, 1975; but see Kerwin & Shaffer, 1994, as an exception).

According to the rules of evidence, information is admissible if it is relevant to the case and has probative value, unless that information was illegally gained, or unless it is too prejudicial, inflammatory, misleading, confusing, or cumulative. If a lawyer or witness deliberately or inadvertently communicates inadmissible information to the jury, and if the opposing attorney objects, the judge has two options: to declare a mistrial or to strike the evidence from the record and admonish the jury to disregard it. Because mistrials are costly, reserved for only the most egregious and harmful breaches of the rules of evidence, judges routinely manage the problem through an instruction to disregard. In this chapter, we examine different theoretical perspectives on this procedure and review mock jury research concerning its impact on jurors exposed to nonevidentiary sources of information. We then examine possible solutions to the problem.

PSYCHOLOGICAL PERSPECTIVES

On the general question of whether people are able and willing to disregard inadmissible evidence upon instruction, there appear to be four relevant bodies of research. One concerns the problem of directed or intentional forgetting, the ability to edit from memory recently acquired information. Thus, subjects might be presented with a list of words, some of which they are told they will have to recall and some of which they will have to forget. As reviewed by MacLeod elsewhere in this book, this research has indicated that people can successfully forget information on cue, depending on how the to-be-forgotten information was encoded, the scope of the instruction, the type of retrieval task, and other factors (see also Johnson, 1994). One must be cautious, however, in generalizing from this laboratory paradigm to the courtroom, where information to be disregarded often has implications for the way other evidence is interpreted (e.g., a defendant's prior crime record is seen as diagnostic of his or her character), and where jurors are expected not to forget the information, necessarily, but to discount it (i.e., attach zero weight) in their decision making.

A second relevant body of research concerns the phenomenon of belief perseverance, the tendency for people's beliefs to persist even after all the evidence on which they were derived has been discredited. For example, Anderson, Lepper, and Ross (1980) had subjects read case studies suggesting that the best fire fighters are either risk takers or cautious types and then generate an explanation for this correlation. Afterward, all subjects were told, supposedly within debriefing, that the information they were given was totally false, manufactured for the sake of the study. When later requestioned about risk-taking and fire-fighting ability, subjects clung to their newly created beliefs even though the evidentiary basis for those beliefs was invalidated. This basic result has been obtained in a wide range of studies (e.g., Anderson & Sechler, 1986; Johnson & Seifert, 1994; Ross, Lepper, & Hubbard, 1975; Schul & Burnstein, 1985). Of relevance to jury decision making, this research suggests that instructions to disregard may fail when the discredited information has already activated the formation of a theory or explanatory structure.

A third relevant body of research concerns the paradoxical effects of thought suppression. In a series of studies on mental control, Wegner (1989) found that people find it very difficult to actively suppress a thought upon instruction, particularly when that thought is vivid or emotionally exciting. In one paradigm, for example, subjects were instructed to think aloud while trying to suppress the image of a white bear. As measured by the number of times subjects rang a bell to signal the intrusion of that image, or the number of times it was mentioned in verbal protocols, results showed that white bears intruded upon consciousness with remarkable frequency (Wegner & Erber, 1992; Wegner, Schneider, Carter, & White, 1987). Research suggests that people are similarly unable to suppress upon instruction the use of salient stereotypes in their social judgments (Macrae, Bodenhausen, Milne, & Jetten, 1994). Indeed, the harder people try to control a thought—particularly one that is emotionally charged (Edwards & Bryan, 1997)—the less likely they are to succeed (Wegner, 1994).

A fourth perspective is provided by psychological reactance theory, which states that people are motivated to protect their freedom to think, feel, and act as they choose (Brehm, 1966; Brehm & Brehm, 1981). According to this motivationally oriented theory, people react against threats to their decision-making freedom by desiring products that are scarce, by engaging in forbidden behaviors, by seeking information that is banned or censored, and by moving in an attitudinal direction opposite to one that is strongly advocated, often resulting in a "boomerang effect," or negative attitude change. In this context, one would predict that instructions to disregard—precisely because they are used to restrict a juror's decision-making freedom—may backfire by arousing psychological reactance. Thus, in one mock jury study, subjects were more likely to use inadmissible testimony when the judge punctuated his ruling with a firmly worded admonishment to disregard than when he did not (Wolf & Montgomery, 1977).

To summarize, at least four areas of research can be brought to bear in understanding the use of jury instructions to disregard. Taken together, these areas suggest a broad range of possible effects. Research on directed forgetting suggests the possibility that jurors are capable of discounting information as requested by the judge. In contrast, research on belief perseverance suggests that such instructions will fail to the extent that the withdrawn evidence leads jurors to construct a theory of the event that is in dispute. Finally, research on the paradoxical effects of thought suppression and psychological reactance suggest a possibility that is even more disconcerting—that admonishments will backfire, increasing rather than decreasing the weight that jurors give to the forbidden information.

MOCK JURY RESEARCH

Do instructions to disregard have the curative, neutralizing effect intended by the courts? Do they serve as a "mental eraser," leading jurors, on command, to discount information to which they had been exposed? Research conducted in a mock jury paradigm has examined the impact of pretrial publicity, presumptuous cross-examination questions, coerced confessions, and witness testimony that is ruled inadmissible by the judge. Across variations in the type of "contaminant" introduced at trial, the basic experimental design requirements are the same. At a minimum, all such studies contain a baseline (no contaminant) control group, an admissible condition in which the item is presented and ruled admissible following an objection, and an inadmissible condition in which the judge strikes the information from the record and admonishes the jury to disregard it. Within the framework of this basic three-group design, instructions to disregard are considered effective to the extent that verdicts in the inadmissible condition resemble those found in the control group and ineffective to the extent that they are more similar to those found in the admissible condition. Building upon this skeletal design, researchers have varied other factors as well, including the type of evidence in dispute, whether that evidence favors the prosecution or defense, and the substance or tone of the judge's admonishment. What follows is a review of the effects on jurors of pretrial publicity, presumptuous cross-examination questions, coerced confessions, and inadmissible testimony, all despite instructions to disregard.

Pretrial Publicity

Many cases find their way into the news media long before they appear in court. Some prominent examples include the recent trials of O. J. Simpson, William Kennedy Smith, Mike Tyson, Susan Smith, Lorena Bobbitt, Dr. Jack Kevorkian, the Los Angeles police officers who beat Rodney King, the Menendez brothers, and Oklahoma City bomb suspects Terry Nichols and Timothy McVeigh. In each instance, the same question arises: Does pretrial exposure to news stories corrupt prospective jurors?

Public opinion surveys consistently show that the more people know about a criminal case, the more likely they are to presume the defendant guilty, even while claiming to be impartial (Constantini & King, 1980/1981; Moran & Cutler, 1991). Mock jury studies have further shown that pretrial publicity biases jurors despite their subsequent exposure to hard evidence, judge's instructions, and deliberation (for a review, see Kerr, 1994). For example, Kramer et al. (1990) played a videotaped reenactment of an armed robbery trial to hundreds of subjects participating in 108 mock juries. Before watching the tape, subjects were exposed to either neutral or prejudicial (factually or emotionally) newspaper clippings on the case. Although subjects were advised to base their decisions solely on the evidence as presented in court, prejudicial publicity had a marked effect: It increased the postdeliberation conviction rate from 33% to 48%. To make matters worse, judges and defense lawyers could not predict from a simulated voir dire which of the jurors were biased by their exposure, a result consistent with other research indicating that voir dire is not an effective remedy (Dexter, Cutler, & Moran, 1992). Moreover, pretrial publicity is even more influential when the news is presented on television rather than in print (Ogloff & Vidmar, 1994).

One standard "remedy" against the biasing effects of pretrial publicity is for judges to admonish the jury, often repeatedly, to ignore all information about the case received from the news media. As reviewed by Kerr (1994), however, at least seven pretrial publicity studies included specific caution-ary instructions in this regard and not a single one demonstrated a remedial effect. In the Kramer et al. (1990) study described earlier, for example, half of the mock jurors were administered a standard jury instruction concerning pretrial publicity, and these subjects exhibited the same biasing effect of prejudicial news exposure as those who did not receive the instruction. Thus, it is clear that in high-profile cases, in which a community is saturated with pretrial publicity, judges should be willing to grant motions for other available remedies (i.e., continuance, change of venue).

Presumptuous Cross-Examination Questions

Just as jurors are biased by news stories, often they receive extralegal information from within the trial itself. The rules of evidence and procedure that guide the questioning of witnesses are designed to facilitate the jury's quest for truth. In theory, this means that methods of direct- and cross-ex-amination should increase the credibility of witnesses who are accurate and honest, while lowering the credibility of those who are inaccurate or dis-honest, thus heightening the jury's fact-finding competence. In practice, however, trial attorneys often engage in ethically questionable practices such as coaching witnesses, leading their testimony in court, distracting the jury at critical moments, and asking questions that invite the introduction of inadmissible testimony (Underwood & Fortune, 1988).

In general, there are two ways in which a lawyer can bias a juror's perception of evidence. One is to ask suggestive questions that elicit mis-leading information from the witness. This method was demonstrated in the classic study by Loftus and Palmer (1974), in which eyewitness reports concerning the speed of an automobile were manipulated by whether the ensuing collision was described by the verb "smashed" rather than by more neutral terms such as "hit," "bumped," or "contacted." A second way in which lawyers can bias the jury is by asking presumptuous questions that imply facts not corroborated by the evidence (e.g., "When did you stop beating your wife"? "Haven't you accused men of rape before?"). Indeed, this strategy was employed in the trial of O. J. Simpson, when defense attorney F. Lee Bailey asked police officer Mark Fuhrman, "Did you plant the bloody glove?"

Is it possible to mislead jurors about a witness through the use of presumptuous questions? To test this hypothesis, Kassin, Williams, and Saunders (1990) presented subjects with a rape trial transcript in which the cross-examiner posed a question to an expert witness implying that he, the expert, had a tarnished professional reputation ("Isn't it true that your work is poorly regarded by your colleagues?" "Hasn't your work been sharply criticized in the past?"). Depending on the condition, the question was met with either an admission ("Yes it is"), a denial ("No, it isn't"), or an objection from the witness's lawyer, after which the question was withdrawn and the jury was admonished to disregard it. The result: Whenever the expert's reputation was questioned (i.e., compared to a control group), ratings of his credibility were significantly diminished. This effect was obtained despite the absence of any corroborating evidence and regardless of whether the accusatory question had produced a denial, an admission, or an objection followed by an instruction to disregard. It is particularly interesting that this effect was obtained even in the objection-disregard condition, where many subjects later reported—in apparent compliance with the judge's admonishment—that they did not actually believe the derogatory implication of the cross-examiner's question.

Coerced Confessions

In criminal justice, confession evidence is the prosecutor's most potent weapon. Confessions to the police, however, are also a recurring source of controversy. Whether a suspect's statement was voluntary or coerced, or whether a suspect was of sound mind, are just two of the issues that trial judges and juries consider on a routine basis. To protect the integrity of the legal system, to guard us against violations of due process, and to minimize the risk that innocent people confess to crimes they did not commit, American courts have erected guidelines over the years for the admission of confession evidence. For example, a confession is typically excluded if it was elicited by physical violence, by a threat of harm or punishment, by a promise of leniency, or in the absence of Miranda warnings (for reviews of recent case law, see Kamisar, LaFave, & Israel, 1994; Mueller & Kirkpatrick, 1995; for reviews of the psychology of confession evidence, see Gudjonsson, 1992; Kassin, 1997; Wrightsman & Kassin, 1993).

In all cases involving a disputed confession, a preliminary hearing is typically held in which the judge determines whether it was voluntary and admissible. In some states, confessions deemed voluntary are admitted into evidence without special instruction. In other states, the jury is directed to make its own independent judgment of voluntariness and to disregard statements found to be coerced. But what if a jury is erroneously exposed to evidence of a coerced confession? Can a judge's admonishment to disregard this potent form of evidence mitigate its persuasive impact when it is divulged at trial but then withdrawn?

In a study designed to test this hypothesis, Kassin and Sukel (1997) had subjects read one of five transcript versions of a murder trial. In a low-pressure version, the defendant was said to have confessed immediately on being questioned. In a high-pressure version, subjects read that the defendant was interrogated with his hands tied painfully behind his back and that the detective had waved his gun in a menacing manner. In half of the cases, the judge ruled that the confession was admissible. In the other half, he ruled that it was inadmissible and issued an admonishment to disregard. There was also a fifth version, a control group in which there was no confession.

In some ways, the results were reassuring. Confronted with a confession elicited through high-pressure interrogation tactics, subjects responded in a legally prescribed manner: They judged the statement to be involuntary and said that it did not affect their decisions. Similarly, subjects for whom the confession was ruled inadmissible were more likely to infer that it was involuntary and claim that it did not influence them. On the all-important measure of verdicts, however, all groups exposed to a confession, compared to the no-confession control group, were more likely to vote guilty. This included those who had received an instruction to disregard. Thus, the conviction rate in the high-pressure inadmissible group was 44%, a significant increase over the 19% rate in the no-confession control group. This result was found even though most subjects in this group knew that the high-pressure confession was involuntary, correctly recalled that it had been stricken from the record, and said that it did not influence their verdicts. These basic results were then replicated in two subsequent mock jury studies, including one conducted in a courthouse with prospective jurors who had just been excused from jury duty. To summarize, it appears that confessions are so prejudicial that jurors do not, and perhaps cannot, fully discount the information even when instructed to do so by the court.

Inadmissible Testimony

In light of the aforementioned mock jury studies on the contaminating effects of pretrial publicity, presumptuous cross-examination questions, and coerced confessions, is it reasonable to expect that jurors can ever disregard inadmissible testimony upon instruction? Members of the legal community are mixed in their beliefs. In *Carter v. Kentucky* (1981), the U.S. Supreme Court argued that admonishment is a "powerful tool" (p. 303) that can be used to "remove from the jury's deliberations any influence of unspoken adverse inferences" (p. 301). Similarly, the Sixth Circuit Court of Appeals recently argued that "a clear and positive instruction to disregard cures error" (*United*

States v. Steele, 1984, p. 588). Yet, many judges over the years have described the practice in highly derogatory terms, as a "mental gymnastic" (*Nash v. United States*, 1932, p. 1007), an "unmitigated fiction" (*Krulewitch v. United States*, 1949, p. 453), a "judicial placebo" (*United States v. Grunewald*, 1956, p. 574), and like an "exorcising phrase intended to drive out evil spirits" (Frank, 1930, p. 184). Paralleling the disagreements in the legal community, research on the effects of inadmissible testimony has yielded somewhat mixed results. In an early experiment, Sue, Smith, and Caldwell (1973) had mock jurors read about the trial of a defendant who was charged with armed robbery and murder. When the evidence was weak and circumstantial, not a single subject voted guilty. In a second condition, however, the state also introduced an illegally obtained recording of a telephone conversation in which the defendant said to a bookmaker, "I finally got the money to pay you off ... when you read the papers tomorrow, you'll know what I mean." The defense argued that because the wiretapping operation was illegal, it should not be allowed into evidence. The judge disagreed, however, and ruled that the tape was admissible. As expected, the conviction rate increased to 26%. In a third condition, the tape was played and the defense objected, but this time the judge ruled that the wiretap was illegal, that the tape was inadmissible, and that the jury should disregard what they heard. In this situation, 35% voted for conviction.

Using the same materials, Carretta and Moreland (1983) presented the wiretap evidence as either admissible or inadmissible. They found that compared to subjects in a baseline control group, those presented with the incriminating wiretap were more likely to perceive the defendant as guilty regardless of admissibility. This pattern was evident not only in predeliberation ratings, but in postdeliberation ratings as well. Indeed, audiotapes of the deliberations revealed that most mock juries exposed to the wiretap evidence discussed it, as well as the judge's ruling, during their deliberations.

Whereas the foregoing studies indicate that instructions to disregard often have no effect on juries, other research suggests that such instructions may even backfire, producing a paradoxical "boomerang effect." This possibility was first demonstrated in an early study in which Broeder (1959) had mock jurors listen to an audiotaped civil case involving an automobile accident. In civil law, juries are not supposed to know whether a defendant is insured for the damages on the assumption that this disclosure will lead them to award large sums to the plaintiff. In a control version of the trial, there was no information concerning the defendant's insurance status. In a second version, the plaintiff's attorney revealed that the defendant had insurance. In the third version, this same disclosure was followed by an objection from the defense, which prompted an instruction to disregard. After all the evidence was presented, juries deliberated on a verdict and on damage awards. In the control condition, mock juries awarded the plaintiff a mean of $33,000. In the insurance-no objection condition, the award increased, as expected, to $37,000. The key question was whether the instruction to disregard served as a mental eraser by bringing awards back down to baseline. The answer was loud and clear: Contrary to expectations, mean jury awards in the insurance-admonishment group increased to $46,000.

To some extent, the judge's admonishment backfired because it drew added attention to the insurance disclosure, heightening its salience and subsequent accessibility in memory. Another problem is that the admonishment may have aroused psychological reactance, a motivation to protect one's decision-making freedom. To examine this possibility, Wolf and Montgomery (1977) presented subjects with a summary of an assault case. Critical testimony favoring the prosecution or defense was ruled either admissible or inadmissible. Among subjects in the latter condition, half were further warned by the judge that the critical testimony "must play no role in your consideration of the case. You have no choice but to disregard it." Interestingly, subjects in this latter situation, compared to those in other conditions, said it was less important to comply with the judge's admonishment.

In the most recent examination of instructions to disregard, Pickel (1995) presented mock jurors with prior conviction evidence that implicated the defendant in a theft trial. That evidence was either ruled admissible, ruled inadmissible with a simple admonishment to disregard, or ruled inadmissible and accompanied by an explanation of this ruling by the judge. The results provided added support for a boomerang effect. As compared to subjects in the baseline control group, those for whom the critical testimony was ruled inadmissible, resulting in a simple admonishment to disregard, complied with that instruction. Yet, subjects who heard the critical inadmissible testimony accompanied by a legal explanation showed an increased conviction rate, similar to that in the admissible condition. As in Wolf and Montgomery's (1977) study, the elaborated admonishment proved counterproductive.

Finally, in sharp contrast to the findings that instructions to disregard are impotent, or worse, that they trigger a boomerang effect, some researchers have found that mock jurors do discount testimony from a witness who is later discredited (Elliott, Farrington, & Manheimer, 1988; Hatvany & Strack, 1980; Weinberg & Baron, 1982). For example, Schul and Manzury (1990) presented subjects with an assault case in which an eyewitness corroborated the victim's story. Sometimes it was also revealed that this witness was completely drunk at the time, thus leading the judge to rule that the testimony was invalid (note that this latter manipulation lacks ecological realism, as judges will almost never "invade the jury's province" by commenting on the credibility of witnesses). The results supported the discounting hypothesis: Compared to a no-eyewitness control group, guilt ratings increased in the credible-witness condition but returned to baseline in the discredited-witness condition. The authors speculated from these results that "court settings activate a schema that leads people to deliberately correct for potential biases" (p. 337).

The Limited Admissibility Rule

Although a certain degree of imperfection is to be expected, there are times when the legal system adds insult to injury by opening its doors to the introduction of inadmissible evidence. If, according to the rules, an item of evidence is allowable for one purpose but not another, the judge shall admit it, restrict its proper scope, and instruct the jury accordingly. This situation arises in a number of ways. For example, the state is normally not permitted to reveal whether the defendant has a criminal record. This rule is based on a legitimate fear that juries will be prejudiced by the defendant's background, presume guilt rather than innocence, and vote to convict on the assumption that "if he did not commit the crime charged he probably has committed or will commit other crimes" (Lempert, 1977). But if the defendant takes the stand, the prosecuting attorney is then allowed to ask about past convictions on cross-examination in an effort to impeach the defendant's credibility as a witness. The judge would then issue a limited instruction to disregard, telling jurors that they may consider the defendant's prior record as it bears on his or her credibility, but that they must not allow that same information to influence their beliefs about the defendant's guilt or innocence. As codified in the Federal Rules of Evidence, this provision is commonly known as the "limited admissibility rule."

Can jurors compartmentalize important evidence in this manner, using it to prove one aspect of the case, but then acting as if it does not exist for another? This rule is viewed by many in the legal system as a lesson in futility. Many years ago, a survey revealed that 98% of the lawyers and 43% of the judges questioned believed that jurors could not comply with such an instruction (Note, 1968). They were right. In a mock jury study, Wissler and Saks (1985) found that subjects who heard that a defendant had a prior criminal record but who were instructed to limit their use of that evidence were significantly more likely to vote guilty even when their judgments of the defendant's credibility as a witness were unaffected by that information. In addition, research shows that deliberating juries spend a good deal of time talking about a defendant's prior record, not for what it implies about his or her credibility as a witness, but for what it suggests about his or her criminal predisposition (Shaffer, 1985). Indeed, mock jurors who are informed of the defendant's record also tend to perceive the remaining evidence as stronger and more damaging than those who are uninformed, even when both groups read the same case (Hans & Doob, 1975).

THE INSTRUCTION TO DISREGARD:
JUSTICE BY JURY

Mock jury research has yielded somewhat inconsistent results. In some studies, subjects were both willing and able to discount evidence that was discredited; yet in most other experiments, the judge's admonishment either did not have the intended curative effect or produced a paradoxical boomerang effect. Part of the problem, to be sure, is that information presented but withdrawn persists by influencing the way jurors interpret other evidence. People simply find it difficult to actively suppress salient information upon instruction, and they react against efforts to restrict their decision-making freedom. In our view, however, the key to the problem stems from the fact that instructions to disregard often call upon juries to set aside information that has probative value, information that would enhance the accuracy of their decision making.

In our view, juries do not share the courts' principles of what constitutes a fair trial. The law defines justice within a "due process" model in which a verdict is just to the extent that it is reached in a manner consistent with the rules of evidence and procedure that regulate the fairness of the process. As legal scholars have long realized, however, due process is not the jury's primary concern (Kadish & Kadish, 1971). Ask a juror what his or her primary objective is, and the answer is "to make the *right* decision." As revealed in numerous cases involving jury nullification, juries throughout history have reached verdicts that they considered fair and equitable, even if inconsistent with the letter of the law (for a review, see Horowitz & Willging, 1991).

The objectives of due process and accuracy are not necessarily incompatible. Indeed, it would not have made sense to develop an adjudication procedure that did not generally achieve accurate results. Based on various assumptions about human behavior, the courts have reasonably determined that certain kinds of information are so inherently prejudicial, unreliable, unfair, or confusing, that they should not be made available to the jury. Granted, such a policy results in occasional verdict errors but, in the long run, accuracy as an objective is well served. It is the "in the long run" part that can be so unsatisfying. Indeed, we would argue that it is precisely because juries want to make correct decisions that they cannot resist the temptation to use information they see as relevant—whether it satisfies the law's technical rules or not.

Various lines of research are consistent with the hypothesis that juries are motivated more by a desire for correct or just outcomes than by a concern for due process. For example, American courts routinely exclude confessions that were elicited by promises or threats made during interrogation, primarily on the ground that such methods violate the due process rights of the accused. Yet, in a series of mock jury studies, Kassin and Wrightsman (1985) found that whereas subjects completely discounted threat-induced confessions, they did not disregard confessions made in response to a promise of leniency. In this latter situation, subjects conceded that the defendant's confession was involuntary according to the law, but they voted for conviction. The reason: People do not perceive an offer of leniency to be sufficiently coercive to elicit a false confession.

Additional research as well indicates that lay people define justice by outcomes rather than by due process. In one study, Pickel (1995) found that mock jurors complied with an instruction to disregard inadmissible hearsay, which is excluded out of concern for its reliability, but they did not disregard the defendant's prior record, an item that has probative value but is excluded because it is prejudicial. In a second study, Thompson et al. (1981) presented subjects with inadmissible evidence that either corroborated or contradicted the defendant's alibi. They found that although subjects were not more likely to vote guilty when the inadmissible evidence favored conviction (compared to a control group), they were significantly less likely to vote guilty when that evidence favored acquittal. With false conviction being the least desirable outcome, subjects were unwilling, regardless of a judge's instruction, to ignore evidence that vindicated the accused. The authors concluded that "jurors tend to decide cases according to their own standards of justice and are not much influenced by what the judge says" (p. 461; see also Greene & Dodge, 1995).

Based on the assumption that juries are motivated primarily by outcome considerations, one would expect selective compliance with admonishments to disregard. If evidence is ruled inadmissible because it lacks validity, jurors should comply with the judge's instruction and disregard that information. However, if that same evidence is excluded because it was obtained in a manner that breached due process (the so-called "technicality" defense), then jurors should allow that information to influence their verdicts regardless of the judge's instruction. In short, jurors may be influenced not by an admonishment per se, but by an explanation of why the critical evidence was being excluded.

In a mock jury study, Kassin and Sommers (1997) tested the hypothesis that jurors would comply with or resist an instruction to disregard inadmissible testimony depending on the reason for its exclusion. Eighty-one subjects read a series of 23 paragraphs, presented on videotape for 30 seconds each, that summarized the evidence, arguments, and instructions of a murder trial. The case involved a man charged with the murder of his estranged wife and male neighbor. The prosecutor charged that the defendant killed his wife and neighbor in a fit of jealous rage after finding them together.

The defendant claimed he merely found the bodies when he returned to his former home to retrieve personal checks and bank documents.

In a control version of the case, the evidence against the defendant was circumstantial, incomplete, and ambiguous. In three other versions, however, a police officer testifying for the state revealed that a wiretap from an unrelated case produced a taped phone conversation in which the defendant could be heard confessing to a friend. In all instances, the defense attorney objected to this evidence. In an admissible testimony condition, the judge overruled the objection and admitted the tape into evidence. In an inadmissible-due process condition, the judge sustained the objection and admonished the jury to disregard the tape recording on the ground that it was obtained illegally, without a proper warrant. In an inadmissible-invalid condition, the judge again sustained the objection, but this time admonished the jury to disregard the tape because it was barely audible and hard to determine what was being said through all the static and background noise.

To examine the online impact of both the critical incriminating evidence and judge's ruling, each subject was given a wireless hand-held dial equipped with a digital display with a numerical setting that ranged from 0 to 100, and had a midpoint of 50. Subjects were instructed to set the dial at 50 and to move it up or down after each paragraph to reflect the extent to which the information led them to see the defendant as guilty or innocent. After the presentation, subjects rendered a verdict, rated their confidence in that judgment, listed the factors most important to their verdict, and answered other case-related questions.

The results provided strong support for the hypothesis. On verdicts, only 24% of the subjects judged the defendant guilty in the baseline control group, compared to 79% in the admissible condition. This highly significant increase in the conviction rate demonstrates the power of the critical wiretap evidence used in this study. What happened when this damaging evidence was ruled inadmissible? The results showed that subjects complied with the judge's ruling, as instructed, when the evidence was excluded because it lacked validity (i.e., the conviction rate was the same as in the control group). When that same evidence was inadmissible because it was illegally obtained, however, subjects exhibited a significant increase in the conviction rate (see Fig. 15.1). This effect is particularly interesting in light of the fact that very few subjects in this condition, compared to those in the admissible group, listed the wiretap evidence among the factors that influenced their verdict.

Turning to the online judgments that subjects made during the trial presentation, the results were highly informative (see Fig. 15.2). As shown in Fig. 15.3, subjects from the four groups reacted similarly to the evidence until the incriminating wiretap was introduced (decision point 9), at which point

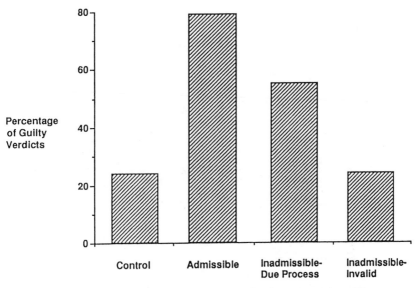

FIG. 15.1. Posttrial conviction rates in the control and experimental conditions (Kassin & Sommers, 1997).

ratings of guilt increased dramatically in the three experimental conditions compared to the control group. At the next point (decision point 10), where the judge ruled on the defense attorney's objection, guilt ratings increased even further when the tape was admissible, decreased slightly when it was ruled inadmissible because it was illegally obtained, and decreased to baseline when it was ruled inadmissible due to a lack of validity. Most interesting, perhaps, is that the four groups differed in the inferences they drew from that point on. Specifically, subjects in the admissible and inadmissible-due process groups saw many of the remaining items of evidence as more suggestive of guilt than did those in the inadmissible-invalid and control groups. This result is consistent with Pennington and Hastie's (1986) contention that jurors engage in integrative processing of the evidence.

To summarize, both online and posttrial judgments supported the hypothesis that jurors would comply with a judge's instruction to disregard inadmissible evidence when that evidence is excluded for a lack of validity, but that they would allow that information to influence their verdicts when the evidence is excluded on the basis of a legal technicality. In the latter situation, subjects appeared to discount the forbidden testimony immediately after the judge's ruling and did not cite that evidence as having swayed their verdicts. Yet, these same subjects saw subsequent items of evidence as more incriminating and exhibited an increased rate of conviction. Clearly, jurors may be influenced not by a judge's ruling per se, but by his or her attribution for that ruling.

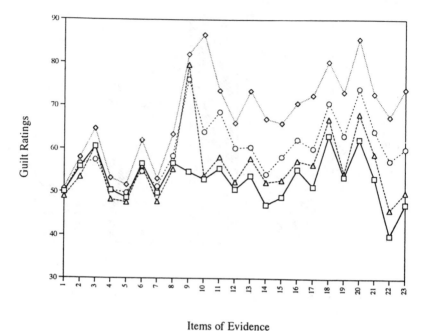

Items of Evidence

—□— Control

·······◇······· Admissible

····○···· Inadmissible-Due Process

----△---- Inadmissible-Invalid

FIG. 15.2. Online ratings of guilt before (points 1–8), during (points 9–10), and after (points 11–23) the critical testimony and instruction.

JURY TRIAL MANAGEMENT: POLICY CONSIDERATIONS

Practically speaking, inadmissible testimony poses a difficult dilemma. On the one hand, trial lawyers are advised, as a matter of strategy, that it is sometimes better to decline the opportunity to object in the jury's presence so as not to draw attention to the damaging information. On the other hand, the lawyer who fails to make a timely objection cannot later cite that problem as a basis for appealing the verdict. As a result, the party damaged by a breach in the rules of evidence is placed in a strategic dilemma, forced to choose between the lesser of two evil options. Indeed, as we have seen, the jury's failure to disregard is a problem that extends across a broad range

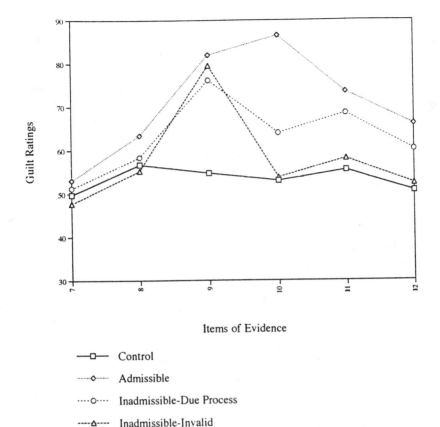

Items of Evidence

—□— Control

······◇······ Admissible

····○···· Inadmissible-Due Process

----△---- Inadmissible-Invalid

FIG. 15.3. On online ratings, the effect can be seen most clearly in ratings made immediately before (7–8) and after (11–12) the manipulation.

of nonevidentiary contaminants (e.g., pretrial publicity, presumptuous cross-examination questions, coerced confessions, and inadmissible testimony) and compromises the objectives of a fair trial (Kassin & Wrightsman, 1988).

Is there anything more that the courts can do to prevent the leakage of evidence not in the trial record? One radical solution is to replace the live trial with videotape as a way to sterilize the presentation of evidence and prevent the jury's contamination. In this procedure, testimony would be videotaped, the judge would then view the tape, rule on objections, and delete all inadmissible testimony, leaving the jury to base its judgment on a clean, carefully edited product (Miller & Fontes, 1979). As interesting as this proposal seems, it may be too drastic a measure to take and may create greater problems than it solves (e.g., jurors may be less attentive to video-tape than to the spontaneous and live event; they would also be limited in their ability to see all that transpires in the courtroom).

Considering less radical proposals for reform, one possibility is for judges to inoculate juries at the start of every trial with a general warning that some of the information they will receive will be inadmissible. In a nonlegal setting, Schul (1993) found that such early warning, when coupled with a subsequent reminder, enabled subjects to suspend the integrative processing of evidence and to think more critically about items later to be discredited. In light of research showing that preevidence jury instructions are generally more effective than postevidence instructions (FosterLee, Horowitz, & Bourgeois, 1993; Kassin & Wrightsman, 1979; Smith, 1991), a special pretrial warning concerning the leakage of inadmissible testimony has interesting potential, particularly if judges get jurors to state during the voir dire that they understand the problem (Tanford, 1990).

A second strategy is for judges to explain to jurors, once the contaminant is introduced, the bases of the ruling and instruction to disregard. To be sure, some of the studies reviewed earlier indicated that strong or elaborated admonishment can backfire. Yet, the study reported in this chapter, coupled with an analysis of the inconsistencies in past research, suggest that jurors will comply with instructions to disregard, at least to the extent that these instructions focus on problems that are substantive rather than procedural. Thus, jurors seem willing to discount information, as requested, to the extent that questions concerning its reliability and validity are raised (e.g., biased news articles, presumptuous cross-examination questions lacking a factual basis, uncorroborated hearsay, and highly coerced confessions).

A variant of this latter approach is to arouse suspicion among jurors concerning the ulterior motives of the attorney, witness, or other source of inadmissible information. Attribution research shows that a state of suspicion concerning an actor's motives triggers critical thinking and facilitates discounting of behaviors with multiple plausible causes (Fein, 1996; Fein, Hilton, & Miller, 1990). To test the hypothesis that suspicion would similarly attenuate the biasing effects of nonevidence in a legal setting, Fein, McCloskey, and Tomlinson (in press) recently conducted two mock jury experiments. In one study, subjects read about a murder case with or without exposure to incriminating newspaper stories about the defendant. Despite the judge's admonishment to disregard, pretrial publicity had the usual contaminating effect on jurors. In a third condition, however, where questions were raised about the motives of the news media for publishing the story (e.g., "to sell papers"), this effect was erased: The conviction rate was as low as that obtained in the baseline control group. A similar pattern of results was obtained in a second study where subjects who read an assault case were biased in their verdicts by damaging inadmissible hearsay. This effect was erased when the defense attorney questioned the prosecutor's motive for knowingly asking a question that invited the disclosure and then the judge explained in his admonishment that lawyers will sometimes invite inadmissible testimony in an effort to sway the jury. As in the first study, this suspicion manipulation brought the conviction rate back down to baseline. To summarize, there are two basic conceptual strategies for controlling the biasing effects of nonevidence and increasing the jury's compliance with instructions to disregard. One involves a general pretrial warning about inadmissible testimony designed to inoculate jurors, perhaps by getting them to suspend the processes of integrative encoding. The second way involves administering a specific treatment to the jurors immediately after they have been exposed. In this approach, the key is for the judge to explain that the prohibited information should be discounted not for strictly procedural reasons, but because it cannot be trusted. In short, it appears that the way to facilitate discounting is either by casting doubt about the specific class of forbidden evidence (e.g., hearsay) or by activating suspicion about the source of that evidence (e.g., the lawyer).

At this point, it remains to be seen whether such strategies are feasible for use in an actual courtroom. Clearly, additional research is needed. For example, it is important to know whether the approaches shown to be effective in mock jury studies, where the baseline control trials are typically weak, would prove too punitive and prejudicial toward an offending party whose case is strong (e.g., if a lawyer has a strong case, does the substantive admonishment on a single item lead jurors to discount other, more probative evidence as well?). Having sufficiently documented the problem, jury researchers are now in a position to investigate the possible solutions.

REFERENCES

Anderson, C. A., Lepper, M. R., & Ross, L. (1980). Perseverance of social theories: The role of explanation in the persistence of discredited information. *Journal of Personality and Social Psychology, 39,* 1037–1049.

Anderson, C. A., & Sechler, E. S. (1986). Effects of explanation and counterexplanation on the development and use of social theories. *Journal of Personality and Social Psychology, 50,* 24–34.

Brehm, J. W. (1966). *A theory of psychological reactance.* New York: Academic Press.

Brehm, S. S., & Brehm, J. W. (1981). *Psychological reactance.* New York: Academic Press.

Broeder, D. (1959). The University of Chicago jury project. *Nebraska Law Review, 38,* 744–760.

Carretta, T. R., & Moreland, R. L. (1983). The direct and indirect effects of inadmissible evidence. *Journal of Applied Social Psychology, 13,* 291–309.

Carter v. Kentucky, 450 U.S. 288 (1981).

Constantini, E., & King, J. (1980/1981). The partial juror: Correlates and causes of prejudgment. *Law and Society Review, 15,* 9–40.

Dexter, H. R., Cutler, B. L., & Moran, G. (1992). A test of voir dire as a remedy for the prejudicial effects of pretrial publicity. *Journal of Applied Social Psychology, 22,* 819–832.

Edwards, K., & Bryan, T. S. (1997). Judgmental biases produced by instructions to disregard: The (paradoxical) case of emotional information. *Personality and Social Psychology Bulletin, 23.*

Elliott, R., Farrington, B., & Manheimer, H. (1988). Eyewitness credible and discredible. *Journal of Applied Social Psychology, 18,* 1411–1422.

Fein, S. (1996). The effects of suspicion on attributional thinking and the correspondence bias. *Journal of Personality and Social Psychology, 70,* 1164–1184.

Fein, S., Hilton, J. L., & Miller, D. T. (1990). Suspicion of ulterior motivation and the correspondence bias. *Journal of Personality and Social Psychology, 58,* 753–764.

Fein, S., McCloskey, A. L., & Tomlinson, T. M. (in press). Can the jury disregard that information?: The use of suspicion to reduce the prejudicial effects of pretrial publicity and inadmissible testimony. *Personality and Social Psychology Bulletin.*

FosterLee, L., Horowitz, I. A., & Bourgeois, M. J. (1993). Juror competence in civil trials: Effects of preinstruction and evidence technicality. *Journal of Applied Psychology, 78,* 14–21.

Frank, J. (1930). *Law and the modern mind.* New York: Tudor.

Greene, E., & Dodge, M. (1995). The influence of prior record evidence on juror decision-making. *Law and Human Behavior, 19,* 67–78.

Greene, E., & Loftus, E. F. (1984). What's new in the news?: The influence of well publicized news events on psychological research and courtroom trials. *Basic and Applied Social Psychology, 5,* 211–221.

Gudjonsson, G. H. (1992). *The psychology of interrogations, confessions, and testimony.* London: Wiley.

Haney, C. (1984). On the selection of capital juries: The biasing effects of the death qualification process. *Law and Human Behavior, 8,* 121–132.

Hans, V., & Doob, A. (1975). Section 12 of the Canada Evidence Act and the deliberations of simulated juries. *Criminal Law Quarterly, 18,* 235–253.

Hatvany, N., & Strack, F. (1980). The impact of a discredited key witness. *Journal of Applied Social Psychology, 10,* 490–509.

Horowitz, I. A., & Willging, T. E. (1991). Changing views of jury power: The nullification debate, 1787–1988. *Law and Human Behavior, 15,* 165–182.

Johnson, H. M. (1994). Processes of successful intentional forgetting. *Psychological Bulletin, 116,* 274–292.

Johnson, H. M., & Seifert, C. M. (1994). Sources of the continued influence effect: When misinformation in memory affects later inferences. *Journal of Experimental Psychology: Learning, Memory, and Cognition, 20,* 1420–1436.

Kadish, M. R., & Kadish, S. H. (1971). The institutionalization of conflict: Jury acquittals. *Journal of Social Issues, 27,* 199–217.

Kalven, H., & Zeisel, H. (1966). *The American jury.* Boston: Little, Brown.

Kamisar, Y., LaFave, W., & Israel, J. (1994). *Modern criminal procedure* (8th ed.). St. Paul, MN: West.

Kassin, S. M. (1997). The psychology of confession evidence. *American Psychologist, 52,* 221–233.

Kassin, S. M., & Garfield, D. A. (1991). Blood and guts: General and trial-specific effects of videotaped crime scenes on mock jurors. *Journal of Applied Social Psychology, 21,* 1459–1472.

Kassin, S. M., & McNall, K. (1991). Police interrogations and confessions: Communicating promises and threats by pragmatic implication. *Law and Human Behavior, 15,* 233–251.

Kassin, S. M., Smith, V. L., & Tulloch, W. F. (1990). The dynamite charge: Effects on the perceptions and deliberation behavior of mock jurors. *Law and Human Behavior, 14,* 537–550.

Kassin, S. M., & Sommers, S. (in press). Inadmissible testimony, instructions to disregard, and the jury: Substantive versus procedural considerations. *Personality and Social Psychology Bulletin.*

Kassin, S. M., & Sukel, H. (1997). Coerced confessions and the jury: An experimental test of the "harmless error" rule. *Law and Human Behavior, 21,* 27–46.

Kassin, S. M., Williams, L. N., & Saunders, C. L. (1990). Dirty tricks of cross-examination: The influence of conjectural evidence on the jury. *Law and Human Behavior, 14,* 373–384.

Kassin, S. M., & Wrightsman, L. S. (1979). On the requirements of proof: The timing of judicial instruction and mock juror verdicts. *Journal of Personality and Social Psychology, 37,* 1877–1887.

Kassin, S. M., & Wrightsman, L. S. (1980). Prior confessions and mock juror verdicts. *Journal of Applied Social Psychology, 10,* 133–146.

Kassin, S. M., & Wrightsman, L. S. (1985). Confession evidence. In S. M. Kassin & L. S. Wrightsman (Eds.), *The psychology of evidence and trial procedure* (pp. 67–94). Beverly Hills, CA: Sage.

Kassin, S. M., & Wrightsman, L. S. (1988). *The American jury on trial: Psychological perspectives.* Washington, DC: Hemisphere.

Kerr, N. L. (1981). Social transition schemes: Charting the group's road to agreement. *Journal of Personality and Social Psychology, 41,* 684–702.

Kerr, N. L. (1994). The effects of pretrial publicity on jurors. *Judicature, 78,* 120–127.

Kerwin, J., & Shaffer, D. R. (1994). Mock jurors versus juries: The role of deliberations in reactions to inadmissible testimony. *Personality and Social Psychology Bulletin, 20,* 153–162.

Kramer, G. P., Kerr, N. L., & Carroll, J. S. (1990). Pretrial publicity, judicial remedies, and jury bias. *Law and Human Behavior, 14,* 409–438.

Krulewitch v. United States, 336 U.S. 440 (1949).

Lempert, R. O. (1977). Modeling relevance. *Michigan Law Review, 75,* 1021–1057.

Loftus, E. F., & Palmer, J. C. (1974). Reconstruction of automobile destruction: An example of the interaction between language and memory. *Journal of Verbal Learning and Verbal Behavior, 13,* 585–589.

Macrae, C. N., Bodenhausen, G. V., Milne, A. B., & Jetten, J. (1994). Out of mind but back in sight: Stereotypes on the rebound. *Journal of Personality and Social Psychology, 67,* 808–817.

Miller, G. R., & Fontes, N. E. (1979). *Videotape on trial: A view from the jury box.* Beverly Hills, CA: Sage.

Moran, G., & Cutler, B. L. (1991). The prejudicial impact of pretrial publicity. *Journal of Applied Social Psychology, 21,* 345–367.

Mueller, C. B., & Kirkpatrick, L. C. (1995). *Modern evidence: Doctrine and practice.* Boston: Little, Brown.

Nash v. United States, 54 F.2d 1006 (1932).

Note. (1968). To take the stand or not to take the stand: The dilemma of the defendant with a criminal record. *Columbia Journal of Law and Social Problems, 4,* 215–223.

Ogloff, J. R. P., & Vidmar, N. (1994). The impact of pretrial publicity on jurors: A study to compare the relative effects of television and print media in a child sex abuse case. *Law and Human Behavior, 18,* 507–525.

Otto, A. L., Penrod, S. D., & Dexter, H. R. (1994). The biasing impact of pretrial publicity on juror judgments. *Law and Human Behavior, 18,* 453–469.

Padawer-Singer, A., & Barton, A. H. (1975). Free press, fair trial. In R. J. Simon (Ed.), *The jury system: A critical analysis* (pp. 123–142). Beverly Hills, CA: Sage.

Pennington, N., & Hastie, R. (1986). Evidence evaluation in complex decision making. *Journal of Personality and Social Psychology, 51,* 242–258.

Pickel, K. L. (1995). Inducing jurors to disregard inadmissible evidence: A legal explanation does not help. *Law and Human Behavior, 19,* 407–424.

Ross, L., Lepper, M. R., & Hubbard, M. (1975). Perseverance in self-perception and social perception: Biased attributional processes in the debriefing paradigm. *Journal of Personality and Social Psychology, 32,* 880–892.

Sandys, M., & Dillehay, R. C. (1995). First-ballot votes, pre-deliberation dispositions, and final verdicts in jury trials. *Law and Human Behavior, 19,* 175–195.

Schul, Y. (1993). When warning succeeds: The effect of warning on success in ignoring invalid information. *Journal of Experimental Social Psychology, 29,* 42–62.

Schul, Y., & Burnstein, E. (1985). When discounting fails: Conditions under which individuals use discredited information in making a judgment. *Journal of Personality and Social Psychology, 49,* 894–903.

Schul, Y., & Manzury, F. (1990). The effects of type of encoding and strength of discounting appeal on the success of ignoring invalid testimony. *European Journal of Social Psychology, 20,* 337–349.

Schuller, R. A. (1995). Expert evidence and hearsay: The influence of "secondhand" information on jurors' decisions. *Law and Human Behavior, 19,* 345–362.

Shaffer, D. R. (1985). The defendant's testimony. In S. Kassin & L. Wrightsman (Eds.), *The psychology of evidence and trial procedure* (pp. 124–149). Beverly Hills, CA: Sage.

Smith, V. L. (1991). Impact of pretrial instructions on jurors' information processing and decision making. *Journal of Applied Psychology, 76,* 220–228.

Smith, V. L., & Kassin, S. M. (1993). Effects of the dynamite charge on the deliberations of deadlocked mock juries. *Law and Human Behavior, 17,* 625–644.

Stasser, G., & Davis, J. H. (1981). Group decision making and social influence: A social interaction sequence model. *Psychological Review, 88,* 523–551.

Sue, S., Smith, R. E., & Caldwell, C. (1973). Effects of inadmissible evidence on the decisions of simulated jurors: A moral dilemma. *Journal of Applied Social Psychology, 3,* 345–353.

Tanford, J. A. (1990). The law and psychology of jury instructions. *Nebraska Law Review, 69,* 71–111.

Thompson, W. C., Fong, G. T., & Rosenhan, D. L. (1981). Inadmissable evidence and juror verdicts. *Journal of Personality and Social Psychology, 40,* 453–463.

Underwood, R. H., & Fortune, W. H. (1988). *Trial ethics.* Boston: Little, Brown.

United States v. Grunewald, 233 F.2d 556 (1956).

United States v. Steele, 727 F.2d 580 (1984).

Wegner, D. M. (1989). *White bears and other unwanted thoughts: Suppression, obsession, and the psychology of mental control.* New York: Viking.

Wegner, D. M. (1994). Ironic processes of mental control. *Psychological Review, 101,* 34–52.

Wegner, D. M., & Erber, R. (1992). The hyperaccessibility of suppressed thoughts. *Journal of Personality and Social Psychology, 63,* 903–912.

Wegner, D. M., Schneider, D. J., Carter, S. R., & White, T. L. (1987). Paradoxical effects of thought suppression. *Journal of Personality and Social Psychology, 53,* 5–13.

Weinberg, H. I., & Baron, R. S. (1982). The discredible eyewitness. *Personality and Social Psychology Bulletin, 8,* 60–67.

Wissler, R. L., & Saks, M. J. (1985). On the inefficacy of limiting instructions: When jurors use prior conviction evidence to decide on guilt. *Law and Human Behavior, 9,* 37–48.

Wolf, S., & Montgomery, D. A. (1977). Effects of inadmissible evidence and level of judicial admonishment to disregard on the judgments of mock jurors. *Journal of Applied Social Psychology, 7,* 205–219.

Wrightsman, L. S., & Kassin, S. M. (1993). *Confessions in the courtroom.* Newbury Park, CA: Sage.

16

"THE JURY WILL DISREGARD ...": A BRIEF GUIDE TO INADMISSIBLE EVIDENCE

William C. Thompson
Juliana Fuqua
University of California, Irvine

During trials, judges often admonish the jurors to disregard something they have seen or heard that fails to qualify as admissible evidence (Tanford, 1990). These admonitions, which are sometimes called "curative instructions," vary in complexity. Sometimes the jurors are told to ignore a particular fact or statement altogether. Sometimes they are instructed to use a piece of evidence conditionally—that is, to draw inferences from it only if they determine that certain conditions are met, and otherwise to ignore it. Sometimes they are instructed to use a piece of evidence for a limited purpose—that is, they are told that they may use it to draw one type of inference, but not another.

These instructions call on jurors to engage in intentional forgetting. Indeed, the requirement that jurors disregard inadmissible evidence is a prime example of a situation in which intentional forgetting is important. It is not surprising, then, that studies on mock jurors' reactions to inadmissible evidence are cited prominently in reviews of the literature on intentional forgetting (Golding & Long, this volume).

This chapter provides a brief overview of the circumstances under which jurors may be instructed to disregard evidence. It is written for the benefit of psychologists who are interested in intentional forgetting and it is designed to help them in two ways. First, it points out a number of interesting psychological questions raised by current legal practices. Second, it provides a framework for understanding the laws of evidence and thereby provides guidance to those who wish to do legally relevant research.

THE LEGAL BASIS FOR ADMISSIBILITY RULES

Jury trials are conducted according to an elaborate set of procedural and evidentiary rules that specify the types of evidence that are and are not admissible (Lempert & Saltzburg, 1977, 1982). Some of these rules have their source in English common law. Restrictions on the use of hearsay, for example, can be traced to common law precedent several hundred years old (Landsman & Rakos, 1991), as can restrictions on the use of character evidence (Wydick, 1987). Other rules are the product of constitutional law. The exclusionary rule (*Weeks v. United States*, 1914; *Mapp v. Ohio*, 1961) restricts the admissibility of evidence gathered in violation of a defendant's rights under the Fourth Amendment. Evidence that violates the defendant's Fifth Amendment privilege against self-incrimination or Sixth Amendment right of confrontation is also excluded.

In the United States, many of these rules have been codified, which means that they are incorporated in statutes. For example, the Federal Rules of Evidence, enacted by Congress in 1975, regulate the federal courts.[1] In each state, there is an evidence code, enacted at the state level, that applies to state courts. Generally the state codes are quite similar to the Federal Rules (indeed, some are identical), although there is variation across jurisdictions on some points. For example, some states are more lenient than others with regard to the admissibility of particular types of hearsay and character evidence.[2]

Rules excluding evidence from admission in court have several purposes (Lempert, 1977; Lempert & Saltzburg, 1977, 1982). One purpose is to screen out evidence that has such limited relevance that it would needlessly prolong the trial without contributing to the proper resolution of the matter at hand. Such evidence is ruled inadmissible because it is deemed insufficiently diagnostic to be worth the trouble of hearing.

A second purpose of exclusionary rules of evidence is to screen out prejudicial evidence—that is, evidence that is so likely to create bias or to

---

[1]The Federal Rules of Evidence were drafted by an advisory committee appointed by Chief Justice Earl Warren in 1965. The committee's mission was to bring clarity and uniformity to legal standards for the admissibility of evidence. A version of the rules was approved by the Supreme Court in 1972, but was thereafter amended by Congress in the course of enacting it into law. The final version is thus a joint product of the Supreme Court's rule-making procedure and the legislative process in Congress. The rules are found in Title 28 of the United States Code (*see*, United States Code Annotated, 1984).

[2]Psychologists who seek to understand particular rules of evidence can look to a number of sources. Law school case books (texts) are helpful. A particularly good one is Lempert and Saltzburg (1977, 1982), which has a social science bent. Another good place to begin is with an annotated code. Most law libraries have annotated versions of the Federal Rules of Evidence and the state codes, which provide indices for finding statutes on particular issues, the text of the statutes, and cross-references to a variety of materials useful for interpreting each statute, such as appellate cases, law review articles, and commentary by the legislative committees that drafted the statutes concerning the justification for each rule.

be misused by the jury that the fact-finding process would be more accurate without it (Kaplan, 1968). One way evidence can be prejudicial is by inflaming the passions of the jury and evoking hostility toward a party without casting much light on the issue at hand. Evidence that a defendant on trial for drunk driving is a pedophile, for example, would probably be considered prejudical because it is likely to generate more heat than light. Evidence can also be prejudicial if jurors tend to overvalue it (i.e., give it more weight than it deserves). Evidence may therefore be excluded because it is thought to be weak or problematic in ways that jurors are unlikely to appreciate. Hearsay evidence, character evidence, and some types of scientific evidence fall in this category.[3]

A third purpose of exclusionary rules is to screen out evidence that cannot be presented without violating the constitutional rights of a criminal defendant. Evidence seized in illegal searches and coerced confessions fall into this category.

Finally, some exclusionary rules of evidence are designed to serve specific public policy goals. For example, when a person is sued for negligence after someone is injured on their property, evidence that the person took subsequent remedial action to prevent future accidents, is inadmissible to prove negligence (e.g., Federal Rules of Evidence, Rule 407, United States Code Annotated, 1984). This rule is justified in part by "a fear that if such evidence were admitted, people would be unwilling to take post-accident precautions, to the general detriment of society" (Lempert & Saltzburg, 1977, p. 187). Similarly, evidence that a party offered an out-of-court settlement is inadmissible to prove liability (e.g., Federal Rule 408) because out-of-court settlements are a favored means of resolving disputes and "individuals would be reluctant to negotiate compromises if they knew evidence of their offers could be used against them in court" (Lempert & Saltzburg, 1977, p. 191). Rules of privilege also fall in this category. The attorney–client privilege, for example, helps assure that people may communicate freely with their attorneys by preventing disclosure of communications between attorney and client. The marital privilege protects the sanctity of the marital relationship by preventing testimony about communications between spouses. The priest–penetant privilege protects the sanctity of the confessional by preventing testimony about it. These policy-oriented rules reflect a legislative judgment that accuracy and completeness of fact finding at trial is less important to society than another goal (Lempert & Saltzburg, 1982).

---

[3]Whether jurors actually overvalue hearsay is an issue psychologists have recently begun to explore (Kovera, Park, & Penrod, 1992; Miene, Borgida, & Park, 1993; Thompson, 1993). Like many rules of evidence, the rules excluding hearsay are based, in part, on the assumption that hearsay is likely to be overvalued and therefore will be prejudicial. Whether such assumptions are warranted is a worthy issue for psychological study.

PROCEDURES FOR DEALING
WITH INADMISSIBLE EVIDENCE

Trials are conducted in a manner designed to prevent the jury from hearing most types of inadmissible evidence. Some questions of admissibility are resolved before trial in hearings on "motions in limine" (i.e., pretrial motions to determine the admissibility of evidence). Lawyers face sanctions if they attempt to present evidence that has been ruled inadmissible. Other questions of admissibility are resolved during the trial when lawyers raise objections. The rules require that testimony of witnesses be elicited in a question-and-answer mode (rather than by narrative) so that the opposing lawyer may object to any question likely to elicit inadmissible testimony (and receive a judicial ruling on the issue) before the answer is given. A degree of skepticism about the ability of jurors to engage in intentional forgetting is reflected in the fact that our system of trial attempts to screen out most inadmissible evidence in advance, rather than simply instructing jurors to ignore it after it is presented.

Despite efforts to prevent it, inadmissible evidence sometimes reaches the jury. The judge then has two options; declaring a mistrial or admonishing the jury to disregard it. Because it is expensive and burdensome to retry cases, judges are reluctant to declare mistrials. The law generally requires that they do so only when the inadmissible evidence is powerfully prejudicial. Consequently, a judicial admonition is by far the most common response when the jury is exposed to inadmissible evidence.

Appellate courts have taken inconsistent positions on the efficacy of judicial admonitions. Justices who favor reliance on admonitions over the option of a mistrial (in a particular case) often argue that jurors can be counted on to ignore evidence when told to do so. For example, in *Bruton v. United States* (1968), a case involving the efficacy of a judicial admonition to ignore a codefendant's confession, which incriminated the defendant, Justice White declared:

> It is a common experience of all men to be informed of "facts" relevant to an issue requiring their judgment, and yet to disregard those "facts" because of sufficient grounds for discrediting their veracity or the reliability of their source. . . . I have no doubt that serious-minded and responsible men are able to shut their minds to unreliable information when exercising their judgment . . . (pp. 142–143)

On the other hand, appellate courts sometimes find judicial admonitions inadequate precisely because of the fear that the jury will be unable to follow them. Thus, the noted jurist Learned Hand once called such admonitions "recommendations to the jury of a mental gymnastic which is beyond not only their powers, but anybody's else" (*Nash v. United States*, 1932, p.

1007). Appellate opinions thus contain a hodgepodge of inconsistent statements about jurors' ability, "treating [jurors] at times as a group of low-grade morons and at other times as men endowed with a superhuman ability to control their emotions and intellects" (Morgan, 1956, p. 105).

Whether such statements are the true basis for a particular ruling, or simply a convenient rationale for a ruling reached on other grounds, is often difficult to assess. Suppose, for example, that after a jury is exposed to inadmissible evidence, the judge chooses to admonish the jurors rather than declare a mistrial, and the resulting jury verdict is appealed. An appellate justice who is reluctant (for any reason) to overturn the verdict can support a ruling affirming it by arguing stoutly that the jurors were able to follow instructions. A justice who wants to overturn the verdict can argue the opposite. It may therefore be difficult to tell whether the resulting statements about jurors' ability reflect the justices' true beliefs, or whether they are simply a form of posturing used to justify a decision reached on other (less defensible) grounds.

The notion that the purported rationale for an appellate opinion may differ from the true rationale was a prominent tenet of the Legal Realist movement (see generally, Monahan & Walker, 1994, pp. 17–30). Jerome Frank, a prominent legal realist and appellate justice, was extremely critical of the notion that jurors can intentionally disregard evidence when so instructed by a judge. Frank called this assumption "a kind of 'judicial lie'" that "undermines a moral relationship between the courts, the jurors and the public; like any other judicial deception, it damages the decent administration of justice" (*United States v. Gruenwald*, 1956, p. 574). It is by no means clear, however, that Frank's jaundiced assessment is widely shared. Some justices (e.g., Justice White, quoted above) appear sincere in their belief that jurors can, at least in some instances, successfully follow instructions to ignore inadmissible evidence.

The following sections describe in more detail the various circumstances under which jurors may be exposed to inadmissible evidence and the legal mechanisms that exist for dealing with it.

Pretrial Publicity and Out-of-Court Communication

Pretrial publicity about a case may expose jurors to evidence that is later ruled inadmissible. It is not uncommon, for example, for the media to report that a defendant confessed in cases where the putative confession is later ruled inadmissible because it was improperly obtained. Inadmissible information about a defendant's prior criminal record is sometimes reported as well. Additionally, the media sometimes report the facts of a case in an inaccurate or biased manner. There has been considerable research on the effects of exposure to such publicity (e.g., Greene, 1990; Moran & Cutler, 1991; Simon, 1980).

Several legal mechanisms exist for dealing with this out-of-court exposure (Hans, 1990; Kramer, Kerr, & Carroll, 1990). During jury selection, potential jurors can be asked what they have heard about the case and those who know too much, or appear to have formed opinions about the case, can be excluded. In cases where pretrial publicity has so tainted the jury pool that it would be difficult to choose an unbiased jury, a change of venue may be granted, but this option is used only in extreme cases because it is burdensome and expensive. In most instances, mere exposure to pretrial publicity about the case is not sufficient grounds for exclusion if the juror professes to have an open mind about the case and promises to consider only evidence admitted in court when reaching a verdict. Whether jurors can accurately assess the extent to which they have been influenced by inadmissible evidence is an interesting psychological question.

At the beginning of the trial, the jurors are admonished to disregard anything heard outside the courtroom. At the beginning of the O. J. Simpson trial, for example, Judge Ito's instructions to the jury included the following:

> You must decide this case solely upon the evidence presented here in the courtroom. You must completely disregard any press, television, radio or other media reports that you may have read, seen or heard concerning this case or the defendant. These reports are not evidence and you must not be influenced in any manner by such publicity.
>
> You are not to discuss among yourselves or with anyone else any subject connected with this trial. You are not to form or express any opinion on the case until the case is submitted to you for your deliberations in the jury room. ... You must not read or listen to any accounts or discussions of the case reported by newspapers or other news media. (*People v. Simpson*, filed Transcript, January 23, 1995, pp. 11525–11526)

During the trial, opportunities for out-of-court exposure to inadmissible evidence continue. Judges typically instruct jurors to report any out-of-court exposure to such information, even if inadvertent, in order that the judge may determine (usually by questioning the jurors) whether it undermines their objectivity. Jurors can be removed from the jury during the trial and replaced by alternates if the judge determines that they have been tainted. Whether judges can accurately assess the degree to which jurors have been influenced by inadmissible evidence is another important psychological question.

Blurting Witnesses

Jurors may also be exposed to inadmissible evidence in the courtroom. Sometimes witnesses unexpectedly blurt out inadmissible facts. Sometimes lawyers are slow to object to an improper question, allowing the witness to present inadmissible testimony before the objection is sustained.

In *State v. Pennell* (1989), for example, the prosecution sought to introduce a then novel form of DNA evidence against a murder defendant. The evidence purported to show a match between the victim and a bloodstain in the defendant's vehicle with respect to genetic characteristics that were estimated to occur at random in only one person in 30 billion. In pretrial motions, the defendant challenged the admissibility of the DNA evidence, arguing (among other things) that there was inadequate scientific validation for the statistical estimate. After an extensive pretrial hearing, the judge agreed and ruled that the prosecution could present evidence that the genetic characteristics of the victim were consistent with those of the bloodstain, but could not present statistics on the rarity of those characteristics. In front of the jury, however, an expert witness for the prosecution, while answering a question about the DNA match, unexpectedly blurted out that such a match would be found between unrelated individuals only one time in 30 billion. The defense demanded a mistrial, arguing that the inadmissible one-in-30 billion statistic was highly damaging to the defendant and was so striking that it would be impossible for the jury to ignore. The judge, however, found it sufficient to instruct the jury that the statistic had been stricken from the record and should be disregarded. The resulting conviction was upheld on appeal.

Although courts generally find that an admonition is an adequate remedy (Tanford, 1990), there are occasional cases in which the inadmissible evidence is deemed so prejudicial that a mistrial is essential. Consider, for example, the situation that arose in a recent Arkansas murder case (*Moore v. State*, 1996). On the witness stand was the prosecution's key witness, Lester Parker (also known as Fleabag), who testified that he had heard defendant Oscar Moore confess to the murder of the victim, Ms. Cannon. Parker was being cross-examined by Moore's attorney when the following exchange occurred.

Q: Now, Fleabag, I don't suppose we could be so lucky as for you to tell us that there was somebody else besides you that heard Oscar Moore on this Saturday night confess to you that he had killed Ms. Cannon?

A: Did.

Q: Oscar Moore, on this Saturday night that he confessed to you that he killed Ms. Cannon, there was nobody else present there, was there?

A: No, but he admitted to killing another woman to his brother. (p. 536)

Because the statement linking Moore to another murder was clearly inadmissible, Moore's attorney asked for a mistrial. Under Arkansas law, which is similar to that in other states, the judge must declare a mistrial "only where the error complained of is so prejudicial that justice cannot be served by continuing the trial or when the fundamental fairness of the trial itself has been manifestly affected" (*Stewart v. State*, 1995, p. 79). After a brief hearing in chambers, the trial judge decided that the inadmissible statement was not sufficiently prejudicial to meet this standard, and therefore simply instructed the jury to ignore Parker's answer to defense counsel's question. After Moore was convicted, however, the verdict was overturned on appeal by the Arkansas Supreme Court, which found that the trial judge had abused his discretion by failing to declare a mistrial "in the face of such a patently inflammatory and prejudicial statement." According to the Supreme Court, Parker's statement was "so prejudicial that it could not be cured by an admonition to the jury" (*Moore v. State*, 1996, p. 537).

The difference of opinion between the trial judge and the Arkansas Supreme Court over the efficacy of an admonition to ignore Parker's statement was apparently based solely on conflicting intuitions. Neither court cited empirical research or psychological theory to support its intuition. It is worth considering whether psychological research and theory, at present, would be helpful in determining which intuition is correct.

Conditional Admissibility

The admissibility of a piece of evidence sometimes depends on proof of a preliminary or foundational fact. For example, in order for the testimony of an alleged eyewitness to be admissible, there must be a foundational showing that the witness actually observed the events about which he will testify. For a deed to be admissible as proof of ownership of property, there must be a foundational showing that the deed is genuine. In order for the confession of an alleged coconspirator to be admitted against the defendant, there must be a foundational showing of the existence of a conspiracy. When evidence requiring a foundation is offered, the judge "makes a preliminary determination of whether the foundation evidence is sufficient. If so, the evidence is admitted" (Advisory Committee's Note on Federal Rule of Evidence 104[4]).

Such evidence is said to be admitted *conditionally* because it may later become inadmissible if the judge's preliminary determination of foundational adequacy turns out to be wrong. For example, if it is later proven that the alleged eyewitness is blind as a bat, that the deed is a forgery, and that the alleged coconspirator never knew the defendant, then this conditionally admissible evidence would become inadmissible for lack of an adequate foundation. If the foundation is so severely undermined that the evidence

---

[4]The advisory committee that drafted the Federal Rules of Evidence provided notes that explain the purpose of each section and how it should be applied. These notes are published in the annotated editions of the Federal Rules that are available in any law library (e.g., United States Code Annotated, 1984).

is clearly inadmissible, the judge may withdraw the evidence from the jury's consideration by instructing them to disregard it. If the adequacy of the foundation is subject to dispute, the judge may instruct the jury to determine for itself whether the foundation is adequate and instruct them to disregard the evidence if they find that it is not.

Whether such instructions are necessary is thought to depend on the nature of the evidence. In some instances, the jury's duty to disregard conditionally admissible evidence (when it is not persuaded of the existence of the preliminary fact on which relevancy is conditioned) is thought to be so clear that an instruction to this effect is unnecessary. For example, if the disputed preliminary fact is the authenticity of a deed, "it hardly seems necessary to instruct the jury to disregard the deed if it should find the deed is not genuine. No rational jury could find the deed to be spurious and, yet, to be still effective to transfer title from the purported grantor" (California Assembly Committee on the Judiciary, Commentary on California Evidence Code Section 403[5]).

In other instances, however, "it is not quite so clear that conditionally admissible evidence should be disregarded unless the preliminary fact is found to exist. In such cases, the jury should be appropriately instructed" (*Id.*) For example, the theory upon which agent's and coconspirator's statements are admissible is that the party is vicariously responsible for the acts and statements of agents and coconspirators within the scope of the agency or conspiracy. Yet, "it is not always clear that statements made by a purported agent or co-conspirator should be disregarded if not made in furtherance of the agency or conspiracy. Hence, the jury should be instructed to disregard such statement unless it is persuaded that the statement were made within the scope of the agency or conspiracy" (*Id.*).

One obvious problem with such instructions is that they are difficult to understand. To ask a juror who is unfamiliar with the concept of conspiracy, for example, to consider statements of an individual only if they were made in furtherance of a conspiracy with the defendant, and otherwise to ignore them, is asking quite a lot. A second problem is that jurors may see little sense in such instructions and may therefore be reluctant to follow them even if they can understand them. Finally, even if jurors try to ignore the inadmissible evidence, it may nevertheless influence their judgment.

Research on the perseverence effect (Nisbett & Ross, 1980, chap. 8; Ross, Lepper, & Hubbard, 1975) seems quite relevant to this last point. Ross and

---

[5]The California Assembly Committee on the Judiciary is the legislative committee that drafted the current version of California Evidence Code Section 403. Like the advisory committee that drafted the Federal Rules, the Judiciary Committee issued commentary on the purpose of the rules and how they were meant to be applied. This commentary is published in annotated versions of the California Evidence Code that are available in most law libraries (e.g., West's Annotated California Codes, 1995).

his colleagues demonstrated that belief in a proposition can persist despite the complete negation of a piece of evidence that initially gave rise to the belief. They theorized that a piece of evidence that is later discredited may exert influence by causing "biased assimilation" of other evidence and by inducing other thought processes that perpetuate belief in a proposition, and that the effects of these processes survive the discrediting of the evidence that initiated them (Nisbett & Ross, 1980, chap. 8). To the extent that these processes occur in jury trials, the effects of conditionally admissible evidence may persist after the foundational facts are refuted. This possibility suggests that judges should exercise caution and apply strict standards when making a preliminary determination of whether the foundation for evidence is adequate.

On the other hand, a jury simulation study in which a key eyewitness was suddenly discredited by evidence that she had not been wearing her glasses and therefore could not have seen what she reported, found evidence of the opposite effect: The defendant was judged less likely to be guilty when this damaging testimony was presented and discredited than when it was never presented (Hatvany, Strack & Ross, 1979, as cited in Nisbett & Ross, 1980). Nisbett and Ross proposed that the perseverance effect may have been overridden in this instance by a powerful "false accusation" script in which the discrediting of a key witness signals the innocence of the defendant. Alternatively, the witness may have been discredited too rapidly, before the mental processes needed for belief perseverance could take hold. In any event, the failure to find belief perseverance in this jury study suggests one should be cautious when drawing inferences about the courtroom from general psychological research.

Special Treatment of Confessions. Although legal scholars have long recognized that it can create problems, conditional admissibility is considered a practical necessity for most types of evidence (Tanford, 1990). To determine the admissibility of each piece of evidence before it is presented would be inordinately time consuming and might disrupt the orderly presentation of testimony. There is one type of evidence, however, for which an exception has been made. In *Jackson v. Denno* (1964), the U.S. Supreme Court ruled that a defendant's confession cannot be admitted conditionally.

A key foundational element for confessions is that they are voluntary. Voluntary confessions are generally admissible; involuntary (coerced) confessions are not. But who makes this determination? Before *Jackson*, it was often the jury. The jurors were instructed to use the confession as evidence only if they determined, based on the evidence, that it was voluntary, and otherwise to ignore it entirely.

In *Jackson*, however, the Supreme Court found that this procedure "poses substantial threats to a defendant's constitutional rights to have an involuntary confession entirely disregarded and to have the coercion issue fairly and reliably determined" (*Jackson v. Denno*, p. 389). In other words, the Supreme Court perceived a danger that the jury would be unable to fully discount an involuntary confession. Psychological research appears to support this judgment. In a series of studies, Kassin and Wrightsman (1980, 1981; Wrightsman & Kassin, 1993) showed that mock jurors give considerable weight to coerced confessions.

After *Jackson*, evidentiary rules were changed to require that the judge rather than the jury make the foundational determination [e.g., Federal Rule of Evidence 104(c); California Rule of Evidence 402(b)]. Confessions can now be admitted only if the judge determines that they were voluntary. However, the standard of proof applied by the judge need only be a "preponderance of evidence" (*Lego v. Twomy*, 1972, p. 486). Hence, the jury may still receive confessions whose voluntariness is in dispute. Kassin and Wrightsman (1993) argued that such confessions may be overvalued by jurors; they suggest that a more stingent criteria for their admissibility is warranted.

Limited Admissibility

Perhaps the most interesting evidentiary rules, with respect to intentional forgetting, are those that permit jurors to use evidence for a limited purpose only. Under these rules, the jury is instructed that an item of evidence may be considered when drawing some inferences, but must be ignored when drawing other inferences (Tanford, 1990). Whether jurors can understand such instructions, and whether they are willing and able to follow them, are interesting psychological questions.

The most common situations in which evidence is admitted for a limited purpose involve character evidence. By longstanding tradition, evidence of a defendant's previous bad behavior is inadmissible when its sole purpose is to prove that he has a "bad character" or criminal propensity and therefore is likely to be guilty (Uviller, 1982; Wydick, 1987). The reasons for this restriction were explained by the U.S. Supreme Court in *Michelson v. United States* (1948):

> The state may not show defendant's prior trouble with the law, specific criminal acts, or ill name among his neighbors, even though such facts might logically be persuasive that he is by propensity a probable perpetrator of the crime. The inquiry is not rejected because character is irrelevant; on the contrary, it is said to weigh too much with the jury and to so overpersuade them as to prejudge one with a bad general record and deny him a fair opportunity to defend against a particular charge. The overriding policy of excluding such evidence, despite its admitted probative value, is the practical experience that its disallowance tends to prevent confusion of issues, unfair surprise and undue prejudice. (pp. 475–476)

Evidence that reflects negatively on a defendant's character may be admissible, however, if it has some purpose other than to merely prove his criminal propensities. If the defendant chooses to testify in his own behalf, for example, evidence of prior crimes can be admitted to impeach his credibility. In theory, such evidence is admitted not to show that the defendant has criminal propensities, but to challenge his truthfulness as a witness. Additionally, every jurisdiction has a rule similar to Federal Rule 404(b), which declares:

> Evidence of other crimes, wrongs, or acts is not admissible to prove the character of a person to show he acted in conformity therewith. It may, however, be admissible for other purposes, such as proof of motive, opportunity, intent, preparation, plan, knowledge, identity, or absence of mistake or accident.

Thus, for example, evidence that the defendant previously assaulted the victim of the present crime might be admissible to show his animosity toward the victim and hence his *motive* to commit the present crime. Evidence that the defendant committed a previous crime might be admissible to prove his *identity* if it was a "signature crime" sufficiently similar to the current charge to support an inference that the same person committed both. Evidence that the defendant committed a previous crime might be admissible to show his *knowledge* if both crimes required similar knowledge, such as knowing how to crack a safe or make a bomb. Whether such evidence is actually admitted or not is decided on a case-by-case basis by the trial judge, who is expected to weigh the probative value of the evidence against its potential for prejudice. In other words, the judge considers whether the evidence is sufficiently important with respect to permissible inferences (e.g., motive, identity, knowledge, etc.) to justify the risk that the jury will use it for impermissible inferences (e.g., the defendant's criminal propensities).

When such evidence is presented, the judge gives the jury "limiting instructions," which say that the evidence is to be used only for permissible purposes, and may not be used to draw impermissible inferences. Several studies have tested the ability of mock jurors to follow such instructions (Tanford & Cox, 1987, 1988; Tanford & Penrod, 1984; Wissler & Saks, 1985). Jurors' judgments in these studies appear to be influenced strongly by impermissible inferences, notwithstanding the limiting instructions.

One practical problem with such instructions is that they are difficult to understand. Because verdicts can easily be reversed on appeal if the judges' instructions are legally inaccurate (but are almost never challenged on grounds that jurors failed to understand the instructions), the primary concern of trial judges is that the instructions be legally accurate, not that they be easy to comprehend. Consequently, instructions are typically cobbled together and read to jurors word-for-word from form books of language previously approved by appellate courts. Even in high profile cases, judges often use boilerplate language that borders on the incomprehensible.

Consider, for example, one of Judge Ito's limiting instructions to the jury in O. J. Simpson's criminal trial. The prosecution presented evidence of previous acts of domestic violence by Simpson against his ex-wife Nicole Brown Simpson, whom he was accused of murdering. The defense sought to exclude this evidence under the propensity rule, but Judge Ito ruled that it was sufficiently important for a permissible purpose, proving Simpson's motive for the crime, to justify its admission. In his closing instructions to the jury, Judge Ito admonished the jury to use the evidence for its limited purpose as follows:

Evidence has been introduced for the purpose of showing that the defendant committed crimes other than that for which he is on trial. Such evidence, if believed, was not received and may not be considered by you to prove that the defendant is a person of bad character or that he has a disposition to commit crimes. Such evidence was received and may considered [sic] by you only for the limited purpose of determining if it tends to show a characteristic method, plan or scheme in the commission of criminal acts similar to the method, plan or scheme used in the commission of the offense in this case, which would further tend to show the existence of the intent, which is a necessary element of the crime charge, the identity of the person who committed the crime, if any, of which the defendant is accused, or a clear connection between the other offense and the one of which the defendant is accused, so that it may be inferred that if the defendant committed the other offenses, the defendant also committed the crimes charged in this case, the existence of the intent, which is necessary—which is a necessary element of the crime charged, the identity of the person who committed the crime, if any, of which the defendant is accused, or a motive for the commission of the crime charged. For the limited purpose for which you may consider such evidence, you must weigh it in the same manner as you do all the evidence—all the other evidence in this case. You are not permitted to consider such evidence for any other purpose. (*People v. O. J. Simpson*, September 22, 1995, Transcript Vol. 229, p. 47124)

To further complicate the jurors' task, Judge Ito then went on to give the jury a conditional admissibility instruction (see previous section of this chapter) with respect to the same domestic violence evidence:

Within the meaning of the preceding instructions, such other crime or crimes purportedly committed by a defendant must be proved by a preponderance of the evidence. You must not consider such evidence for any purpose unless you are satisfied that the defendant committed such other crimes or crimes [sic]. The prosecution has the burden of proving these facts by a preponderance of the evidence. Within this limited context, preponderance of the evidence means evidence that has more convincing force and the greater probability of truth than that opposed to it. If the evidence is so evenly balanced that you are unable to find that the evidence on either side of an issue preponderates, your finding on that issue must be against the party who has the burden of proving it. You should consider all the evidence bear [sic] upon— bearing upon every issue, regardless of who produced it. (Vol. 229, p. 47126)

It seems doubtful that most lay jurors, after hearing intructions of this nature read to them once, would fully comprehend what they should and should not do with the evidence. Hence, jury comprehension is a threshold issue with respect to the efficacy of limiting instructions. Whether jurors are willing and able to use evidence for a limited purpose (as the limiting instructions ask) is a moot issue if the jurors cannot understand the instructions.

Courts generally acknowledge that limiting instructions have limited efficacy, but are willing to tolerate the danger that jurors will use evidence for an impermissible purpose when it is sufficiently important for a permissible purpose. Inadmissible evidence of some types is considered so prejudicial, however, that a limiting instruction is not enough. Special procedures must be invoked to prevent the jury from hearing the evidence at all.

In *Bruton v. United States*, (1968), for example, the U.S. Supreme Court found that a limiting instruction was inadequate to prevent a jury from being prejudiced by inadmissible testimony concerning a codefendant's confession. Bruton and a codefendant named Evans were tried jointly for the robbery of a postal facility. A postal inspector testified that Evans had confessed to the crime and had named Bruton as his accomplice. Because this testimony was hearsay, it was inadmissible as evidence against Bruton. It was admissible against Evans, however, under an exception to the hearsay rule that allows confessions to be used against the confessor. The judge dealt with this situation by giving the jury a limiting instruction, telling them that the evidence of a confession "if used, can only be used against the defendant Evans" and that the jury must "not consider it in any respect with respect to the defendant Bruton, because insofar as he is concerned, it is hearsay" (p. 125, n. 2). In his final instructions to the jury, the judge reiterated that if the confession was considered, the jury "should consider it as evidence in the case against Evans, but ... must not consider it and should disregard it, in considering the evidence in the case against the defendant Bruton" (p. 125, n. 2).

After he was convicted, Bruton complained on appeal that the limiting instruction did not adequately protect him from prejudice resulting from the jury's exposure to evidence that was inadmissible against him. The Eighth Circuit Court of Appeal disagreed and upheld the conviction. "To overturn Bruton's conviction we would be required to speculate that the jury, presumably composed of prudent and intelligent men, disregarded the court's instructions and their oaths" (*Bruton v. United States*, 1967, p. 362). Quoting earlier opinions of the U.S. Supreme Court, the Court of Appeal declared that the possibility that the jury was confused by the limiting instruction "amounts to nothing more than unfounded speculation ..." (p. 362). The Court of Appeal went on to say that "[o]ur theory of trial relies upon the ability of a jury to follow instructions" and that "[w]e must assume the jury was capable of assessing the evidence and following the instructions of the court as they are bound to do by their oath" (p. 362).

Thereafter, however, the conviction was reversed by the U.S. Supreme Court, which expressed greater skepticism about the efficacy of the limiting instruction:

> The naive assumption that prejudicial effects can be overcome by instructions to the jury ... all practicing lawyers know to be unmitigated fiction. ... A jury cannot "segregate evidence into separate intellectual boxes" ... It cannot determine that a confession is true insofar as it admits that A has committed criminal acts with B and at the same time effectively ignore the inevitable conclusion that B has committed those same criminal acts with A. (*Bruton v. United States*, 1968, pp. 129, 131)

After Bruton, a confession can no longer be admitted in a joint trial if it incriminates a codefendant. The confession must either be excluded outright, or "sanitized" to remove reference to the codefendant before it is presented to the jury. Another option, of course, is to sever the two defendants and try them separately, in which case the confession is admissible in the trial of the defendant who confessed, but not in the trial of the other defendant.

CONCLUSION

Why should psychologists be interested in legal rules on the admissibility of evidence? This brief review suggests three important reasons. First, study of the legal rules may be a useful hypothesis-generation technique. Legal materials are filled with intriguing assumptions about the way in which lay jurors evaluate evidence. In the implicit assumptions of a legislature or the common-sense conclusions of a court, psychologists who look carefully will see testable hypotheses, many of which are fresh and interesting.

A second reason for study of legal rules is that it helps identify gaps in our knowledge. One test of psychology's development as a science is its ability to address practical questions in a sophisticated and useful manner. Admissibility rules raise a plethora of psychological questions. Psychologists should find it useful to consider how well they can answer those questions at present, and what additional steps must be taken to provide better answers in the future.

Finally, there is the possibility that psychologists have something useful to say to legal professionals. Our research and theory may support some of the psychological assumptions that underlie the framework of admissibility rules and may raise doubts about others. By making our findings available to legal professionals, and by explaining their relevance to evidentiary issues, psychologists can assist in the development of a more rational basis for the law.

When offering such assistance, however, psychologists should exercise a degree of humility in order to avoid the tendency toward overgeneralization that is often found in the field of psychology and law (Bermant, McGuire, McKinley, & Salo, 1974; Konecni & Ebbesen, 1979, 1981, 1982; Pennington & Hastie, 1981; Thompson, 1993; Vidmar, 1979). Questions about the influence of inadmissible evidence, the efficacy of judges' instructions, and related issues, are unlikely to have single, simple answers. Contextual factors, such as the nature of the case and the precise fact pattern, may be very important. To draw meaningful conclusions and to make useful recommendations while taking such factors into account will be as challenging as it is important.

REFERENCES

Bermant, G., McGuire, M., McKinley, W., & Salo, C. (1974). The logic of simulation in jury research. *Criminal Justice and Behavior, 1*, 224–233.

Bruton v. United States, 375 F.2d 355 (1967).

Bruton v. United States, 391 U.S. 123 (1968).

Greene, E. (1990). Media effects on jurors. *Law and Human Behavior, 14*, 439–450.

Hans, V. P. (1990). Law and the media: An overview and introduction. *Law and Human Behavior, 14*, 399–408.

Jackson v. Denno, 378 U.S. 368 (1964).

Lego v. Twomy, 404 U.S. 477 (1972).

Kaplan, J. (1968). Decision theory and the factfinding process. *Stanford Law Review, 20*, 1065–1106.

Kassin, S. M., & Wrightsman, L. S. (1980). Prior confessions and mock jury verdicts. *Journal of Applied Social Psychology, 10*, 133–146.

Kassin, S. M., & Wrightsman, L. S. (1981). Coerced confessions, judicial instruction, and mock juror verdicts. *Journal of Applied Social Psychology, 11*, 489–506.

Konecni, V. J., & Ebbesen, E. B. (1979). External validity of research in legal psychology. *Law and Human Behavior, 3*, 39–70.

Konecni, V. J., & Ebbesen, E. B. (1981). A critique of theory and method in social-psychological approaches to legal issues. In B. D. Sales (Ed.), *The trial process* (pp. 481–498). New York: Plenum Press.

Konecni, V. J., & Ebbesen, E. B. (Eds.). (1982). *The criminal justice system: A social psychological analysis*. San Francisco: Freeman.

Kovera, M. B., Park, R. C., & Penrod, S. D. (1992). Jurors' perceptions of eyewitness and hearsay evidence. *Minnesota Law Review, 76*, 703–722.

Kramer, G. P., Kerr, N. L., & Carroll, J. S. (1990). Pretrial publicity, judicial remedies, and jury bias. *Law and Human Behavior, 14*, 409–438.

Landsman, S., & Rakos, R. F. (1991). Research essay: A preliminary empirical enquiry concerning the prohibition of hearsay evidence in American courts. *Law and Psychology Review, 15,* 65–85.

Lempert, R. O. (1977). Modeling relevance. *Michigan Law Review, 75,* 1021–1100.

Lempert, R., & Saltzburg, S. (1977). *A modern approach to evidence* (1st ed.). St. Paul, MN: West Publishing Co.

Lempert, R., & Saltzburg, S. (1982). *A modern approach to evidence* (2nd ed.). St. Paul, MN: West Publishing Co.

Mapp v. Ohio, 367 U.S. 643 (1961).

Michelson v. United States, 335 U.S. 469 (1948).

Miene, P., Borgida, E., & Park, R. (1993). The evaluation of hearsay evidence: A social psychological approach. In N. J. Castellan (Ed.), *Individual and group decision making: Current issues* (pp. 151–166). Hillsdale, NJ: Lawrence Erlbaum Associates.

Monahan, J., & Walker, L. (1994). *Social science in law: Cases and materials* (3d ed.). Mineola, NY: Foundation Press.

Moore v. State, 323 Ark. 529, 915 S.W.2d 284 (1996).

Moran, G., & Cutler, B. L. (1991). The prejudicial impact of pretrial publicity. *Journal of Applied Social Psychology, 21,* 345–367.

Morgan, E. (1956). *Some problems of proof under the Anglo-American system of litigation.* New York: Columbia University Press.

Nash v. United States, 54 F.2d 1006 (1932).

Nisbett, R., & Ross, L. (1980). *Human inference: Strategies and shortcomings of social judgment.* Englewood Cliffs, NJ: Prentice-Hall.

Pennington, N., & Hastie, R. (1981). Juror decision-making models: The generalization gap. *Psychological Bulletin, 89,* 246–287.

People v. O. J. Simpson, No. BA 097211 (Sup. Ct. Los Angeles County).

Ross, L., Lepper, M. R., & Hubbard, M. (1975). Perseverance in self-perception and social perception: Biased attributional processes in the debriefing paradigm. *Journal of Personality and Social Psychology, 32,* 880–892.

Simon, R. J. (Ed.). (1980). *The jury: Its role in American society.* Lexington, MA: Lexington Books.

State v. Pennell, No. IN88-12-0051–IN88-12-0053 (Sup. Ct. New Castle County, Del., ruling as of November 6, 1989).

Stewart v. State, 320 Ark. 75, 894 S.W.2d 930 (1995).

Tanford, J. A. (1990). The law and psychology of jury instructions. *Nebraska Law Review, 69,* 71–111.

Tanford, S., & Cox, M. (1987). Decision processes in civil cases: The impact of impeachment evidence on liability and credibility judgments. *Social Behavior, 2,* 165–182.

Tanford, S., & Cox, M. (1988). The effects of impeachment evidence and limiting instructions on individual and group decision making. *Law and Human Behavior, 12,* 477–497.

Tanford, S., & Penrod, S. (1984). Social inference processes in juror judgments of multiple-offense trials. *Journal of Personality and Social Psychology, 47,* 749–765.

Thompson, W. C. (1993). Research on jury decision making: The state of the science. In N. J. Castellan (Ed.), *Individual and group decision making: Current issues* (pp. 203–218). Hillsdale, NJ: Lawrence Erlbaum Associates.

United States v. Gruenwald, 232 F.2d 556 (1956).

United States Code Annotated. (1984). St. Paul, MN: West Publishing Co.

Uviller, H. R. (1982). Evidence of character to prove conduct: Illusion, illogic and injustice in the courtroom. *University of Pennsylvania Law Review, 130,* 845–913.

Vidmar, N. (1979). The other issues in jury simulation research: A commentary with particular reference to defendant character studies. *Law and Human Behavior, 3,* 95–106.

Weeks v. United States, 232 U.S. 383 (1914).

West's Annotated California Codes. (1995). St. Paul, MN: West Publishing Co.

Wissler, R. L., & Saks, M. J. (1985). On the inefficacy of limiting instructions: When jurors use prior conviction evidence to decide guilt. *Law and Human Behavior, 9,* 37–48.

Wrightsman, L. S., & Kassin, S. M. (1993). *Confessions in the courtroom.* Beverly Hills, CA: Sage.

Wydick, R. C. (1987). Character evidence: A guided tour of the grotesque structure. *U.C. Davis Law Review, 21,* 123–195.

17

INTENTIONAL FORGETTING IN PERSPECTIVE: COMMENTS, CONJECTURES, AND SOME DIRECTED REMEMBERING

Robert A. Bjork
University of California, Los Angeles

This is a remarkable book. Over the years, I, like other authors in this volume, have felt the need to start articles and talks on intentional forgetting with the argument that forgetting is not simply a failure of humans as information-processing devices, but, rather, that forgetting is an essential component of *any* information-processing system, living or artificial; that there must be some means to forget, or erase, or inhibit, or segregate out-of-date information. To illustrate that argument, it has also seemed necessary to point to examples of everyday situations where forgetting is consistent with our goals, especially the need to update our memories. In this volume as well, Colin MacLeod's impressive overview of directed-forgetting research begins in similar fashion, as does the E. L. Bjork, R. A. Bjork, and Anderson chapter on "Varieties of Goal-Directed Forgetting."

Why do such preambles seem necessary? One reason, I think, is that we are aware that the typical person in our audiences—even many of our professional colleagues—assumes, at least tacitly, that remembering is good and forgetting is bad. A second reason, related to the first, is that we realize that the notion of *intentional* forgetting is a strange one, at least outside of Freudian/psychodynamic contexts. Forgetting does not seem like something we would *want* to do in the first place, and it does not seem like something we *could* do, even if we wanted to. The observation, familiar to all of us, that it seems impossible *not* to think of something, such as an elephant, when instructed to do so (cf. the work of Wegner and his colleagues; e.g., Wegner, 1994), gets interpreted as a kind of evidence that forgetting is not something over which we have any control.

An incident from early in my own involvement in research on intentional forgetting illustrates the point. In 1967, and again in 1968, I gave talks on intentional forgetting at Indiana University, the second of which I titled "Intentional Forgetting, Part 2: Forget Part 1." I began that talk with a disclaimer, saying that I didn't really mean what the title said, but that I couldn't resist using it. At that point, someone in the audience said, "Well, it's too late now." The reason that comment was funny then, and is funny now, is because it presumes the speaker was able to do a preposterous thing, that is, to forget on demand.

One reason I find this book remarkable is that its chapters, collectively, demonstrate that our justifying preambles have, in a sense, been too weak. The picture of intentional forgetting that emerges from this volume—in human, animal, social, legal, and clinical contexts—is that intentional forgetting is as variegated, as complicated, and nearly as prevalent as intentional remembering—and also inextricably intertwined with intentional remembering.

This book is also remarkable in its timeliness. As Golding and Long point out in their broad overview chapter, the various approaches to the study of intentional forgetting have been largely isolated from each other. With some noteworthy exceptions, the separate research traditions represented in this volume have not so much passed like ships in the night as run side by side like ships in the night. In certain instances, the lack of communication is understandable, possibly even justifiable, because the underlying issues diverge substantially across those separate traditions, but in other instances, the lack of cross-fertilization seems a missed opportunity to broaden our separate perspectives and to share empirical findings and procedural innovations in a timely way.

In the first of the major sections that follow I give my perspective on the history of research on directed forgetting in human memory. I then comment on ignoring, disregarding, and discounting information in social and legal contexts; on motivated forgetting in clinical contexts; and on other approaches to the study of intentional forgetting.

DIRECTED FORGETTING IN HUMAN MEMORY: A PERSONAL PERSPECTIVE

Directed Forgetting as a Puzzle

My involvement in directed-forgetting research began as an effort on my part to control for memory load. As a graduate student at Stanford University, I was intrigued by some results reported by Bennet Murdock in 1963. Murdock presented short lists of paired associates to subjects and, at the end of each list, tested for the recall of one of the pairs in each list by presenting its stimulus member as a cue for recall of its response member. Holding constant the number of pairs presented prior to a tested pair, Murdock manipulated (across lists) the number of subsequent pairs in the list; and, conversely, holding constant the number of subsequent pairs, he also manipulated the number of prior pairs in a list. As the number of pairs that either preceded or succeeded a tested pair increased, performance on that pair decreased, which Murdock attributed to increasing within-list proactive and retroactive interference, respectively.

What seemed unclear to me was whether the decrease in recall as a function of the number of prior pairs should actually be attributed to proactive interference of the classic interference-theory type. Given that subjects had to learn the proactive pairs as they were presented, because any one of them might be tested at the end of the list, there were reasons to expect increased proactive interference as the number of such pairs increased. However, the number of prior pairs also increased a subject's memory load, that is, the total number of pairs that were a potential target of the end-of-list test. It occurred to me that one might be able to control for memory load with a signal to subjects that they could forget the presignal pairs in a given list; that is, a signal that the pair to be tested at the end of the list would *not* be a presignal pair. As long as some lists were to contain such a signal and others were not, in unpredictable fashion, the subjects would still need to try to learn the to-be-forgotten pairs *as* they were presented, which would be sufficient reason to expect proactive interference of the classic type. With respect to a subject's memory load of pairs that were candidates to be tested at the end of a list, however, such a signal would let the subject eliminate the presignal pairs.

As tends to be true of our autobiographical memories for events during our graduate careers, particularly those happening relatively early in our graduate careers, I have a clear image of the reaction of my graduate advisor and mentor, William Kaye Estes, to the notion of signaling subjects to forget (by means of a background color change). His reaction was, as I recall it, best described as bemused. He nonetheless encouraged me to go ahead with the experiment, and quite strongly. Looking back, however, I think he mostly thought that running such an experiment would do me no harm and might even advance my general education as a researcher.

When I later showed Professor Estes my actual results, I am not sure either of us knew quite what to think. I had expected, as a young mathematical modeler, to be able to tease out the relative contributions of memory load and "genuine" proactive interference, but what I found was no proactive interference effects at all of the to-be-forgotten pairs. In that sense, subjects seemed able to forget when instructed to do so. Initially, if briefly (see MacLeod's review), we even had to entertain the possibility that some kind of erasure mechanism might be operating. Such a possibility seemed unlikely, but was suggested not only by the elimination of proactive inter-ference, but also by subjects' apparent inability to recall to-be-forgotten pairs. When, near the very end of the experiment (and contrary to the assurances I had given the subjects), I presented the stimulus member of a to-be-forgotten pair as a test for its associated response (without informing subjects that I was doing so), recall of the correct response was negligible.

A second experiment, carried out in collaboration with Gordon Bower, also produced results that seemed surprising and puzzling at the time. We again presented short lists of paired associates, some of which (in unpre-dictable fashion) contained cues to forget the pairs presented prior to the cue, but we occasionally repeated the stimulus member of a to-be-forgotten (TBF) pair as the stimulus member of a to-be-remembered (TBR) pair, but with a new response (in essence, an A–B, A–D manipulation at the level of individual TBF and TBR pairs). When such TBR pairs were tested, we found that recall was actually better than corresponding pairs where the stimulus term was not a repetition of a to-be-forgotten stimulus. That result, if still a bit surprising, is more interpretable now (see MacLeod's review of the work by Timmins, 1973, and by Geiselman & Bagheri, 1985, on repetition effects in directed forgetting) than it was then.

Those two experiments, referred to as "early pilot studies" in the Bjork (1970) article, comprised my earliest work on directed forgetting. My inter-ests in directed forgetting then simmered for a couple of years, while I attended to such matters as fitting Markov learning models and completing a doctoral dissertation, but were rekindled shortly after I arrived at Michigan in 1966 as a beginning assistant professor. David LaBerge, however, who had been my advisor during my one year of graduate work at the University of Minnesota, learned about my initial results when he visited Stanford, and he decided to pursue the forget-cue procedure. With the assistance of Ross Legrand, and with little or no input from me, he carried out a follow-up experiment using a procedure designed to eliminate—or at least greatly reduce—opportunities for rehearsal. After concluding that the results were interesting and generally consistent with what I had found earlier, he sent me an initial write-up of the experiment, which, to my surprise, had me listed as first author. My contributions to the version that we eventually published (Bjork, LaBerge, & Legrand, 1968) were modest, but David LaBerge, over my objections, continued to insist that I should be first author.

Directed Forgetting as a Tool

As is captured so well in MacLeod's review, the earliest research focused on directed-forgetting phenomena as a kind of puzzle that was interesting for its own sake. At Michigan, a number of faculty members (particularly Elizabeth Bjork, David Krantz, Arthur Melton, and Walter Reitman), postdoctoral visitors (particularly David Elmes and Addison Woodward), and graduate students (particularly Arthur Glenberg, Robert Jongeward, and Alexander Pollatsek) shared my interest in and curiosity about directed forgetting. We generated new procedures and results at a rapid rate, and new results and procedural variations from other laboratories also began to appear in abundance, as MacLeod summarized so well in his review of the "golden age" period.

Looking back at that period, I realize now that the way I came to view directed-forgetting research was heavily influenced by my collaborators and colleagues at Michigan, and by the information-processing zeitgeist that then prevailed in the Human Performance Center where I had my office. The influence of two colleagues in particular, Walter Reitman and Arthur Melton, warrants mention.

Walter Reitman was very interested in directed forgetting from the very first moment that I mentioned some of my results to him, but *why* he was so interested seemed strange to me. He found directed forgetting interesting from a control-process standpoint, and he thought it important to do certain experiments in which subjects were *asked* to control their forgetting/remembering strategies in various ways. He was also interested in such unsavory things as getting verbal reports from subjects as to their own metacognitive operations. Given my own training, such approaches seemed to smack of mentalism or introspectionism. At one point, we cotaught a graduate seminar—a seminar that was unusually well attended; one attraction, apparently, being the opportunity to watch Walter and me argue with each other, which we did frequently and with considerable vigor. The term *directed forgetting* was coined in one of those seminar sessions and soon became our preferred term; it had, as we viewed it then, an attractive double meaning—that the forgetting in question was "directed" in the sense of being cued or instructed and was also "directed" in the sense of being aimed at the to-be-forgotten information.

Walter Reitman's influence on me, if by no means immediate, was eventually substantial. In fact, as I mention at the end of these comments, I think that issues of control, intent, and resource allocation are among the important remaining issues in the study of directed forgetting in humans (see also the comments on intentionality in the E. L. Bjork, R. A. Bjork, & Anderson chapter in this volume).

Arthur Melton's influence was also substantial, but of a quite different character. He influenced me to look at directed forgetting in the broader context of forgetting and interference processes, and in my interactions with him, I came to realize that certain of the questions suggested by directed-forgetting phenomena were very similar to those faced by the interference theorists of another era. (See the E. L. Bjork, R. A. Bjork, & Anderson chapter in this volume for an example of some of those similarities.)

The information-processing approach of that era, based as it was on a kind of flow-chart analogy between how humans process information and the processing architecture of the typical digital computer, influenced my thinking and the thinking of most memory researchers. As I stressed elsewhere (Bjork, 1989), for example, the computer metaphor led one to think in terms of explanatory mechanisms such as scanning, grouping, sorting, tagging, and so forth, and not in terms of mechanisms like inhibition. During that period, I took pains in colloquium talks to disabuse my audience of the idea that directed-forgetting results had anything to do with actual inhibition or erasure, or with clinical phenomena, such as repression.

Partly as a consequence of the prevailing information-processing zeitgeist, my orientation gradually shifted across my years at Michigan from trying to understand the dynamics of directed forgetting, *per se*, to viewing cues to forget and remember as tools to study processes such as rehearsal and the differentiation of items in human memory. In my 1972 review of the directed-forgetting literature, for example, I noted that the widespread interest in the directed-forgetting paradigm seemed motivated, at least in part, by the impression that it revealed "some curious and previously unappreciated abilities," but I argued that the paradigm was important "not primarily because it raises new questions or illustrates surprising capacities, but rather because it has the potential of contributing new leverage on some old and important problems in the study of human memory" (p. 218). Looking back at my own directed-forgetting publications during the 1970s—that is, publications of experimental studies where a directed-forgetting manipulation was involved—the label *directed forgetting*, or some equivalent expression, often does not even appear in the titles of those articles (see Bjork, 1975, 1978; Bjork & Geiselman, 1978; Bjork & Landauer, 1979; Woodward, Bjork, & Jongeward, 1973).

Basically, I argued in 1972 that directed-forgetting procedures constituted a new tool for memory researchers. It is interesting that now, a quarter century later, MacLeod concludes his review in this volume with the assertion that directed forgetting is "an established technique in the set available to memory researchers"—a technique that "as we develop new tests of memory and new ideas about its operation ... will no doubt be called on to help in answering questions along the way" (p. 52).

The Search for a Missing Mechanism

With respect to the goal of understanding directed forgetting *per se*, virtually all of the basic phenomena that had been reported as of the mid 1970s, the point at which I moved from Michigan to the University of California, Los Angeles, seemed consistent with the two-process theory I had advocated earlier (Bjork, 1970). According to that theory, subjects, in response to a forget cue, "devote all further rehearsal, mnemonic, and integrative activities exclusively to the R-items; and they differentially group, organize, or code R-items in a way that functionally segregates them from F-items in memory" (Bjork, 1972, p. 229). On certain empirical grounds, however, and in terms of a kind of plausibility argument that applied to certain experimental situations, I began to feel ever more strongly that those two processes were not the sole mechanisms involved in directed forgetting. My misgivings were shared by Edward Geiselman, who joined me at UCLA, first as a postdoctoral fellow, then as a faculty colleague.

We were suspicious about the theory in two general respects. First, as we argued in the Geiselman, Bjork, and Fishman (1983) article, the theory emphasized mechanisms of selective remembering, not selective forgetting, and an accumulating body of diverse findings seemed to imply that some kind of active forgetting process was triggered by cues to forget. Certain effects of repeating or re-exposing TBF items, for example, seemed most readily interpreted as evidence that those items, in response to the initial cue to forget, had been inhibited (see Bjork, Abramowitz, & Krantz, 1970, and E. L. Bjork, R. A. Bjork, & Glenberg, 1973, as cited in Bjork, 1989; Reed, 1970; Timmins, 1973). The early work of Weiner and his colleagues (e.g., Weiner & Reed, 1969), with linkages to motivated forgetting, such as repression, also suggested that active inhibition might be involved (see MacLeod's summary), as did the results obtained by Johnson (1971), who examined the pupillary response to forget cues. And there seemed to be parallels between certain posthypnotic-amnesia phenomena, where active forgetting was more clearly involved, and corresponding directed-forgetting phenomena.

Second, in certain cases where the two-process theory was logically consistent with the results, it seemed implausible that subjects could actually execute the presumed selective-rehearsal and selective-grouping operations in the time available (often only 1 sec or so). In an experiment by Jongeward, Woodward, and Bjork (1975), for example, sets of four words were presented, one word at a time at a 2.3-sec rate; there was then a 3-sec rehearsal period; and, finally, a 1-sec cue to remember the first two, the last two, all, or none of the words in that set. Thus, for a total of 12.2 secs, subjects had to process the words in a given set without knowing which of those words, if any, they would be asked to remember or forget, and they then had 1 sec to interpret quite a complicated cue before the next set of four words began. They were also instructed to restrict any rehearsal activities to the current set of words, which they said, during the debriefing, they were only too happy to do. At the end of lists consisting of eight such four-word sets, the subjects recalled about 35% of the TBR words and intruded less than 5% of the TBF words.

In an initial effort to find the "missing mechanism," Bjork and Geiselman (1978), using a variation on the item-by-item cuing procedure, obtained evidence that the momentary retrieval of TBR items in response to a remember cue, together with the absence of such a retrieval of TBF items in response to a forget cue, played a critical role in the differentiation of TBR and TBF items in memory. That mechanism, however, seemed more descriptive than explanatory, and also seemed special purpose in nature; that is, it was not clear how that mechanism might explain some of the other results that seemed to suggest that a forget cue triggered an inhibitory process.

Our next approach was to examine the effects of a forget cue on the incidental memory of to-be-judged items that had been interleaved with the to-be-learned items (Geiselman et al., 1983). The fact that a cue to forget or remember the to-be-learned items had the same effects on the to-be-judged items as on the to-be-learned items themselves, even though subjects were not trying to learn the to-be-judged items (and, hence, had no reason to rehearse those items either before or after a cue of either type), provided strong evidence for an active forgetting process of some kind. The details of our results implicated retrieval inhibition as that process (for excellent summaries of our results and arguments, see the chapters by MacLeod and E. L. Bjork, R. A. Bjork, & Anderson in this volume).

Our initial evidence suggesting that retrieval inhibition was the "missing mechanism" in directed forgetting led Ed Geiselman and his students to test the retrieval-inhibition idea in various ways, as summarized in MacLeod's chapter, and led me to reinterpret some earlier unpublished results (see Bjork, 1989). At the point that the existing data seemed convincing that retrieval inhibition was, indeed, a mechanism in directed forgetting, Harold Gelfand, who was then visiting UCLA, raised an interesting question: What are the necessary conditions for retrieval inhibition to happen? Is it something that simply happens, in magic-wand fashion, when subjects are presented an explicit and unambiguous cue that information presented prior to the cue is wrong, or was presented in error, and should be forgotten? Or is it necessary that some type of new to-be-learned material is presented—something that will serve to replace the to-be-forgotten material?

To address those questions, we (Gelfand & Bjork, 1985, as cited in Bjork, 1989) asked subjects to recall a first list of words they had earlier been instructed to forget (or to remember). The critical experimental manipulation involved what happened *after* the instruction to forget or remember that list and *before* the recall of that list was then tested. During that interval, which was fixed in duration, the subjects either did nothing (while the experimenter fumbled around with some folders), or carried out an incidental-learning task involving a list of adjectives, or learned a second list. It was only in the condition where a second list was learned to replace the to-be-forgotten list that we found evidence of retrieval inhibition. Thus, from those results, it appears that retrieval inhibition is a by-product of new learning, and not simply a product of an intent or instructional set to forget.

Gelfand and Bjork's results continue to influence my own thinking about the dynamics of directed forgetting, particularly having to do with the updating of memory, and with the linkage of directed-forgetting phenomena to other phenomena, such as "unlearning" in retroactive interference. Those results are also suggestive of mechanisms that might underlie the repression of real-world memories (see the speculations of E. L. Bjork, R. A. Bjork, & Anderson in this volume). Were I to construct my own table of "Principal Findings," analogous to MacLeod's Table 1.2, the fact that retrieval inhibition is apparently a by-product of new learning would be high on the list.

By the end of the 1980s, I had not only come to believe—in marked contrast with my views of an earlier era—that inhibitory processes were involved in directed forgetting, but that inhibition, particularly retrieval inhibition, is a prevalent and adaptive mechanism in human memory more generally (see Bjork, 1989). About that same time, other results from other paradigms in research on attention, language, and memory soon began to implicate inhibitory mechanisms as well. From that point to the present, in collaboration with a number of individuals at UCLA, especially Michael Anderson, Elizabeth Bjork, Laura Da Costa, John Shaw, and Bobbie Spellman, we have taken a broader look at the role of inhibition in human memory (see, e.g., Anderson, Bjork, & Bjork, 1994; Anderson & Spellman, 1995; E. L. Bjork, R. A. Bjork, & Anderson in this volume; Shaw, Bjork, & Handal, 1995).

Procedures, Precedents, and Processes in Directed Forgetting

In his review of directed-forgetting research in this volume, MacLeod covers findings that derive from two basic procedures: the *item procedure*, in which individual items are cued one at a time; and the *list procedure*, in which there is a single cue to forget one of two sets of items, where those sets are defined temporally and/or by item type. He rightly credits Muther's (1965) study—of which I was unaware during much of my own early work—with being the first to employ the item-by-item procedure in directed forgetting. If I can lay any claim at all to having been the first to use a directed-forgetting procedure, that claim is limited to the standard version of the list procedure, where an explicit cue to subjects to forget the items studied prior to the cue is presented before the items they are then asked to learn, if any.

If I was unaware of Muther's work, I was well aware, at least by some early point in my work at Michigan, of John Brown's (1954) study,[1] which

---

[1]In a footnote, MacLeod mentions that the same John Brown, in his 1958 article, used a short-term forgetting procedure virtually identical to that used by Peterson and Peterson a year later in their well-known 1959 article. As an historical footnote of sorts, I should perhaps reveal that I deserve substantial credit for the term "Brown–Peterson paradigm," which was

MacLeod cites as an early precursor of work on directed forgetting. On each of a series of trials, Brown instructed subjects, either before (preinput cuing) or after (postinput cuing) the presentation of two interleaved or successive sets of items, whether to recall one or both of those sets, and, if both, in what order. Although it now seems fair to cite Brown's study as a precursor of the work of Epstein and his colleagues on postinput cuing, I did not, at the time, think of Brown's experiment as a directed-forgetting experiment. Rather, I thought of it, as Brown did, as an experiment on effects of set-to-learn and output interference.

The various ways one might interpret Brown's early experiment raises the issue, I think, of what should and should not be called directed forgetting—and, hence, what should and should not be called an experiment on directed forgetting. We have reached a level of procedural and process sophistication, in my opinion, where there is some need to sharpen our terminology. In particular, I think precuing procedures warrant another name of some kind ("directed ignoring"?), and I think only a subset of postcuing procedures should qualify as directed-forgetting procedures. If every experiment where subjects are told, implicitly or explicitly, that they need not try to learn or remember some of what is to be presented, or are told they need not recall some of what they have tried to learn, is to be thought of as an experiment on directed forgetting, the term becomes so broad as to become meaningless from a process standpoint. Most of our laboratory paradigms in the study of human memory involve either preinput instructions to subjects that some to-be-processed items need not be learned, as in the case of digit shadowing and other rehearsal-preventing distractor activities, or postinput instructions to recall only a sample of what was learned, as in the case of cuing the recall of one of a set of paired associates, or both.

At a minimum, I think the term *directed forgetting* should be reserved for situations in which (a) there has been a prior attempt, however brief or extended, to learn the material that is now to be forgotten and (b) there is an explicit (or totally unambiguous implicit) cue to forget that material.

Beyond that minimal definition, it may prove increasingly necessary to distinguish among the procedures that *do* qualify as directed-forgetting procedures. As MacLeod concludes in his review, it has become apparent, especially given the work of Basden, Basden, and Gargano (1993; see Basden & Basden, this volume), that the item and list procedures invoke quite different processes, or at least a different weighting of the three processing mechanisms—selective rehearsal, selective grouping, and retrieval inhibi-

---

introduced in the late 1960s and is now standard. Not that I, as a new assistant professor, had any real influence on the field during the late 1960s; rather, *I* was the one who convinced Art Melton that John Brown, as well as the Petersons, deserved credit for that procedural innovation, and Art Melton *did* have an influence on the field.

tion—that have been implicated in research on directed forgetting. Within the list-procedure category, I also think the mechanisms involved differ quite dramatically depending on whether the cue to forget a set of items studied earlier is presented *before* or *after* the set of items that are to be remembered (and recalled). In particular, I think the fact that a forget cue of the former type, that is, one presented prior to the to-be-remembered items, is the much more effective of the two (see, e.g., Bjork, 1970) is attributable, in part, to the critical role the *subsequent* learning of the to-be-remembered items plays in the inhibition of the to-be-forgotten items (see my earlier comments on Gelfand & Bjork's, 1985, results).

Stated in a different way, I think directed-forgetting procedures should no longer be thought of as *a* tool in the study of human memory dynamics, but, rather, as a set of tools, where different procedures are the tools of choice to gain leverage on somewhat different problems. Thus, if it is one's goal to understand the "inhibitory regulation of working memory" (Hasher & Zacks, 1988; Zacks & Hasher, 1994), for example, and how that process may change with aging, the item procedure seems a particularly useful tool (see, however, Zacks, Radvansky, & Hasher, 1996, where some inferential leverage is gained by using both the item and list methods). If, on the other had, one's primary goal is to understand interference and inhibition processes in the updating of human memory, the list method seems the tool of choice. In short, as MacLeod documents so well in his review, directed forgetting as a process is multifaceted; and, I would add, as a research instrument directed-forgetting procedures are multifaceted as well.

INTENTIONAL FORGETTING IN SOCIAL AND LEGAL CONTEXTS

The six chapters in this volume on intentional forgetting in social and legal contexts, together with Golding and Long's overview of those topics, provide a thorough review of an interesting and impressive body of research. The cognitive approach and social/legal approach to the study of intentional forgetting are, by a considerable margin, the two approaches to the study of intentional forgetting that are most heavily represented in this volume. Unfortunately, those two lines of research, as Golding and Long point out, have been largely isolated from each other. They assert, in particular, that research on intentional forgetting in the social/legal tradition has been mostly uninformed by developments in the research on directed forgetting in humans, but the converse is at least as true, in my opinion.

To some extent, the isolation of the cognitive and social/legal traditions is understandable, even defensible. The issues that provide the historical motivations to use instructions to forget, ignore, disregard, suppress, and discount information in the social and legal research traditions are somewhat different from those motivating research in the cognitive tradition, though there are clear points of intersection. In general, however, I think research on intentional forgetting in social and legal contexts would profit from a full understanding of the theoretical and procedural developments in research on directed forgetting in humans, and I think there are innovations and results in the social/legal research tradition that have clear implications for those of us concerned with the basic mechanisms of directed forgetting in humans.

A point that recurs with some frequency in the chapters on intentional forgetting in social and legal contexts is that instructions to disregard, ignore, and so forth are frequently unsuccessful in achieving their stated purpose. That is, subjects' judgments or impressions or attitudes are frequently unaffected by such instructions, or even show "boomerang" effects. Where the authors *do* make allusions to the directed-forgetting literature, they often say that such findings seem at odds with the successful directed forgetting typically obtained with standard directed-forgetting procedures using simple verbal materials. What strikes me, however, is how consistent the results from the social/legal domain are with the results in the directed-forgetting domain—provided that the experimental conditions are comparable.

As far as whether the conditions of intentional forgetting are the same from one situation to another, a number of considerations seem important, some of which I discuss below. In that context, I point to some noteworthy parallels in the findings obtained in the cognitive and social/legal domains. My comments are necessarily brief. For a perceptive, systematic, and thorough effort to link and organize the cognitive and social-judgment literatures on intentional forgetting, the interested reader should see Johnson's review (1994). My view of the relations between the paradigms and phenomena in the cognitive and social/legal domains has much in common with her analysis.

Forgetting Versus Ignoring, Disregarding, and Discounting

If, as I mentioned earlier, there is an issue as to what should and should not be considered directed forgetting in human memory research, there is a far broader and more complicated issue as to what should and should not be considered intentional forgetting in social and legal contexts. One aspect of the issue is whether the subjects in a given experiment are, in fact, actually asked to forget something that was said or that happened earlier, or, instead, are asked to be suspicious of that event, or to pretend it never happened, or to discount its relevance or importance.

Terminology in the social/legal research literature—if not always the discussions, analyses, and interpretations in that literature—reflects a sensitivity to the issue of what constitutes intentional forgetting. Terms such as *ignore, disregard, discredit, discount,* and *suppress* have shades of meaning that seem generally well understood. The basic point, however, is that the typical instruction administered in social/legal experiments on intentional forgetting does not actually ask the subject to forget something, but, rather, to give that "something" little or no weight in some decision or judgment.

Instructed Forgetting Versus Intentional Forgetting

A second consideration is whether *whatever* the subject is being asked to do is consistent with the subject's own goals. In the typical directed-forgetting experiment in the human memory domain, the subject's own goals tend to be consistent with following the experimenter's instructions. Under normal circumstances, subjects prefer to have fewer things to remember, to be able to focus rehearsal and mnemonic activities on to-be-recalled information, and to do whatever will help them perform well, all of which are goals fostered by instructions that some items can be forgotten.

In certain social/legal paradigms, however, an instruction to disregard may not be something the subject wants to hear, and may not be consistent with what the subject views as his or her most important task. For example, a juror who is told that some testimony or evidence that seems highly pertinent to the case is inadmissible and should be disregarded, may, consciously or unconsciously, weigh the goal of arriving at the most accurate verdict as more important than honoring the judge's instruction to disregard (forget). In a variety of other real-world and experimental situations as well, the forgetting asked for may be consistent with the asker's goals, but may not fit well with the goals of the recipient of that request. For example, when the stated reason for an instruction to forget or disregard is that the information in question is "confidential," there may well be such a conflicting agenda (see, e.g., Golding, Fowler, Long, & Latta, 1990).

Of course, such considerations are hardly news to social psychologists. In the context of research on intentional forgetting, however, such considerations seem important for two reasons. First of all, in the literature on instructions to ignore, disregard, and discount in social and legal experiments, as summarized in this volume, there is a striking, if unsurprising pattern: The more the information that is the target of such instructions is discredited, proven to be false, and so forth, the more evidence there is that subjects actually follow those instructions in their judgments or recall performance.

That pattern makes me wonder whether in research on hindsight effects, where subjects, in making a judgment or prediction of some kind, seem unable to set aside some outcome information they now know, even when asked to do so (see Golding and Long's review), the results might differ if there were a way to change the task so that *ignoring* what one now knows is consistent with one's own self-esteem or the opinion of others. As Campbell and Tesser (1983) conjectured, hindsight biases may derive in part from motivational factors—in particular, the fact that having good foresight is an attribute that impresses others. Given that there *are* situations in the world, however, where we know more about something than we might like other people to know we know (about television soap operas, for example; or even, in some subcultures, mathematical reasoning), it might be possible to construct a judgment situation where subjects are more motivated to ignore just-presented outcome information.

A second consideration, and one that may be more important from a theoretical standpoint, is that the *intent* to forget may have an active, intrinsic, and direct effect on to-be-forgotten items in memory. That is, in addition to the indirect effects of intent to forget, such as reducing or eliminating a subject's inclination to continue to think about, rehearse, or integrate to-be-forgotten information with to-be-remembered information, the intent to forget may play an active role of some kind in the inhibition of to-be-forgotten information. It is an open research question, but there are some human-memory results (see E. L. Bjork, R. A. Bjork, & Anderson, this volume) suggesting that inhibition may require the allocation of resources, which, in turn, would require the intent to allocate those resources; the work of Macrae and his colleagues on the role of effort and resource allocation in the suppression of stereotype information also suggests such a possibility (e.g., Macrae, Bodenhausen, Milne, & Wheeler, 1996; for a summary, see Bodenhausen, Macrae, & Milne, this volume).

Direct Versus Indirect Measures of "Forgetting"

Typically, in the social/legal research tradition, whether an instruction to disregard, ignore, or discount some information has an effect on subjects' memory for that information is assessed not by a test of the subjects' later ability to recall that information, but by some other measure, such as whether that instruction alters a legal or social judgment, evaluation, or impression of some kind. The absence of any such effects is taken as evidence that the instruction was ineffective. At one level of analysis, such a conclusion seems unassailable. Often, however, that conclusion is accompanied by a claim, overt or implied, that the instruction also had no effect on subjects' episodic recall of the event or information in question. That claim might also be true, but the lack of an effect of the instruction on judgments and impressions does not necessarily constitute evidence for that claim.

The problem is that judgments, evaluations, and impressions are frequently *indirect* tests of memory, which are often sensitive to prior events when direct measures, such as recall, are not (see, e.g., Richardson-Klavehn & Bjork, 1988). That is, such tasks typically do not refer the subject back to the episodic events of interest; rather, they require an overall decision or judgment of some kind (for a more complete discussion, see Johnson, 1994). Of particular relevance are the recent findings in the human-memory literature that an instruction to forget can impede recall of the to-be-forgotten information without lessening the effect of that information as measured by indirect tests, such as word-fragment completion (see MacLeod's summary of those findings in this volume). It is entirely possible, therefore, that in certain of the social and legal experiments where an instruction to disregard has been declared completely ineffective, as measured by some type of judgment-task performance, a test of recall of the to-be-disregarded information would have shown impaired recall.

Whether, and under what circumstances, such a dissociation might appear is a matter of considerable theoretical and practical interest. If an instruction to forget or to disregard can impair recollection of the event or information that is the target of that instruction, without lessening its impact as measured by other means, there are circumstances where the impact of to-be-forgotten information on certain judgments may be larger than the impact of comparable to-be-remembered information. Using a variation on the "false fame" paradigm of Jacoby and his colleagues (e.g., Jacoby, Kelley, Brown, & Jasechko, 1989), we recently found support for such a conjecture (E. L. Bjork, R. A. Bjork, Stallings, & Kimball, 1996). When a nonfamous name was made familiar by virtue of its having been presented earlier in the experiment on a list of such names, subjects were more likely to attribute that familiarity, falsely, to real-world fame when that earlier list was to be forgotten than when it was to be remembered.

When Intentional Forgetting Succeeds and Fails: Other Considerations

When considered together, the cognitive and social/legal research literatures suggest that there are a number of procedural determinants of whether instructions to forget or to disregard succeed or fail. In her review, Johnson (1994) attempted to characterize in detail the conditions that yield successful and unsuccessful intentional forgetting. At a somewhat more global level, I am struck by the importance of the following factors.

The Relatedness of What Is to Be Forgotten and to Be Remembered.
In general, instructions to disregard or to ignore in social/legal contexts seem ineffective when the to-be-forgotten information has already been integrated with the information to be remembered. In the directed-forgetting literature, an instruction to forget also tends to be ineffective when to-be-

forgotten and to-be-remembered items are closely related and/or integrated with each other (see, e.g., Golding, Long, & MacLeod, 1994). Certain findings that derive from item-by-item cuing procedures seem like exceptions to that rule, but with the item-by-item procedure, to-be-forgotten items may never be encoded at a level that would integrate them with to-be-remembered items, even if the items themselves have a natural relationship.

The Temporal Positioning of Instructions to Forget or Disregard. Both literatures suggest that, in a sense, we can reach a point where it is too late to instruct someone to forget or to disregard. Instructions to forget or to disregard become less effective as time passes because presentation of the information to be forgotten or disregarded passes, especially when that delay is filled with the presentation and processing of information that is to be remembered.

The Reexposure of To-Be-Forgotten Information. Another point of consistency is that reexposure to information that was earlier to be forgotten or disregarded can have dire consequences with respect to the goal of forgetting or disregarding successfully. Such reexposures can reinstate that information and its interference with subsequent recall of information to be remembered and/or its influence on subsequent judgments where that information is to be disregarded.

The Replacement of To-Be-Forgotten Information With To-Be-Remembered Information. Finally, although the conclusion seems more tentative, it appears that giving subjects a set to replace to-be-forgotten information with new to-be-remembered information may play an important role in successful intentional forgetting. Gelfand and Bjork's (1985) results, as mentioned earlier, suggest that new (replacement) learning plays an important role in the inhibition of old to-be-forgotten information, and findings in the social/legal context also suggest that to-be-disregarded information is more effectively nullified in subsequent judgments if alternative information is provided as a replacement for that information.

MOTIVATED FORGETTING IN CLINICAL CONTEXTS

From an historical standpoint, one might expect that the oldest tradition of research on intentional forgetting would be in the context of research on clinical disorders. Conceptually, the notion that intentional or motivated forgetting plays a role in psychodynamic disorders, as in the repression mechanisms hypothesized by Freud and others, traces back a century or so. From an empirical research standpoint, however, the use of explicit instructions to forget or to remember appears to be a very recent innovation (the exception being in the case of hypnosis, where the use of explicit instructions to hypnotized subjects to forget what happened while they were hypnotized has a very long history; see, e.g., Nagge, 1935).

An early body of controlled research on "motivated forgetting" examined whether materials with a negative valence were forgotten more rapidly than were neutral or positive materials (see, e.g., Ratliff, 1938). The forgetting examined in those experiments was not motivated in the sense of being instructed, but, rather, was motivated in the sense of satisfying a presumed (theory-based) need to forget or repress negative or unpleasant memories. It is a fair summary of that early research, I think, to say that the evidence of more rapid forgetting of negatively valenced materials in those controlled studies was, overall, unconvincing. In an interesting and potentially important development, the motivated-forgetting approach has been resurrected by Cloitre and other researchers, but now augmented by the use of explicit directed-forgetting procedures.

Directed-Forgetting Procedures as a Tool in Clinical Research

As summarized by Cloitre (this volume), directed-forgetting procedures are emerging as a potentially fruitful tool in clinical research. At several different locations, groups of researchers recently carried out a number of experiments in which subjects with certain clinically diagnosed disorders, or subjects who are high or low on certain measured personality traits, or subjects who have a history of trauma of some specific kind, are given explicit instructions to forget or to remember words or phrases that are related or unrelated to those disorders, traits, or traumas (those groups are Cloitre and her collaborators, and McNally and his collaborators, as cited by Cloitre; and Brewin, Myers, Power, and their collaborators in England—see, e.g., Brewin, in press; Myers, Brewin, & Power, 1996). The logic behind these experiments (see Cloitre's discussion) is that subjects who have a certain disorder, or who possess a certain trait, or who have been the victim of a particular trauma, such as rape, are likely to show a pattern of recall performance that is diagnostic and, from a theoretical standpoint, informative. As Cloitre clarifies, there are theory-based reasons, depending on the disorder, trait, or trauma of interest, to expect that relevant materials might be better or more poorly recalled than neutral materials, and that such differences might interact with whether those materials were to be forgotten or to be remembered.

Two aspects of this new line of research make it seem especially promising to me. First, as Cloitre points out—and something that had not occurred to me prior to reading her discussion—directed-forgetting procedures engage attentional, rehearsal, retrieval, and inhibitory processes in a way that makes enhanced or impaired recall of to-be-remembered materials potentially as informative as enhanced or impaired recall of to-be-forgotten materials. That is, one might think the sole observation of interest would be whether, compared to the recall of neutral materials or the performance of control subjects, the recall of to-be-forgotten materials that have personal valence for a given subject is impaired or facilitated. As Cloitre points out, however, there are also theory-based reasons to expect that the levels of recall of to-be-remembered neutral and valenced materials might differ as well, and that such differences, if any, especially when viewed against the levels of performance on corresponding to-be-forgotten materials, have the potential to be diagnostic and informative.

A second reason the approach seems promising at this early stage is that the initial results do reveal some substantial differences in the recall of materials to be forgotten and to be remembered as a function of subject type, and whether those materials are neutral or subject relevant in some way. Those differences, thus far, have not always corresponded with the experimenters' expectations and predictions, but that fact may simply illustrate that the approach has the potential to inform and refine theorizing. And, as Cloitre points out, researchers may have only scratched the surface thus far with this new methodology; any systematic differences that might appear on comparisons between the list and item-by-item directed-forgetting procedures have the potential to be diagnostic, as do possible differences on direct and indirect measures of retention.

Inhibition and Recovery of Traumatic Memories

E. L. Bjork, R. A. Bjork, and Anderson conclude their chapter in this volume with some speculations on the possible relevance of inhibitory processes identified in laboratory paradigms to the forgetting and recovery of real-world traumatic memories. They carefully label their comments as "speculations," because whether the phenomena and processes identified in highly constrained and emotionally quite neutral laboratory settings are generalizable to the memory of real-world traumas is open to serious question at this point. Certain parallels are tempting and suggestive, however, as these authors outline.

It is not appropriate here to reiterate those possible connections, but a couple comments seem in order. First, and quite the opposite of what I thought years ago, the processes triggered by directed-forgetting procedures in the laboratory may bear some meaningful and instructive relations to the real-world processes of inhibition and recovery that are of interest to clinical researchers. Second, and related to the first point, there is much to be gained by a dialogue between cognitive scientists interested in forgetting mechanisms and clinical researchers interested in the memory dynamics that characterize certain disorders. It seems clear now that the research paradigms and theoretical characterizations of memory processes developed by cognitive psychologists are of potential importance to clinical researchers. It also seems clear that the work of clinical researchers has the potential to inform the theoretical work of cognitive scientists, in much the same way, perhaps, that research on patients with organic amnesias of one kind or another has isolated and illustrated certain memory processes more clearly than is observable in standard experimentation with normal subjects.

OTHER APPROACHES TO INTENTIONAL FORGETTING

In this section I comment on the other approaches to the study of intentional forgetting that are represented in this volume. Where my comments are brief, it is not because there is little to say, but because my perspective, in terms of how the issues and phenomena that characterize a given approach relate to the issues and phenomena in research on directed forgetting in adult waking humans, is already well represented by the authors of one or more of the prior chapters in this volume.

Directed Forgetting in Animals

The body of research on directed forgetting in animals, which is summarized and analyzed by Grant and by Zentall, Roper, Kaiser, and Sherburne in this volume (and by Roper & Zentall, 1993, in an earlier review), is impressive in two respects. First, it is a body of research marked by careful analysis and clever experimentation. Second, it is impressive in terms of the sheer amount of research that has been completed over the last 20 years or so; I am particularly struck by Zentall, Roper, Kaiser, and Sherburne's statement that "directed forgetting is perhaps the most thoroughly examined animal memory phenomenon that has been studied for its cognitive implications" (pp. 3–4).

The early research on directed forgetting in animals was stimulated by the early research on directed forgetting in humans, but the specific experimental procedures, appropriately enough, soon came to differ in some important ways from those used with humans. The most common procedure used by animal researchers, the matching-to-sample procedure, where cues following a given stimulus sample serve to signal whether comparison stimuli will or will not follow that sample (remember and forget cues, respectively), does not correspond in its details to any of the procedures used with humans. The authors mention that the procedure is closest to the item-by-item procedure used with humans, but the differences are substantial in how and when TBR and TBF items are tested in the two cases.

At a more general level, however, in terms of process-model considerations, there does seem to be a meaningful correspondence between the matching-to-sample procedures used with animals and the item-by-item procedures used with humans. In both instances, the procedures seem particularly well suited to examining the role of rehearsal/maintenance processes in distinguishing between TBR and TBF items, which has been a major focus of the research on directed forgetting in animals. What I cannot help wondering, however, given some of my own interests, is whether animals could take advantage of cues to forget in the sense of updating memory, that is, in the sense of replacing TBF stimuli with TBR stimuli.

To address that question, it seems plausible that the directed-forgetting version of Sternberg's memory-scanning task, introduced long ago by Bjork, Abramowitz, and Krantz (1970; as cited in Bjork, 1989), and resurrected more recently by other researchers (see Neumann, Cherau, Hood, & Steinnagel, 1993; Neumann & DeSchepper, 1992; Zacks et al., 1996), could be adapted to animals. The standard memory-scanning paradigm consists of a series of trials, on each of which a small set of items is presented one at a time. After each such set of to-be-remembered items, a probe item is presented, to which the subject is to respond "yes" or "no" as quickly as possible depending on whether the probe item does or does not match one of the items in that set. In the directed-forgetting version of the task, some lists, in unpredictable fashion, contain a signal to subjects to forget the items presented prior to the signal, that the judgment to be made is whether the probe matches one of the items that will follow that signal. In effect, the forget cue is a signal to the subject that the list is starting over. Human subjects can indeed start over, or "forget," in the sense that their "yes" response times are unaffected by the presence (or number) of presignal to-be-forgotten items in a given list. Their "no" responses are slower, however, when the probe is a to-be-forgotten item than when it is an item not presented at all on that trial.

What makes adapting the paradigm to animals seem feasible are some results obtained by Wright and his collaborators (e.g., Wright, Santiago, Sands, Kendrick, & Cook, 1985). Using pigeons, monkeys, and humans as subjects, Wright and his colleagues found strikingly similar effects of probe delay and serial input position on the memory-scanning performance of each species (percent correct judgments, not reaction time, was the measure of interest). The search sets consisted of four visual stimuli in each case, but the materials were scaled to each species (simple pictures for pigeons, more complicated pictures for monkeys, and kaleidoscope patterns for humans), as was the range of probe delays (0 to 10 sec for pigeons; 0 to 30 sec for monkeys; and 0 to 100 sec for humans). Their actual results, though very interesting, are not what is important for present purposes; it is the fact that those results were similar across species that suggests that the directed-forgetting version of the memory-scanning task may be adaptable to animals.

Posthypnotic Amnesia

Golding and Long provide a concise and informative summary of research on posthypnotic amnesia—that is, on the effects of instructions to hypnotized individuals that, after awakening, they will be unable to recall the events that occurred during hypnosis. In the modern era of research on posthypnotic amnesia, there has been a productive interaction between researchers interested in posthypnotic amnesia and researchers interested in directed forgetting in waking humans, in part because those researchers have sometimes been the same people. One issue that has motivated recent research on posthypnotic amnesia, in fact, is whether the mechanisms are the same as those identified in nonhypnotic directed forgetting. As Golding and Long mention, there is currently a difference of opinion on that matter among researchers.

Whether the mechanisms are basically the same or differ in some important way, there are some striking similarities between the empirical phenomena that characterize posthypnotic amnesia and analogous effects of directed forgetting in waking subjects. In both cases, for example, there is disrupted and disorganized retrieval of to-be-forgotten items when subjects are asked to try to recall those items; and subjects exhibit a kind of source amnesia for where and when the TBF items that are recalled were presented. Also, in both cases, the influence of to-be-forgotten events and information on indirect measures of memory is nonetheless preserved, and TBF items are as readily relearned as TBR items.

Thought Suppression

In the influential work by Wegner and his colleagues on thought suppression (e.g., Wegner, 1994; Wegner, Schneider, Carter, & White, 1987), the basic procedure involves asking subjects *not* to think about some target item, such as a white bear or the Statue of Liberty. As a means of trying to comply with that instruction, subjects typically initiate a process of self-distraction; that is, they try to keep their minds focused on some *other* salient thought or personal experience. That strategy intermittently fails, however, apparently because subjects, owing to some kind of nonvolitional monitoring process, intermittently check whether they are complying with the instruction. There is also evidence that attempting to suppress a thought can make it hyperaccessible as measured by other means and that, after a period of suppression, there can be "rebound" effects where thoughts that were suppressed become more accessible than they would have been without a period of attempted suppression.

It is not feasible or appropriate here to summarize the myriad variations on that basic procedure that have now been explored, nor to describe fully the details of the phenomena that have been obtained. Golding and Long provide a brief overview in their chapter, and Bodenhausen, Macrae, and Milne summarize a series of interesting experiments on a related topic, stereotype suppression, in their chapter. There are some comparisons of the basic methodologies of thought-suppression and directed-forgetting experiments that merit comment, however, and some speculations on the relationship of the processes that underlie thought suppression and directed forgetting also seem warranted.

At one level, an instruction not to think about something, such as a white bear, seems quite similar to an instruction to forget something that was just presented for study. There are some substantial differences, however. In the directed-forgetting case, for example, the instruction refers to a well-defined episodic event, not a concept or experience or stereotype that already exists in memory. Also, it is the experimenter-provided task of learning the items that *are* to be remembered that diverts attention from the to-be-forgotten items, not a subject-generated effort to think of something other than the to-be-suppressed thought. Another difference is that subjects in directed-forgetting experiments are not asked to monitor how well they are avoiding the retrieval of to-be-forgotten items (although, it occurs to me, they *could* be asked to do so), whereas subjects in thought-suppression experiments are typically asked to indicate, by ringing a bell or some other means, when the to-be-suppressed thought has intruded into consciousness.

Possibly because of such differences, the phenomena and presumed processes in research on thought suppression and directed forgetting have not seemed to be all that closely related, although some similarities have been noted. In a chapter on thought suppression as a mental-control technique, for example, Wegner, Eich, and Bjork (1994) stressed that the success of both thought suppression and directed forgetting depends, in part, on avoiding environmental cues that point to or re-present the "suppressed" or "forgotten" thought or information. In general, however, the processes implicated in research on thought suppression have not seemed to inform research on directed forgetting, and vice versa.

Recently, however, Martin Conway (personal communication, 1996) pointed out that thought suppression and directed forgetting may be more closely related than researchers in either area have tended to think. As background for Conway's conjecture, I need first to summarize Wegner's (1994) "ironic processes" theory of thought suppression (see also Golding & Long's summary in this volume). Wegner argues that two processes are involved: one intentionally initiated, effortful, and resource demanding; the other involuntary and less demanding of cognitive resources. In thought-suppression experiments, the first process takes the form of distracting one's self by thinking about other matters, and is initiated as a means of complying with the instruction to suppress the thought in question. The other process, a monitoring process, is one that runs in the background, but intermittently and involuntarily captures consciousness, so to speak. Its function is to check whether the goal of the first process is being achieved; in the thought-suppression context, however, that involves accessing the very thought that is to be suppressed. An important assumption of Wegner's theory is that the intentional process is more demanding of central cognitive resources; thus, under cognitive-load or secondary-task conditions, it suffers more than does the relatively automatic monitoring process, leading to less effective thought suppression.

Conway's conjecture is that directed forgetting itself may involve a similar interplay of processes and that, in particular, directed forgetting may itself require central resources. That conjecture is prompted by several considerations. First, the results obtained by Gelfand and Bjork (1985), discussed earlier, suggest that *both* the intent to forget (i.e., the allocation of central resources to that goal) *and* new learning of to-be-remembered information are necessary to suppress or inhibit to-be-forgotten information. Second, as E. L. Bjork, R. A. Bjork, and Anderson speculate in this volume, the mechanism that underlies the repression of traumatic memories may be retrieval-induced (or learning-induced) retrieval inhibition; thus, for example, victims of abuse may be motivated to retrieve positive or neutral memories of an abusive family member, which, eventually, would inhibit access to the recall of abuse incidents.

In Conway's view, "retrieval inhibition is exactly the mechanism needed to create Freud's 'screen memories.'" The intention to suppress thoughts or to forget prior events would have much in common and, in fact, would interact in certain ways. Drawing on Wegner's ideas, Conway speculated that "when control-process resources are depleted, repressed materials may be brought to mind by a monitoring process, especially in the presence of relevant environmental stimuli, and at that point directed forgetting could be used to again repress the offensive materials." As an example, he described the behavior of a serial killer interviewed by Christianson and Engelberg (1997), who, "when reminded of his murders, would immediately pick any reading materials to hand (e.g., the label of contents on some tinned food), and intensely and repetitively read that material until the 'memories passed.'" (See Conway, 1997, for more examples.)

Directed Forgetting in Development and Aging

A final approach that merits comment is the use of directed-forgetting procedures to examine issues in the development of information-processing abilities, or in how those abilities change with aging. In their overview chapter, Golding and Long summarize the literature on directed forgetting in retarded and normal children and adolescents, much of it contributed by Bray and his colleagues; they also summarize the findings in research on directed forgetting in elderly subjects.

To document the usefulness of directed-forgetting procedures as a tool in research, there may be no better examples than the research on intentional-forgetting processes in development and aging. In terms of identifying what memory-control processes, such as selective rehearsal, are and are not available at a given point in normal or retarded development, directed-forgetting procedures have proved fruitful and instructive. And in terms of identifying changes in the management of attentional and working-memory resources that accompany aging, especially having to do with the inhibitory control of those resources (see Hasher & Zacks, 1988; Zacks & Hasher, 1994; Zacks et al., 1996), directed-forgetting procedures have also proved an especially useful tool.

With respect to using directed forgetting as a tool, the recent work of Zacks et al. (1996) illustrates an important point: Theoretical leverage can be gained by using more than a single directed-forgetting procedure. In a series of experiments, Zacks et al. tested younger and older subjects using both the item-by-item and the list methods of directed forgetting. In addition, with the list method, where some lists contained a cue to subjects to forget the items in the list presented prior to the cue, they examined both the recall of postcue items (Experiment 2) and the speed at which subjects could identify whether an end-of-list probe item had or had not occurred among the postcue items (Experiment 3); the latter case is the directed-forgetting version of the memory-scanning paradigm, which I described more fully in my comments on directed forgetting in animals.

Among their other results, Zacks et al. found that older subjects, with item-by-item cuing, were less able than younger subjects to exclude to-be-forgotten items from recall. With the list method, however, they *were* able to exclude to-be-forgotten items; that is, with "start-over" cuing in a list context, the older subjects, like the younger subjects, did not show proactive interference owing to the presence or number of to-be-forgotten items in their recall of, or reaction time to, to-be-remembered items.

For present purposes, it is not important exactly what that finding, and the other findings obtained by Zacks et al., may imply as to the information-processing capabilities that are and are not preserved in aging (for a full discussion, see their article). The important point is that the pattern of effects across different directed-forgetting procedures is *likely* to differ in certain ways in a given situation, and those differences are likely to be instructive. As MacLeod documents in his review chapter, and as I argued earlier in this chapter, the different ways of administering instructions to remember and to forget can put somewhat different demands on subjects, which, in turn, can trigger somewhat different processing strategies and mechanisms.

Finally, the research by Zacks and her colleagues illustrates yet another important point: The use of directed-forgetting procedures as a tool in research on special populations such as the elderly has the potential to inform theory development more generally. In their use of the directed-forgetting version of the memory-scanning paradigm, they replicated—for both younger and older subjects—a pattern of results that Bjork et al. (1970; as cited in Bjork, 1989) found puzzling: "Yes" response times to to-be-remembered probes were an increasing function of the size of the to-be-remembered set, but independent of the number of to-be-forgotten items in the list; and "no" response times to to-be-forgotten probes were slower than "no" response times to items that had not appeared at all in the list, but were also independent of the number of to-be-forgotten items in the list.

That pattern is puzzling because the "yes" response times suggest that subjects can restrict their memory scanning to the to-be-remembered set, which then predicts that the two types of "no" responses should not differ. Furthermore, given that the two types of "no" responses *do* differ, it would seem that the "no" responses to to-be-forgotten items should vary with the number of to-be-forgotten items. As a possible interpretation of that puzzling pattern, I speculated in my 1989 paper that "no" responses to to-be-forgotten probes might be slowed not because the scanning of the to-be-remembered set was any slower once such probes were encoded, but because to-be-forgotten items were inhibited, resulting in a slower encoding of to-be-forgotten probes. I put that hypothesis forward in a very tentative and qualified way, but Neumann and his colleagues (Neumann & DeSchepper, 1992; Neumann et al., 1993) replicated the same pattern of results and interpreted other aspects of their results as consistent with an inhibited-encoding interpretation.

For reasons that Zacks et al. document, however, such a view would seem to predict that the difference in response time to the two types of "no" probes, that is, to-be-forgotten probes and nonpresented probes, should be larger for the younger subjects, the opposite of what they found. Whether their arguments against the inhibited-encoding view, and in support of an alternative interpretation they favor, are totally convincing or not, their results provide a convincing demonstration that the results of directed-forgetting experiments in the context of development, aging, clinical disorders, and so forth, have the potential to inform theory development more broadly.

CONCLUDING COMMENTS

I have grown accustomed to thinking of directed-forgetting procedures as a new and somewhat novel approach in research on human memory. In the context of this volume, however, as Golding and Long point out, research on directed forgetting in human memory is the old and established field. It is not true in every instance, but the historical roots of much of the work reviewed in this volume go back to the early work on directed forgetting. For those of us who, 30 years or so ago, began tinkering with instructions to people to forget things, and trying to defend why doing that made any sense at all, it would have been hard to imagine that any book like this one might exist some day, let alone a book with the range and wealth of findings and ideas that are reported in this volume.

So what does the future hold? On the one hand, I am convinced by this volume that directed-forgetting procedures, as a research tool, will prove increasingly useful in a variety of contexts. On the other hand, I think there is much that remains to be understood about the basic mechanisms that underlie the intentional ignoring, forgetting, suppressing, or discounting of information, prior events, or current thoughts. Toward that end, we need to refine our characterization of such processes, which, though closely related, may involve somewhat different mechanisms and may serve somewhat different functions in our interactions with the world.

With respect to directed forgetting in humans, I think there is much that remains to be understood about the inhibitory mechanisms that now appear implicated by recent findings. Do central control processes play a direct role in such inhibition? Or is retrieval inhibition solely a by-product of new learning or the retrieval of competing information? And in what ways are the inhibitory mechanisms in directed forgetting similar to or different from the inhibitory mechanisms that are intrinsic to human attention? Some of the answers to those questions may come, in part, from neuroscience approaches to human memory. The results of research on frontal-lobe functions and the interplay of the hippocampus and neocortex suggest, to me at least, that directed-forgetting tasks, in combination with imaging techniques, might prove revealing.

Finally, whatever twists and turns future research on intentional forgetting might take, one thing is clear: Intentional forgetting, as I said at the outset of this chapter, is inextricably intertwined with intentional remembering. If our goal is to understand fully how information is selected, encoded, learned, and remembered, we also need to understand how information is ignored, inhibited, discounted, and forgotten.

REFERENCES

Anderson, M. C., Bjork, R. A., & Bjork, E. L. (1994). Remembering can cause forgetting: Retrieval dynamics in long-term memory. *Journal of Experimental Psychology: Learning, Memory, and Cognition, 20,* 1063–1087.

Anderson, M. C., & Spellman, B. A. (1995). On the status of inhibitory mechanisms in cognition: Memory retrieval as a model case. *Psychological Review, 102,* 68–100.

Basden, B. H., Basden, D. R., & Gargano, G. J. (1993). Directed forgetting in implicit and explicit memory tests: A comparison of methods. *Journal of Experimental Psychology: Learning, Memory, and Cognition, 3*, 603–616.

Bjork, E. L., Bjork, R. A., Stallings, L., & Kimball, D. R. (1996, November). *Enhanced false fame owing to instructions to forget.* Paper presented at the meetings of the Psychonomic Society, Chicago.

Bjork, R. A. (1970). Positive forgetting: The noninterference of items intentionally forgotten. *Journal of Verbal Learning and Verbal Behavior, 9*, 255–268.

Bjork, R. A. (1972). Theoretical implications of directed forgetting. In A. W. Melton & E. Martin (Eds.), *Coding processes in human memory* (pp. 217–235). Washington, DC: Winston.

Bjork, R. A. (1975). Short-term storage: The ordered output of a central processor. In F. Restle, R. M. Shiffrin, N. J. Castellan, H. R. Lindeman, & D. B. Pisoni (Eds.), *Cognitive theory* (Vol. 1, pp. 151–171). Hillsdale, NJ: Lawrence Erlbaum Associates.

Bjork, R. A. (1978). The updating of human memory. In G. H. Bower (Ed.), *The psychology of learning and motivation* (Vol. 12, pp. 235–259). New York: Academic Press.

Bjork, R. A. (1989). Retrieval inhibition as an adaptive mechanism in human memory. In H. L. Roediger & F. I. M. Craik (Eds.), *Varieties of memory and consciousness: Essays in honor of Endel Tulving* (pp. 309–330). Hillsdale, NJ: Lawrence Erlbaum Associates.

Bjork, R. A., & Geiselman, R. E. (1978). Constituent processes in the differentiation of items in memory. *Journal of Experimental Psychology: Human Learning and Memory, 4*, 347–361.

Bjork, R. A., LaBerge, D., & Legrand, R. (1968). The modification of short-term memory through instructions to forget. *Psychonomic Science, 10*, 55–56.

Bjork, R. A., & Landauer, T. K. (1978). On keeping track of the present status of people and things. In M. M. Gruneberg, P. E. Morris, & R. N. Sykes (Eds.), *Practical aspects of memory* (pp. 52–60). London: Academic Press.

Brewin, C. R. (in press). Clinical and experimental approaches to understanding repression. In D. Read & D. S. Lindsay (Eds.), *Recollections of trauma: Scientific research and clinical practice.* New York: Plenum Press.

Brown, J. (1954). The nature of set-to-learn and intra-material interference in immediate memory. *Quarterly Journal of Experimental Psychology, 6*, 141–148.

Brown, J. (1958). Some tests of the decay theory of immediate memory. *Quarterly Journal of Experimental Psychology, 10*, 12–21.

Campbell, J. D., & Tesser, A. (1983). Motivational interpretations of hindsight bias: An individual difference analysis. *Journal of Personality, 51*, 605–620.

Christianson, S.-A., & Engelberg, E. (1997). Remembering and forgetting traumatic experiences: A matter of survival. In M. A. Conway (Ed.), *Recovered memories and false memories* (pp. 230–250). Oxford, England: Oxford University Press.

Conway, M. A. (1997). Past and present: Recovered memories and false memories. In M. A. Conway (Ed.), *Recovered memories and false memories* (pp. 150–191). Oxford, England: Oxford University Press.

Geiselman, R. E. (1977). Effects of sentence ordering on thematic decisions to remember and forget prose. *Memory & Cognition, 13*, 323–330.

Geiselman, R. E., & Bagheri, B. (1985). Repetition effects in directed forgetting: Evidence for retrieval inhibition. *Memory & Cognition, 13*, 51–62.

Geiselman, R. E., Bjork, R. A., & Fishman, D. (1983). Disrupted retrieval in directed forgetting: A link with posthypnotic amnesia. *Journal of Experimental Psychology: General, 112*, 58–72.

Gelfand, H., & Bjork, R. A. (1985, November). *On the locus of retrieval inhibition in directed forgetting.* Paper presented at the meetings of the Psychonomic Society, Boston, MA.

Golding, J. M., Fowler, S. B., Long, D. L., & Latta, H. (1990). Instructions to disregard potentially useful information: The effects of pragmatics on evaluative judgments and recall. *Journal of Memory and Language, 29*, 212–227.

Golding, J. M., Long, D. L., & MacLeod, C. M. (1994). You can't always forget want you want: Directed forgetting of related words. *Journal of Memory and Language, 33*, 493–510.

Hasher, L., & Zacks, R. T. (1988). Working memory, comprehension, and aging: A review and a new view. In G. H. Bower (Ed.), *The psychology of learning and motivation* (Vol. 22, pp. 193–225). San Diego, CA: Academic Press.

Jacoby, L. L., Kelley, C., Brown, J., & Jasechko, J. (1989). Becoming famous overnight: Limits on the ability to avoid unconscious influences of the past. *Journal of Personality and Social Psychology, 56*, 326–338.

Johnson, D. A. (1971). Pupillary responses during a short-term memory task: Cognitive processing, arousal, or both? *Journal of Experimental Psychology, 90*, 311–318.

Johnson, H. M. (1994). Processes of successful intentional forgetting. *Psychological Bulletin, 116*, 274–292.

Jongeward, R. H., Woodward, A. E., & Bjork, R. A. (1975). The relative roles of input and output mechanisms in directed forgetting. *Memory & Cognition, 3*, 51–57.

Macrae, C. N., Bodenhausen, G. V., Milne, A. B., & Wheeler, V. (1996). On resisting the temptation for simplification: Counterintentional effects of stereotype suppression on social memory. *Social Cognition, 14*, 1–20.

Murdock, B. B. (1963). Short-term retention of single paired associates. *Journal of Experimental Psychology, 65*, 433–443.

Muther, W. S. (1965). Erasure or partitioning in short-term memory. *Psychonomic Science, 3*, 429–430.

Myers, L. B., Brewin, C. R., & Power, M. J. (1996). *Repressive coping and the directed forgetting of emotional material.* Manuscript submitted for publication.

Nagge, J. W. (1935). An experimental test of the theory of associative interference. *Journal of Experimental Psychology, 18*, 663–682.

Neumann, E., Cherau, J. F., Hood, K. L., & Steinnagel, S. I. (1993). Does inhibition spread in a manner analogous to spreading activation? *Memory, 1*, 81–105.

Neumann, E., & DeSchepper, B. G. (1992). An activation based fan effect: Evidence for an active suppression mechanism in selective attention. *Canadian Journal of Psychology, 46*, 1–40.

Peterson, L. R., & Peterson, M. J. (1959). Short-term retention of individual verbal items. *Journal of Experimental Psychology, 58*, 193–198.

Ratliff, M. M. (1938). The varying functions of affectively toned olfactory, visual and auditory cues in recall. *American Journal of Psychology, 51*, 695–701.

Reed, H. (1970). Studies of the interference processes in short-term memory. *Journal of Experimental Psychology, 84*, 452–457.

Richardson-Klavehn, A., & Bjork, R. A. (1988). Measures of memory. *Annual Review of Psychology, 39*, 475–543.

Roper, K. L., & Zentall, T. R. (1993). Directed forgetting in animals. *Psychological Bulletin, 113*, 513–532.

Shaw, J. S., Bjork, R. A., & Handal, A. (1995). Retrieval-induced forgetting in an eyewitness paradigm. *Psychonomic Bulletin and Review, 2*, 249–253.

Timmins, W. K. (1973). Repetition of intentionally forgotten items. *Journal of Verbal Learning and Verbal Behavior, 12*, 168–173.

Wegner, D. M. (1994). Ironic processes of mental control. *Psychological Review, 101*, 34–52.

Wegner, D. M., Eich, E., & Bjork, R. A. (1994). Thought suppression. In D. Druckman & R. A. Bjork (Eds.), *Learning, remembering, believing: Enhancing human performance* (pp. 277–293). Washington, DC: National Academy Press.

Wegner, D. M., Schneider, D. J., Carter, S. R., III, & White, T. L. (1987). Paradoxical effects of thought suppression. *Journal of Personality and Social Psychology, 53*, 5–13.

Weiner, B., & Reed, H. (1969). Effects of the instructional sets to remember and to forget on short-term retention: Studies of rehearsal control and retrieval inhibition (repression). *Journal of Experimental Psychology, 79*, 226–232.

Woodward, A. E., Bjork, R. A., & Jongeward, R. H. (1973). Recall and recognition as a function of primary rehearsal. *Journal of Verbal Learning and Verbal Behavior, 12,* 608–617.

Wright, A. A., Santiago, H. C., Sands, S. F., Kendrick, D. F., & Cook, R. G. (1985). Memory processing of serial lists by pigeons, monkeys, and people. *Science, 229,* 287–289.

Zacks, R. T., & Hasher, L. (1994). Directed ignoring: Inhibitory regulation of working memory. In D. Dagenbach & T. H. Carr (Eds.), *Inhibitory processes in attention, memory, and language* (pp. 241–264). Orlando, FL: Academic Press.

Zacks, R. T., Radvansky, G. A., & Hasher, L. (1996). Studies of directed forgetting in older adults. *Journal of Experimental Psychology: Learning, Memory, and Cognition, 22,* 143–156.

AUTHOR INDEX

SUBJECT INDEX

A

Animals, 471–473
  associationist approach, 265–266
  cognitive processing in animals, 265–266
  double-sample procedures, 249–253,
      274–281
    ambiguity, 275
    reallocation procedure, 277–281
    sample memory, 276–277
    symmetry of effect on matching, 277
  F-cue effect, 243–253
    double-sample trials, 249–253
    experiments, 243–253
  instructional deficits, 281–283
  mechanism responsible for directed forgetting,
      281
  memorial account, 255–261
    R-probe testing, 257–258
    successively presented discriminative
        stimuli, 255–257
  nonmemorial account, 253–255
    response-pattern compatibility account,
        254–255
  omission procedures, 267–270
    delay cues, value of, 269–270
    successive matching, 268–269
  rehearsal, 242
    in delayed matching-to-sample, 242
  substitution procedures, 271–274
    failure to learn meaning of F-cue,
        272–273
    maintenance of sample rehearsal, 272
    response compatibility, 272–273
  trace decay model, 239–242
    stimulus duration, influence of,
        240–241
    stimulus repetition, influence of,
        240–241

B

Attitudes
  corrective advertising, 71
  debriefing, 66–67
  impression formation, 67–70
  persuasive messages, 70
  propositions, 70
  sleeper effect, 70–71

B

Bias
  hindsight bias, 73–77, 465–466
  juror bias, 414
  and social information, 307–310
  and suspicion, 336–339
  Bruton v. United States, 375 F.2d 355, 448, *450*
  Bruton v. United States, 391 U.S. 123, 438, 448,
      449, *450*
  Carter v. Kentucky, 450 U.S. 228, 420, *431*

C

Children
  inhibition, 80
  passive-active strategy, 79
Clinical disorders
  borderline personality disorder, 397,
      402–404, 409
  childhood trauma, 401–407, *see also*
      Traumatic memories
  cognitive characteristics, 395–396
  motivated forgetting, 468–469
  obsessive–compulsive disorder, 396–399, 408
  panic disorder, 397, 399–401, 408–409
  post-traumatic stress disorder, 396–397,
      409–410
    and adult rape victims, 407–408
    and childhood sexual assault, 404–407

495